*We dedicate this book to Marge Granzella -
a dear friend and a teacher of children.*

Series Editor: Virginia Lanigan
Editorial Assistant: Nicole DePalma
Cover Administrator: Linda Knowles
Composition and Prepress Buyer: Linda Cox
Manufacturing Buyer: Megan Cochran
Marketing Manager: Ellen Mann
Editorial-Production Service: P.M. Gordon Associates
Text Design and Production: Meral Dabcovich/Visual Perspectives
Photo Researcher: Susan Duane

This book is printed on recycled, acid-free paper.
ISBN: 0-205-13788-1
Printed in the United States of America.

10 9 8 7 6 5 4 3 2 1 99 98 97 96 95 94

PHOTO CREDITS

Jeffrey W. Meyers/Stock Boston: pp. 2, 185; Richard S.Orton/The Picture Cube: pp.
134, 170; Courtesy of Robert B. Ruddell: p. 226; Robert Frerck/Woodfin Camp &
Associates: p. 243; Jerry Howard/Stock Boston: p. 279; Robert Finken / The Picture
Cube: pp. 291, 392, 554; Frank Siteman/The Picture Cube: p. 368; Jean Claude
LeJeune/Stock Boston; p. 454; Jacob A. Riis/Museum of the City of New York:
p.596; Elizabeth Crews/Stock Boston: p.652; Bob Kramer/The Picture Cube: p. 717;
Will Faller: pp. 20, 206, 335, 430, 462, 536, 579, 684, 709; Jim Pickerell: pp. 7, 56,
94, 254, 310, 349, 417, 643, 664; Stephen Marks: pp. 45, 476, 501, **623/632**; Robert
Harbison: pp. 70, 117; Frank Siteman; p.:516.

II

Teaching Children to Read and Write:
Becoming an Influential Teacher

Robert B. Ruddell
University of California, Berkeley

Martha Rapp Ruddell
Sonoma State University

Allyn and Bacon

Boston ■ London ■ Toronto ■ Sydney ■ Tokyo ■ Singapore

CONTENTS

CHAPTER 3

UNDERSTANDING THE BEGINNING STEPS: EARLY READING AND WRITING DEVELOPMENT

CHAPTER 4

DEVELOPING READING COMPREHENSION: USING INSTRUCTIONAL STRATEGIES TO DEVELOP HIGHER LEVEL THINKING 134

CHAPTER 5

BUILDING VOCABULARY AND COMPREHENSION CONNECTIONS

CHAPTER 6

USING LITERATURE AND READER RESPONSE TO ENHANCE ATTITUDES AND COMPREHENSION   254

CHAPTER 7
GUIDING CHILDREN'S WRITING   310

CHAPTER 8
USING WORD ANALYSIS STRATEGIES TO
DEVELOP READER INDEPENDENCE :
TRANSFORMING PRINT TO MEANING   368

CHAPTER 11

EVALUATING CHILDREN'S PROGRESS IN READING AND WRITING 536

CHAPTER 12

EXAMINING INSTRUCTIONAL APPROACHES: BASAL READER, LITERATURE-BASED, WHOLE LANGUAGE, AND SUPPLEMENTARY PROGRAMS 596

PREFACE

TO THE STUDENT:

We wrote this book for you. We wrote it because we wanted to make available to you, in a manner at once comprehensive and comprehensible, the knowledge you will need to be an influential teacher of reading and writing. We included a broad base of information to allow you to make informed decisions about your belief system, your own knowledge base, and your evolving theories about how children acquire and develop literacy. And we have not forgotten the real world of classrooms in this text: We have included many, many instructional strategies for guiding children's literacy development in ways consonant with current beliefs, knowledge, and theories. Further, we've provided for various levels of understanding and application in the text because we know that beliefs, knowledge, theories, and teaching skills, grow and change.

In writing each chapter, we drew extensively on our own elementary school teaching experience, our university teaching experience with students who are preparing to become teachers, and our teaching and in-service work with experienced teachers throughout the United States. Our research and writing on influential teachers and literacy learning also informed the writing of this book. Above all, we have attempted to write a "reader-friendly" text—one that speaks to you by involving you, as we illuminate the latest theory, apply theory to the classroom through instructional strategies, and extend ideas with examples and illustrations.

Each chapter begins and ends with a Double Entry Journal (DEJ)—an interactive strategy that is designed to stimulate your thinking and draw on your previous experience and knowledge base. The before-reading DEJ provides a focus on the chapter topic and activates prior knowledge. The after-reading DEJ builds on your knowledge but combines it with the new ideas and strategies introduced in the chapter. To do the DEJ activity, you will need a notebook for recording your responses. The idea is to record responses before reading (the DEJ at the beginning of each chapter) on a *left-hand* page. Then after reading (the DEJ at the end of each chapter) do your DEJ responses on the *right-hand* page facing the page where you recorded your before-reading responses. In this way you can "cook" ideas you had before reading, extend and elaborate on them after reading, and make connections between your before- and after-reading responses. You will find that a simple spiral notebook will work nicely for DEJ writing, although you may prefer to integrate your DEJ responses with your class notes; just remember to use facing pages. Be sure to share your thinking with a class partner if at all possible.

You will find the **How to Do** feature throughout the text. How to Do provides a summary of selected instructional strategies introduced in the book (Chapters 3, 4, 5, 6, 7, 9, and 10). How to Do generally follows extended discussions of instructional strategies and is intended to give you a no-nonsense, step-by-step list of things you need to plan, prepare for, and/or consider in order to use the strategy successfully in your classroom. You will be able to develop lesson plans easily from the How to Do summaries.

You will also find **Building Tables** at the very end of chapters that introduce instructional strategies. Building Tables show how you can combine various strategies (the Building Tables grow, or "build," successively from chapter to chapter; hence, their name). Building Tables tell you (1) the focus of each strategy introduced in a chapter, (2) how the strategy is best used (small groups, large groups), (3) what strategies you already know (from former chapters) that this strategy combines well with, (4) preparation requirements (light, moderate, extensive), (5) additional resource needs, and (6) the page on which the How to Do for that strategy appears.

We encourage you to turn to the brief chapter summaries found at the end of Chapter 1 to get a quick overview of the book, the chapters, and the topics covered. We hope that you will find this book to be interesting, informative, and useful.

To the Instructor:

In this book, we urge each reader to become an influential teacher of reading and writing—a teacher who will change the lives of children. We believe the text chapters provide a balanced amalgam of theory and practice. We wanted to provide not only detailed, practical teaching strategies and suggestions but also the research and theory base underlying these suggestions. It was fortuitous for us that this book was in progress during the time we completed editing *Theoretical Models and Processes of Reading—Fourth Edition* (Ruddell, Ruddell, & Singer, 1994). In order to identify the multidisciplinary range of pieces to be included in that volume, we did an extensive and exhaustive review of the most recent reading and literacy research. This process resensitized us to the critical need in our profession to "bridge build" between research and classroom practice. We believe we have accomplished this in *Teaching Children to Read and Write: Becoming an Influential Teacher.*

As we mentioned earlier, a brief survey of the text appears in chapter summaries at the end of Chapter 1. These summaries reveal that the topics in the text range from building comprehension and word analysis strategies to enjoying literature and reader response, from understanding the nature of early literacy acquisition and the writing process to developing various classroom organization and management strategies, from discussing language and cultural diversity to examining the major instructional approaches, from evaluating reading and literacy progress to continuing professional change and growth.

In what we hope your students will find as a "reader-friendly" text, we speak as directly as possible to them and make every attempt to encourage them to interact with the text through the Double Entry Journal, personal examples and illustrations, recall and analysis of their own early reading and writing experiences, the How to Do summaries, and the Supporting Activities and Building Tables at the end of chapters. The *Instructor's Manual* is designed specifically for you and provides chapter summaries, objectives, and teaching and evaluation suggestions.

We hope that your use of this book in your class creates a partnership that enables us to share responsibility with you for developing influential reading and writing teachers. We ask for your support in providing comments on features of the book that work well for you and features that can be improved. We thus encourage you to correspond with us or to contact us in person at professional literacy conferences such as IRA, NRC, NCTE, or AERA. We sincerely hope that you will find the book challenging and interesting for your students and of value in your own teaching.

R.B.R.
M.R.R.
Oakland, California
October 1994

ACKNOWLEDGMENTS

We cannot publish this text without acknowledging and thanking the many individuals who are part of it. Our public school students—those children we taught in years past—were very much in our thoughts as we wrote. Some of these students lived a small coal-mining town in the Appalachian Mountains where one of us taught; others traveled the world with their military families and stopped off in Leavenworth, Kansas, long enough for sixth grade with the other of us. Still others lived and grew up in cities and rural towns in Missouri and Pennsylvania. We have maintained contact with a few of the "kids" over a period of three or four decades and marvel at their accomplishments. As all experienced teachers know, our students taught us as much as (if not more than) we taught them. We owe them a great deal, and here and now express our heartfelt appreciation.

We thank our teachers and mentors as well, those who influenced and enlarged our worlds: Mrs. Humphrey, Mrs. Rodgers, Mr. Cofer, Mr. Waddell, Eddie Kennedy, Ruth Strickland, David Russell, Tony Manzo, and Jane Davidson. Our mothers, Nellie Hogshead Ruddell and Velma Rapp Jones, were two of our most important and influential teachers.

We thank teachers throughout this country. Our combined travel and speaking engagements have given us opportunities to speak to teachers in every state of the nation. Whenever possible, we visited their classrooms to learn from them and their students. In the course of this we were privileged to watch many influential teachers at work. To these teachers across the nation, we express our grateful thanks.

Our university students—preservice teachers and experienced teachers who have returned to graduate school—contributed in an important way to this work. Their questions, insights, and responses have been invaluable to our thinking. They listened, commented, and prodded us at times. You will find selected examples of teaching and conversations from their classrooms in various parts of the book. Our special thanks go out to these students who have not only supported but critiqued our ideas by testing them in their classrooms.

We also wish to thank the reviewers of the manuscript as our work progressed. Their careful reading and reactions have without question added to the quality of our final chapter editing. They include:

Carmela Abbruzzese, Regis College (Massachusetts)

Marlys Ann Boschee, University of South Dakota

Alan Block, University of Wisconsin–Stout

Arlinda Eaton, California State University–Northridge

Susan Daniels, University of Akron (Ohio)

Susan Lara, University of Texas at Permian Basin

Ronald Oldham, Bemidji State, (Minnesota)

We are especially indebted to our good and long-time friend and master editor, Tab Hamlin. Not only does he thoroughly understands reading and literacy instruction but he is highly effective in using his writing wizardry to clarify murky sentences and paragraphs to help them communicate meaning. A special thanks to you, Tab.

We were most fortunate to have a wonderful support and editorial staff at Allyn and Bacon. These individuals include Virginia Lanigan, Education Editor, who constantly encouraged and supported our efforts throughout the process; Nicole De Palma, Virginia's patient editorial assistant; Mary Beth Finch, production editor; and Janice Buyer, copy editor.

Of course, we acknowledge our children—Amy, Bobby, and John— and grandchildren—Sarah, Ryan and Kenny—whose love and pride are always constant. Kenny, Ryan, Sarah, and John contributed their writing to our text.

And finally, to—and for—each other, we give thanks. Through all the planning sessions, the days and weeks pounding out words and ideas at our respective computers, the disagreements and negotiations toward rapprochement, and even when tempers and voices rose—we hung in there and, ultimately, were able to laugh at intensity, fatigue, and little snits. It worked. And, for now, the job is done.

Robert B. Ruddell is Professor of Eduction in the Division of Language and Literacy at the University of California at Berkeley. He teaches graduate and teacher credential program courses in reading and literacy development and is the Director of the Advanced Reading-Language Leadership Program.

Bob began his teaching career at the age of eighteen in a one-room country school in the Appalachian Mountains, has taught at all grade levels, and served as a supervisor of reading in a county schools office. He has lectured and conducted workshops for teachers in each of the fifty states of the nation and in England, Sweden, Germany, Ivory Coast, Australia, and Canada.

He is the recipient of the International Reading Association's William S. Gray Citation of Merit recognizing lifetime achievement and leadership contributions to the field of reading and literacy development. He is President of the Reading Hall of Fame and has served on the IRA Board of Directors. He is co-author of *Theoretical Models and Processes of Reading*. His articles have appeared in *The Reading Teacher* and *Language Arts* as well as in a variety of research journals and yearbooks. His research and teaching interests are focused on the development of comprehension and critical thinking, reader motivation, and the study of Influential Teachers.

He received his M.A. degree from West Virginia University and George Peabody College for Teachers and his Ed.D. from Indiana University. Bob enjoys international travel, reading suspense and mystery novels, and a good game of golf or tennis.

Martha Rapp Ruddell is Professor of Education at Sonoma State University in Rohnert Park, California. She teaches in the elementary and secondary teacher credential programs and the graduate Reading and Language M.A. program. Marty has ten years of teaching experience in second grade and middle school and senior high language arts, English, and Title I reading.

She is the author of a college text, *Teaching Content Reading and Writing*, and co-author of *Theoretical Models and Processes of Reading*. She has published articles in such journals as the *Journal of Reading, Reading Teacher*, and *Teacher Education Quarterly*. Marty spends significant time in elementary and middle school class-rooms supervising student teachers and maintaining partnerships with teachers and schools. She does professional presentations and conducts in-service programs throughout the United States and in England, Australia, Canada, and Sweden. Her current research interests include vocabulary development, portfolio assessment, and electronic journaling with student teachers.

She received a B.S.E. degree in Elementary Education from Central Missouri State University; an M.A. degree in Reading at Northeast Missouri State University; and a PH.D. degree in Reading and Social Psychology at the University of Missouri, Kansas City. Marty loves to read, dance, travel, and do *New York Times* crossword puzzles.

CHAPTER 1

BECOMING AN INFLUENTIAL
READING AND WRITING TEACHER

INTRODUCTION

This book has three major goals. The first is to increase your understanding of children's reading and writing development. The second is to extend your understanding by examining the most recent theories and research about the nature of children's reading and writing development. The third goal is to introduce you to classroom-based instructional strategies and approaches that will help you become an effective teacher who will have a major influence on your students' personal and academic success. This first chapter discusses these goals in detail. In addition, it outlines the remaining chapters that develop and implement these goals.

Successful achievement in reading and writing is vital to most of our personal and professional goals, regardless of our age. These basic literacy skills, however, are taken for granted by most of us. As you considered your early reading and writing experiences in school (in the Double Entry Journal exercise above) you may have experienced a flood of memories from kindergarten, first, and second grades; on the other hand, you may have little memory of how and when you learned to read and write. Whatever the case, you have learned to read and write and to do both well.

Regardless of our memories about learning to read, most of us have a clear recollection of some aspect of early reading experiences: the first full-length book we read by ourselves, a book that was special to us for one reason or another, or a book with particularly vivid characters and story events. The books in the following list were identified by several of our students as carrying special meaning for them. Do any of them create special memories for you?

The Secret Garden by Francis Hodgson Burnett
The Yearling by Marjorie Kinnan Rawlings
Ramona the Pest by Beverly Cleary
The Cat in the Hat by Dr. Seuss (Theodore S. Geisel)
The Moon-Spinners by Mary Stewart
James and the Giant Peach by Roald Dahl
The Lion, the Witch, and the Wardrobe by C. S. Lewis
Little House on the Prairie by Laura Ingalls Wilder
The Bears on Hemlock Mountain by Alice Dalgliesh
Charlotte's Web by E. B. White

Your own special book list may be different from this one, but in all probability you do remember books that carry very personal meaning for you at a particular time in your life.

Most of us have little memory of the process so essential to reading success in the early and middle grades, but we do have fond memories of early experiences with books, experiences that occurred at a time when we were already well on the road to becoming "expert" readers and writers.

THREE GOALS OF THIS TEXT

Let us look again at the goals of this text.

1. The *first* goal is to increase your understanding of children's reading and writing development.
2. The *second* goal is to extend your understanding in a meaningful way by examining the most recent theories and research about the nature of reading and writing.

3. The *third* goal is to introduce classroom-based instructional strategies and approaches that will help you become a highly effective teacher of reading and writing, and an influential one as well.

MORE ABOUT THE FIRST GOAL

You will increase your understanding of children's reading and writing development by exploring language, reading, and writing acquisition—from early experiences in the home through the elementary school years. The major focus of this discussion will center around understanding your students as hypothesis testers and meaning makers. Children come to school fully equipped to explore their world. They are constantly examining their surroundings, testing ways in which this world fits into their already developed understandings, and adjusting their ideas to assimilate the new into the old (Piaget, 1952; Ruddell & Ruddell, 1994; Sulzby, 1991). Reading and writing development are rooted in oral language; that is, children construct and reconstruct meaning as they talk with adults at home and teachers and peers at school, and as they explore environmental print (e.g., signs, logos, words like "EXIT," etc.) and new language forms (Dyson, 1986; Sulzby & Teale, 1991; Vygotsky, 1978). From this oral language base, children acquire language knowledge that supports their reading and writing development. Your purpose as teachers is to help children become effective readers and writers.

MORE ABOUT THE SECOND GOAL

Your thorough grasp of the most recent theories and research related to reading and literacy processing will become critical to the daily decisions you make as you teach your students. Contrary to popular belief that theory and practice are separate and incompatible entities, the fact is we all use our own (and others') theories daily as we go about our lives. Theories are nothing more nor less than informed hunches about how things work. Theories help us make the world "make sense." Consider for a moment your theory about how governmental institutions operate—the post office, the Department of Motor Vehicles, the state teacher-credentialing office, for example. Our theories about how these institutions function affects all of our decisions and actions in dealing with the institutions themselves—our "practice," if you will.

This same clear and direct relationship between theory and practice holds true just as surely in the classroom as it does with respect to government institutions. Your theory of how children acquire and develop literacy directly influences your classroom practice. As we explore current language and literacy theory and research, not only will you have opportunity to see what others are thinking about these processes, but you will construct personal theories that will guide your own classroom practice.

The knowledge base in language and literacy today is vastly different from that of even a decade ago. Recent work in the disciplines of psycholinguistics, sociolinguistics, and the anthropology and sociology of language has provided a wealth of information that holds valuable implications for reading and writing instruction (Bloome, 1991; Gumperz, 1981; Menyuk, 1991; Ogbu, 1983). This work has led to many new understandings of the way in which human beings process information, organize and retain knowledge, and generate new knowledge. Most of our current theories of literacy development feature the role of *schemata,* knowledge modules and mental categories that help us assimilate, store, and retrieve new and old information (Anderson, 1985; Schallert, 1991). Current theories also include information about how readers and writers transact with text (Rosenblatt, 1994), and how we translate theoretical knowledge to instructional strategies in classrooms (Beck & McKeown, 1991; Haggard, 1989; Ruddell, 1992). We are now more fully aware of the importance of family language and cultural interaction styles and the way in which these styles influence our students' responses, or lack of responses, in the classroom (Au, 1980; Heath, 1982). Just as important, we have instructional knowledge and strategies readily available to help students from varied language and cultural backgrounds to succeed in the classroom (Tierney, Readence, & Dishner, 1990).

MORE ABOUT THE THIRD GOAL

This theoretical and research knowledge base serves to guide the creation and use of strategies and approaches that will become the tools of instruction for your classroom. A personal goal of great importance to your literacy teaching success is to integrate current language and literacy theory—the knowledge base—into personal theories and beliefs about language and literacy development, and to apply these theories in your own classroom practice. Whether you realize it or not, you already have a rather elaborate belief system about the nature of teaching and reading and writing instruction.

Your belief system has been formed from many sources—early home learning experiences, learning experiences throughout your own schooling, and influential teachers you may have been fortunate enough to have had in kindergarten through the college or university levels (Ruddell & Kern, 1986). A brief checklist entitled "Identifying My Personal Belief System— Teaching Reading and Writing Skills" is found at the end of this chapter. Turn to this checklist and indicate your agreement or disagreement with each item as you begin the process of defining your personal belief system about reading and writing instruction and teaching.

As you read this text, you can expect your current belief system (i.e., your theories) to change and grow. As they do, you will find that your ideas about classroom practice, likewise, change. To guide you in this process, this book develops major chapter topics on literacy development. These range from emergent literacy and comprehension development to reader motivation, writing development, and classroom organization.

Each of the major instructional topics is accompanied by classroom-based teaching strategies grounded in current theory and research and effective classroom practice. These selected strategies have a clear instructional goal or goals, a plan for implementation, opportunity for instructional monitoring, and opportunity for the development of self-directed monitoring by your students. These teaching strategies can become valuable instructional tools in your classroom.

The point of view and ideas developed in the following chapters are meaning based, strategy oriented, and designed to equip you with an array of highly functional instructional strategies that will enable you to become an effective teacher of reading and writing. You will develop an understanding of widely used instructional approaches, including the basal reader approach, the literature-based approach, and the whole language approach. The major goal, however, is to provide instructional understandings and strategies that will be of value to you, regardless of the "approach" you eventually use with the students in your classroom.

Planning Together

MEMORIES OF ONE OF MY INFLUENTIAL TEACHERS*

Name of influential teacher _____

Grade level _____

Subject area taught _____

Personal appearance characteristics _____

_____

Teaching style or teaching characteristics _____

_____

_____

*We have found over the years that some people cannot identify an influential teacher in their K–12 school experience; often these individuals can, however, identify an influential teacher from within their family or from college or university experience.

TABLE 1-1

Becoming an Influential Teacher

Strong emphasis will be placed throughout the discussion in this book on encouraging you to become an *influential* teacher. "But," you ask, "What *is* an influential teacher?" An influential teacher is a special teacher whom we recall in a vivid and positive way from our academic experience—from kindergarten through our college years—and who has had a major influence on our personal or academic success (Ruddell & Haggard, 1982; Ruddell & Kern, 1986). Search your memory for a moment for such a teacher or teachers from your own elementary and secondary school years. In all probability, you will identify at least one such teacher, and possibly as many as five or six. In most cases, you will find that you not only remember the name of influential teachers but also the grade level they taught, and even their personal attributes, physical characteristics, and teaching styles. Influential teachers in all likelihood have had a major impact at some point on your academic achievement or your personal life. Use the space in Table 1-1 to assist you in recalling one of your influential teachers.

What Influential Teachers Do

Studies of influential teachers (Ruddell & Haggard, 1982; Ruddell & Kern 1986; Ruddell & Harris, 1989; Ruddell, Draheim, & Barnes, 1990), find that these teachers:

1. use highly motivating and effective teaching strategies,
2. help students with their personal problems,

3. create a feeling of excitement about the subject matter content or skill area they teach,
4. reflect a strong sense of personal caring about the student, and
5. demonstrate the ability to adjust instruction to the individual needs of the student.

BELIEFS OF INFLUENTIAL TEACHERS

In-depth interviews with influential teachers, ranging from kindergarten through the university level, indicate a number of common features that these teachers believe to be important to their teaching (Ruddell & Haggard, 1982; Ruddell & Kern, 1986). These features are presented in Table 1-2.

Now, take a few moments and reflect on the teaching characteristics that you recalled about your influential teacher(s) and compare your recollections with the five characteristics identified in Table 1-2. What characteristics did you find that were similar to those of your influential teacher? Which were different? Why do you think these similarities and differences are present?

STUDENTS' PERCEPTION OF INFLUENTIAL TEACHERS

Table 1-2 shows what influential teachers believe about themselves. Research also reveals students' perceptions of these influential teachers. This research suggests that between kindergarten and grade twelve, high achievers have, on the average, 3.2 influential teachers, while low achievers have only 1.5 such teachers. Regardless of achievement level, however, high and low achievers perceive their teachers in almost identical ways. Their perceptions include the following: Influential teachers use clearly formulated instructional strategies with clear instructional goals, plans, and monitoring for student feedback; these features are readily apparent and consistently used throughout their teaching lessons. Influential teachers also have in-depth knowledge of reading and writing processes as well as content knowledge, and they understand how to teach these processes effectively in their classrooms. They also frequently tap internal student motivation stimulating intellectual curiosity, exploring students' self-understanding, using aesthetic imagery and expression, and motivating the desire to solve problems. Influential teachers place little emphasis on external student motivation, such as using achievement pressure to "please the teacher."

These influential teacher characteristics represent the bedrock of good teaching. This chapter and those that follow will emphasize these characteristics and develop classroom-tested instructional strategies designed to help you understand critical reading and writing processes and to teach these processes effectively in your classroom. The goal is not only to assist you to become an outstanding reading and writing teacher but to become an *influential reading and writing teacher* as well.

SHARED BELIEFS OF INFLUENTIAL TEACHERS ABOUT TEACHING

1. Personal Characteristics:
— energy, commitment, passion
— warmth and caring
— flexibility
— high expectations of self

2. Understand Learner Potential:
— sensitive to individual needs, motivations, and aptitudes
— understands "where students are"
— high demands on learners

3. Attitude Toward Subject:
— enthusiasm
— goal to create intellectual excitement
— consider alternative point of view

4. Life Adjustment:
— concern with student as a person
— attentive to academic problems and personal problems

5. Quality of Instruction:
— makes material personally relevant
— stresses basic communication: clear writing, comprehension of text material, critical thinking
— teaching is logical and strategy oriented:
(a) clear statement of problem
(b) use of familiar concrete examples
(c) extension to more abstract examples
(d) analysis of abstract concepts involved
(e) application of concepts to new contexts
— goal to identify issues that should be considered before conclusions are reached
— need to engage students in the process of intellectual discovery

TABLE 1-2

YOUR TEACHING EXPECTATIONS

You have undoubtedly given careful thought to your choice of teaching as a career. Whether you teach in a metropolitan inner-city classroom with students who speak widely diverse dialects or languages, or in a suburban—or possibly rural—classroom where the language forms used are more homogeneous, you will most certainly find students in any given classroom who differ considerably in reading and writing achievement. Parental interest and participation in schools will vary from close cooperation and assistance to none.

Socioeconomic conditions will also vary, with family incomes ranging from affluence to poverty. Extraordinary diversity typifies U.S. schools; however, for too many children, life at home makes life at school difficult at best. A recent report from the Select Committee on Children, Youth and Families (Farrell, 1991) indicates that

- One in five children lives in poverty.

- One in four lives with only one parent.

- Five hundred thousand children are born each year to teen-age mothers unprepared for parenthood.

- Some 8.3 million children lack health insurance.

- Forty percent are at risk of failing in school.

For many children these factors define the reality they face at home and in school. Such factors define equally the reality that teachers often face as they plan for and direct learning experiences for children.

THE NATIONAL PICTURE OF ELEMENTARY READING INSTRUCTION

A quick "snapshot" impression of reading across the nation can be developed from the recent *NAEP 1992 Reading Report Card for the Nation and the States* (Mullis, Campbell, & Farstrup, 1993). This study describes reader experiences, achievement, and instructional emphasis at grades four, eight, and twelve. The following information, based on approximately 6,300 fourth-grade students and their teachers in over 527 schools, brings the fourth-grade reader into focus and provides insight into reading instruction at the elementary school level.

Achievement Differences

- Large differences were found in reading proficiency of fourth-graders across ethnic groups and type of community. White and Asian/Pacific Islander students achieved higher than African-American, Latino, and Native American students; advantaged urban students achieved much higher than disadvantaged urban or rural students.

Instructional Approaches

- Instruction for 85 percent of fourth-grade students was based in part on a basal reader approach, with 36 percent of the classrooms relying solely on this approach. Some aspect of whole language instruction was used with 82 percent of the students and literature-based reading instruction received moderate emphasis in 88 percent of the classrooms.

11

- Moderate (50 percent) or heavy (11 percent) emphasis on phonics instruction was found in 61 percent of the classrooms.

- According to the fourth-grade teachers, two-thirds of the students read silently and were provided time to read self-selected books almost daily.

Instructional Time Allocation

- Time allocated to reading instruction included thirty to forty-five minutes per day for approximately one-third of the students, sixty minutes for about one-half; the remaining students received ninety minutes or more.

Workbooks and Skill Sheets Use

- Workbook and skill sheet assignments were used daily or weekly for 81 percent of the students. Writing about reading was used with 72 percent of the students on a daily or weekly basis.

Television vs. Reading

- Students were found to prefer television to books, with 60 percent of the fourth-graders watching three or more hours of television each day while only 44 percent reported reading for pleasure on a daily basis. Those students who watched television four hours or more per day (44 percent) were found to have the lowest average reading proficiency.

Decreasing Reading Interest with Age

- Interest in reading decreased as students progressed through the grades. Forty-four percent of the fourth-grade students reported reading for fun almost every day, but this was the case for only 25 percent of the eighth and twelfth graders.

Findings from a previous, but similar, nationwide study, *Learning to Read in Our Nation's Schools* (Langer, Applebee, Mullis, & Foertsch, 1990) supports many of these findings. This study, based on approximately 4,500 fourth-grade students in over 300 schools, provides important insight into students' home environments, access to reading materials, skill emphasis, grouping practices, and teacher autonomy.

Home Environment Support

- The higher achieving fourth-graders reported home environ-ments that emphasized academic achievement reflected by higher levels of attendance in preschool and kindergarten, more home-work, and more required reading.

Access to Reading Materials

- Fourth-graders who had access to reading material in their homes, such as books and magazines of their own, had higher reading proficiency than students who did not report access to such materials.

Specific Skill Instruction

- According to the fourth-grade teachers, 50 percent of their students received daily comprehension skill emphasis, 28 percent received word analysis skill emphasis, 40 percent received vocabulary instruction, and 38 percent had opportunity to read aloud. Fifty-seven percent of the teachers reported that they read daily to their students.

Reading Groups

- For reading instruction, 79 percent of the fourth-graders were assigned to ability-based reading groups. Approximately one hour was spent each day in reading instruction with about 30 minutes in small groups. Even so, 28 percent of the students were never or rarely asked to discuss their reading in small groups.

Who Decides What to Teach

- Teachers report considerable autonomy in decisions about sequence of classroom instruction, but little in their choices of what to teach. Teachers working in low socioeconomic urban schools reported more limited autonomy than other teachers.

MAKING SENSE OF THE FINDINGS

These findings support the close connection between the fourth-grade students' reading success in the classroom, their home literacy experiences and socioeconomic conditions, and instructional practice in schools. It thus becomes very important to recognize and meet the specific instructional needs of children from varied cultural backgrounds and socioeconomic conditions. While the fourth-grade teachers appear to have provided emphasis on comprehension, word analysis skills, and vocabulary development, using various instructional approaches, it is clear that very heavy reliance is still placed on the use of workbooks and worksheets. The most recent of the two studies (Mullis, Campbell, & Farstrup, 1993) indicates that teachers are emphasizing greater integration of reading and language processes by encouraging students to write about reading. It would appear, however, on the basis of the earlier nationwide study (Langer, Applebee, Mullis, &

Foertsch, 1990) that higher-level reasoning activities, such as discussing and analyzing what students have read, received minimal emphasis. These findings indicate that much more emphasis is needed in providing opportunity to develop higher-level reasoning skills and the use of small group and teacher-directed discussions involving both reading and writing experiences. These two studies highlight the importance of developing reading proficiency as an important goal of instruction, but the findings related to decreasing reading interests across grades four, eight, and twelve emphasize the equally critical need to build strong reading interest and motivation so that students will maintain the desire to read.

A Preview of Chapters Ahead

Your commitment to meeting the range of student needs in your classroom is the first important step in becoming an influential reading and writing teacher. The discussion in chapters that follow is designed to support this commitment by introducing and developing new knowledge and instructional strategies that will lead to effective reading and writing instruction.

Reading and Writing Processes

The next chapter, Chapter 2, "Coming to Know the Reading and Writing Processes: Understanding Meaning Making," will introduce you to reading and writing processes. You will examine the development of language background knowledge in the preschool and elementary school years. Your understanding of reading as an interactive meaning construction process which directly involves the reader's previous experience and background knowledge is central to the chapter. The importance of reader motivation, reading comprehension strategies, and meaning monitoring strategies in comprehending and using printed text are also emphasized.

Your role as the classroom teacher becomes central to the development of reading and writing competencies as you come to understand the nature of these processes and create the classroom environment for teaching reading and writing.

Beginning Reading and Writing Steps

Chapter 3, "Understanding the Beginning Steps: Early Reading and Writing Development," develops the nature of reading and writing instruction for the kindergarten and first-grade student. This includes introducing your students to the culture of the classroom, concept development, oral language experiences, and early reading and writing development.

Of central importance to this chapter is understanding that the kindergarten and first-grade student is a meaning maker and hypothesis tester. The discussion includes developmental differences in students at these levels, and influences of the home and school environment on meaning making.

Instructional strategies are introduced for developing language and concepts critical to instruction and group participation, creating picture and print awareness in early reading, composing and recording ideas, forming sense of story and narrative, building positive attitudes toward reading and writing development, and using informal reading and writing assessment. Specific activities range from the use of language experience charts and big books to shared book experiences and the Directed Listening-Thinking Activity (DL-TA).

While Chapter 3 is of critical importance to you as the kindergarten and first-grade teacher, it is also of importance should you teach in the later grades, not only in order to understand the previous instructional experiences your students will have had but to provide effective instruction for those students who will still be achieving at the beginning levels in your classroom.

READING COMPREHENSION

Chapter 4, "Guiding Reading Comprehension: Using Instructional Strategies to Develop Higher-Level Thinking," provides an important introduction and guide to your reading comprehension program from kindergarten through grade six. Emphasis is placed on levels of thinking, comprehension skills, and questioning and discussion strategies designed to foster higher-level thinking. Two widely used group reading approaches, the Directed Reading-Thinking Activity (DR-TA) and the Directed Reading Activity (DRA) are introduced.

Five key instructional strategies are developed to target specific aspects of comprehension instruction. These include the PreReading Plan (PReP) to activate prior knowledge; the Question-Answer Relationships (QAR) to focus on thinking demands and information sources in questions; the Reciprocal Questioning (ReQuest) and Reciprocal Teaching strategies to develop teacher modeling in forming questions, setting purpose, and integrating information; and the Group Mapping Activity (GMA), which uses graphic representations to help students integrate and synthesize information.

This chapter focuses for the most part on comprehension development using narrative text, while comprehending expository text is emphasized in Chapter 9. The important need to develop comprehension and higher-level thinking skills has been spotlighted again and again, in national commission reports and national survey evaluation research (Goodlad, 1990; Langer et al., 1990; The Holmes Forum, 1991). The discussion in this chapter provides a foundation enabling you develop a highly effective comprehension and higher-level thinking program for your students.

VOCABULARY DEVELOPMENT

Chapter 5, "Building Vocabulary and Comprehension Connections," develops an understanding of vocabulary instruction and the importance of connecting new concepts to students' prior knowledge. Key principles of vocabulary instruction are developed to assist you in understanding the relationship between vocabulary and comprehension and in determining whether they should be developed before, during, or after the story. The importance of teaching vocabulary in context and the development of the reader's independent meaning construction is emphasized throughout the chapter. Specific instructional strategies include Teaching Vocabulary in Context (TVC), concept webs, semantic maps, semantic feature analysis, Vocabulary Self-Collection Strategy (VSS), and vocabulary logs and journals.

The discussion in this chapter stresses the importance of active learning and personal motivation as critical elements in successful vocabulary instruction. Vocabulary teaching should not only enhance children's comprehension of text but should also develop high interest and curiosity about new words.

USING CHILDREN'S LITERATURE

Chapter 6, "Using Literature and Reader Response to Enhance Attitudes and Comprehension," introduces you to children's literature and the importance of reader response as the catalyst for highly motivated reading. The use of an aesthetic instructional stance designed to build internal reader motivation, such as intellectual curiosity and self-understanding, is emphasized.

This chapter develops an understanding of how to select high-interest children's literature and organize the classroom literature and reading center. The strengths and limitations of the literature-based instruction, basal reader instruction, and combined approaches to using children's literature are introduced. Specific instructional strategies developed include reading aloud, storytelling, reader response and literature response journals, sharing responses about books, Sustained Silent Reading (SSR), Readers Theatre, the Investigative Questioning Procedure (InQuest), and thematic units. The informal evaluation of children's progress in responding to literature is developed.

The important role of children's literature in the elementary-grade reading program becomes clear as you understand the nature of reader motivation and reader response. This discussion is especially important in light of the many state literature initiatives that have developed throughout the country (*Handbook for Planning an Effective Literature Program*, 1987).

INTEGRATING WRITING WITH READING

Chapter 7, "Guiding Children's Writing," explores children's writing development from their very early writing and experimentation with written language through continued writing experiences and instruction in elementary school. The chapter presents a process writing approach and discusses at length how to implement the writing workshop and project-based or theme cycle-based writing. The chapter also addresses instructional issues regarding children's spelling and handwriting development.

Word Analysis Skill Strategies

Chapter 8, "Using Word Analysis Strategies to Develop Reader Independence: Transforming Print to Meaning," builds your understanding of word analysis skill strategies essential for the elementary grades. The effective, and eventual automatic, use of letter-sound correspondences, letter patterns, syllable units, and context clues is critical for rapid and independent reading by your students. The discussion stresses the importance of reading instruction that introduces word analysis skills in a natural print context which provides the student immediate feedback and focuses attention on meaning.

This chapter is important to you if you use a basal reader anthology approach that has sequenced word analysis skills and prewritten instructional activities. But it is especially important if you elect to design and tailor your own word analysis program using a literature-based or whole language instructional approach.

Content Area Reading and Reference Skill

Chapter 9, "Developing Children's Literacy Abilities in Content Areas," explores ways for teachers to guide children's reading and writing in subject areas. Specific instructional strategies are emphasized including a combination of the content Directed Reading-Thinking Activity (Content DR-TA), Group Mapping Activity (GMA), and the Vocabulary Self-Collection Strategy (VSS). Additional strategies include the Know-Want to Know-Learned Plus (K-W-L Plus), the Directed Inquiry Activity (DIA), and elements of the writing workshop.

The central focus of this chapter is that children construct meaning as they read and write; content learning is thus increased as children pursue topics of interest and respond in writing to text. Writing here is viewed as more than simply a means for recording what is learned; rather, it is a means for extending the learning itself. Theme cycles, project-based learning, the Foxfire approach, and visual literacy projects are recommended as ways to bring reading, writing, and subject matter learning into an integrated whole. A final discussion in this chapter explores study skills as important, but not in themselves sufficient, components in content area learning.

Language and Cultural Diversity

In Chapter 10, "Understanding Language, Cultural, and Achievement Diversity in the Classroom," attention is given to our attitudes toward students who have dialects and languages different from our own. The discussion then develops specific classroom-based strategies and activities that have been effectively used in teaching reading and writing skills to bilingual students from diverse and different language and cultural backgrounds. These include sheltered English and vocabulary journals (to develop background and conceptual knowledge), the Directed Listening-Thinking

Activity and Reciprocal Teaching (to construct and monitor meaning), and Literature Response Journals and the use of multicultural/multiethnic literature (to motivate individual and group response).

This chapter also emphasizes your important role in working with students who have special needs, ranging from physical diversity to giftedness.

EVALUATION AND ASSESSMENT

Chapter 11, "Evaluating Children's Progress in Reading and Writing," will help you become proficient in using informal observations in your teaching to meet the instructional needs of students. Special attention is given to the instructional use of information gathered from informal group discussions and classroom reading and writing experiences. The discussion develops the use of the informal reading inventory and miscue analysis and the use of portfolio evaluation, a relatively new evaluation approach. Key recommendations are presented to assist you in effective communication with parents regarding their children's progress.

Formal achievement testing, including values and limitations, is also discussed. The central focus of this discussion, however, is on the effective use of observations to provide information that can be used to plan and enhance the reading and literacy growth of your students.

THREE INSTRUCTIONAL APPROACHES

In Chapter 12, "Examining Instructional Approaches: Basal Reader, Literature-Based, Whole Language, and Supplementary Programs," you will be introduced to the three major approaches to literacy instruction used across the nation. This discussion develops the background and philosophy that underlie each of these approaches and shows how they work in the classroom. You will use your knowledge developed in the previous chapters as you come to understand these major approaches to reading instruction and learn how to adapt each to your classroom. The chapter coverage includes discussion of lesson plans, student literature anthologies, workbooks, core literature selections, and the use of previously discussed strategies and activities such as language-based stories, recording and sharing children's stories, oral story sharing, the writing workshop.

You will also find specific criteria identified to assist you in the selection of supplementary reading and writing programs, computer software programs, and in the adoption of textbooks.

This chapter will be of particular value in the event you find that one of these instructional approaches is mandated by your school or school district. It is thus of critical importance that you be familiar with the use of the basal reader, literature-based, and whole language instructional approaches. It is also important for you to understand how to integrate these approaches. For example, should you be in a school using a basal reader approach, you will need to understand how you can supplement this approach using concepts, ideas, and strategies from the literature-based and whole-language approaches.

CLASSROOM ORGANIZATION AND MANAGEMENT

Chapter 13, "Organizing and Managing Classrooms for Literacy Learning," presents classroom organization and management recommendations for early, beginning, and continuing readers. This chapter is also closely linked to Chapter 12 and develops organization and management structures for each of the three major approaches (basal reader, literature-based, and whole language). The chapter emphasizes that classroom organization and management in guiding children's reading and writing development involve far more than discipline; further, the chapter asserts that what teachers believe about how children learn has a powerful influence on organization and management issues—e.g., physical arrangement of the room, materials and equipment in the room, orchestration of classroom schedules and events, time allocation and use, and establishment of classroom rules and routines.

CONTINUING PROFESSIONAL GROWTH

In Chapter 14, "Continuing Professional Change and Growth: Reaching the Influential Teacher Goal," you are encouraged to remain open to new ideas that will continue to enhance your teaching effectiveness in reading and writing development. This discussion explains the process of personal change and growth and encourages you to reflect on your own teaching philosophy and belief system. The importance of developing a personal support system through personal knowledge and ingenuity, influential peer teachers, your principal, and supportive parents is stressed.

We also encourage you to continue your professional growth and connections through in-service and staff development, professional organizations, and continuing education. Finally, this chapter is designed to assist you in identifying your areas of greatest strength and your need-emphasis areas that will lead to the professional goal of becoming an influential teacher—a teacher who will have a significant influence on the personal and academic lives of your children.

THE CHALLENGE—BECOMING AN INFLUENTIAL TEACHER

We have now set the goal for you to become an influential reading and writing teacher. Your personal motivation and drive to achieve this goal will take the form of a personal commitment to the children you teach. The plan leading to this goal will be implemented through the content of your courses and your instructors, and will be supported by the ideas, experiences, and instructional strategies developed in this text. Your direct experience with

An Influential Teacher

students in real classrooms will enable you to develop and implement many of these ideas and further define your personal instructional belief system. It will be important for you to monitor constantly the ideas and strategies presented in your courses and in the chapters that follow by testing them against the reality of your experiences with students. You will develop confidence in yourself and in your emerging teaching belief system as this process continues.

A TEACHER'S BELIEF

The following statement from one teacher expresses the enthusiasm, vitality, and caring that are so important in becoming an influential teacher.

> *I've been teaching for 15 years and each year gets better and better. I want to be where I am. I love the students. I think that they are the best show in town and I tell them that over and over again. I keep my youth and optimism because of them. They contribute far more to my life than anybody can possibly imagine.*
>
> *What I give, I'm sure, is minimal next to what I receive. Teaching for me is an avocation, not a vocation. I feel that people who are burnt out ought to get out. They don't belong with children.*

Children are the best that any society has. They are the future and they deserve the best of everything. If we, as teachers, can't give them that, then we should find other work to do. The salaries certainly don't compensate for the commitment involved—but, I am a teacher.

DOUBLE ENTRY JOURNAL

Go back to the Double Entry Journal exercise you completed before reading this text. Look at your recollections of early reading and writing experiences in school. Consider also the question we asked in the middle of the chapter: for you to identify influential teachers. Jot down the names of your primary-grade teachers and what you remember about them. Were any of these teachers on your list of influential teachers? Why or why not? What do your early experiences reading and writing in school tell you about your primary-grade teacher's views (theories) about children's learning? List those beside each teacher's name. How do these views coincide with or differ from your own? Share your ideas with a friend.

Supporting Activities

1. Recall your earliest memories of reading a full-length book and describe what you remember about the experience and the book. Do you recall your emotional response to this literature? Identify your book and share your memories with a class partner and/or briefly record them in a diary or journal.

2. Briefly examine each of the items in the Personal Belief System checklist on p. 23, indicating your level of agreement or disagreement. Compare your responses with a class partner and explore your reasons for agreement or disagreement on each item.

3. Return to your notes on your memories of your influential teacher (or teachers). Consider the way in which this teacher (or teachers) may have influenced your personal beliefs about teaching effectiveness. How are your beliefs similar? How are they different?

4. Briefly review our discussion of "The National Picture of Elementary Reading Instruction." Do these findings surprise you? Why or why not? How can we more effectively develop higher-level reasoning skills in our classroom instruction? Share your ideas with a class partner.

IDENTIFYING MY PERSONAL BELIEF SYSTEM:
TEACHING READING AND WRITING SKILLS

	Agree			Disagree	
1. Teaching reading is, for the most part, helping students understand the relationship between letters and sounds.	1	2	3	4	5
2. Using home and life experiences of the student is very important in helping students comprehend text.	1	2	3	4	5
3. It is important to make reading material personally relevant to each student.	1	2	3	4	5
4. Reading and writing are two very different skills and should not be taught in conjunction with each other.	1	2	3	4	5
5. High achievement expectation is important if students are to achieve at the optimal level.	1	2	3	4	5
6. Monitoring and feedback on student reading and writing responses is important for student success.	1	2	3	4	5
7. Students who speak a second language will have more difficulty learning to read than those who speak only English.	1	2	3	4	5
8. Nonverbal responses of students deserve little consideration in small group discussion.	1	2	3	4	5
9. Reading motivation can best be developed by providing clear signals indicating what response the teacher wants.	1	2	3	4	5
10. Clear, definite teaching goals and plans are critical for good reading and writing instruction.	1	2	3	4	5
11. Student comprehension can be greatly enhanced by engaging students in the process of intellectual discovery.	1	2	3	4	5
12. Exhibiting a positive attitude toward reading and writing or skills being taught is the mark of a good teacher.	1	2	3	4	5

Anderson, R. C. (1985). Role of the reader's schema in comprehension, learning, and memory. In H. Singer & R. B. Ruddell (Eds.), *Theoretical models and process of reading* (3rd ed.) (pp. 372–384). Newark, DE: International Reading Association.

Applebee, A. N., Langer, J. A., Jenkins, L. B., Mullis, I. V. S., & Foertsch, M. A. (1990). *Learning to write in our nation's schools: Instruction and achievement in 1988 at grades 4, 8, and 12.* National Assessment of Educational Progress. Princeton, NJ: Educational Testing Service.

Au, K. H. (1980). Participation structures in reading lessons: Analysis of a culturally appropriate instructional event. *Anthropology and Education Quarterly, 11,* 91–115.

Beck, I., & McKeown, M. (1991). Conditions of vocabulary acquisition. In R. Barr, M. L. Kamil, P. Mosenthal, & P. D. Pearson (Eds.), *Handbook of reading research, Volume II* (pp. 789–814). New York: Longman.

Bloome, D. (1991). Anthropology and research on teaching the English language arts. In J. Flood, J. M. Jensen, D. Lapp, & J. R. Squire (Eds.), *Handbook of research on teaching the English language arts* (pp. 46–56). New York: Macmillan.

Dyson, A. H. (1986). Children's early interpretations of writing: Expanding research perspectives. In D. B. Yaden & S. Templeton (Eds.), *Metalinguistic awareness and beginning literacy* (pp. 201–218). Portsmouth, NH: Heinemann.

Farrell, J. A. (1991, July 5). Congress united on tax breaks for children: Right, left agree parents need help. *San Francisco Examiner,* p. 8.

Goodlad, J. I. (1990). *Teachers for our nation's schools.* San Francisco, CA: Jossey-Bass Publishers.

Gumperz, J. J. (1981). Conversational inference and classroom learning. In J. L. Green & C. Wallat (Eds.), *Ethnography and language in educational settings.* Norwood, NJ: Ablex.

Haggard, M. R. (1989). Instructional strategies for developing student interest in content area subjects. In D. Lapp, J. Flood, & N. Farnan (Eds.), *Content area reading-learning: instructional strategies* (pp. 70–88). Englewood Cliffs, NJ: Prentice-Hall.

Handbook for planning an effective literature program. (1987). Sacramento, CA: California State Department of Education.

Heath, S. B. (1982). Questioning at home and at school: A comparative study. In G. Spindler (Ed.), *Doing the ethnography of schooling* (pp. 105–131). New York: Holt, Rinehart & Winston.

Langer, J. A., Applebee, A. N., Mullis, V. S., & Foertsch, M. A. (1990). *Learning to read in our nation's schools: Instruction and achievement in 1988 at grades 4, 8, and 12.* National Assessment of Educational Progress. Princeton, NJ: Educational Testing Service.

Menyuk, P. (1991). Linguistics and teaching the language arts. In J. Flood, J. M. Jensen, D. Lapp, & J. R. Squire (Eds.), *Handbook of research on teaching the English language arts* (pp. 24–29). New York: Macmillan.

Mullis, I. V. S., Campbell, J. R., & Farstrup, A. E. (1993). *NAEP 1992 reading report card for the nation and the states.* Washington, DC: Office of Educational Research and Improvement.

Ogbu, J. U. (1983). Literacy and Schooling in subordinate cultures: the case of black Americans. In D. P. Resnick (Ed.), *Literacy in historical perspective* (pp. 129–153). Washington, DC: Library of Congress.

Piaget, J. (1952). *The origins of intelligence in children.* New York: International University Press.

Purcell-Gates, V. (1988). Lexical and syntactic knowledge of written narrative held by well-read-to kindergartners and second graders. *Research in the Teaching of English, 22*(2), 128–160.

Rosenblatt, L. M. (1994). The transactional theory of reading and writing. In R. B. Ruddell, M. R. Ruddell, & H. Singer (Eds.), *Theoretical models and processes of reading* (4th ed.) (pp. 1057–1092). Newark, DE: International Reading Association.

Ruddell, R. B. (1992). A whole language and literature perspective: Creating a meaning making instructional environment. *Language Arts, 69,* 612–620.

Ruddell, R. B., Draheim, M., & Barnes, J. (1990). A comparative study of the teaching effectiveness of influential and noninfluential teachers and reading comprehension development. In J. Zutell & S. McCormick (Eds.), *Literacy theory and research: Analyses from multiple paradigms,* 39th Yearbook of the National Reading Conference (pp. 153–163). Chicago, IL: National Reading Conference.

Ruddell, R. B., & Haggard, M. R. (1982). Influential teachers: Characteristics and classroom performance. In J. A. Niles & L. A. Harris (Eds.), *New inquiries in reading research and instruction,* 31st Yearbook of the National Reading Conference (pp. 227–231). Rochester, NY: National Reading Conference.

Ruddell, R. B., & Harris P. (1989). A study of the relationship between influential teachers' prior knowledge and beliefs and teaching effectiveness: Developing higher order thinking in content areas. In S. McCormick & J. Zutell (Eds.), *Cognitive and social perspectives for literacy research and instruction,* 38th Yearbook of the National Reading Conference (pp. 461–472). Chicago, IL: National Reading Conference.

Ruddell, R. B., & Kern, R. B. (1986). The development of belief systems and teaching effectiveness of influential teachers. In M. P. Douglas (Ed.), *Reading: The quest for meaning* (pp. 133–150). Claremont, CA: Claremont Graduate School Yearbook.

Ruddell, R. B., & Ruddell, M. R. (1994). Language acquisition and literacy processes. In R. B. Ruddell, M. R. Ruddell, & H. Singer (Eds.), *Theoretical models and processes of reading* (4th ed.) (pp. 83–103). Newark, DE: International Reading Association.

Schallert, D. L. (1991). The contribution of psychology to teaching the language arts. In J. Flood, J. M. Jensen, D. Lapp, & J. R. Squire (Eds.), *Handbook of research on teaching the English language arts* (pp. 30–39). New York: Macmillan.

Sulzby, E. (1991). The development of the young child and the emergence of literacy. In J. Flood, J. M. Jensen, D. Lapp, & J. R. Squire (Eds.), *Handbook of research on teaching the English language arts* (pp. 273–285). New York: Macmillan.

Sulzby, E., & Teale, W. (1991). Emergent literacy. In R. Barr, M. L. Kamil, P. B. Mosenthal, & P. D. Pearson (Eds.), *Handbook of reading research, Volume II* (pp. 727–757). New York: Longman.

The Holmes Forum (1991). *The Holmes Group.* East Lansing, MI: The Holmes Group.

Tierney, R. J., Readence, J. E., & Dishner, E. K. (1990). *Reading strategies and practices, A compendium.* Boston: Allyn & Bacon.

Vygotsky, L. S. (1978). *Mind in society.* Cambridge, MA: Harvard University Press.

CHILDREN'S LITERATURE REFERENCES

Burnett, F. H. (1911). *The secret garden.* New York: Lippincott.

Cleary, B. (1968). *Ramona the pest.* New York: William Morrow.

Dahl, R. (1961). *James and the giant peach.* New York: Alfred A. Knopf.

Dalgliesh, A. (1952). *The bears on Hemlock Mountain.* New York: Charles Scriber's Sons.

Lewis, C. S. (1950). *The lion, the witch, and the wardrobe.* New York: Macmillan.

Rawlings, M. K. (1938). *The yearling.* New York: Charles Scribner's Sons.

Seuss, Dr. (1957). *The cat in the hat.* Boston: Houghton Mifflin.

White, E. B. (1952). *Charlotte's web.* New York: Harper & Row.

Wilder, L. I. (1935). *Little house on the prairie.* New York: Harper & Row.

COMING TO KNOW READING
AND WRITING PROCESSES:
UNDERSTANDING MEANING MAKING

DOUBLE ENTRY JOURNAL

Think for a moment about all the things you do as you read and write. Create two lists, one labeled "Reading" and the other one "Writing." Jot down everything you do while reading and writing. Now think about your very earliest literacy experiences—reading and writing you did even before you went to school perhaps. What did you do then as a reader and writer? Make two more lists for your "Early Reading" and "Early Writing." How was your early reading and writing the same as or different from your reading and writing today?

INTRODUCTION

Educators, philosophers, psychologists, and others have long been interested in how children learn to read and write. Nearly a century ago, Edmund Huey called reading the "most remarkable specific performance that civilization has learned in all its history" and challenged researchers and theorists to explain what people actually do when they read and comprehend language (1908).

Since Huey's pioneering work, we have made important progress toward understanding language and literacy processes. We now possess considerable knowledge about the nature of literacy acquisition and development, and have much information about effective language and literacy teaching practices (Anderson, Hiebert, Scott, & Wilkinson, 1985; Barr, Kamil, Mosenthal & Pearson, 1991; Flood, Jensen, Lapp, & Squire, 1991; Singer & Ruddell, 1985). Further, we understand that language knowledge and comprehension processing ability start at birth and grow rapidly through the preschool and elementary school years.

CHAPTER PURPOSE

Our purpose in this chapter is to develop an understanding of the knowledge processes that underlie language and literacy development and are thus of central importance to reading and writing instruction. Many of the ideas presented here will be revisited and developed in greater depth through instructional examples and teaching strategies in later chapters.

First, we'll explore expert reader competencies. Second, we will survey early language acquisition and explore the relationship of language acquisition and literacy development. Third, we will explore how background knowledge is organized and stored. Fourth, we will examine the role of learner motivation on persistence in reading and writing. Fifth, we will discuss comprehension strategies readers use to process and understand different types of text. And finally, we will conclude the chapter through a synthesis of the important principles underlying literacy instruction. In this conclusion, we will examine an interactive teaching model or representation of the reading and writing processes. The principles and the teaching model will serve as the underpinning for your teaching and the framework for our discussion of reading and writing instruction in the subsequent chapters.

EXPERT READER COMPETENCIES

Let us begin our discussion with the assertion from Chapter 1 that you are an expert reader. As a result, you have developed special competencies that enable you to construct meaning from print. This can be quickly illustrated. Read the following passage with the goal of comprehension or making meaning. Before you read the passage, however, look at the four questions that follow it. Be ready to discuss the last question. As you read the passage, reflect on the processes that you are using in your attempt to understand the passage content.

The Wimmy Wuggen and the Moggy Tor

Once upon a time, a wimmy Wuggen zonked into the grabbet. Zhe was grolling for poft because zhe was very blongby.

The wimmy Wuggen grolled and grolled until zhe motted a moggy Tor.

Zhe glind to the moggy Tor, "Ik am blongby and grolling for poft. Do yum noff mehre ik can gine some poft?"

"Kex," glind the Tor, "klom with ne wimmy Wuggen. Ik have lodz of poft in ni bove."

Now, respond to the following questions:

1. Where did the wimmy Wuggen zonk?
2. Why was zhe grolling for poft?
3. Did the moggy Tor help the Wuggen? Why do you think so?
4. What would you do if you were the wimmy Wuggen? Why?

A careful look at your responses will reveal some interesting insights about the processes you used as you read and made sense of the passage.

WORD ANALYSIS

Because you are an expert reader, the word analysis process you used in transforming the print to meaning was largely an automatic one. You moved swiftly from left to right across the page, activating your well-integrated knowledge of letter-sound and letter-pattern–sound-pattern relationships. You easily processed the print in the words, using your familiarity with English spelling patterns. Capital letter and sentence markers were also processed at an automatic level to identify meaning-bearing units, as were quotation marks signaling conversational units.

MEANING CLUES

You were highly effective in using two types of meaning clues from your expert language background. The first clue is found in relational meanings (e.g., *a* and *the* signaling that a noun will follow, *-ed* and *-ing* signaling a verb, etc.). The second clue involves instant grasp of word meaning from the sentence context based on your knowledge of syntax, or sentence structure. In the sentence, "Zhe was grolling for poft because zhe was very blongby," you were able to infer that *grolling* is a verb, and *poft* is a noun. You may also have inferred that *grolling* could mean *looking* and *poft* could mean food, at least as a hypothesis. You may have held this inference in mind and tested it as you continued reading.

STORY SCHEMATA

The story title, "The Wimmy Wuggen and the Moggy Tor," activated your background knowledge of a story schema. The title suggested the possibility that this was a story narrative (as opposed to an informational article or essay, for example) and that it involved two main story characters, the *wimmy Wuggen* and the *moggy Tor*. This assumption was reinforced with the opening words, "Once upon a time." These words triggered the expectation of a folktale schema, with story features such as simple characterization (e.g., good vs. bad) and folktale story plot; in fact, this story structure may have paralleled an old favorite folktale such as "The Fox and the Chicken." But perhaps it did not. In that case, it became necessary for you to use your general folktale schema to predict the possible story outcome.

INTERNAL AND EXTERNAL MOTIVATION

Your motivation for constructing meaning for "The Wimmy Wuggen and the Moggy Tor" came from two sources. The first is the internal motivation of intellectual curiosity—to see if you really could make sense of the story. The second is external motivation, which may be driven by the expectation that your instructor and/or your peers will read the story and be ready to discuss the last question (and you wouldn't be ready if you hadn't read the story yourself).

HYPOTHESIS FORMATION

The interactive nature of reading and language processing is evident in your use of various aspects of your language background to form tentative hypotheses. Some of these hypotheses were about words, e.g., *grolling, poft.* Some were about sentences, "Ik have lodz of poft in ni bove." And some had to do with story schema, e.g., folktale characteristics. These hypotheses were tested as the meaning-making process continued. Eventually, you reached some level of meaning closure for the text.

COMPREHENSION STRATEGIES

Finally, your response to each of the four questions involved different comprehension strategies. Each question required a different level of comprehension processing and thinking. You also monitored your responses to the questions by testing their "correctness" against the information in the passage and your story expectations, based on your background knowledge.

Question 1 from the list involved use of sentence structure and simple recall or rereading of the story to identify "*into the grabbet.*" The second question required inference, relying on the possibility that the word "*blongby*" might translate to "*hungry,*" or simply using the word "*because,*" signaling causation to identify "*because zhe was blongby.*"

Your response to the third question required story inference and interpretation in which you may have used your prior knowledge of a story like "The Fox and the Chicken" to predict or conclude the event of the Wuggen's unhappy end and the Tor's gastronomic enjoyment. If this prior knowledge was not present, you may have used an alternative folktale schema to predict a happy outcome for both, with the Tor providing poft, i.e., food, for the Wuggen. The fourth question required more involved thinking of a problem-solving nature, as you applied the story information in a personal way, placing yourself in the role of the wimmy Wuggen, using your expectations based on the story structure, activating your belief about the intent of the muggy Tor at this point in the story, and then explaining what you would do and why.

SIX KEY COMPONENTS OF EXPERT READER COMPETENCIES

This brief introspective reading experience demonstrates how expert readers use six key components in the reading process:

1. Expert readers use print-to-meaning word analysis knowledge, consisting of letter-sound and letter-pattern–sound-pattern relationships, as well as visual meaning markers, to assist in constructing meaning. This process is for the most part automatic.

2. Expert readers possess language knowledge that enables them to infer meaning from relational and lexical elements within and across sentences.

3. Expert readers possess a literacy background and prior story knowledge that they draw upon to identify a story schema, such as folktale, which is helpful in inferring word and story meaning basic to understanding the story and story outcome.

4. Expert readers possess reading motivation, both internal and external, supporting their persistence and continued reading in the process of making meaning.

5. Expert readers' processing of text is interactive and involves meaning making using word, sentence, and story structure. This enables them to reach meaning closure and arrive at a conclusion about the story.

6. Expert readers are effective in drawing on comprehension strategies that enable them to use different levels of thinking (from simple recall to high-level inference) and monitor meaning construction in light of background knowledge, reading objective, and expected outcome.

READING EXPERTISE

This discussion focuses on the abilities and functioning of expert readers who have developed the art and skill of meaning making through years of print, language, and literacy experience. But what level of reading and writing expertise can be expected of children in kindergarten and grades one through six? This will depend on a variety of factors, ranging from the literacy environment in students' homes and communities to instructional experiences that students have encountered at school. Whatever the influence of such factors, however, you can be sure that your classroom of thirty to forty students will contain children with widely varying literacy abilities and achievements. Your role will be to adjust your instructional program to meet the learning needs of each of your students.

CHILDREN'S KNOWLEDGE BASE FOR LITERACY DEVELOPMENT

ORAL LANGUAGE DEVELOPMENT

Acquiring language is one of the most complex tasks human beings will ever accomplish, yet as adult, experienced language users we have little or no memory of how we accomplished it. Despite its complexity the process of language acquisition is a very natural one. It is most strongly influenced by the language used at home, and is well under way in infancy.

DEVELOPING SOUND OR PHONOLOGICAL CONTROL

By the time they enter school, children have mastered the great majority of sounds that comprise the phonological system of their native language (Ervin & Miller, 1963; McCarthy, 1954; Templin, 1957). In English language acquisition, the vowel sounds are acquired first, and in fact most vowels and several initial and final consonants, such as /m, n, p, t /, and /f/, have developed by age three. A few consonants, such as /v/ and /th / develop as late as age six or seven (Templin, 1957). Most native English-speaking children, however, can produce the great majority of English sounds by age five or six.

Children's sound systems appear to be acquired largely independent of vocabulary items (Miller, 1967). Children rely initially on sound contrasts between consonants and vowels, for example /p/ and /ă /, and consonant contrasts such as /p/ and /b/. The use of these contrasts will be familiar to you if you have observed very young children forming sounds, babbling, and playing with language. By using a comparatively small number of contrasts, children come to learn most of the sounds of the language in their homes.

DEVELOPING GRAMMATICAL AND LANGUAGE PATTERN CONTROL

Grammatical Control

In addition to mastery of the sound system, children's grammatical sense is also well along by the time they enter the early grades. The learning process in early language development seems to include some degree of imitation, but more important the ability to generalize—to apply language principals to whole categories of language structures—for example, learning how to create plural nouns. In the process, children overgeneralize when dealing initially with irregular English language forms. So, after learning to form the plural "blocks" from "block," children generalize to "toys" and "dogs"; some weeks later, they (over)generalize to "foots" for *feet*, "mans" for *men*, and "sheeps" for *sheep*. When they begin to use the past tense of regular verbs, such as *walked* and *watched*, children subsequently overgeneralize in the use of irregular verb forms such as "breaked" for *broke* and "runded" for *ran* (Miller & Ervin, 1963).

The order of acquisition for this aspect of language growth appears to be highly consistent and patterned as children progress through four developmental stages. These stages are (1) little or no use of a particular word form, (2) sporadic use, (3) overregularization (or overgeneralization), and (4) adult-like use (Anderson & Freebody, 1985; Brown, 1973; Cazden, 1968; DeVilliers & DeVilliers, 1973). The important point here is that *children's ability to generalize and extend these generalizations in creating other language forms is basic to language learning* and, further, that overgeneralization is a natural part of this process.

Syntactical Control

The control of language patterns progresses rapidly by the preschool and primary-grade levels. Children at these levels are not only able to comprehend complex sentences but also to produce expanded, elaborated, and transformed sentences (Chomsky, 1969; Fraser, Bellugi, & Brown, 1963; Loban, 1976; O'Donnell, Griffin, & Norris, 1967; Strickland, 1962).

Children's progress in forming sentences moves from single words ("doggie"), to telegraphic speech ("See doggie"), to a high degree of control by the age of four or five years ("Ooh, look at the doggie"). Telegraphic speech such as "Where go?" "Where Mommie?" "Want cookie," "No bib," and "See doggie" illustrate normal syntactic patterning in early language development. Such utterances consist of "pivot" words, like *where, want,* and *see,* and "remainder" words, such as *go, Mommie, cookie,* and *doggie.* The pivot words occur with high frequency and correspond to adult word classes such as determiners, e.g., *that,* and adverbs, e.g., *where.* The remainder words occur with much lower frequency and will later correspond to noun, verb, and adjective classes in adult language (Ervin & Miller, 1963).

Following the development of two-word utterances children's telegraphic speech expands rapidly, so that within one or two years their sentences reach a high degree of complexity, with control over prepositions, conjunctions, plural forms for nouns, and tenses for verbs. Grammatical operations now provide for use of questions, negatives, and infinitives (Miller, 1967).

Development of children's syntactical control, however, extends well into and even beyond the elementary grades. Menyuk (1963) and Chomsky (1969) have identified developmental components in children's syntax extending from nursery school into the early elementary grades. Menyuk noted that even in first grade some patterns such as "if" and "so" clauses, and perfect tenses are still in the process of development. DeStefano (1978) has demonstrated that throughout the elementary years, children's syntax continues to develop from multiple conjoined sentences such as, "I have a cat and he's black and he likes hot milk" to an embedded form, "My black cat likes hot milk." The developmental sequence for oral language syntax moves from simple constructions and run-on forms to more complex sub-ordination-type patterns (O'Donnell, Griffin, & Norris, 1967).

The developmental process for syntactical control, as with grammatical control, appears to be stagelike. Menyuk (1984) suggests three stages of syntactic development: (1) acquiring the ability to comprehend and produce sentences; (2) judging the correctness of the sentence forms; and (3) making corrections based on the intended meaning.

DEVELOPING VOCABULARY AND LEXICAL CONTROL

Piaget's Cognitive Stages

Children's vocabulary and conceptual development make enormous progress during the preschool years. During this period, youngsters form hundreds of concepts from common qualities or properties of objects and connect these features with the object name or vocabulary label. Piaget (1967) and Piagetian theorists (Sinclair-deZwart, 1969) view conceptual development and language as stemming from thought that originates as children move through four cognitive stages. These are: (1) the *sensorimotor stage*, ages 0–2, in which children have no concept of cause and effect; (2) the *preoperational thought stage*, ages 3–7, in which children use egocentric language and have some understanding of cause and effect; (3) the *concrete operations stage*, ages 9–11, in which egocentrism is reduced and children use logic and cause-and-effect reasoning in concrete problem situations; and (4) the *formal operations stage*, ages 12 and higher, in which children understand viewpoints of others and use abstract language and concepts.

Conceptual development in children, according to Piagetian thought, thus appears to move along a continuum from concrete, through semiconcrete or functional, to abstract levels (Feifel & Lorge, 1962). Russell and Saadeh's early work (1962) provides support for such a continuum in its contrast of student conceptual responses at grades three, six, and nine. Russell and Saadeh conclude that third-grade children favor concrete responses (e.g., "light" defined as a lamp turned on), while the older children favor functional and abstract responses (e.g., "light" defined as a bright object). In her extensive work on child language, Ervin-Tripp (1967) emphasizes that conceptual maturation moves from concrete referents to hierarchies of superordinates that may have rather vague features, e.g., *mammal, vertebrate*, to nonvisible referents, e.g., *politics, energy*.

Concept formation, using these mental operations that follow a general biological timetable, occurs in close proximity to and strongly influences language and lexical development. Children's direct experiences in exploring their environment, and their verbal interactions with peers and adults for the purpose of making sense of their experiences, contribute in a most important way to their language development.

Vygotsky's View—The Importance of Modeling and Social Interaction

While there is strong support for conceptual stages of development, as discussed above, it is important to remember that language learning and concept development are motivated and influenced by the social interactions of children with their peers and adults. Language learning is a social event strongly influenced both by social interactions and mental maturation. The interaction of these two factors accounts for the extraordinary growth of children's language (Genishi & Dyson, 1984).

As Vygotsky (1986) observes, preschoolers call a *cow* a *cow* because it has horns, a *calf* a *calf* because its horns are small, while a *dog* is called a *dog* because it is small and has no horns. He emphasizes that adult modeling and opportunity for children to interact verbally with adults are very important in the development of such concepts. Verbal interaction with mature speakers provides opportunities to test tentative notions about word meanings. Vygotsky conceptualized the "Zone of Proximal Development" (ZPD) to describe the distance between what an individual is able to do independently and what she or he is able to do with assistance. He considers social interaction to be critical within the ZPD, and states, "What a child can do in cooperation today, he can do alone tomorrow" (Vygotsky, 1986, p. 101).

Eventually, children conceptualize the arbitrary nature of language itself as they understand that word labels are assigned to concepts. For example, they grasp the concept that *dog* represents a pet that has four legs, a wagging tail, and barks. They also understand that some labels may represent several concepts, depending upon contextual use, e.g., *run*. The development of language as a representation of meaning is strongly influenced by the social and communication experiences of children.

Learning New Vocabulary

The motivation to learn new vocabulary is driven by the dual factors of the child's intellectual curiosity and the social nature and use of language. This is evident in Haggard's (now M. Ruddell) study of conditions that influence independent word learning (1980). Haggard identified four specific conditions in elementary school children's acquisition of new words. These consisted of (in order of frequency): (1) the word had an appealing sound or was perceived to be "adult," e.g., "I learned the word *fickle* because it rhymed with *pickle*"; (2) the word occurred in an incident involving strong emotion that often involved mispronunciation and/or embarrassment, e.g., *centrifugal* (pronounced "cen-tra-fu´-gal"), *horizon* (pronounced "hor´-a-zone"); (3) the word had immediate usefulness, frequently in a very personal sense, e.g., *room mother*, *appendectomy*; and (4) the word was common in peer-group usage, e.g., *wretched* from a class of children that called one child "Wretched Ritchie." In two of these categories, social interactions are prominent (numbers 2 and 4); in the other two, aspects of social interactions are implicit.

Another finding of this study that emphasizes social interactions is that once the meaning of a new word is determined, learners rehearse using the new word in a safe environment, such as among family and friends or in a classroom where word learning and exploration are valued, to complete the acquisition of the new word. The social nature of language learning is thus a strong motivating factor in children's language acquisition. This social motivation and opportunity for language interaction with others, combined with the mental maturation of children, leads to the rapid acquisition and control of language.

Written Language Acquisition and Language Development

Emergent Literacy

Our knowledge of written language acquisition has increased enormously over the past decade and has led to revised views of preschool children's language competence (Clay, 1983; Ruddell & Haggard, 1985; Ruddell & Ruddell, 1994) and their concepts about written language (Harste, Burke, & Woodward, 1982). Recent research has examined children's emergent literacy—the early writing and reading behaviors that signal the beginning of children's development into conventional writing and reading processes (Sulzby, 1991; Sulzby & Teale, 1991). Children begin with pictorial representation in their attempt to connect speech with written language and to understand the relationship between graphic symbols and sounds (Clay, 1975, 1983; Dyson, 1982; Ferreiro, 1978, 1986).

Whether they use standard symbols or not, preliterate youngsters produce writing that is contextually appropriate, ranging from vertically aligned grocery lists to paragraphed letters to a grandparent. Harste, Burke, and Woodward's seminal work (1982) demonstrated that children's writing and print awareness develops before formal schooling and, in fact, much earlier than we had previously thought. What we formerly considered to be scribbling and "looking at books," we now understand to be children's early literate behaviors. Harste, Woodward, and Burke, (1984) note distinctions between children's early writing and drawing (see Figure 2-1). They suggest that the separation of oral language development from written language development is an artificial one, and view literacy as part of a continuum of speech acts available to the functioning adult in a literate society. Thus, children's oral language development provides the foundation for their emergent literacy development.

Based on their extensive study of preschool children's written production, Harste, Burke, and Woodward (1982) conclude that (1) written language is

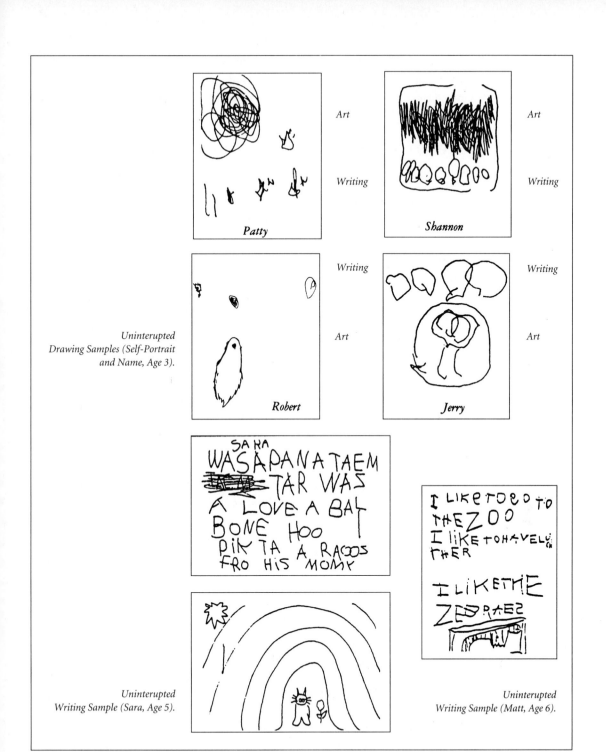

FIGURE 2-1

Children's Written Language Samples Illustrating Development Growth. (Reproduced with permission from Harste, Woodward, & Burke, 1984, pp. 94 and 96.)

learned naturally, just as is the case with oral language, (2) children in literate societies are involved at an early age in understanding and controlling print; and (3) children's perceptions of print are organized, systematic, and identifiable.

INVENTED SPELLING AND PATTERNS OF SPELLING GROWTH

Yet another facet of the recent work on emergent literacy is the study of children's invented spelling. Invented spelling is typical of most children at the preschool and kindergarten levels and extends well into the early grades as children gain control over the spelling system. Some people prefer the term "temporary spelling" to emphasize the transitory nature of invented spellings (Gillet & Temple, 1990). Invented spelling is found to be systematic, rule governed, and consistent in nature (Chomsky, 1971, 1979; Henderson & Beers, 1980; Read, 1971, 1975; Temple & Gillet, 1989). Charles Read's extensive work on the origin of invented spellings indicates that many invented spelling rules grow directly from children's attempts to map speech to print.

In addition, patterns of invented spelling development have been identified which children use as they progress toward conventional spelling (Temple & Gillet, 1989). The first pattern is *prephonemic spelling*. As illustrated in Figure 2-2, prephonemic spelling is made up of letters and letterlike forms arranged on horizontal lines, indicating awareness that words are made from letters. It is typical of kindergarteners, and many first-graders.

The second pattern is *early phonemic spelling* (see Figure 2-2), consisting of letters and letterlike forms in short consonant strings, indicating discovery of the alphabetic principle. This is typical of kindergarteners the very beginning reader, and most first-graders.

Then comes the third pattern, *letter-name spelling*, in which letters names are used to represent sounds in words (e.g., "h" used to represent "ch" because it is the only letter in the alphabet with the "ch" sound in its name, "aich"), indicating clear awareness of a symbol-sound relationship without a clear understanding of the full extent of that relationship. This pattern is also illustrated in Figure 2-2, and is typical of beginning readers who can read a little and most first- and many second-graders.

The fourth pattern is *transitional spelling*, in which letters are used to represent all sounds, and long and short vowel sounds are represented correctly, indicating that the spelling system is near completion. It is typical of more advanced readers who are still not fluent.

In pattern five, *derivational spelling*, letters are used to reflect rule-governed spelling patterns for vowel marking and consonant doubling. Stage five, however, also shows lack of awareness of relational patterns in words derived from the same base (as is seen in more mature spelling). Pattern five is typical of children and adults who have some fluency, but who have not read widely. Our awareness of these patterns is of value in understanding children's spelling progress and their growth in representing words in written form. While movement through the patterns is stagelike, children tend to move back and forth between patterns and/or exhibit elements of more than one pattern at a time.

WRITING GROWTH IN THE ELEMENTARY YEARS

The Early Primary Grades

Children's writing development increases steadily throughout the elementary school years, with early writing bearing close resemblance to spoken language (Hunt, 1970; Loban, 1976; O'Donnell, Griffin, & Norris, 1967). The content of kindergarten and first-grade children's writing is very egocentric in nature and is focused on the social self, family, friends, and their environment (Calkins, 1986). Dyson notes that writing activities in the early primary grades frequently involve talk that supports the meaningful intent of drawing and writing (1982). She expresses the view, based on her extensive observations of children, that they are constantly in the process of negotiating meaning in the context of the classroom. Her "multiple worlds perspective" suggests that the children's writing world is only one of many worlds they are actively constructing (Dyson, 1988). Writing, in essence, involves meaning negotiation within the social context of teacher and peers in the classroom.

Stories written by children in the primary grades move from simple descriptions to simple narratives characterized by chronology (Calkins, 1986). Gradual change occurs in story complexity as children move from writing all they can remember about a topic to simple characterization and sense of story plot.

The Intermediate Grades

During the intermediate grades, children demonstrate an increased awareness of characterization and plot in their writing. Calkins (1983, 1986) notes that, in grades four through six, children begin to develop revision ability and the effective use of narration and description in their writing. As with oral language development, written language control becomes more complex. Children move from the use of multiple sentences connected by *and* and *but* to sentences that combine the meaning of these conjoined sentences into one through subordination and embedding. They shift from writing everything down to thinking through a story idea and then expressing it in writing. Many children in grades five and six start to develop a "writer's voice" and an awareness of audience in their narrative and expository writing (Calkins, 1986).

41

CHARACTERISTICS OF PREPHONEMIC SPELLING

Phillip

Phillip, Kindergartner

—— **FIGURE 2-2** ——

Children's Invented Spelling. (Reproduced with permission from Temple & Gillet, 1989, pp. 41 and 43.)

Stages of Writing Development

An extensive research review by Danielewicz (1984) indicates that children progress through stages of writing development. In the first stage, they *unify* spoken and written language, making few distinctions between the two. In the second stage, they *distinguish* between spoken and written language by reducing coordinating conjunctions, such as *and* and *but*. In the third stage, children *strip* features of spoken language from written production. In the fourth and last stage, they *add* features typically associated with written language. Written language development thus extends from preliterate writing through formal written forms.

While the stages of development are not sharply defined, a clear progression is noted in children's differentiation between spoken and written

I love my mother. Me and my mother. Me and my dog.

I L AM. MA M. MAM DOG

I like my mother. Me and my mother. Me and my dig.

My TEETH

Last nit I pold oht my lustuth and I put it ondr my pelr. And wan I wok up I Fid a two dilr bel. The End.

language, syntactic complexity, the function and use of writing, story elements and sense of story, and development of voice and audience awareness.

FACTORS INFLUENCING ORAL AND WRITTEN LANGUAGE DEVELOPMENT

Various background variables influence children's verbal control and language development. Vygotsky (1986) highlights the importance of the availability of adults for dialogue with children in language acquisition. Courtney Cazden's work with two- and three-year-old children (1965) supports Vygotsky's view. She found that adult responses of full grammatical sentences to children's telegraphic speech resulted in children's increased performance in grammatical development.

Milner's work with high- and low-achieving first-grade readers (1963) also supports the Vygotskian perspective. Milner found that high-achieving children engaged in conversation more often with their parents, were read to more often by high-esteemed adults, and had more books available than did low-achieving children. Templin (1950) examined writing development of normal and hearing-impaired children. She found that children with hearing loss used more words in their explanations of natural phenomena than did hearing children of the same age, grade, and intelligence. This finding suggests that the hearing-impaired children needed more words to express a concept because they could not express their ideas through elaborated sentences and more abstract vocabulary. The opportunity to interact through oral language experiences by means of hearing would appear to exert direct influence on performance in written language.

HOME AND COMMUNITY INFLUENCES

A number of studies have examined the relationship between language growth and social interaction in the home and community. These findings suggest that children from homes in which "children are to be seen and not heard" are less verbally assertive with adults (Ward, 1971). In such homes there is only limited child-initiated interaction. Children from most middle-class homes, however, are more assertive and even "forward" with adults, and use language for clarification and extension of experience (Brown, 1973; Brown & Bellugi, 1961). Speidel (1982) found that in middle class homes, questioning routines are used to give information and teach concepts, e.g., "See the cow? What is the cow doing?" This was in marked contrast to Hawaiian Creole-speaking homes where questions are used to notify children of a mistake or an error (Gallimore, Boggs, & Jordan, 1974).

Other findings also support the view that children have greater opportunity for success in literacy acquisition when the home language interaction patterns and literacy attitudes are similar to those in the school. Labov (1970) observes that children from African-American low income homes are highly verbal, but that rules of address, politeness, and adult-child verbal

Reading Time at Home

interaction are quite different from those of the school (1970). Gallimore, Boggs, and Jordan (1974) found that Hawaiian Creole-speaking children were "manifestly competent" in home and community, where information giving and concept development are transmitted during group conversation or verbal play, but not at school where information-sharing rules are more formal and distinctly different. These findings highlight the need for and importance of understanding the different interaction patterns that children bring to the classroom. We will return to this issue in Chapter 10, where we suggest ways to adjust instruction to meet the needs of all children.

LEARNING FUNCTIONS OF LANGUAGE

An important aspect of language learning for children is the acquisition of a wide range of language functions that serve different literacy purposes in the home, community, and school settings. Halliday's extensive work (1973, 1978) describes a variety of language functions speakers use depending on their intention. These include the following:

1. **Instrumental** ("I want"): satisfying material needs.
2. **Regulatory** ("do as I tell you"): controlling the behavior of others.
3. **Interactional** ("me and you"): getting along with other people.

4. **Personal** ("here I come"): identifying and expressing the self through linguistic interaction.
5. **Heuristic** ("tell me why"): learning and exploring reality, the world around and inside one.
6. **Imaginative** ("let's pretend"): creating a world of one's own, whereby the [child's] reality is created.
7. **Informative** ("I've got something to tell you"): communicating content and new information.

Halliday proposes that acquisition of the complete range of language functions is necessary for full communication.

Flexibility and effectiveness of language functioning develop as children acquire different language functions, which include what is appropriate to talk about, when, with whom, how, and with what speech patterns (Smith, 1981). Within the school setting, at least three classroom language functions appear to be necessary (Ruddell & Haggard, 1985; Ruddell & Ruddell, 1994). These are briefly described for oral and written language forms in Table 2-1, with Halliday's specific functions noted for each.

Once a variety of language functions is acquired, children can switch function or register in order to adjust to the needs of a given situation. Of particular importance is the flexible and appropriate use of functions unique to various literacy forms in the school (DeStefano, 1978), such as written language functions ranging from personal notes to project reports (Olson, 1977).

Children from language- and book-enriched backgrounds appear to achieve control over a wider range of language functions earlier than children from less enriched backgrounds (Langer, Applebee, Mullis, & Foertsch, 1990). As teachers, we must be sensitive to the influence of home and culture on children's language use, and we must understand that often language-rich homes and communities may be language- and literacy-rich in ways we do not understand or in ways different from classroom and school norms (Gallimore, Boggs, & Jordan, 1974; Heath, 1982, 1983; Moll, 1992). Children will vary dramatically in the language and literacy experience they bring to the classroom and in their understanding and control over functions of language critical to success in school. Our awareness of these differences will enable us to plan learning experiences that support children's language and literacy achievements and develop their effective control over language functions important to classroom success.

READING ACQUISITION AND LANGUAGE DEVELOPMENT
WORD ANALYSIS AND MEANING

Language background knowledge is closely allied with reading acquisition, as children encounter meaningful symbols and contextually based

CLASSROOM LANGUAGE

FUNCTION	ORAL FORM	WRITTEN FORM
Informal Personal Exchange	Greetings	Personal notes to friends
	(Interactional, Personal)	
	Communications of feelings	Unedited written experiences
	(Instrumental, Interactional, Personal)	
	Control of others' behavior	Memos and directions
	(Instrumental, Regulatory)	
Formal Information Exchange	Classroom discussion	Edited experience stories
	(Informational, Heuristic)	
	Classroom lectures	Edited reports
	(Informational)	
	Public talks	School textbooks
	(Informational)	
Literary Exchange	Drama and theater	Poetry, narrative, drama
	(Imaginative, Informational, Heuristic)	

TABLE 2-1

Classroom Language Functions (Halliday's language functions are noted in parentheses)

print in picture books and storybooks and throughout their environment, e.g., traffic signs, fast-food logos, toothpaste containers. Many children have developed a strong sense of print and meaning awareness based on their experiences with storybooks, comic strips, cereal boxes, television advertisements, and the like (Purcell-Gates, 1988; Sulzby & Teale, 1991). Some children can print and read their own names, write the letters of the alphabet, and recognize a limited number of words that carry special meaning for them, e.g., *I, my, birthday.* Still others are reading conventional print upon entry to kindergarten or first grade.

Early Word Analysis Development—Grades K–1

In kindergarten and grade one, children extend their understanding of the relationship between print and its oral language counterparts. Refining the idea that print represents language, and in turn meaning, is critical to early reading acquisition (Strickland & Feeley, 1991). This concept enables beginning readers to make application of print predictions using the language knowledge they already possess. They come to understand that oral language is represented by print, that the print is arranged from left to right on the page, that words are represented by printed letters and separated by blank spaces between them. As mentioned in our previous discussion of invented spelling, beginning awareness of the oral language and print connection occurs before children enter school.

As children progress through the primary grades, they acquire word-analysis skills that provide for deciphering print into its oral counterpart and meaning. This involves the understanding letter-sound relationships, e.g., *c-a-p* /k ă p/, as well as larger letter-pattern and sound-pattern unit relationships such as the final e marker which signals a different sound of the previous vowel, e.g., *c-a-p-e* /k ā p/. Of critical importance at this stage is the opportunity to use word analysis skills in a natural language context, either oral or written (Goodman, 1985). This enables children to integrate the word analysis skills in the sentence context and test deciphered words for meaning, e.g., "The wind was cold and the boy put the *cap* on his head" in contrast to "The man waved the red *cape* at the angry bull."

Recent study of the word analysis process indicates that early successful readers learn to separate the sounds or phonemes in spoken words to assist them in finding the match between the sounds and letters or letter-patterns in printed words (Bryant & Bradley, 1985; Liberman & Shankweiler, 1979; Liberman, Shankweiler & Fischer, 1974; Rodgers, 1967). This process, known as *phonemic segmentation*, is an important step in the word analysis process and will be developed in greater detail for instruction in Chapter 8.

As children move through the primary grades, they begin to develop word analysis generalizations that follow English spelling patterns and are able to apply these in the analysis of new words, e.g., vowel-consonant pattern as in *at*, consonant-vowel-consonant pattern as in *mat*, consonant-vowel-consonant-*e* pattern as in *mate*. Gibson and Levin (1975) suggest that children appear to perceive regularities in the letter and sound patterns and transfer this knowledge to unfamiliar words that follow the same patterns.

Language functions also influence the word analysis process. For example, *hafta*, *gonna*, and *wanna* are quite appropriate and functional in informal conversational settings. In written language, however, these are usually represented as *have to*, *going to*, and *want to* (Lindsay, 1969), and these more formal representations occur with some frequency in primary-grade texts.

Such is also true for the contractions *I'll*, *she'll*, and *he'll*, which appear in the written equivalents *I will*, *she will*, and *he will* in most children's textbooks. As noted in Table 2-1, the language function shifts from an informal personal exchange to a more formal informational exchange. This requires a different language function mode for children in the early grades.

Continuing Word Analysis Development—Grade Two and Beyond

As children progress through grades two and three and into the intermediate grades, they develop the ability to analyze larger words into pronounceable units using syllable generalizations. This process is a complex one. It requires visual analysis of the word to locate the pronounceable units, then the blending of these units into the oral representation, the sound, of the word. The use of meaningful context is also important at this stage, as the word is tested for meaning in the context of the sentence and text (Ehri, 1991).

Many children become highly fluent readers by grade three and reach a stage of near automatic word analysis processing, requiring little conscious thought, for a large number of words. These readers rely heavily on predictions based on the sentence and text meaning. Some readers, however, will not have reached a high level of fluency even at grades four, five, and six. Because of the heavy reading requirements at these grades in content texts, these readers will experience major reading difficulty unless given special attention. We will address this issue in later discussions, especially in Chapters 8 and 11.

Oral Language Variation

The use of varied dialects by some children and the presence in classrooms of many children for whom English is a second language requires special understanding and attention in school. It is important to understand that dialects are highly regular language systems (Labov, 1970, Ruddell, 1974). This regularity is evident in the *l*-lessness common to the nonmainstream African-American dialect (also known as Black English), which results in consistent production of specific homonyms, so that *toll* becomes *toe*, and *fault* becomes *fought*. The simplification or loss of consonant clusters in the final positions of words results in *past* becoming *pass*, *meant* becoming *men*, and *hold* becoming *hole*.

It is just as important to understand interactions between children's first language and English. Because of sound variations between English and Spanish, some Hispanic children may have difficulty with such vowel contrasts as those between the words *bit* and *beat*, and *bet* and *bait*, and with such initial consonant contrasts as *sue* and *zoo*. For similar reasons, Navajo children may have difficulty with initial consonant distinctions in words like *vote* and *boat*, and *chip* and *gyp*.

These variations in the sound system of dialects or languages spoken by children may result in meaning confusions of many kinds. This will be especially true when word analysis skills are taught using words in isolation, and reinforces the importance of using a meaningful sentence or story context.

Just as important is the attitude you hold toward varied language forms. It is very easy to assume that dialect forms are somehow inferior to standard English and are slanglike rather than rule-governed and systematic. As illustrated above, nothing could be further from the truth. Lack of knowledge about children's first language or dialect may create both language and cultural chasms that are difficult to bridge. It is of vital importance that we do not stereotype children who use dialects or whose first language is not English as less intelligent and/or less informed. More will be said about this issue in Chapter 10.

READING COMPREHENSION AND LANGUAGE DEVELOPMENT

Children's background language knowledge serves as the foundation for reading comprehension. Their home and school environments provide constant opportunity to form new concepts, develop understanding of story sense, build explanations of how things work, and see and use written language in many informal and formal settings. These opportunities serve to expand and enrich children's linguistic knowledge (Cazden, 1965, 1968). The comprehension of printed text thus relies heavily on children's already well-developed language knowledge and their ability to connect key meaning elements in sentences and larger units of discourse.

As we have discussed, children entering kindergarten and the early grades have made enormous progress in developing concepts and word knowledge. They have also progressed in syntactical or sentence structure knowledge, and early understanding of story or text structure knowledge. Most children are able to use picture clues and understand and comprehend stories presented orally. Their early notion of story progresses from unorganized lists of information to sequences and simple narratives. They also develop a sense of story chronology using a chain of related events that reflects a general sense of story plot (McNeil, 1987; Applebee, 1978). Sense of story becomes further refined as children move through the primary and intermediate grades. It will eventually emerge into a full narrative form, due in part to their extensive encounter with narrative reading in their classrooms.

As children gradually acquire word analysis abilities in the first and second grade, they shift from focus on correct identification of words (Bussie, Chittenden, Amarel, & Klausner, 1985) to the use of sentence structure and story sense in creating meaning. At this stage, they make predictions and develop meaning expectations using the background knowledge they have acquired in oral language interactions.

Children's knowledge of text structure and meaning expectations, however, will differ markedly depending on their prior language experiences with text structure. Various researchers (Clay, 1979; Durkin, 1966) have found that children who have been read to before entering school are more likely to succeed at an earlier level in learning to read. These children approach print with high meaning expectations. They possess knowledge and familiarity with story structure and the language of text.

Heath (1982, 1983) studied children from three different communities which she labeled "Gateway, (a mainstream urban community)," "Roadville (a white mill community)," and "Trackton (a black mill community)." She found that children from these communities held vastly different attitudes toward written language. They transferred their community and home literacy patterns to learning behaviors at school. Gateway children received early initiation to books, written and oral narrative, book-reading behaviors, and questioning routines. Roadville children were expected to accept the power of print through association with alphabet letters and workbook-like activities. Trackton children lived in a highly oral community where storytelling and verbal attention-getting skills were prized, and few children's books and book-reading activities were found in the home. Heath concluded that Gateway children entered school not only familiar with book-reading routines, but with well-developed comprehension strategies as well.

Story Reading at Primary and Intermediate Grades

Reading interests for youngsters at the primary grades include picture books and highly repetitive and predictable books, fairy tales, folktales, modern fantasy, and humor (Feeley, 1981). Children at this level have special interest in story characters of their own age, and in family and animal-oriented narratives. Reading interests of children at ages nine through eleven focus on narrative adventure and fantasy while their expository interests range from space exploration and computers to sports and biography (Burgess, 1985). At this age, reading interests are strongly influenced by peers' recommendations and continued reading of a favorite author.

In grades four, five, and six, many children develop a more refined sense of narrative, including expectations of characters, story setting, and problems and goals. They are interested in episodes forming the story plot, attempts to resolve problems, and story resolution. A strong predictive sense develops in narrative reading (Whaley, 1981). These children are well along in mastering word analysis skills and are near automatic processing in the recognition of words. At this stage, children begin to connect their purpose or objective in reading to an appropriate reading strategy. This may range from reading to locate specific story information to understanding the story plot. They are also more attuned to whether this strategy is working through the use of comprehension monitoring, a form of metacognitive awareness.

Content Area Reading

The role of expository reading in science, social studies, and other areas expands dramatically for children at the intermediate grade levels. This requires development of an understanding of text organization that differs markedly from the highly familiar narrative text structure. New text organization patterns in expository text include descriptive and informational, cause and effect, problem and solution, and comparison and contrast. Understanding these new patterns presents a challenge to many children. Up to this point, they have largely encountered only descriptive and information-type reading. The new patterns become important organizational guides for intermediate-grade readers as they recognize and use one or more of them in creating meaning from expository text.

Accompanying these new text structures in the content area reading is a rapidly expanding vocabulary load. This is especially the case in science, social studies, and mathematics. For example, words such as *vertebrate* and semantically related vocabulary items such as *mammal*, *bird*, *fish*, *amphibian*, and *reptile* will need to be acquired. The teacher's role becomes very important in helping students connect these new concepts to their related background knowledge.

Children's knowledge of and familiarity with the syntactical, lexical, and text structure elements will directly influence their success in comprehending text as they construct meaning. Their background language knowledge and their knowledge of and familiarity with different text forms will be of critical importance to forming and testing predictions, and constructing meaning from narrative and expository text. Both the home and school environments exert strong influence on children's literacy acquisition by providing experiences in comprehending various text forms and in establishing the importance and value of literacy.

How Background Knowledge Is Organized and Stored

Schema Theory

Our overview of children's language and literacy development demonstrates that rapid language and comprehension growth occurs during their preschool and elementary school years. This background includes knowledge of the sound, word analysis, lexical, syntactical, and text structure systems and how to use them. In addition, children's experiences in different home and community cultures influence their knowledge and values related to the functions and uses of oral and written language forms. This knowledge background differs from child to child depending on the home, community, and school experiences encountered. But how is this knowledge organized, and how is it stored and used to construct meaning?

Schema theory provides insight into the organization and storage of background experiences and knowledge. As mentioned in Chapter 1, *schemata* (plural for *schema*) are knowledge structures in our memory that organize our environment and experience, and allow us to adapt to new experiences (Rumelhart, 1981; Rumelhart & Ortony, 1977; Wadsworth, 1971). Schemata can be thought of as information packets or knowledge modules that are used to organize and make sense of concepts formed from our experiences (Adams & Collins, 1985), such as "going to the grocery store." Schemata grow from general experience to form specific knowledge modules defined by a related group of concepts. Personal concrete experiences and interactions with others are important to this development and lead to abstract representation of these encounters. Schemata are thus created from contexts and experiences but take the form of abstract representations that are independent of the original context and experiences (Shanklin, 1982). For example, the "going to the grocery store" schema may represent an overarching knowledge module that a grocery store is a business establishment where we buy food that has been prepared or grown by someone else and is taken home to use in meal preparation.

Knowledge within schemata appears to be organized in a hierarchical fashion (Schank & Abelson, 1975). Below the global concept "going to the grocery store" are more specific schemata such as going to a large food market or to a small "Mom and Pop" store. The explanatory power of schema theory is found in the idea that the first level of any schema provides for an abstraction and conceptual framework for all of the particular events that fall below the overarching schema but are within its domain (Adams & Collins, 1985).

Schemata may include several kinds of knowledge structures. The schema "going to the grocery store" consists of knowledge structures that embody the *concepts* used to identify the bread, vegetables, and other groceries. It also includes knowledge structures that embody the *procedures* used in shopping, such as how to find certain grocery items, and how to pack groceries so that the fresh bread does not get crushed.

New information is added to schemata by connecting the new information to the overarching conceptual framework. For example, we may connect certain foods to the "grocery store" schema as we shop for fresh fish at the local fish market or for fresh vegetables and fruits at a roadside stand on a hot summer day. We may also use our schema to infer, or instantiate, certain information that is not explicitly provided in the text or in a given situation. We may expect, for example, that in a large chain food market there will be several lines of people with food carts or baskets waiting for one of several clerks who uses an electric code reader to tabulate our food cost, then he or she collects our money and places our groceries in paper or plastic bags to assist us in carrying the food home. Or in shopping for bread at the local bakery we may expect to find fresh bread and other baked goods, accompanied by a delicious aroma of baking cookies, and a single clerk who calculates the cost, collects our money, and carefully places the bread and other baked goods in a grocery bag for transporting them to our home.

LEARNING AND COMPREHENDING
FROM THE SCHEMA THEORY PERSPECTIVE

Schema theory perspective views the mind as a highly complex set of cognitive structures that serve to organize and relate experiences in memory. Learning process then involves organizing, building, and reorganizing information by forming schemata and incorporating new information into them. The comprehension process is driven by the child's desire to make sense of experience. It involves the use of strategies that provide for connecting and using relevant schemata.

A property common to both learning and comprehension is the inferencing process using background knowledge schemata. This process helps us reach meaning closure by "filling in the meaning gaps" as we make sense of what we perceive in a given experience, whether this be a trip to the grocery store, a classroom discussion, or reading a fairy tale (Harste, Woodward, & Burke, 1984).

When the schema theory perspective is combined with the previously discussed work of Halliday (1978), Vygotsky (1986), and Piaget (1963, 1967), it becomes clear that the development of a background knowledge schema is influenced by children's social and cultural experiences as well as their cognitive development stages. Children are thus active theory builders and hypothesis testers from infancy, as they construct meaningful schemata. These schemata represent the clusters of concepts and procedures that have developed based on children's experiences in their unique home and community cultures. Children actively search for meaning through inference by applying the schemata they have developed on the basis of their experience. An important part of our role as teachers is to assist students throughout the elementary school years in creating new schemata and in refining and expanding those that are already formed.

LEARNER MOTIVATION AND THE USE OF BACKGROUND KNOWLEDGE

In our previous discussion, we cited strong support to demonstrate that children's motivation to learn language and to use it effectively at home is social in nature (Harste, Woodward, & Burke, 1984; Genishi & Dyson, 1984; Vygotsky, 1986). The desire to engage in social interaction is inherent in children from their earliest years. This desire provides high motivation for children to develop and use background knowledge to communicate with parents, siblings, and peers. In the family unit, language plays an important social interaction function conveying a sense of belonging, love, and self-esteem (Mathewson, 1985). Central to the social desire to use language is the importance of making meaning—understanding and communicating

ideas with other human beings. This social aspect of communication is critical in forming positive attitudes and values toward reading and literacy use.

SOCIAL ENVIRONMENT OF THE SCHOOL

This same motivational drive continues as children enter school and encounter their teacher and other youngsters of similar age and similar interests. The social environment of the school, however, is distinctly different from that of the home for most children. Now the child is one of many, and the attention of the teacher is spread across the class. New rules are present, as demanded by the organization of the classroom. New language functions must be learned, such as how to engage in a discussion with small and large groups of peers. And new concepts are encountered, ranging from understanding the role of community helpers to developing reading and writing skills.

A critical part of our role as teachers is to understand children's dual motivations: (1) the need to engage in social interaction and (2) the desire to communicate, to understand, and to make sense of school experiences. A central objective of our instruction is to support and maintain these motivations in our classrooms. If we can do this effectively, we set the stage for children to use their already developed background knowledge of language and to form and maintain a positive attitude toward reading and literacy instruction.

INFLUENCE OF ATTITUDE AND MOTIVATION

Children's attitude or their state of positive readiness toward literacy learning is directed by their motive for participating in the learning experience. The motive in effect becomes the individual child's purpose or objective for learning. This motive or objective serves to activate the prior knowledge schemata related to the objective and to establish the child's expectations for the content use. The positive acceptance of the motive or objective also influences and supports persistence in reaching the objective.

It is important to note that this purpose or objective may be internal to the child, external in nature, or a combination of both (Ruddell, 1992). If internal, it will be formed and directed by the child, as is the case in a child's selection of *Charlotte's Web* to be read with the purpose of personal enjoyment and escape. On the other hand, the objective may be external and teacher-selected and -directed, as in having students read and discuss an excerpt from *Charlotte's Web* for the purpose of developing comprehension.

USING BOTH EXTERNAL AND INTERNAL MOTIVATION

Ideally in directed instruction the objective, which has been identified by the teacher, will be developed with the children in a way that also activates their internal motivation and interest. For example, we may attempt to use children's internal motivation toward problem resolution for comprehension

Developing Internal Motivations for Reading

development. We can do this by encouraging students to identify with the gentle and caring spider, Charlotte, as they read to discover how she attempts to save her friend Wilbur from Zuckerman's smokehouse. The story reading would be followed by a discussion of the students' responses and insights into Charlotte's method and motivation to save Wilbur and how this might differ from their own resolution of the problem.

The development of high student motivation and positive attitudes toward reading is critical to students' success. The discussion in Chapter 1 described characteristics of influential teachers and identified their concern with using highly motivating teaching strategies, understanding "where students are," making material personally relevant, and using a process approach to intellectual discovery. Influential teachers effectively account for and use student motivation and background knowledge in teaching. We will return to this in Chapter 6, as we place special emphasis on using internal instructional motivation and building positive attitudes toward reading.

BACKGROUND KNOWLEDGE AND COMPREHENSION STRATEGY USE

Our discussion to this point has emphasized that background knowledge is developed and stored in the form of schemata and is used in the comprehension and production of oral and written language. How is this background knowledge activated and used to comprehend in the reading process?

Several strategic processes are involved in the complex and split-second mental task that results in our meaningful comprehension of text. These processes interact constantly, influencing each other as meaning is constructed. They do not operate in stepwise fashion. This is demonstrated as we reflect on the processing you used to read the "The Wimmy Wuggen and the Moggy Tor" passage earlier in this chapter.

SELECTING AND ACTIVATING BACKGROUND KNOWLEDGE

As we have discussed, your motivation to read serves to define the purpose or objective for reading a specific text selection. This may be based on your own self-directed internally motivated objective: for example, your intellectual curiosity leads you to want to understand the unusual story about the Wuggen and the Tor. Or it may be based on an externally motivated objective identified by the teacher, such as, "What would you do if you were the wimmy Wuggen? And why?" In the instructional setting, both types of motivation will ideally be used. Your reading objective is also shaped by the intended use of the reading experience, for example, to be ready to discuss what you would do if you were the wimmy Wuggen and explain why.

The reading objective is used to identify and activate the two types of background knowledge schemata: First, the relevant content knowledge, for example, a folktale schema; and second, process knowledge, such as how to make inferences about story outcomes.

We select a particular processing strategy based on our reading objective and expected use of the constructed meaning. The strategy will be refined as we discover a narrative text, a folktale genre, and the need to make inferences to understand such words as *grolling* and *poft*. The strategy will need to incorporate the use of inferences and predictions about story characters (such as evidence suggesting the nature of the relationship between the Wuggen and the Tor) and about the story outcome, in order to reach conclusions related to the initial questions and the anticipated follow-up discussion.

ACTIVATING AND APPLYING MONITORING STRATEGIES

As we begin to read the text, our initial comprehension objective also serves to activate our comprehension monitoring strategy, which is metacognitive in nature. **Metacognition** involves our awareness of our thinking process as we construct meaning (Brown, 1985). Our self-monitoring and self-correcting strategies may include evaluative reading, hypothesis testing, and self-questioning. For example, we may ask ourselves, "What reason do I have to believe that the Tor will help the Wuggen?" Our comprehension monitoring is used throughout our encounter with the text constantly to evaluate the constructed meaning represented in our mind. This meaning monitoring is essentially a check for understanding, in which we evaluate the consistency between our new meaning construction and our prior knowledge. This process is directed by our original comprehension objective.

Assuming our meaning construction makes sense and is consistent with our prior knowledge and comprehension objective, we will proceed with the planned strategy we have selected. For example, if the text is written about a topic for which we have rich background knowledge, such as a folktale, our reading rate may increase and allow us to focus on the overall meaning of the text and our initial objective. If, on the other hand, we do not understand the text or the meaning seems inconsistent with our prior knowledge or objective, we may shift our text-processing strategy to a new one. If the vocabulary, syntax, and text organization are difficult and complex to understand, as may be the case with a legal document, we may need to reduce our reading rate and concentrate on smaller units of meaning, then attend to the overall meaning and reading objective. If the text is extremely difficult and we find that we are comprehending very little, we may even decide to discontinue reading. The nature of our success in reading will influence our motivation, attitude, and persistence toward the reading material and the reading process.

USING THE CONSTRUCTED MEANING—EXPECTED OUTCOMES

Following the reading experience, we often use our newly constructed meaning in some manner. This may consist of participation in a teacher-directed discussion with our peers related to the narrative or expository text we have been reading, a written response in our personal reading journal, or opportunity to think through a personal problem after reading a favorite novel that triggered a unique solution to the problem. Ideally, our initial reading objective has been connected to the expected use from the outset. If this is the case, we have in all probability constructed meaning and organized it in such a way that key ideas can be used in our anticipated discussion, reading report, or thoughts about our personal problem.

Now, take a few moments and reread the brief passage, "The Wimmy Wuggen and the Moggy Tor" (pages 30–31). Think about the processes you used in your initial reading. Note the interactive nature of your background knowledge content and the processing strategies you used. What was your motivation to read the passage, and what objective or objectives did you select? What background knowledge was activated as you began to read? What comprehension process strategies did you use in your attempt to understand the passage? Did these strategies differ as you responded to each of the four questions? If so, how? What monitoring strategies did you use as you constructed meaning? How did you use your constructed meaning for the story? Which of these processes seemed to interact with each other as you arrived at meaning closure for the story?

Your introspective responses to these questions will highlight the nature of the process that you use in constructing meaning from any text.

The Comprehension Process—A Synthesis

It is clear that the meaning construction process is a highly interactive one. Each of us purposefully uses our background knowledge and monitoring strategies to construct our personal meaning representation from an author's text language. One of your important roles as teacher is to assist your students in the development of meaning construction. As shown in Figure 2-3, you are central in defining the instructional objective, with concern for motivation and expected outcomes, and in communicating this objective to the children using your instructional background knowledge. This directly involves your concept schemata, your teaching strategies, and your attitudes and values toward the content and toward your individual students.

The children in turn will interpret the objective, including the expected outcomes, and use this information to activate their background knowledge schemata. Your instruction must be designed to facilitate this process to insure that background concepts and text processing schemata are activated and related to the text content or discussion as your students begin the meaning construction process. Instruction will also need to be concerned with developing and maintaining positive motivation toward the reading experience. Negotiation of meaning between you and the children becomes a vital aspect of your teaching. You establish the initial reading objective, with concern for internal and external motivation. You direct the instructional experience. And you provide instructional monitoring and discussion feedback for your students.

The comprehension process thus involves:

- Purposeful reading guided by internally and externally motivated objectives and expected use.

- Activation of background knowledge content including lexical, syntactic, and story structure schemata.

- Activation of background knowledge processing strategies for effective meaning construction.

- Mobilization of attitudes and values related to the text content and expected use of the constructed meaning.

- Activation of monitoring strategies to check the meaning construction as directed by the objective.

- Interactive use of these processes to construct meaning.

In an expert reader such as you, these processes have become fine-tuned. They require little conscious thought as you read narrative and expository text that is of high interest and in which you have excellent background knowledge. You become much more conscious of these processes as you encounter text in which your background knowledge is less well defined. In

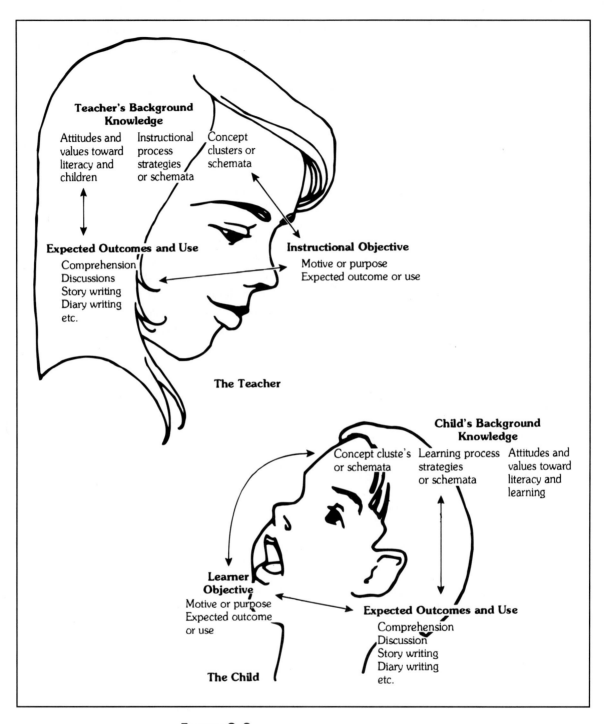

Teacher's Background Knowledge

Attitudes and values toward literacy and children

Instructional process strategies or schemata

Concept clusters or schemata

Expected Outcomes and Use

Comprehension
Discussions
Story writing
Diary writing
etc.

Instructional Objective

Motive or purpose
Expected outcome or use

The Teacher

Child's Background Knowledge

Concept cluste's or schemata

Learning process strategies or schemata

Attitudes and values toward literacy and learning

Learner Objective

Motive or purpose
Expected outcome or use

Expected Outcomes and Use

Comprehension
Discussion
Story writing
Diary writing
etc.

The Child

FIGURE 2-3

The Meaning Construction Process—Meaning Negotiation Between Teacher and Child either case, however, you have carefully honed comprehension processing and monitoring strategies that enable you to construct meaning from text. Your role as teacher is to develop many of these same processes with your children from kindergarten through the elementary school grades. We will place special emphasis on comprehension development and meaning construction in the chapters that follow.

Reading and Writing Processes
A Summary

This chapter has developed the idea that early language and literacy acquisition provide the foundation for children's reading and language development in elementary school.

Five significant factors appear to characterize early language acquisition and subsequent development of language and reading comprehension (Ruddell & Haggard, 1985; Ruddell & Ruddell, 1994).

First, children are active participants in their own language and literacy development. This greatly facilitates their ability to reach generalizations and gain control over their knowledge of word, sentence and text structure. The driving force behind their growth is the need to construct meaning—to make sense of their world.

Second, children's perceptions of print and productions of oral and written language are systematic and organized—even when overgeneralization creates language forms that do not conform to conventional English.

Third, children acquire and use literate behaviors in their very early years, well before entry into school, the onset of formal literacy instruction, and the acquisition of conventional literacy. Children enter school with a high degree of language competence that continues to develop and grow throughout their school experience.

Fourth, language acquisition and literacy development are influenced by children's language and world knowledge, social interactions, and language environment. Congruence between home and school language and literacy experiences increases children's opportunity for success in learning to read and write.

And fifth, home and community environments, interactions, and experiences are often language-rich in ways not fully explored or understood.

We have examined the way in which background knowledge is developed and stored in the form of knowledge structures, or schemata, in memory. These knowledge structures are organized in a hierarchical manner, are central to meaning construction, and account for clusters of related concepts and processes used in meaning construction.

Children's motivation, both internal and external, is a critical component in the learning and comprehension process. The motive or objective in constructing meaning from text activates related background knowledge schemata for both concepts and processes.

The reading comprehension process involves purposeful meaning construction which is guided by the readers' objective and intended use. The objective serves to identify and activate a relevant content schema and the reader's stored background knowledge. Active comprehension processing strategies or plans are critical in constructing meaning and are guided by the reader's objective. Self-directed monitoring strategies are also essential to check meaning construction against background knowledge and reading purpose.

The process is highly interactive once the meaning construction process is under way; the reader's comprehension strategies are adjusted by the monitoring of meaning, enabling him or her to reach the comprehension objective and intended use. The concepts developed in this chapter will form the basis of discussions in the chapters that follow. In the next chapter, we will turn our attention to early reading and literacy instruction for the kindergarten and first-grade student.

DOUBLE ENTRY JOURNAL

Create the beginning of your own literacy history. Go back to the notes you jotted down before reading this chapter, add to them based upon information from this chapter and other memories that information may have triggered, and talk to people who were around you in your years before and during elementary school. Write out your early literacy history and look at how fascinating your progress was. If you're comfortable doing so, share your history with a friend. Continue adding to your literacy history as you continue through this book and course.

Supporting Activities

1. Identify one of your favorite cartoons, such as "Dennis the Menace" by Hank Ketcham, or "The Far Side" by Gary Larson, and use your understanding of schema theory to explain the humor of your cartoon. Share your ideas with a class partner. How can background knowledge schema explain the difficulty in understanding humor for students who speak English as a second language?

2. Reexamine Sarah's (age 5) and Matt's (age 6) uninterrupted writing samples and illustrations in Figure 2-1. Can you interpret their invented spelling text? Be sure to use their illustrations to assist you. Check your interpretation with that provided below for Sarah* and Matt.** How would you classify each of these responses based on the classroom language functions found in Table 2-1?

3. Request a morning or afternoon observation with an elementary school teacher and his or her children in a classroom at your favorite grade level. Identify and briefly describe examples of teacher-child or child-child interactions that illustrate children's strong motivation to (1) engage in social interaction and (2) communicate, understand, and make sense of their classroom experiences. How can instruction be designed to use these motivations to foster children's literacy development?

4. Based on our discussion in this chapter and your personal insights, write a brief (one to two pages) definition of the reading process. Be sure to account for the role of comprehension as well as attitudes and motivation in your definition. After completing your definition, share your key ideas with a class partner. Keep your definition in a convenient location in your notebook and add new ideas to it as you progress through your readings and class discussions.

*Sarah: "Once upon a time there was a lovable bunny who picked a rose for his mommy."
**Matt: "I like to go to the zoo. I like to have lunch there. I like the zebras."

REFERENCES

Adams, J., & Collins, A. (1985). A schema-theoretic view of reading. In H. Singer & R. B. Ruddell (Eds.), *Theoretical models and processes of reading* (3rd ed.) (pp. 404–425). Newark, DE: International Reading Association.

Anderson, R. C., & Freebody, P. (1985). Vocabulary knowledge. In H. Singer & R. B. Ruddell (Eds.), *Theoretical models and processes of reading* (3rd ed.) (pp. 343–371). Newark, DE: International Reading Association.

Anderson, R., Hiebert, E. H., Scott, J. A., & Wilkinson, I. A. G. (1985). *Becoming a nation of readers: The report of the commission on reading.* Washington, DC: The National Institute of Education.

Applebee, A. N. (1978). *The child's concept of story.* Chicago: The University of Chicago Press.

Barr, R., Kamil, M. L., Mosenthal, P. B., & Pearson, P. D. (1991). *Handbook of reading research: Vol. II.* New York: Longman.

Brown, A. (1985). *Metacognition: The development of selective attention strategies for learning from texts.* In H. Singer & R. B. Ruddell (Eds.), *Theoretical models and processes of reading* (3rd ed.) (pp. 501–526). Newark, DE: International Reading Association.

Brown, R. (1973). *First language: The early stages.* Cambridge, MA: Harvard University Press.

Brown, R., & Bellugi, U. (1961). *Three processes in the child's acquisition of syntax.* In E. H. Lenneberg (Ed.), *New directions in the study of language* (pp. 131–162). Cambridge, MA: MIT Press.

Bryant, P., & Bradley, L. (1985). *Children's reading problems.* New York: Oxford University Press.

Burgess, S. A. (1985). Reading but not literate: The childread survey. *School Library Journal, 31,* 27–30.

Bussie, A. M., Chittenden, E. A., Amarel, M., & Klausner, E. (1985) *Inquiry into meaning: An investigation of learning to read.* Hillsdale, NJ: Erlbaum.

Calkins, L. M. (1983). *Lessons from a child.* Portsmouth, NH: Heinemann.

Calkins, L. M. (1986). *The art of teaching writing.* Portsmouth, NH: Heinemann.

Cazden, C. B. (1965). *Environmental assistance to the child's acquisition of grammar.* Unpublished doctoral dissertation, Harvard University.

Cazden, C. B. (1968). The acquisition of noun and verb inflections. *Child Development, 39,* 433–448.

Chomsky, C. S. (1969). *The acquisition of syntax in children from 5 to 10.* Cambridge, MA: MIT Press.

Chomsky, C. S. (1979). Approaching reading through invented spelling. In L.B. Resnick & P.A. Weaver (Eds.), *Theory and practice of early reading* (pp. 43–65). Hillsdale, NJ: Erlbaum.

Clay, M. (1975). *What did I write?* Portsmouth, NH: Heinemann.

Clay, M. (1979). *Concepts about print tests.* Portsmouth, NH: Heinemann.

Clay, M. M. (1983). Getting a theory of writing. In B. M. Kroll & G. Wells (Eds.), *Explorations in a development of writing* (pp. 259–284). New York: Wiley.

Clay, M. (1985). *The early detection of reading difficulties.* Portsmouth, NH: Heinemann.

Danielewicz, J. M. (1984). *Developmental differences between children's spoken and written language.* Unpublished manuscript, University of California, Berkeley.

DeStefano, J. S. (1978). *Language, the learner and the school.* New York: Wiley.

DeVilliers, J. G., & DeVilliers, P. A. (1973). A cross-sectional study of the development of grammatical morphemes in child speech. *Journal of Psycholinguistic Research, 2,* 267–278.

Durkin, D. (1966). *Children who read early.* New York: Teachers College Press.

Durkin, D. (1978–1979). What classroom observations reveal about reading comprehension instruction. *Reading Research Quarterly, 14,* 481–533.

Dyson, A. H. (1982). Reading, writing, and language: Young children solve the written language puzzle. *Language Arts, 59,* 829–839.

Dyson, A. H. (1988). Negotiating among multiple worlds: The space/time dimensions of young children's composing. *Research in the Teaching of English, 22*(4), 355–390.

Ehri, L. C. (1991). Development of the ability to read words. In R. Barr, M. L. Kamil, P. Mosenthal, & P. D. Pearson (Eds.), *Handbook of reading research: Volume II* (pp. 383–417). New York: Longman.

Ervin, S. M., & Miller, W. R. (1963). Language development. In H. Stevenson (Ed.), *Child psychology: The 62nd yearbook of the national society for the study of education* (pp. 108–143). Chicago: University of Chicago Press.

Ervin-Tripp, S. M. (1967). Language development. *Review of Child Development Research* (pp. 55–105). New York: Russell Sage Foundation.

Feeley, J. T. (1981). What do our children like to read? *NJEA Review, 54*(8), 26–27.

Feifel, H., & Lorge, I. B. (1962). Qualitative differences in the vocabulary responses of children. *Journal of Educational Psychology, 43,* 170–174.

Ferreiro, E. (1978). What is written in a written sentence? A developmental answer. *Journal of Education, 160,* 25–39.

Ferreiro, E. (1986). The interplay between information and assimilation in beginning literacy. In W. H. Teale & E. Sulzby (Eds.), *Emergent literacy: Writing and reading* (pp. 15–49). Cambridge, UK: Cambridge University Press.

Flood, J., Jensen, J. M., Lapp, D., & Squire, J. R. (1991). *Handbook of research on teaching the English language arts.* New York: Macmillan.

Fraser, C., Bellugi, U., & Brown, R. (1963). Control of grammar in imitation comprehension and production. *Journal of Verbal Learning and Verbal Behavior, 2,* 121–135.

Gallimore, R., Boggs, J. W., & Jordan, C. (1974). *Culture, behavior and education: A study of Hawaiian-Americans.* Beverly Hills, CA: Sage Press.

Genishi, C., & Dyson, A. H. (1984). *Language assessment in the early years.* Norwood, NJ: Ablex.

Gibson, E. J., & Levin, H. (1975). *The psychology of reading.* Cambridge, MA: MIT Press.

Gillet, J. W., & Temple, C. (1990). *Understanding reading problems* (3rd ed.). New York: HarperCollins.

Goodman, K. S. (1985). Unity in reading. In H. Singer & R. B. Ruddell (Eds.), *Theoretical models and processes of reading* (3rd ed.) (pp. 813–840). Newark, DE: International Reading Association.

Haggard, M. R. (1980). Vocabulary acquisition during elementary and post-elementary years: A preliminary report. *Reading Horizons, 21,* 61–69.

Halliday, M. A. K. (1973). *Explorations in the functions of language.* London, UK: Edward Arnold.

Halliday, M. A. K. (1978). *Language as social semiotic.* London, UK: Edward Arnold.

Harste, J. C., Burke, C. L., & Woodward, V. A. (1982). Children's language and world: Initial encounters with print. In J. Langer & M. T. Smith-Burke (Eds.), *Reader meets author: Bridging the gap* (pp. 105–131). Newark, DE: International Reading Association.

Harste, J. C., Woodward, V. A., & Burke, C. L. (1984). *Language stories and literacy lessons.* Portsmouth, NH: Heinemann.

Heath, S. B. (1982). What no bedtime story means: Narrative skills at home and school. *Language and Society, 2,* 49–76.

Heath, S. B. (1983). *Ways with words: Language, life and work in communities and classrooms.* Cambridge, UK: Cambridge University Press.

Henderson, E., & Beers, J. (Eds.). (1980). *Developmental and cognitive aspects of learning to spell.* Newark, DE: International Reading Association.

Huey, E. B. (1968). *The psychology and pedagogy of reading.* Cambridge, MA: MIT Press. (Originally published by Macmillan in 1908)

Hunt, K. W. (1970). Syntactic maturity in school children and adults. *Monographs of the Society for Research in Child Development, 35.*

Labov, W. (1970). The logic of nonstandard English. In F. Williams (Ed.), *Language and poverty: Perspective on a theme* (pp. 153–189). Chicago: Markham.

Langer, J. A., Applebee, A. N., Mullis, I. V. S., & Foertsch, M. A. (1990). *Learning to read in our nation's schools: Instruction and achievement in 1988 at grades 4, 8, and 12.* Princeton, NJ: Educational Testing Service.

Liberman, I., & Shankweiler, D. (1979). Speech, the alphabet, and teaching to read. In L. Resnick & P. Weaver (Eds.), *Theory and practice of early reading: Volume II* (pp. 109–132). Hillsdale, NJ: Erlbaum.

Liberman, I., Shankweiler, D., Fischer, F. W., & Carter, B. (1974). Explicit syllable and phoneme segmentation in the young child. *Journal of Experimental Psychology, 18,* 201–212.

Lindsay, M. R. (1969). *A descriptive exploration of the growth and development of spontaneous oral vocabulary of elementary school children.* Unpublished doctoral dissertation, University of California, Berkeley.

Loban, W. D. (1976). *Language development: Kindergarten through grade twelve.* Urbana, IL: National Council of Teachers of English.

McCarthy, D. A. (1954). Language development in children. In L. Carmichael (Ed.), *Manual of child psychology* (pp. 492–630). New York: Wiley.

McNeil, J. D. (1987). *Reading comprehension: New directions for classroom practice* (3rd ed.) Glenview, IL: Scott Foresman.

Mathewson, G. C. (1985). Toward a comprehensive model of effect in the reading process. In H. Singer & R. B. Ruddell (Eds.), *Theoretical models and processes of reading* (3rd ed.) (pp. 841-857). Newark, DE: International Reading Association.

Menyuk, P. (1963). Syntactic structures in the language of children. *Child Development, 34,* 407–422.

Menyuk, P. (1984). Language development and reading. In J. Flood (Ed.), *Understanding reading comprehension* (pp. 101–121). Newark, DE: International Reading Association.

Miller, W. R. (1967). *Language acquisition and reading.* Unpublished manuscript, University of California, Berkeley.

Miller, W. R., & Ervin, S. (1964). *The development of grammar in child language.* Monographs of the Society for Research in Child Development, *92,* 9–34.

Milner, E. (1963). A study of the relationship between reading readiness in grade one school children and patterns of parent-child interaction. *The 62nd Yearbook of the National Society for Study of Education* (pp. 108–143). Chicago: University of Chicago Press.

Moll, L. C. (1992). Literacy research in community and classrooms: A sociocultural approach. In R. Beach, J. L. Green, M. L. Kamil, & T. Shanahan (Eds.), *Multidisciplinary perspectives on literacy research* (pp. 211–244). Urbana, IL: National Council of Teachers of English.

O'Donnell, R. C., Griffin, W. J., & Norris, R. C. (1967). *Syntax of kindergarten and elementary school children: A transformational analysis.* Champaign, IL: National Council of Teachers of English.

Olson, D. R. (1977). From utterance to text: the bias of language in speech and writing. *Harvard Educational Review, 47,* 257–281.

Piaget, J. (1963). *The origins of intelligence in children.* New York: Norton. (Originally published by International Universities Press in 1953)

Piaget, J. (1967). The genetic approach to the psychology of thought. In J. P. DeCecco (Ed.), *The psychology of language, thought and instruction.* New York: Holt, Rinehart & Winston.

Purcell-Gates, V. (1988). Lexical and syntactic knowledge of written narrative held by well-read-to kindergartners and second graders. *Research in the Teaching of English, 22*(2l), 128–160.

Read, C. (1971). Preschool children's knowledge of English phonology. *Harvard Educational Review, 41,* 1–34.

Read, C. (1975). *Children's categorization of speech sounds in English.* Champaign, IL: National Council of Teachers of English.

Read, C. (1986). *Children's creative spelling.* Boston, MA: Routledge and Kegan.

Rodgers, T. (1967). *Linguistic considerations in the design of the stanford computer based curriculum in initial reading* (Report No. 111, USOE grant OE5-10-050). Stanford University: Institute for Mathematical Studies in the Social Sciences.

Ruddell, R. B. (1974). *Reading-language instruction: Innovative practices.* Englewood Cliffs, NJ: Prentice-Hall.

Ruddell, R. B. (1992). A whole language and literature perspective: Creating a meaning making instructional environment. *Language Arts, 69,* 612–620.

Ruddell, R. B., & Haggard, M. R. (1985). Oral and written language and the reading process. In H. Singer & R. B. Ruddell (Eds.), *Theoretical models and processes of reading* (3rd ed.) (pp. 63–68). Newark, DE: International Reading Association.

Ruddell, R. B., & Ruddell, M. R. (1994). Language acquisition and literacy processes. In R. B. Ruddell, M. R. Ruddell, & H. Singer (Eds.), *Theoretical models and processes of reading* (4th ed.) (pp. 83–103). Newark, DE: International Reading Association.

Rumelhart, D. E. (1981). Schemata: The building blocks of cognition. In J. T. Guthrie (Ed.), *Comprehension and teaching: Research reviews.* Newark, DE: International Reading Association.

Rumelhart, D. E., & Ortony, A. (1977). The representation of knowledge in memory. In R. C. Anderson, R. J. Spiro, & W. E. Montague (Eds.), *Schooling and the acquisition of knowledge.* Hillsdale, NJ: Erlbaum, 1977.

Russell, D. H., & Saadeh, I. Q. (1962). Qualitative levels in children's vocabularies. *Journal of Educational Psychology, 43,* 170–174.

Schank, R., & Abelson, R. (1975). *Knowledge structures.* Hillsdale, NJ: Erlbaum.

Shanklin, N. K. (1982). *Relating reading and writing: Developing a transitional model of the writing process.* Bloomington, IN: Monographs in Teaching and Learning, School of Education, Indiana University.

Sinclair-deZwart, H. (1969). Developmental psycholinguistics. In D. Elkind & J. H. Flavell (Eds.), *Studies in cognitive development.* New York: Oxford University Press.

Singer, H., & Ruddell, R. B. (1985). (Eds.). *Theoretical models and processes of reading* (3rd ed.). Newark, DE: International Reading Association.

Smith, F. (1981). Demonstrations, engagement and sensitivity: A revised approach to language learning. *Language Arts, 58,* 103–112.

Speidel, G. E. (1982). Responding to language differences. *Oral language in a successful reading program for Hawaiian children* (Report No. 105). Honolulu, HI: Kamehameha Early Education Program.

Strickland, D. S., & Feeley, J. T. (1991). The learner develops: Development in the elementary school years. In J. Flood, J. M. Jensen, D. Lapp, & J. R. Squire (Eds.), *Handbook of research on teaching the English language arts* (pp. 286–302). New York: Macmillan.

Strickland, R. G. (1962). *The language of elementary school children: Its relationship to the language of reading textbooks and the quality of reading of selected children* (Bulletin 38). Bloomington, IN: School of Education, Indiana University.

Sulzby, E. (1991). The development of the young child and the emergence of literacy. In J. Flood, J. M. Jensen, D. Lapp, & J. R. Squire (Eds.), *Handbook of research on teaching the English language arts* (pp. 273–285). New York: Macmillan.

Sulzby, E., & Teale, W. (1991). Emergent literacy. In R. Barr, M. Kamil, P. Mosenthal, & P. D. Pearson (Eds.), *Handbook of reading research: Vol. II* (pp. 727–757). New York: Longman.

Temple, C., & Gillet, J. W. (1989). *Language arts: Learning processes and teaching practices* (2nd ed.). Glenview, IL: Scott, Foresman and Company.

Templin, M. C. (1950). *The development of reasoning in children with normal and defective hearing.* Minneapolis, MN: University of Minnesota Press.

Templin, M. C. (1957). *Certain language skills in children* (Institute of Child Welfare Monographs). Minneapolis, MN: University of Minnesota Press.

Vygotsky, L. S. (1986). *Thought and language.* (rev. ed.; A. Kozulin, Trans. & Ed.). Cambridge, MA: MIT Press.

Wadsworth, B. J. (1971). *Piaget's theory of cognitive development.* New York: David McKay.

Ward, M. C. (1971). *Them children: A study in language learning.* New York: Holt, Rinehart and Winston.

Whaley, J. F. (1981). Story grammar and reading instruction. *The Reading Teacher, 34,* 762–771.

CHAPTER 3

UNDERSTANDING THE BEGINNING STEPS: EARLY READING AND WRITING DEVELOPMENT

Yetta Goodman (1984) has suggested that we could never possibly tell children all they must know in order to learn to read. Think about that for a moment. Then make a list of all the things you think children need to know to learn to read and write. Share your list with a friend.

INTRODUCTION

Children come to school expecting to become literate. This expectation is so universal that if we were to poll a group of children getting ready to start school, chances are the first thing they would tell us that they are going to do when they go to school is "learn to read." Very young children enter kindergarten and the early grades with a vast resource of knowledge about language and literacy that will support them as they learn to read and write. They are experienced information-seekers who constantly explore their surroundings—asking questions, experimenting, and observing. Throughout this process, children's knowledge about language and literate behavior grows, and changes, rapidly. As part of their daily interactions with adults, family, friends, and home and other environments, children construct their own concepts about literacy and what it means to learn to read and write. In fact, many children expect to become fully literate on their first day of school.

What we now know is that most children enter school well on their way toward literacy. Recall our discussion in Chapter 2 in which we characterized children's early language and literacy acquisition. That characterization suggests that most children come to school primed for literacy. Following is a review of our discussion from Chapter 2:

1. *Children are active participants in their own language and literacy development;* the driving force behind their growth is their need to construct meaning—to make sense of the world.

2. *Children's perceptions of print and productions of oral and written language are systematic and organized*—even when overgeneralization creates language forms that do not conform to conventional English.

3. *Children acquire and use literate behaviors in the very early years,* well before entry into school, the onset of formal literacy instruction, and the acquisition of conventional literacy.

4. *Language acquisition and literacy development are influenced by children's language and world knowledge, social interactions, and language environment.* Congruence between home and school language and literacy experiences increases children's opportunity for success in learning to read and write.

5. *Home and community environments, interactions, and experiences are often language-rich in ways not fully explored or understood.*

The goal of this chapter is to develop an understanding of how teachers create learning environments and implement literacy instruction to assist children in successful early reading and writing experiences in school.

First, we will examine the characteristics of a classroom environment that facilitates reading and writing development. Second, we will provide an overview of important developmental patterns of early reading and writing growth. Third, we will present instructional strategies and teaching activities designed to enhance early reading and writing acquisition; these strategies and activities will range from attention to the language of instruction and group participation to building positive attitudes about literacy through story sharing. And, finally, we will emphasize the importance of ongoing assessment, through daily observation, in evaluating children's language and literacy learning.

CREATING READING AND WRITING CLASSROOMS

The kind of classroom you create—whether it is literacy-rich or not, for example—is dependent in large part on how you think about and act on your beliefs about literacy. So you must first examine and identify your beliefs about literacy learning and then implement these beliefs through instruction. We have just reviewed five major conclusions that can be drawn about children's early language and literacy development. These conclusions, along with information in Chapter 2, this chapter, and others, should serve to anchor and support your belief system. In addition to a belief system, it is important that you understand the requisite conditions for optimal learning and how children construct and negotiate meaning in classrooms.

CONDITIONS FOR OPTIMAL LEARNING

Brian Cambourne and Jan Turbill (1987), Australian language educators, have identified seven optimal conditions for literacy learning. While Cambourne originally intended these conditions to explain language acquisition in the home (1984), he and his colleagues have extended them to reading and writing development in the classroom (Brown & Cambourne, 1987). According to Cambourne and Turbill, classrooms that provide optimal conditions for learning are those in which

1. *Children are immersed in language.* Written text is everywhere—on signs and bulletin boards, in books, magazines, papers, and texts. Children's drawing and writing are displayed on classroom bulletin boards; story-reading time, sharing time, and many other language-rich activities fill the classroom day.

2. *Children and teachers are actively involved in meaningful demonstrations of language in action.* The classroom is filled with the buzz of conversations as work and play progress. Classroom activities and events are alive with working noise. Teachers and students alike are active questioners, and teachers use questions to activate background knowledge and encourage predictions, both during and after reading.

3. *Language is employed for real-life purposes, providing opportunity for children to use literacy for personal, social, and school needs.* Cooperative planning of class events—a class birthday party or field trip—recording plans on wall charts, and following up with necessary action is commonplace. Children (and teachers) keep diaries, logs, and journals. Calendars, weather records, seating charts, and all manner of useful documents and charts are displayed throughout the room.

4. *Children assume responsibility for their own learning.* Children have many opportunities to work cooperatively creating, planning, and

carrying out projects, both large and small; self-selecting books they want to read and topics they want to write about; and working in classroom centers. Children are personally accountable for using free time productively.

5. *Adults hold expectations that all children will learn.* The prevailing attitude is that *everyone* will succeed. Teachers, and other adults in the classroom and school, set clear expectations for children's accomplishments and provide a supportive environment in meeting these.

6. *Approximation is encouraged.* Perfection is not the issue here. We routinely smile and reward infant approximations of conventional speech—"da-da" for "daddy," "bongie" for "bottle"—yet we persist in telling children in school they're wrong. We must smile and reward language learners of all ages as they acquire more sophisticated language forms and literacy achievements. For example, in storytelling, we may encourage children to predict story outcomes and to revise and refine their predictions as the story progresses. The point is to provide a psychologically safe setting for children to approximate, and to try again with planned instructional support. Cambourne and Turbill call this a franchise to "have a go" (1987, p. 7). Approximations in such an environment are no longer wrong; they're simply one more step toward being right.

7. *Feedback is given to the learner as an ongoing process.* Language learners need lots of feedback from which to evaluate their progress, draw new or revised conclusions, and move forward. Again, we seem to do this naturally with preschool children—when we respond to "da-da" with "Yes, that's daddy," for example. Children in classrooms need feedback as well, from teachers, other adults, and their peers.

These seven conditions for literacy instruction serve to define the nature of reading and writing classrooms and to guide learning events in them. Effective implementation of instructional strategies and activities to guide learning, however, will require that you understand how children negotiate meaning as they come to understand and participate in classroom tasks.

NEGOTIATING MEANING—UNDERSTANDING CLASSROOM TASKS

Successfully negotiating meaning in classrooms requires understanding of the complex social unit that classrooms represent. To begin with, teachers have instructional goals and objectives they wish to meet. Children, however, may not hold, or even perceive, these objectives. As Dyson (1984) has emphasized:

...Literacy is not simply a set of skills; it is a social activity. No matter what the instructional objectives of specific tasks, children do not focus on objectives, but on tasks as activities—as whole experiences—that include materials to be used, a series of actions to be followed, and a way of talking during and about the activity...

Meaning negotiation is more complex than we may initially think.

Types of Meaning

Pauline Harris (1989) has examined the meaning-negotiation process in her research with first-grade children. Her work is based on two areas of thought: (1) Kelly's (1955) view that we construct our own reality based on background knowledge and what we anticipate in a specific environment and (2) Erickson's (1982) study of the "pedagogical encounter," the transaction of meaning between the individual child and the instructional environment. Harris concludes that four types of meaning must be considered as children negotiate and construct meaning in learning events. These are:

- *Personal meanings*—meanings based on children's background knowledge, their behavior-response style, actions and strategies used in talking about their experiences, and their expectations about the learning experience.

- *Group meanings*—meanings based on understanding the group agenda, which consists of objectives, expectations, and behaviors for the individual working as part of a group, and expectations of the group as a whole.

- *Task meanings*—meanings involving both academic and social meanings. Academic meanings consist of children's subject matter knowledge, text structure knowledge, and understanding of directions and instructions; social meanings include understanding of relationships between teacher and child, working in small and large groups, who speaks and when, turn-taking, classroom rules, and location of materials.

- *Text meanings*—meanings constructed from knowledge of word analysis, syntactic patterns, and illustrations; understanding of story features, including characters, settings, story sequence, and plot; and understanding of "metabook" meanings, such as authorship, format of illustrations, and number of pages.

The interactions for these four types of meaning are shown in Figure 3-1 and are based on Harris's research (1989, p. 143).

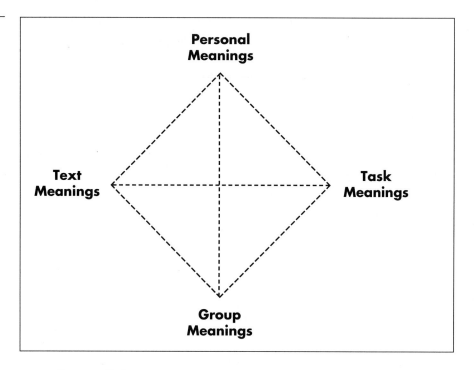

FIGURE 3-1

Meaning Negotiation in Classroom Interaction Using Personal, Group, Text and Task Meanings. (Reproduced with permission from Harris, 1989, p. 143.)

Harris's view of meaning types and the interactions suggested in Figure 3-1 provide a glimpse of what students must do in order to negotiate meaning successfully in classrooms. Our goal is to encourage and help children learn to orchestrate meaning relationships between and among task, text, personal, and group meanings. In doing this, we help them understand the instructional objective and our expectations, and to participate effectively in completing the learning experience.

Meaning Breaks

It is clear, however, from Figure 3-1, that meaning breaks may occur at a number of places in the instructional experience. Such breaks explain why some children have difficulty negotiating meaning and participating in classroom instruction. Based on her observations of instruction, Harris notes (1989, p. 142):

> *The extent to which individual children connected text [meaning] and task [meaning] varied, and while all children used books to do their assigned activities, the books were used to different degrees of meaning. Part of the varying degrees to*

*which children connected themselves with texts, and connected
text and task together, arose from text and task being two separate constructs. For example, if a child focused upon the
social or visual aspects of tasks, then attention to comprehension and deeper meanings of the related texts seemed lessened.
On the other hand, if a child could attend to both the academic and social task demands, as well as to text meanings, then
the child, ideally, could construct an integrated meaning from
the overall encounter. Only one child, Christine, in this study
appeared to achieve such integration: she was a child who, in
addition to being a fluent reader, showed parallel sequencing
of her thought processes, in relation to the text, the task, and
what the rest of her group was doing. She thus positioned herself to text and task demands in a balanced manner, and effectively negotiated the multiple meanings in her encounters.
Other children in the study showed less balanced approaches,
with focus upon certain aspects of text or task, and their participation and understanding for the deeper meanings of text
and task appeared to be undermined as a result.*

Ambiguity, Classroom Tasks, and Meaning Negotiation

Children of all ages face ambiguity daily in classrooms. The ambiguity
may be *intended*—for example, when the teacher deliberately assigns open-
ended, complex tasks; or it may be *unintended*—when children produce
responses or products that do not match the teacher's expectation. Whether
the ambiguity is intended or unintended, children generally disambiguate
classroom tasks in one of two ways: (1) by reducing the task to low-level, rote
responses (Doyle & Carter, 1984; Haggard, 1989; Ruddell, 1991) or (2) by
redefining, or reconstructing the task itself (Haggard, 1989; Murphy, 1988).

Doyle and Carter (1984) define ambiguity as ". . . the extent to which a
precise and predictable formula for student action in generating a product
can be defined" (p. 130). Susie Murphy's study of unintended ambiguity
(1988) found that students' unexpected responses to procedural reading
tasks occurred most frequently because the children did not understand
what the task was asking them to do. In the face of such ambiguity, the children constructed their own definition of the task, thus arriving at answers
unanticipated by the teacher and text materials. Children asked to do highly
open-ended tasks—such as group or individual projects—are often quite
persistent in asking questions for the purpose of reducing the ambiguity.
"How long is it supposed to be?" "What kind of report do you want?"
"How do you want us to do it?" are typical of such questioning. In extreme
cases, children may refuse to work until more information is forthcoming.

A critical element in children's tolerance for ambiguity is the degree of *risk*
present—the degree to which they face heavy consequences for failure to meet
task demands (Doyle & Carter, 1984). When both ambiguity and risk are high,

children have scant recourse but to reduce one or the other, and since they have little control over *risk* (consequences for failure to meet task demands), they most often seek to reduce the ambiguity. If we are to encourage children to accept ambiguity, then, we need to reduce class risks. Classroom conditions we discussed earlier create environments where risk is low, where approximations are valued and children are willing to try new ideas and behaviors and develop their personal strategies for handling ambiguity (Ruddell, 1991)—to "have a go," as it were. In such environments, children not only develop higher tolerance for ambiguity but have the opportunity for ongoing discussion and meaning negotiation. Their experiences constructing personal, text, task, and group meanings are thus more likely to be successful.

Sensitivity to Children's Understandings

Our role as teachers requires that we be sensitive to children's responses to ambiguity and risk, and further that we understand the way in which task meaning, text meaning, personal meaning, and group meaning function in harmony and influence children's meaning construction. This will enable us to negotiate meaning more effectively with children as we engage them in learning events. We may find for example, that the children's *task meaning* understandings present a problem, that they understand task functions only vaguely—words such as *right* and *left*, *up* and *down*, or *underline* and *circle*. Some individual children may not be able to work cooperatively in a small group or tolerate even moderate levels of open-endedness in group or individual tasks. Other children's understanding of *text meaning* may be inadequate if needed word analysis skills are not in the child's knowledge store or if concepts in the text are too difficult.

Children's *personal meaning* may not match intended meanings because of knowledge or cultural differences, or children may be unable to focus attention on a specific idea. Their *group meaning* will need to include understanding of group goals and agendas and the ability to listen to and understand divergent viewpoints if they are to function effectively in the instructional episode. Understanding of the these aspects of the classroom social unit and the way in which they function in meaning negotiation will be of great help in creating and directing effective learning episodes and in troubleshooting meaning negotiation problems when breakdowns occur in classrooms.

EARLY LITERACY DEVELOPMENT—PATTERNS AND GOALS

In the past decade, considerable study of children's early literacy experiences has yielded extraordinary insights into how children become literate (Harste, Woodward, & Burke, 1984; Morrow, 1993; Sulzby, 1985, 1994; Sulzby & Teale, 1991). In this section we will discuss early reading development; we will explore early writing development later in this chapter and at length in Chapter 7.

DEVELOPING A LINGUISTIC REPERTOIRE

Elizabeth Sulzby's work has focused on children's early reading of favorite storybooks. Her original sample of children were preschool and kindergarten age and had not been exposed to formal reading instruction. Sulzby developed a tree diagram from this study (see Figure 3-2) that appeared to suggest that children progressed in a stage-like manner from picture reading to independent reading. More recently, however, (1994) she conceptualizes these reading patterns as the "linguistic repertoire" that children acquire and move in and out of on their way toward conventional reading, refining old patterns and adding new ones in the process. The repertoire includes two broad categories. First, picture-governed story attempts, in which children treat the picture as the main source of the story meaning; and second, print-governed attempts, in which they consider the printed language as the story meaning source. These categories include a variety of patterns that children move between and among on their way to conventional reading (Sulzby now prefers "conventional" to "independent"). Below is a short explanation of the patterns in the linguistic repertoire:

Story Not Formed—Oral. Individual pictures in storybooks are treated as independent and isolated meaning units as reflected in the children's oral interpretation of the picture. No attempt is made to build a story.

Story Formed—Oral Language-Like. Pictures are used to form a story "of sorts" as the child looks at each picture. The language used provides some dialogue for the characters and may include comments and observations about the pictures.

Story Formed—Written Language-like—Print Not Watched. Pictures are used to weave a story using language with intonation and words that sound like written language. Written language-like reading includes storytelling that closely follows the pattern of the book on a page-for-page basis, and eventually approximates and even matches the text of the book.

Print Watched—Refusal. Print is used to some extent in the story-reading attempt. This pattern includes initial refusals to try to read that may occur suddenly and are often accompanied with the child's explanation of why he or she cannot read. The child has come to understand that people read the print rather than the pictures.

Print Watched—Aspectual. Here the child also focuses on specific aspects of print such as a few known words, or attempts to sound out words.

Holistic—Strategies Imbalanced. Print is used in an integrated and more meaningful way. Early in this pattern, the child may omit unknown words, substitute words, or depend on remembered text rather than the written text.

Holistic—Independent Reading. The child's reading becomes more conventional; the child will read at times with ease and fluency and at other times with numerous reading miscues. When miscues occur, however, the

TREE STRUCTURE OF CATEGORIES OF CLASSIFICATION SCHEME FOR EMERGENT READING OF FAVORITE STORYBOOKS

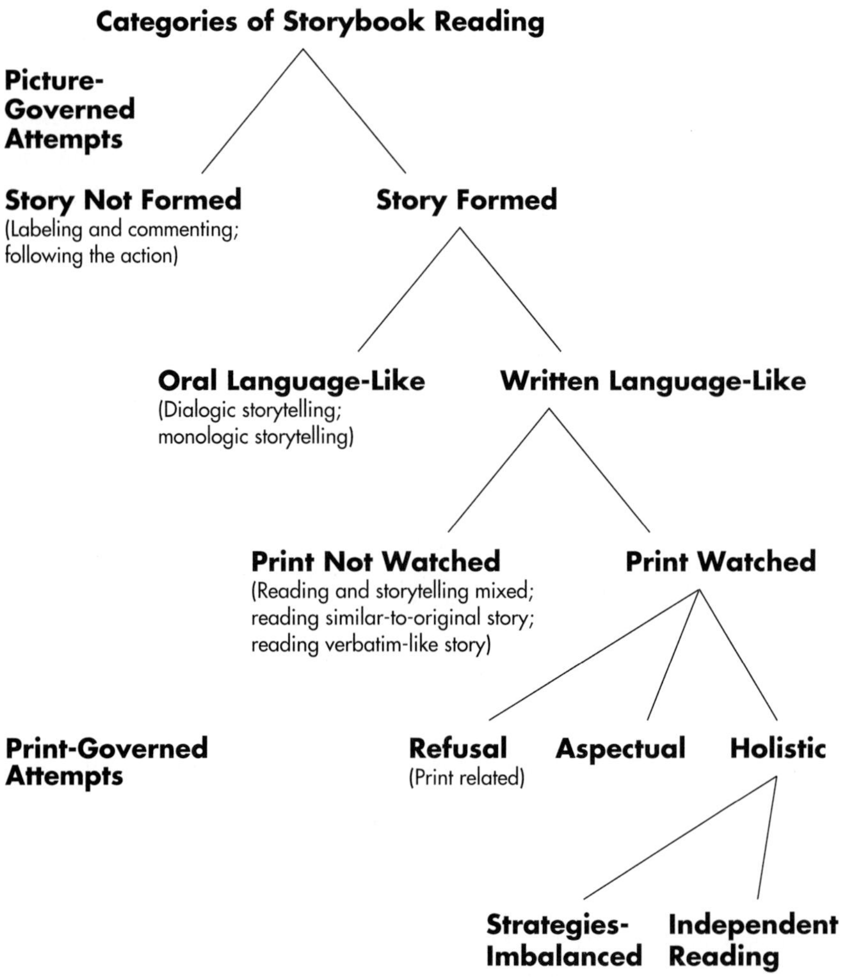

Categories of Storybook Reading

Picture-Governed Attempts

Story Not Formed
(Labeling and commenting; following the action)

Story Formed

Oral Language-Like
(Dialogic storytelling; monologic storytelling)

Written Language-Like

Print Not Watched
(Reading and storytelling mixed; reading similar-to-original story; reading verbatim-like story)

Print Watched

Print-Governed Attempts

Refusal
(Print related)

Aspectual

Holistic

Strategies-Imbalanced

Independent Reading

This figure includes independent reading attempts only: the child is making the reading attempts without dependence upon turn-taking reading or interrogation by the adult.

FIGURE 3-2

Developmental Stages in Storybook Reading for Preschool and Kindergarten Children. Reproduced with permission from Sulzby, 1985, Figure 1.)

child self-corrects, based on the meaning inferred from the text. This stage gives clear evidence of predicting and self-correcting.

In her discussion of conventional reading (1994, p. 279), Sulzby comments,

> [Children] also seem to show a particular knack for mimic-ry of a whole activity, of 'acting as if' they were accomplished performers when clearly they still lack certain skills or accomplishments of their elders. They seem to use their social sense of what linguistic usages and forms 'work' in a particular social context.

Her point here is that our observations of children must take into account their ability to "act as if" and not overestimate their literacy abilities. Just as importantly, we should realize that "acting as if" is a marvelous support, or scaffolding, strategy for acquiring new skills and behaviors. Figure 3-3 shows an example of a three-year-old reading. Can you identify Jennifer's linguistic repertoire?

DEVELOPING LITERACY AWARENESS

The linguistic repertoire Sulzby proposes suggests that children use pictures and text to create meaning as they move toward conventional reading. This process is greatly enhanced by home and school learning environments where children have opportunities to participate in storytelling and story reading and where adults and older siblings demonstrate a strong interest in and place value on reading and literacy use (Durkin, 1966; Soderbergh, 1977; Bussie, Chittenden, Amarel, & Klausner, 1985; Purcell-Gates, 1988).

For example, Durkin found in her research on children who read before entering school (1966) that between 47 and 83 percent of their parents reported that reading materials, paper, pencil, and chalkboards were readily available at home. By contrast, only 14 to 23 percent of the parents of nonearly readers reported that such materials were available in the home. A logical connection is found between early picture and print experiences and reading as children draw pictures, label and title their pictures, and learn to write their own names, the alphabet, and beginning stories (Graves, 1982; Calkins, 1986).

Children entering kindergarten will vary greatly in their understanding of the "conventions of reading" (Mason, 1984), as well as the "arbitrary rules that govern the act of reading (e.g., knowing that one reads from left to right [in English], that punctuation is important, and what spaces between letters mean) . . ." (Mason, 1984, p. 511) and the labels and concepts used in reading instruction. Research on children's knowledge about printed text reveals marked growth during the kindergarten year. For example, the percentage of children understanding alphabet knowledge has been found to increase from 44 to 75 percent. Letter-name identification has increased from 38 to 56 percent, the ability to use rhyming words from 13 to 63 percent, and knowledge of locational terms such as *top* and *bottom* from 65 to 80 percent (Hardy, Stennett, & Smythe, 1974). Downing and Oliver's work (1973–1974), with

From the time Jennifer was a year old, she was read to regularly by her mother. At three years, three months of age, Jennifer was visited by a researcher (R), who asked her to read *Are you My Mother?* (Eastman, 1967), a book that had been read to her many times. In an enthusiastic manner and with a reading intonation, she read the entire book, a portion of which follows:

Jennifer	*Text*
Out pop the baby birdie.	Out came the baby bird.
He says, "Where is my mother?" (aside to R) He's looking for it.	"Where is my mother?" he said. He looked for her.
Looked up; did not see her.	He looked up. He did not see her.
And he looked down; he didn't see it.	He looked down. He did not see her.
So he said he's gonna go look for her.	"I will go and look for her," he said.
------------------------------------	------------------------------------
Came to a kitten and he said, "Are you my mother?"	He came to a kitten. "Are you my mother?" he said to the kitten.
"N…and he didn't say anything. He just looked and looked.	The kitten just looked and looked. It did not say a thing.
Then he came to a hen and he said, "Are you my mother?" "No."	The kitten was not his mother, so he went on. Then he came to a hen. "Are you my mother?" he said to the hen. "No," said the hen.

FIGURE 3-3

Jennifer's Storybook Reading. Can you identify Jennifer's linguistic repertoire in storybook reading? (Reproduced with permission from Teak & Sulzby, 1989, p. 2.)

five, six, and seven year old children demonstrates the need to develop concepts such as *syllable, word,* and *sentence*. This is understandable because of the dominance of oral language in the child's life. A spoken sentence, for example, may represent a single meaning unit in the child's mind—in effect one long word. Such important terms and concepts are frequently not understood by children even after a year in kindergarten, and yet they are used routinely in early reading instruction.

Just as important is developing children's emerging understandings about what constitutes literate acts. A number of studies over the years

(Johns, 1972; Kita, 1979; Reid, 1966) have suggested that, for many children, "reading" is associated solely with school or mechanical tasks—doing workbook exercises, sounding out words, rendering print into oral language, and so forth. Other children think meaning resides in pictures; still others simply don't know what reading is about.

Mason (1984) emphasizes the importance of early reading experiences that develop a functional understanding of the relationship between printed words and the meaning they represent. Such print experiences need to use concepts and experiences familiar to children. Children must also learn the classroom conventions, rules, and labels that are critical for directing instruction and for their understanding of how to do instructional tasks.

The importance of early literacy instruction that connects children's prior experiences and background knowledge with their classroom literacy experiences is evident in the recommendations for Literacy Development in Prefirst Grade found in Table 3-1. This statement was prepared by the Early Childhood and Literacy Development Committee of the International Reading Association.

GOALS OF INSTRUCTION IN EARLY READING AND WRITING DEVELOPMENT

Based on the previous discussion, we wish to suggest five instructional goals for early literacy instruction. These consist of:

First, developing in children an understanding of the conventions of reading, the language of instruction, concepts about literacy, and group-participation conventions that will enable them to participate effectively in individual and group instructional activities;

Second, developing children's awareness and understanding of picture and print concepts that form the basis for early reading and writing;

Third, developing children's sense of observing, recording, and writing with the aim of building understanding of how thoughts and experiences can be represented in print;

Fourth, developing their sense of story and narrative features, which will serve as the basis for understanding narrative text;

And fifth, developing positive attitudes toward early reading and writing through shared book and story experiences.

INSTRUCTIONAL STRATEGIES AND ACTIVITIES FOR EARLY LITERACY ACQUISITION

We will consider each of the instructional goals in the context of the classroom. Our intent is to provide instructional strategies and activities that illustrate how these goals may be implemented in your classroom instruction.

RECOMMENDATIONS

1. Build instruction on what the child already knows about oral language, reading, and writing. Focus on meaningful experiences and meaningful language rather than on isolated skill development.
2. Respect the language the child brings to school, and use it as a base for language and literacy activities.
3. Ensure feelings of success for all children, helping them to see themselves as people who enjoy exploring both oral and written language.
4. Provide reading experiences as an integrated part of the communication process, which includes speaking, listening and writing, as well as art, math and music.
5. Encourage children's first attempts at writing, without concern for the proper formation of letters or correct conventional spelling.
6. Encourage risk-taking in first attempts at reading and writing, and accept what appear to be errors as part of children's natural growth and development.
7. Use reading materials that are familiar or predictable, such as well-known stories, as they provide children with a sense of control and confidence in their ability to learn.
8. Present a model for children to emulate. In the classroom, teachers should use language appropriately, listen and respond to children's talk, and engage in their own reading and writing.
9. Take time regularly to read to children from a wide variety of poetry, fiction, and nonfiction.
10. Provide time regularly for children's independent reading and writing.
11. Foster children's affective and cognitive development by providing them with opportunities to communicate what they know, think, and feel.
12. Use developmentally and culturally appropriate procedures for evaluation, ones that are based on the objectives of the program and that consider each child's total development.
13. Make parents aware of the reasons for a broader language program at school and provide them with ideas for activities to carry out at home.
14. Alert parents to the limitations of formal assessments and standardized tests of prefirst-graders' reading and writing skills.
15. Encourage children to be active participants in the learning process rather than passive recipients by using activities that allow for experimentation with talking, listening, writing, and reading.

TABLE 3-1

Recommendations for Literacy Development in Prefirst Grade

Source: Reproduced with permission from Strickland & Morrow, 1989, p. 161.

CONVENTIONS OF READING: THE LANGUAGE OF INSTRUCTION, CONCEPTS ABOUT LITERACY, AND GROUP PARTICIPATION

Specific language of instruction and group participation concepts that need to be developed in kindergarten and grade one include the following:

1. Direction words such as *left* and *right* ; *top* and *bottom* ; *over* and *under*, *into* and *out of* ; and *beside* and *between.*

2. Ordering words such as *front* and *back*; *beginning, middle,* and *end*; *first, second, third,* etc.

3. Color words such as *red, green, orange, yellow, blue, black,* and *white*; and geometric shape words such as *circle, square, triangle,* and *rectangle.*

4. Instructional directions such as *make a circle around*; *draw a line under*, and *draw a picture of.*

5. Feeling- and sensory-based words such as *happy* and *sad*; *sweet* and *sour*, *soft* and *rough*; *bright* and *dark*; and *quiet* and *noisy.*

6. Group participation, attention, and task-sequencing directions such as *all eyes looking at me*; *now listen carefully*; *next we will. . . .*; *find your favorite book*; and *put your materials away.*

Many of these instructional concepts will develop in the natural occurrence of classroom events. It is important however, that you:

- Sensitize yourself to the idea that some children will not understand these seemingly basic concepts.

- Realize that these concepts are important for understanding instructional directions and participating in individual and small group activities.

- Carefully observe children who have difficulty in understanding instructional tasks that include these concepts.

- Develop these concepts in meaningful high-interest classroom activities.

- Use every opportunity in all areas of instruction to develop and use these concepts.

Developing Directional Concepts

Directional concepts frequently provide difficulty for many kindergarten and first-grade students. These concepts can be readily developed through game and play activity. For example, the concepts of *right, left, in,* and *out* may be developed in a group game using the old folk song "Here We Dance Looby Loo"(an alternative version of this song is known as the "Hokey-Pokey"). Have the children hold hands in a circle with you as you sing the song together following the directions. You will need to model the movements for directions along with those children who already have directional concepts established.

> Here we dance looby loo,
> Here we dance looby light,
> Here we dance looby loo,
> All on a Saturday night.
> I put my *right* foot *in,*
> I put my *right* foot *out,*
> I give my *right* foot a shake, shake, shake,
> And turn myself about (*left* foot, *right* hand, *left*
>   hand, head, whole body).

You can also use directional terms when working with individual and small groups of children. As you discuss a picture during story sharing, you can point to an object in the illustration and ask, "What is that at the *top* (or bottom, left, or right) of the page?" This type of informal learning can be used to develop a wide variety of concepts in an inductive fashion. *Richard Scarry's Biggest Word Book Ever!* (1985) provides marvelous illustrations using giant-sized pages that serve this purpose well.

Your own ingenuity becomes important as you create opportunities to develop instructional concepts throughout the day. Children will enjoy planning a trail through the classroom. You can encourage them to choose key points on the trail to go *up, over, across,* etc. After the route has been determined, you may have the children identify the points on the trail and record each point on a chart as they name it. Your chart might look something like this:

> Our Trail
> <u>up</u> the big box
> <u>across</u> the rug
> <u>over</u> Pedro's desk
> <u>around</u> the aquarium
> <u>under</u> the table

You may then help the children make tagboard signs for each point on the trail. After attaching the signs to the appropriate objects on the trail, the children can use string to trace the trail as the signs are read.

Developing Geometric Shape Language

Awareness of geometric shape language can be developed by having children trace and cut two or more large paper circles, squares, rectangles, and triangles, from different colored construction paper. They can then create familiar objects and paste these on white art paper. For example, a circle placed on the side of a triangle forms an ice cream cone, a square with a triangle on top forms a house, a rectangle and two small circles form a car.

After the geometric pictures are completed, each child can describe the object to the rest of the class, using the geometric shape vocabulary. For example, "This is an ice cream cone. A brown *triangle* is the cone. The red *circle* on top is the strawberry ice cream, and the white *circle* is a scoop of vanilla." It will undoubtedly help for you to model the explanation activity first and do some group practice before asking children to do it individually.

Identifying Class Participation Rules

Group cooperation can be greatly enhanced early in the school year by identifying and discussing classroom participation rules that are important to everyone (we'll discuss these at length in Chapter 13). A final list can be recorded on chart paper and displayed in the room. Such a list may include items such as the following:

Our Classroom Sharing Rules

1. Listen carefully to directions.

2. Take turns in sharing ideas.

3. Listen to what each person has to say.

4. Don't interrupt when someone else is talking.

5. Raise your hand to let other people know you have something to say.

Easy reference can be made to your agreed-on list to help remind the children of the importance of cooperation in group sharing. Children will need to understand how to enter into, take turns, and share ideas in discussion.

Developing Language of Instruction

You will find attention-direction phrases helpful as you introduce, explain, and conclude instructional activities. These include such phrases as *all eyes looking at me*, pausing until everyone's attention is focused and followed by, *now listen carefully, first we will…, put all of your things away.* Frequent opportunity exists throughout the school day for developing these oral signals for group directions.

Many language of instruction and group instruction concepts can be developed in an exciting and enjoyable way through story sharing and individual exploration using a variety of children's books. These books are especially designed for introducing new concepts to children. Children's favorites include:

Mitsumasa Anno, *Anno's Counting Book*
Eric Carle, *The Very Hungry Caterpillar*
Donald Crews, *Bicycle Race*
Donald Crews, *Freight Train*
Gail Gibbons, *Dinosaurs*
Gail Gibbons, *Flying and Playgrounds*
Tana Hoban, *Big Ones, Little Ones*
Tana Hoban, *Count and See*
Tana Hoban, *Is It Larger? Is It Smaller?*
Tana Hoban, *Is It Red? Is It Yellow? Is It Blue?*
Betsy and Giulio Maestro, *Where Is My Friend? A Word Concept Book*
Anne Rockwell, *Boats*
Anne Rockwell, *Things That Go*
Nancy Tafuri, *Who's Counting?*
Brian Wildsmith, *Brian Wildsmith's 1, 2, 3*

Spend time in your school library to look through these and other books with high potential for developing instructional concepts in your classroom.

Developing Concepts About Reading

Certainly, one of the critical aspects of developing children's concepts about reading (and writing) is, as Cambourne and Turbill suggest, to immerse them in a print-rich environment and provide opportunity daily for reading and writing to be a natural part of classroom events. This includes having paper and pens or pencils available in the play area for authentic order-taking in restaurant play, as well as recording experiences on charts and in journals and logs, and reading to children every day. *Lots* of time for free reading—even in classrooms where the majority of children are not yet reading conventionally—is also required. Add to this language- and literacy-rich environment by encouraging children to think about and reflect on their own literacy processes. Below is a transcript of a discussion in Jenny Sirell's kindergarten class about what good readers do. Notice how children bring their experience into this discussion and how they contribute to each other's concept of what makes a good reader.

T: What do you think makes someone a good reader?

S1: They know how to read the words and they read a lot.

S2: They tell funny stories.

S3: They look at the words and sound them out.

S4: They think about reading.

T: How?

S4: I don't know—they just think about the story they're reading and stuff.

T: Do you know a good reader?

S1: My mom's a good reader. She reads all the time . . . so does my dad.

T: So good readers read a lot! What do they read?

S1: I don't know . . . stuff like newspapers, magazines . . .

S5: My dad always reads in the bathroom.

T: How do you think they learned to read?

S4: They went to kindergarten.

T: Yes, that's true but what do you think they learned in kindergarten when it came to reading? [Begins listing children's ideas on chart paper.]

S5: They learned how to sound out words.

T: What else?

S1: They looked at the pictures.

S4: They guessed. They made up a story.

T: Good—anything else?

S2: They read the story over 'til they memorized it.

S3: They learned their stories from their moms and dads and practiced.

T: Wow! You guys know a lot about what it takes to be a good reader. Now, I have another idea. What do you think your brain is doing when you read? I mean, is it sending messages to your body? Are your eyes doing something? Are your lips doing something? Are your ears doing something? Is your nose doing something? [children laugh] Are your hands doing something?

S1: Well, your eyes are looking at the words so your brain is saying, "Hey, these are words." And your lips are moving telling your brain what the words are and your ears are listening to the words.

T: Do your hands move?

S3: Yeah, to turn the page, silly.

T: Oh, so your brain tells your hands when to turn the page?

S3: Yeah.

S5: Sometimes I point at the words I say when I read.

T: Why?

S5: 'Cause that way I remember what word I'm on.

T: So it sounds like your brain is doing a lot of important things. What I'd like you to do is draw a picture of your brain reading. Think of all the things it takes to be a good reader you just told me and all the things your brain does while you're reading. You can draw pictures inside your brain or write words if your pictures aren't saying enough.

In this delightful interchange, not only did children learn from one another, but the teacher also learned about children's knowledge bases and had the opportunity to extend those. Stop occasionally and ask your students what makes a good reader or what makes a good writer. List their ideas and probe their thinking as Jenny did. Extend their thinking with the kind of individual activity Jenny used, and refer to students' ideas periodically in class discussion.

PICTURE AND PRINT AWARENESS

The development of picture and print awareness goes hand in hand with development of children's concepts about reading and writing and the language of instruction. Most children enter school with rich picture and print experiences from their environment—television, movies, magazines, newspapers, comics, cereal boxes, billboards, and so forth. Others have additional experience observing adults writing grocery lists, notes, and letters, and reading newspapers, books, and magazines. For these children, environmental experiences have already formed an excellent picture and print-awareness background.

However, this is not the case with all children. It is particularly not the case with those youngsters who have had very limited opportunities to explore and talk about pictures and print, to read or be read to at home, and to see adults reading and writing.

Specific concepts related to early picture and print awareness include the following:

1. **Picture knowledge:** *pictures (drawings, illustrations, and photographs) represent ideas and meaning,* and *pictures may be used in sequence to tell a story or to explain new ideas.*

2. **Print knowledge:** *print represents ideas and meaning* through written language; *each word is made up of letters* that represent or stand for sounds; *print is organized by words* identified by the blank spaces between them; each line of *print is read on the page in a left-to-right direction*; the *lines of print are read from top to bottom* on the page; and *special punctuation marks are used* to indicate the beginning and end of sentences (.), to ask questions (?), to provide special emphasis (!), and to show that someone is talking (" ").

3. **Page knowledge:** *pages have top and bottom positions,* and *when two pages are side by side, the left page is read first.*

4. **Book knowledge**: *books have fronts and backs; pages are organized from left to right* in a book; and *pictures and print in books can be used to tell a story or explain new ideas.*

Concepts About Print

Marie Clay, a New Zealand educator, has developed a Concepts About Print Test (1979), that is used to evaluate children's early print awareness. Most of the concepts identified above are evaluated in the test. As the examiner reads from a small book (*Sand* or *Stones*), the child is asked to "help" (any small book that has both print and pictures may be used). Questions are asked to identify print awareness related to book, sentence, and words. For example, as the book is handed to the child with the spine of the book facing the child, the examiner asks, "Show me the front of this book." Then the examiner opens the book to a place where print is on one page and a picture is on the other and asks, "Show me where I begin reading." Other tasks require the child to show where on the page one begins reading, how one moves from top to bottom of pages, and what words and letters are. Throughout, the examiner observes and records the child's responses, and notes the strategies used by the child in responding to the questions. Valuable instructional information regarding children's book and print awareness knowledge can be obtained through similar observations using storybooks or specially prepared print in your classroom. As you develop picture and print concepts with your children keep the following in mind:

- Children's language background and meaning awareness are critical to successful development of picture and print awareness.

- Instructional activities and strategies used in developing picture and print conventions should carry meaning for children.

- A classroom environment that surrounds children with pictures and print provides opportunity for active and direct involvement in the use of oral and printed language.

Developing Picture-and Print-Awareness Concepts

Many picture- and print-awareness concepts are developed through environmental print in the classroom, language experience charts, Big Book reading, oral storytelling using picture book illustrations, and direct hands-on book experiences.

Extensive use and display of environmental print in the classroom can be very important in developing the concept of letter, word, sentence, and story (Allen, 1976). Here are several ways to create a print-rich environment:

1. Place large alphabet posters in a location easily visible to the children.
2. Print word labels on tagboard and tape them to familiar objects in the

classroom, such as *desk, chalkboard, bookcase, door, piano, aquarium, fish,* etc.

3. Print the name of each child on tagboard and place it on the child's desk. Have small groups of children compare their names, noting what different letters are used in each.

4. Use newspaper photographs or poster-sized illustrations representing high-interest content such as community helpers in action, animals, or a playground scene as the basis for oral language discussion. Then develop written word labels for individuals, animals, or objects in the pictures and discuss these. Mount the pictures and word labels on the classroom bulletin board.

5. Ask the children to draw a picture of a family member or a special pet. Label each child's picture using the name provided by the child and display it on the bulletin board.

In short, surround and immerse your children in environmental print and language of all types.

Connecting Picture Awareness to Meaning

A good beginning point in connecting picture awareness to meaning is the use of wordless storybooks in which the illustrations alone tell the story. Early on, children are able to infer and create the story relying on the illustrations. Excellent books of this type include Pat Hutchins's *Rosie's Walk* and *Changes, Changes;* Ezra Jack Keats's *Skates;* Mercer Mayer's *A Boy, a Dog, and a Frog* and *Frog Goes to Dinner;* and Jan Ormerod's *Sunshine* and *Moonlight.*

Language-Experience Charts

Language-experience charts based on children's home and school experiences provide excellent opportunity to develop print awareness and understanding that print represents meaning (Goodman, Bird, & Goodman, 1991). The great advantage of this instructional activity is its flexibility. You and your children can create a written record of any experience by simply using large chart paper and a marker pen. For example, after a walk around the school, a field trip to the zoo or aquarium, or a half-hour spent working in the class garden, you can create a chart that captures the key events in the experience as revealed in the children's discussion. Here is one example from a first-grade classroom, based on a school trip to Marine World Africa USA.

Our Trip to Marine World

We went to marine world.

We saw dolphins and killer whales.

We went on the elephant ride.

We saw tigers in the water.

We then went to the ski show and
there was a man skiing on bare feet!

We had a good time.

Then we rode the bus back to school.

This story of the children's experiences provides any number of opportunities for activities to develop picture and print awareness. These include:

- Have each child draw a picture of his or her favorite experience during the event. Have the child dictate a title for the picture or a sentence about it. Record the title or sentence under the picture.

- Have individual children identify specific letters or words on the experience chart story by cupping hands around the letter or word.

- Make tagboard cards for individual words, specific letters, and punctuation marks, e.g., *We, we, dolphin, s, tiger, s, ., !.* Have individual children match the words, letters, and punctuation marks as you read the sentence containing these. Read the words and sentences together with the children.

- Display the language-experience story and children's individual pictures on the classroom bulletin board.

Big Books

Big books provide another excellent opportunity for children to develop concepts about books and picture and print awareness within an exciting and meaningful language context. Big books are common in most primary classrooms today and are most often giant-sized reproductions of standard-sized books. The illustrations and print are large enough for children to see as you work both in large and small groups.

As the big book is introduced, you can draw the children's attention to the front and back, to the left-to-right organization of the pages, and to top and bottom picture orientation. You can also highlight the role of the illustrations and that of the printed text in understanding the story, as you reinforce the idea that the printed language is used in reading the story.

The large-sized print in big books enables you to direct children's attention for a "read along." Don Holdaway (1979) stresses the importance of using enlarged books in shared reading experiences and in directing the children's attention by tracking the print with a pointer or your hand. In this way the concepts of left-to-right organization of print, organization of lines of print from top to bottom of the page, the use of special punctuation marks, and the idea that print represents meaning are embedded in a meaningful story context.

Using Big Books

Many big books are readily available from publishers. Three that teachers and children especially like are Bill Martin's *Brown Bear, Brown Bear, What Do You See?* and Mem Fox's *Hattie and the Fox* and *Mrs. Wishy-Washy* from the Wright Group Story Box.

Oral Story Reading

Oral story reading using standard-sized books provides many of the same opportunities as those found in the big book shared reading experience. Make sure that the children have an unobstructed view of the illustrations in the book and that you have the story clearly in mind, so that you can direct the children's attention to the illustrations and print organization. Although standard-sized books do not have the advantages of oversized print and pictures, you nevertheless can draw children's attention to print and illustrations with them. As you can see, this kind of story reading provides many informal opportunities to build picture-and print-awareness concepts with the children as you share the story with them.

Alphabet Books

ABC books are excellent for developing letter-name knowledge and initiating the connection between letters and sounds. Most of these delightfully illustrated books display capital and small letters accompanied by high-interest illustrations and printed words that begin with the letter. For example, Theodore Geisel (in *Dr. Seuss's ABC*) develops the letter *b* in the following way:

BIG B little b (p. 6)

What begins with B? (p. 7)

After turning the page we see the words *Barber, baby, bubbles,* and a *bumblebee* (p. 8) with whimsical illustrations on the opposite page (p. 9).

This type of book not only develops alphabet-name knowledge but also begins to develop initial consonant sound-letter relationships. Several excellent ABC books include the following:

Mitsumasa Anno, *Anno's Alphabet*

Mary Azarian, *A Farmer's Alphabet*

Muriel Feelings, *Jambo Means Hello: Swahili Alphabet Book*

Bert Kitchen, *Animal Alphabet*

Dr. Seuss, *Dr. Seuss's ABC*

Tracey Cambell Pearson, *A Apple Pie*

Rhyming Books

Rhyming books provide a high level of interest and also help to develop recognition of rhyming endings. This in turn has important value in early reading instruction. Many children's favorites are found in the following poetry collections:

Marc Brown, *Finger Rhymes*

Nancy Larrick, *When Dark Comes Dancing: A Bedtime Poetry Book*

Jack Prelutsky, *Read-Aloud Rhymes for the Very Young*

Caroline Royds, *Poems for Young Children*

Clyde Watson, *Catch Me & Kiss Me & Say It Again*

Guiding the development of picture and print awareness is a vital aspect of your early reading and literacy program, particularly for children who have had limited early literacy experiences. In Chapter 8, "Using Word Analysis Strategies to Develop Reader Independence: Transforming Print to Meaning," we will develop the connection between print awareness and word analysis skills.

DEVELOPING A SENSE OF OBSERVING AND WRITING

Children's curiosity and social nature provide a natural opportunity for you to encourage them to pursue their observations through discussion. This in turn leads to helping them begin to compose and record their ideas. With your guidance, they come to understand how their observations and thoughts can be represented in written language. The objectives such guidance and instruction provide include the following:

1. To show how thoughts and ideas are represented through drawing and writing.
2. To help students understand the use of familiar and new vocabulary to create descriptions of people, animals, objects, and events.
3. To develop the understanding that events occur in a time sequence, which we can show by the order used in presenting our ideas in writing and by special words such *as next, then, after that,* and *finally.*
4. To build familiarity with conventional ways to record ideas in written form, using titles, capital letters, and punctuation.

The activities and strategies suggested below develop the above objectives in an integrated fashion. As you read about these activities and strategies, keep the following key ideas in mind.

- Make sure the activities and strategies are developed in a context that has meaning for the children.
- Use the children's own curiosity, interests, and background knowledge.
- Make sure the children know that you expect them to be successful in the activity.
- Provide positive response and feedback to children as they participate in the activity.

An effective way to engage kindergarten and first-grade children at a high level of interest is to encourage expression through art forms. These can then serve as the basis for composing and recording ideas. For example, finger painting, brush painting, or simple drawing provides a way of representing self, a family member, a pet, or a favorite storybook character. Bear in mind that this type of activity will require careful preparation of materials, including art paper, paints and brushes, and wet paper towels for cleanup.

Start the activity by considering and discussing topics such as self or family. Encourage each child to develop an idea of key interest through a picture. When the picture has been completed, ask each child to share his or her picture by describing it to a small group or to the class. Then have the child dictate a *title* for the picture. Write the title on a piece of lined tagboard or a separate piece of paper and staple or tape the tagboard to the bottom of the picture. This is an opportunity for brief discussion about the meaning of the word title and why the title is placed at the bottom or top of the child's work. Titles may range from word groups to simple sentences, e.g., *Me*; *Mom*; *Dad*; *My Rabbit*; *Our House*; *The Three Bears*; *The Baby Bear*; *My Mommy Is Watering the Flowers*.

Describing Favorite Animals

Many opportunities for descriptive writing can be developed from a visit to a nearby park, children's animal farm, or zoo.

After the field trip, have the children talk about the animals they enjoyed most and how animals are different. Encourage them to describe their favorite animal's size, color, shape, and distinguishing features, and how the animal might feel to touch. Then have each child draw a large picture of the favorite animal on art or butcher paper. Provide help in writing the child's description of the animal on the drawing.

Have each child share his or her animal drawing and description with the class. For example, one kindergarten child's description of the giraffe from the class zoo visit read as follows, "A giraffe is very tall. He is yellow

with spots. He has a very long neck and skinny long legs." The animal pictures and descriptions can then be placed on the bulletin board with a title such as, "Animals Are Different."

"Mystery Box" to Develop Descriptive Language

Kindergarten and first-grade children are intrigued and motivated by activities that involve a sense of mystery. One such activity, the "mystery box object," is highly effective in developing descriptive language. The mystery box is prepared by using a closed cardboard box with circular holes cut in opposite sides. The holes need to be large enough for a child to insert his or her hands, but not large enough for anyone to see the object that is inside. A diameter of three to four inches is suggested. Place an object in the box that can be easily identified by texture and touch, for example, an apple or a pencil. One child is then asked to put his or her hands into the holes, describe the shape and feel of the "mystery box object" to the class, and try to guess what it is. Students in the class may also try to guess the name of the object based on the description. When the object has been identified, replace it with another and have a different student feel and describe it.

To encourage the use of descriptive language, select objects that children are familiar with, but that have many different textures. For example, you may use a pine cone, a seashell, a small rock, a pencil, an orange, and a small square piece of felt cloth. These will provide opportunity for such touch descriptions as *rough, smooth,* and *soft*. These objects will also provide for incorporating such shape and size descriptions as *square, round, long, short, big, small, soft,* and *hard.* Encourage descriptive language that includes texture, shape, and size. Each child's mystery box descriptions can be recorded on chart paper for the class.

Our Mystery Box Objects

	My Description	My Mystery Object
Amy	rough, round, pointed end	pine cone
Mike	smooth, long, sharp end	pencil
Marcus	soft, fuzzy, thin, round	felt circle

After this language experience chart has been read with the class, each child can draw a picture of his or her mystery object. Using the chart, the name of the object can then be printed under the picture, and the drawing can be titled, "My Mystery Object."

Descriptions Based on Sight and Sound

The use of descriptions based on visual and auditory awareness is an effective way to develop children's observation skills and to build cause-and-effect relationships. One activity that provides for visual and sound descriptions and their causes is a "listening observation" walk around the playground, around the school block, or in a nearby park. Before the walk, encourage the children to predict what sounds they think they may hear on the walk. Record these on the chalkboard or chart paper. During the walk, the children should listen carefully and try to observe what makes the sound they hear.

After returning to class, encourage the children to identify the sounds they heard and discuss their observations of what produced the sounds. Record this information on the chalkboard or chart paper, and compare it with the predicted sounds made before the walk. Finally, to develop a sense of time sequence, encourage the children to think about when they heard the sound during the walk. Number the sounds to show their order of occurrence in the walk, as illustrated above. Here is a chart from one first-grade teacher's classroom, based on a walk around the school block.

Our Listening Walk Around Our School

Sounds We Heard	What Made the Sound
(3) buzzing	a lawn mower
(5) hammering	a carpenter
(2) barking	a dog
(1) banged shut	our classroom door
(4) chirping	birds

Making a Language-Experience Story

The above activity can easily be extended into a brief language-experience story using vocabulary that shows a time sequence. Help the children to create a brief story about the listening walk by using each of their observations in a sentence. Develop the observations using the number order recorded on the chart.

Begin your language-experience story by saying something like the following: "Let's write a story about our listening observation walk. How should our story begin?" *Then accept whatever opening sentence the children provide.* Continue eliciting their participation by prompts like, "Okay, what should go next?" and "Now what do we want to say?" Throughout this process, be sure to record exactly what the children say. You will undoubtedly guide a number of discussions in which children negotiate among themselves to arrive at the final wording or content of a sentence.

After the story is recorded, read the story back to the students to give them an opportunity to evaluate the story itself. Say, "Now I'm going to read the story back to you. After I'm finished, tell me if you'd like to make any changes or additions." Read the story, invite discussion for revision and editing, and read the story again after revisions are made. Check to make sure the story in its final form meets with class approval.

The time sequence words and each sound and its cause are then underlined to focus the children's attention on these key concepts. Now read the story aloud, inviting the class to choral read along with you. Point to words as you read. Do this several times and then ask if anyone would like to read the story singly or if anyone would like to point to and pronounce words he or she knows in the story. Following these activities, the children may illustrate the story; the next day, a typed, "real-print" version of the story should be distributed to each child. The following story illustrates a final language-experience story.

> ## Our Listening Walk Around Our School
>
> We went on a listening walk around our school.
>
> We listened for sounds and what caused them.
>
> The <u>first</u> sound was <u>our classroom door</u>, which <u>banged shut</u>.
>
> The <u>next</u> sound was a <u>barking dog</u>.
>
> <u>Then</u> we heard a <u>lawn mower buzzing</u>.
>
> <u>After that</u> we heard a pretty <u>bird chirping</u>.
>
> <u>Finally</u>, we saw a <u>carpenter hammering</u> nails.
>
> He was building new steps.
>
> We <u>finished</u> our walk and came back to our classroom.

Pantomiming Feelings and Descriptions

As children begin to formulate sensory descriptions from their experiences, they find pantomime activities of great interest. Pantomime can provide opportunity to search for ways of expressing descriptions through direct action. For example, a pantomime activity may be developed around the topic of "Our Faces and Bodies Tell How We Feel," using descriptive words that show different emotions.

Start the activity by writing the title "Our Faces and Bodies Tell How We Feel," on the chalkboard. Encourage the children to identify words we can use to tell about different facial and body expressions. Elicit words such as *happy, joyful,* and *playful,* and write these on the chalkboard. Then identify contrasting emotion words such as *unhappy, sad,* and *painful* and place these on the board.

After a discussion of the words, tell the class that they are going to act some of these words out and explain the following activity. You or a child will first whisper one of the words to another child who acts out the word without speaking. The rest of the class tries to guess what word is being pantomimed. When the correct word is identified, underline it on the chalkboard. Continue through the series of words, giving other children the opportunity to do the pantomiming. The activity may be concluded by asking each child to draw a picture that illustrates his or her favorite word. Then write the word that the picture illustrates at the bottom of each drawing. Display the titled drawings on the bulletin board, chalk rail, or classroom walls.

Extending Pantomime

The development of descriptive language using pantomime may be extended by establishing make-believe characters whom the children pantomime. For example, one child may pantomime a curious baby black bear; a second child could pantomime a slow brown turtle. Whisper the animal descriptions to the children. As the children pantomime their animals, the other children attempt to guess what kind of animals they are and describe what the animals are doing. Culminate the activity by recording the children's descriptions on large chart paper, and encourage each child to tell why a particular description was used.

Recording Oral Description: Invented Spelling

Throughout kindergarten and the first grade, children make frequent requests for help in writing descriptions and stories. Initial language-experience activities, in which the teacher does the writing, will shift gradually so that children assume greater responsibility for writing their own accounts. It is important from the beginning that children use their own invented spelling in writing titles for pictures, or in writing their own accounts and beginning stories.

As we discussed in Chapter 2, many kindergarten and first-grade children will use various patterns of invented spellings, ranging from prephonemic spelling, to more advanced letter-name spelling, to transitional spelling. The critical point is to remember that children's invented spellings are temporary and often represent more than one invented spelling pattern. This requires understanding and flexibility on your part *and from parents.* If you are going to encourage children's invented spelling in your classroom, you will need to do two things.

First, you need to identify your own ideological stance with regard to children's spelling and decide how you will handle children's requests for spelling assistance during writing. Make no mistake about it, *children will ask you to give them "correct" spellings for words.* Your response to these requests will influence the willingness of children in your classroom to try spelling on their own. Here are possible responses and their effects:

1. *Spell the word for the child.* This will discourage invented spellings and reinforce children's search for "correct" spellings.

2. *Say to the child, "Spell it the way you think it should be spelled" or "Spell it as best you can."* This will encourage invented spellings, but may also create discomfort or even extreme frustration for the child. Some may refuse to attempt any spelling.

3. *If the child persists in requesting the spelling or refuses to attempt his/her own spelling, say the word (without exaggeration) and ask, "How do you think the spelling starts? What letter would you use?" Then accept*

whatever letter the child proposes. Say, "Good. What letter comes next?" This will reduce frustration and help convince the child that attempting to spell on your own is not risky business in this classroom.

4. *Later, if you wish, you can write the conventional spelling above or underneath the child's spelling and say, "Here's how we usually spell_____. Look how close you came."* This gives children information about conventional spelling that allows them to continue moving toward it.

5. *Later still, invented spellings may be converted to conventional ones during revision and polishing stages of the writing process.* This serves to place conventional spelling in its rightful perspective—something we attend to and are serious about in any writing that moves beyond early drafting stages.

Whatever your decision about how spelling is to be handled in your room, see to it that every adult in the room understands and adheres to that position. We cannot begin to describe the confusion and difficulties in classrooms where one adult asks children to "spell it the way you think it should be spelled" while another adult gives them "correct" spellings.

If you decide that invented spelling will be encouraged in your classroom, you must then inform parents early in the year about your spelling program and your approach to children's spelling inventions. You must explain to them the natural, developmental appropriateness of invented spellings. You will also need to reassure them that invented spelling is temporary and that it leads ultimately to conventional spelling. You should give them strategies for encouraging their child's experimentation with print and spelling. Use, or adapt, the letter in Figure 3-4 to send to parents—with a copy to the principal. (We understand that you may not wish to *say* that you don't use a traditional spelling book in your class, even though we hope you'll try—see Chapter 7). Adapt the letter as you wish.

The main idea in a classroom where spelling invention and experimentation are encouraged is to give children lots of opportunity for constructing their own theories about how written English works. To do this, they must be free to represent their ideas fluently in pictorial and written form, to spell and write and draw without fear of being "incorrect," and to have many opportunities to see conventional spelling and participate in converting their inventions to conventional spellings.

Developing Individual Word Banks

You can also effectively enhance children's independence and help children become confident spellers by developing individual word banks. Words children have learned may be written on strips of lined paper and stored in individual word banks for continued use. File boxes make perfect word banks

Dear Parents,

In our classroom, we will be doing a lot of writing this year. You will notice on papers that come home and in writing your child does at home that some of the words are written in nonconventional ways. This is called "invented spelling" and occurs because children are naturally curious about how language works. One of the ways they express their curiosity is by experimenting with spelling forms and word representations.

Here are some things you need to know about invented spelling:

1. Invented spelling is *temporary* (some people even call it "temporary spelling") and constantly changing. This is because children's concepts about how print works are constantly changing and becoming more sophisticated. Rest assured, that just as your child discarded unconventional spoken language forms as he or she learned conventional ones, so shall your child discard invented spelling when the time is right.

2. Invented spelling leads children toward conventional spelling. Children learn about how print works by experimenting and trying out their current theories. Your child will discard invented spelling as this knowledge grows.

3. I *do* teach spelling in this class, but I don't consider children's invented spelling "misspellings," nor do I use traditional spelling books. Here's how I teach spelling:

   a. I frequently direct children's attention to sounds in words and their representations in print.

   b. I frequently show children conventional spelling of their inventions and point out how close children came to the conventional spelling.

   c. I assist children in revising, refining, and polishing selected pieces of writing for publication. In the process of doing this, I teach conventional spelling.

   d. Each week the children select ten words that they want to learn and know more about. Conventional spelling is part of what we learn about these words, and, by the end of the year, we will have created our own spelling book.

Here are some things you can do to support your child's growing concepts about how print works and his or her willingness to experiment with print:

1. When your child asks you how to spell a word, encourage him or her to spell the way s/he thinks it should be spelled.

2. If your child continues to ask for help, say the word and ask, "How do you think the word starts? What letter would you use?" *Then accept whatever letter the child proposes.* Say, "Good. Now what do you think comes next?" and so on.

3. Later, you can write the conventional spelling above or below the child's invented spelling and say something like, "Look how close you came."

4. Have your child read accounts or stories s/he's written to you. You'll be surprised at how easily and fluently those invented spelling are read.

If you have any questions about invented spelling, feel free to call me, come see me, or bring them up during our discussion at Back-to-School-Night.

Sincerely,

This letter may be reproduced or adapted without permission.

—— **FIGURE 3-4** ——————————————————————

Invented Spelling Letter for Parents

(4"x 6" or 5"x 8"), and file cards may be used for recording words instead of strips of cut paper. As the number of slips in the box grows beyond twenty or twenty-five, alphabet dividers can be added for easy word access. Word banks should be stored in or near the children's desks for quick reference use. A major value of word banks is for children to have a growing collection of words they know and spell conventionally. Word banks also ease children's spelling burden and concern and allows them to focus on their ideas and thoughts and express them in written form. It further reinforces children's familiarity with the alphabet and alphabetical order.

Descriptions in Children's Literature

Children's books are a wonderful resource of imagery in illustrations and descriptive language. As you share literature with children, encourage them to identify illustrations and sentences that are rich in their description of character and setting. Reread these sections and examine the illustrations

and descriptive language used by the illustrator and author. The following picture and storybooks are some of children's favorites with image-evoking descriptions:

Aliki, *Feelings*

Ludwig Bemelmans, *Madeline*

Lenore Blegvad, *Anna Banana and Me*

Don Freeman, *Corduroy*

Katharine Holabird, *Angelina Ballerina*

Shirley Hughes, *Alfie Gives a Hand*

Albert Lamorisse, *The Red Balloon*

Leo Lionni, *Fredrick*

Robert McCloskey, *Make Way for Ducklings*

Ron Maris, *My Book*

H. A. Rey, *Curious George*

Richard Scarry, *Richard Scarry's What Do People Do All Day?*
Dr. Seuss, *The Cat in the Hat*
Michele Steptoe, *Snuggle Piggy and the Magic Blanket*

The development of children's sense of observation, composing, and recording will heighten their descriptive language ability. It will further reinforce children's understanding that their thoughts and ideas can be recorded through drawing and writing.

DEVELOPING A SENSE OF STORY AND NARRATIVE

Many children have developed some sense of story by the time they enter kindergarten and first grade. This story sense has been developed in part through story reading and story listening with parents, other adults, and siblings. Children's experiences in watching favorite movies and television may also contribute to a sense of story. They are aware that characters interact with each other and they have a general sense that there is a plot leading to some outcome or resolution, which is usually positive.

The concepts basic to the development of a sense of story and narrative include:

1. Developing the idea that stories have characters, settings, events, and a plot.
2. Developing a sense of sequence as story events unfold.
3. Developing simple inferences and predictions about story events and story outcomes.
4. Developing the ability to retell and create simple stories through dictation, drawings, or writing and sharing these stories with other children.

These story-sense concepts can often be integrated into a single instructional activity. To do this, your instructional strategies should account for:

- using high interest stories;

- actively involving the children in the story-reading and story-telling experiences through questions and observations;

- providing opportunities for children to make inferences and predictions at key points in the story; and

- encouraging the children to retell and create new stories and to share these experiences with other youngsters in the classroom.

Using Shared Book Experiences

An excellent instructional strategy for developing sense of story and narrative is the shared book experience (Holdaway, 1979; Lynch, 1986). This strategy provides opportunity to introduce the concept of story through high-interest literature and to develop active thinking through the social dynamic found in a small group interaction.

Don Holdaway (1979) has discussed the shared book experience as one that is similar in many ways to the bedtime story experience. Stories are introduced in a secure, nonthreatening, and motivating environment that provides for optimal exploration and learning. This approach is closely related to language-experience activities such as those previously discussed in this chapter.

The central instructional tool in the shared book experience is the big book. As discussed earlier, this is a giant-sized version of a children's book that can be clearly seen by children from ten to fifteen feet away. A wide variety of these books are now available from publishers. Criteria for selecting Big Books for your class include high student interest, a predictable story line, high-quality illustrations, and variety that ranges from repetitive patterns to simple narrative.

Using *Brown Bear* in a Shared Book Experience

The development of a sense of story through the shared book may be illustrated using the Big Book *Brown Bear, Brown Bear, What Do You See?* Written by Bill Martin, Jr., with brilliant illustrations by Eric Carle (Holt, 1983), this delightful book is a cumulative patterned story. It starts with the title question "Brown Bear, Brown Bear. What do you see?" and the beginning of the patterned response "I see a redbird looking at me." The question is repeated with a new animal: "Redbird, redbird. What do you see?" Redbird responds, "I see a yellow duck looking at me." The story continues with blue horse, green frog, purple cat, white dog, black sheep, goldfish, mother, and children. The ending poses the question, "Children, children, what do you see?" with a reiteration of all the characters presented and the patterned refrain, "That's what we see."

Introduce the book by examining the cover with your children. As you read the title, *Brown Bear, Brown Bear, What Do You See?*, use the pointer to point to words and ask children what they think the book will be about. Encourage and accept a wide variety of responses.

You may briefly examine the inside title pages to note that this story is written by Bill Martin, Jr. and that the pictures have been drawn by Eric Carle. The key point is to establish the idea that real people write and illustrate stories, and that we too can create and illustrate our own stories.

Read (using the pointer), "Brown Bear, Brown Bear. What do you see?" Ask, "What do you think the brown bear sees?" and accept responses. Turn the page and read, "I see a redbird looking at me." Then read, "Redbird, redbird. What do you see?" and again ask, "What do you think Redbird sees?" Continue through the story in this manner. Rather soon the children will use the repeated pattern of the text and the picture clues to chant along with as you read each sequence.

After the initial reading, reread the entire story without discussion and with everyone chiming in. The predictable text and rhythm of the book provides excellent opportunity for retelling and elaboration as children create their own book. The patterned story, "_____ _____ what do you see?" and the repetitive response involving the next character, "I see a _____ _____ looking at me" becomes the framework upon which children build their own stories using new animals and actions.

The children's stories may be illustrated and story pages stapled or sewn together to create their books. The story-making experience should be followed with the opportunity for each child to share his or her story with a small group or the class. Each storybook can then be displayed on the bulletin board or in a special location in the classroom. We recommend Jane Davidson's *Illustrating and Making Books* (1991), a short, inexpensive guide for bookmaking. Figure 3-5 illustrates some of the book forms she demonstrates.

The Special Value of Predictable Books

Brown Bear, Brown Bear is a well-known predictable book. There are many others. Predictable books provide excellent opportunity to develop children's story sense, predicting abilities, and ability to draw inferences. Although many of them are not in Big Book size, they nevertheless are easy to use with individual children, small groups, or the entire class. The key to their use is: first, developing the predictable pattern through a shared oral reading; second, involving the children in using and responding to the pattern; and third, extending the book experience to retelling the story or creating a new story using the pattern.

The books listed on page 111 are children's favorites. You will enjoy using them as you develop a sense of story and encourage children to make predictions and draw inferences.

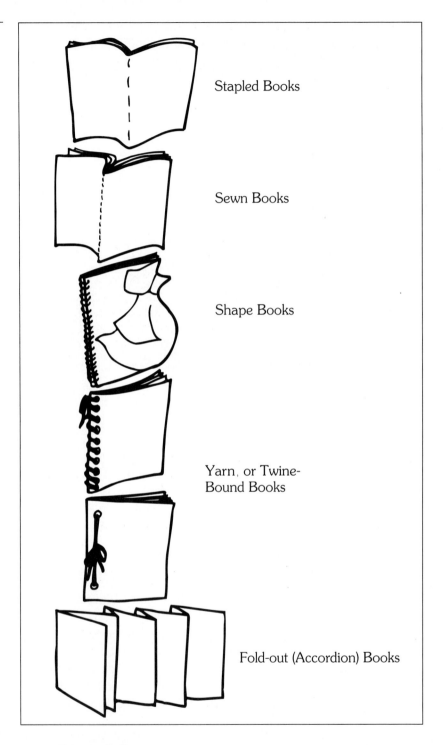

Stapled Books

Sewn Books

Shape Books

Yarn, or Twine-
Bound Books

Fold-out (Accordion) Books

FIGURE 3-5

Making Your Own Books. (Adapted with permission from Davidson, 1991.)

Janet and Allan Ahlberg, *Each Peach Pear Plum*

Margaret Wise Brown, *Goodnight Moon*

P.D. Eastman, *Are You My Mother?*

Ed Emberly, *Drummer Hoff*

Paul Galdone, *The Gingerbread Boy*

Paul Galdone, *Henny Penny*

John Ivimey, *Three Blind Mice*

Robin Koontz, *This Old Man: The Counting Song*

Arlene Mosel, *Tikki Tikki Tembo*

Rodney Peppe, *The House That Jack Built*

Harry Stevens, *Fat Mouse*

Olive Wadsworth, *Over in the Meadow*

Brian Wildsmith, *Cat on the Mat*

Brian Wildsmith, *Toot Toot*

These predictable books encourage children's active participation and involvement in the reading experience. For example, you will find children joining you in Paul Galdone's *Henny Penny* as the cumulative sequence develops to "So Henny Penny, Chicken Licken, Turkey Lurkey, and Foxy Loxy went to see the king." Opportunities abound for using predictable books, ranging from the initial introduction of the book and follow-up book-making to the children's selection of them for independent reading time and story retelling with a student partner.

The Directed Listening-Thinking Activity (DL-TA)

An excellent strategy for developing sense of story plot through predictions and inferences is the Directed Listening-Thinking Activity (DL-TA) (Stauffer, 1976). The DL-TA can be used with small or large groups of children. In the DL-TA, the teacher reads a story to the class stopping at planned points to ask children to make predictions about the story and comment on what has happened thus far. Using a DL-TA requires that you read the story carefully (or that you already know the story well) before using it with children. During prereading identify stop-points where you will stop to ask children to make predictions and support their predictions from a combination of information in the story and their own knowledge base. These stop-points will usually occur: (1) after the title, (2) after the story introduction (usually a paragraph or two), (3) at one or two points of high interest or suspense in the story, and (4) just before the story ending.

The main questioning pattern is quite simple: After reading the story title, you ask, "With a title like that, what do you think this story will be about? Why do you think so?" After the stop-point predictions during the story you ask, "What do you think will happen now (or next)? Why do you think so?" And at the final suspense stop-point you ask, "How do you think the story will end? Why?" *Please note that these questions do not ask for specific information from the text* (e.g., "Where was Henny Penny going?"). They are deliberately open-ended to allow children freedom to think about the story in their own ways. These questions encourage speculation, prediction-making, and discussion about differing individual interpretations.

It is very important in using the DL-TA that you accept students predictions and inferences as long as the students have some logical justification for the predictions. For the story title question ("With a title like that, what do you think this story will be about?") responses can be expected to be somewhat diverse, depending on how general or specific the story title is. Your stop-point questions throughout the story ("What do you think will happen now? Why do you think so?") provide for confirmation or revision of earlier predictions. These questions will also produce responses that become more focused on the story plot as the story develops. As new information is provided, the children will make more refined predictions and draw more story-specific inferences.

The DL-TA provides an excellent opportunity to use the social dynamic of the group. As children make and justify different story predictions, new ideas and possible story outcomes will emerge from the group. As different predictions develop, it will be helpful for you to ask the group questions such as, "Which of these predictions do you agree with?" This kind of questioning will encourage the children to consider various plot options and outcomes and reexamine their own predictions.

The following brief DL-TA outline is based on Nonny Hogrogian's *One Fine Day*. This beautifully illustrated Armenian folktale tells of a sly, thirsty fox who steals milk from an old woman. The woman chops off the fox's tail and demands that her milk be returned in exchange for it. The story progresses in a cumulative problem-solving plot. The fox must journey to the cow for milk, to the field for the cow's grass, and to the stream for the field's water. He must go on to the maiden for the water jug, to the peddler for the maiden's blue bead, to the hen for the peddler's egg, and to a kind old miller for the chicken's grain. All ends well as the old woman sews the fox's tail back in place, and he joins his friends on the other side of the forest.

The DL-TA is a valuable instructional strategy for developing inferences and predictions about story events and outcomes and can be easily used as a springboard for other activities. The development of characterization, setting, events, and story plot may be extended in many activities. For example, the children may be encouraged to find a favorite character, draw a picture of that character and add a title when it is finished. Several children may take different parts of the book and illustrate the story in order to create their own version of the story with a cover page and title. The pages may then be stapled together to make their own book, which can be shared with

DL-TA LESSON—*ONE FINE DAY*

1. Read the title as the book is introduced. "The title of this book is *One Fine Day* by Nonny Hogrogian. With a title like that, what do you think this story will be about? Why do you think that?"

2. Read the story to the point where the fox has lapped up most of the milk. Then stop (bottom of page 4) and ask, "What do you think will happen now? Why do you think so?"

3. Read the story to the point where the old woman chops off the fox's tail (bottom of page 6). The fox is in distress, and the old woman says, "Give me back my milk and I'll give you back your tail." Then ask, "Now what do you think will happen? Why?"

4. Read several episodes of the story to establish the manner in which the fox is solving the problem, e.g., to the cow for the old woman's milk, to the field for the cow's grass, etc. Stop at the point the fox needs the maiden's jug, and the maiden needs a blue bead (bottom of page 13). Then ask, "Now what do you think will happen? Why?"

5. Continue sharing the story episodes until the last episode, as the fox reaches the kind miller and begins to cry (bottom of page 19). Ask the students, "How do you think the story will end? Why?"

6. After the children's predictions are made and explained, you may narrow the predictions to two or three and ask the children, "Which of these predictions do you agree with?" After a show of hands, finish reading the story, following it with a brief discussion of the ending and how it may be similar to or different from the children's predictions.

7. An excellent way to conclude the story is to reread the final part of the story using the cumulative episodes (top of page 21) and encourage the children to read in chorus with you, "So he gave him the grain to give to the hen to get the egg to pay the peddler ..."

HOW TO DO . . . .

A DL-TA

1. Select the story to be read. Preread the story (even if you already know it). You may even wish to practice reading it aloud.

2. Determine stop-points. Stop first after the title. Stop second after the opening (one or two paragraphs). Stop one or two more times during the story at points of high interest or suspense. Stop just before the story end or resolution is reached.

3. Prepare questions to be asked at stop-points ("With a title like that, what do you think this story is about?" or "Now what do you think will happen?"). *Be sure* to ask "Why?" or "What makes you say that?" after children make predictions or draw conclusions.

4. On the last stop, ask, "How do you think the story will end?" and "Why?"

the class. Or children may assume the role of different characters and act out the story as you reread it to them.

DEVELOPING POSITIVE READING AND LITERACY ATTITUDES

As we orchestrate instructional experiences in the classroom, we need to remember that there should be a place and time for children simply to enjoy stories and share their reactions to them. Opportunities to experience good children's literature through story listening, story reading, and story sharing help children build positive attitudes toward literacy development. This also helps to create the desire to explore the world of books as children pursue topics of special interest and share books.

As you plan your effort to build positive reading and literacy attitudes through story enjoyment and personal sharing, keep in mind the following suggestions:

- Create a special place in your classroom for storytelling, story sharing, and independent book exploration.

- Select books that are of special interest to your children, and take into account the children's background knowledge and level of maturity.

- Establish a daily book sharing and story experience time.

- Read to children every day.

The Reading Center

The creation of a reading center in your classroom will greatly facilitate children's enjoyment of good books and other reading. The reading center should be furnished and decorated in such a way as to make it attractive and inviting, and if possible should be near the writing center (see Chapter 13). A discarded rug from your home or a parent's home is very useful. So are several oversized pillows. Two or three low bookshelves (which can be easily reached by the children) can also serve as partitions. A low round table and chairs provide a homelike feeling.

Use the rug to define the reading center area. The book shelves can be placed at one side of the rug to separate the area from the rest of the room. Place the table and chairs at one corner of the rug and the oversized pillows at the opposite corner. An adult-sized rocking chair adds a special touch and can be effectively used during sharing to provide good picture book visibility for the children. High-interest posters related to books and reading can be used to decorate one back wall of the book corner, with the other wall used as bulletin board space for display of children's drawings and stories. A felt storyboard and story puppets will be of value for storytelling and dramatization of stories. Figure 3-6 shows one way to organize a reading center.

Library Corner

FIGURE 3-6

Creating a Reading Center. (Reproduced with permission from Morrow, 1989, p. 97.)

Selecting Books for the Reading Center

In addition to purchasing books, you will undoubtedly use the school library as a primary source of books for your classroom and children. You need to be highly knowledgeable about the school library and to establish a warm working relationship with the librarian. You will need to spend time exploring the library to build your knowledge of the books that are available and their locations, and develop procedures for bringing your children to the library regularly. You will also want to make arrangements for checking out books throughout the year for your classroom.

A good plan is to use twenty to thirty books for a period of four weeks, returning them at the end of that time and checking out a new collection. This procedure will enable you to plan for four weeks. It will also let your children know that a specific group of books will be in your classroom for a set time period.

Your book selection—whether purchases or loans from the school library—will need to account for children's interests and backgrounds. Initial selections for kindergarten and first grade may include the following types of books:

- *Alphabet picture books*, which include letters and illustrations of objects with names that begin with each alphabet letter.

- *Concept and informational books*, which describe objects, colors, shapes, and abstract ideas such as sizes and textures.

- *Nursery rhyme books*, which contain old favorite nursery rhymes and illustrations.

- *Wordless storybooks*, which use illustrations to tell the story without words.

- *Predictable books*, which develop a story through repetitive and highly structured patterns that provide for easy anticipation and prediction of text.

- *Easy-to-read books*, which use limited and controlled vocabulary, often with rhyme, and creative story lines.

- *Picture storybooks*, which develop story through pictures and print.

- *Fairy tales and folktales*, which provide for retelling of traditional fairy and folk stories using pictures and print.

- *Narrative storybooks*, which develop creative high-interest story lines with limited use of illustrations.

As you look for books that match the interest of your children, keep in mind the following special topics: Adventure, Animals, Bedtime,

Behavioral Problems, Boys, Cats, Dance, Death, Dinosaurs, Divorce, Dogs, Family Problems, Fantasy, Fear, Friendship, Girls, Grandparents, Growing Up, Health, History, Holidays, Humor, Manners, Mice, Music, Pigs, Rabbits, Science, Siblings, and Sports. These topics can be of value as you examine books in your school library and as you talk with your school librarian. We will return to the use of children's literature in Chapter 6.

Scheduling Story Time

It is extremely important to establish a time each day for story reading, storytelling, and book exploration. Many teachers find a twenty- to thirty-minute time period immediately after the lunch and/or recess is ideal for this purpose. This time serves to reestablish children's rapport with the classroom. It allows them to relax, enjoy, and become refocused for the remainder of the school day.

Other teachers, however, use part of the last hour of the school day reading to children. Regardless of your choice, the key point is to have a regular daily time for book and story sharing time. This serves to prioritize the

Story Reading and Sharing at School

value of reading and story sharing and to build positive attitudes toward reading and literacy development.

Preparing for Story Reading and Sharing

Your preparation for story reading and story sharing is of vital importance to the success of this activity. The following suggestions will be of value.

- Be sure to read and examine the book you have selected in advance. Think about how you will present the story, including a good stop-point should you have limited time.

- Practice using expression when you read. Use your voice to fit the dialogue and the characters.

- Use pacing to emphasize suspenseful parts, to build a high level of interest as the story progresses.

- Slow down your reading presentation and think of the mental images you are creating in the minds of your children through the language of the story.

- Be sure all children are seated comfortably and can see the storybook pictures that you are sharing.

- Use storytelling aids to heighten interest. For example, you may bring a small toy mouse to class when you share a book such as *Alexander and the Wind-Up Mouse* by Leo Lionni. A felt board or puppets may also be used to develop actions of key story characters or to retell a story.

- Help your children understand that books are written and illustrated by real people. Encourage writing to the author through the publisher and enclose a self-addressed, stamped envelope for the author's convenience in responding.

- Encourage your children to interact with the story content, either during or following the story, as you determine.

- Create an atmosphere of informality and enjoyment for your children during book sharing time.

You will find that Jim Trelease's *The New Read-Aloud Handbook* (1989), Eden Ross Lipson's *Parent's Guide to the Best Books for Children* (1988), and Dorothy Strickland and Lesley Mandel Morrow's *Emerging Literacy: Young Children Learn to Read and Write* (1989) have many suggestions, ideas, annotations, and categorized book lists that will enhance your teaching.

Remember that the enjoyment of children's literature will build positive attitudes and motivation toward reading and provides the early foundation for establishing life-long readers.

Evaluating and Using Publisher-Developed Programs

It is entirely possible that your school or school district is in the process of adopting or has adopted a publisher-developed program for early literacy development. Should this be the case, the following questions will be helpful to you in selecting and using such materials:

- Do the objectives of the published program account for the five key early reading and literacy goals discussed in this chapter (page 83)?

- Do the objectives and instructional activities reflect an understanding of the latest research in early reading and writing development, such as the seven conditions for optimal instruction (Cambourne & Turbill, 1987) discussed earlier in this chapter (pags 74–75)?

- Are the objectives of the program developed through instructional activities and strategies that are appropriate and suitable for the range of needs and interests of children?

- Do the instructional materials and activities hold potential for developing meaning-centered instruction with high motivation and interest for children?

- Does the program include high-quality children's stories and illustrations that appeal to children?

- Is the teacher's guide written clearly and developed in a format that can be used with ease?

- Do you believe you can use the program effectively and integrate it into your classroom?

- Is the program organized in such a way that you can use it flexibly by selecting units or portions of it instead of having to follow the program lesson by lesson and unit by unit to the end as dictated by the publisher?

- Does the program recognize the importance of observations and ongoing assessment of individual children?

Your Decision-Making Power

It is important to understand that as the teacher you hold a great deal of decision-making power in the selection and use of materials. Published materials are essentially tools to facilitate your instruction. *You* are the one who understands best the needs of your students and makes decisions about what instruction will be most effective. You, then, choose the lesson materials from what is available to you. We will discuss program use in depth in Chapter 12. We now turn to the assessment of your children's progress.

ASSESSMENT OF PROGRESS THROUGH INFORMAL CLASSROOM OBSERVATIONS

So far in this chapter, we have identified learning conditions and meaning negotiations necessary for early reading and writing instruction. We have listed five instructional goals, and we have discussed a wide range of instructional activities and strategies to be used in developing early reading and writing abilities with kindergarten and first-grade children. We will now turn to the assessment and evaluation of our children's progress through classroom observations.

The purpose of assessment is twofold. First, it provides information on students' progress. Second, it yields information that enables us to adjust instruction to meet the needs of individual children.

A CHANGE IN ASSESSMENT AND EVALUATION PROCEDURES

Over the past two decades, assessment and evaluation in kindergarten and first grade have changed in a significant way, from reliance on formal testing to informal, ongoing teacher observations. In past years, formal readiness tests played a central role in group placement and achievement testing in kindergarten and first grade. The most widely used of these tests and the skills evaluated are shown in Table 3-2.

A brief examination of the content of these tests reveals that they place a major emphasis on print and sound awareness. While these tests provide some information on children's achievement, they are very limited in the skills and knowledge background evaluated and are designed to be used at the beginning and end of the school year. At best, they serve to provide some insight into children's visual recognition of letters, sounds, and comprehension of sentences. This information may verify observations that you have already made about your children's progress.

The major shift in assessment at the early grades places emphasis on a much broader array of reading and writing concepts within the learning context of the classroom. As teachers, we thus assume greater assessment responsibility. We must now consider assessment and evaluation as an integral part of our instruction.

In effect, this viewpoint holds that the most effective assessment will take place in the natural context of daily instruction, as children participate in reading and writing events. As we make observations about their learning in real instructional situations, we gain information about children's progress that is of much greater value than is the case with a readiness achievement test.

OBSERVATIONAL ASSESSMENT

Initially, observational assessment may seem to be formidable. The process can be simplified, however, when we place observational assessment

TEST	SKILLS EVALUATED
Clymer-Barrett Prereading Battery	Reading letters, word matching, discrimination of beginning and ending sounds, form completion, and sentence copying.
Gates-MacGinitie Readiness Skills Test	Listening comprehension, auditory discrimination, following directions, letter recognition, visual-motor coordination, auditory blending.
Harrison-Stroud Reading Readiness Profiles	Visual discrimination, use of context, context and auditory clues, auditory discrimination, using symbols.
Lee-Clark Reading Readiness Test	Discrimination of letters, picture selection based on verbal description, discrimination of printed words forms.
Metropolitan Readiness Test	Word meaning, listening in sentence context, matching letters and forms, alphabet knowledge, numbers and draw-a-man test.
Murphy-Durrell Diagnostic Reading Readiness Test	Auditory discrimination, visual discrimination, letter-name knowledge, and learning rate.

TABLE 3-2

Reading Readiness Tests and Skills Evaluated

in the context of daily classroom teaching. There are four essential steps you can take to implement effective observational assessment:

1. Sensitize yourself to the frequent opportunities in the classroom day for observation of children's literacy abilities, and understand the importance of this assessment.

2. Be aware of the concepts and knowledge you wish to assess based on the instructional goals you have.

3. Develop a systematic way to observe and record children's progress.

4. Consider ways to use this information in planning instruction to meet specific student needs.

Every instructional event presents an opportunity to note some aspect of your students' progress. This may be as simple as a child's understanding or not understanding directions that are essential to completion of an instructional task, or as complex as understanding or not understanding a sequence of events to comprehend the story plot. Day in and day out, we have multiple opportunities to observe children's progress in various learning situations. These situations may extend from understanding the language of instruction and group participation to story comprehension and enjoyment of story sharing.

Based on the discussion in this chapter, a number of specific instructional concepts and behaviors can be identified for observational assessment of children's early reading and writing development. The five instructional goals introduced on page 83 serve to form a framework for the assessment we are recommending. The checklist in Table 3-3 is based on these five categories and includes specific reading and writing concepts and the behaviors associated with them.

USING THE CHECKLIST

This checklist is best used by organizing your thinking and observations around the five general categories, A, B, C, D, and E. As you become familiar with these basic categories, you will find that the five items under each category will serve to define that category in a easily understood way. Make copies of the checklist, one for each student, and keep them on your desk or in a convenient place in your room. Select three or four students each day for observation. By concentrating on a small number of students each day, you will be able to note the progress of all of your students over a two-week period. It is important to establish a personal goal to complete your observations at least once each month.

Note each child's progress by circling the appropriate letter on the checklist. Specifically note success areas: this will remind you what children know about how print and language work. It is also helpful to make a brief note indicating the nature of the instructional activity the child was participating in during your observation.

You may also wish to design another checklist tailored to your own teaching objectives. Many observation opportunities are present beyond reading and writing events. Indeed, such opportunities extend to all parts of the school day, including individual and group play activities. The point is to sensitize yourself to the importance of making regular observations of children to identify their progress, and to use this information in designing and shaping your instructional program. You will also find these observations very helpful during parent conferences and discussions. Observation checklists then become part of children's portfolios. We will discuss portfolios at length in Chapter 11.

Student Name _____ **Grade** _____

Dates Observed _____

Instructions: Circle the appropriate letter to assess your student's progress.
R = Rarely; O = Occasionally; U = Usually

A. Understands Language of Instruction and Group Participation

1. Knows direction words, ordering words, color words, feeling- and sensory-based words _____ R O U

2. Can follow instructional directions _____ R O U

3. Can participate and cooperate in group activities and is tolerant of other children's viewpoints _____ R O U

4. Understands how to ask questions to clarify a task meaning or text meaning problem _____ R O U

5. Understands how to ask questions to clarify a personal or group problem _____ R O U

B. Understands Picture- and Print- Awareness Knowledge

6. Knows that pictures and print represent ideas and meaning _____ R O U

7. Understands that pictures used in sequence can tell a story _____ R O U

8. Knows concept of letter, word, sentence, and role of special punctuation marks _____ R O U

9. Knows that print is read in left-to-right direction, that lines are read from top-to-bottom, and that pages have top and bottom positions and are organized from left-to-right _____ R O U

10. Understands that pictures and print can be used to tell a story and explain ideas _____ R O U

C. Knows How to Use Observing, Recording, and Writing Knowledge

11. Understands that thoughts and ideas can be recorded through drawing and writing _____ R O U

12. Writes fluently to produce stories and descriptions _____ R O U

13. Can use written conventions such as story titles and capital letters _____ R O U

14. Understands specific vocabulary that reflects order and sequence of events _____ R O U

15. Can use ideas to create or recreate experiences based on classroom and field trip experiences _____ R O U

D. Demonstrates Sense of Story and Narrative

16. Understands that a story has characters, settings, events, and plot _____ R O U

17. Can follow and understand events in story sequence _____ R O U

18. Can develop inferences and predictions about story events and outcomes and support these using story content or background knowledge _____ R O U

19. Can comprehend and retell a story to other children or the teacher _____ R O U

20. Can and does read—conventionally or otherwise _____ R O U

E. Demonstrates Positive Attitude Toward Reading and Literacy Activities

21. Enjoys story reading and story-sharing time _____ R O U

22. Shows enthusiasm toward exploring picture and storybooks _____ R O U

23. Likes to share personal stories and books with a friend or small group _____ R O U

24. Enjoys small group discussion of ideas related to books which have been shared or read during story sharing _____ R O U

25. Enjoys creating new stories based on a shared story _____ R O U

Special observation notes:

This checklist may be used without permission.

TABLE 3-3

Early Reading and Writing Assessment Checklist

Early Reading and Writing Development

A Summary

Our discussion in this chapter has focused on three areas critical to early reading and writing development: First, creating optimal reading and writing learning conditions in the classroom; second, implementing instructional goals through a variety of activities and strategies; and third, developing ongoing assessment based on your daily observation of children's progress.

Our discussion has emphasized the importance of your developing sensitivity to the way children negotiate meaning; this is critical to helping children understand and actively participate in instructional experiences. Essentially, it involves adjusting instruction to the individual needs, one of the main characteristics of the influential teacher discussed in Chapter 1.

Instruction must also develop children's understanding and ability to negotiate various meanings in learning how to "do school." These include learning the language of instruction, knowing how to participate and work cooperatively in small groups, developing a rich concept of literacy processes, understanding how to do instructional tasks, and understanding the unique features of printed text that contribute to meaning.

INSTRUCTIONAL AND ASSESSMENT STRATEGIES

The instructional activities and strategies introduced in our discussion are designed to help you develop five critical areas in early reading and literacy development. These include: (1) understanding the language of instruction, developing concepts about reading and writing, and becoming adept at group participation; (2) developing picture and print awareness; (3) knowing how thoughts and ideas can be represented in print through observing, recording, and writing; (4) developing a sense of story and narrative; and (5) building positive attitudes toward reading. How you select and use activities and strategies will be determined in large part by your belief about early reading and writing development and knowledge about your students.

Your knowledge of students' progress will be based to a great extent on observations in real learning situations. This will range from developing an understanding of the background knowledge and meanings children bring to your classroom on the first day of school to their reading and writing progress throughout the school year. The observation checklist in Table 3-3 presented will be helpful in this regard and accounts for the five instructional goals discussed in the chapter.

In the next chapter, we turn our attention to the development of reading comprehension, extending some of the ideas in the present chapter to create a positive and interactive learning environment to enhance children's meaning-making and thinking processes.

DOUBLE ENTRY JOURNAL

Now that we've discussed early reading and writing at some length, go back to the list you made earlier of the things children need to know in order to read and write. Organize your list, creating categories of some type. Add to your list based upon what you read. Now look at your list and decide which of the items on it are things teachers can teach. Put an asterisk by those. Share your new lists and categories with a friend.

Supporting Activities

1. Briefly review the seven conditions for optimal instruction presented at the beginning of this chapter. Arrange to visit an elementary school classroom at a grade level of your preference during reading and language arts instruction. Identify and briefly discuss classroom experiences during directed instruction that reflect these conditions. Were there some conditions that you did not observe? If so, speculate on why this might be the case.

2. After reviewing the Directed Listening-Thinking Activity (DL-TA) presented earlier in this chapter, locate a children's story that you believe can be effectively presented using this comprehension strategy. Carefully read the story, identify the episode "prediction stop-points," and then present the story to primary-grade students at the appropriate level. Briefly

reflect on this experience and describe the children's predictive responses. You may wish to use a tape recorder to assist you in this process. What insights did you derive from their responses? What changes would you make in using this story again with the DL-TA strategy?

3. Observe one kindergarten or first-grade child working in his or her classroom story or reading center. Briefly describe how he or she selected the books chosen. What strategies were used in exploring and reading the book selected? In your conversation with the teacher, identify her or his beliefs about the way in which the center contributes to literacy development in the classroom. Are these beliefs consistent with your observations? Also explore how new books are obtained for the center.

4. Refamiliarize yourself with the "Early Reading and Writing Assessment Checklist" found in Table 3-3. Pay particular attention to the five major categories, A through E. Photocopy the checklist. Arrange an observation in a kindergarten or first-grade classroom during reading and language arts instruction. With the teacher's assistance, select one child and observe this child for the entire period using the checklist. Briefly describe your insights and instructional recommendations for this child based on your observations using the major categories in the checklist.

REFERENCES

Allen, R. V. (1976). *Language experiences in communication.* Boston: Houghton Mifflin.

Brown, H., & Cambourne, B. (1987). *Read and retell.* Portsmouth, NH: Heinemann.

Bussie, A. M., Chittenden, E. A., Amarel, M., & Klausner, E. (1985). *Inquiry into meaning: An investigation of learning to read.* Hillsdale, NJ: Erlbaum.

Calkins, L. M. (1986). *The art of teaching writing.* Portsmouth, NH: Heinemann.

Cambourne, B. & Turbill, J. (1987). *Coping with chaos.* Portsmouth, NH: Heinemann.

Cambourne, B., (1984). *Basic conditions for language development.* Paper presented at the meeting of the 10th National Australian Reading Association Conference, Sydney, Australia.

Clay, M. M. (1972). *Reading: The patterning of complex behaviour.* Portsmouth, NH: Heinemann.

Clay, M. M. (1979). *Concepts about print tests.* Portsmouth, NH: Heinemann.

Clay, M. M. (1985). *The early detection of reading difficulties* (3rd ed.). Portsmouth, NH: Heinemann.

Cullinan, B. E. (1989). Literature for young children. In D. S. Strickland & L. M. Morrow (Eds.), *Emerging literacy: Young children learn to read and write* (pp. 35–51). Newark, DE: International Reading Association.

Davidson, J. L. (1991). *Illustrating and making books.* Cortland, IL: Prairie Publications.

Downing, J., & Oliver, P. (1973–74). The child's conception of "a word." *Reading Research Quarterly, 9,* 568–582.

Doyle, W., & Carter, K. (1984). Academic tasks in classrooms. *Curriculum Inquiry, 14,* 129–149.

Durkin, D. (1966). *Children who read early.* New York: Teachers College Press.

Dyson, A. H. (1984). Learning to write\learning to do school: Emergent writers' interpretations of school literacy tasks. *Research in the Teaching of English, 18,* 233–265.

Erickson, F. (1982). Taught cognitive learning in its immediate environments: A neglected topic in the anthropology of education. *Anthropology & Education Quarterly, 13,* 148–180.

Goodman, K. S., Bird, L. B., & Goodman, Y. M. (1991). *The whole language catalog.* Santa Rosa, CA: American School Publishers.

Goodman, Y. (1984). The development of initial literacy. In H. Goelman, A. Oberg, & F. Smith (Eds.), *Awakening to literacy* (pp. 102–109). Portsmouth, NH: Heinemann.

Graves, D. (1982, December). *Let's take another look at the development of young writers.* Paper presented at the National Reading Conference, Clearwater Beach, FL.

Haggard, M. R. (1989). Reducing ambiguity: How students and teachers make sense of school. In S. McCormick & J. Zutell (Eds.), *Cognitive and social perspectives for literacy research and instruction.* The Thirty-Eighth Yearbook of the National Reading Conference (pp. 445–451). Chicago: National Reading Conference.

Hardy, M., Stennett, R., & Smythe, P. (1974). Development of auditory and visual language concepts and relationship to instructional strategies in kindergarten. *Elementary English, 51,* 525–532.

Harris, P. (1989). *First grade children's constructs of teacher-assigned reading tasks in a whole language classroom.* Unpublished doctoral dissertation, University of California, Berkeley.

Harste, J. C., Woodward, V. A., & Burke, C. L. (1984). *Language stories and literacy lessons.* Portsmouth, NH: Heinemann.

Holdaway, D. (1979). *The foundations of literacy.* New York: Ashton Scholastic.

Johns, J. (1972). Children's concepts of their reading and their reading achievement. *Journal of Reading Behavior, 4,* 56–57.

Kelly, G. (1955). *The psychology of personal constructs.* New York: W. W. Norton.

Kita, J. (1979, November). *Children's conceptions of reading and writing.* Paper presented at the annual meeting of the National Reading Conference. San Antonio, TX.

Lipson, E. R. (1988). *The New York Times parent's guide to the best books for children.* New York: Times Books.

Lynch, P. (1986). *Using big books and predictable books.* Richmond Hill, Ontario: Scholastic-TAB.

Mason, J. M. (1984). Early reading from a developmental perspective. In P. D. Pearson, R. Barr, M. L. Kamil, & P. Mosenthal (Eds.), *Handbook of reading research* (pp. 508–543). New York: Longman.

Morrow, L. M. (1993). *Literacy development in the early years.* Boston, MA: Allyn & Bacon.

Murphy, S. B. (1988, February). *The problem with reading tasks: Watching children learn.* Paper presented at the Eastern Educational Research Association, Miami Beach, FL.

Purcell-Gates, V. (1988). Lexical and syntactic knowledge of written narrative held by well-read-to kindergartners and second graders. *Research in the Teaching of English, 22,* 128–160.

Reid, J. (1966). Learning to think about reading. *Educational Research, 9,* 56–62.

Ruddell, M. R.-H. (1991). Students' metacognitive response to ambiguous literacy tasks. *Reading Research and Instruction, 31,* 1–11.

Ruddell, R. B., & Haggard, M. R. (1985). Oral and written language acquisition and the reading process. In H. Singer & R.B. Ruddell (Eds.), *Theoretical models and processes of reading,* (3rd ed.) (pp. 63–80). Newark, DE: International Reading Association.

Soderbergh, R. (1977). *Reading in early childhood: A linguistic study of a preschool child's gradual acquisition of reading ability.* Washington, DC: Georgetown University Press.

Stauffer, R. G. (1976). *Teaching reading as a thinking process.* New York: Harper & Row.

Strickland, D. S., & Morrow, L. M. (1989). *Emerging literacy: Young children learn to read and write.* Newark, DE: International Reading Association.

Sulzby, E. (1985). Children's emergent reading of favorite storybooks: A developmental study. *Reading Research Quarterly, 20,* 458–481.

Sulzby, E. (1994). Postscript. In R. B. Ruddell, M. R. Ruddell, & H. Singer (Eds.), *Theoretical models and processes of reading* (4th ed.)(pp. 278–279). Newark, DE: International Reading Association.

Sulzby, E., & Teale, W. (1991). Emergent literacy. In R. Barr, M. L. Kamil, P. B. Mosenthal, & P. D. Pearson (Eds.), *Handbook of reading research, Volume II* (pp. 727–757). New York: Longman.

Teale, W. H., & Sulzby, E. (1989). Emergent literacy: New perspectives. In D. S. Strickland & L. M. Morrow (Eds.), *Emerging literacy: Young children learn to read and write* (pp. 1–15). Newark, DE: International Reading Association.

Trelease, J. (1989). *The new read-aloud handbook.* New York: Penguin Books.

Vygotsky, L. S. (1986). *Thought and language* (rev. ed.: A. Kozulin, Trans. & Ed.). Cambridge, MA: MIT Press.

Alphabet Books

Anno, M. (1975). *Anno's alphabet.* New York: Crowell.

Azarian, M. (1981). *A farmer's alphabet.* New York: Godine.

Feelings, M. (1974). *Jambo means hello: Swahili alphabet book.* New York: Dial.

Kitchen, B. (1984). *Animal alphabet.* New York: Dial.

Pearson, T. C. (1986). *A apple pie.* New York: Dial.

Dr. Seuss (1963). *Dr. Seuss's ABC.* New York: Random House.

Big Books

Fox, M. (1987). *Hattie & the fox.* Scarsdale, NY: Bradbury.

Martin, B. (1983). *Brown bear, brown bear, what do you see?* New York: Holt.

Scarry, R. (1985). *Richard Scarry's biggest word book ever!* New York: Random House.

Wright Group Story Box (1984). *Mrs. Wishy-Washy.* San Diego, CA: Wright Group.

Concept Development Books

Anno, M. (1977). *Anno's counting book.* New York: Crowell.

Carle, E. (1969). *The very hungry caterpillar.* New York: Philomel/Putman.

Crews, D. (1978). *Freight train.* New York: Greenwillow.

Crews, D. (1985). *Bicycle race.* New York: Greenwillow.

Gibbons, G. (1985). *Flying and playgrounds.* New York: Holiday.

Gibbons, G. (1987). *Dinosaurs.* New York: Holiday.

Hoban, T. (1972). *Count and see.* New York: Macmillan.

Hoban, T. (1976). *Big ones, little ones.* New York: Greenwillow.

Hoban, T. (1978). *Is it red? Is it yellow? Is it blue?* New York: Greenwillow.

Hoban, T. (1985). *Is it larger? Is it smaller?* New York: Greenwillow.

Maestro, B., & Maestro, G. (1985). *Where is my friend? A word concept book.* New York: Crown.

Rockwell, A. (1982). *Boats.* New York: Dutton.

Rockwell, A. (1986). *Things that go.* New York: Dutton.

Tafuri, N. (1986). *Who's counting.* New York: Greenwillow.

Wildsmith, B. (1965). *Brian Wildsmith's 1, 2, 3.* New York: Franklin Watts.

Image-Evoking Description Books

Aliki (1984). *Feelings.* New York: Greenwillow.

Bemelmans, L. (1939). *Madeline.* New York: Viking.

Blegvad, L. (1985). *Anna Banana and me.* New York: McElderry.

Freeman, D. (1968). *Corduroy.* New York: Viking.

Holabird, K. (1983). *Angelina Ballerina.* New York: Crown.

Hughes, S. (1984). *Alfi gives a hand.* New York: Lothrop.

Lamorisse, A. (1957). *The red balloon.* New York: Doubleday.

Lionni, L. (1967). *Fredrick.* New York: Pantheon.

Lionni, L. (1969). *Alexander and the wind-up mouse.* New York: Knopf.

McClosky, R. (1941). *Make way for ducklings.* New York: Viking.

Maris, R. (1983). *My book.* New York: Puffin.

Rey, H. A. (1941). *Curious George.* Boston: Houghton Mifflin.

Scarry, R. (1968). *Richard Scarry's what do people do all day?* New York: Random House.

Dr. Seuss (1957). *The cat in the hat.* New York: Beginner Books.

Steptoe, M. (1987). *Snuggle piggy and the magic blanket.* New York: Dutton.

Poetry Collections

Brown, M. (1980). *Finger rhymes.* New York: Dutton.

Larrick, N. (1983). *When dark comes dancing: A bedtime poetry book.* New York: Philomel/Putman.

Prelutsky, J. (1986). *Read-aloud rhymes for the very young.* New York: Knopf.

Royds, C. (1986). *Poems for young children.* New York: Doubleday.

Watson, C. (1978). *Catch me & kiss me & say it again.* New York: Philomel.

Predictable Books

Brown, M. W. (1947). *Goodnight moon.* New York: Harper.

Eastman, P. D. (1960). *Are you my mother?* New York: Random House.

Emberly, E. (1967). *Drummer Hoff.* Englewood Cliffs, NJ: Prentice-Hall.

Galdone, P. (1968). *Henny Penny.* New York: Clarion.

Galdone, P. (1975). *The gingerbread boy.* New York: Clarion.

Hogrogian, N. (1971). *One fine day.* New York: Macmillan.

Ivimey, J. (1986). *Three blind mice.* New York: Clarion.

Koontz, R. (1988). *This old man: The counting song.* New York: Dodd, Mead.

Mosel, A. (1968). *Tikki Tikki Tembo.* New York: Holt.

Peppe, R. (1985). *The house that Jack built.* New York: Delacorte.

Stevens, H. (1987). *Fat mouse.* New York: Viking.

Wadsorth, O. (1985). *Over in the meadow.* New York: Viking.

Wildsmith, B. (1982). *Cat on the mat.* New York: Oxford.

Wildsmith, B. (1988). *Toot, toot.* New York: Oxford.

Read-Aloud and Reference Books

Lipson, E. R. (1988). *Parent's guide to the best books for children.* New York: Times Books.

Strickland, D., & Morrow, L. M. (1989). *Emerging literacy: Young children learn to read and write.* Newark, DE: International Reading Association.

Trelease, J. (1989). *The new read-aloud handbook.* New York: Penguin Books.

Wordless Storybooks

Hutchins, P. (1968). *Rosie's walk.* New York: Macmillan.

Keats, E. J. (1973). *Skates.* New York: Franklin Watts.

Mayer, M. (1967). *A boy, a dog, and a frog.* New York: Dial.

Ormerod, J. (1981). *Moonlight.* New York: Lothrop, Lee & Shepard.

Ormerod, J. (1981). *Sunshine.* New York: Lothrop, Lee & Shepard.

CHAPTER 3	DL-TA	
FOCUS ON	Developing sense of story	
GUIDES STUDENTS	Before and during reading	
USE TO PLAN	Lessons	
MAY BE USED	Whole class, small groups	
MAY BE COMBINED WITH (KNOWN STRATEGIES)	Shared Book Experience	
MATERIALS PREPARATION	Light	
OTHER PREPARATION	Moderate	
OUTSIDE RESOURCES	Not needed	
HOW TO DO	Page 114	

Building Tables "grow" or build, successively from chapter to chapter. They tell you (1) the focus of each strategy introduced in a chapter; (2) how the strategy is best used; (3) what strategies from previous chapters combine well with new ones; (4) preparation requirements; (5) additional resources needed; and (6) the page on which a strategy's How-to-Do appears.

DEVELOPING READING COMPREHENSION: USING INSTRUCTIONAL STRATEGIES TO DEVELOP HIGHER-LEVEL THINKING

INTRODUCTION

Reading comprehension is the act of constructing meaning while interacting with text. Comprehension is, in fact, an incredibly complex mental process: When we read, our comprehension strategies direct the split-second activation of many thousands of neurons and integrate our prior knowledge and experience with information in text to create meaning. Comprehension is more, however, than simply a mental process. Comprehension is affected by who we are, how we relate to the world and others in it, our accumulated store of factual and intuitive knowledge, and even how we feel on a given day.

You have only to experience a brief excerpt from a favorite children's book to become consciously aware of the complexity of this process. In the following excerpt from *Charlotte's Web* (White, 1952), Wilbur, Fern's pet pig and the runt of the litter, has been sold to the Zuckermans who live just down the road. Wilbur has just settled down for a nap near the barn door when he hears a thin voice calling to him.

"Salutations!" said the voice.

Wilbur jumped to his feet. "Salu-*what*?" he cried.

"Salutations!" repeated the voice.

"What are *they*, and where are *you*? screamed Wilbur. "Please, *please*, tell me where you are. And what are salutations?"

"Salutations are greetings," said the voice. "When I say 'salutations,' it's just my fancy way of saying hello or good morning. Actually, it's a silly expression, and I am surprised that I used it at all. As for my whereabouts, that's easy. Look up here in the corner of the doorway. Here I am. Look, I'm waving!"

E. B. White has just introduced, or reintroduced, us to Charlotte, the gentle spider in *Charlotte's Web* (1952, pp. 35–36). Charlotte's role in life seems to be that of constantly helping Wilbur, who in turn appears to make her own life a little brighter.

Comprehension of this delightful story may occur on different levels for different readers. The six-year-old child, listening to the story for the first time, will have one level of understanding and emotional response to the story conclusion; a teenager or adult, returning to a favorite book from childhood, will have another; and a young parent reading the book to his or her child may respond to *Charlotte's Web* in yet another way. Each individual constructs her or his own personal meaning for the text, and so responds individually as Charlotte weaves the last word in her web and prepares her new egg sac before departing.

Individual constructions of meaning occur just as surely in the classroom as they do when we listen to or read stories on our own. In classrooms, teachers guide children's reading and comprehension development for the purpose of increasing children's ability to construct full, rich meaning from text. The teacher's role in guiding children's reading comprehension development is a critical one: This development will directly affect children's achievement, academic success, and reading enjoyment, both in their many years of schooling and throughout their lifetime.

PROGRESS IN COMPREHENSION

In Chapter 2, we described the rapid progress children make in acquiring vocabulary, language control, and sense of story on entrance to kindergarten and grade one, areas essential to effective comprehension (Pearson & Fielding, 1991). This progress continues throughout the primary and intermediate grades, as children expand their conceptual knowledge, their ability to understand sentences and story structure, and their interests, and as they develop specific reading strategies that enable them to comprehend stories and expository material.

During the elementary years, children also become increasingly sophisticated in their ability to understand what makes text easy or hard, to connect their reading purpose to a reading strategy, and to monitor their own comprehension. Danner's research (1976) with children at grades 2, 4, and 6 indicates that sixth-grade children are more effective than children at the earlier grades in understanding that topic sentences assist them in organizing and remembering the content of the text. Forrest and Waller (1979) demonstrate that sixth-grade children, in contrast to third-graders, vary their reading strategy when reading stories for different purposes, such as enjoyment, making up a title, skimming for information, and studying.

Children in the later grades also experience more success in monitoring their comprehension than do younger children (Myers & Paris, 1978; Wixon, 1979); younger children do not appear to possess comprehension "fix up" strategies, as do older children, even when they are aware of a comprehension problem (Myers & Paris, 1978).

These findings suggest a number of clear developmental differences across the elementary grades in children's comprehension processing of written text. These differences may be due to a combination of factors, including increased experience reading text, increased mental and social maturation, or little instructional emphasis in these areas in the early grades. The findings may also be interpreted to suggest that reading instruction in the elementary grades should, indeed, emphasize self-monitoring of comprehension and connecting reading purpose to reading strategy and text to be read.

COMPREHENSION: PROCESS AND STRATEGIES

Our goal in this chapter is to extend your understanding of comprehension processes and strategies. *First,* we will review the key features of the comprehension process and identify our central goal in comprehension instruction and related objectives. *Second,* we will address comprehension instruction in the classroom through a classroom-based comprehension framework emphasizing higher-level thinking, comprehension skills, and questioning strategies. And *third,* we will introduce specific instructional approaches and strategies designed to develop comprehension and higher-level thinking.

COMPREHENSION DEVELOPMENT IN THE CLASSROOM

The overriding goal for comprehension instruction is the development of reading comprehension abilities that enable children to construct, interpret, apply, and transform meaning effectively using narrative and expository text. Central to this goal is building higher-level thinking processes that go far beyond the mere recall of factual information. Such a goal requires that teachers understand the essential features of the comprehension process and the role they play in creating instructional conditions for guiding children's comprehension development.

ESSENTIAL FEATURES FOR COMPREHENSION

In Chapter 2, we identified six essential features that define the comprehension process in the context of the classroom. These are:

1. *Purposeful reading* guided by clear objectives and expected use;

2. *Activation of background knowledge content* related to the story or expository content;

3. *Activation of background knowledge processing strategies* appropriate for the reading purpose;

4. *Mobilization of attitudes and values* related to the text content;

5. *Activation of monitoring strategies* to provide for a check on meaning construction; and

6. *Interactive use of these processes* to achieve the reading purpose and expected use.

The key to successful comprehension instruction is to incorporate these six features into instructional objectives and teaching strategies. These features are critical, not only for comprehension but in negotiating meaning between teacher and child as well. You may recall how we illustrated the meaning construction process in Chapter 2. You will see the illustration again here (Table 4-1) as you think about reading comprehension as a meaning construction process.

THE TEACHER'S ROLE IN COMPREHENSION INSTRUCTION

It is very important to remember that instruction must emphasize active meaning negotiation and comprehension processing and must provide children with a wide variety of opportunities for social interactions that are directly connected to their reading experience. Interaction of this kind will provide for higher-level comprehension processing, interest, and motivation (Singer, 1980). The following comprehension objectives define your role in comprehension instruction and are closely allied to the comprehension features we just discussed in the previous section:

The teacher's role in comprehension instruction involves

1. *Negotiating a clear understanding of the reading purpose* and *expected use* of the reading experience with the children;

2. *Activating and helping children use their background knowledge* by connecting this knowledge to the content of the reading material;

3. *Developing text-processing strategies and an understanding of when to use these strategies* based on the reading purpose and the nature of the reading text;

4. *Helping children relate their prior attitudes and values* to the content of the text and the reading experience;

5. *Teaching children to become aware of the importance of checking meaning construction* against prior knowledge and information in the text; and

6. *Building the understanding that reading purpose, background knowledge, processing strategy, prior attitude toward content and instruction, and meaning monitoring must operate in harmony* for effective comprehension.

These objectives clearly demonstrate that development of children's comprehension relies heavily on involving children actively in the thinking process, ranging from activating background knowledge, to building and using text-processing strategies, to monitoring their own meaning constructions. The teaching model you present to your children as you use various questioning strategies, as you respond, and as you engage them in discussions is important in shaping their understanding and expectations about reading comprehension and meaning construction (Palincsar, 1984; Pearson & Fielding, 1991).

TYPES OF TEACHER QUESTIONS

A surprisingly large number of teachers fail to engage children in active thinking that involves higher-level comprehension processing—comprehension processing that goes beyond the factual recall of information. Our early research (Ruddell & Williams, 1972), and others' work (Durkin, 1978–1979; Guszak, 1967) reveals that, both in the primary and intermediate grades, approximately 70 percent of teacher questions are at the factual or literal comprehension level. Frank Guszak (1967) observed teachers at grades two, four, and six in reading groups and social studies lessons, and noted that over two-thirds of the questions they used were related to the factual make-up of stories and expository text. When teachers did ask open-ended questions, most could be answered by "yes" and "no" (e.g., "Did you like this story?"). This kind of factual approach to discussion may actually lead students away from complex understanding of events, interactions, and ideas in narrative and expository text.

Dolores Durkin's extensive observational study of teachers using basal readers (1979) indicated that most questions teachers used were factual and served to test and assess children's recall of story content, rather than to instruct. Instruction that did take place was usually of a form in which little elaboration occurred. Durkin characterized the teachers she studied as "interrogators" and "mentioners." John Goodlad (1984) found from his nationwide study of over one thousand classrooms, covering a wide range of grade levels, that "frontal teaching," in which the teacher stands or sits in front of students and talks, is the norm in classrooms at all levels. He concluded that students are rarely engaged in active learning from one another, or through productive interactions using higher-level thinking with their teachers.

CHILDREN'S ACTIVE INVOLVEMENT

Comprehension development relies heavily on the cognitive processes that occur when teachers activate children's background knowledge and processing and monitoring strategies and direct them toward a purposeful reading objective (Hansen, 1981; Fielding, Anderson, & Pearson, 1990). Taba has referred to this process as "cognitive commerce" (Taba, 1965; Taba & Elzey, 1964). Children's active involvement in teacher and peer interactions that connect prior attitudes and values to the reading content also greatly increases their motivation and interest (Mathewson, 1985; Ruddell & Speaker, 1985). Our research on influential teachers, in kindergarten through third grade, indicates that these teachers are highly effective in actively engaging children across a wide range of thinking levels in story-based discussions (Ruddell, 1990).

THE INSTRUCTIONAL FRAMEWORK: THINKING LEVELS AND COMPREHENSION SKILLS

The framework presented in Table 4-1 is intended to assist you in building your own mental conceptualization of the comprehension process. The framework was developed from an extensive research review (Ruddell, 1974,

	LEVELS OF THINKING			
COMPREHENSION SKILLS	FACTUAL	INTERPRETIVE	APPLICATIVE	TRANSACTIVE
1. Identifying Details	X	X		
2. Sequence of Events	X	X		
3. Cause and Effect	X	X	X	X
4. Main idea	X	X	X	X
5. Predicting Outcomes	X	X	X	X
6. Valuing	X	X	X	X
7. Problem Solving	X	X	X	X

TABLE 4-1

An Instructional Framework for Comprehension Development

1978) and has been refined and revised from our further research and work with classroom teachers in the elementary grades (Ruddell, Draheim, & Barnes, 1990). This instructional framework identifies four levels of thinking at the top of the table, and seven frequently used comprehension skills appropriate at each level of thinking (shown at the left side of the table).

We will illustrate the four levels of thinking and specific comprehension skills using the following excerpt from *Charlotte's Web*. Before reading the following excerpt, however, briefly examine the four questions that follow the passage. As you read the passage, try to track your thinking and comprehension processes as directed by the questions. It will be helpful to recall that at this point in the book, Wilbur has grown a bit rotund, and sheep has spread the rumor to the other barnyard animals that Wilbur will soon become smoked bacon and ham in Zuckerman's smokehouse. Charlotte is gravely concerned about Wilbur and decides to act. We enter Chapter 11, entitled "The Miracle" (p. 77).

> The next day was foggy. Everything on the farm was dripping wet. The grass looked like a magic carpet. The asparagus patch looked like a silver forest.
>
> On foggy mornings, Charlotte's web was truly a thing of beauty. This morning each thin strand was decorated with dozens of tiny beads of water. The web glistened in the light and made a pattern of loveliness and mystery, like a delicate veil. Even Lurvy, who wasn't particularly interested in beauty, noticed the web when he came with the pig's breakfast. He noted how clearly it showed up and he noted how big and carefully built it was. And then he took another look and he saw something that made him set his pail down. There, in the center of the web, neatly woven in block letters, was a message. It said:
>
> SOME PIG!
>
> Lurvy felt weak. He brushed his hand across his eyes and stared harder at Charlotte's web…

Now, briefly respond to the following questions:

1. What was written in Charlotte's web?
2. Why did Lurvy, the hired hand, feel weak?
3. How would you have reacted, had you been the very first person to see the words in Charlotte's web that morning?

4. How do you think Charlotte felt as she observed Lurvy examining the web that morning?

The Four Levels of Thinking

Do you find that these questions require different mental processing as you respond? The answer is obviously yes. These questions have been designed to represent the four levels of thinking presented in Table 4-1. Each level is briefly defined below:

1. The **factual level**, illustrated in the first question, involves memory and recall of information directly from the text. This information is stated explicitly in the text and essentially involves "reading and recalling information in the lines," i.e., "SOME PIG!" No higher-level mental processing is required. The comprehension skill of **identifying details** is used in this question.

2. The **interpretive level**, illustrated in the second question, requires inference and the manipulation of text-based information. This information is implied in the text. Processing it might be thought of as "reading between the lines," e.g., "Lurvy was surprised to see words written in the web because he had never seen words in a spider's web before." Responding to this question involves the comprehension skill of **cause and effect**.

3. The **applicative level**, illustrated in the third question, involves integrating text-based information with personal knowledge schemata. This information and this knowledge are applied to develop a personalized meaning, which essentially requires "reading beyond the lines." This level is illustrated in the responses, "Well, I might call Mr. Zuckerman to see if he sees the same thing that I do" or "We could call a newspaper reporter and a photographer to write a story on this web" or other possible responses appropriate to the story context. The third question involves the comprehension skill of **predicting outcomes**.

4. The **transactive level**, illustrated in the fourth question, involves the use of text-based knowledge, personal knowledge schemata, and values (Rosenblatt, 1985; Ruddell, 1990). The reader is encouraged to empathize or identify with a character and more fully enter the story. This level can be thought of as "reading with the character" in narrative text. In expository text the transactive level is reached when the reader transforms the text in a personal way that creates a strong internal response to text. For example, as a reader hears and feels the majesty and poetry of Martin Luther King, Jr.'s "I Have a Dream" speech, or the young scientist's excitement as she finds in text the key to the answers she's seeking, or as any of us experience that center-of-

being "click"—the visceral response when ideas constructed from text astound or awaken us. Responses from our *Charlotte's Web* example illustrating the transactive level include "I think Charlotte was happy to see that Lurvy was so surprised when he read the words in her web" or "She thinks her plan to save Wilbur is going to work" or other responses that reasonably fit the story context and your children's personal experiences. This question involves the comprehension skill of **valuing.**

Using All Four Levels of Thinking

As you consider the emphasis you wish to place on these four levels of thinking, you will find that it is very easy to create factual-level questions such as identifying details. This is one reason teachers rely heavily on the use of questions at this level, and it explains in part why these questions are so common in basal reader teacher guides. Factual questions simply ask for story information in question form.

Not only are factual questions easy to create, they can also be answered quickly. Unfortunately, however, they provide very limited opportunity for developing discussions that build higher-level thinking. Our observations of influential teachers indicate that these teachers use *factual-level* questions and discussions only about 20 percent of the time, in contrast to noninfluential teachers who rely on the factual level about 70 percent of the time (Ruddell, 1990). Questions at the interpretive, applicative, and transactive levels take more effort and time to construct, but these questions are central to building higher-level thinking. The influential teachers were found to use the *interpretive level* about 55 percent of the time in contrast to 25 percent use for noninfluential teachers. The *applicative level* was used 22 percent of the time and *transactive level* was about 3 percent of the time by the influential teachers. Noninfluential teachers used the applicative level only 2 percent of the time and did not use the transactive level at all. Emphasis on questions that require active mental processing of story-based information and personal schemata at the interpretive, applicative, and transactive levels is of paramount importance in our teaching.

Comprehension Skills and Thinking Levels

The comprehension skills identified at the left side of Table 4-1 are to some extent self-defined. You have no doubt become familiar with these skills in your past instructional experience. Even so, a brief definition of each comprehension skill follows, using examples based on our excerpt from *Charlotte's Web*. Again, note the relationship between each comprehension skill and the thinking level involved, as indicated by the "X" in Table 4-1.

1. Identifying details requires the student to recall specific information from the text. This skill involves either memory or visual scanning for the sort of text-based information elicited by such questions or directives as, "What was Lurvy doing in the barnyard that morning?" or "Read the first page of the story to find out what was written in the web." Such questions and directives will, for the most part, involve the factual level of thinking. These questions do little to build higher levels of thinking, but they may serve to troubleshoot difficulty when a child is unable to respond at a higher level because specific details are not understood. Caution must be used in such troubleshooting, however, in that some children will comprehend text effectively, focusing on overall story meaning, even though they may have missed a number of story details. Their understanding of the story may not be revealed if you use only identifying-detail-type questions that focus on the factual level in story discussion, rather than questions that allow story understandings and higher levels of thinking to emerge.

2. Sequence of events relates to the order in which ideas or actions occur in the text. This comprehension skill will be used primarily in building factual and interpretive levels of thinking. For example, the question, "What did Lurvy do right after he saw the words in the web?" is at the factual level, because this information is stated directly in the story and requires only information recall. The interpretive level of thinking is illustrated by, "What do you think Lurvy will do now?," which requires story inference using the information presented to this point in the story.

3. Cause and effect requires explanation of causes of story events and outcomes. If the causal information is stated directly in the text, the factual level of thinking is used in information recall, as in answering the question "What made Lurvy set his pail down?" The skill of cause and effect can, however, be used to develop any of the higher levels of thinking; questions at the higher levels will frequently start with *what, why,* and *how.* We are essentially asking "*What* happened and *why*?" "*What* factors were involved in the cause?" "*How* are these related to the effect?" The interpretive level is illustrated by the question "Why do you think Charlotte wrote the words 'SOME PIG!' in her web?"

4. Main idea focuses on the central thought of the text and requires synthesis and interpretation of information and may be used with each of the four levels of thinking. If your question is based on the main idea stated in a topic sentence, as is often the case in science and social studies material, the student may simply recall this information in responding at the factual level of thinking. The following question however, asked after reading the first page of Chapter 11 of *Charlotte's Web,* or possibly the entire chapter, illustrates a main idea question at the interpretive level, "Why do you think this chapter is called 'The Miracle'?" This question requires the child to integrate the story content and synthesize it in relation to the central thought of the text. Main idea questions will develop, for the most part, the interpretive, applicative, and transactive levels of thinking.

5. Predicting outcomes requires thinking that integrates story details, character traits, and sense of story plot in order to consider immediate and long-range story event outcomes. This comprehension skill can be used to develop interpretive, applicative, and transactive levels of thinking. The question we presented earlier, "How would you have reacted, had you been the very first person to see the words in Charlotte's web that morning?," is at the applicative level of thinking. Response to this question requires use of the text-based information *and* personal background knowledge to explain how *you* would have reacted and why.

6. Valuing involves the use of personal attitudes and values in interpreting character motives and traits, and eventually, identification of the author's motive. This skill also uses the previously discussed comprehension skills, ranging from identification of details to predicting outcomes. Valuing-type questions can be used to develop interpretive, applicative, and transactive levels of thinking. For example, "Why did Charlotte want to help Wilbur in our story?" is a valuing question at the interpretive level. This question requires the integration of information to define Charlotte's character and the connection of this character to Wilbur's predicament. "Why do you think Charlotte selected the specific words 'SOME PIG!' to write in her web?" is an applicative-level question. This question focuses on the student's personal interpretation of the central story character and the relationship between character traits and the selection of the specific words. At the transactive level we may ask a question such as, "Pretend for a moment that you are Charlotte. What words would you have selected to write in the web, and why?" This question encourages the child to place him- or herself in Charlotte's role, empathize with her situation, think of Wilbur's position in the story and the story events to this point, and integrate this information with personal values to identify the word or words for the web.

7. Problem solving involves active manipulation and transformation of information. This complex skill utilizes all the other comprehension skills, ranging from identifying details and sequence of ideas to valuing and predicting outcomes. To use the problem-solving skill, the student must identify the problem and relevant information, formulate possible hypotheses, test these hypotheses and search for solutions, and develop explanations and conclusions. This comprehension skill builds interpretive, applicative, and transactive thinking levels.

In a sense, we can think of reading, discussing, and understanding *Charlotte's Web* as a problem-solving process. It is important to help children form hypotheses about the story plot as they develop an understanding of Charlotte, Wilbur, and Templeton in E. B. White's narrative. An example of a problem-solving question sequence at the applicative level, posed at the end of our Chapter 11 excerpt, is simply, "What do you think will happen next? Why do you think that?" And near the conclusion of the chapter, "How do you think this story will end?" As we will see in our discussion on comprehension strategies, these questions are the stock and trade of the Directed Reading-Thinking Activity (DR-TA). Problem-solving questions are similar in nature to predicting-outcomes-type questions discussed above. Both require the student to hypothesize, integrate, synthesize and arrive at and verify conclusions, using larger segments of information across the text.

These four levels of thinking and seven comprehension skills form the basis of comprehension instruction. Look again at Table 4-1 on page 141. It will help you to conceptualize the way the four levels operate in concert with the seven comprehension skills. The importance of considering the four levels of thinking and the seven comprehension skills simultaneously is to understand that these two dimensions of the framework must operate in concert. A given comprehension skill, such as cause and effect, may operate at a factual thinking level, if the cause-and-effect relationship is stated explicitly in the text and requires only recall of cause and effect information; *or* it may operate at an interpretive thinking level, if the child must use and integrate the text-based information to infer the cause-and-effect relationship. Once this concept is clear, you possess an invaluable tool for developing children's comprehension of literature and content area text material.

Questioning and Discussion Strategies

At this point we have developed an understanding of the importance of building levels of thinking using specific comprehension skills. We now turn to the use of questioning and discussion strategies that will assist you in orchestrating comprehension skill development with the four levels of thinking. Use of these questioning strategies can greatly increase the potential for developing higher-level thinking as you involve your students in discussions. An understanding of the following four strategies will greatly facilitate your ability to initiate and direct discussions that provide for active comprehension building.

1. **Focusing** is a strategy often used to initiate a discussion, or, when discussion tends to stray from the topic to refocus attention on the initial question. The focusing-type question is designed to activate background knowledge and develop a reading purpose. For example, at

the beginning of our chapter excerpt, we might ask "Charlotte is really worried about Wilbur ending up in Zuckerman's smokehouse; what do you think she might do to help him?" This is a focusing question at the applicative-thinking level, and it involves the predicting outcomes comprehension skill.

2. **Extending** is used to elicit additional information on the same topic of discussion at the same level of thinking. The following questions are generic in nature but illustrate questions and responses using the extending strategy:

"Is there anything else you could say about that?"

"Who has another thought about this idea?"

"Keep going, that sounds interesting."

3. **Clarifying** is a strategy in which the question or response encourages explaining or refining a response. Clarifying differs from extending by encouraging the child to deal with a vague response and work to refine it. For example, we may say,

"Could you explain your point again?" or

"Oh, I see what you mean, it could have been . . . [so and so]."

The clarifying strategy may also be used to elicit information on the *same topic* at a *lower level* of thinking. We may need to shift from an interpretive-level question to a factual level question to assist the child in integrating important information into the thinking process. For example, if no response is given to the interpretive-level question "Why do you think Charlotte built her web and wrote the words "SOME PIG!" in it?" we may need to go the factual level. In this case, we may ask the factual-level question "Do you think Charlotte was trying to trick Mr. Zuckerman? Why do you think so?" The purpose here is to recall and re-establish Charlotte's belief stated in the previous chapter that "The way to save Wilbur's life is to play a trick on Zuckerman. If I can fool a bug, I can surely fool a man." (p. 67) After establishing this information, we then return to the original interpretive-level question.

4. **Raising** is the attempt to solicit additional information on the same topic at a higher comprehension level. For example, after receiving a positive response to the factual-level question "What was written in Charlotte's web?," we may then raise to an interpretive level by asking, "Do you think Charlotte's plan will save Wilbur? Why do you think so?"

The Strategies in Use: An Example

The following interchange between one of our influential teachers and her kindergarten and first-grade students illustrates the use of these strategies (Ruddell, Draheim, & Barnes, 1990). Note that the specific questioning strategy, the thinking level, and the comprehension skill used in each segment of the discussion are identified in the transcript. This discussion occurred at the conclusion of the story *Alexander and the Wind-Up Mouse* by Leo Lionni (1969). The story centers around the theme of friendship and caring as Alexander, a real mouse, is very concerned about his friend Willy, a toy mouse, who is broken and about to be thrown away. The teacher and students are examining the story illustration collage at the end of the story showing Alexander and Willy.

A child asks, "Which one is Willy?"

T: Can't you tell? (*Focusing, factual level, identifying details*)

C1:   No.

T: I don't know. It's hard to tell. How could you tell them apart? (*Focusing, interpretive level, identifying details*)

C1:   Because he's a wind-up mouse.

T: Anything else about them that was different? (*Extending, interpretive level, identifying details*)

C2:   Yes, he had a key.

T: Yes, anything else? (*Extending, interpretive level, identifying details*)

C3:   Round—wheels.

T: Yes, maybe.

C4:   Kind of like an egg.

T: Sort of.

C4:   His ears were like two drops of tears.

T: Well, that's a good description. Can you think of anything else about the way Mr. Lionni chose to make the mice? (Wait time, 5 seconds) Here's Alexander. Here's Willy (shows picture of each). (*Extending, interpretive level, cause and effect*)

C3:   One's rounder.

C2:   One of them is smooth, and the other one's rough.

T: Why do you suppose one's smooth and one's rough? (*Raising, applicative level, cause and effect*)

C3:   Because one's a toy.

T: Which one would that be, the smooth one or the rough one? (*Clarifying, interpretive level, cause and effect*)

C2:   The smooth one.

T: That's probably the one I would choose—because I would think of a toy — (interrupted).

C4:   Because a real mouse would have fur.

T: And so he wouldn't be very smooth would he? (*Extending, interpretive level, cause and effect*)

149

C3: No, he would be rough with hair sticking out.

This interaction illustrates the skillful use of focusing-, extending-, clarifying-, and raising-type questions. The levels of thinking emphasized include factual, interpretive, and applicative, using the comprehension skills of details and cause and effect.

By contrast, the interchange below uses limited strategies and places heavy emphasis on the factual level of thinking.

This teacher is in the process of concluding the story discussion, also using *Alexander and the Wind-Up Mouse*.

T: What did you like about the story? (*Focusing, factual or interpretive level, identifying details*)

C1: I liked the part where he found the pebble.

T: You like where he found the pebble. Where did he find it, Timmy? (*Extending, factual level, identifying details*)

C1: By a box.

T: Where? (*Extending, factual level, identifying details*)

C1: By a box.

T: By a box. What were some of the things that were in the box? (*Extending, factual level, identifying details*)

C2: Dolls—(interrupted).

T: There were old toys in that box. Why had they been placed there? (*Extending, factual level, cause and effect*)

C3: Because they were old and couldn't work.

T: And they couldn't work. What did they plan to do with them, Henry? Henry, what did they plan to do with old toys? (*Extending, factual level, sequence of events*)

This discussion uses a very limited repertoire of questioning strategies, primarily extending. The children's thinking level is limited to the factual level using comprehension skills of recall of details, cause and effect, and sequence of events. (Note that while the first question allowed for interpretive response, none were forthcoming and no further encouragement to go beyond the factual level occurred.) While a variety of comprehension skills are used, these are of limited value because of the exclusive focus on the factual level, which simply involves recall of literal information from the story.

The effective use of questioning strategies is important for developing higher-level thinking. *Focusing* establishes a mental set, a purpose for reading, and activates the child's background knowledge. *Extending* elicits additional information on the same topic at the same thinking level. *Clarifying* encourages the child to explain, clarify, or reconceptualize a response at the same level of thinking, or to recall important factual-type information at a lower thinking level in order to clarify the response. *Raising* builds the topic of discussion to a higher comprehension level.

Our emphasis, however, on the interpretive, applicative, and transactive levels of thinking is of critical importance if we are to develop higher-level thinking in our comprehension instruction.

Four Additional Strategies

It is also important to become aware of four additional strategies that must be used with sensitivity and discretion in teaching.

5. **Receiving** is a strategy that we use to acknowledge a response, with no elaboration. Receiving can be positive, using eye contact, a nod of the head, a brief smile, or a brief positive statement. The teacher in the first example above uses receiving in a positive way, as revealed in voice intonation, by responding, "Yes, maybe" and "Sort of." A commonly used positive receiving statement is "Right, good thinking." Receiving can also be negative, exemplified by direct eye contact and a frown, or a curt response such as "You're not listening." The frequent use of positive receiving is important to establish a classroom atmosphere that encourages risk taking and active learning.

6. **Controlling** is the strategy used to dominate discussion; controlling provides little opportunity for verbal interaction. This strategy may be used by the overeager child who does not understand the importance of turn-taking and sharing in group interaction, and who provides a rapid response to your every question before anyone else can participate. Many teachers also use the controlling strategy frequently. The teacher in the second example above uses a controlling strategy in the very last question, as she repeats "Henry, what did they plan to do with the old toys?" Questions such as the following are controlling in nature. Note how they all limit or control the students' responses.

"That was a really good story, wasn't it?"

"I think Charlotte's plan will work, don't you?"

"Who would you like to be in this story? Would you like to be Templeton?"

7. **Ignoring** occurs when a question or response is purposefully not received, either by teacher or child. Most of us have experienced this strategy at some point in our educational experience. The lack of acceptance of a child's response may be due to any number of factors, such as limited time or a negative attitude toward a specific child. Frequent use of the ignoring strategy is very detrimental to the child's self-concept and greatly reduces the desire to participate in group discussion and interactions.

8. **Wait time** is a strategy used to promote reflection and thinking on the part of the child. We have a tendency to fear "silent spaces" in our classroom and tend to fill all silent space with observations,

comments, and even answers to our own questions. Wait time can be quite effective: after you ask a question, just provide five or six seconds of reflection time before you initiate discussion. At first, this will seem like an eternity, but it will result in productive thinking on the part of the children.

A second effective use of wait time is to pause for from two to five seconds after a student has responded to provide time for additional thoughts. Wait time was effectively used in the first teacher's transcript above after the questions "Yes, anything else?" and "Can you think of anything else about he way Mr. Lionni *chose* to make the mice?"

You can quickly assess your use of each of these eight questioning-and-response strategies in your comprehension instruction by tape recording one of the directed reading lessons in your classroom. Simply list the eight strategies down the left margin of a blank sheet of paper and, as you listen to your recording, note the number of times you use each strategy. Then listen to your lesson once again as you become more conscious of the strategies you use in relation to the responses of specific children and the way in which they construct meaning.

COMPREHENSION APPROACHES AND STRATEGIES FOR THE CLASSROOM

We will now turn to specific instructional approaches and strategies that serve to build higher-level thinking and comprehension skills in classrooms. Our discussion of the four levels of thinking, comprehension skills, and question-and-discussion strategies will serve as the foundation for understanding and using these specific comprehension approaches and strategies.

We will explore two different avenues to comprehension instruction in the classroom. *First,* we will present two major and widely used approaches that serve to direct group reading instruction using full-length stories, book chapters, or chapters from content areas such as science or social studies. These approaches are the Directed Reading-Thinking Activity (DR-TA) and the Directed Reading Activity (DRA). *Second,* we will introduce four strategies that are useful in building levels of thinking and comprehension skills by targeting specific aspects of the comprehension process. These strategies serve to help children: (1) activate background knowledge before reading (PreReading Plan—PReP); (2) identify reading purpose and sources of information needed in comprehending text (Question-Answer Relationships—QARs); (3) learn how to ask and respond to questions through modeling (Reciprocal Questioning—ReQuest; and Reciprocal Teaching); and (4) integrate and synthesize information using the entire story or chapter (Group Mapping Activity—GMA).

Group Reading Approaches: The Directed Reading-Thinking Activity (DR-TA) and the Directed Reading Activity (DRA)

The Directed Reading-Thinking Activity (DR-TA)

The DR-TA approach, developed by Stauffer (1969, 1976), is designed for group comprehension instruction. This approach has received attention and wide use by teachers over the last decade because of its emphasis on developing higher-level thinking and because of its ease of use with children's stories and book chapters. The approach involves active comprehension and interchange of children's ideas stimulated by higher-level-thinking-type questions. The DR-TA is highly effective in using the social dynamic of small or large group instruction. Individual and group story predictions are developed based on individual background and text-based information. Jane Davidson's research (1978a) provides strong indication that teachers using this approach do focus more on higher-level-thinking comprehension development than do teachers who rely on the DRA approach (presented later in the chapter), which is commonly used with stories in basal reader programs.

The goals of the DR-TA are to help children set a reading purpose, make predictions using personal background and text-based knowledge, synthesize information directed by reading purpose, verify and revise predictions, and reach story conclusions. Vocabulary is not introduced at the outset of the discussion, as is the case with the DRA.

The DR-TA involves two key phases. The first is directing and guiding children's thinking processes throughout the story. The second involves extension and follow-up activities based on student needs identified in the first phase. Skill development may range from idea synthesis through conceptual story mapping (see the discussion of the Group Mapping Activity later in this chapter) to emphasis on word-analysis skills.

To use the DR-TA efficiently requires that you establish a classroom atmosphere that encourages and values thinking and risk-taking. The environment in your classroom must create a sense of trust that will encourage students to form hypotheses and make predictions about story content. The group dynamic should encourage diverse predictions and allow ample opportunity for children to connect predictions to the story content. You will find that a wide range of predictions will be proposed by children, and that youngsters who are rather shy or even withdrawn will become engaged in making story predictions and active thinking.

DR-TA: The First Phase. The first phase of the DR-TA involves a three-step cycle:

- *first*, making predictions using text information and personal background knowledge;

■ *second,* reading to verify or alter predictions based on new text information and background knowledge;

■ and *third,* providing support and proof of predictions based on text and personal knowledge.

We will use a small group discussion with eight students in a sixth-grade classroom to illustrate these steps. The teacher has read the story in advance and has identified several predetermined stop-points where students will be asked to make predictions, verify predictions, develop new predictions, and provide support and proof for their predictions. The teacher's stop-points occur after the title, the second paragraph, the bottom of the first page, a high-interest point midway through the story as the climax develops, and a stop-point immediately preceding the story conclusion.

The students are familiar with the DR-TA approach. Each student has a single folded page of paper to cover the text below the stop-point directed by the teacher (unless the stop occurs at the bottom of a page). The teacher has asked the students to open their books to the story entitled "Slipstream," by Sheila Hodgson, in their literature anthology *Wingspan* (Ruddell, Monson, & Sebesta, 1981). The story is about a seemingly indifferent but money-driven charter pilot, and his copilot who are flying a tour group from England to a jazz festival in the Channel Islands when severe fog is encountered. Attempts to land at alternate fields are blocked by the presence of a phantom plane on each landing strip; the phantom plane is the type used in World War II. Both men hear a familiar jazz tune, sounds not coming from a radio in the aircraft. The plane must crash-land in the English Channel, and everyone is rescued unhurt. The investigation that follows reveals a major structural defect in the plane that would have caused it to be blown apart had it landed on the ground. (The phantom plane and mysterious music in the story create a Twilight Zone genre. This may be connected to the World War II time period when orchestra leader Glenn Miller disappeared on a flight crossing the Channel.)

The following discussion ensues after teacher (**T**) and students (**S**) read the title, "Slipstream," and author, Sheila Hodgson:

T: With a title like "Slipstream," what do you think this story will be about? (*This focusing-type question* at the *interpretive thinking level* is designed to encourage predicting outcomes by activating personal background knowledge and to stimulate story predictions in the group.)

S1: I think it will be about an airplane flight, because a slipstream has to do with airplanes and our book is called *Wingspan.*

S2: Your mind is floating in a slipstream of air.

S3: I think the story will be about two people and one who moves very fast in a dangerous direction and the other one gets sucked into this.

T: Those are interesting predictions. Now let's read the first two paragraphs of the story to find out what happens. (*Receiving* strategy is used with these divergent responses followed by refocusing on the reading purpose.)

(The students then placed their line marker after the second paragraph of the selection and proceeded to read.)

> He had not liked the job. He was a man in his
> late forties, a charter pilot accustomed to strain and
> indifferent to people. Half the shares in the com-
> pany belonged to him. He was a director of Sonic
> Flights. He worked long hours in his own interest
> and took whatever came in the name of profit.
> He did not like the job.

(The teacher observed the students reading, noting their progress. A few students finished reading quickly, the teacher acknowledged this with eye contact and a nod of the head. A few seconds later, all students finished the two paragraphs.)

T: What do you think now? (*Extending, interpretive level, predicting outcomes*)

S1:   The story is about this pilot and he's going on one last flight and quit his job.

T: Why do you think that? (*Extending*)

S1:   He doesn't like his job.

S2:   I think something will happen to put him on the line and it will be dangerous.

S3:   It'll have to do with money because he's a part of Sonic Flights.

T: Let's read to the bottom of the page to find out.

(The students read the text to the bottom of the page.)

> It was perhaps the time of year, misty
> December running up to Christmas. It could have
> been the passengers, a noisy mob on their way
> from London to a jazz festival in the Channel
> Islands. Captain Armitage disliked jazz and
> ignored the swinging scene. He saw to it that the
> tour manager paid heavily in advance. He got his
> clearance from ground control and the aircraft
> swung lazily into the gray sky.

They were over the Channel when the fog dropped down, lapping round in thick billows. Armitage sighed. He was not afraid of the calculated risk. But he knew that a quick turnaround, a rigid time schedule, made all the difference between profit and loss. Captain Armitage had no intention of showing a loss.

"Ladies and gentlemen. This is your captain speaking." It always paid to make soothing noises to the customers. "Owing to adverse weather conditions we shall be approximately ten minutes late in arriving. Sonic Flights apologizes for any inconvenience." The loudspeaker crackled regretfully and fell silent.

"Late?" said the copilot, a young man with bleak eyes. "You're not going to try and land in this?"

T: Now what will happen and why? (*Extending, interpretive level, predicting outcomes*)

S1: Something bad.

S2: I don't think he'll land. Something will happen so that he'll change his mind.

S3: He's a money-making machine and he'll try to land. He cares more about making money than his passengers.

S5: But if the passengers all die, the pilot will die, too.

S4: Well, I think there's a problem between the captain and the copilot. The copilot will stop him from landing.

T: How many of you think he will land? (Three students raise their hands.) How many of you think he won't try to land? (Five students raise their hands.) (*Clarifying* strategy encourages all students to synthesize information and reach a tentative conclusion.)

T: Let's read the next two pages, to the bottom of page 109, to find out what happens. (*Refocusing* on comprehension purpose, reading to verify, reject, or form new hypotheses about story plot.)

(The teacher continued the same pattern of interaction at this stoppoint using discussion, verification, and proof. The students were asked to read the next two pages and stop at the bottom of page 111, which immediately preceded the story conclusion.)

In this section of the text, the phantom World War II aircraft continues to block their landing; syncopated jazz music is heard by Armitage, the pilot, and his copilot; their fuel is finally consumed; they crash-land in the English Channel and are rescued. This section ends with the following text:

Weeks later, both men were summoned to appear before an investigatory committee. There was a report in from the salvage party. The chairperson held it up.

"You gentlemen were luckier than you know."

(The following discussion occurred.)

T: OK, now how do you think the story will end? (*Raising, applicative level, predicting outcome*)

S1: I think they were saved from a big crash.

T: Why do you say that? (*Clarifying, interpretive level, predicting outcome*)

S1: It says "You gentlemen were luckier than you know." where we stopped. So, there must have been something wrong with the plane.

S4: Yeah, and the World War II plane was always ahead of them to keep them from landing.

S3: The phantom plane saved them from a big crash.

T: Good, what other ideas do you have? (*Extending*)

S2: It's sort of like the opposite of the movie I saw called "Back to the Future," where they go back in time.

S5: Maybe someone from another time came back to rescue them, like in the "Twilight Zone."

T: Those are all very good ideas. Now finish the story. (*Receiving*)

(The students completed the story followed by a brief discussion of the conclusion, which served to verify their conclusions.)

Note that the DR-TA approach relied on interpretive, applicative, and transactive levels of thinking, with the major emphasis on predicting outcomes. The factual level was used only insofar as the students would quickly reread a section during the discussion to verify a specific idea. The discussion began with a wide range of divergent predictions, but as the story progressed, predictions and speculations began to converge on a narrower range based on text-based and personal knowledge. Most of the students in the group contributed directly to the discussion, and all students were involved in making a decision between and among possible predictions. As we examine this discussion, it becomes clear that the individual contributions began to converge toward a group conclusion the further the story progressed. This is the dynamic thinking interchange that Taba (1965) refers to as "cognitive commerce." The teacher created high motivation by stimulating the students' intellectual curiosity as they read, discussed, and continued to read toward the story conclusion. The students' reading rate increased progressively as the story moved toward conclusion.

The DR-TA can be used with stories in basal readers and with chapters from multiple copies of children's literature selections. It is especially good for introducing the first chapter of a novel. Key points to keep in mind in using the DR-TA include choosing high-interest quality literature, becoming familiar with the story or chapter you plan to use, and identifying in advance four to six discussion stop-points in the text (Ruddell, 1988, 1993). Stop-points in the body of the text should be at points that may lead to new predictions in the story plot and speculations about story characters, events, and ideas. The questioning pattern at the stop-points is basically simple and consists of questions such as the following:

1. **After the title**—"With a title like that, what do you think this story will be about? Why do you say that?"
2. **After each stop-point in text**—"What do you think now? What makes you say that?" "Which of these predictions to you agree with? Why do you say that?"
3. **Before the story conclusion**—"How do you think the story will end? Why?"
4. **After the story**—"Why did the story end this way?" "How would you have ended the story?"

You may find when you first begin using the DR-TA that you are a little uncomfortable with these broad, open-ended questions. That's because you are so used to the traditional classroom questioning routine in which many specific (and often factual) questions are asked. Resist the temptation to fall into (or back into) the pattern of grilling children about every conceivable idea the text might stimulate; give the broad, open-ended questions a chance to work. You'll soon find that you don't *need* to ask about story details because children use those details naturally in their response to your prompts, "Now what do you think?" and "What makes you say that?"

This approach closely parallels the Directed Listening-Thinking Activity (DL-TA), which we discussed in Chapter 3. The DL-TA provides for development of the same thinking levels. The only difference is that in the DL-TA you read the story to children using key stop-points and discussion. At any grade level, such an oral presentation has the advantage of allowing children to think about and discuss a story or text that they cannot read comfortably for themselves.

In summary, the key features of the DR-TA in comprehension development are as follows:

1. It establishes clear purpose for reading.
2. It involves the students in active comprehension by calling on their personal background knowledge and text knowledge.
3. It develops higher-level thinking using predictions and speculations, reading to verify, revising predictions or forming new ones, and reaching conclusions.

4. It uses the social dynamic of group interaction to propose and discuss options and outcomes.

5. It arrives at decisions and conclusions based on text and personal knowledge.

DR-TA: The Second Phase. The second phase of the DR-TA approach, following the directed reading and discussion phase, is follow-up extension activities (Ruddell, 1988, 1993). This phase is based on your observations of the students during directed reading and discussion. It may involve emphasis on vocabulary development (e.g., in the earlier example, words such as "charter," "hallucination," "salvage," and "obsolete," were all used in the context of the story). Emphasis on word analysis may also be important for some students based on your observations during the lesson. Other follow-up activities may include the use of the Group Mapping Activity (discussed later in this chapter), which is intended to help each student summarize, synthesize and integrate the story using personal story representation through mapping.

The Directed Reading Activity (DRA)

The DRA is the primary instructional approach that has been used in most basal reading programs over the past half-century (Betts, 1946). While minor modifications have been made during this time, the main purposes of the DRA remain the same: to remove barriers to comprehension by preparing students for reading, to emphasize word recognition and comprehension

---

HOW TO DO . . . .

A DR-TA

1. Select the story or text to be read.

2. Determine stop-points. Stop after the title, after the first or second paragraph, and then at points of high suspense or interest. Stop once more just before the end of the story. Use no more than four or five stop-points in any given story.

3. Prepare questions to be asked at stop-points. Remember not to ask a lot of factual questions. Instead, ask broad, open-ended questions (e.g., "With a title like that, what do you think the story will be about?" "Now what do you think?") followed by prompts for children to reveal their thinking and logic (e.g., "Why?" "What makes you say that?").

4. Obtain/prepare cover sheets for children to use to cover text that occurs after indicated stop-points (if needed).

skill development, and to guide students' reading through a given selection. In all probability, you were taught to read at some point in your elementary school years by a teacher who relied on a basal reader teaching guide that used the DRA approach.

The approach consists of five steps. These are listed next.

DRA Step One: Preparation for Reading. This step includes activating students' prior knowledge related to the story, introducing new vocabulary and concepts, and building interest and motivation to read the selection.

DRA Step Two: Guided Silent Reading. The teacher provides a purpose-setting statement or question to guide students' reading. The teacher may encourage the students to read the selection in its entirety, guided by the purpose-setting question or statement, or the teacher may elect to use guided reading questions, frequently provided in the Teacher's Guide, to direct discussion on a page-by-page or story section basis.

DRA Step Three: Comprehension Development and Discussion. This should always start with the purpose-setting question or questions used in the first step followed by discussion questions that promote more in-depth understanding of story characters, story plot, or story concepts.

DRA Step Four: Purposeful Rereading. The purpose of this step is to give children frequent opportunities for oral reading *after they have read the text silently.* It often occurs spontaneously as children support answers to questions ("It says right here . . . "). Or, reading aloud may follow from the teacher's direction for children to read orally a favorite part of the story, a passage that describes a character, or a conversation in the story that was particularly interesting. Readers Theatre, in which children choose "parts" and read characters' dialogue with a narrator reading the story line, is the ultimate in oral rereading experiences.

DRA Step Five: Follow-Up Activities and Skill Extension. The skills involved may include word analysis, vocabulary, comprehension, literature concepts, or writing development. The activities may either introduce or provide practice with specific skills and concepts. Frequently, in basal reading programs, the follow-up activities are used in workbook or skillbook formats. These activities are often used with small groups of students who are reading at a similar ability level.

A DRA Lesson Plan

The following lesson plan for the story "Slipstream" illustrates the key steps in the development of the DRA approach as found in a basal reader Teacher's Guide (see Figure 4-1). The first step, preparation for reading, is represented by the Story Summary, Background Information, Key Words and Meanings, and motivation and key reading purpose sections. Step Two, guided silent reading, uses the Key Reading Purpose to focus the students'

SLIPSTREAM

Text pages 107-112
Workbook pages 32-33
Lesson Activity Master 8

INSTRUCTIONAL MATERIALS

map of British Isles, showing the English Channel and the Channel Islands
any recording of Glenn Miller's music, especially any with cuts of "Moonlight Serenade" or "In the Mood" (optional)
encyclopedias and other references
duplicator master prepared by teacher (optional)

LESSON OBJECTIVES

The student should be able to:

1. identify sequence of events at the interpretive level **(Comprehension)**

2. locate information in encyclopedias and other references **(Research and Study Skills)**

3. demonstrate fluency in the invention of solutions to an open-ended story **(Creativity)**

STORY SUMMARY

Captain Armitage, charter pilot, is flying a group from England to a jazz festival in the Channel Islands when foggy weather makes it impossible to land. He is ordered to return to base. The return flight goes smoothly, but, as the plane approaches the runway, he sees another aircraft parked directly across his path. Fortunately, he pulls his plane up and overshoots the parked plane. The control tower doesn't understand what is happening and orders him to try another approach. It happens again. Armitage and his co-pilot try to land at several other fields only to have the same experience. They recognize the aircraft that blocks each runway as an American plane dating from the Second World War. Furthermore, from time to time, both men hear faint sounds of a familiar jazz tune, sounds not coming from a radio aboard the aircraft. When the fuel is gone, Captain Armitage crash-lands in the English Channel. Fortunately, everyone is picked up unhurt. During the investigation that follows, the salvage party reports a structural defect in the plane which would

have caused it to be blown apart if the plane had landed on dry land. Armitage decides that they were saved by his instinct. His co-pilot, however, remembers the jazz tune, does some research, and discovers that an American jazz musician disappeared over the Channel at Christmas many years ago. He is not convinced that Armitage is correct in his explanation of the incident.

BACKGROUND INFORMATION

Students may be interested to learn that the famous orchestra leader Glenn Miller disappeared on a flight during the Second World War. Miller was famous for his "big band" sound though he was not really noted as a jazz musician. The reference to a jazz musician in the story may refer to him. Students interested in music, especially bands, may want to do some research on Glenn Miller.

KEY WORDS AND MEANINGS

Some of the words listed below will be familiar to most students through library books, textbooks, and other media. Present to your students only those words that you believe they will not be able to read independently.

adverse	light aircraft
calculated risk	obsolete
charter	overshooting
diverting	salvage
grammar school	slap
hallucination	syncopated
indifferent	technology

Introduce the Key Words by duplicating and distributing Lesson Activity Master 8. Ask the students to read the words aloud. After each word has been pronounced, ask students to volunteer ideas about the meaning of the word. Tell them that they may use the Glossary for any clues that give them difficulty. Then let them complete the activity independently. Answers are in parentheses.

FIGURE 4-1

Directed Reading Activity Lesson Plan. (Reproduced with permission from Ruddell, Monson, & Sebesta, 1981, pp. 89–95.)

Find the definition for each of the following words. Then put the letter for that definition in the space in front of the word it defines. The first one is done for you.

WORDS		DEFINITIONS
(h)	adverse	a. to save
(j)	calculated risk	b. to rent or hire
(b)	charter	c. the study of the mechanical arts
(k)	divert	d. go beyond the target
(f)	grammar school	e. no longer in use
(m)	hallucination	f. elementary school
(i)	indifferent	g. a slang term meaning suddenly straight, directly
(n)	light aircraft	h. unfavorable or harmful
(e)	obsolete	i. not caring
(d)	overshoot	j. a chance
(a)	salvage	k. turn away from a direction
(g)	slap (slang definition)	l. in an irregular rhythm used in jazz music
(l)	syncopated	m. something that is seen or heard that really isn't there
(c)	technology	n. a small plane

MEANINGFUL READING

MOTIVATION AND KEY READING PURPOSE

You might introduce the selection by showing the students a map of England, the English Channel, and the northern coast of France. Ask a student to locate the English Channel and the Channel Islands. Then ask students to imagine a light aircraft caught in a heavy fog over the Channel Islands. The pilot has been ordered to return to England. The plane moves on through the thick fog, seeming to be the only thing alive in the sky. Ask students what thoughts and feelings they would have if they were flying the plane. Finally, ask them what they think might happen to them while up in the sky in this situation.

Key Reading Purpose: Tell the students to read the story to find out what strange experiences the pilots of a small plane have and what explanations are given for their mysterious adventure.

90

Slipstream

by Sheila Hodgson

He had not liked the job. He was a man in his late forties, a charter pilot accustomed to strain and indifferent to people. Half the shares in the company belonged to him. He was a director of Sonic Flights. He worked long hours in his own interest and took whatever came in the name of profit.

He did not like the job.

It was perhaps the time of year, misty December running up to Christmas. It could have been the passengers, a noisy mob on their way from London to a jazz festival in the Channel Islands. Captain Armitage disliked jazz and ignored the swinging scene. He saw to it that the tour manager paid heavily in advance. He got his clearance from ground control and the aircraft swung lazily into the gray sky.

They were over the Channel when the fog dropped down, lapping round them in thick billows. Armitage sighed. He was not afraid of the calculated risk. But he knew that a quick turnaround, a rigid time schedule, made all the difference between profit and loss. Captain Armitage had no intention of showing a loss.

"Ladies and gentlemen. This is your captain speaking." It always paid to make soothing noises to the customers. "Owing to adverse weather conditions we shall be approximately ten minutes late in arriving. Sonic Flights apologizes for any inconvenience." The loud-speaker crackled regretfully and fell silent.

"Late?" said the copilot, a young man with bleak eyes. "You're not going to try and land in this?"

107

FIGURE 4-1 CONTINUED

162

Armitage grunted. He disliked Chris David, a grammar school type who knew too much technology. A creep who flew by mathematics. Armitage flew on a wing and a prayer.

"We have a bad report."

He would never have employed Chris David, but staff were hard to get at the money Armitage was prepared to pay.

The fog curdled, clots of acid vapor clinging to the tail. They seemed to be the last thing left alive.

"Don't want to disappoint the kids," said Captain Armitage heartily. The aircraft shook and muttered; it seemed to hang without movement among the yellowing clouds. The air parted and lightened, then darkened and closed in on them again. Nine hundred meters below, the ground control for the Channel Islands spoke. The voice sliced upward through the fog and ordered the pilot to return to England.

"Ladies and gentlemen. This is your captain speaking." The loudspeaker gave no hint of Armitage's sour anger. "I am sorry to tell you that weather conditions make it impossible to land. We are therefore flying back to base. Another attempt will be made later in the day."

"Next time I'll walk," said one of the passengers. Jeering applause greeted the remark. A laugh ran through the cabin.

Over the coast the fog thinned to a dirty mist. By the time they approached the airfield the visibility was fair to good. The controller cleared him to land. Armitage swept down the glide path—and stared.

Parked straight across the runway was a light aircraft.

He jerked the nose up, lifted sharply, and circled the gray sky. Armitage had seen some crazy things in the past, had done some himself—but this was not funny.

108

This was going to lead to a full inquiry. He felt himself shaking. It was a full minute before he even heard the controller's voice.

"Ariel five seven, why are you overshooting?"

Armitage replied with some violence. Beside him he could hear Chris David gasp.

"Did you see that?" cried Armitage. "Did you see that? Ground control must be crazy. What are they playing at down there?" He repeated the question into the mike. There was a crackling, and then:

"Ariel five seven, why are you overshooting?" The voice sounded puzzled.

It occurred to Armitage that his sight was playing tricks. He was forty-eight and had never felt better. But he treated his body as he did the plane, pushing his demands to the limit. He made a mental note to have his eyes tested after Christmas. He gave instructions to switch over to the instrument-landing system and approach the glide path a second time. As they dropped through the clouds the runway rose smoothly in front of them. And there it was again.

A light aircraft slap across their route.

Armitage yelled. He swung the machine up and away. The control tower cried harshly from below.

"Ariel five seven, Ariel five seven! Do you read? Why are you overshooting. Ariel five seven?"

He became aware of Chris David's flat, astonished eyes.

"We're diverting to Keston."

"Why?"

"Because," said Armitage grimly, "whatever is going on down there, I want no part of it." He ignored the copilot's protests. The engines droned on and the cabin shuddered. Then another sound split the thin air. After a while—

109

"For pity's sake!" It was too much. "Who's playing music? I've got enough on my mind. Tell those clowns back there to shut up."

"Nobody's playing music."

Yet he could hear it. A jazz beat, now loud, now soft. Fear sucked at his throat. He was overworked. He was under pressure.

"When we get to Keston," said Armitage in a tight voice, "you'd better bring her down."

The control tower at Keston was expecting them. The controller sounded tense and authoritative. There was no fog here. At less than three hundred meters David gasped, seized the controls—and flung the aircraft skywards.

"What did you see?" asked Armitage. But he knew the answer.

They flew on to three more airfields. At each, the pattern was the same. Unrest began to spread through the cabin. David went back to reassure the passengers. It was not easy. It was not easy to explain that they were not landing because he and the captain saw—thought they saw—

A kind of syncopated throbbing shook the air, the wail of some jazz instrument. Armitage glanced over his shoulder. All the passengers were strapped in.

110

"About that music—" said Chris David.

Armitage nodded.

They began to analyze it, drawn together by the fellowship of fear.

After the last attempt at landing Armitage exclaimed, "It's the same aircraft! You realize that?"

David looked at him.

"Whatever airfield we try, we're blocked by the same aircraft! It's not possible." Armitage loosened his collar. It was very hot. "That plane down there dates from the Second World War. It's obsolete. It's American, too."

"We are," said Chris David carefully, "having some kind of hallucination." He gave a dry cough.

Armitage dried his hands. Sweat was trickling down his palms. "All the same, we've got to do something, and fast. We're running out of fuel."

Down below, a full-scale alert had been sounded. Four airfields reported the incident. The flight had been checked. The passengers had been identified.

High above, Armitage cruised on through space. When the fuel was gone, he came to a decision. He spoke to Chris David. Then he crash-landed in the English Channel.

They were picked up within the hour, unhurt. For one brief moment David saw Armitage standing on the deck of the rescue ship. His eyes were fixed on the sky. His head was tilted as if he were straining to hear a fading voice.

"All right?" cried David.

Captain Armitage nodded. He tried to hum, but the music had gone.

Weeks later, both men were summoned to appear before an investigatory committee. There was a report in from the salvage party. The chairperson held it up.

"You gentlemen were luckier than you knew." He

111

FIGURE 4-1 CONTINUED

tossed the report on the table. "There was a serious fault in your undercarriage."

"Oh?"

"It is not," said the chairperson, "the purpose of my committee to pass judgment on your maintenance. But I have to tell you this. If you had come down on dry land, you would have blown apart."

What had saved them? Luck? Fate?

"Instinct," Captain Armitage said as they were leaving the building. "A trained pilot develops a kind of extra sense. He can tell."

"I don't know," Chris David frowned. "I did a bit of research—out of curiosity. You see, I remembered the name of the tune."

"What tune?"

"The tune we both heard!"

"I didn't hear any tune," said Armitage. And he really believed it.

Chris David clutched his arm. "There was an American musician who disappeared over the Channel. It was during the war at Christmastime. You know the man?"

"No," said the Captain. He hailed a taxi. He did not believe in ghosts, and he was not interested in jazz musicians.

1. Describe the first two landing approaches Armitage tried to make when he was ordered to return to England.
2. Why do you think Captain Armitage and Chris David saw the same plane blocking their way on the different landing strips?
3. Get together with two other students, one playing the part of Armitage and the other playing Chris David. You be the investigator. Role play the investigation.

112

ANSWERS TO QUESTIONS ON STUDENT TEXT PAGE 112

Correct answers are provided for factual questions. Suggested responses are provided for those questions and activities that are open-ended.

1. As Armitage approached the glide path he saw a light aircraft parked across the runway. He abruptly lifted the plane up and circled the field. He switched over to his instrument-landing system and made a second attempt. As he approached the runway, he saw the aircraft again and was forced to lift his plane.

2. Students might suggest that Captain Armitage and Chris David saw the ghost of an American musician who disappeared over the Channel during World War II at Christmas time.

3. Students might suggest a scene such as the one that follows.

Investigator: Captain Armitage, why did you refuse to land after receiving ground clearance?

Armitage: Because I saw an aircraft parked across the airfield.

Investigator: You saw this aircraft both times you approached the airfield?

Armitage: I did.

Investigator: And you, Mr. David? What did you see as Captain Armitage approached the runway?

David: I didn't see anything, sir.

Investigator: Then why did you refuse to land at Keston?

David: Because I saw the same plane that Captain Armitage had seen.

Investigator: Did either of you consider the possibility of a mirage? You know, it's quite possible Mr. David, that after Captain Armitage told you what he thought he saw. . .

David: I know sir, the power of suggestion is great. We did discuss this possibility; and we both came to the conclusion that even though we might be hallucinating, it still wasn't worth chancing a crash.

Investigator: As it turned out you still made a crash landing in the Channel.

Armitage: But that was because we had run out of fuel, sir.

UNIT 2—A BIT OF SKY

FIGURE 4-1 CONTINUED

164

Investigator: Well gentlemen, this is quite a story you have told me. I can't say it is very believable. However, you were extremely lucky. The report from the salvage party says you had a serious fault in your undercarriage. If you had come down on dry land instead of the Channel, you would have blown apart.

FOLLOW-UP DISCUSSION AFTER READING

When students have read the selection choose questions from the following to guide a discussion.

1. Why do you think the author included a description of misty, foggy weather at the beginning of the story? (valuing—author's motive identification, interpretive)

2. Was Captain Armitage the kind of person who would enjoy telling about his mysterious experience? Why or why not? (valuing—character trait identification, applicative)

3. What happened the second time Captain Armitage tried to land the plane? (He saw the same aircraft across the runway that he had seen when he tried the first landing.) (identifying details, factual)

4. Why was the charter flight bound for the Channel Islands? (The passengers were on their way to a jazz festival.) (identifying details, factual)

5. Why was the destination of the passengers important in the story? (main idea, interpretive)

6. How did Captain Armitage react the first time he saw the aircraft across the runway? (valuing—character trait identification, interpretive)

7. How did Armitage react when his co-pilot saw the same plane across the runway at Keston? Why do you think he changed? (cause and effect, interpretive)

8. What role did the sound of jazz music play in this story? Why is it important? (main idea, interpretive)

9. Which man, Captain Armitage or Chris David, do you think had the most likely answer for the strange happenings? Why? (valuing—personal judgment, interpretive)

ACTIVITIES FOR SKILL DEVELOPMENT AND EVALUATION

From the suggestions below, choose activities to meet the needs of your students. Evaluate student achievement throughout the lesson. Activities marked with [E] are especially suited for evaluation. Activities marked with [I] may be completed independently.

Objective 1: Comprehension: To identify sequence of events at the interpretive level.

Activity. **[I]** Discuss the term *flight log* with the students. Ask them how a flight log might be kept and why it might be useful. Explain that a flight log is one of the first things investigators look for when a plane crashes or makes an unusual landing. Tell the students that the flight log often gives some idea of what might have caused the problems. Then duplicate and distribute the following lesson.

MAKING A FLIGHT LOG

Read the following information. Then complete the flight log in the same brief style as that provided below.

Suppose that you are Captain Armitage recording the flight log for that charter flight to the Channel Islands. Since you don't know the specific date and time period of the flight, you will have to make up that information. Use actual facts of the flight from information found in the story. That information as well as your own ideas will help you finish the flight log. You might begin like this:

December 15, 19____. 8 a.m. (0800 hours): Cleared for take-off to Channel Islands. Fog developing over the Channel.

(1000 hours): Advised by Channel Island control tower that weather conditions too poor to land. Returning to base.

_____
_____
_____
_____
_____
_____
_____
_____
_____

(See Workbook pages 32–33.)

SLIPSTREAM (107–112)   93

FIGURE 4-1 CONTINUED

165

Objective 2: Research and Study Skills: To locate information in encyclopedias and other references.

Activity. Introduce the lesson by reminding the students that in the story "Slipstream," Chris David, Captain Armitage's co-pilot, heard jazz music playing as he tried to land the plane. You might also point out to the students that after that happening, Chris did some research and found out that an American jazz musician, Glenn Miller, had died in an airplane crash over the English Channel in 1944.

Ask the students if they know what jazz is. Accept any reasonable answers. Then tell students that they are going to find out a little about the history of jazz.

Divide the students into several groups, and appoint a group leader for each. Assign each group a few questions chosen from those given below. Tell each group leader to assign one or more questions to each student in his or her group. Tell the students that they may use encyclopedias or other references to answer the questions. After each group has completed the assignment, allow time for sharing information. Answers will vary. Brief answers are given in parentheses.

1. When, where, and how did jazz begin? (late 1800's; New Orleans; combined religious and folk music)

2. What is ragtime? Who made it famous? (energetic piano music; Scott Joplin)

3. Who was W.C. Handy? What famous song did he write? (a jazz composer, known for his "Blues" music; "Saint Louis Blues")

4. What is improvisation in jazz? (music that is composed as it is played)

5. What is syncopation in jazz? (shifting the beat of the music)

6. When and where was the Golden Age of Jazz? (during the 1920's in the United States)

7. Who was Bessie Smith? (black blues singer of the 1920's and 1930's)

8. Who was "Fats" Waller? (a black jazz composer and piano player who composed "Honeysuckle Rose")

9. Why is Louis Armstrong famous? What was his nickname? (He was an accomplished black trumpet player and singer. His nickname was Satchmo.)

10. What was the "swing era"? (when bands played happy, relaxed jazz music for vocalists during the 1930's and mid 1940's)

11. Who started the "swing era"? (Duke Ellington)

12. Who was the "King of Swing"? (Benny Goodman)

13. When was boogie-woogie played? Name a song of this type. (during the late 1930's to 1940's; "Boogie Woogie Bugle Boy")

14. What was "bop" or "bebop"? (complicated jazz of the 1940's)

15. What is a combo? (a small group of jazz musicians)

16. What is a synthesizer? (electronic musical instrument of the 1970's)

17. Why do you think some jazz musicians had such names as "Fats", "Count", "King", and "Duke"? (titles given by their fans; sometimes related to physical characteristics)

Objective 3: Creativity: To demonstrate fluency in the invention of solutions to an open-ended story.

Activity. Have students discuss some of the strange things that happened on Captain Armitage's flight from London to the Channel Islands. Ask students to propose different explanations as to why Armitage and David saw a plane blocking different runways and why they heard jazz music in mid-flight. Encourage students to come up with as many explanations as possible. Their ideas can

94

———— **FIGURE 4-1 CONTINUED** ————

be realistic or in the realm of fantasy and the supernatural.

Although the story doesn't really provide any concrete explanations to the strange phenomena that take place, there are several clues in the story that could be used in the students' proposed solutions: For example, Clue 1. The plane that Armitage and David saw was an obsolete World War II American plane. Clue 2. An American musician disappeared over the English Channel during World War II.

Once students have proposed several explanations, ask each one to write his or her own ideas in paragraph form. Later, let students share their ideas with the rest of the group.

EXTENDED READING FOR STUDENTS

COBALT, MARTIN, *Pool of Swallows* (Nelson, 1974). Mystery in which pools that rise suddenly into swirling floods turn out to have a logical explanation. ● ● ●

GARFIELD, LEON, *Black Jack* (Pantheon, 1968). A sequence of absolutely unbelievable events told in such a way that they seem possible. ● ●

MAYNE, WILLIAM, *The Battlefield* (Dutton, 1967). Set in Yorkshire, England, the mystery in this story has to do with some unusual carved stone which appears to be very old. ●

TOWNSEND, JOHN ROWE, *The Intruder* (Lippincott, 1970). A story by a well-known author, set in England, with a compelling sense of mystery. ● ●

NOTES

FIGURE 4-1 CONTINUED

reading. Step Three, comprehension development and discussion, relies on the three questions at the end of the story, found in the students' anthology, and Follow-Up Discussion after reading. The fourth step, purposeful rereading, may be used at your discretion, should you elect to ask your students to locate and read parts of the story from the Follow-Up Discussion after reading. Step Five, follow-up activities and skill extension, is represented by the activities for Skill Development and Evaluation section.

The effective use of the DRA with basal reading programs requires that you be selective in choosing from the questions and activities provided in the Teacher's Guide. Most publishers provide a wide range and variety of questions and activities for each of the five steps described above. The suggested questions and instructional ideas are developed by the author(s) and publisher for a nationwide market without specific knowledge about you or your students. Clearly, basal readers attempt to provide something for everyone, thus resulting in a very detailed, and extensive, lesson plan for each selection. If you attempt to use every question and every activity provided in most Teacher's Guides for a particular story selection, you can easily spend two or three weeks teaching just that story. This is neither practical nor productive. The point here is that you have the freedom and the responsibility to choose selectively among the questions and activities and use only those that most effectively meet your instructional philosophy and the needs of your students.

Also bear in mind that you do not have to use the teaching suggestions in the Teacher's Guide at all. It is perfectly all right for you to use basal story selections with your own choice of instructional approach. Many basal reader stories can easily be used with the DR-TA and various other instructional strategies. The basal reader collection is a useful source of multiple copies of stories for instruction and discussion; applying alternate strategies such as the DR-TA simply requires that you become familiar with the stories and make the needed adaptations.

DR-TA and DRA: A Comparison

As you have seen, the DR-TA and the DRA lesson discussions above are based on the same story, "Slipstream." A comparison of the DR-TA and the DRA reveals a number of similarities and several critical differences.

Similarities include the following:

1. Both group reading approaches activate background knowledge and build interest in the story.
2. Both approaches provide structure in directing the reading of the selection.
3. Both approaches use follow-up discussion of the reading selection.
4. Both approaches use follow-up activities to develop new concepts and to review and reinforce known concepts based on the instructional needs of your students.

HOW TO DO . . . .

A DRA

1. Select the story and estimate the number of days you'll need to complete the preparation for reading, guided silent reading, and follow-up extension activities.

2. Choose the vocabulary words to be presented and prepare materials for presentation (sentence strips for pocket chart, duplicated handout, sentences written on board and so forth).

3. Decide the purpose-setting question or statement (use or adapt the one from the Teacher's Guide).

4. Decide what comprehension questions to use (choose from those in the Teacher's Guide or write your own).

5. Identify skills to be developed, activities for developing the skills, and prepare materials or equipment necessary for activities (choose from activities in the Teacher's Guide or develop your own).

6. Determine extension and follow-up activities (choose or adapt from the Teacher's Guide).

7. Prepare any handouts, materials, or equipment needed.

The main differences between the two approaches are:

1. The DR-TA approach relies on story context for initial vocabulary introduction and does not introduce vocabulary and new concepts before the story is read. Note that the DR-TA closely parallels the DL-TA (Directed Listening-Thinking Activity), in which the story is presented orally, as discussed in Chapter 3. These closely related approaches rely on story context and high student motivation to carry vocabulary meaning. Vocabulary and new concepts are developed in follow-up activities after the story as needed. A vocabulary strategy useful for this purpose, the Vocabulary Self-Collection Strategy (VSS), will be discussed in Chapter 5.

2. The DR-TA provides constant emphasis on active comprehension and the development of higher-order thinking levels through predicting and speculating, revising predictions based on new information, and providing reasons for responses.

3. The DRA, as used in basal reading programs, provides preselected vocabulary, purpose-setting questions, guided reading questions, and follow-up comprehension questions and activities. This is convenient for you as the teacher, but it demands that you be selective in choosing vocabulary and questions appropriate for your students. The use of the DRA with a basal reader program requires that you take control of the Teacher's Guide and select and adapt the suggestions and approach to meet the needs of your students.

4. The DRA approach can be adapted for use with most literature and content reading selections. This requires that you preselect the vocabulary concepts, establish the reading purpose, guide reading questions, and provide follow-up activities as the strategy steps above are followed or modified.

Using DR-TA and DRA in Concert

The DR-TA and DRA approaches can be effectively used in concert with each other to build higher levels of thinking and comprehension skills. Many teachers who use a basal reading program alternate these two approaches, depending on the story line and the instructional objectives. Of course, this requires that you become familiar with the selection and identify key stop-points for discussion as you prepare to teach a basal reader story using the DR-TA.

Making Predictions

Teachers who rely heavily on full-length children's books, often referred to as "trade books," can easily apply the DR-TA to selected chapters. This approach can be alternated with the DRA as you introduce difficult vocabulary and concepts before reading, set the reading purpose, develop guided reading and discussion, and develop follow-up activities. The key point to keep in mind is your own flexibility in using and adapting these approaches to build high reader motivation and develop higher-level thinking and comprehension skills.

STRATEGIES USED TO TARGET SPECIFIC COMPREHENSION PROCESSES

The instructional strategies in this section of the chapter provide additional flexibility in your instructional program. These strategies are designed to focus on specific comprehension processes and can be used in conjunction with the DR-TA or the DRA.

Activating Background Knowledge: The PreReading Plan (PReP)

The activation and use of background knowledge relevant to the reading material is a critical aspect in the reading comprehension process. Judith Langer (1981, 1982) developed the PreReading Plan (PReP) to help students identify and extend their prior knowledge about a topic before reading. PReP is appropriate for children at every elementary grade level. Its value is in refining children's knowledge of a topic through group discussion in building anticipation toward the reading experience. The PReP strategy has the potential to stimulate and involve all levels of thinking—factual, interpretative, applicative, and transactive. An added value of PReP is to help you gain information about the knowledge your students possess on a given topic in order to determine whether there is need for further instruction before reading. The strategy is appropriate for narrative as well as expository material.

The PReP strategy consists of two parts, the instructional phase and the response analysis phase. The instructional phase of the PReP strategy involves three steps that explore children's understanding of the key topic of the story or expository material.

PReP Step One: Initial Association with the Key Topic or Concept. The purpose of this step is to encourage free association and divergent thinking. It resembles the initial phase of the DR-TA, when we pose the question "With a title like that, what do you think this story will be about?" In using the PReP strategy, however, you will first identify the key topic or story concept that you wish to explore. Statements and questions such as the following are used with the key topic or concept based on the text (Langer, 1982):

"Tell me anything that comes to mind when . . . (you hear this word, see this picture, etc.)."

"What do you think of . . . ?"

"What might you see, hear, feel . . . ?"

"What might be going on . . . ?"

For example, on the topic of underwater exploration, PReP was used to explore children's understanding of problems they might expect to find in deep-water exploration. They were shown a picture depicting deep-sea life and asked "What comes to mind when you look at this picture?" The children's responses reflected different perspectives and different levels of prior knowledge and experiences; responses ranged from "fish and plants," to "divers might get cold or lost if a flashlight breaks," to "divers are in danger because water isn't like land, without air."

As the students develop ideas, you record their responses on the board. The objective is to identify any information the students have about the central concept of the text, along with related knowledge and experiences they may have.

PReP Step Two: Reflections on the Initial Associations. This step is intended to provide opportunity for children to explain their initial responses and to understand those made by their peers. You simply ask, "What made you think of . . . (the initial response provided)?" This question is also designed to help students evaluate the way in which their ideas may be related to the text topic, i.e., problems of deep-water exploration.

PReP Step Three: Reformulation of Knowledge. This step occurs after the students have had the opportunity to explain their initial ideas. The question "Based on our discussion, do you have any new ideas about . . . (the picture, the word, the topic)?" makes provision for children to probe their memories and evaluate their ideas, while at the same time speculating on the text to be read. The intent here is to provide opportunity for children to revise, integrate, and add new ideas before the reading experience. The discussion environment for PReP should be an accepting one in which inquisitive minds flourish.

A Recommended Variation. Tierney, Readence, and Dishner (1990) recommend one important variation in using the PReP strategy. This variation provides children with more context for the story or expository reading material and requires that you have students read the title and a paragraph or two of the text material before developing associations with the topic in step one. By doing this, you provide a context for the story or expository reading material and, as a result, activate background knowledge more relevant to the reading material. (It has the disadvantage of limiting children's associations to the stimulus word or picture, however.) This should be followed by focusing attention on the key topic or concept, using the questions in step one, as described above. This modification is a useful adaptation of PReP and may be used alternately with the original form.

The Response Analysis Phase of PReP. The response analysis phase of PReP is of value in providing you with information related to the instructional needs of your students. Langer (1982) suggests that observations should be used from all three phases of the PReP strategy to determine whether students have sufficient prior knowledge to be successful in the reading experience. Students with *little knowledge* about a concept will tend to respond with words that may describe ideas or experiences associated with the key topic but that are not quite relevant. *Some knowledge* will be reflected in examples and definition of characteristics, e.g., "fish and plants," "divers might get cold or lost if a flashlight breaks." *Much prior knowledge* takes the form of definitions, analogies, or concept linking that shows evidence of concept integration, e.g., "divers are in danger because water isn't like land, without air." Students with little knowledge about the key topic of discussion will probably need direct instruction on key concepts before the reading experience. Students with some or much prior knowledge can be expected to read the text with adequate or good comprehension following the PReP experience.

HOW TO DO . . . .

PReP

1. Decide what key concept you wish to focus students' attention on before reading the story or text.

2. Choose the stimulus word, picture, or event to focus students' attention on the topic. Prepare any materials you need.

3. Prepare your stimulus question, e.g., "What do you think of when I say 'friendship'?" "What comes to mind as you look at this picture?"

4. Record students' responses on the chalkboard as they respond to the stimulus question.

5. After children have responded, point to specific responses recorded on the chalkboard and ask individuals, "What made you think of this when I said '(initial stimulus question)'?"

6. Extend the original question. "Based on our discussion, do you have any new ideas about (concept)?"

7. Guide students into the reading. "Our story is about . . . ; what do you think we might find in the story?"

Connecting Reading Purpose to Text and Personal Information Sources: Question-Answer Relationship (QAR)

The Question-Answer Relationship (QAR) strategy (Raphael, 1982, 1986) is a way to help children (1) understand the thinking demands of questions and (2) learn how to use information sources in responding to questions. The strategy can be effectively used with children from grades one through six.

The QAR strategy classifies questions into four categories of information sources that incorporate the factual, interpretive, applicative, and transactive thinking levels that we discussed earlier in the chapter. The first type of information is stated explicitly in the text—**Right There**—and requires recall or location of information at the factual level of thinking. The second information source—**Think and Search**—is also text-based but must be inferred or concluded from various factual statements in text and uses the interpretive level of thinking. The third information source—**Author and You**—is based on the combination of information from text and from students' background knowledge. This QAR requires use of the interpretative, applicative, or transactive levels of thinking. The fourth source—**On My Own**—relies heavily on the reader's background knowledge and uses the applicative or transactive levels of thinking. The QAR strategy thus helps students understand and analyze the thinking demands of questions and the procedures required in developing answers.

The instructional principles used in teaching the strategy are well supported and consist of (1) provision for immediate feedback to students; (2) moving from short text passages to longer more involved text; (3) initiation of the strategy with factual questions in which answers are explicitly stated in the text and progression to questions based on longer text passages that require interpretative, applicative, or transactive level thinking; and (4) provision for supportive group instruction at the outset, followed by activities that require greater student independence.

The following discussion provides a four-step introduction to the QAR strategy (Raphael, 1982, 1986). This concentrated introduction is best developed over a one-week period. It may then be followed by additional review and maintenance over the next several weeks as determined by your observations of children's needs.

QAR Step One: Day One, Introducing QAR. This step is designed to develop an awareness in the students of the connection between questions and the mental procedures used in responding to them. The following categories of question-answer relationships are used:

- **Right There**—signals that the answer is stated directly "in the book" and requires simple recall or location using the factual level of thinking;

- **Think and Search**—signals that the answer "is in the book" but must be "put together" from the text information using the interpretive level of thinking;

- **Author and You**—signals the answer is not in the text but must be formed "in my head," from the information the author provides and from the student's own background knowledge using the interpretive, applicative, or transactive levels of thinking;

- **On My Own**—signals that the answer is not in the text and must be created, "in my head," from the student's background knowledge using the interpretive, applicative, or transactive levels of thinking.

In the Book QARs

Right There
The answer is in the text, usually easy to find. The words used to make up the question and words used to answer the question are **Right There** in the same sentence.

**Think and Search
(Putting It Together)**
The answer is in the story, but you need to put together different story parts to find it. Words for the question and words for the answer are not found in the same sentence. They come from different parts of the text.

In My Head QARs

Author and You
The answer is *not* in the story. You need to think about what you already know, what the author tells you in the text, and how it fits together.

On My Own
The answer is not in the story. You can even answer the question without reading the story. You need to use your own experience.

FIGURE 4-2

Illustrations to Explain QARs to Students. (Reproduced with permission from Raphael, 1986, p. 519.)

The chart shown in Figure 4-2 will be helpful in introducing the four types of QARs. You may wish to make a similar chart for your classroom or for use on an overhead transparency. Another option consists of writing the labels for the four key types of QARs on the chalkboard using two major headings "In the Book QARs" (i.e., Right There and Think and Search) and "In My Head QARs" (i.e., Author and You and On My Own).

After introducing the four types of QARs using the categories in the chart, you will need to illustrate each one, using text and related questions. This should be done in a group discussion, limiting the text to be read to four or five sentences. In the following discussion, based on a third-grade lesson, the focus is on applying the Right There and Think and Search QARs (Raphael, 1986, p. 518):

Sample text:

> Mom put a large plate of meat on the table. Then she went back into the kitchen. She came out with more food. She had a plate filled with carrots. She also had a plate filled with potatoes.

Questions

1. What food did Mom put on the table?
2. What meal were they eating?

The following discussion is in response to the first question, emphasizing Right There:

T: What food did Mom put on the table?

C1:   Meat.

C2:   Potatoes.

T: How do you know that this food was on the table? Can you prove it in any way?

C3:   It says so in the story.

C4:   What does it say about the food in the story?

C3:   It says there was meat, potatoes, and carrots.

T: Can you point to where in the story it tells you? (Student points to words *carrots, meat,* and *potatoes.*)

T: Great! That information was in the story you just read. That is one place you can go to find answers to questions—in the stories and books that you read.

(Note that the teacher focuses on locating Right There information in response to the question, using the text at a factual level of thinking.)

The following discussion is in response to the second question, emphasizing Think and Search:

T: (in response to students saying the text is about dinner) How do you know? Does the text tell you that it is dinner?

C: (in unison)　　　No!

T: Then how do you know?

C1: You don't eat meat with carrots and potatoes for breakfast!

C2: That's what you eat for dinner.

T: How do you know that? What helped you decide on that?

C3: Because that's what I eat for dinner sometimes.

T: You used a good source of information for that answer—your own experiences. Many times it is important when we're reading and answering questions to think about information up here (points to her head), in our heads.

(Later Discussion)

T: When you found the information in the text to tell what kinds of foods mother brought in, did you find all the information in the same sentence? Where did you find the answer information?

C1, 2, 3: (simultaneously) In the first sentence. At the end. In the whole story.

T: Exactly! You are all partially right. The information is in many places. For a complete answer, you had to think of all the different parts to the answer, search through the text, and put it all together! That's why this kind of QAR is called a Think and Search. Sometimes we can find all the information we need to answer a question right there in the same sentence, but many times we think and search for information that we have to put together to give a complete answer.

The teacher continues to emphasize strategies useful for seeking information and uses the Think and Search label in this conclusion. This Think and Search QAR emphasizes an interpretive level of thinking.

After developing the Right There and Think and Search QARs, you will then move to develop the Author and You and On My Own QARs using the text in a similar way. Again, only a few sentences should be used in a small group discussion. In the discussion, emphasize the source of information for each QAR.

The Author and You QAR uses both the information that the author provides and student background knowledge. For example, returning to our earlier excerpt from *Charlotte's Web,* the question "Why did Charlotte want to help Wilbur in our story?" makes no sense unless the reader understands Charlotte's caring nature and her role to that point in the story. This Author and You QAR requires that the text information provided by the author and the student's background knowledge be used at the interpretive level of thinking. By contrast, the On My Own, QAR is illustrated in the question "How would you have reacted had you been the very first person to

177

see the words in Charlotte's web that morning?" The response to this question relies heavily on the reader's background knowledge applied to the context of the story and uses the applicative level of thinking.

QAR Step Two: Day Two, Review and Practice. This lesson should begin with a review of each of the four QARs using the chart, overhead projector, or chalkboard outline. For this review, prepare in advance two passages, at least two paragraphs in length, and four accompanying questions for each passage using each type of QAR. Duplicate copies of the passage and questions to distribute to the class. The following passage illustrates the first review passage and the QAR questions. (In the sample that follows, we've noted the QAR categories and possible answers to the questions. You would not include these with your questions.)

Nothing to Do!

"Mother, I'm so bored! What can I do?" wailed Holly.

"Why don't you play with your father's new computer?" her mother replied. She had to shout because the robot was vacuuming the rug. Robots did all the work in the factories and offices, too.

"I'm tired of playing with the computer," Holly said. "Sometimes it seems as if everyone has nothing to do except to try to think of something to do," she mumbled to herself. "Maybe I can change all that with a little mischief!" An idea suddenly came to her, and she raced away to gather her friends together.

Questions

1. Why did Holly have to shout to her mother?
   Possible Answer: The robot was vacuuming the rug.
   QAR: Right There (factual level)
2. What did Holly want?
   Possible Answer: Something new to do.
   QAR: Think and Search (interpretive level)
3. What do you think Holly will do next?
   Possible Answer: She might unplug all the robots.
   (answers will vary)
   QAR: Author and You (applicative level)
4. What would you do to entertain yourself if you lived with Holly?
   Possible Answer: (Answers will vary)
   QAR: On My Own

Have the children read the passage and answer the questions in small group settings. Emphasize to them the importance of identifying the QAR category each question represents and discussing their reasons for choices. Monitor the small group discussions and encourage groups to focus on the reasoning behind their responses. The key to this second step is for children to establish clearly the relationship between each question and the source of information that must be used in constructing the answer, i.e., "in the book," or "in my head."

The second passage, which can be modeled after the above passage, may then be read independently by each student. The children answer the questions and identify the type of QAR for each, i.e., Right There, Think and Search, Author and You, or On My Own independently. Groups then convene for children to share and discuss their independent responses. At grades one and two, you may wish to do both passages orally in whole class or with groups.

QAR Step Three: Day Three, Extension to Longer Passages. The purpose of this lesson is to review again the QAR strategy and then apply it to a longer text. You will need to select two short stories or science or social studies passages that are several paragraphs long. Divide each passage into two or three brief coherent sections. For each passage, prepare two or three questions to be used after each section, with a total of five or six questions. The full set of questions for each passage should represent the four different QAR categories.

The first passage should be used with children working together in a small group discussion to identify and review each of the QAR categories and to consider their responses to each question. The following brief text illustrates.

Lost in the Woods

Can you imagine being lost in the woods for six days? That is what happened to Mark Steiner, who was lost when he was only nine years old. His parents, together with hundreds of volunteers, searched and searched for him. When they found Mark, he was very ill and had to remain in the hospital for many weeks. This was a frightening experience for a child. Mark never wanted to go hiking or camping in the woods again.

Questions

1. How old was Mark when he was lost?
   QAR: Right There (factual level)

2. How long do you think Mark was lost in the woods?
   QAR: Think and Search (interpretive level)

3. What would you do if you were lost in the woods?
   QAR: On My Own (applicative level)

Then one day as Mark was walking his dog, the dog broke off the leash and ran into the woods. Without thinking Mark followed. It wasn't until he found the dog that Mark realized where he was—in the woods. And it wasn't so bad!

That was just the beginning. Now Mark is an expert camper and Boy Scout. In fact, last year he visited the very same woods in which he had been lost!

Questions

1. Why do you think Mark became an expert camper?
   QAR: Author and You (interpretive level)
2. Why did Mark go back to visit the place where he was lost?
   QAR: Author and You (applicative level)

The second passage, prepared in a similar way, may then be completed independently by the students. The follow-up discussion should emphasize the connection between each QAR search category and the students' responses.

QAR Step Four: Day Four, Application to Classroom Reading. The above introduction to the QAR strategy will enable most children to apply the QAR search categories to their classroom reading material. Use a story from your basal reader or a chapter from a literature selection or textbook for which you have multiple copies. Design five or six questions for the selection, using each of the four QAR categories. After the children read the selection silently, discuss the story using your questions and the QAR strategy.

This strategy not only helps your students with classroom reading, but it also equips them with the instructional language and search processes that will be valuable in directing their thinking in group discussions and in individual work. As we've suggested, the QAR strategy is also easily integrated into teaching and discussion of expository reading material in science, social studies, and other subject areas. As children become familiar with QARs, you will find that you can use them to provide helpful comprehension search clues for children's responses to your questions. When you observe a student having some difficulty with a question, you may simply prompt, "That's a Right There question," or "That's a Think and Search question," or "That's an Author and You question," or "That's an On My Own question." It is also important for you to use and review QARs when you're not specifically teaching them. In any discussion, you can respond, "Good, Devon. That was an Author and You question, wasn't it?" You will find that children soon will use the same helpful language as they evaluate their own thinking and/or assist their peers in responding to questions.

HOW TO DO . . . .
QAR

1. Prepare a QAR chart using an illustration like the one in Figure 4-2.

2. Prepare two short passages with questions that use all four categories in the chart.

3. *Day One*: Introduce the QAR chart, display the illustration, and give lots of examples of each category of QAR.

4. *Day Two*: Review and practice using QARs. Have children work in small groups to read, answer the questions, and decide on QAR categories for the first passage. Share group decisions in whole class discussion.

5. Distribute the second passage and have children read, answer the questions, and choose QAR categories independently (or do this passage in small groups). Share responses in small groups and whole class.

6. *Day Three*: Prepare longer passages with more questions for children to do first in small groups and then independently.

7. *Day Four*: Gradually introduce QAR discussion in various discussion throughout the school day.

Asking Questions and Setting Reading Purpose Through Modeling: Reciprocal Questioning (ReQuest); Reciprocal Teaching

The purpose of the ReQuest strategy and the Reciprocal Teaching strategy is to develop children's active reading comprehension. These strategies are designed to accomplish this goal by helping students learn to ask questions, set reading purposes, and integrate and synthesize information. Both strategies also serve to improve students' ability to self-monitor their comprehension processes (Palincsar, 1984).

Reciprocal Questioning (ReQuest)

The ReQuest strategy, designed by Anthony Manzo (1969; Manzo & Manzo, 1990), is valuable for developing students' ability to create questions, build comprehension, and self-monitor responses. ReQuest uses reciprocal questioning as the teacher and students take turns in assuming the role of the questioner. The teacher's questions serve as a model of question-asking behavior for students and guide them toward formulating a purpose for reading the full text. The ReQuest strategy can be effectively used across all grade levels. To implement this strategy, start by giving each student a copy of the story or content area reading material to be read. Then use the following seven steps.

ReQuest Step One: Introduction. Introduce the procedure using such language as:

> "The purpose of this lesson is to improve your understanding of what you read. We will all read silently just the first paragraph of the story. Then we will take turns asking questions about the paragraph and what it means. You will ask questions first, then I will ask questions. Try to ask the kind of questions a teacher might ask in the way a teacher might ask them."
>
> "You may ask me as many questions as you wish. When you are asking me questions, I will close my book. When I ask questions, you close your books." (Adapted from Manzo, 1969, p. 125)

ReQuest Step Two: Initial Reading and Student Questioning. You and the children will read the first paragraph silently. (See the text excerpt from *Charlotte's Web* presented earlier in the chapter. Note that, because of dialogue, the first paragraph is " 'Salutations!' said the voice.") After reading the paragraph, close your book, and the students will then proceed to ask you any question they wish about the paragraph. You will initially find that students may ask questions of a factual nature, e.g., "What did the voice say?" or "How do you spell 'salutations'?" or "What does 'salutations' mean?" This initial pattern of questioning, however, will soon incorporate higher-level questions, following your model.

ReQuest Step Three: Teacher Questioning and Modeling. After students have finished asking questions, it is your turn to ask them questions about the first paragraph. They then close their books, using a paper marker. You might ask, "Why do you think Charlotte introduced herself by saying 'Salutations!'? or "Why do you think Charlotte introduced herself to Wilbur at this point in the story?" Although you have prepared questions in advance, you will undoubtedly ask some questions that follow logically from questions the students have asked earlier. It is important to help students understand that each question deserves to be answered and that "I don't know" responses must be supported. That is, if you or your students are uncertain of the answer, you, as well as your students, need to explain why the question cannot be answered.

ReQuest Step Four: Continued Reciprocal Questioning. Silently read the next paragraph or segment of text and follow the pattern in steps two and three as questions are asked by your students, with your book closed, and then by you, with their books closed. Starting with the second question-answer exchange, you should demonstrate in your questions how the information in this segment connects to the information in previous segment(s), e.g., "What does the word *they* refer to when Wilbur says 'What are *they* and where are *you*'?'"

ReQuest Step Five: Setting a Purpose for Reading. Continue reading until sufficient information is provided to allow students to get the gist of the story so that they can make outcome predictions. Then ask, "What do you think is going to happen in the rest of this selection? Why do you think so?" Encourage students to engage in active predictions for the story or text outcome at this point. After making predictions, have students turn their prediction statements into questions. Thus, the prediction "I think that, somehow, Wilbur and Charlotte become friends" becomes the question "How do Wilbur and Charlotte become friends?" There may be several different predictions and purpose-setting questions generated as individual reading purposes are established. Write these prediction questions on the chalkboard or have students record their prediction questions on paper for later reflection. Do *not* reshape and change children's questions to fit what you know to be the outcome of the story. Questions not answered by the story may be just as legitimate as those that are; you can handle this eventuality later in discussion.

ReQuest Step Six: Silent Reading. Ask your students to read to the end of the text to see if their predictions are correct.

ReQuest Step Seven: Follow-Up Discussion. After children finish reading the selection, initiate discussion by asking the prediction question(s), e.g., "How did Wilbur and Charlotte become friends?" This is an important first question because it demonstrates that the purpose-setting question is the first issue you want to address after reading. If you fail to ask this question first, children will learn that the whole exercise leading up to the reading is just instructional noise of no real importance in the lesson; they will then, in subsequent ReQuest lessons, ignore the lead-up questioning and purpose-setting question with impunity. If the story did not answer the question asked, now is the time to acknowledge—"Our story didn't really answer this question, did it? What question did it answer? Okay. Let's answer that one"—and then continue with discussion. After children are experienced ReQuest users, you may want to let them work in pairs or small groups to discuss their prediction questions, provide explanations, and compare these with the text outcomes.

As you use ReQuest with your students, it is important to remember that your questions provide the model for their question-asking behavior. By emphasizing interpretive, applicative, and transactive questions, you will soon find that children ask similar-type higher-level questions.

You may also model your thinking processes in responding to student questions. For example, in response to a student's question "Why did Charlotte want to save Wilbur?" you may observe "That question really makes me think. Okay, in order to answer that question I need to think about Charlotte's character. She's really a caring person. She knows Wilbur may end up in Zuckerman's smokehouse and has to figure out a way to save him. She wants to save Wilbur because she cares about Wilbur and thinks that's the right thing to do."

The ReQuest strategy can be used effectively both with groups and with individual students. In each case, it provides excellent insight into the student's background knowledge and reading and reasoning processes.

Reciprocal Teaching

The reciprocal teaching strategy is similar to the ReQuest strategy in using teacher modeling to shape students' question and predictions. This strategy, developed by Palincsar (1984), is designed to develop students' comprehension and comprehension-monitoring ability. Like ReQuest, reciprocal teaching has potential use across all grade levels. The following four skill processes are integral to the strategy (Palincsar & Brown, 1986):

1. **Predicting**—hypothesizing what the author will discuss next in the text.
2. **Question Generation**—forming a question based on information in the text and on background knowledge.
3. **Clarifying**—focusing attention on parts of the text that are not clearly understood, searching for the reason for the text difficulty, and taking steps to restore meaning.

HOW TO DO . . . .

ReQuest

1. Select the story and decide the length and number of initial reading segments.

2. Preread the story and determine the aspects of the story your questioning will develop. List some higher-level questions that you wish to use (but remember not to use them if the children ask them first).

3. Identify any follow-up activities for the story and prepare any materials needed.

4. Introduce the ReQuest procedure to the children and use it with a story.

Reading and Thinking Together

4. Summarizing—identifying the most important idea in the paragraph or to a given point in the text.

The strategy relies heavily, as does ReQuest, on teacher modeling using cognitive "scaffolds" or supports (Bruner, 1990; Wood, Bruner, & Ross, 1976), to develop these four comprehension skill processes. This essentially means that the teacher, or a student acting in the role of the teacher, provides a temporary and carefully designed instructional and modeling scaffold to support learners as they build a working understanding of the four central procedures. As students gain independence using the procedures in text comprehension, the teacher's role is gradually decreased, in effect removing the instructional scaffolding support. As is the case with ReQuest, the teacher and students take turns in leading the discussion.

The procedure for introducing and developing the Reciprocal Teaching strategy is described below (Palincsar, 1984, p. 254). The strategy is introduced and modeled in Steps One and Two, and transfer of responsibility to the students is developed in Steps Three through Five.

Reciprocal Teaching Step One: Introducing the Procedure. Provide your students a short story or content-based passage several pages in length. Read the title and ask for predictions based on the title, just as was the case with the DR-TA strategy. Ask the children to read a brief introductory section of the passage, which you have predetermined, to provide story or subject matter context. Explain to the children that, today, you will be the teacher, but several days from now they will take turns being the teacher and directing the discussion.

Reciprocal Teaching Step Two: Introducing and Modeling the Skill Processes. Introduce each of the four skill processes described above—predicting, question generation, clarifying, summarizing—using the context of the text just read.

- Ask and discuss the predicting questions that you have prepared for this portion of the reading passage. You may wish to design one of these questions at a factual comprehension level and one or two at the interpretive or applicative levels. Your questions should also serve to activate the children's background knowledge related to the text content. (Predicting and question generation)

- Model clarification of answers to help the children become aware of comprehension problems, difficult vocabulary, or new concepts. The clarifying strategy, discussed earlier in the chapter, is also of value in helping students understand how to "fix up" a meaning problem, using information in the text, background knowledge, or information from their own or other students' responses. (Clarifying)

- Model a brief summary for the section read after discussing and clarifying meaning problems. (Summarizing)

- Offer a prediction about what the next section may be about. Remember that you have multiple purposes here: to help the children develop an understanding of the four skill processes involved through your modeling; to help them understand how these processes enable them to comprehend the text; and to provide a discussion leader model to help the children when they assume the teacher's role. (Predicting and question generation)

Reciprocal Teaching Step Three: Preparing Students to Assume the Teacher's Role. As the children become familiar with the four skill processes and their application to comprehending text, begin to guide and prepare your students to assume the role of teacher. For example, to help students form questions, you may ask "What question did you think I might ask?" or "If you were the teacher, what question would you ask?" To help students understand and use summarizing skills you may observe "Remember that a summary includes the main idea of the part we just read; it doesn't include lots of details." To help students encourage participation by members of the group, you may model the use of extending type questions, e.g., "Who has a thought about this question?" or "Who has another prediction?" At this stage, you are starting to remove your instructional scaffolding and transfer the discussion responsibility to your students.

Reciprocal Teaching Step Four: Guiding Students as They Assume the Teacher's Role. After the children have become familiar with the skill processes and comfortable with group discussion, identify a student to assume the role of teacher. As this is done, it is important to provide praise and feedback to the student leader and to students in the group, e.g., "That was an excellent question" or "That question really requires us to think" or "Another way you might have asked that question is . . . " or "You could also summarize the passage by saying…"

The following first-grade classroom discussion illustrates reciprocal teaching using text related to aquanauts and underwater exploration. The teacher read the story orally to the children who had been previously introduced to the four skill processes central to the strategy. Note the children's effective use of the skill processes of question generation, summarizing, and clarifying, and the teacher's use of positive receiving and scaffolding as she models and develops a prediction (Palincsar & Brown, 1986, p. 771).

C1: My question is, what does the aquanaut need when he goes under water?

C2: A watch.

C3: Flippers.

C4: A belt.

C1: Those are all good answers.

T: Nice job! I have a question too. Why does the aquanaut wear a belt? What is so special about it?

C3: It's a heavy belt and keeps him from floating up to the top again.

T: Good for you.

C1: For my summary now: This paragraph was about what aquanauts need to take when they go under the water.

C5: And also about why they need those things.

C3: I think we need to clarify gear.

C6: That's the special things they need.

T: Another word for gear in this story might be equipment: The equipment that makes it easier for the aquanauts to do their job.

C1: I don't think I have a prediction to make.

T: Well, in the story, they tell us that there are "many strange and wonderful creatures" that the aquanauts see as they do their work. My prediction is that they'll describe some of these creatures. What are some of the strange creatures you already know about that live in the ocean?

C6: Octopuses.

C3: Whales?

C5: Sharks!

T: Let's listen and find out. Who'll be our teacher?

This discussion served to activate the children's background knowledge and to model setting a purpose for the reading. The new knowledge encountered in the text can now be effectively linked to the background information that surfaced in the discussion.

Reciprocal Teaching Step Five: Using Reciprocal Teaching in Alternative Ways. Finally, consider alternative uses for the reciprocal teaching strategy. This may take the form of peer tutoring using reciprocal teaching or the use of the strategy with beginning readers where you present the text orally.

Reciprocal teaching has been shown to be an effective strategy for improving students' comprehension ability. The strategy provides for active comprehension and high-level interaction as students gradually assume responsibility for questioning, predicting, summarizing, and clarifying.

HOW TO DO . . . .

RECIPROCAL TEACHING

1. Select a short story or content-based passage that the children can read comfortably.

2. Prepare introductions for the four skill processes—predicting, question generation, clarifying, and summarizing, i.e., develop questions for prompting students' predictions, prepare questions that you might ask about the text, find a section of the text that needs clarification and decide how to clarify, and prepare a summary statement.

3. Introduce the activity and story or passage using predicting prompts much like opening questions of a DR-TA. Alert children that today you will be teacher; later, they will assume the teacher's role.

4. Introduce the skill processes; model each using the introductions you prepared (step 2, above). Discuss each skill process explicitly and provide numerous models of each.

5. Begin asking children to supply teacher-type questions, e.g., "What questions might I ask here?" or "If you were the teacher, what questions would you ask?"

6. Begin asking children to assume the teacher's role. Provide guidance and feedback to them.

Learning to Integrate and Synthesize Information: Group Mapping Activity (GMA)

The Group Mapping Activity (GMA), developed by Jane Davidson (1978b, 1982), is an instructional strategy that is useful for building comprehension through the integration and synthesis of story ideas and concepts. Mapping can be used effectively from kindergarten through grade six. This strategy is used after your students have completed reading a literature selection or expository material in science or social studies. (GMA can also be used to create Study Maps; see Chapter 9.)

The GMA strategy asks children to create a graphic representation that illustrates their personal interpretation of the relationship between story characters and plot in narrative or ideas and concepts in expository reading material. This representation takes the form of a map or diagram based on their personal understanding of the text. Following the completion of their mapping, the students are asked to share their map and interpret their graphic representation of the text. Sharing maps is the "group" part of this instructional strategy, and it is here, during the sharing, that children's story understandings are elaborated and extended. The following two steps explain the development of the GMA strategy.

GMA Step One: Creating Maps. After students have finished reading a literature or content area selection the following directions are used. (You will need to have prepared two maps, each on a single sheet of paper, similar to those in Figures 4-3a and 4-3b, to use with the directions.)

> "I would like you to map your interpretation of the story on a sheet of paper. A map is a diagram of what you think the story is about. There is no right or wrong way to draw a map. You may use lines, words, circles, squares, or any other shapes for your map. Here are some samples of the way a map might look. It can look like this (hold up your first prepared map for three or four seconds, see Figure 4-3a) or it can look like this (hold up your second map for a few seconds, see Figure 4-3b). Or it can look any way you want it to look. Now create your map from the story ideas in your mind. Don't look back at the story right now." (Adapted from Ruddell & Haggard, 1986)

When you show your two prepared maps, do so for only a few seconds; you want the children to get an idea of what maps look like, but you don't want them to get the idea that their maps have to look just like yours. You may wish to set a time limit of five to ten minutes for your students to create their maps, but this will vary depending on them and the time available.

GMA Step Two: Displaying and Sharing Maps. After your students have completed their maps, ask all of them to hold up their maps for the entire

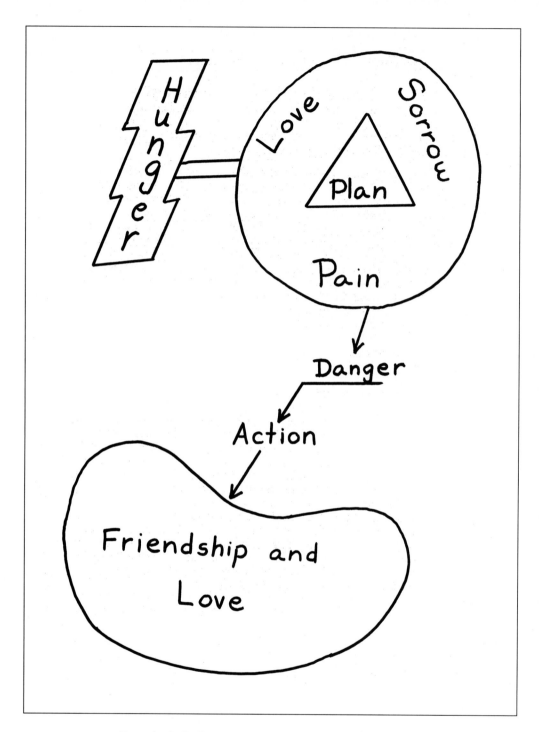

FIGURE 4-3 A

Sample Maps for Introducing the Group Mapping Activity. (Reproduced with permission from Ruddell Haggard, 1986, pp. 5 and 6.)

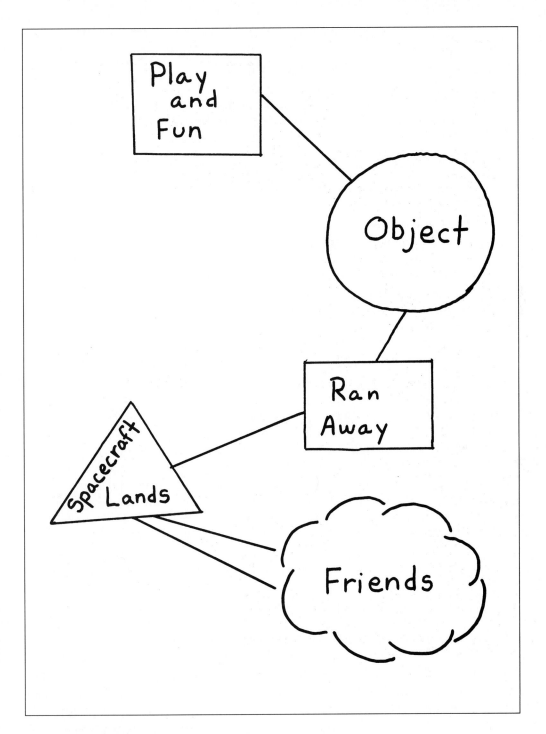

FIGURE 4-3 B

Sample Maps for Introducing the Group Mapping Activity. (Reproduced with permission from Ruddell Haggard, 1986, pp. 5 and 6.)

group to see what others have drawn. It helps to say "Now hold up your maps so we can see how different they are." Allow a few moments for the students to look at one another's maps.

Invite an individual student to share his or her map with the group. The following language is helpful in this regard: "Who would like to share his or her map with the rest of the group? I would like you to tell about your map and share your reasons for mapping the story the way you did." As the map is shared, use prompts that encourage your students to explore relationships between the story characters, events, and story plot using the map, e.g., "Why did you decide to put an arrow pointing from that character to this other one?" In addition, you want to encourage discussion and interaction between and among your students.

The following story map (see Figure 4-4) was created by Carey, a third-grade student, after reading Chapter 9, "Paws on the Snow," from *The Bears on Hemlock Mountain* by Alice Dalgliesh (1952). This story describes the adventures of Jonathan, who is sent over Hemlock Mountain to borrow Aunt Emma's big iron pot to prepare stew for a family celebration. On his way home, he must travel over Hemlock Mountain again. It is just starting to get dark, and he hears the "Crunch! Crunch! Crunch!" of the bears' feet in the snow. The bears are coming closer. Jonathan turns over the big iron pot and crawls under it—just in time. He hears his father's voice calling him from a distance as the story nears the end.

Carey shared her map by explaining that the two long lines showed Jonathan's trip from his home (bottom left triangle marked "help") over Hemlock Mountain to Aunt Emma's house to get the iron pot (left top with iron pot upside down). She explained that the most exciting part of the story was shown in the box labeled "danger." This box shows the three bears (triangles) and Jonathan (small triangle) who is safe under the iron pot (small half-circle). Jonathan's father has come from home (marked "help") searching for Jonathan and has scared the three bears off into the woods (three triangles at bottom right of page). She felt sure Jonathan would now be rescued.

Carey's map and her explanation of the map illustrates excellent integration and synthesis of characters, events, and story climax and the expected resolution. The mapping experience assists in this understanding through the integrated visual representation of the story. In addition, sharing the map in class provides important elaboration of story understandings and serves as a model for mapping and story interpretation for other students.

After the first student has shared his or her map, continue with other student volunteers as time permits. Identify peer partners at this point and have each of the students share his or her finished story map with the partner. Be sure to encourage your students to explain why they chose to draw their map in a particular way and how it represents the story.

Conclude the GMA by emphasizing that each student mapped the story in a special way that helps us understand the story characters and events, and how

 Map the Story

The Bears on Hemlock Mountain

In the space below, draw a STORY MAP to show what you think this story is about. You may use lines, circles, squares, or any other shapes to make your Story Map.
REMEMBER: a map is not a picture. It is your way of showing what happens in the story.

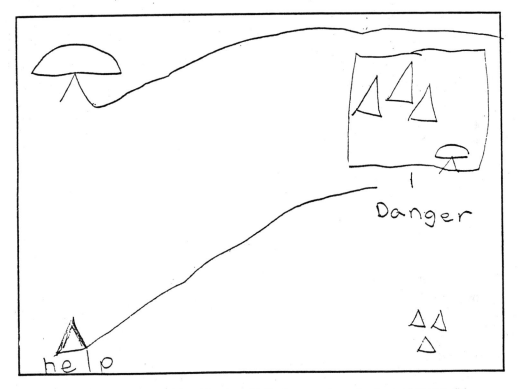

Now, share your Story Map with a friend and tell why you chose to draw what you did.

Shared with _C a r e y_ .

FIGURE 4-4.

Carey's Sample Map Using the GMA Strategy

these are connected to the story plot. It is important to recognize children's thinking and mapping efforts through such statements as "That map shows good thinking!" or "I really like the way in which you mapped our story."

Troubleshooting the GMA. You may find that when you first use the GMA strategy some children will experience frustration in not having a specified structure to follow for their story maps. It helps to show the "dummy" maps you prepared in advance; it also helps to reassure them by saying "You can make your map look any way you want it to look." For the most reluctant children, encourage them by asking, "How would you like to start your map?" as you work individually with them. Continue to encourage children to create their own individual maps. Ask them not to look back at the story at this point, because they will get bogged down in detail if they do. Then be very sure you demonstrate the point that there is no "right" way to map by your acceptance of widely divergent maps when they are displayed and shared. After just the first mapping experience, the children will understand that they are free to create their own mapping structure; they will also have many new ideas for experimenting with other structures and mapping approaches from having seen other children's maps.

You will also notice that children, and very young ones especially, often create maps that are picture-like rather than abstract representations. In Figures 4-5 and 4-6, we present two of Alita's maps. Alita's first map (Figure 4-5) was for the same chapter of *The Bears on Hemlock Mountain* as was Carey's in Figure 4-4, and was completed early in the second month of second grade. Later in the month, she mapped *Flibbity Jibbet and the Key Keeper* (Ruddell & Haggard, 1986), shown in Figure 4-6, in a much more abstract and representational way. Notice also Alita's lonely invented spellings: "were" for "where;" "fineds" for "finds."

Group Mapping: How It Helps. Group mapping encourages children to think in new ways about what they have read. Marjorie Siegel (1994) describes *transmediation* as a process in which one sign system (in our case, visual representation called "mapping") is used as a way of knowing, or understanding, another sign system (written language). Transmediation occurs when two sign systems are linked by a meaning (Siegel, 1994), and Siegel has found that students given the opportunity to represent text visually arrive at new and important meanings, insights, and understandings about the text as the result of this experience. She suggests that allowing students to use visual representation to interpret text invites children to think metaphorically. Davidson (1982, p. 56) notes that "the act of mapping requires students to make intellectual commitments about their perceptions of the meaning of a passage as they draw relationships, details, or ideas from information in the text." You will find that your children's maps will provide "a window on the mind" as they reveal important insights into their thinking and comprehension processes.

FIGURE 4-5

Alita's Map of *The Bears on Hemlock Mountain*

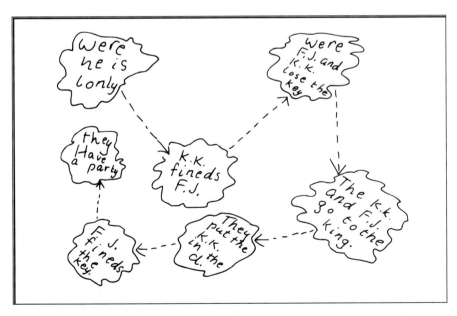

FIGURE 4-6

Alita's Map of *Flibbity Jibbet and the Key Keeper*

HOW TO DO . . . .

A GMA

1. Prepare "dummy" maps like those in Figures 4-3a and 4-3b.

2. After the reading, ask children to construct maps. Use the following means to clarify the mapping task:

    a. "A map is a diagram of what you think the story is about. There is no right or wrong way to map. You may use words, shapes, or lines on your map."

    b. Show "dummy" maps, saying, "A map may look like this . . . like this. . . or like this."

    c. "Do not look back at the story while you're mapping. You may look back at it later."

3. Have students display maps "so we can see how different they are."

4. Ask students to share their maps by telling how they mapped and why they chose to do it that way. Use prompts and questions to clarify and extend their thinking.

Comprehension Development
A Summary

Your responsibility in developing children's comprehension and higher-level thinking abilities is one of the most important, if not the most important, charge that you assume as a teacher. Our goal in this chapter was to introduce and reinforce the idea that comprehension instruction must involve and foster active meaning negotiation and comprehension processing, directed by a clear reading purpose and expected use. Instruction must not only develop text-processing strategies that assist children in comprehending the narrative or expository text being read, but it must also activate their background knowledge and involve their attitudes and values. In addition, teachers must help children learn to monitor their own meaning construction and develop strategies for "fixing up" meanings when comprehension goes awry. These various features of active comprehension must operate in concert in order for children to comprehend narrative and expository text effectively.

Thinking Levels and Comprehension Skills

Understanding the factual, interpretive, applicative, and transactive levels of thinking is of critical importance in creating and using questions and discussions that stimulate rich comprehension of text. The instructional framework for comprehension development presented in this chapter stresses the importance of integrating these levels of thinking with specific comprehension skills, ranging from identifying details and sequence of events to valuing and problem solving. Questioning and discussion strategies, particularly focusing, extending, clarifying, and raising, assist teachers in orchestrating the comprehension skills to develop higher-level thinking. Your understanding and effective use of the receiving, controlling, ignoring, and wait-time strategies is of great importance in establishing a positive classroom climate for productive interactions and discussion.

Group Reading Approaches

The group reading instructional approaches (DR-TA and DRA) are two valuable tools designed to integrate the levels of thinking and comprehension skills in your classroom. The Directed Reading-Thinking Activity (DR-TA) and the Directed Reading Activity (DRA) are widely used and valuable approaches for reading instruction. The DR-TA activates students' background knowledge and incorporates active comprehension as students make story predictions, verify or alter predictions, and provide support for predictions while reading. The DRA, commonly used in basal readers, makes provision for prereading vocabulary development and uses guided reading throughout and following a story. Your use of the DRA, as developed in basal reading programs, requires flexible and selective use of activities and questions that stimulate higher-level thinking. Both the DR-TA and the DRA approaches can be effectively incorporated in your reading instruction and may be used with various materials. The DR-TA and DRA provide useful structures for guiding children's comprehension development and encouraging higher-level thinking.

Strategies for Specific Aspects of Comprehension

We also introduced five strategies in the chapter designed to target specific aspects of the comprehension process. These strategies add enormous flexibility to your teaching. The PreReading Plan (PReP) activates prior knowledge before reading and helps identify those students who may need special instruction before encountering the reading material. The Question-Answer Relationships (QARs) strategy helps students focus on the thinking demands of questions and use specific information sources in creating responses for questions. The Reciprocal Questioning (ReQuest) and Reciprocal Teaching strategies use teacher modeling to help students understand how to ask questions, set a reading purpose, and integrate information. The Group Mapping Activity (GMA) emphasizes the integration and synthesis of information after reading through graphic representations that express students' personal interpretation of narrative or expository text.

Implementing the Chapter's Objectives

The two directed group reading approaches and the five strategies that target specific comprehension skills are powerful means for guiding comprehension development. We present the teacher's role objectives once again below along with suggestions for how these strategies contribute to the objectives themselves:

The teacher is responsible for

1. Negotiating with children a clear understanding of the purpose and expected use for reading (DR-TA, DRA, PReP, ReQuest, Reciprocal Teaching).

2. Activating and helping children use their background knowledge (DR-TA, DRA, PReP, ReQuest, Reciprocal Teaching).

3. Developing text processing strategies and an understanding of when to use these strategies (QARs, ReQuest, Reciprocal Teaching, DR-TA).

4. Helping children relate their prior attitudes and values to the content of the text (GMA, PReP, ReQuest, Reciprocal Teaching, DR-TA, DRA).

5. Teaching children to become aware of the importance of checking meaning construction (QARs, ReQuest, Reciprocal Teaching, DR-TA, DRA).

6. Building the understanding that reading purpose, background knowledge, processing strategy, prior attitude toward content, and meaning monitoring must operate in harmony for effective comprehension (DR-TA, DRA, ReQuest, Reciprocal Teaching, GMA).

As you introduce and use these instructional strategies in your teaching it is of vital importance that you engage your students in active comprehension to build higher-level thinking and comprehension skills. In the next chapter, we will turn our attention to vocabulary development, an integral part of the comprehension process.

DOUBLE ENTRY JOURNAL

Now that you've finished reading the chapter, go back to the list you generated before reading. Create a new list of things you need to do to guide children's comprehension development, working from your earlier one and what you learned reading the chapter. On your new list, write your reasons for each item and note instructional approaches that you think will assist in carrying out each.

Supporting Activities

1. Spend some time observing a teacher whom you consider to be a very good one as she or he guides children's comprehension development. What are some key feature of this teacher's approach? What kinds of questions and discussion strategies does he or she use? How might you incorporate some aspects of this teacher's approach in your own teaching?

2. Ask someone to videotape or audio tape your own teaching. Analyze your teaching using the four levels of thinking presented in Table 4-1. To what extent do you emphasize the higher thinking levels (interpretive, applicative, transactive)? Which questioning strategies do you rely on most heavily (see Questioning and Discussion Strategies)? What suggestions do you have for improving your emphasis on higher-level thinking through questioning strategies?

3. Observe a group of children as they read and discuss a story or other text. What do you notice about the very best readers in the group? What do these children do when they don't know a word or have trouble understanding text? What do they do *really well*? What do you notice about the children who are not doing so well? What do they do if they don't know a word or have trouble understanding text? What do they do well? Discuss your findings with someone else in this class.

4. Interview three or four teachers. Ask them what *they* think the teacher's role is in guiding children's comprehension development. What two or three things do they consider to be *most* important in reading instruction?

5. Using stories from a basal text or children's literature, develop lesson plans for applying the one or more of the instructional strategies from this chapter: DR-TA, DRA, PReP, QAR, ReQuest, Reciprocal Teaching, GMA. Try combining two or more of the strategies for one lesson (see the Building Table at the end of this chapter).

REFERENCES

Betts, E. A. (1946). *Foundations of reading instruction.* New York: American Book.

Bruner, J. S. (1990). *Acts of meaning.* Cambridge, MA: Harvard University Press.

Danner, F. W. (1976). Children's understanding of intersentence organization in the recall of short descriptive passages. *Journal of Educational Psychology, 68,* 174–183.

Davidson, J. L. (1978a). The DR-TA: A reading-thinking strategy for all levels. In R.T. Vacca & J. A. Meagher (Eds.), *Reading as a language experience* (pp. 37–43). Storrs, CT: University of Connecticut.

Davidson, J. L. (1978b, April). *Mapping: A dynamic extension of the DR-TA.* Paper presented at the meeting of the IRA Language-Experience Special Interest Group, San Antonio, TX.

Davidson, J. L. (1982). The group mapping activity for instruction in reading and thinking. *Journal of Reading, 26,* 52–56.

Durkin, D. (1979). What classroom observations reveal about reading comprehension instruction. *Reading Research Quarterly, 15,* 481–533.

Fielding, L. G., Anderson, R. C., & Pearson, P. D. (January 1990). *How discussion questions influence children's story understanding* (Tech. Rep. No. 490). Urbana, IL: University of Illinois, Center for the Study of Reading.

Forrest, D. L., & Waller, T. B. (1979, March). *Cognitive and metacognitive aspects of reading.* Paper presented at the meeting of the Society of Research in Child Development, San Francisco.

Goodlad, J. I. (1984). *A place called school: Prospects for the future.* New York: McGraw-Hill.

Guszak, F. J. (1967). Teacher questioning and reading. *The Reading Teacher, 21,* 227–234.

Hansen, J. (1981). The effects of inference training and practice on young children's reading comprehension. *Reading Research Quarterly, 16,* 321–417.

Langer, J. A. (1981). From theory to practice: A prereading plan. *Journal of Reading, 25,* 2.

Langer, J. A. (1982). Facilitating text processing: The elaboration of prior knowl-edge. In J. Langer & M. Smith-Burke (Eds.), *Reader meets author/Bridging the gap* (pp. 149–162). Newark, DE: International Reading Association.

Manzo, A. V. (1969). The ReQuest procedure. *Journal of Reading, 13,* 123–126.

Manzo, A. V., & Manzo, U. (1990). *Content area reading: A heuristic approach.* Columbus, OH: Merrill.

Mathewson, G. C. (1985). Toward a comprehensive model of affect in the reading process. In H. Singer & R. B. Ruddell (Eds.), *Theoretical models and processes of reading* (3rd ed.) (pp. 841–857). Newark, DE: International Reading Association.

Myers, M., & Paris, S. (1978). Children's metacognitive knowledge about reading. *Journal of Educational Psychology, 70,* 680–690.

Palincsar, A. S. (1984). The quest for meaning from expository text: A teacher-guided journey. In G. G. Duffy, L. R. Roehler, & J. M. Mason (Eds.), *Comprehension instruction: Perspectives and suggestions.* New York: Longman.

Palincsar, A. S., & Brown, A. L. (1986). Interactive teaching to promote indepen-dent learning from text. *The Reading Teacher, 39,* 771–777.

Pearson, P. D., & Fielding, L. (1991). Comprehension instruction. In R. Barr, M. L. Kamil, P. Mosenthal, & P. D. Pearson (Eds.), *Handbook of reading research Vol. II* (pp. 815–860). New York: Longman.

Raphael, T. E. (1982). Question-answering strategies for children. *The Reading Teacher, 36,* 186–190.

Raphael, T. E. (1986). Teaching question-answer relationships, revisited. *The Reading Teacher, 39,* 516–523.

Rosenblatt, L. M. (1985). The transactional theory of literary work: Implications for research. In C. R. Cooper (Ed.), *Researching response to literature and the teaching of literature: Points of departure* (pp. 33–53). Norwood, NJ: Ablex.

Ruddell, M. R. (1988). Developing critical thinking with the directed reading-think-ing activity. *The Reading Teacher, 41,* 526–533.

Ruddell, M. R. (1993). *Teaching content reading and writing.* Boston: Allyn & Bacon.

Ruddell, R. B. (1974). *Reading-language instruction: Innovative practices.* Englewood Cliffs, NJ: Prentice-Hall.

Ruddell, R. B. (1978). Developing comprehension abilities: Implications from research for an instructional framework. In S. J. Samuels (Ed.), *What research has to say about reading instruction* (pp. 109–120). Newark, DE: International Reading Association.

Ruddell, R. B. (1990, December). *A study of the effect of reader motivation and com-prehension development on students' reading comprehension achievement in influential and noninfluential teachers' classrooms.* Paper presented at the annual meeting of the National Reading Conference, Orlando, FL.

Ruddell, R. B., Draheim, M., & Barnes, J. (1990). A comparative study of the teach-ing effectiveness of influential and noninfluential teachers and reading comprehension development. In J. Zutell & S. McCormick (Eds.), *Literacy theory and research: Analyses from multiple paradigms* (pp. 153–162). Chicago: National Reading Conference.

Ruddell, R. B., & Haggard, M. R. (1986). *Thinking about reading: Focus on story comprehension.* Cleveland, OH: Modern Curriculum Press.

Ruddell, R. B., Monson, D. L., & Sebesta, S. L. (1981). *Wingspan, Teacher's edition.* Boston, MA: Allyn & Bacon.

Ruddell, R. B., & Speaker, R. B. (1985). The interactive reading process: A model. In H. Singer & R. B. Ruddell (Eds.), *Theoretical models and processes of reading* (3rd ed.) (pp. 751–793). Newark, DE: International Reading Association.

Ruddell, R. B., & Williams, A. (1972). *A research investigation of a literacy teaching model: Project DELTA.* Department of Health, Education and Welfare, Office of Education, EPDA Project No. 005262.

Siegel, M. (1994, April). The curricular possibilities of transmediation: Strategy framework and metaphor. In C. Panofsky (Chair), *Vygotsky and beyond: Semiotic mediation and its significance for literacy teaching and performance.* Symposium conducted at the meeting of the American Educational Research Association, New Orleans, LA.

Singer, H. (1980). Active comprehension: From answering to asking questions. In C. M. McCullough (Ed.), *Inchworm, inchworm: Persistent problems in reading education* (pp. 222–232). Newark, DE: International Reading Association.

Stauffer, R. G. (1969). *Directing reading maturity as a cognitive process.* New York: Harper & Row.

Stauffer, R. G. (1976). *Teaching reading as a thinking process.* New York: Harper & Row.

Taba, H. (1965). The teaching of thinking. *Elementary English, 42,* 534–542.

Taba, H., & Elzey, F. F. (1964). Teaching strategies and thought processes. *Teachers College Record, 65,* 524–534.

Tierney, R. J., Readence, J. E., & Dishner, E. K. (1990). *Reading strategies and practices: A compendium.* Boston, MA: Allyn & Bacon.

Wixon, K. (1979). Miscue analysis: A critical review. *Journal of Reading Behavior, 11,* 163–175.

Wood, D., Bruner, J., & Ross, G. (1976). The role of tutoring in problem solving, *Journal of Child Psychology and Psychiatry, 17,* 89-100.

Dalgliesh, A. (1952). *The bears on Hemlock Mountain.* New York: Charles Scribner's Sons.

Hodgson, S. (1981). Slipstream. In R. B. Ruddell, D. L. Monson, & S. L. Sebesta (Eds.), *Wingspan* (pp. 107–112). Boston, MA: Allyn & Bacon.

Lionni, L. (1969). *Alexander and the wind-up mouse.* New York: Alfred A. Knopf.

White, E. B. (1952). *Charlotte's web.* New York: Harper & Row.

CHAPTER 4	DR-TA	DRA	PReP
FOCUS ON	Making and supporting predictions	Removing comprehension barriers; Guided reading	Concept associations
GUIDES STUDENTS	Before and during reading; Before writing	Before, during, and after reading	Before reading or writing
USE TO PLAN	Lessons	Lessons	Lessons
MAY BE USED	Whole class, small groups	Whole class, small groups	Whole class, small groups, individuals
MAY BE COMBINED WITH (KNOWN STRATEGIES)	GMA	PReP, QAR, GMA	DRA, QAR, GMA
MATERIALS PREPARATION	Light	Moderate	Not needed
OTHER PREPARATION	Moderate	Moderate to extensive	Not needed
OUTSIDE RESOURCES	Not needed	Useful	Not needed
HOW TO DO	Page 159	Page 169	Page 173

Building Tables "grow" or build, successively from chapter to chapter. They tell you (1) the focus of each strategy introduced in a chapter; (2) how the strategy is best used; (3) what strategies from previous chapters combine well with new ones; (4) preparation requirements; (5) additional resources needed; and (6) the page on which a strategy's How-To-Do appears.

QAR	ReQuest	Reciprocal Teaching	GMA
Analysis of question-answer relationships	Question-asking, meaning construction	Prediction, Clarification, Summarization, Reprediction	Organizing information
After reading	Before reading	Before reading, during reading	After reading, before writing
Lessons	Lessons	Lessons	Lessons, units
Whole class, small groups, individuals	Whole class, small groups, individuals	Whole class, small groups, individuals	Whole class, cooperative groups, partnerships
DRA, GMA	GMA	GMA	DL-TA, DR-TA, DRA, PReP, QAR, ReQuest
M oderate	Little	M oderate	Moderate
Moderate to extensive	Moderate	Moderate	Moderate
Moderate to extensive	Useful	Not needed	Not needed
Page 181	Page 184	Page 196	Page 196

BUILDING VOCABULARY AND
COMPREHENSION CONNECTIONS

INTRODUCTION

Vocabulary knowledge develops rapidly from preschool years through adulthood; in fact, it is estimated that children expand their vocabulary at the rate of 2,700 to 3,000 words per year or, on the average, about seven words each day (Beck & McKeown, 1991; Just & Carpenter, 1987; Nagy & Herman, 1987; Nagy, Anderson, & Herman, 1987; Nagy, Herman, & Anderson, 1985). This rapid growth is driven by children's intellectual curiosity and general maturation (Piaget, 1967) and is fueled by the social use of language with peers and adults (Vygotsky, 1986; Genishi & Dyson, 1984). Children integrate new word knowledge into their working vocabulary by "trying on" new words, exploring words, and using these words with peers and adults at home and school.

It is important to note, however, that children vary greatly in the rates at which they acquire new vocabulary. Findings (Beck & McKeown, 1991; Graves, Brunetti, & Slater, 1982; Graves & Slater, 1987) suggest, for example, that the vocabulary of primary-grade children at the upper socioeconomic level is twice the size of children at lower socioeconomic levels.

Vocabulary knowledge has long been considered to be critical to children's successful reading comprehension. As children increase their stock of word meanings, they also broaden their thinking and become aware of new semantic and conceptual relationships; this broadened awareness, in turn, increases reading comprehension. Well over fifty years of research (Davis, 1944, 1968; Anderson & Freebody, 1981; Beck & McKeown, 1991; Johnson, Toms-Bronowksi, & Pittelman, 1981; Beck, Perfetti, & McKeown, 1982; Ruddell, 1994) supports this position. The strong research-based linkage between vocabulary and comprehension is, however, not always reflected in instructional practice. We have a disturbing number of studies indicating that vocabulary instruction is a very small part of elementary reading instruction (Graves, 1987). In her observational study, Dolores Durkin (1979) reported the startling finding that out of 4,469 minutes of observed reading instruction only 19 minutes were allocated for teaching vocabulary, with an additional 4 minutes of vocabulary review.

In this chapter, we look at the relationship between vocabulary and comprehension and explore ways instruction can guide children in acquiring and developing vocabulary. The chapter emphasizes further how vocabulary instruction can and should be an integral part of literacy learning. The chapter emphasizes further the many ways for teachers to encourage children's independent word learning.

VOCABULARY AND COMPREHENSION

To illustrate at least part of the complex relationship between vocabulary and comprehension we present Lewis Carroll's opening words in the whimsical poem "Jabberwocky," from *Through the Looking Glass* (1987, original publication 1871). Reflect as you read on the critical role of vocabulary knowledge in the comprehension of this poem.

> Twas brillig, and the slithy toves
>
> Did gyre and gimble in the wabe:
>
> All mimsy were the borogroves,
>
> And the mome raths outgrabe.

Though little vocabulary meaning is present here, conventional English letter and sound patterns, and a familiar grammatical system using word order, connecting words, and inflectional endings are clearly present in the poem. The meaning, however, is somewhat of a mystery and left to individual interpretation. The next stanza begins to shape our understanding, comprehension, and imagery using vocabulary that is more familiar.

> Beware the Jabberwock, my son!
>
> The jaws that bite, the claws that catch!
>
> Beware the Jubjub bird, and shun
>
> The frumious Bandersnatch!

Graeme Base's beautifully illustrated *Jabberwocky* (1987) places a visual interpretation on Carroll's poem, which in effect defines many of the creative nonsense word labels such as *slithy toves, borogoves, vorpal sword, Tumtum tree,* and *Jabberwock.* This text clearly illustrates that vocabulary knowledge and reading comprehension are not only interactive but interdependent in nature. In classrooms, vocabulary instruction must become a critical part of reading instruction and will have a strong impact on children's reading comprehension.

Goals and Objectives of Vocabulary Instruction

Goals in vocabulary development are threefold. *First,* vocabulary instruction must develop children's background knowledge of concepts and word labels that enable them to comprehend narrative and expository text. *Second,* vocabulary instruction must teach children how to understand new word meanings independently. And *third,* instruction must build positive attitudes toward vocabulary learning and encourage independent word learning.

The specific objectives derived from these goals, which have guided the development of the vocabulary strategies introduced in this chapter, include the following:

1. **To help children develop new vocabulary knowledge in the context of narrative and expository reading material** through strategies that involve them in active learning and comprehension;

2. **To guide them in connecting new vocabulary knowledge to prior background knowledge** that they already possess;

3. **To help them understand the importance of checking new vocabulary meaning** in the context of the story or exposition;

4. **To develop and activate vocabulary processing strategies** that will be of value to children as they independently determine the meaning of new words;

5. **To lead children toward positive attitudes, values, and interests related to narrative and expository reading material**, thus increasing motivation and independence in vocabulary learning.

The implementation of these goals and objectives is central to vocabulary instruction.

Vocabulary Development in the Classroom

Michael Graves (1987) describes six vocabulary learning tasks: (1) learning to read known words, (2) learning new meaning for known words, (3) learning new words representing known concepts, (4) learning new words representing new concepts, (5) clarifying and enriching the meanings of known words, and (6) moving words from receptive to expressive vocabularies. He points out further that children need not only to learn new words, they also need to learn how to learn words and how to learn about words (1987).

Graves's tasks are represented slightly differently in Priscilla Drum and Bonnie Konopak's (1987) illustration of the situational context for learners that each of these tasks represent (see Table 5-1). Drum and Konopak's illustration illuminates the task categories somewhat by showing the prior knowledge the learner has for each task and the learning goal.

Graves recommends, as do Drum and Konopak and Beck and McKeown (1991), that, in order to address these different task categories in learning new words and learning how to learn words, vocabulary instruction must include multiple approaches. Beck, McKeown, and Omanson (1987) recommend a program of "rich instruction" for teaching vocabulary and developing children's independent vocabulary-learning abilities. To develop a rich instructional vocabulary program, you need to include the following four approaches:

1. direct instruction to develop meaning in the immediate context of the material being read;
2. direct teaching of selected words that are not only essential in comprehending the material being read but also have broad utility beyond that context;
3. presentation of word learning strategies to encourage children toward increasingly independent indentification of meanings of unknown words through meaning context and classroom resources, using a reference aid such as the dictionary; and
4. wide and extensive reading to develop vocabulary learning from context.

A successful, rich vocabulary instructional program will incorporate each of these various approaches. The instructional strategies discussed later in this chapter will include all of them.

STUDENT'S STATE	LEARNING GOALS	EXAMPLE
1. Knows word meaning aurally	Decoding for reading	Can describe an 234*elephant* accurately but cannot read the word
2. Knows word meaning but does not express it	Production in writing and speech	Can understand *chaos* but not sufficiently familiar to use it
3. Knows meaning but not word	New label for old concept	Knows the idea of fear and hiding but does not know the word *cringe*
4. Knows partial meaning of word	Extend the attributes for a label	Knows the word *guerrilla* means a soldier but does not know the tactics or the type of soldier connoted
5. Knows different meaning for word	New concept for old label	Knows that *force* means strength but does not know the vector meaning
6. Knows neither the concept nor the label	New concept and new label	Knows nothing about atomic structure, including the term *ion*

TABLE 5-1

Prior Student State for Learning Word Meanings
Source: Reproduced with permission from Drum & Knonpak, 1987, p. 76

PRINCIPLES USEFUL IN VOCABULARY INSTRUCTION

The Importance of Active Learning

The key to successful vocabulary instruction is to get students actively involved the vocabulary learning process (Beck & McKeown, 1991; Haggard, 1982, 1986; Ruddell, 1994). Active involvement *not* only ensures mental engagement in the process, it also builds high interest in vocabulary study. Children's active participation is *not* stimulated by asking them to memorize fifteen or twenty isolated definitions over the week and take a vocabulary test on Friday! Instead, instruction that uses active mental processing encourages students to "reason with words" and to integrate new information into their background knowledge.

Reasoning with Words: Meaning Context. Planning for active involvement should incorporate three types of word reasoning. *First, a new word needs to be developed and understood in the meaning context in which it is found.* Texts differ greatly with respect to how "reader-friendly" they are in presenting new vocabulary. For example, the meaning of *picket-lines* is used in a reader-friendly context, through definition and example, as Chapter 3 opens in *Little House on the Prairie* (Wilder, 1935, p. 19).

> Pa made camp as usual. First, he unhitched and unharnessed Pet and Patty, and he put them on their picket-lines. Picket-lines were long ropes fastened to iron pegs driven into the ground. The pegs were called picket-pins. When horses are on picket-lines they could eat all the grass that the long ropes would let them reach. But when Pet and Patty were put on them, the first thing they did was to lie down and roll back and forth and over. They rolled till the feeling of the harness was all gone from their backs.

On the other hand, the meaning of *vibrations* in the following excerpt from *Sharks* (Berger, 1987, p. 12) is found in a less friendly text, and will require further explanation if it is to be fully understood.

> Sharks can quickly pick up the movement of a wounded fish, for example. Suppose someone hooks a fish. The fish flings itself about in the water to get off the hook. A shark can sense the fish's vibrations at great distances. It heads straight for the struggling fish, and often before the catch can be pulled out of the water, the shark has bitten off a mouthful.

The meaning of *vibrations* in this context suggests a rapid frantic-like flinging to and fro movement, and further assumes that a child's background knowledge will provide for this understanding. To develop children's understanding of this word we may wish to demonstrate through hand actions what *vibration* in this context might "look like," guide children in formulating a definition, and quickly check the definition in a glossary or dictionary. In this way, teachers thus become "context sensitive" to new vocabulary as we identify words that need to be given special attention. Many new words developed in friendly text will require no teaching; on the other hand, new vocabulary that appears in unfriendly text will need to be explained and discussed in that context.

Comparison and Contrast. *Second, a new word needs to be related to semantically similar words and word groups through comparison and contrast to refine, connect, and integrate meanings.* For example, discussion of *picket-line* might explore how its meaning in this context is similar to, or different from, the meaning of a picket fence. Or in an entirely different semantic sense how *picket-line* could be examined with regard to *protest, strike, walkout,* and *demonstrator.* Children could further explore the relationship between Laura Ingalls Wilder's use of *picket-line* and a strike *picket line.*

In regard to the second excerpt above, discussion may focus on the way in which *vibrate,* the base word for vibration, is similar to and different from the words *quiver, shake,* and *shiver.* Because these words have strong visual properties, children could also act out their understanding of each word and use it in the context of the original sentence as they "try on" the meaning. In this manner, we begin to refine the special meaning of *vibration* as used in the context of the way sharks locate food.

Varied Contexts. *Third, the meaning of new words can be enhanced and connected to other semantically related words by creating new and varied contexts and interpretations.* Meaning clues and connections between the new words *miser, Spartan,* and *frugal* are evident in the following friendly text.

> The miser led a Spartan existence. His tiny room contained only a single bed and a rough board desk. He was a frugal person spending very little for clothing or food. A shaggy grey beard framed his long face and his ragged clothes hung on his thin long frame.

After discussing the meanings of these new words based on the context, we may then engage students in developing meaning connections between these words and their prior knowledge using the following questions: "How are the words *Spartan* and *frugal* related in describing a *miser*?" "What are all the characteristics you think a *miser* might have, and why?"

The value of this type of active involvement in vocabulary learning resides in refining and building semantic connections between the new vocabulary information and children's prior vocabulary knowledge. Children's active involvement in word reasoning will be of prime importance in the instructional strategies developed later in this chapter.

Personal Motivation and Vocabulary Development

Your awareness of children's personal motivation and growing independence in learning new vocabulary can be valuable in stimulating vocabulary development. A brief review of our discussion from Chapter 2 reveals four motivations for elementary-grade children's word learning (Haggard, 1980):

1. The word has an appealing, interesting sound and is "adultlike" in usage, e.g., *fickle, delicious.*

2. The word has immediately usefulness, e.g., *monitor, perturbed.*

3. The word involves strong emotion, e.g., mispronunciation and possible embarrassment, using the words *fatigue* and *centrifugal.*

4. The word is common in peer group usage, e.g., *wretched* as in "Wretched Richie."

Central to these motivations is the social nature of vocabulary learning. They explain in part why children have such a strong interest in those Mesozoic reptiles with the wonderfully intriguing names such as *brontosaurus* (thunderlike lizard), *stegosaurus* (rooflike lizard), *tyrannosaurus* (tyrantlike lizard), and ichthyosaurus (fishlike lizard). Children have absolutely no trouble learning these words. Many kindergarten and first-grade youngsters possess an amazing knowledge of sharks from the *great white* to *the hammerhead shark.* We also may be surprised at their recollection and knowledge in identifying and discussing the Ninja turtle foursome—*Michelangelo, Donatello, Raphael,* and *Botticelli.* These words not only have a fascinating sound and adultlike appeal for children, but can be used immediately in conversations with peers and adults.

Also keep in mind Haggard's (1980) finding that word learners need a safe environment for rehearsing new words—for moving words from their receptive to expressive vocabularies. Haggard reported that one woman in the study practiced using new words over and over on her friends and family and said, "I know when my eyes don't light up anymore when I say it, that the word is really mine!"

Identifying New Vocabulary for Teaching

Selecting vocabulary words to teach is an important part of reading instruction. Selection is important if for no other reason than the fact that there are usually more words that *could* be taught than there is time for teaching them or cognitive capacity for children to learn them. In addition, no two children know, or need to know, *exactly* the same list of words. So, you have a responsibility to select words carefully to make the most of the learning episode. The following questions are useful in making vocabulary selection decisions:

- Is the new vocabulary central to the meaning of the story or expository material?

- Which new words, in the context of the reading selection, will present problems for those students who have limited background knowledge?

- Which vocabulary is developed in a reader-friendly context to the extent that it does not need to be taught (as was the case with the word *picket-line* in the previous excerpt from *Little House on the Prairie*)?

■ Which vocabulary is used in unfriendly text, in a context that does not illuminate meaning and will therefore require introduction and/or explanation (as was the case with the word *vibration* in the excerpt on the feeding habits of sharks)?

After reading and examining the text material and identifying potential vocabulary items based on these criteria, you will then need to decide at what point in instruction the new words will be introduced and developed. The three main options are discussed below:

1. **Before reading the selection.** This decision reflects your belief that the words are absolutely essential for children's comprehension of the story, that the words appear in unfriendly text, and that student background knowledge is not sufficient for independent understanding. This decision also reflects your belief that words selected to be taught constitute potential barriers to comprehension—that children don't already know the words and will need to have prior discussion and information about them in order to read and understand the text.

2. **During reading of the selection.** This option is used when you are reasonably certain that your students will understand the words from the friendly text context and/or personal background knowledge. Vocabulary instruction during reading is directed toward developing students' abilities to understand new words independently. It should guide students in using various reference sources, or asking someone when they are uncertain about new vocabulary. Vocabulary development during reading thus focuses primarily on developing students' ability to construct meaning from the text independently and use reference resources in the classroom.

3. **After reading the selection.** This decision indicates that the words identified may appear in a friendly text, which your students can use to understand new vocabulary while reading, or that the students' background knowledge is sufficient to understand the text. Your decision to develop vocabulary meanings after reading reflects your belief that small group discussion time is needed to connect new meanings in the reading text to related concepts in order to deepen and enrich vocabulary learning. Most important, this decision reflects your understanding that long-term acquisition and development of vocabulary requires the kind of elaborated discussion that can occur only after reading.

From this discussion, we think you can see that there are some clear distinctions between vocabulary instruction that occurs before, during, and after reading. Before-reading vocabulary instruction is short, sweet, and to the point; its purpose is to make sure children have some understanding of words they are going to encounter in text because you believe the children don't already know those words. Before-reading instruction is directed at immediate recall of word meanings while reading; it is not sufficiently extended to "set" the words in memory. Additional practice and follow-up activities are necessary for long-term retention of new words. Much of during-reading vocabulary instruction is actually primed before the reading itself; that is, you discuss with students strategies to use for figuring out the meaning of unknown words independently. Students then apply those strategies while reading. Other during-reading instruction occurs when someone says "What does _____ mean?" and the teacher, or another student, gives a definition. After-reading vocabulary instruction is focused both on long-term retention of newly learned words (i.e., "setting" them in memory) as well as developing students' independent word learning abilities. After-reading instruction requires substantial time for exploration of words and word meanings, practice using new words, and lots of discussion about words.

Using Basal Reader Vocabulary

If you use a basal reader program, its Teacher's Guide will in all probability follow the Directed Reading Activity (DRA) strategy discussed in Chapter 4, where significant emphasis is placed on teaching words before reading. In basal programs, the authors and/or editors of the program will already have identified new vocabulary to be taught with each story (these are listed at the beginning of a selection in the guide). The identification of these new words will be based, for the most part, on the judgment of the guide writers, who will apply their own standards in choosing words for the list, standards that may differ widely from yours. In addition, it is impossible for even the most experienced guide writer to have personal knowledge of your students and their needs. For these reasons, you will want to make the final decision on which words should be taught (and these may include words not identified by the guide writers) and to decide whether these words should be introduced before or after reading. Vocabulary development during reading will rely primarily on the students' use of context and special reference resources. Again, the final selection of new vocabulary should be based on your familiarity with the story, and on your judgment as to vocabulary that is most central to the reading text, the friendly or unfriendly nature of the new vocabulary context, and, most important, the background knowledge possessed by your children.

Summary of Vocabulary Instruction Principles

The following principles are of critical importance to vocabulary instruction in your classroom:

1. Use a variety of approaches for teaching vocabulary to create a program of rich instruction. Include direct teaching of vocabulary, use of

immediate context to determine meanings, use of classroom vocabulary resources, and extensive and wide reading of children's literature and content materials.

2. Use instruction that provides for active learning by teaching your children to "reason with words," using the meaning context in which the words are found.

3. Develop new words by relating them to semantically similar words through contrast and comparison, and by creating new contexts and interpretations, which will lead to the integration and connection of word meanings.

4. Remember that vocabulary learning is a social process as you incorporate children's personal motivations to learn new words, including sound and "adultlike" appeal, immediate usefulness, and peer group use.

5. Base your selection of new vocabulary for instruction on the importance of the vocabulary in comprehending the story or content material, your students' background knowledge, and the friendly or unfriendly nature of the text material.

6. Consider the objectives of your instruction to determine whether to develop vocabulary before, during, or after reading. Such objectives might include developing vocabulary knowledge of your students, helping them to use reading context to construct meaning, connecting new vocabulary meanings to semantically related words, and giving them increased opportunity to identify their personal vocabulary as they learn to reason with words.

These principles for vocabulary teaching will be integrated in the discussion of the specific vocabulary strategies in the next section of this chapter.

Vocabulary Strategies for the Classroom

The following strategies have been selected to develop children's vocabulary knowledge, to build processing strategies leading to independence in constructing meaning for new words, and to create positive attitudes toward an increasing independence in vocabulary learning. It is important to keep the six principles of vocabulary learning in mind as you think about and begin to use these strategies. The strategies provide instructional flexibility enabling you to develop vocabulary before, during, or after reading.

Teaching Vocabulary in Context (TVC): Before-Reading Vocabulary Instruction

Teaching vocabulary in context (TVC) will most often be used to introduce vocabulary before reading the story, but may also be used in follow-up vocabulary reinforcement. **The first step involves identifying the new**

vocabulary to be taught. The criteria for selecting new words discussed earlier will need to be applied as you consider the background knowledge of your students, concepts central to the text, and the friendly or unfriendly nature of the reading context.

Briefly reexamine the story "Slipstream" found in Chapter 4, which we used to introduce the Directed Reading Activity (DRA). As you review the story, you will recall that charter pilot Captain Armitage was flying a tour group from England to a jazz festival in the Channel Islands. Bad weather forced the return of the flight to England and to various airfields. Armitage found each landing strip was blocked by the same "phantom aircraft." The investigation following the crash landing revealed a structural defect in the plane that could have been fatal to all on board if they had landed at one of the airfields. The vocabulary identified, in the Teacher's Guide, for this story included the following:

adverse	light aircraft
calculated risk	obsolete
charter	overshooting
diverting	salvage
grammar school	slap
hallucination	syncopated
indifferent	technology

In teaching this story, your first decision will be to identify which (if any) of these words you believe important for introduction as you consider your students' background knowledge and the context in which the words are used. Based on your rereading of the story, what other words would you select for teaching before reading? For example, other possible words might include *slipstream, jazz,* and *undercarriage.*

Keep in mind that before-reading vocabulary instruction must be kept short so that it doesn't use up all the time you have for introduction of the story or text; if it does, the children will have little opportunity or reason for getting interested in the story or text to be read. Limit your selection to four or five words and teach those words in no more than five to eight minutes.

The second step in using this strategy is to establish a meaningful story context for introduction of the vocabulary items. In order to establish a story schema and connect the new vocabulary to children's background knowledge, it is important to provide a brief introduction to the story. This should include the title and a few ideas related to the central story theme. For example, "Our story today is entitled 'Slipstream.' This story is about a pilot, Captain Armitage, who is flying a group of tourists from England to a vacation island—but they can't land due to fog. He encounters strange and mysterious events in the flight." The point is to provide sufficient information to enable the students to form a general story schema that will help link the new vocabulary introduced to their own background knowledge.

The third step is to introduce and discuss those words that you believe are central to understanding the story and that are new to your students. The first rule here is that new words should be presented embedded in the text in which children will encounter them in reading. Write the words you have selected on the board in the sentences (or sentence fragments) in which they first appear in the story. For example, for the words *adverse* and *calculated risk* (from "Slipstream"), write on the board

> Owing to *adverse* weather conditions we will be approximately ten minutes late.
> He was not afraid of the *calculated risk*.

You may want to write the sentences on chart paper before the instruction begins. Alternatively, you may simply list the words on the board or chart paper with information that tells students where to find the words in the text:

adverse—page 107, paragraph 5 (see page 162, Student Text)
calculated risk—page 107, paragraph 4 (see page 162, Student Text)

Read the sentences aloud and ask students to speculate about the meaning of the vocabulary words. Write their ideas quickly on the chalkboard and record other ideas that surface in the discussion. For example:

adverse—	sounds like bad
	bad weather causing them to be late
	must mean something bad or against you
	stormy
calculated risk—	a risk is something you dare
	calculate = add up
	a risk you think about

After some discussion of each word, arrive at an agreed-upon definition that the class or group accepts. If necessary, check the definition in the glossary or dictionary. The value of presenting the word in the context of the

219

text is that you make it easier for children to discern the meanings intended in the context of this particular reading material. This in an important aspect of the teacher's role in vocabulary development (Readence, Bean, & Baldwin, 1989).

You should expect that several of the words you present will be easily defined from a combination of context information and students' prior knowledge. Others will not and will require, ultimately, that you tell students the meaning. You need to have ready definitions of all the words so that you can give them when the pooled knowledge of the class is not sufficient for developing an adequate definition.

Expect also that the children will already know some of the words you selected to teach (none of us is ever perfect at predicting what words students do and do not know). If this happens, *do not continue teaching the word as though the children didn't know it.* Check that they've really got the meaning, congratulate them on their wonderful vocabularies, and move right on to the next word.

Introducing vocabulary before reading does consume discussion time. For this reason it is important to select those four or five words most central to the story or content material (and which the children do not know) and to keep the discussion short. Remember, you'll have an opportunity to talk more about words after reading.

The fourth step is to evaluate your students' vocabulary knowledge and determine possible need for follow-up instruction. Your introduction of vocabulary, as discussed above, will provide an excellent opportunity to assess your students' background knowledge (Moore & Moore, 1986).

HOW TO DO . . . .

TEACHING VOCABULARY IN CONTEXT (TVC)

1. Preview the story or material to be read and select four or five words to be taught.

2. Write the words in text sentences on the chalkboard or a chart (or list words on the board with locational information).

3. Read the sentences aloud and ask students to speculate on the word meanings.

4. Record the children's ideas on the board.

5. Arrive at an agreed-upon class definition of each word (check a dictionary/glossary if necessary).

DEVELOPING INDEPENDENCE IN USING CONTEXT: DURING-READING VOCABULARY INSTRUCTION

Context-Structure-Sound-Reference (CSSR) System

A main objective in vocabulary development is to help students acquire strategies that will lead to independence in constructing meaning for new words in a story or in expository reading material. The following process is important in helping children answer the question "What do you do when you come to a word you do not know?" This strategy was first suggested by William S. Gray in 1946 and is based upon the notion that one should begin the process of figuring out a new word with the information most likely to pay off—context. Context is then followed by using word structure and pronunciation to assist in meaning construction; finally, one seeks the aid of a reference source when all else fails. We have widened the dictionary step to include many reference sources, and call the strategy CSSR—Context, Structure, Sound, Reference (Ruddell, 1993).

Develop the following four sequential steps in discussion with your children. Your intent is to assist them in becoming strategic readers—readers who have a functional system for dealing with unknown words (Ruddell, 1993). Following the discussion, create a summary wall chart of the steps for easy reference.

WHEN YOU COME TO A WORD YOU DO NOT KNOW, CHECK

1. **CONTEXT—read to the end of the sentence in which the word is found.** Are there meaning clues in the sentence? Are there meaning clues in other parts of the paragraph or story to this point? Using these clues do you think you know what the word means? Does it make sense? If so, go right on reading.

If Not

2. **STRUCTURE—look at parts of the word for meaning clues.** Do you recognize any roots or prefixes you know? Do any of the endings help? Combine this information with the context clues. Does it make sense? If so, go right on reading.

If Not

3. **SOUND—try to pronounce the word and check for meaning.** Often we may not recognize the meaning of a word in print but when we hear it we know the meaning. Do you know this word? Use this information with the context of the sentence. Does it make sense? If so, go right on reading.

If Not

4. REFERENCE—check a reference. Are there any margin notes to help explain the meaning? Does the glossary in the text define the word? Look it up in a dictionary. Ask someone. Combine that information with information from context. Does it make sense? Go right on reading.

An interesting and important part of making the CSSR system work is understanding that the goal is for readers to exit the system as soon as they can. So if they construct useful, sensible meaning from context, then they don't go any further—there is no need to do any more of the steps. It is important when teaching children about the system and how to use it that you emphasize (1) making sense, so that meanings fit the context; and (2) going right on reading when useful meaning is obtained.

Throughout other vocabulary instruction and word-analysis instruction (see Chapter 8), children will have opportunities to learn about and practice various aspects of the CSSR system—getting meaning from context; using word roots and other affixes (prefixes, suffixes) that are meaning-bearing; sounding words out; and using various reference sources. All children do not automatically understand, however, that the specific skills should be applied in a functional *system*. The very best readers probably use a CSSR-like system intuitively; many children do not. We have fairly strong evidence to suggest that the least-able readers do not know how to get meaning from context (Jenkins, Slocum, & Matlock, 1989); further, least-able readers often begin by trying to sound words out and have no idea

HOW TO DO . . . .

CONTEXT-STRUCTURE-SOUND-REFERENCE (CSSR) SYSTEM

1. Prepare a chart showing the parts of the CSSR system.

2. Walk children through the system elaborating on and discussing each part.

3. Using a short passage and four words, demonstrate how to use the system. Make sure each of the four words illustrate at least one part of the system.

4. Find opportunities in other learning events to teach or reinforce students' understanding of the system parts. Remind students frequently of the CSSR system.

5. Direct students to apply the CSSR system as they read independently.

6. Debrief children after reading as to how the CSSR system worked.

where to go if pronunciation does not yield meaning (which it frequently does not—try, for example, to get meaning by sounding out *egregious, doughty,* or *portcullis*). If children are to acquire a functional system for understanding new words it is important that you tell them about the system, display the system in the room, and remind them often to use the system when they are reading independently.

USING STORY AND PERSONAL CONTEXT: AFTER-READING VOCABULARY INSTRUCTION

The Vocabulary Self-Collection Strategy (VSS) (Haggard, 1982, 1986; Ruddell, 1993) is intended to foster long-term acquisition and development of vocabulary. VSS has two major characteristics: (1) It focuses on words children *want and need* to know, words important to them and for which they have shown interest and curiosity, and (2) it simulates word learning that occurs naturally in children's lives and thus guides them in becoming independent word learners.

Using Vocabulary Self-Collection Strategy (VSS)

VSS begins after children have read and discussed a story or text. It is initiated by the teacher asking students to nominate one word or term that they would like to learn or to know more about, one they think should appear on a class vocabulary list. The teacher also gets to nominate one word. Students are required to tell

1. **Where they found the word** by reading the sentence in which the word appears;
2. **What they think the word means in this context;** and
3. **Why they think the class should learn it.**

In most classrooms, this part of VSS is most efficiently done with the children in nominating teams of from two to five students, depending on the number of words the teacher wishes to have in the nominated pool (a good rule of thumb is eight to ten words, with a target of five to six words for the final class list). Don't forget that the teacher nominates one of the original pool words as well. Generally, three to five minutes is sufficient time for groups to go back to the story or text and find words, prepare their definitions from text, and develop a rationale for learning each word; it is often useful to rush students a bit, keeping them on task and leaving little time for extraneous discussion, and then extending the time if it is really needed. You would be wise to predetermine your selection (and, in fact, have two or three on deck in the event of duplication with student choices) in order to be free to monitor group functioning and answer any questions that might arise.

As soon as groups are ready, a spokesperson from each group presents a nominated word, tells where it was found, what the group believes it means, and why it was chosen. The teacher writes the words on the board and leads discussion to define each, first from context as nominators tell what they think their word means, and then, if needed, from any references available in the room. Discussion should include contributions from other class members as well, so that definitions are extended and personalized.

The focus is always on the meaning of the word in the specific context of the immediate content topic or text; however, conversation is likely to range across other meanings or context which are part of students' prior knowledge and experience. These other meanings serve as useful comparisons and contrasts to the topic-specific meaning under discussion. After all words/terms have been nominated, a final class list is established by eliminating duplicates, any words or terms the class feels it already knows, and any that do not appear to be appropriate (the teacher, at this time, spot-checks to see if any words introduced prior to the reading appear, or need to appear, on the final class list).

During this process, words chosen for the class list are circled (or identified in some way), and eliminated words simply left alone so that nothing is erased from the board. Chosen words are then redefined and written with definitions in vocabulary journals or any ongoing unit or lesson documents; e.g., entered in appropriate places on Study Maps (see Chapter 9) (Haggard, 1986). Words not chosen for class study may be recorded by students who wish to include them on their own personal vocabulary lists.

VSS Follow-Up

VSS is not complete without follow-up activities to reinforce initial learning. After the selection process, you will need to develop activities for extended use and practice of the words. These activities should (1) allow students to use words in a meaningful way, (2) allow students to associate new words with known words and concepts, (3) develop associations with other words, (4) encourage higher-order thinking, (5) lead students to many different resources, and (6) acknowledge and capitalize on the social nature of learning (Ruddell, 1993). It is important to understand that without the follow-up activities it is very unlikely that much long-term retention of words will occur. In the upcoming section Developing Word Meanings, we suggest a number of activities to follow VSS.

Advantages of VSS

One of the first and most readily apparent advantages of using the VSS is how easily it is implemented and how quickly children like collecting their own words. VSS requires no special equipment or materials and can be used with literature, basal reader, and all content area texts. Further, VSS words can be collected from a videotape, electronic media (computers), a filmstrip, a demonstration, or a field trip as well as from books and other written texts. It only takes time and a little teacher effort to develop follow-up activities.

HOW TO DO . . . .

VOCABULARY SELF-COLLECTION STRATEGY (VSS)

1. After reading (or other learning event), ask student pairs or groups to find a word or term that they would like to know or learn more about. Students are to be prepared to

a. tell where they found it in the text and read the word in the sentence,

b. tell what they think the word/term means, and

c. tell why they think the word/term should be on the class vocabulary list.

2. Accept word nominations with discussion of possible meanings and reasons for learning (items a through c above). Encourage extension and refinement of meanings through collaboration and pooling of information.

3. Nominate the word you wish to have on the list and supply all of the requisite information (items a through c above).

4. Narrow class list to predetermined number (if needed).

5. Refine definitions as needed for each word/term.

6. Direct students to record final list words and definitions (as developed in class discussion) in vocabulary journals, on maps, or where you wish.

7. Develop VSS lesson activities for reinforcement.

8. Provide time for students to complete lesson activities assignments.

9. Incorporate vocabulary items into end-of-unit or spelling test as appropriate.

More important, VSS makes word learning and sensitivity to words a vital part of classroom life. Children really like talking about and playing with words, and they are surprisingly adept at choosing words that are important for their own learning (Fisher et al., 1992; Haggard, 1982). The biggest issue here is *time.* When children are vitally interested and excited about words (about anything, actually) time tends to fly, because children want to keep talking. You can expect to have to monitor time carefully in order to move the lesson forward. But the rewards are worth it. Mary Paff, a student in one of our classes tells of a fifth-grade boy in Mary Paff's class who had been difficult, uninvolved, and unhappy in class since the beginning of the school year. Quite unexpectedly, he became a bright-eyed dynamo during VSS lessons, eager to contribute and actively involved in the discussion. After the class had been doing VSS for three or four weeks, he turned to Mary one day as they were walking out to the playground and said, "I've got a good vocabulary, don't I?" Yes, and he's found a place to shine in school.

One Last Word About VSS

Teachers are always a little worried that, given the opportunity to choose their own vocabulary words, children will pick the easiest words they can find for VSS just to go through the motions. They won't. Students love VSS and will choose the words they need and want to know—words with wonderful sounds and images (*cavernous maw*, *Lilliputians*), words that intrigue and interest them. Easy words are already known—and boring. VSS is also easily combined with spelling instruction (see Chapters 3 and 7) in such a way that VSS words become class spelling words each week. VSS creates active, interested word learners.

DEVELOPING WORD MEANINGS: INSTRUCTION TO SUPPORT WORD LEARNING

In the introduction to this chapter, we talked about the application of children's newly acquired vocabulary to a broadening understanding of semantic relationships. This leads to children's understanding of word

Vocabulary Self-Collection

meaning connections and, in turn, increased comprehension of what they read. The following discussion deals with strategies designed to help accomplish this goal.

These strategies may be used before or after reading or any time during the school day. Many of them are excellent for use with CSSR and/or as VSS follow-up activities. Their purpose is to develop depth of meaning for vocabulary and concepts and to build meaning connections to known words. These activities involve information in text and graphic representations for extending meanings.

Using Meaning Clues in Context

We need to develop children's awareness of contextual meaning clues that they can use in constructing meaning of unfamiliar vocabulary. Direct teaching of context clues may occur before or after reading, but it must occur. What is important to understand here is that children must be taught how to use context. As we mentioned earlier, we have strong evidence that many children do not know how to use context effectively to construct meaning for words (Stanovich, 1991); however, teaching children how to use context increases their ability to do so (Jenkins, Matlock, & Slocum, 1989).

One of the easiest and most productive ways to develop children's ability to use context is through the Interactive Cloze activity (Meeks & Morgan, 1978). Interactive Cloze is based on the notion of "closure"—the ability of the human mind to complete incomplete stimuli (Taylor, 1953). A cloze activity involves a short passage with selected words deleted; the purpose of the activity is for students to use information from the undeleted parts to replace the deleted words. In the Interactive Cloze activity, children work together to accomplish this task.

The Interactive Cloze begins with a short passage in which a few carefully selected words are deleted (see Figure 5-1). The first and last sentences of the passage are left intact. For very young children no more than three to five words should be deleted. At the upper grades, as many as eight to ten deletions are fine. Choose deletions with the goal of stimulating lots of talk and interaction.

Allow children to work individually or in pairs to replace the deleted words. When everyone has finished, organize the children into groups of four or five and ask them to compare their responses. Children must tell why they chose the replacements they did. Each group is to arrive at agreement on the replacement for each deletion. After all groups have finished, read through the passage and have groups compare their replacements for deleted words; it helps to have the passage duplicated on an overhead transparency or written on the board for this part of the exercise. Following this, read the original passage for final comparison.

From this very simple activity, a great deal of instruction and practice using context occurs. In order to determine their replacements children must look at the context to see what possible words make sense for the deletions. Individual replacements are made on the basis of meaning each student constructs for the text, including prior knowledge about text and the topic. Reasons for replacements are shared as children compare and debate individual choices and arrive at group consensus prior to class discussion. Later, these are shared with the whole class.

Interactive Cloze is a good activity to follow discussion of the CSSR system because it teaches and reinforces getting meaning from context. Your role is to monitor small group discussion and then highlight in whole class discussion how the context directed the search for meaningful word replacement. As children become skilled at doing Interactive Cloze, you may increase the length of passages and the number of deletions.

Developing Synonyms

Synonyms are words that have almost the same meaning as one or more other words. Clues for linking synonyms are provided by the surrounding sentence context and children's background knowledge. The development of synonym meaning is illustrated by the following examples:

1. After reading the story, "The Little Wee Woman and the Great Big Cow," a Scottish folktale adapted by Gay Seltzer (Ruddell & Haggard, 1986, p. 13), a second-grade teacher made the following observation.

The Key Keeper was lonesome. Even though he lived in the King's castle, and was liked by everyone, he was still _____. All day he would go about the _____ with his big keys, up and down the long _____. He would go _____ through the crooked halls, locking and unlocking the heavy doors for the King and the King's helpers.

After everyone had gone to his room and the doors were _____ for the night, the key Keeper would go alone to his room to eat his supper. He was lonesome.

FIGURE 5-1

Interactive Cloze Passage from *Flibbety Jibbet and the Key Keeper* (appropriate for 2nd – 3rd Grades)

"*Little* and *wee* are *synonyms* because they mean almost the same thing. Let's think of as many words as we can that are synonyms for *little* and *wee*." The words *little* and *wee* were placed on the chalkboard, and the class generated and discussed additional words. These included *tiny, small, short, miniature, toy,* and *itty-bitty*. The children then played with the synonyms—putting various combinations of them together to create new titles for "The Little Wee Woman."

2. In the story "Why Wasn't I Asked to the Party?" by Elizabeth Starr Hill (Ruddell & Haggard, 1987, p. 52), the central character, Jan, figures out a way to get invited to the party. The text then reads, "A buoyant feeling rose in her. Things might be made to work out right after all." The class discussion of *buoyant feeling,* using the context of the two sentences in the story, led to the conclusion that such a feeling makes you "feel cheerful" and "like you are floating on air." The children were then asked to identify and discuss experiences that gave them a *buoyant feeling*. This discussion was followed by the children's use of the word in a sentence that began, "I had a buoyant feeling when _____ Other words that mean almost the same thing are _____ . and _____ ."

Developing Similes

Similes are figures of speech that create mental images by comparing two unlike things, such as "She is like a rose." Similes use the words *like* and *as* in this comparison. Again the context of the text is critical to meaning construction, as illustrated in the following examples.

1. After reading the story, "Laurie and the Cowardly Lion" by Betty Broadbent Carter (Ruddell & Haggard, 1986, p. 74), a second-grade teacher reread the following sentences from the story and wrote them on the board.
   Her stomach was flip-flopping *like a fish out of water.*
   Arthur tore out of his house *like a tornado.*

She then explained that the author of the story describes story events by using comparisons that help us picture the events in our minds. The class discussed comparisons used in each sentence and then created new comparisons to complete the sentence stems.

Her stomach was flip-flopping like _____
The train flashed by like _____

2. The following activity was developed by a sixth-grade teacher after the children had completed reading a chapter in John Fitzgerald's *Tom Spots a Card Shark* (Haggard & Ruddell, 1986, p. 24). She observed,

229

You can make meaning by comparing two unlike things. A simile is a figure of speech in which two unlike things are compared. This comparison is useful to a writer in creating meaningful images in a story. The words *like* and *as* are used in simile comparisons. Here are two examples from our story:

"When it came to money he was *like a bloodhound on the trail of a fugitive*" and "Mr. Walters looked as surprised *as a man who opens a can of beans and finds peas inside instead.*"

The class discussed the two similes and then completed the following sentences creating their own comparisons and images.

My dog has a nose as _____

My friend has legs as _____

My bike sounds like _____

My cat's fur feels like _____

The students then shared their similes by discussing them in partner teams.

Concept Webs

A Concept Web is a simple diagram or map used to develop and connect a key concept to children's prior knowledge and understandings and to connect the concept to information presented in the reading text. This strategy can be used from kindergarten on up. The concept or concepts should be of central importance to the narrative or expository material being read.

Write the concept on the board and circle it. Then discuss it with the children, eliciting information about the concept from their background knowledge. Build the web by drawing lines to connect semantically related concepts and ideas as strands around the concept.

The use of concept webbing is illustrated by a third-grade teacher's application of it to the central characters in *Mufaro's Beautiful Daughters* by John Steptoe (1987). This sensitively illustrated West African tale is about a villager, Mufaro, who has two beautiful but very different daughters. Nyasha is considerate and helpful, while Manyara is greedy and ambitious. When the great king decides to choose a wife, Mufaro sends his daughters. On the journey, their true nature is revealed. This knowledge strongly influences the king's decision and the story outcome.

The teacher selected two concepts central to and underlying this story and the story characters, Nyasha and Manyara. These concepts were *kind* and *selfish*. The two words were written on the board. Then the students, using their prior knowledge and the story context, suggested other words to make the strands of the webs. The concept webs that resulted are shown in Figure 5-2.

The concept webs for *kind* and *selfish* serve to connect the children's prior knowledge with the character traits of Nyasha and Manyara. When the

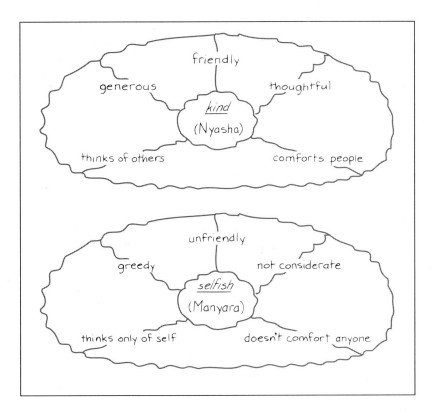

— **FIGURE 5-2** —

Third-Grade Concept Webs for Central Story Concepts in *Mufaro's
Beautiful Daughters*

webs were made, the discussion was extended to contrast specific vocabulary
items and meanings in them such as *kind* and *selfish*, *generous* and *greedy*,
and *friendly* and *unfriendly*.

Concept webs give children an important strategy for developing and
integrating knowledge, whether this knowledge is in the context of a literary
experience or content area reading—science or social studies, for example.
The concept web shown in Figure 5-3 was developed by a fourth-grade class
after reading the book *Sharks* written by Gilda Berger and illustrated by
Christopher Santoro (1987). This web serves to summarize key features and
habitat for a wide variety of sharks ranging from the *dwarf shark* to the
whale shark. After the discussion, the children created drawings of sharks
based on the information from their web and the book and labeled each by
name. The teacher then displayed their work on the bulletin board under
the caption *Sharks I Know*.

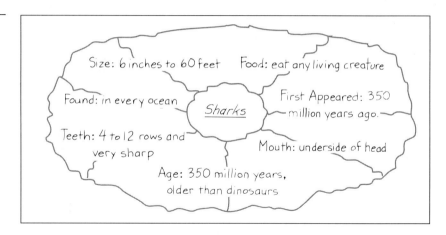

Size: 6 inches to 60 feet   Food: eat any living creature

Found: in every ocean   Sharks   First Appeared: 350 million years ago.

Teeth: 4 to 12 rows and very sharp

Mouth: underside of head

Age: 350 million years, older than dinosaurs

—— **FIGURE 5-3** ——

Fourth-Grade Concept Web for Sharks

Semantic Maps

Semantic Maps are similar to Concept Webs but are used to develop more complex relationships. These maps are graphic representations that can be used to help students understand the relationships between concepts, story characters, plot development, and key ideas in the reading text; as such, they are not unlike the story maps produced from the Group Mapping Activity (GMA) (see Chapter 4). Semantic maps can be used across the grades but will vary in complexity depending on the grade level. Semantic maps can be used before reading to activate student's background knowledge related to a concept or topic and introduce new concepts, or after reading, to summarize and integrate ideas.

Creating the Map. Semantic mapping begins when you write the central concept on the board, e.g., *spring*. The children then brainstorm ideas about, or related to, *spring*. You record the ideas in random order on the board, probing and extending children's responses as it is reasonable to do so. When no new ideas are forthcoming, guide the class in organizing the ideas by classifying or categorizing them. Then ask the children to construct individual maps (or a group map) showing the classifications and connections.

The map-creation phase involves active discussion and comprehension as children are encouraged to connect ideas and integrate ideas using the scaffolding of the map categories. The last phase of the mapping involves the children in text rereading, and verification of understandings leading to map revisions and extensions. The process is highly effective in helping children organize and integrate new concepts with their background knowledge.

There are some differences between semantic mapping and the GMA
discussed in Chapter 4, particularly with regard to the amount of teacher
direction used in organizing and creating the maps. Recall that the GMA uses
children's personal graphic representation after reading to interpret relationships between story characters and plot or between ideas and concepts in
expository reading material. Semantic maps can be more structured in showing relationships which move from main idea to secondary categories and
supporting details (Hanf, 1971). The teacher may assume a more active role
in directing semantic mapping and construction of the final maps; however,
the teacher may choose to be less directive in semantic mapping (as with the
GMA) and allow children to organize their maps as they wish.

A First-Grade Map. The following semantic map was created in a first-
grade classroom after reading the basal reader story *Kate and the Zoo*
(Heimlich & Pittelman, 1986). The Directed Reading Activity (DRA) was
used to develop the story through vocabulary introduction and story discussion. After story discussion, the following steps were used to create the
semantic map in Figure 5-4.

1. The title of the story *Kate and the Zoo* (main idea) was printed on the
   chalkboard and a circle was drawn around it.

2. The five topic headings (secondary categories) were printed on lines
   drawn from the main idea, e.g., "Things Kate sees at the zoo" (factual),
   "How Kate feels" (interpretive), etc.

3. The children were involved in a discussion of ideas remembered from
   the story (supporting details). After responding, each child was asked
   under which category that information would be written. That information was added to the map and other children were encouraged to add
   new information under the same heading.

4. The discussion process continued, using each heading as the children
   contributed supporting ideas to the map.

5. The following day, the map was reviewed and the story was reread for
   the purpose of adding new information. This information was added
   following the story rereading.

6. The completed map was duplicated and a copy was given to each first-
   grade student. The students were then asked to take the map home and
   use it to retell the story to their parents.

This semantic mapping lesson took place early in the school year and was
one of the children's first experiences in creating semantic maps. For this reason, the teacher assumed a more active role in structuring the lesson by identifying topic headings and developing supporting details related to each.

As we've suggested earlier, an alternative approach, or less-structured
approach after children have experience creating semantic maps, is to write
the main topic on the chalkboard, lead a brainstorming discussion with

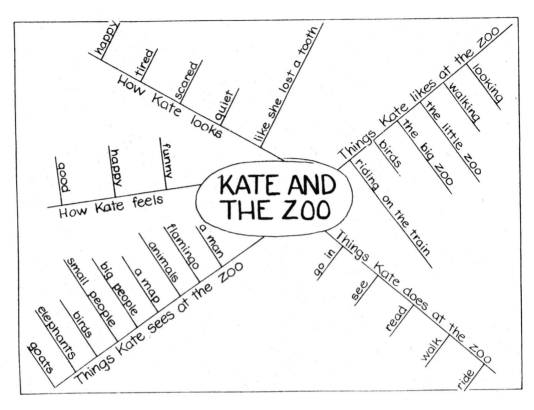

FIGURE 5-4

First-Grade Semantic Map for *Kate and the Zoo*. (Reproduced with permission from Heimlich & Pittelman, 1986, p. 11.)

children about the topic, list children's ideas on the chalkboard or chart paper, and then have the children decide the topic (or category) headings. The children then construct individual maps using these topic headings.

Semantic Mapping at the Upper Grades. Semantic mapping can be effectively used as a before-reading *and* after-reading vocabulary development strategy. The semantic map in Figure 5-5 illustrates a before-reading map, and Figure 5-6 illustrates extended work on the same map after reading (Heimlich & Pittelman, 1986). These maps were created by students at the upper grades over a three-day period using the central theme of *sharks*. It is interesting to contrast the more complex development of these semantic maps with the third-graders' concept web on *sharks* presented earlier in this chapter.

The instructional procedure follows that previously discussed. During the first day of instruction, the main idea and central concept, *sharks*, was written on a transparency and used with an overhead projector. Idea brainstorming followed, and details were recorded as students' background knowledge (supporting ideas) about sharks was activated. After idea generation was completed, the secondary categories, such as *characteristics* and *habitat*, were created by the students and their teacher. The supporting ideas were then organized under the main categories.

Students were then asked to read the story following the DRA. After reading the story, the new information about sharks was identified and added to the map, using a different color marker, to highlight the new information.

In the second day of instruction, the semantic map in Figure 5-5 was used to review the information about sharks. Students were then asked to identify vocabulary or ideas on the map that they would like to investigate. This information was recorded and served as the basis for pursuing research using the classroom and school library resources. Research questions included "What are sharks' natural enemies?" and "Are all sharks dangerous?" The students then pursued answers to their questions either individually or in partner pairs.

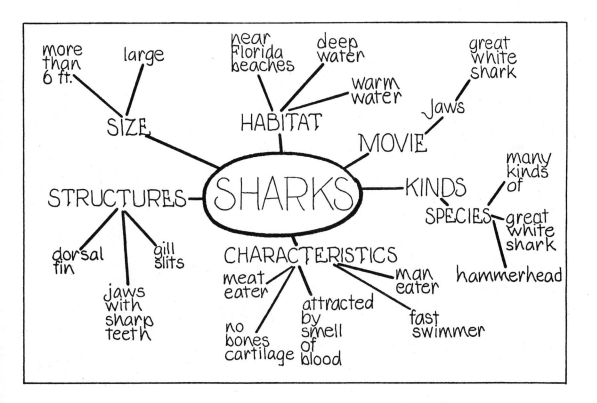

FIGURE 5-5

Before Reading—Semantic Map on Sharks. (Reproduced with permission from Heimlich & Pittelman, 1986, p. 32.)

235

The third day of instruction started with a review of the semantic map followed by a discussion and sharing of information based on children's independent research. This new information was then added to the semantic map under the most appropriate category using yet a different color marker. The use of different color markers, or chalk, is valuable in helping students identify which information is based on their prior background knowledge (day one—introduction), which is based on their reading (day one—discussion), and which comes from their research (days two and three). The completed semantic map from the third day of discussion is shown in Figure 5-6.

Semantic mapping represents a valuable instructional activity for developing new vocabulary and integrating new concepts with prior knowledge. It is particularly useful as a follow-up to VSS.

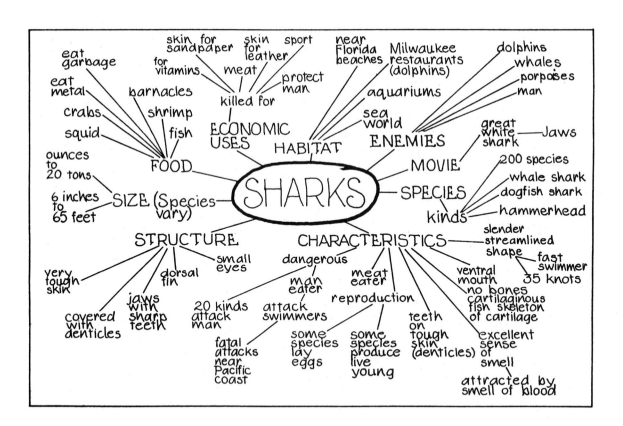

FIGURE 5-6

After Reading and Researching—Semantic Map on Sharks. (Reproduced with permission from Heimlich & Pittelman, 1986, p. 33.)

HOW TO DO . . . .

CONCEPT WEBBING AND SEMANTIC MAPPING

1. Determine a major concept or topic central to the reading or area of study, e.g., *spring, friendship, electricity.*

2. Write the name of the concept or topic in the center of the chalkboard, overhead transparency, or easel chart page.

3. Ask children to brainstorm their knowledge and ideas about the topic.

4. Record their ideas on the board. If webbing, draw lines to show connections and relationships.

5. After no more ideas are forthcoming, invite children to develop categories or classifications for the ideas and create their own semantic maps from their classification scheme, or

6. Guide the class in developing categories for organizing the ideas and lead the group in developing a semantic map from the information on the board.

Semantic Feature Analysis (SFA)

Semantic Feature Analysis (SFA) is an instructional strategy used to develop vocabulary knowledge by establishing shared meaning relationships between words. Words that share semantic features define a central concept or semantic category. For example, a *kitten* and a *goldfish* are both in the same semantic category of "pets" because they are both special animals who live with us, must be fed and cared for daily, receive love, and give us enjoyment and comfort. But *kittens* and *goldfish* obviously differ in appearance (fur and fins, respectively), in what they eat, and in the way they breathe. Further, kittens and goldfish are very different from their genetic relatives the *tiger* and the *shark*. Our understanding of the semantic features for the category "pets" serves as the basis for understanding and differentiating the concept labels *kitten, goldfish, tiger,* and *shark.*

Semantic Feature Analysis (SFA) begins with a grid constructed for a concept (e.g., "pets") in which elements or exemplars of the concept are listed vertically (e.g., kitten, goldfish, dog, bird, snake, rat) and features of one or more exemplars are listed horizontally (e.g., 4-legged, swims, learns tricks, cute, found in wild, etc.). See Figure 5-7 for an SFA grid for the concept "pets." Distribute a copy of the grid to the class and ask children to decide individually which feature matches each word; they are to put a plus

	4-legged	swims	learns tricks	cute	found in wild	
kitten						
goldfish						
dog						
bird						
snake						
rat						

—— **FIGURE 5-7** ——

Semantic Feature Analysis for "Pets"

(+) for features that do match and a minus (-) for those that do not. After children have completed the grid, put them into pairs or small groups to compare their responses; later, have small groups share and lead a discussion with the whole class. Children may then add more exemplars of the concept and more features to continue the analysis.

You can expect conflicts and differences of opinion in the children's discussion of SFA grids; you need to be aware that such differences will arise and be prepared to handle them. One way is to have students go back to their SFAs and change their coding system by adding an asterisk (*) for "sometimes matches." Another way is to alert children before their discussion that they will likely disagree with one another at some point and remind them of their responsibility to listen to each other in the face of such differences.

Semantic feature analysis is also useful for building understanding of central characters in children's literature. The SFA in Figure 5-8 is based on a sixth-grade classroom analysis of the four main characters in Patricia MacLachlan's Newbery Award–winning book *Sarah, Plain and Tall* (Pittelman, Heimlich, Berglund, & French, 1991, p. 52). This book tells the story of Sarah, who answers an ad for a mail-order bride. She leaves her home in Maine and travels to the plains to marry Papa, a widower, who has two children, Anna and little Caleb.

This analysis focuses on the feelings and emotions of the characters based on the children's reading of the first two chapters of the book. As the next chapter of the book was developed, the class expanded the character

Feelings	Characters / Anna	Caleb	Papa	Sarah
sad	+	+	+	?
lonesome	+	+	+	?
anxious	+	+	+	+
anticipating	+	+	+	+
curious	+	+	+	+
worried	+	+	—	—
happy	+	+	+	?

FIGURE 5-8

Semantic Feature Analysis of Central Characters After Reading Chapters 1 and 2 of *Sarah, Plain and Tall.* (Reproduced with permission from Pittlelman, Heimlich, Berglund, & French, 1991, p. 52.)

features using the emotions portrayed by the characters. Each child was then asked to select a favorite character and use that character's "voice" (features) in writing a letter to another book character. Envelopes were then addressed to that character and randomly delivered to each student in the class. In turn, students receiving the addressed letter assumed that character's voice and wrote a return letter.

Semantic feature analysis is useful in any subject area. Figure 5-9 illustrates the use of SFA in studying planets in Earth's solar system. This analysis was used by the teacher in a before-reading vocabulary activity to help students identify their prior knowledge about the solar system and to prepare for an information search as they read the text. The value of SFA in subject-area study is the manner in which it illuminates relationships and connections within and across concepts.

PLANETS IN EARTH'S SOLAR SYSTEM

	CLOSER TO THE SUN THAN EARTH	LARGER THAN EARTH	HAS MOON	HAS RINGS	INNER PLANET	ORBITS THE SUN
Earth	−	−	+	−	+	+
Jupiter	−	+	+	−		−
Mars	+	−	+	−	+	+
Mercury	+	−		−	+	+
Neptune	−	+		−		−
Pluto	−	+		−		−
Saturn	−	+		+		−
Uranus	−			−		−
Venus	+	−	+	−	+	

+ = student believes feature is true of that planet
− = student believes planet lacks that feature
Matrix items will later be checked against reading material

—— FIGURE 5-9 ——

Prereading Semantic Analysis on Planets in Earth's Solar System–As Filled Out by an Individual Student. (Reproduced with permission from Cunningham & Cunningham, 1987, p. 509.)

Vocabulary Logs or Journals

Vocabulary Logs or Journals provide a systematic way for children from kindergarten through the upper grades to record and learn new words and concepts. Words entered into the children's logs may be based on the VSS, words of high personal interest discovered in content areas such as science and social studies, or words from newspapers, magazines, and television. At the beginning levels, the log or journal may take the form of children's collected words with definitions, as well as words in sentence contexts that are personally illustrated. The collection may also include magazine and newspaper pictures depicting new vocabulary words which are pasted in the log and labeled.

At the intermediate grades, the log may include vocabulary items consisting of individual and class definitions and sentence contexts, and labeled magazine or newspaper clippings representing a personal collection of vocabulary items. The log or journal may also be used to record notes when key vocabulary items and concepts are researched using dictionary and encyclopedia resources.

Graphic representations showing word connections and word relationships also deserve space in vocabulary logs. These will become a regular part of your instruction as you use concept webs, semantic maps, and semantic feature analysis. Some children will wish to copy the final web, map, or analysis grid from the chalkboard summary into their logs or journals. You will need to provide time for them to do this.

Vocabulary logs provide a natural reservoir of new words. As you become comfortable in using VSS and apply the strategy to vocabulary study in literature, science, social studies, and other areas, the children's vocabulary logs will become especially useful. By recording vocabulary, and definitions, and by using these words in context, children will begin to form their own dictionary reference resource for spelling and writing.

Organizing the Vocabulary Log or Journal. You will need to consider several of the following options:

1. **Alphabetical organization.** This organization will provide alphabetical listing, with words added in a dictionary-like fashion on a daily basis. The value of this organization is ease in locating words for writing and reports. The disadvantage is that vocabulary discussions that are semantically related lose their meaning connection when alphabetized. A bit more time is necessary to record words in alphabetical order, particularly in the early grades.

2. **Chronological organization.** This system provides for daily or weekly vocabulary entries, without concern for a systematic organization. The value of the system is found in word groupings that may be connected by common meanings. This will be the case when working with concept webs, semantic maps, and semantic features analysis. This system also works particularly well in using VSS when a group of words are selected for specific study over a period of several days. The limitation is in difficulty of quickly locating a word, although many children will become highly effective in quickly finding vocabulary items using this system.

3. **Subject matter organization.** This approach provides for specific sections of a log devoted exclusively to reading, science, social studies, mathematics, and so on. The value of this approach is found in quick

location of words used and continuity in the collecting vocabulary in a subject matter area. The disadvantage is found in fragmenting vocabulary across subject-matter boundaries and additional time required in locating specific vocabulary items.

4. **Combination of approaches.** This system, for example, could be organized by subject matter area with words entered by alphabetical order. Easy and quick location is the key advantage but fragmentation by content area will require location time.

Whatever system of organization you or your students elect to use for your children's vocabulary logs, the main point to keep in mind is that the organization of log and journal entries should support your teaching style, your children's motivation to acquire vocabulary, and ease of word location.

Materials for Vocabulary Logs. After deciding on an organizational system, it is important to provide your children with (or help them acquire) materials to use the system. These may take the form of a spiral-bound or solid-spine notebook simply labeled "*Vocabulary Log*" or "*Vocabulary Journal*." A three-ring notebook with dividers and filler paper using the heading "*Vocabulary Collection*" and top of page headings for name, date, new word, and definition will work well with any organizational scheme— alphabetic, chronological, subject matter, or combination.

Your children's vocabulary logs or journals will greatly assist in the vocabulary acquisition process as new concepts and labels are developed. As children are encouraged to reflect on their log entries over several weeks, they will develop a sense of achievement. Your periodic response to their journal entries, written in the margin of their logs, will provide not only feedback to the children but also insight into their vocabulary growth.

Word Sleuthing and Vocabulary Development

Word sleuthing stems naturally from, and should be very much a part of, VSS, although you don't have to do VSS in order for your students to become word sleuths. In science, at the early grades, word sleuthing may include the study of animal families and names of young animals, e.g., *bear/cub, horse/foal, elephant/calf, fox/kit,* and *rabbit/nestling.* In social studies, study of governments and leaders at the intermediate grades may include new terms for leaders and rulers in different countries, e.g., *shogun* (Japanese military commander), *viceroy* (governor of a colony or dominion), and *sultan* (ruler of a Muslim state). Other opportunities will arise each week in the classroom as new topics are explored in each area of your curriculum from reading and language arts to music and science.

Encourage children's interests in the study and collection of words in their home environment by including such word sleuthing in VSS activities. This will range from identifying interesting words in newspapers and

New Experiences–New Words

news programs, to new vocabulary encountered in television commercials and magazine advertisements. The key point is to build high interest and motivation in word sleuthing and a positive attitude toward investigating new vocabulary and concepts. The vocabulary log or journal serves as an important collection and recording tool for words found at home and in the community. The ideas below may help you create word sleuths in your classroom.

Word Borrowing. A brief discussion of the important contributions to our language from other languages and cultures will encourage your children to explore the source of these "borrowed" words and may not only develop positive interest in word sleuthing but also in the study of different cultures. As you examine these borrowings, note how they may be grouped into such categories as animals, foods, clothing, household objects, customs, and the environment. Such categories can prove useful as you develop new vocabulary though strategies such as Concept Webs, Semantic Maps, and Semantic Feature Analysis.

From the time of early settlements in this country, our language has contained a number of Native American "loanwords." These come largely from the Algonquian stock (which included Arapaho, Blackfoot, Cheyenne, Cree, Delaware, Fox, Micmac, Chippewa, and Penobscot tribes). These borrowed words include *opossum, moose, skunk,* and *woodchuck,* animals that were unique to the North American continent. Vegetation names such as *hickory, pecan,* and *persimmon,* and social custom and family member words such as *powwow, caucus and papoose* are other borrowings from Native Americans (Pyles, 1964).

Our language has served as a unifying element for immigrants from various countries who found a second language essential for daily interaction. In return, the immigrant populations also contributed new vocabulary to the language. From New Amsterdam came the Dutch words *coleslaw, cookie, boss, sleigh, waffle,* and *Santa Claus.* From the Pennsylvania German came *fat-cakes* (donuts), *smearcase* (cottage cheese), *dunk* (to dip), and *hex* (to cast a spell on). By way of the Canadian border, through French explorers, the words *prairie, chowder, buccaneer,* and *levee* entered the language, and the Spanish words *mosquito* (little fly), *negro* ("black," an adjective that was converted to a noun), *armada,* and *alligator.* More Spanish words came into our language as the interaction between the pioneers and Mexican and Spanish-speaking people of the West and Southwest increased. These words included *burro, chili, pronto, patio, tornado,* and *cafeteria.*

Other borrowings that are thoroughly incorporated into our language include the African words *banjo, goober* (peanut), *chigger, hoodoo,* and *voodoo.* The Italian contributions include the words *balcony, opera, piano, umbrella,* and *volcano,* while Persian words consist of *caravan, khaki, shawl, sherbet, chess, lemon, turban,* and *borax.* The Greeks contributed *acrobat, magic, barometer, elastic,* and *tactics,* and the Russian language gave us words such as *ruble, steppe,* and *vodka* (Baugh, 1957; Pyles, 1964). From the Chinese, we have borrowed the words *dim sum, wonton,* and *foo young,* and from the Japanese *haiku, aikido, origami,* and *sumo.*

Developing interest in the source and origin of words can lead to a long-term interest in vocabulary building. Borrowed words should be the topic of frequent vocabulary self-collections. High motivation in using classroom resources such as the dictionary, thesaurus, and encyclopedia may develop from the study of borrowed words.

New Words and New Meanings Related to Technology and Advertising. Children's word study can be easily connected to the technological age by examining new coinings and combinations and new meanings attached to familiar words used to label discoveries and inventions. Such words include *astronaut,* derived from Greek, literally meaning "star" (*astro*) "sailor" (*naut*), *space docking, rapid transit, jumbo jet,* and *freeway.* Computer-based words such as *menu, program, byte, floppy, hard disk, online, compact disc* and *superhighway* are prime candidates for exploration.

Discussions can also be developed as children consider the reasoning behind the trade names of commercial products. Consider, for example, the automobile names *Probe, Stealth, Thunderbird, Infiniti, Saturn,* and *Maxima,* and the cleaning detergent products *Vanish, Pledge, Comet,* and *Brillo.* What relationship exists between the names of these automobiles and cleaning products and the image which the manufacturer hopes to create in the mind of the buying public? Another interesting point for young word sleuths is how many "common words" began as product names, (Kleenex, Xerox, Ping-Pong, etc.). By developing a classroom unit related to the use of words in advertising, children will come to understand the power of language in influencing their perception of products ranging from cereals to automobiles. By sensitizing children to vocabulary found in their daily environment, you will encourage word sleuthing and contribute to children's spontaneous and continued vocabulary learning. Vocabulary logs and journals will provide a sense of growth and accomplishment in acquiring new words and concepts.

Building Vocabulary Knowledge
A Summary

Vocabulary knowledge is a critical part of the comprehension process. In this chapter, we presented three goals for vocabulary learning: developing and connecting new vocabulary to children's background knowledge, developing children's strategies for constructing meaning for unknown words, and building positive attitudes toward and increasing independence in vocabulary learning. The specific objectives for our instructional program grow directly from these goals.

Principles of vocabulary instruction stress the importance of active learning and rich instruction as children are encouraged to construct meaning by "reasoning with words." Personal motivation is critical to vocabulary development if we are to instill the desire in children to develop concepts over their lifetime and become increasingly independent word learners.

Careful consideration must be given to the selection of new vocabulary for direct teaching as well as systematic instruction in how to construct meaning for unknown words. The strategies developed in our discussion provide important options in teaching vocabulary before reading (TVC), during reading (CSSR), and after reading (VSS). Follow-up activities provide practice and opportunity for children to gain in-depth, complex understanding of words and concepts.

DOUBLE ENTRY JOURNAL

Look back at your list of things you do when you come to a word you do not know. How closely does your system match the CSSR system we discussed in this chapter? How do your word-learning strategies support your vocabulary growth? What are some ideas from this chapter you want to try in your classroom?

Supporting Activities

1. Early in this chapter we identified three types of word reasoning that are important for active mental involvement designed to enhance vocabulary learning. Briefly review this discussion on meaning context, connection to semantically similar words, and creating new meaning contexts. Arrange for an observation of an elementary classroom at your level of interest. As instruction proceeds, examine the way in which the teacher develops new vocabulary. Briefly describe how new words are introduced and developed. What evidence is present to indicate that semantic connections are being made between new vocabulary and the children's prior vocabulary knowledge? What changes would you make had you taught the same vocabulary lesson?

2. Obtain a teacher's guide for a widely used reading program at the grade level that is of greatest interest to you. Locate an interesting story, and after carefully reading the story, examine the vocabulary that is recommended for teaching before the story is read. The four questions discussed earlier in the chapter (see "Identifying New Vocabulary for Teaching") will be of value to you in this process. What recommended

vocabulary would you select for introduction? What recommended vocabulary would you not teach? Are there other vocabulary items that you believe should be taught that are not in the recommended list? Discuss your thinking with a class partner.

3. Follow the same process for identifying a story in a basal reader that is described in question number 2. Review the earlier discussion on instructional strategies (Concept Web, Semantic Feature Analysis, Vocabulary Self-Collection, Vocabulary Journal) and select one strategy that you believe could be used effectively in developing vocabulary for this story. Write an instructional plan using the strategy you have selected. Share your ideas with a class partner.

4. Use a newspaper that you have read today, or during the last several days, and identify two vocabulary items that you believe would be appropriate for introduction to children at the grade level of highest interest to you. Briefly describe how you would introduce these words accounting for use of context, prior background knowledge, and high interest.

REFERENCES

Anderson, R. C., & Freebody, P. (1981). Vocabulary knowledge. In J. T. Guthrie (Ed.), *Comprehension and teaching: Research reviews* (pp. 77–117). Newark, DE: International Reading Association.

Baugh, A. C. (1957). *A history of the English language.* New York: Appleton-Century-Crofts.

Beck, I. L., & McKeown, M. G. (1991). Conditions of vocabulary acquisition. In R. Barr, M. L. Kamil, P. Mosenthal, & P. D. Pearson (Eds.), *Handbook of reading research: Volume II* (pp. 787–814). New York: Longman.

Beck, I. L., McKeown, M. G., & Omanson, R. C. (1987). The effects and uses of diverse vocabulary instructional techniques. In M. G. McKeown & M. E. Curtis (Eds.), *The nature of vocabulary acquisition* (pp. 147–163). Hillsdale, NJ: Erlbaum.

Beck, I. L., Perfetti, C. A., & McKeown, M. G. (1982). The effects of long-term vocabulary instruction on lexical access and reading comprehension. *Journal of Educational Psychology, 74,* 506–521.

Cunningham, P. M., & Cunningham, J. W. (1987). Content areas reading-writing lessons. *The Reading Teacher, 40,* 506–512.

Davis, F. B. (1944). Fundamental factors in reading comprehension. *Psychometrika, 9,* 185–197.

Davis, F. B. (1968). Research in comprehension in reading. *Reading Research Quarterly, 3,* 499–545.

Drum, P. A., & Konopak, B. C. (1987). Learning word meanings from written context. In M. G. McKeown & M. E. Curtis (Eds.), *The nature of vocabulary acquisition* (pp. 73–87). Hillsdale, NJ: Erlbaum.

Durkin, D. (1979). What classroom observations reveal about reading instruction. *Reading Research Quarterly, 14,* 481–533.

Fisher, P. J. L., Blachowicz, C. L. Z., Costa, M., & Pozzi, L. (1992, December). *Vocabulary teaching and learning in middle school cooperative literature study groups.* Paper presented at the annual meeting of the National Reading Conference, San Antonio, TX.

Genishi, C., & Dyson, A. H. (1984). *Language assessment in the early years.* Norwood, NJ: Ablex.

Graves, M. F. (1987). The roles of instruction in fostering vocabulary development. In M. G. McKeown & M. E. Curtis (Eds.), *The nature of vocabulary acquisition* (pp. 165–184). Hillsdale, NJ: Erlbaum.

Graves, M. F., Brunetti, G. J., & Slater, W. H. (1982). The reading vocabularies of primary-grade children of varying geographic and social backgrounds. In J. A. Harris & L. A. Harris (Eds.), *New inquiries in reading research and instruction* (pp. 99–104). Rochester, NY: National Reading Conference.

Graves, M. F., & Slater, W. H. (1987, April). *The development of reading vocabularies in rural disadvantaged students, inner-city disadvantaged students, and middle-class suburban students.* Paper presented at the annual meeting of the American Educational Research Association, Washington, DC.

Gray, W. S. (1946). *On their own in reading.* Chicago: Scott, Foresman.

Haggard, M. R. (1980). Vocabulary acquisition during elementary and post-elementary years: A preliminary report. *Reading Horizons, 21,* 61–69.

Haggard, M. R. (1982). The vocabulary self-collection strategy: An active approach to word learning. *Journal of Reading, 26,* 203–207.

Haggard, M. R. (1986). The vocabulary self-collection strategy: Using student interest and world knowledge to enhance vocabulary growth. *Journal of Reading, 29,* 634–642.

Haggard, M. R., & Ruddell, R. B. (1986). *Thinking about reading: Level F.* Cleveland, OH: Modern Curriculum Press.

Haggard, M. R., & Ruddell, R. B. (1987). *Thinking about reading, series 2: Level C.* Cleveland, OH: Modern Curriculum Press.

Hanf, M. B. (1971). Mapping: A technique for translating reading into thinking. *Journal of Reading, 14,* (270), 225–230.

Heimlich, J. E., & Pittelman, S. D. (1986). *Semantic mapping: Classroom applications.* Newark, DE: International Reading Association.

Jenkins, J. R., Matlock, B., & Slocum, T. A. (1989). Two approaches to vocabulary instruction: The teaching of individual word meanings and practice in deriving word meaning from context. *Reading Research Quarterly, 24,* 215–235.

Johnson, D. D., Toms-Bronowski, S., & Pittelman, S. D. (1981). *A review of trends in vocabulary research and the effects of prior knowledge on instructional strategies for vocabulary acquisition* (Program Report No. 95). Madison, WI: Wisconsin Center for Education Research.

Just, M. A., & Carpenter, P. A. (1987). *The psychology of reading and language comprehension.* Newton, MA: Allyn & Bacon.

Meeks, J. W., & Morgan, R. F. (1978). Classroom and the Cloze procedure: Interaction in imagery. *Reading Horizons, 18,* 261–264.

Moore, D. W., & Moore, S. A., (1986). Possible sentences. In E. K. Dishner, T. W. Bean, J. E. Readence, & D. W. Moore (Eds.), *Reading in the content areas: Improving classroom instruction* (2nd ed.) (pp. 174–179). Dubuque, IA: Kendall Hunt.

Nagy, W. E., Anderson, R. C., & Herman, P. A. (1987). Learning word meanings from context during normal reading. *American Educational Research Journal, 24,* 237–270.

Nagy, W. E., & Herman, P. A. (1987). Breadth and depth of vocabulary knowledge: Implications for acquisition and instruction. In M. G. McKeown & M. E. Curtis (Eds.), *The nature of vocabulary acquisition* (pp. 19–35). Hillsdale, NJ: Erlbaum.

Nagy, W. E., Herman, P. A., & Anderson, R. C. (1985). Learning words from context. *Reading Research Quarterly, 20,* 233–253.

Piaget, J. (1967). The genetic approach to the psychology of thought. In J. P. DeCecco (Ed.), *The psychology of language, thought and instruction.* New York: Holt, Rinehart & Winston.

Pittelman, S. D., Heimlich, J. E., Berglund, R. L., & French, M. P. (1991). *Semantic feature analysis.* Newark, DE: International Reading Association.

Pyles, T. (1964). *The origins and development of the English language.* New York: Harcourt Brace Jovanovich.

Readence, J. E., Bean, T. W., & Baldwin, R. S. (1989). *Content area reading: An integrated approach* (3rd ed.). Dubuque, IA: Kendall Hunt.

Ruddell, M. R. (1993). *Teaching content reading and writing.* Boston, MA: Allyn & Bacon.

Ruddell, M. R. (1994). Vocabulary knowledge and comprehension: A comprehension-process view of complex literacy relationships. In R. B. Ruddell, M. R. Ruddell, & H. Singer (Eds.), *Theoretical models and processes of reading* (4th ed.) (pp. 414–447). Newark, DE: International Reading Association.

Ruddell, R. B. (1986). Vocabulary learning: A process model and criteria for evaluating instructional strategies. *Journal of Reading, 29,* 581–587.

Ruddell, R. B., & Haggard, M. R. (1986). *Thinking about reading: Level C.* Cleveland, OH: Modern Curriculum Press.

Ruddell, R. B., & Haggard, M. R. (1987). *Thinking about reading, series 2: Level E.* Cleveland, OH: Modern Curriculum Press.

Stanovich, K. E. (1991). Word recognition: Changing perspectives. In R. Barr, M. L. Kamil, P. Mosenthal, & P. D. Pearson (Eds.), *Handbook of reading research: Volume II* (pp. 418–452). New York: Longman.

Taylor, W. L. (1953). Cloze procedures: A new tool for measuring readability. *Journalism Quarterly, 30,* 360–368.

Vygotsky, L. S. (1986). *Thought and language.* Cambridge, MA: MIT Press. (Originally published in 1962)

CHILDREN'S LITERATURE REFERENCES

Base, G. (Illustrator) (1987). *Jabberwocky*. Cleveland, OH: Modern Curriculum Press.

Berger, G. (1987). *Sharks*. New York: Doubleday.

Carroll, L. (1987). *Through the looking glass*. Cleveland, OH: Modern Curriculum Press. (Original publication, 1871)

MacLachlan, P. (1985). *Sarah, plain and tall*. New York: The Trumpet Club.

Steptoe, J. (1987). *Mufaro's beautiful daughters*. New York: Lothrop, Lee & Shepard.

Wilder, L. I. (1935). *Little house on the prairie*. New York: Harper & Row.

CHAPTER 5	TVC	CSSR	VSS
FOCUS ON	Preteaching vocabulary	Developing a functional system for learning new words	Acquiring and developing vocabulary
GUIDES STUDENTS	Before reading	During reading	After reading or writing
USE TO PLAN	Lessons	Lessons, units, yearly activities	Lessons, units yearly activities
MAY BE USED	Whole class, small groups	Whole class, small groups, individuals	Whole class, cooperative groups, partnerships
MAY BE COMBINED WITH (KNOWN STRATEGIES)	DRA, QAR, GMA	DR-TA, DRA, ReQuest	DL-TA, DR-TA, DRA, PReP, ReQuest, GMA
MATERIALS PREPARATION	Light	Light to moderate	Not needed
OTHER PREPARATION	Light	Light	Moderate
OUTSIDE RESOURCES	Useful	Useful	Necessary
HOW TO DO	Page 220	Page 222	Page 225

Building Tables "grow" or build, successively from Chapter to Chapter. They tell you (1) the focus of each strategy introduced in a chapter; (2) how the strategy is best used; (3) what strategies from previous chapters combine well with new ones; (4) preparation requirements; (5) additional resources needed; and (6) the page on which a strategy's How-to-Do appears.

CONCEPT WEBS	SEMANTIC MAPS	SFA
Concept and word associations	Concept and word associations	Concept and word relationships
Before, after reading; before writing	Before, after reading; before writing	After reading, before writing
Lessons	Lessons	Lessons
Whole class, small groups	Whole group, cooperative groups, partnerships, individuals	Whole group, cooperative groups, partnerships
DL-TA, DR-TA, DRA, PReP, ReQuest, VSS	DL-TA, DR-TA, DRA, PReP, ReQuest, VSS	DL-TA, DR-TA, DRA, QAR, VSS
Not needed	Not needed	Moderate to extensive
Not needed	Not needed	Not needed
Useful	Useful	Useful
Page 237	Page 237	

253

USING LITERATURE AND READER RESPONSE TO ENHANCE ATTITUDES AND COMPREHENSION

INTRODUCTION

Literature experiences can open gateways for readers—gateways leading to new encounters, people, places, and ideas, and often to rich and enchanted lands. These experiences, at the primary grades, will range from children's imaginative travels with Max in *Where the Wild Things Are* (Sendak, 1963) to empathy with Charlotte and her central role in rescuing Wilbur in *Charlotte's Web* (White, 1952). At the intermediate grade levels, children experience love and adventure with Billy, Old Dan, and Little Ann in *Where the Red Fern Grows* (Rawls, 1961) and the awakening of friendship and a sense of belonging for Mary and Colin in *The Secret Garden* (Burnett, 1911).

Literature programs need to be part of the "how to" of reading by developing reading skills, but they must go far beyond the "how to" by contributing to the "want to" of reading as well by building positive attitudes and the desire to read. The "want to" of reading must be cultivated with just as much care and thoughtful teaching as is the "how to" of reading.

Students' active involvement in responding to literature is critical to the development of positive reading attitudes and high-level comprehension. As

Albert Grande (1965, p. 12) so aptly noted in the mid-1960s, "Literature, as an expression of human strife, conflict, feelings, and ideas, must engage the student's active response, evoking his (or her) fund of intellectual and emotional experience… . It would be unfortunate not to relate the individual student's personal experience to his (or her) interpretation of literature."

The power of personal involvement in your own childhood experiences with literature can be demonstrated through a moment of reflection. Think for a moment of one book that you encountered between kindergarten and grade six that has special memories for you. What was the title of the book, and who was the author? What do you remember about the story? How did you respond to it? Do your memories reveal close identification with the central story character? What impact did the book have on you? The following thoughts are shared by a former student, Pat Derkum, as she describes her favorite childhood series of books, written by Laura Ingalls Wilder (1935).

> *I received the full set of the* Little House on the Prairie *books at the end of first grade. They came in a nice yellow box, and were the first "grown-up" books I had ever owned ("grown-up" meaning they were not picture books). While I could not really read them at this point in my life, I consider this time as the time I was truly hooked on books for life. I was so proud of these books and the way they smelled in their new box. The gift of these books made me realize that I was a reader of books. Not only was I a reader, but an owner of books, and that was almost as exciting.*

> *I have many good memories of sitting next to my mom on the couch while she read these books aloud. Together we lived with Laura in the Big Woods, on the prairie, etc. I remember picturing the invasion of the locusts, and the one-room school houses. While I listened to, and later read, these books aesthetically, I believe efferent knowledge "snuck around" the corners. How else but through these books could I have understood what it was like in the pioneer times?*

> *Later on, of course, I read these books for myself many times. The covers are shabby now, but the box still holds them all. Over the years, I developed a real identification with Laura. I wore my hair in pigtails like she did, and my favorite dress was a prairie type dress with an apron attached. Being a timid person, I empathized with Laura when she could not control the big boys in her classroom, as big boys intimidated me, too.*

*In conclusion, this set of books has not had an earth shat-
tering effect on me as a person, and hasn't changed my life in
any major way. Yet the* Little House *books enriched my life
more than any other children's books, because I identified
with Laura so much. Also, since they were my first "real"
books, and I was so proud of the fact that they were mine, I
think that they helped start my love for books in general.*

These ideas clearly reveal the reader's close identification with the central
story character, Laura, and her excitement and awareness of becoming an
"owner" and a reader of books. Her memories of reading with her mother,
and even the smell of the new books, evoke positive associations with reading and literature. The aim of our discussion in this chapter is to assist you
in building these same attitudes in children through the literature experiences in your classroom.

GOALS OF A LITERATURE PROGRAM

As teachers actively involve and immerse students in children's literature, five goals are uppermost in importance. These are:

1. To provide children with a range of literature experiences that builds on
   and extends their knowledge base, including an awareness of people and
   other living things, of events, and of ideas not present in their own life
   experience.
2. To bring children's prior knowledge, life experience, and values into
   sharper focus through active comprehension by examining and contrasting the many aspects of life represented through literature *via* language.
3. To provide children with pleasure (in an aesthetic sense) through the joy
   of language; and to encourage the appreciation of life experience by isolat-
   ing, magnifying, or contrasting, "slices of life" for aesthetic observation.
4. To develop children's self-understanding through insight into their own
   behavior as they encounter a broad range of human behavior.
5. To develop children's awareness of language as a powerful means of
   human expression as they experience the skillful use of imagery, drama,
   humor, and pathos.

All of these goals assume that teachers are, themselves, eager consumers
of childrens's literature; knowledgeable from first-hand experience about a
wide range of poetry, books, stories, biographies, and informational texts
appropriate for the children they teach; and absolutely committed to the

principles and values upon which literature programs rest. Effective literature programs require that teachers read from the libraries their children use and that teachers demonstrate daily their own love of reading and responding to literature. Ellen Jackson, a kindergarten teacher we know, is this kind of teacher. In Ellen's classroom, poetry infuses the classroom day: Ellen recites poetry, the children chant and recite poetry, poems are sent home in the daily "take-home" packets, children commit poems to memory—well over eighty during the school year; and at the end of the year, children bind all of the poems they learned into a Poetry Book that they take home to save.

Ellen just completed a study of the effect of her approach. She interviewed children and parents and found that her kindergarten children, well into fourth, fifth, and sixth grades, remembered vividly their poetry learning experiences in her class and still returned to their Poetry Books with pleasure. First-, second-, and third-grade students continued to read their Poetry Books at home.

SPECIFIC OBJECTIVES

A well-designed literature program should account for specific objectives that closely parallel the literature goals identified above. These include the following:

1. **Fostering high motivation toward reading** by exploring new characters and peoples, living things, and events and ideas that connect to but also go beyond children's own life experiences.
2. **Developing new concepts, background knowledge, and active comprehension** using a broad range of literature selections and sharing these through classroom discussions.
3. **Enjoying the aesthetic pleasure derived from experiencing literature** that uses language and illustrations to portray life and bring "slices of life" into sharper focus.
4. **Developing understanding of self** through identification with central story characters and their experiences.
5. **Understanding the power of language to convey human experiences and emotions** (ranging from happiness to sadness and from love to anger) through narration, exposition, and poetry.
6. **Increasing reading fluency and higher-level thinking** through many experiences with literature.

IMPORTANCE OF THE BASIC LANGUAGE-DEVELOPMENT PRINCIPLES

While literature holds the potential to develop these objectives, you, as teacher, play the critical role in creating the classroom environment necessary to reach them. The discussion that follows will focus on four critical aspects in the development of your literature program: (1) understanding of the reader motivation process; (2) understanding the role of instructional stance in developing reader motivation; (3) selecting and using literature in your classroom; (4) selecting and using effective approaches and strategies for teaching literature; and (5) evaluating children's responses to literature.

THE READER MOTIVATION AND RESPONSE PROCESS

Understanding students' motivational processes in exploring literature is of central importance to understanding reader response in literature instruction. Children's desire to read, the "want to" of reading, involves the development of positive attitudes toward reading and self. Central to reader motivation is the development of each child's positive self-concept as a reader and as a person. As Carl Rogers (1961) observed, the self-concept is not developed independently but is a product of the individual's interaction and integration with other people including parents, siblings, friends, and teachers. One could even question whether our "self" could be developed at all if there were no opportunities to contact and interact with others.

READER IDENTIFICATION

What role, then, can literature experiences play in the development of a favorable and expanded self-concept and to development of reading motivation and response to literature? Literature experiences serve to expand the child's familiarity with "other selves," aspirations of others, and activities of others. The contrasting of self with others, regardless of whether these "others" are real or fictional, can enhance the understanding and development of one's own "self." This first step in building high motivation and self-concept is that of **reader identification** (Ruddell, 1990; Russell, 1970), in which the child is able see his or her self "living through" a literary character. In effect, the reader responds by entering into the story plot with the character and story.

The reader identification process is illustrated when we reflect on our identification with Charlotte, Wilbur, or Templeton in *Charlotte's Web* (White, 1952). We may ask, for example, to what extent each of these characters represents our own "self" and causes us to reflect on our own perception of self, as we enter into and transact with the story. A strong theory base supports the idea that reader identification is a very real psychological event (Mathewson, 1985; Rosenblatt, 1991; Ruddell, 1990; Russell, 1970). Through reader identification children (and all of us) experience what the character experiences in his or her adventures. As the story plot develops and the character is acted upon by external forces and circumstances and responds to them in the story, the child may imagine "self" experiencing

259

similar responses and actions. This may involve encountering major difficulties and disappointments or solving problems.

CATHARSIS

As the story plot unfolds and the character achieves significance, the
child may experience similar emotional responses and reactions. This is the
second step in the reading motivation process and is known as **catharsis**.
Catharsis produces a response of relief, a reduction of the reader's feeling of
tension, and, in effect, a venting of emotions. You may reflect on this process
yourself, by asking, "How did I feel and respond as Charlotte saved Wilbur
from the smokehouse by weaving those mysterious words *SOME PIG!* in her
web?" What emotions did you experience as Charlotte entered the autumn
of her own life?

INSIGHT

Through identification with the central character and through experiencing and solving problems similar to the reader's own, resulting in story
catharsis, the reader begins to achieve a deeper understanding and improved
perception of self. This process constitutes the third step in the readers
response and is known as **insight**. This may be illustrated in our understanding of Charlotte's nurturing role as a mother figure, and Wilbur's com-
placent and childlike approach to life, or in a new understanding of
Templeton's frustrations, as we reexamine and understand our self-perceived role in life and our reactions to the daily frustrations that we
encounter.

The congruence or "fit" of our life experiences with those of a central
story character not only leads to our newly discovered "self" in the literary
work but also serves to develop a more positive attitude toward the literature being read. This may be tested in an introspective way by asking, "Have
I returned to a book such as *Charlotte's Web*, or other favorite books, a second time either for sections that are enlightening or inspiring or to experience the complete work again?" Later in this chapter, our discussion on
strategies and approaches for teaching literature will rely on this process in
developing reader motivation.

THE ROLE OF INSTRUCTIONAL STANCE IN READER MOTIVATION

The development of reader motivation and response through identification, catharsis, and insight is strongly influenced by our instructional stance
or attitude toward literature. Louise Rosenblatt (1991) has identified two

approaches, or stances, from which readers engage text; these stances have very different purposes and exert important influence on the way in which readers respond to text. The first is an **aesthetic stance**, which draws the reader into the text. The second is an **efferent stance**, which shifts the reader's thinking to content and the analytical search for information to be retained.

THE AESTHETIC STANCE

The aesthetic stance involves a *transaction* between the reader and the text as the reader crosses over and enters into "the journey" of the work to experience the story, the event, or the ambiance created by text (Rosenblatt, 1985, 1988). It goes beyond a simple interaction with the text and involves a shared, or reciprocal, process between reader and text. In the transaction, the reader synthesizes "ideas, sensations, feelings, and images from his or her past linguistic, literary, and life experiences" to form a new experience. Rosenblatt calls this process and the new experience the *evocation* (Rosenblatt, 1985).

A critical aspect of teaching literature is to recognize the relationship between the instructional stance a teacher assumes and the outcomes of the literary event. An aesthetic instructional stance focuses attention on reading that leads to identification with story characters, personal interpretation and connection to prior life experiences, and transaction with the story. This stance encourages children to enter into the text and experience "the journey." The following question-prompts illustrate the aesthetic instructional stance:

1. *Evoking past experience:* What do you think the story (or chapter) will be about (after reading title)? What do you think is happening in this illustration (cover or early illustration)? What do you think about this situation and why?

2. *Relating child's experience to the story:* Has anything happened to you that is like _____ (incident in the story)? Tell me about it. If you were _____ (central character in the story), what do you think could happen to you? Have you ever done anything like _____ (central character) did in the story? Tell me about it.

3. *Story discussion:* If you had been _____ (central character) when _____ (critical story event) happened, how would you have felt and reacted? How do you think _____ (central character) felt when _____ (critical event) happened? Why do you think _____ (central character) did _____ (critical event) at that point in the story?

4. *Story identification, catharsis, insight:* Was there someone in the story who did what you would like to do? Who was it? Why would you like to do that? Which character would you choose to be from all those in the story? Why? What do you think happens to _____ (central character) after the story ends?

261

5. *Author discussion:* Imagine for a moment that you are talking to the author of this book; what questions would you ask? What do you think was the author's reason for having the story end the way it did? Do you know any other books written by this author?

THE EFFERENT STANCE

An efferent instructional stance emphasizes very different objectives and focuses attention on reading for content and information to be "taken away" from the text. We frequently rely on the efferent stance in teaching subject-matter content for the purpose of increasing children's knowledge and assisting them in remembering information after reading (Rosenblatt, 1991). Rosenblatt makes the strong point, however, that informational text does not *have* to be read from an efferent stance; in other words, the stance does not inhere in the *text*, but rather in the reader's approach to the text. Informational and expository text may be read from an aesthetic stance; further, informational expository text read from an efferent stance may be read well beyond the literal level of comprehension.

Questions such as the following illustrate the efferent stance.

1. *Evoking past experience:* What do you know about _____ (central character)? What does this picture tell us about _____ (central character)?

2. *Relating child's experience to the text:* Have you ever seen (or touched) a _____ (central topic or concept)? Have you ever traveled to _____ (central topic or concept)? What reaction did you have when this happened?

3. *Information discussion:* How would you describe _____ (central character, topic, or concept)? What idea did you find that was most interesting to you in the book?

4. *Information insight:* What new ideas did you learn from this book? What idea would you like to know more about? How could you find out more about this idea?

5. *Author discussion:* If you could talk to the author, what would you like to ask? Do you know any other books written by this author?

ADOPTING INSTRUCTIONAL STANCES

Aesthetic and efferent stances are both legitimate and useful instructional approaches that are appropriately adopted depending on instructional objectives. If the goal, however, is to encourage active reader response in a literature program and to develop children's positive attitudes toward reading, it is then important that the aesthetic instructional stance be predominant. This means that instead of asking who was in a story and what the main character did to solve his or her problem, teachers ask questions that encourage children to identify and empathize with the character and to enter the story and reading experience fully. For example, aesthetic stance questions would be those such as "How did you feel when that happened?" "Why do you think Max did that?" "What would you have done when Sarah came?" "How do you think Karana got the courage to go on?" as children read *Where the Wild Things Are* (Sendak, 1963), *Sarah, Plain and Tall* (MacLachlan, 1985), and *Island of the Blue Dolphins* (O'Dell, 1960). Our objective with these questions is to evoke an understanding of family, love, loss, courage, loneliness, and friendship, as children identify and transact with characters and events. In the process they gain understanding of "other selves," both imaginary and realistic, and deeper insight into themselves. Certainly, they encounter new information and ideas, but these are not the main focus of the reading event; rather, the focus is on aesthetic response—transacting with and living through the story.

Many classroom teachers (and many publisher-produced reading programs) use the efferent instructional stance as the principal avenue in developing literature experiences. This is evident in the frequent use of the DRA strategy (Directed Reading Activity), discussed in Chapter 4, which emphasizes vocabulary introduction and guided reading questions that focus on specific story content. As noted in our discussion in Chapter 4, often the efferent questions asked in a DRA are not *good* efferent questions; approximately 70 percent of the questions asked in elementary school classrooms are at the literal recall level (Guszak, 1967). Such questions compound the issue with regard to efferent and aesthetic reading: Not only are teacher questions focused almost solely on factual and content knowledge, but they most frequently require children to recall specific bits of literal information. In teaching subject knowledge—science, social studies, for example—the value of literal questioning is dubious; with literature, it is absolutely counter to the goal of appreciation and deep understanding.

Teachers can encourage an aesthetic stance in using literature by helping students transact with text through close identification with central story characters and text topics. To assist in this process, it is important to recognize several types of personal reader motivations that can be used to build each student's identification with a literature selection. Your ability to do this will depend not only on your knowledge of children and their interests but also on your knowledge of children's literature. Your goal will be to connect students with the literary work through discussions that link students' background knowledge, personal interests, and responses to the story characters, plot, language, and format and illustrations (Mathewson, 1976, 1985).

INTERNAL READER MOTIVATION

There are at least six types of **internal reader motivations** that provide insight into why children read, and your awareness of these motivations is important in creating the aesthetic instructional stance you wish to adopt to guide children's approach to text (Mathewson, 1985; Ruddell, 1990; Russell, 1970; Squire, 1989). Most quality pieces of children's literature hold potential for using one or more of the following internal reader motivations.

1. **Problem resolution** motivation allows the student to see himself or herself as successful in problem solving or problem resolution, as was the case with Charlotte in *Charlotte's Web* (White, 1952). Books with high potential for problem resolution identification include *Alexander and the Wind-Up Mouse* (Lionni, 1969), *The Bears on Hemlock Mountain* (Dalgliesh, 1952), *It's Not the End of the World* (Blume, 1972), *Mufaro's Beautiful Daughters* (Steptoe, 1987), and *Island of the Blue Dolphins* (O'Dell, 1960).

2. **Prestige** motivation enables the child entering the story to become a person of significance, and no longer a boy or girl in a world grown too large. The reader becomes an individual with adultlike status who exerts control over his or her surroundings; both Charlotte and Wilbur offer this motivation in their experiences throughout *Charlotte's Web*. Books such as *Henry the Explorer* (Taylor, 1966), *Tico and the Golden Wings* (Lionni, 1964), *Where the Wild Things Are* (Sendak, 1963), and *The Man from Snowy River* (Paterson & Macarthur-Onslow, 1981) provide this type of motivation.

3. **Aesthetic** motivation involves the elevation of an aesthetic sense, ranging from appreciation of the beauty of nature to the enjoyment of family interaction and harmony. This motivation is also present throughout *Charlotte's Web* and in such books as *On the Banks of Plum Creek* (Wilder, 1937), *When I Was Young in the Mountains* (Rylant, 1982), *My Place* (Wheatley & Rawlings, 1987), and *Sarah, Plain and Tall* (MacLachlan, 1985).

4. **Escape** enables the reader to leave the realities of daily existence through involvement with text. This may take the form of identification with a character of similar age and experience or with an explorer or traveler as the child's "self" travels to faraway places doing unfamiliar and exotic things. E. B. White's work draws us into the story to the extent that we release our immediate environment, worries, problems, and concerns as we become one with Charlotte, Wilbur, or Templeton. Books such as *Now We Are Six* (Milne, 1927), *Where the Wild Things Are* (Sendak, 1963), *Ramona Forever* (Cleary, 1984), *Matilda* (Dahl, 1988), and *The Lion, the Witch and the Wardrobe* (Lewis, 1950) provide a wonderful avenue of escape from everyday reality.

5. **Intellectual curiosity** is an important motivation as the curious mind works to untangle mysteries and explore our present and other

worlds. Books such as *The Eleventh Hour: A Curious Mystery* (Base, 1988), *The Great Valentine's Day Balloon Race* (Adams, 1980), *Navajo Coyote Tales* (Morgan, 1988), and *The Train to Bondi Beach* (Hathorn, 1981) lead the reader into discovery and exploration. This motivation is also important as children read and explore information books, ranging from underwater exploration to space.

6. **Understanding self** is a motivation that provides a powerful drive to delve into the self, to understand our personal drives, hopes, and aspirations and those of the people in our immediate life. Books of this type include *Dear Phoebe* (Alexander, 1984), *Alexander and the Terrible, Horrible, No Good, Very Bad Day* (Viorst, 1972), *Millicent and the Wind* (Munsch, 1984) *Tales of a Fourth Grade Nothing* (Blume, 1972), *Everybody Needs a Rock* (Baylor, 1974), and *The Secret Garden* (Burnett, 1911).

Many of the literature selections identified here have potential to fit into more than one internal motivation category. The use of this motivation, however, will be based on the background experience and interests of individual children and your awareness of these experiences and interests. For example, all children experience various daily frustrations at home and school. The motivation of understanding self through identification with story characters who experience similar frustrations and problems can be effectively used with Alexander in *Alexander and the Terrible, Horrible, No Good, Very Bad Day* (Viorst, 1972) and Ramona in *Ramona Quimby, Age 8* (Cleary, 1981).

The use of these internal reader motivations assumes, for the most part, that you will adopt an aesthetic instructional stance which will lead to identification with story characters and story content. Your awareness and use of these internal motivations will encourage children to "step into the story" experience, and live through the story.

EXTERNAL MOTIVATIONS

External reader motivations are also present in literature experiences, including such motivations as *teacher expectations* and *peer recommendations and influence.* The expectations you hold for children have a powerful effect on children's behavior and achievement in school. Your expectations with respect to literacy experiences direct and guide students' responses to text and continuing relationships with books and reading. Peer influence on reading literature selections is likewise important. Children can and do spontaneously share favorite authors and high-interest books such as Judy Blume's *It's Not the End of the World* (1972) and *Then Again, Maybe I Won't* (1971), and C. S. Lewis's *The Lion, the Witch, and the Wardrobe* (1950), but they tend to do so more frequently in a classroom or other environment that encourages such sharing.

Our observations of influential teachers as they introduce literature reveal that they effectively use both internal and external reader motivations. It is important to note, however, that in teaching literature influential teachers place major emphasis on an aesthetic instructional stance, with minor emphasis on teacher expectations and the efferent instructional stance (Ruddell, 1991). The use of the aesthetic stance and children's internal motivations leads to higher interest and active meaning construction on the part of the child.

SELECTING LITERATURE AND ORGANIZING CLASSROOM RESOURCES

We now turn to the important questions of choosing the literature students will read and providing the resources needed to implement your classroom literature program. These issues require careful consideration. Your selection of fiction and nonfiction books must account for the broad range of interests and ability levels of your students. Your resources will need to include a collection of full-length children's trade books (nontextbooks) for your classroom literature and reading center. They will also need to include the school library, and of great importance, the school librarian.

SELECTING CHILDREN'S LITERATURE FOR YOUR CLASSROOM

The selection of a classroom literature collection should be guided by your attempt to provide high-quality books that "fit" the interests, maturity, and reading ability levels of your students. The following criteria, in the form of questions, will be helpful in choosing quality trade books for your classroom.

1. Will the story or information content appeal to the interest and maturity of the students in my classroom?
2. Is the book written at a level that my students can read with ease?
3. Does the book, if fiction, include such features as vivid characterization, compelling illustrations, and high-interest plot, using language and style that will encourage children's identification with the characters and draw them into the story?
4. If nonfiction, does the book develop opportunity to discover new worlds and people, other living things, events, and ideas, to expand the background knowledge and experiences of the children?
5. Do I personally enjoy the selection, and can I "place" the book with one or more of my students using the internal reading motivations discussed above?
6. Is the selection appropriate for my instructional goals, for example, reading for pleasure, or reading to develop important information or content as a part of a unit or theme development?

7. Does the book have potential for a variety of uses in my classroom, such as pure enjoyment, independent reading, or reading aloud?

In creating your classroom collection, you may want or need to rely heavily on your school library. You will also find the public library of value for supplementing your literature collection for short periods of time. Over the years, however, you will want to develop your personal collection of favorite children's books for classroom use. A great variety of children's literature is now available in inexpensive paperback form. You should have multiple copies (six to ten) of a number of paperback titles available for group reading and response.

Keep a continuing list of books that you want to add to your classroom collection as you encounter new books in the school library, the public library, book stores, and book displays at professional conferences. This list should be kept current and complete—author, title, publisher, ISBN (International Standard Book Number—used for ordering a book), and price, if possible—and ready to submit on a purchase order on very short notice. Our experience suggests that when school funds suddenly become available at the end of the school year (or during the summer), the teachers whose completed purchase orders are on the principal's desk are the ones who get the books.

CHILDREN'S READING INTERESTS AND RESPONSES

Not unexpectedly children's reading interests and responses gradually shift across grade levels, and even though time and the world change, children's reading interests at different age and grade levels remain relatively stable.

The Early Grades

In kindergarten and grades one and two, children like to read picture books, picture storybooks, predictable books, fairy tales, folktales, modern fantasy, and humor. These books frequently center on animals, nature, family, and child characters of the children's ages (Consuelo, 1967; Monson & Sebesta, 1991; Nelson, 1966). At this level, the children are also interested in general-information-type materials, including history, and science information books. In grades three and four, children's interest in nature and animals continues, but strong interest develops in adventure stories that include personal experiences familiar to the children (Graham, 1986).

Children respond to literature in the primary grades by focusing on the story action as a pattern of events, rather than on such features as point of view or the theme of the story (Applebee, 1978). First- and some second-grade children favor retelling and brief story synopsis with global-type evaluation responses, such as "It's good." When asked to explain why they like or dislike a story, their responses usually involve a single incident such as "I liked it because the troll fell in the water" (Applebee, 1978). Third-graders tend to use special categories for evaluating a story, such as "dreary" or "interesting" (Martinez & Roser, 1991).

THE INTERMEDIATE GRADES

In grades four through six, children develop a strong interest in narrative adventure and fantasy. Informational-type reading ranges from ocean and space topics to computers and sports (Burgess, 1985). You will find that reading preferences for boys and girls start to differ somewhat during these grades. Boys show a stronger preference for topics related to mystery and nonfiction, while girls prefer animal stories, westerns, fairy tales, and realistic fiction (Landy, 1977; Lynch-Brown, 1977; Row, 1968; Shores, 1954; Wolfson, Manning, & Manning, 1984). At these grade levels, children's reading interest in specific books is strongly influenced by peer sharing and peer recommendations.

Children's responses to stories at the intermediate grades become more elaborated and complex. They tend to use a more detailed synopsis and retelling in story response discussion than is the case at the primary grades. They have a more advanced sense of narrative, which includes expectations of characters, story setting, and story goals. They also demonstrate growing concern for analyzing the structures of stories and creating generalizations about story meaning. By grade six, children begin to provide tentative explanations of symbolic and thematic features of stories (Applebee, 1973; Cullinan, Harwood, & Galda, 1983).

Research on children's interests across the grades reveals that at all levels they prefer books that have well-developed characterization in which characters confront problems and seek solutions, and plots that focus on characters with different points of view (Abrahamson, 1979; Abrahamson & Shannon, 1983; Ingham, 1982). Children also prefer books that provide for predictability, security, and, perhaps not surprisingly, a happy ending (Ingham, 1982).

A BRIEF OVERVIEW OF TYPES OF CHILDREN'S LITERATURE

As you select children's literature for your classroom, you will want a simple organizational system to help you keep track of the books you select and to ensure that you account for a wide range of books in your selection process. It will also be of value in enlisting the help of your librarian and other resources in identifying specific books.

Various classification systems have been used for children's literature, depending on the instructional need or focus, including reading ability levels, subject areas, and social themes. The most general organizational system used in school libraries is shown in Table 6-1. The examples shown will assist you in defining the categories.

FICTION

REALISM—MIRRORS REALITY

1. **Modern**, e.g., *The Boy Who Wouldn't Say His Name; When I Was Young in the Mountains; Millicent and the Wind; Ramona Quimby,* **Age 8**; *A Pair of Red Clogs; Good-Bye to Budapest; Where the Red Fern Grows.*

2. **Historical**, e.g., *Sarah, Plain and Tall; Little House on the Prairie; Johnny Tremain; Ishi, Last of His Tribe; Island of the Blue Dolphins.*

FANTASY—FREE FROM BONDS IMPOSED BY EXISTENCE

1. **Modern**, e.g., *Where the Wild Things Are; Danny and the Dinosaur; Flossie & the Fox; Charlotte's Web; The Little Prince; Charlie and the Chocolate Factory; The Lion, the Witch, and the Wardrobe.*

2. **Traditional**, e.g., *Mufaro's Beautiful Daughters; Stories to Solve: Folktales from Around the World; The People Could Fly* **(folktale)**; *Cinderella; Puss in Boots* **(fairy tale)**; *Once a Mouse; North Wind and the Sun* **(fable)**; *The White Archer; Myths of the World* **(myths)**; *Stone Soup; Legend of the Milky Way* **(legend)**.

NONFICTION

1. **Biography/Autobiography**—detailed account of a specific life, e.g., *And Then What Happened, Paul Revere?; Anne Frank: The Diary of a Young Girl.*

2. **Informational**—exploration of new and interesting concepts and ideas, e.g., *I Like Caterpillars; The Sense of Wonder; Sharks; Why Do Volcanoes Erupt?*

3. **Poetry**—anthologies and single-author books of rhymes, verse, and songs, e.g., *The Real Mother Goose; Where the Sidewalk Ends; A Child's Garden of Verse.*

TABLE 6-1

Classifying Children's Books for Easy Reference

One value of this classification system is that it provides a sense of organization to help familiarize you with a wide range of children's literature. You can also acquire one or more general references that provides brief descriptions of children's books. Such easy-to-use references not only provide general categories but also themes and topics useful in matching books to children's interests, ranging from "Grandparents" to "Growing Up" and from "Holidays" to "Humor." Examples of such references are:

Betsy Hearne (1990). *Choosing Books for Children.* New York: Dell.

Kids' Favorite Books (1992). Newark, DE: International Reading Association.

Sharon Dreyer (1985). *The Bookfinder: When Kids Need Books.* Circle Pines, MN: American Guidance Service.

Charlotte Huck (1979). *Children's Literature in the Elementary School,* Third Edition. New York: Holt.

Eden Ross Lipson (1988). *The New York Times Parent's Guide to the Best Books for Children.* New York: Times Books.

Dianne L. Monson (1985). *Adventuring with Books, 1985: A Booklist for Pre-K–Grade 6.* Urbana, IL: National Council of Teachers of English.

Jim Trelease (1989). *The New Read-Aloud Handbook.* New York: Penguin.

The librarian at your school or in the nearby public library can be of great help in your book selection process. Also, don't forget to seek guidance from the children's book-award lists.

SPECIAL BOOK CATEGORIES

Picture and Picture Storybooks

Picture books and picture storybooks can also be classified according to our system. Picture storybooks use pictures alone, or pictures and text, to tell the story; however, characterization, setting, and plot would be incomplete without the pictures. These books most commonly deal with topics that would be considered modern fantasy or are realistic in nature. Stories using only pictures are illustrated by *Rosie's Walk* (Hutchins, 1968), *A Boy, a Dog, and a Frog* (Mayer, 1967), and *Sunshine* (Ormerod, 1981). Examples of picture storybooks, using both picture and print, include *Brown Bear, Brown Bear, What Do You See?* (Martin, 1983), *One Fine Day* (Hogrogian, 1971), and *Corduroy* (Freeman, 1968). The importance of pictures in these books is clearly evident, as for example when the text states, "He waited," while the picture portrays the excitement, fear, or loneliness intended by the author.

As discussed in Chapter 3, informational-type picture books may be used to introduce new concepts, such as the alphabet or numbers, e.g., *Anno's Alphabet* (Anno, 1974), *Jambo Means Hello: Swahili Alphabet Book* (Feelings, 1974), and *Brian Wildsmith's 1, 2, 3* (Wildsmith, 1965), or the new ideas and concepts as presented in *Dinosaurs* (Gibbons, 1985) and *Is It Larger? Is it Smaller?* (Hoban, 1985).

Poetry

As you familiarize yourself with the children's books available in your classroom and library, be sure that you do not overlook poetry. Think for a moment about poetry you enjoyed in your own childhood. While fantasy throws off the constraints of realism, poetry allows ideas just to be. Thoughts, images, and feelings can be presented as elaborately, briefly, simply, or abstractly as desired. Through *content*, poetry can reach out to young children as they enjoy humor and animal adventures as well as their most vital interest which is *me*. A poem like John Ciardi's "And off He Went Just as Proud as You Please," which captures our preference for our own name, is always enjoyable. Dorothy Aldis's "Everybody Says" suggests another way we can look at ourselves as individuals. For the older child, identification with strong character traits can be an important avenue to growth and understanding of self as illustrated in Leonard Clark's "Charles."

Imagery is the second gift of poetry. While prose can also create imagery for the reader, poetry often does so more powerfully. A classic example is Carl Sandburg's "Fog." Children's imaginations can be easily aroused with a question such as "What color do you think of for the day Monday?" or "What color do you think of when you picture a fierce wind blowing?" Mary O'Neill evokes these and many other images in the poem "Hailstones and Halibut Bones."

And finally, *rhythm* plays an important role in poetry's contribution to children. Regardless of age, we respond to a pulsating beat. The work of A. A. Milne captures a special beat and rhythm for very young children in "Happiness"; in "Disobedience" the child exerts a certain amount of control over Mother, using a satisfying rhythm. Sightly older children respond to the rhythm and humor in "The King's Breakfast."

Other forms of poetry that deserve consideration include narrative poetry, which tells a story; lyric poetry, written in a rhythmic style like a song; and free verse, which is not governed by the rules of rhyme or rhythm. Children will also enjoy special poetic forms such as haiku, which creates sudden and sparkling imagery. The limerick is, of course, devoted to nonsense humor, and your students will delight in the many works of Edward Lear.

A must for your classroom is a poetry anthology from which you can read and share poems with your children on a frequent basis. Excellent examples of such anthologies are:

Stephen Dunning, Edward Luders, and Hugh Smith (Eds.) (1967). *Reflections on a Gift of Watermelon Pickle.* New York: Lothrop, Lee & Shepard.

Kenneth Koch and Kate Farrell (1985). *Talking to the Sun: An Illustrated Anthology of Poems for Young People.* New York: Holt.

Lee Bennett Hopkins (1987). *Pass the Poetry Please.* New York: Harper.

Nancy Larrick and Wendy Lamb (1991). *To Ride a Butterfly.* New York: Bantam.

Again, you will find your school librarian of help in identifying such poetry anthologies.

Rhymes and Jingles

Rhymes and jingles, which are separate from poetry in the formal literary sense, represent a part of folklore. These range from Mother Goose rhymes to Gelett Burgess's "Purple Cow." Older readers will be challenged by the tongue-twister qualities of George Strong's "The Modern Hiawatha." Like folktales, many rhymes and jingles reflect the culture from which they come. A wonderful multicultural collection of these is *Skipping Around the World* by Francelia Butler (1989). Helping children record some of their jump rope and clapping-game rhymes can serve several purposes. It legitimizes and gives recognition to a kind of "poetry" they already know. It offers opportunities for comparison of different versions of the same rhyme pattern, which can be used as a model for new rhymes to be created.

ORGANIZING THE CLASSROOM READING CENTER

As your create your center, think again about the literature goals and objectives presented earlier in this chapter. Uppermost in your mind should be creating a center that will contribute to your instructional goals—and to children's voluntary reading—by providing a variety of high-interest books in an attractive physical environment that promotes individual and small group reading and response (Morrow, 1991).

In Chapter 3, we discussed the creation of a special book and story sharing center in the classroom. You may want to reread that discussion now as you consider how you will house your classroom literature collection to make it most usable and attractive. The following suggestions extend and add to the recommendations we made in Chapter 3:

1. Select an easily accessible area that can be sectioned off by using movable or portable partitions. The area should be large enough to be used comfortably by five or six students. A corner of your classroom will work well for the center by providing two walls for visual displays.

2. Place colorful posters related to books, reading, or art on one wall of the center. Attractive posters can be obtained from the Children's Book Council (67 Irving Place, New York, NY 10003) and the American Library Association (50 East Huron Street, Chicago, IL 60611).

3. Use the center's bulletin board to display children's literature-related art and written responses. These may take the form of drawings of a favorite story character or a key story event, individually designed book "advertisements," or letters to book authors.

4. Provide a cassette player or recorder, headphones, and recorded stories together with the associated books for listening and reading.

5. Develop a collection of children's books representing a wide range of literary experiences at different reading levels, using the classification categories presented in Table 6-1. Call on your school library and the public library to help in this effort. Set a goal of from five to eight books per child for the book collection (Huck, 1976).

6. Add magazines, newspapers, television guides, and other reading materials that you and your children use and read daily.

7. Add books children wrote, illustrated, and published to your reading center.

As you develop your reading center, you will need to devote extra time, energy, and thought to your selection and collection of children's books. The most critical element will be the identification of a wide range of fiction, nonfiction, informational, and poetry books that fit the reading interests and reading levels of your children. Keep in mind the six internal reader motivations discussed earlier in this chapter as you provide for individual reader motivations in your literature center collection.

You should work toward a good collection of children's literature that will remain in your classroom. Probably, you will find that some children's books are already present in your classroom at the beginning of the school year. Almost certainly, though, you will want to expand this collection. Some ways to do this include getting contributions from parents, sponsoring (or persuading parents to sponsor) fund-raisers for book purchase, and, if you are fortunate, drawing on school monies designated for the purchase of children's literature. Many excellent children's books are now available in paperback form at a low price. You should encourage children to enroll in a paperback book club. This will start a personal book collection for each child, which may also be shared with other children in the class over the year.

Favorite Children's Books

The list of children's books in Table 6-2 is based on a recent literature survey we conducted of favorite books used by elementary teachers and their students. The most frequently selected books at each grade are identified and are suggestive of the range of titles that you will want to include in your literature center collection. *Books We Love Best* (Bay Area Kids, 1991) is a collection of book reviews written by children.

ENLISTING HELP FROM THE LIBRARIAN AND THE SCHOOL LIBRARY

As we pointed out in Chapter 3, your school librarian and the school library represent two very important resources for expanding your classroom

GRADE LEVEL	BOOK TITLES
Kindergarten	*Alligators All Around: An Alphabet* (Sendak); *Bringing the Rain to Kapiti Plain: A Nandi Tale* (Verna); *Cinderella* (Perrault); *Mother Goose: A Treasury of Best-loved Rhymes* (Piper); *Peter and the North Wind* (Littledale); *The Very Hungry Caterpillar* (Carle); *Why Mosquitoes Buzz in People's Ears* (Aardema).
Grade 1	*Anansi the Spider: A Tale from the Ashanti* (McDermott); *Frog and Toad* (Lobel); *Little Bear* (Minarik); *Mr. Rabbit and the Lovely Present* (Zolotow); *Rosie's Walk* (Hutchins); *The Three Little Pigs* (Galdone); *The Very Busy Spider* (Carle).
Grade 2	*The House on East 88th Street* (Waber); *Miss Nelson Is Missing!* (Allard); *Miss Rumphius* (Cooney); *Owl Moon* (Yolen); *The Story of Ferdinand* (Leaf); *A Taste of Blackberries* (Smith); *Where the Wild Things Are* (Sendak).
Grade 3	*Charlie and the Chocolate Factory* (Dahl); *The Case of the Elevator Duck* (Berends); *The Hundred Dresses* (Estes); *Mufaro's Beautiful Daughters* (Steptoe); *Ramona Quimby, Age 8* (Cleary); *The Story of Jumping Mouse* (Steptoe); *Superfudge* (Blume).
Grade 4	*Bridge to Terabithia* (Patterson); *Dear Mr. Henshaw* (Cleary); *In the Year of the Boar and Jackie Robinson* (Lord); *Island of the Blue Dolphins* (O'Dell); *Mrs. Frisby and the Rats of NIMH* (O'Brien); *Sarah, Plain and Tall* (MacLachlan); *The Velveteen Rabbit* (Williams).
Grade 5	*The Dark Is Rising* (Cooper); *The Indian in the Cupboard* (Banks); *Johnny Tremain* (Forbes); *My Side of the Mountain* (George); *Robin Hood—Prince of Outlaws* (Miles); *The White Mountains* (Christopher); *Witch of Blackbird Pond* (Speare).
Grade 6	*Are You There, God? It's Me, Margaret* (Blume); *Hatchet* (Paulsen); *James and the Giant Peach* (Dahl); *The Lion, the Witch, and the Wardrobe* (Lewis); *Mrs. Frisby and the Rats of NIMH* (O'Brien); *The Secret Garden* (Burnett); *Where the Red Fern Grows* (Rawls).

TABLE 6-2

Teachers' Favorite Books for the Classroom Reading Center

book collection. The librarian can be a useful and knowledgeable resource not only for you but for your children as well. Arrange a tour of the library early in the school year to introduce your children to the library and to help them become familiar with book location and checkout procedures. Your working relationship with the librarian becomes very important as you identify groups of books you may wish to check out in developing thematic units on topics ranging from *families* and *friendship* in the primary grades to *Western expansion* or *space exploration* at the intermediate levels.

You will also want to arrange for the checkout of thirty to forty books for your literature center, books that cover a broad range of interests and reading levels and include fiction as well as informational nonfiction. Arrange with the librarian to keep these books in your classroom from two to four weeks. Then exchange them for new titles. Don't forget the public library in your area.

Many school librarians are skilled in the art of storytelling or are knowledgeable about storytellers who are willing to visit your classroom. Or the librarian may wish to have your class visit the library for the storytelling experience. In such a case, ask the librarian to have follow-up literature available for checkout and later use in your classroom.

HELPING CHILDREN CHOOSE BOOKS INDEPENDENTLY

Children's interest in books is a major factor in book selection. This will become evident as they identify books they would like to read in the reading center or the school library. Sometimes children are not very good at choosing books within their comfortable reading range and are averse to reading books the teacher recommends. Jeanette Veatch (1968) recommends a simple technique to help such children identify books they can read with relative ease. You can easily teach this "five-finger test" to your children:

1. Choose a book you think will be of interest.
2. Open the book to a page that is largely print.
3. Start reading from the top of the page, and each time you run into a word you don't know, put up a finger. A word you don't know is a word you can't say, or a word for which you don't know the meaning. If the word is the name of a person or place, you don't have to count it.
4. Read to the end of the page and see how many fingers you have up.
5. Decide how hard the book is for you. If you have
   zero to one fingers up the book is *easy*,
   two to five fingers up the book is *medium*,
   six or more fingers up the book is a *challenge*.
6. If the book is an easy book or a challenge book, it can still be a good choice for you. It is important, however, that you select a medium book for your independent reading.

This simple technique provides a general idea of difficulty and gives children an independent way to determine the readability of a book.

DESIGNING A BOOK CHECKOUT SYSTEM

To encourage independent reading at home and during school, you will need to devise a simple book checkout system for your literature and reading center. In the primary grades, the children may bring a self-selected book to you at a specified daily checkout time. This time might occur immediately after recess or lunch, for example. Using a 3- by 5-inch card, just note the date, the child's name, and the book title, and file the card under the child's name. Once this procedure is established (over a three- or four-week period), most children will be able to make their own checkout cards, copying the date from the chalkboard, and the book title from the book, and will be able to file the card under their own names in the checkout box. At the upper primary and intermediate grades, you may wish to amend the process by having cards filed under the book author's name.

Your reading center can play an important role in helping children develop positive attitudes toward literature, new background knowledge, and reading enjoyment. We cannot overstress the paramount importance of these positive attitudes. If they are firmly established, they will affect the individuals' entire life.

INSTRUCTIONAL STRATEGIES FOR TEACHING LITERATURE

We now turn to the development of a range of instructional strategies that are valuable in using literature and reader response to enhance children's positive attitudes and active comprehension. The strategies selected are designed to create high reading interest, motivation, and active comprehension. As each strategy is developed, reflect on the importance of the *reading response process* (identification, catharsis, and insight), the *instructional stance used* (aesthetic or efferent), and the role of students' *internal reading motivations*, as discussed earlier in this chapter. To use the reader response process, stance, and motivations in your teaching, you will need to account for four questions in your instruction:

1. What are the key interests and motivations of my children based on what I know about them and have observed in my classroom?

2. Based on these interests, what literature selections would hold high appeal and interest for them?

3. What role do the internal reading motivations (problem resolution, prestige, aesthetic, escape, intellectual curiosity, and understanding self) play in building reader identification and interest in a particular literature selection?

4. What instructional strategy or strategies will be most effective in developing the literature experience?

READING ALOUD: STORY AND POETRY SHARING

Reading literature and poetry aloud to children is an important way to increase children's enjoyment in literature and to provide opportunity for active comprehension and reader response. Reading aloud is a traditional classroom practice appropriate for all grades. It serves as an unparalleled opportunity for you to model fluent oral reading and for children to observe your active involvement and enjoyment in reading. A major value of reading aloud is its flexibility. Not only does it cross grade levels, but it also serves a variety of different instructional purposes, varying from pure enjoyment of the beauty of language to making picture and story predictions (Trelease, 1989; Vandergrift, 1965).

When and What to Read Aloud

Reading aloud works best if you can schedule regular and specific times each day for it, ranging from five to fifteen minutes, depending on your purpose. Some teachers schedule reading aloud at the beginning of the school day, and at various reentry points during the day (after recess and lunch, for example) to establish a mood and create a sense of classroom unity while sharing quality literature. Other teachers use the reading-aloud experience as a regular part of initiating and developing a literature, social studies, or science unit of study. Whatever your choices, the best rule of thumb we can give you is to read aloud to your students as often as you can every day, share poetry at every opportunity, and every read-aloud experience need not be preplanned—read aloud spontaneously on many occasions.

The reading-aloud experience may be as self-contained as sharing a poetry selection, e.g., "Hailstones and Halibut Bones," sharing a picture storybook, e.g., *Where the Wild Things Are* (Sendak, 1963), or reading the beginning paragraphs of a new book as an introduction of it to your children, e.g., *Island of the Blue Dolphins* (O'Dell, 1960). The reading-aloud experience may also be an extended and ongoing one as you present serial installments of a specially selected book over several weeks. Good candidates for extended reading aloud are *Ramona Quimby, Age 8* (Cleary, 1981) and *Charlotte's Web* (White, 1952) in the primary grades, or *From the Mixed-Up Files of Mrs. Basil E. Frankweiler* (Konigsburg, 1967) and *The Lion, the Witch, and the Wardrobe* (Lewis, 1950), at the intermediate-grade levels.

Preparing to Read Aloud

Our comments about spontaneous reading notwithstanding, reading aloud deserves some amount of thought and preparation on your part. Identify the piece of literature or poetry you want to read aloud. Select a reading that you like and that you can reasonably expect children will like as well. You may wish to involve the children in helping you select the books and poetry for reading aloud. Prepare for the reading by becoming thoroughly familiar with the work. Read the story silently and familiarize yourself with the characters, the setting, the events in the plot, and the story outcome; practice reading poetry aloud to capture the rhythm and sounds of words. Identify the mood and feeling tone you wish to create. Read at least a part of narrative works orally, to gain a sense of voice quality and timing that will assist you in creating the appropriate story mood.

Prepare your children for the story or poem with a brief background as to why you have selected it. You may also wish to share a bit of information on the author. Make sure your children are as comfortable as possible. If illustrations are important to the story, make sure that the children can see the pictures from their seated location. Some teachers find that a story-reading atmosphere is effectively established by lighting a candle or by gently ringing a special story-reading bell.

When you read, use appropriate voice and intonation variation to establish characters, story setting, and plot development. Let your imagination and sense of story help create and sharpen these aspects of your oral reading. Use a reading pace that matches your own visualization of the story. Let your enthusiasm for the story be evident in your reading. Expect minor distractions when reading to the total class and even when reading to small groups. Some children will enter into the story with total concentration, but others like to doodle and draw or may comment on story events and whisper to other children. Such comments may be received and acknowledged with a slight nod and a smile, thus drawing a specific child back into the group. The nod and smile also indicate that you too are enjoying the story. Use children's interest and response to the story as a barometer to indicate if the content and the length of the story, chapter, or poem are appropriate.

Decide on the nature of reader response you desire at the conclusion of the story, chapter, or poem. This may range from discussion of favorite characters and plot to sharing of personal experiences and insights obtained from the story. Response groups and response journals, as discussed below, may also be effectively used at the read-aloud conclusion. If you are reading a book, each chapter may provide a natural break, or you can simply conclude a reading with a predicting question, such as "What do you think will happen next? Why do you think that?" At the next reading, a brief synopsis of what has gone before will help to reestablish the story schema for your children. Keep in mind that an important part of the

The Storyteller Arrives!

oral reading experience is the enjoyment of the story as children visualize story characters, setting, and the unfolding of the story plot.

Reading stories and poetry aloud can provide a high level of interest, pleasure, modeling, and active thinking for your children. An excellent reference to further assist you in read-aloud literature is Jim Trelease's *The New Read-Aloud Handbook* (1989). This book contains a variety of suggestions for parents and teachers and has an excellent annotated bibliography of children's books. Your knowledge of children's books will support you mightily in this.

STORYTELLING

The most natural and personal means of conveying a story is simply to tell it. Storytelling can be effectively used at all elementary grade levels and is a way that you can give of yourself and share a personal appreciation for literature using stories you especially like. Leland Jacobs, a wonderful storyteller himself, emphasized that a good storyteller enters into the story, lives in it, and in effect loses self in the story (Jacobs, 1965). Most of us have been held spellbound by stories told by grandparents, aunts or uncles, a family friend, a former teacher, or by a storyteller around a campfire. Reflection on these experiences will reveal that the storyteller used a clear sense of characterization and plot, language precision designed to create sharp visual images, and a sense of timing and pacing as the story unfolded.

Preparing for Storytelling

As is the case in story reading, the storyteller must carefully prepare for the story presentation. Begin by identifying the story you want to tell and the purpose of the storytelling experience. Choose a story that you like and that you think your students will also like. The story should have a plot that is compact and that establishes the central story problem early. The setting should be sufficiently detailed to enable the listener to create clear mental images. The characters should be limited to only a few, and their features and behavior should be established early, to provide easy identification and to help children enter into the story. The story resolution should hold the listeners until the very end (Jacobs, 1965).

Folktales such as *The Three Little Pigs* or *Three Billy Goats Gruff* contain these characteristics. There is also a sense of predictability and story rhythm, which allows the listener to participate in the telling, as illustrated in "He huffed, and he puffed, and . . ." Other appropriate story forms include cumulative tales such as *Henny-Penny* (Galdone, 1968) and *One Fine Day* (Hogrogian, 1971). An excellent collection of African-American folktales, *The People Could Fly*, (Hamilton, 1985) is also available. Fairy tales, myths, and legends also provide a wide array of stories for classroom telling. And don't forget classic children's stories with storytelling potential. These will range from *Make Way for Ducklings* (McCloskey, 1941) to *Little Toot* (Gramatky, 1939).

Prepare to tell your story by reading it carefully and visualizing its pattern. How will you develop the setting and the characters? How does the beginning of the story develop, and how does the plot unfold? How will you end the story? Next, decide whether you will commit the story to memory or tell it in your own words using key phrases, rhymes, or appealing language descriptions used by the author. Finally, you will need to decide how you will introduce the story. This may be as simple as "This is a story about …" or it may need to be a more detailed introduction, which establishes the source of the story and how it came about. Finally, decide on what type of reader response you wish to have at the conclusion of the story.

Tell the story to your students using appropriate voice and intonation patterns that create the story mood. Eye contact and sensitivity to group response are important as the story develops and will provide important clues to gauge children's interest and motivation. During the presentation, you may find that some children will ask about the meaning of an unknown word, make observations, and orally anticipate what is going to happen. It is best to answer these questions and comments by slightly altering your story, thus showing that you are responding to their concerns. Build the story to its conclusion as you complete your presentation.

Involve children in your planned reader response. This response may simply consist of children's observations about the story and how the characters or plot connect to their own experiences or in telling what parts of the story they enjoyed most and why. The story may also be used as the basis for capturing their thoughts in their response journals or encouraging some students to pursue similar stories in independent reading.

Resources for Storytelling

Storytelling workshops are often sponsored by community groups and can be of great value in helping you develop this special ability. A number of storytelling organizations, classes, and conferences are now available, and at literacy conferences sponsored by professional organizations (the International Reading Association and National Council of Teachers of English) and their affiliates, storytelling sessions are common. Also keep in mind community storytellers who may be available to visit in your classroom. You will find the following resources of value as you select and refine storytelling for your classroom:

Leland B. Jacobs (1965). *Using Literature with Young Children.* New York: Teachers College Press.

Anne Pellowski (1987). *The Family Story-Telling Handbook: How to Use Stories, Anecdotes, Rhymes, Handkerchiefs, Paper, and Other Objects to Enrich Your Family Traditions.* New York: Macmillan.

HOW TO DO . . . .

STORYTELLING

1. Select the story you wish to tell; check for strong plot lines and a manageable number of characters.

2. Read the story over a number of times, visualizing its pattern.

3. Look for repeated language patterns and rhythms.

4. Block the story into parts for learning. Decide what, if any, language from the story you wish to include in your presentation.

5. Decide how you will introduce the story, including any environmental arrangements.

6. Decide what, if any, response you want from the children after the storytelling event.

7. Continue rereading the story and begin practicing your own presentation.

8. Practice telling the story aloud until you feel comfortable and confident.

9. Tell your story to your students.

LITERATURE RESPONSE JOURNALS

We have emphasized the importance of discussions that provide opportunity for children to respond to literature and to share their ideas and reactions. (For more information about reading response groups, see Chapters 9, 12, and 13. We will focus on individual literature in this discussion.) Opportunities for literature response can also be provided through Literature Response Journals writing. A Literature Response Journal is a place in which students record their responses to what they read, providing opportunity for the teacher to write back to them. Literature Response Journals can be effectively used from the primary grades, as children begin to record ideas in picture and written form, through the intermediate grades. A major advantage of Literature Response Journal writing is the permanent nature of the written response. Such writing enables students not only to share and record ideas but also to revisit responses periodically to reflect on, extend, and refine their ideas and thinking.

The Literature Response Journal has been described as "a sourcebook, a repository for wanderings and wonderings, speculations, questionings . . . a place to explore thoughts, discover reactions, let the mind ramble—in effect, a place to make room for the unexpected" (Flitterman-King, 1988). It is also, simultaneously, a way for teachers to gain insight into children's meaning construction process and the way in which they actively engage in responding to literature.

Using Literature Response Journals

To initiate Literature Response Journals, you will need to purchase or have children bring folders or spiral or three-ring notebooks to serve as the journals themselves. Introduce literature journals by establishing the purpose and response atmosphere for journal writing. Nancy Atwell (1984) aptly describes this initiation process:

> This folder (or response journal) is a place for you and me to talk about books, reading, authors, and writing. You're to write letters to me, and I'll write letters back to you.
>
> In your letters to me, talk with me about what you've read. Tell me what you thought and felt and why. Tell me what you liked and didn't like and why. Tell me what these books meant to you and said to you. Ask me questions or for help, and write back to me about my ideas, feelings, and questions.

This introduction assumes an aesthetic instructional stance, discussed earlier in this chapter, and clearly establishes the view that students' personal feelings and ideas will be valued in the journal entries. In addition, there is a clear indication that the teacher and student will react to each other's responses and exchange ideas in the response journal.

Periodically provide several question prompts that will help children initiate their journal responses. These prompts should be open-ended in nature and rely on the higher levels of thinking (interpretive, applicative, and, especially, transactive) discussed in Chapter 4. Ten such prompts (for use with fiction) are listed below (Farnan, 1992):

1. Who was your favorite character? Why?
2. Which character did you dislike most? Why?
3. Are you like any character in the story? Explain.
4. If you could be any character, who would you be? Explain.
5. What does this story remind you of in your life?
6. What kind of person do you think the author of this story is?
7. How do you respond to this story so far?
8. Do you share any feelings of the characters in the story? Explain.
9. What is the most important word, phrase, or paragraph in the story? Explain.
10. If you were a teacher, would you want your students to read this story? Tell why.

Note that these prompts encourage the reader to respond by constructing meanings based on personal interaction and transaction with the text. A similar list of prompts can be created for use with nonfiction, information-content books. Prompts like these are equally appropriate for literature response discussions. You may wish to design a literature response chart using several of these prompts to assist your children in discussions and journal writing. It is very important, however, that the prompts *not* be used in a formulaic manner. Each child should be able to select any one or more of the prompts in the initial development of literature response writing.

Respond to your students' Literature Response Journal writing on a regular basis. Your written response should be for the purpose of exchanging ideas and thoughts with children about the literature, *not* for the correction of spelling and criticism of grammar. It is important that you search for positive features in children's responses but also that you be honest when ideas are not understood. Donald Graves (1990) comments that early in this process children may write neutral accounts and summaries of what they read, and only later begin to write true response in which they talk about the effect of the literature on their lives or connect ideas from text to insights or ideas they have. He marvels at how rich such true response is (and how different it is from neutral accounts), often sustaining dialogue between teacher and students on a single topic for several weeks. Approach this response effort in a positive vein as you exchange ideas with each young reader.

Patterns of Literature Response

As children become comfortable in using the response journals, you will find individual response modes developing. Hancock (1992) has identified

283

five patterns in children's response journals at the sixth-grade level. These are: (1) character interaction (talks to or offers advice to characters); (2) character empathy (reacts to emotions expressed by characters); (3) prediction and validation (expresses belief about what will happen and confirms or denies original thinking); (4) personal experiences (connects own life experience to main characters of story events); and (5) philosophical reflections (reveals personal values and convictions). You may wish to comment on patterns you observe in your children's writing and encourage them to try other patterns of response.

Encourage your students to reread their response journals frequently and search for insight into their own literature response patterns. For example, you may ask "How do you react to the main character in you favorite stories? Do you react in the same way and if so, why? What other ways could you respond to the main character?" "How do you connect your own personal experiences to the story characters and plot?" "What do you reveal about yourself as you respond to key characters and story events?" Discuss these insights with your students and encourage optional response patterns if only one response pattern seems to dominate.

As children become experienced using literature journals consider encouraging them to share journal responses with a partner. They may want to have a separate peer-response journal, or incorporate their partner dialogue into a three-way exchange that includes your responses as well. Prepare children in advance, however, for the highly confidential nature of journal exchange. Children must be willing to protect the privacy and the confidential nature of each person's response, and must understand that everyone has the right to decline an invitation to do peer-journaling. In all likelihood you will find that your children respond very positively to Literature Response Journals. You may also be surprised at the insights you gain into their meaning construction and literature response processes.

BOOK REPORTS OR SHARING RESPONSES ABOUT BOOKS

Book reports have been used by teachers over the years as a way of ensuring that children read books. This is still the case in many classrooms. Most of us, in our elementary school years, experienced the dreaded Book Report Due Day. The night before Due Day, we finished reading, or possibly skimming, the book in order to do the report. This often involved writing the name of the author, the book title, and in the intermediate grades the publisher and copyright date, at the top of the page, followed by a detailed summary of the book. Enterprising students learned how to mine book-jacket text in creating summaries. Some students didn't even bother to skim the book and edit book-jacket blurbs; they lifted blurbs verbatim and turned them in—early experiences in plagiarism. Reports were turned in to our teacher and returned to us the next week with red-lined punctuation, spelling, and grammar corrections. Little if any comment was made on any ideas about the book that we might have inserted in the report; this is understandable, since very few personal comments were made.

Most children abhor book reports, and rightly so. Book reports are the epitome of teaching as inquisition (Durkin, 1978–1979)—in which children must "prove" they have consumed text—and the antithesis of what we should be doing with books in school. What we should be doing is engaging in "grand conversations" (Eeds & Wells, 1989) about books children have read and enjoyed. We simply must shift from forcing children to report on books for the express purpose of proving that the books were being read, to listening to children's ideas and responses to books that are shared in a variety of social settings where the reader becomes the informed expert.

As an alternative to traditional book reports, consider other ways for children to share their reading interests and responses. Start by making sure that children are reading books they like and can read comfortably. Clarify with the children that the purpose of book sharing is just that—to share their ideas and responses about books they have read with others. Then design book-sharing activity options that actively involve children through oral discussions, written discussions, and art work. Nine suggestions for book-sharing activities follow:

1. **Partner book sharing**—based on children's Literature Response Journals, which may involve targeted sharing, for example sharing responses to only the first chapter of the book to pique new reader interest.

2. **Small-group book sharing**—with three or four children, in which each child brings a favorite book and describes a favorite character or part of the book.

3. **Individual or partner letters to the book author or illustrator**—for the purpose of sharing enjoyment of a book character, or the entire book, or asking a question about a specific character, or questions about how the book was written and illustrated.

4. **Individual or partner illustrations of a favorite character from a favorite book**—for a bulletin-board display entitled "My Favorite Book Character."

5. **Individual, partner, or small-group book advertisement**—using book characters and key story event to "sell" the book to other children (if you have not read the delightfully funny scene of Ramona's book report commercial in *Ramona Quimby, Age 8* [Cleary, 1981] we recommend that you do—as soon as possible). Prepare billboard advertisements for a bulletin-board display entitled "Will You Buy It?"

6. **A partner or small-group "Television Book Review Panel"**—prepare to discuss "pros" and "cons" of two of their most favorite and two least favorite books.

7. **Individual- or partner-designed "Mystery Book Jacket"**—with clues to story in artwork or written form with book author and title hidden on inside of the book jacket, for a bulletin-board display entitled "Do You Know This Book?"

8. **Self-stick note responses**—in which children respond to passages they select in a story, write their response on a self-stick note, and attach the note on the page next to the passage. Later, children select several passages and their responses to share with a partner or small group. This may be used in groups where children are reading different books or where they are all reading the same book.

9. **Bookmark response and sharing** (Goldenhersh, 1992)—in which you prepare bookmarks that invite children to respond to their reading in some way. ("If you were to create a dance from this story, what would it be like?" "If you wanted to interview a character from this book, which one would it be and why?" "What song does this book remind you of?"). Children prepare their responses and share them with a partner or group.

If you suddenly have the urge to have your children complete a book report, then focus the assignment by using one of the Literature Response Journal prompts discussed earlier. Your response to the report should address your children's thoughts and ideas, with little or no emphasis on spelling, punctuation, and grammar. The strategies discussed here for sharing ideas and response to books will build high interest and motivation as individual children, partners, or small groups of children actively discuss books.

SUSTAINED SILENT READING (SSR)

Sustained Silent Reading (SSR) is an instructional strategy that involves reading *every day*, by *everyone* in the classroom, including the teacher. The strategy has been used effectively in schools over the past three decades and is appropriate for all grade levels (Hunt, 1971; McCracken, 1971; McCracken & McCracken, 1978). SSR is designed to build positive attitudes toward reading and to give children a daily opportunity to read material of their choice. Reading material in SSR is wholly student-chosen and includes books, magazines, and other reading material. The time period for SSR will range from five to fifteen minutes depending on grade level.

Preparing for SSR

Prepare your children for using SSR one or two days before actually using it. Your discussion should emphasize that a special reading time will be set aside for everyone in the classroom to read their favorite book or reading material. At the kindergarten and primary grade levels, designate five to ten minutes, and, for the intermediate grades, ten to fifteen minutes. Use this preparation time to ensure that each child has a book or other reading material selected from your reading center collection, from the school

library, or from home. We have no objection to comic books, but some
teachers and schools do, especially if the comic contains violence. Selections
can range from picture and picture storybooks in the early grades to realistic
and modern fiction at the intermediate grades. Informational books, magazines, and newspapers are good candidates for some children.

Bookmarks are valuable to identify the stopping and starting points for
SSR. To make simple markers, cut strips of construction paper and give one
to each child. Have the child write his or her name on it. Don't neglect one
for you, too. Be sure that you have selected your own favorite book for SSR.

Establish the rules for SSR, and review these just before you initiate the
strategy (Tierney, 1990). SSR rules are as follows:

1. Everyone in the room reads during SSR.
2. There will be no interruptions during SSR. If you have questions or
   comments, you will need to wait until everyone is finished reading. SSR
   is *silent* reading. Talking and whispering do not count as SSR.
3. You will not be asked to report on what you have read.
4. SSR reading time will be for _____ minutes, every day starting
   at _____ and ending at _____ .

By making a simple wall chart with these four rules you will provide a helpful reminder for children in initiating SSR. You should also consider that a
few children will have misplaced their book as you begin. Be prepared by
having a few substitute books ready for immediate use.

Implementing SSR

On the first day of SSR, remind children of the rules, open your book, give
the signal to start, and begin reading. Using a kitchen timer to keep track of
SSR time will release you from the timekeeper role and allow you to participate fully in SSR. When the alarm sounds to conclude SSR, each child—and
you—places the bookmark in the book and closes it in preparation for continuing instruction. On occasion you may wish to provide one or two additional
minutes to allow your children to find a good stopping point in their reading.

Don't forget that your role during SSR is an important one—modeling
reading as you enjoy your favorite book. This is a powerful message to children
and is completely subverted if you use SSR time to grade papers, prepare for
the next class activity, or any other nonreading task. An occasional sweep of the
eyes around the room is sufficient for monitoring student activity during SSR.

At the outset of SSR, you will find that some children have difficulty concentrating on reading. This may require adjustment of the interest and reading difficulty of the book or reading material. For some children SSR will provide opportunity to reread, examine, and explore illustrations or photographs
in their books. Should you find that several children initially have difficulty in
following the class rules, you may simply ask that everyone close their books.
A brief review of the SSR rules may be necessary before proceeding.

After you have used SSR for several days and have the routine established, you may wish to provide opportunity for a few minutes of response time. This is an excellent opportunity for children to use their Literature Response Journals to record ideas and impressions related to their book. Sharing responses with a predesignated class partner also works well. However, it is very important that children do not view response time as violation of the rule "You will not be asked to report on what you read during SSR." Be sure to discuss and clarify that issue; you may find that inviting responses works best after SSR is well established in your room.

Some teachers find that the SSR "no talking or whispering" rule is too restrictive, and, in fact, prohibitive of children's natural inclination to read and talk about books together. In fact, a *Newsweek* "Buzzwords" column (Zeman, 1991) reported some time ago that students have changed the acronym referent of SSR from "Sustained Silent Reading" to "Sit down, Shut up, and Read!" If you find the silence rule restrictive, you may adjust it and encourage children to read and whisper-discuss books in pairs during SSR (we guess the strategy then becomes SSSR—Sustained Sort-of-Silent Reading!).

The key to the successful implementation of SSR is using SSR daily with children and by modeling reading enjoyment in the process. By doing this consistently, teachers build positive attitudes toward reading and encourage students' enjoyment of self-selected reading material.

READERS THEATRE

Readers Theatre can be used to create interest and enthusiasm about literature. In Readers Theatre, children do not dramatize stories; rather, story characters come to life through children's voices as they read character parts in dramatic play form and use minimal actions to accompany their reading. Readers Theatre presents a wonderful opportunity to develop a first-hand understanding of characterization, setting, plot, and story resolution. The script is essentially formed by altering the literature selection in such a way that a narrator relates descriptive passages and the reader/actors speak character parts. In Readers Theatre children have the opportunity to enter and become part of the work as they interpret the script. Readers Theatre can be used with children across the elementary grades, but is most effectively and easily used after children have gained some degree of reading fluency.

Introduce the notion of Readers Theatre to children by telling them that actors sit in a group and read a play script without costumes, props, or actions. Briefly explore the idea of television or movie scripts and how these scripts are similar to the dialogue between story characters in narrative text. Discuss ways in which a classroom Readers Theatre production would be similar to and different from a television or movie production.

Consider possible stories that you might use for Readers Theatre in your classroom. Encourage your children to talk about favorite stories that contain interesting characters, plenty of dialogue, a story plot with high suspense, and a special ending. Write the titles of these stories on the board and locate several of them. Examine each story, or chapters in the story, that could be used for your Readers Theatre production. Some ideas for the primary grades are storybooks such as *Miss Nelson Is Missing!* (Allard & Marshall, 1977) and *Hi, Cat!* (Keats, 1970). At the upper primary and intermediate grades, possible chapter selections range from *Harriet the Spy* (Fitzhugh, 1964), e.g., Chapter 11, "The Miracle," to *The Lion, the Witch, and the Wardrobe* (Lewis, 1950), e.g., Chapter 2, "What Lucy Found There."

To begin adaptation of the story, or story chapter, into a script for your classroom production, each child should have a copy of the story to be used, and since some amount of writing or other marking of the text is necessary, duplicated copies of the text work best here. Have the children work in their small group to decide what parts of the descriptive text should be narrated; they may wish to make some deletions or minor revisions to shorten the narrated text and can mark their editing on their individual copies of the story. Have them decide who will serve as the narrator, if one is needed, the key characters and their reading parts, what simple props (e.g., hats) would help carry the story, and any sound effects to be used. Write these roles and special needs on the chalkboard and the name of the child who will carry out each assignment. Consider what story introduction will be needed to establish the story if a chapter excerpt is used. Decide which part of the room could best be used as a stage if this will help carry the story. Place the props in that section of the room.

Prepare for the production by having each child read his or her story part silently. Since spoken parts are embedded in the text and not separated in the manner of scripts, it helps to let children use colored highlighter pens to mark the speaking parts. Then have the narrator and actors practice by reading the story aloud. Encourage children to use voice intonation and expression to convey the feelings, emotions, and mood intended in the story, and to determine how the props for the production will be used.

Perform the production as planned. The other children in your class, who are not in the production, can be the audience. It is important to help the audience understand that in Readers Theatre we need to use our imaginations to help create the characters and story setting in our minds. After the performance, explore how different roles were portrayed, how the production might be revised and refined, and how the audience reacted. Again, this is an excellent opportunity for the children to use their Literature Response Journals to capture impressions and ideas related to the presentation and to the story itself. Readers Theatre can be effectively used not only with contemporary stories but also with traditional fantasy, such as folktales, fables, and fairy tales. A useful resource in expanding your understanding of Readers Theatre is *Readers Theatre: Story Dramatization in the Classroom* (Sloyer, 1982).

HOW TO DO . . . .

READERS THEATRE

1. Introduce, explain, and discuss the concept of Readers Theatre with your students. Be sure to distinguish Readers Theatre from dramatization.

2. Consider stories for adaptation to a Readers Theatre production. Select several from which children may choose.

3. Reproduce copies of the selected story so that each member of the group has his/her own copy.

4. Guide children as they mark the story to create the narrator part; assist them in deciding how much of the descriptive content of the story should be part of the narrator's role.

5. Guide the group's determination of any minimal props or sound effects needed. Record these on the board.

6. Have students choose roles and go through the story as a group, each marking her/his speaking parts with a colored highlighter pen.

7. Give the group opportunity to practice reading, both in the group and with children independently working on their own parts.

8. Do the performance. Lead a follow-up discussion with the group and the audience.

INVESTIGATIVE QUESTIONING PROCEDURE (INQUEST)

InQuest (Shoop, 1986) is an instructional strategy designed to encourage children to enter a story by playing the role of the central character or that of an "investigative reporter" who interviews the central character about story events. The children respond to the story by taking either the point of view of the central character or that of a reporter. The teacher identifies a stop-point in the story at which an important story event has occurred. The children then imagine a news conference at the scene of the event. One student assumes the role of the major character and is interviewed by the other student "investigative reporters." The goal here is to explore ways in which character traits, story setting, story events, and story plot fit together to form a story. The strategy has been used effectively with children from grades three through six.

Introduce InQuest by leading a discussion on the topic of "Questions Used by the Investigative Reporter in Story Interviews." The objective of this discussion is to help students understand how to form questions that will reveal information about story character traits and motivation, story setting, and events, and how these are connected to the plot. Shoop (1986) suggests that students may be encouraged to observe television excerpts of investigative reporting and study the type of questions asked. She recommends that the following questioning principles are important to elicit in the discussion:

1. Questions that get longer responses are most desirable.
2. Questions that receive yes/no answers can be followed by "why?" to obtain more information.
3. Interview questions often elicit information, a reflection, an evaluation, or a prediction.
4. A good interview should have a variety of question types.

Identify a literature selection, from your basal reader or from a full-length story, that contains a central and interesting character and has clear plot development. You will need multiple copies of the selection so that all readers will have one. Identify a story event that represents a point of critical

Reading for Pleasure Using Sustained Silent Reading

action in the story. For example, in *Charlotte's Web* (White, 1952), a good InQuest stop-point occurs when Lurvy, the hired hand, takes Wilbur's breakfast to the barnyard early one morning and discovers the words "SOME PIG!" neatly woven in a spider's web (p. 77).

Ask your students to read the story and stop at the place you designate. Ask them to keep in mind the questions they would like to ask the character at this point (in this case, Lurvy). Tell them that a news conference has been called and they are the investigative reporters representing your school paper. Role-play the news conference.

The first several times you use InQuest with your children, you may wish to play the role of the character or that of a reporter, in order to model responses and questions. As your children become familiar with the news conference setting, ask for a student volunteer to play the character to be interviewed. The other children in the group are to assume the role of investigative reporters. Remind the student being interviewed that he or she is to take the point of view of the character and answer the reporters' questions using the information revealed up to that point in the story. Remind the "reporters" that their questions should be designed to elicit information about previous story events leading up to the event. For example, areas for exploration might include how Lurvy discovered the words in the web, his interpretation of how the words got there, the possible role of a spider named Charlotte, the significance of the words "SOME PIG!" and what this discovery may mean to Lurvy and the Zuckerman family, and the possible impact of this apparent miracle on the barnyard animals.

When the interview has been completed, lead a follow-up discussion for debriefing. Consider the type of questions asked, the kind of follow-up questions that were used, and the information obtained. Identify some examples of good interview questions and procedures used by your students as you work toward refining the question formation process. This follow-up discussion should encourage children to consider how evaluating information and forming predictions while reading can be of value in understanding character motivation, story events, and story plot.

You will find that InQuest can be used effectively in both full-length literature selections and story chapter excerpts such as those found in basal reading programs. The InQuest strategy offers a valuable instructional tool to build self-monitoring in meaning construction while encouraging the reader to enter into the world of a central story character.

THEMATIC UNITS: INTEGRATING LITERATURE AND CONTENT AREAS

Developing thematic literature-based units offers many opportunities to integrate literature with other content areas of the curriculum. A thematic unit is quite simply an instructional plan that relies on key topics or concepts that can be used to integrate literature and content area information. The use of thematic units will not only build high motivation and interest for your children but will offer rich opportunity to develop new concepts related to various curriculum areas such as social studies, science, and mathematics.

In using a thematic approach, it is important to strike a balance between the aesthetic stance and the efferent stance in instruction. While you will maintain an objective of encouraging children to identify with story characters, and transact with and respond to the literature, you will also have a second objective, that of exploring new ideas and developing concepts related *to* curriculum content.

To develop a thematic unit, begin by identifying the specific objectives that you wish to accomplish. These may range from building reading motivation and response through identification with the main story characters, to learning about a specific concept related to ecosystems and nature (science), historical events and cultural differences (social studies), or endangered species and economics (mathematics, science, and social studies). Consider a unifying theme that will enable you to integrate a specific literature selection or selections with your content objectives. Themes may be viewed from either a **topical perspective** or a **conceptual perspective**. For example, at the primary grades, a topical perspective might be related to such topics as "my family" or "foxes," while at the intermediate grades a topic theme might consist of "the American Revolution" or "space travel." A conceptual perspective, on the other hand, might deal with a theme on the importance of love and friendship at the early grades, or our relationship to and responsibility for preserving nature and natural resources at the intermediate grades. Various themes will suggest themselves as you consider the topics and concepts in the content areas of social studies, science, math, art, and music in your classroom curriculum.

Select specific literature and informational-type books from your reading center and school library that are related to your central theme. Brainstorm ideas about ways in which you can use your theme to integrate your literature selections with your content area materials. If possible, share your ideas and interests with another teacher who may have similar interests at the same grade level in your school.

Start slowly, as you first identify a few literature selections and explore integrating these with one area of your content area subject, such as social studies or science. Consider how the story can be used to help the content become more interesting and bring increased depth to the study. For example, the use of historical fiction and biography can provide motivation and insight in the study of the American Revolution. A book like *Early Thunder* (Fritz, 1987) can build an understanding of the conflict the early colonists experienced between loyalty to the king and rebellion, through the eyes of a 14-year-old boy living in Concord, Massachusetts in 1775 (Johnson & Ebert, 1992). Assess the instructional problems and successes you encounter in this first attempt. Refine your ideas, increase your literature selections, develop new integrated activities, and expand the thematic integration process into other areas of your choice.

Topical Thematic Units

An example of a topical unit developed for inner-city second-grade students by Julie Stevenson (1990) illustrates the integration of this unit into various areas of her curriculum. This is a topical thematic unit on "foxes," designed to build students' motivation and interest toward reading and simultaneously to develop meaning-construction strategies and new content information. The unit was also intended to expand concepts developed in a basal reading story on foxes that was used in her classroom.

This topic unit relied on three literature selections, *Flossie and the Fox* by Patricia McKissack, *Rosie's Walk* by Pat Hutchins, and *One Fine Day* by Nonny Hogrogian. The instructional strategies used in developing the unit included read-aloud story sharing, Literature Response Journals, Readers Theatre, the Directed Reading-Thinking Activity (DR-TA), and the Group Mapping Activity (GMA). The content areas emphasized and the related instructional activities are illustrated in Figure 6-1. The culminating event for the unit involved the creation of a big book about foxes based on the children's dictation to the teacher and illustrated by the children.

Conceptual Thematic Units

An example of a conceptual thematic unit, designed for intermediate-grade students by Catherine Gross (1989), illustrates critical features of this approach. The unit is based on the literature selection *Julie of the Wolves* (1972), by Jean Craighead George. This story sensitively describes the adventures, hardships, loneliness, and adjustment of thirteen-year-old Julie, an Eskimo girl, also known as Miyax. Her journey across the barren tundra to Point Barrow, her acceptance by the wolves, her discovery of her father, and her struggle to adapt to a different culture form the core of the novel. Supporting materials for the unit included *The Call of the Wolves* (Murphy, 1989), *Alaska Wildlife: A Coloring Book* (Holen, 1988), *Zoo Books: Wolves* (Wildlife Education, 1989), and informational books on the wilderness, survival skills, and life in the arctic.

The three basic concepts developed in this unit included:

1. Young people from different cultures have similar feelings and needs for love and caring in a family, as well as needs to be independent and competent.
2. Society changes, and old ways sometimes clash with new ways.
3. Respect for all living things is important if we are to maintain a balance of nature in our environment.

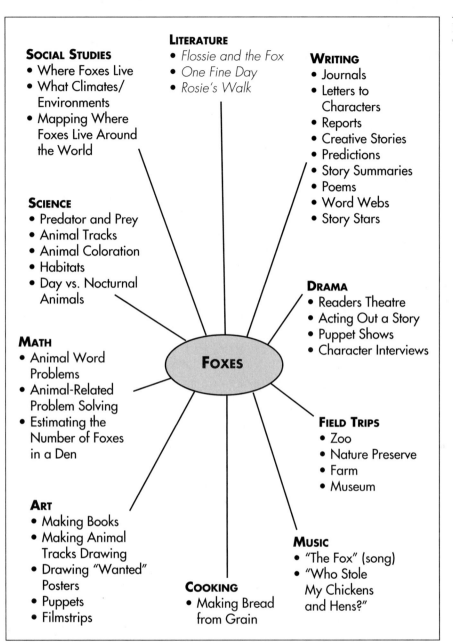

LITERATURE
- *Flossie and the Fox*
- *One Fine Day*
- *Rosie's Walk*

SOCIAL STUDIES
- Where Foxes Live
- What Climates/ Environments
- Mapping Where Foxes Live Around the World

SCIENCE
- Predator and Prey
- Animal Tracks
- Animal Coloration
- Habitats
- Day vs. Nocturnal Animals

MATH
- Animal Word Problems
- Animal-Related Problem Solving
- Estimating the Number of Foxes in a Den

ART
- Making Books
- Making Animal Tracks Drawing
- Drawing "Wanted" Posters
- Puppets
- Filmstrips

FOXES

WRITING
- Journals
- Letters to Characters
- Reports
- Creative Stories
- Predictions
- Story Summaries
- Poems
- Word Webs
- Story Stars

DRAMA
- Readers Theatre
- Acting Out a Story
- Puppet Shows
- Character Interviews

FIELD TRIPS
- Zoo
- Nature Preserve
- Farm
- Museum

MUSIC
- "The Fox" (song)
- "Who Stole My Chickens and Hens?"

COOKING
- Making Bread from Grain

FIGURE 6-1

Second-Grade Topical Thematic Literature Unit on Foxes

The instructional strategies used in developing this unit included Literature Response Journals, DR-TA, GMA, Semantic Mapping, and VSS. The curriculum integration included the following areas:

Social Studies—the geography of Alaska, Eskimo customs and culture, the history of Alaska, including statehood;

Science—study of habits and culture of wolves, endangered species, and ecosystems;

Math—construction of graphs of past and present wolf population, charting variations in snowfall at various seasons, use of wilderness supply catalogs to plan for and order expedition supplies;

Art—construction of posters to create awareness of endangered wildlife, design of stamps of wildlife, construction of models of huts, igloos, and totem poles, and drawings of Eskimo clothing;

School Events—planning an assembly related to endangered species, reading stories to kindergarten and first grade that feature wolves;

Field Trips and Community Speakers—trip to the zoo and science museum to study wolves, inviting speakers from organizations to discuss endangered wildlife, inviting storytellers to present Eskimo folktales and legends.

The development of this type of conceptual unit requires multiple copies of the central literature selection, in this case *Julie of the Wolves*. The literature selection and the above content areas are integrated into the instruction and discussions to develop the three central concepts of the thematic unit.

HOW TO DO . . . .

THEMATIC UNITS

1. Identify the instructional objectives for the unit (i.e., "What do I want my students to know or be able to do when the unit is finished?").
2. Consider a unifying theme. The theme may be topical or conceptual.
3. Select literature and informational books for use in developing the theme.
4. Determine the activities, events, and projects useful in achieving unit objectives. Guide the class in carrying out the activities, events, and projects.
5. Evaluate the effectiveness of the unit as a whole.

The development of thematic units that integrate literature and the content areas requires planning and creative effort on your part. You will find, however, that the motivation, interest, and conceptual development of your students will be greatly enhanced by this integrated thematic approach.

EVALUATING CHILDREN'S PROGRESS IN RESPONDING TO LITERATURE

Evaluation of children's responses to literature is an ongoing process throughout daily instruction over the school year. Evidence of growth will be based on observations of the children as they engage in, transact with, and respond to literature experiences. These observations provide information that enables teachers to adjust teaching and instruction. The following questions will be of help in your informal evaluation.

1. Do my students enjoy listening to stories read aloud and told in the classroom? Do they ask for certain books to be read again over and over?

2. Do they exhibit strong interest and enthusiasm in reading and exploring and checking out new literature from the classroom reading center and from the school library?

3. Do they enjoy identifying and exploring informational-type books from the classroom reading center or the library?

4. Do my students look forward to entering their ideas in their Literature Response Journals and to participating in discussions of stories in class? Do they respond to my written responses and observations in their journals?

5. Do they informally exchange information about story characters and story plots? Do they share ideas about content from information-type books?

6. Do they enter into response discussions eagerly and enthusiastically?

7. Do they exhibit an understanding of and empathy with story characters in our reading response discussions and journals? In their discussions and journals, do they show growth in the application of story-based insights to their own life?

8. Are children becoming more fluent readers? Are they growing more independent in choosing books to read?

9. Do they ask to take books home to read and share with a parent or sibling?

10. Do they exhibit a sense of pride in literature-related activity projects, such as book posters, mystery book jackets, or other literature-related writing, which will be displayed in the classroom?

Your observations based on these questions will provide important clues indicating the success of your literature instruction and program.

Literature and Reader Response
A Summary

Our discussion in this chapter has focused on the use of children's literature and reader response experiences to enhance children's positive attitudes and motivation toward reading and active comprehension. The use of high-interest literature and opportunity for response to literature are critical toward this end. We have discussed the nature of the reader response process, which involves reader identification, catharsis, and insight. Awareness of the six internal reader motivations, ranging from problem resolution to understanding of self, also helps teachers connect children to the literature they will find of high interest.

The role of instructional stance is basic to successful literature instruction. We have emphasized the importance of the aesthetic instructional stance designed to help children identify with story characters, enter into and transact with the story, and provide opportunity for story response and idea sharing. The efferent instructional stance should assume a minor role in reader-response-oriented instruction but becomes important in idea and concept development.

The selection of literature and informational books for your classroom reading center is central to effective literature instruction. Your familiarity with and knowledge of children's literature and informational books will enable you to connect these books with children's reading interest. Your school library, the librarian, and your public library will become important literature resources.

Our discussion of literature instruction presented a range of instructional approaches and teaching strategies designed to encourage reader motivation, reader response, and active comprehension. These strategies place children's thinking and the literature experience at the heart of instruction. Your understanding of these various strategies, ranging from Reading-Aloud and Literature Response Journals to Readers Theatre and InQuest, will provide you an invaluable set of instructional tools for your classroom. Your use of thematic units, both topical and conceptual, can be of great value in integrating literature with the content areas and can enhance your student's reading motivation and concept development.

Evaluation of students' progress in the classroom literature program through informal observations is viewed as an ongoing daily process. This is a critical part of instruction as you revise, refine, and fine-tune your instruction toward the goal of building positive attitudes and active comprehension through reader response to literature.

In Chapter 1, we pointed out that "Successful achievement in reading is vital to most of our personal and professional goals." A key element in building such success is helping children find joy in reading. A child who enjoys reading will become a good reader. Taking advantage of the enormous wealth of good children's literature is the most direct way to build this joy. This chapter has been directed toward that goal.

DOUBLE ENTRY JOURNAL

Go back to your list of the last five books you read. For each, identify your predominant stance in your reading. Speculate as to why you read the book from that stance. What internal reader motivations can you identify? How many of the last five books you read were children's books? Share your responses with a partner.

Supporting Activities

1. Reflect on the books you have read, ranging from your earliest experiences with children's literature to reading in your adult life. Identify one book (in all probability there will be several) that has had a major impact on your life at the time you read the book. Briefly describe this impact on your personal life. Now identify the internal or external motivations (see Reader Motivations discussion in the chapter) that were critical in this influence. Share your responses and ideas with a class partner.

2. Briefly explain how the process of identification, catharsis, and insight influences children's motivation to read. How is a child's prior knowledge and experience connected to the identification and motivation process?

3. What role does instructional stance play in helping students establish a reading purpose and motivation to read? Briefly explain how a predominately aesthetic instructional stance differs from a predominately efferent instructional stance. Which stance would you use with the following books: Maurice Sendak's *Where the Wild Things Are,* E. B. White's *Charlotte's Web,* Whitfield's *Why Do Volcanoes Erupt?* and Wildlife Education books such as *Zoo Books: Wolves?* Why? Share your ideas with a class partner.

4. We have discussed a variety of instructional strategies designed to enhance your teaching of literature (reading aloud, storytelling, Literature Response Journals, Sharing Responses About Books, Sustained Silent Reading, Readers Theatre, InQuest, and the use of Thematic Units). Select and review one of these strategies that has strong appeal to you. Identify and carefully read a children's book (or books) that you believe can be introduced to children using your selected strategy. Briefly describe your instructional plan for using this strategy and your literature selection to a small group of children at the grade level of your choice. Arrange to teach a small group of children at the appropriate grade level and implement your plan. Did the children's responses follow your expectations? What changes would you make in your teaching this strategy the next time?

5. Evaluation of the children's progress in responding to literature is an important part of the instructional program. Briefly create an evaluation plan by designing specific questions to form a checklist that will enable you to evaluate children's attitude, motivation, and response to literature. Arrange for an observation of a classroom at the grade level appropriate for your evaluation and use your checklist. What evidence did you find related to instruction designed to enhance attitudes, motivation, and response to literature? What implications for instruction do you have? What additional items would you add to your checklist based on your observation?

Abrahamson, R. F. (1979). *Children's favorite picture storybooks: An analysis of structure and reading preferences* (ERIC Documents Reproduction Service No. ED 174 977).

Abrahamson, R. F., & Shannon, P. (1983). A plot structure analysis of favorite picture books. *Reading Teacher, 37*, 44–48.

Applebee, A. (1973). *The spectator role: Theoretical and developmental studies of ideas about and responses to literature with special reference to four age levels.* Unpublished doctoral dissertation, University of London, London, England.

Applebee, A. (1978). *The child's concept of story.* Chicago: University of Chicago Press.

Atwell, N. (1984). Writing and reading literature from the inside out. *Language Arts, 61*, 240–252.

Burgess, S. A. (1985). Reading but not literate: The childread survey. *School Library Journal, 31*, 27–30.

California State Department of Education. (1987). *Handbook for planning an effective literature program: Kindergarten through grade twelve.* Sacramento, CA: California State Department of Education.

Consuelo, Sr., M. (1967). What do first graders like to read? *Catholic School Journal, 67*, 42–43.

Cullinan, B., Harwood, K., & Galda, L. (1983). The reader and the story: Comprehension and response. *Journal of Research and Development in Education, 16*, 29–37.

Durkin, D. (1978–1979). What classroom observations reveal about reading comprehension instruction. *Reading Research Quarterly, 15*, 481–533.

Eeds & Wells, D. (1989). Grand conversations: An exploration of meaning construction in literature study groups. *Research in the Teaching of English, 23*. 4–29.

Farnan, N. (1992). Promoting connections between reader and text: A reader response approach. *The California Reader, 25*, 6–8.

Flitterman-King, S. (1988). The role of the response journal in active reading. *The Quarterly of the National Writing Project and the Center for the Study of Writing, 10*, 4–11.

Goldernhersh, B. L. (1992). *Read it with bookmarks.* Belleville, IL: Classroom Catalyst Press.

Goodman, K. S., Bird, L. B., & Goodman, Y. M. (1991). *The whole language catalogue.* Santa Rosa, CA: American School Publishers.

Goodman, K. S., Shannon, P., Freeman, Y. S., & Murphy, S. (1988). *Report card on basal readers.* Katonah, NY: Richard C. Owen.

Graham, S. A. (1986). Assessing reading preferences: A new approach. *New England Reading Association Journal, 21*, 8–12.

Grande, A. (1965). *Authentic existence and the teaching of literature.* Unpublished doctoral dissertation, University of Pittsburgh, Pittsburgh, PA.

Graves, D. H. (1990). *Discover your own literacy.* Portsmouth, NH: Heinemann.

Gross, C. H. (1989). *An inservice presentation of a literature-based integrated unit for teaching content-area reading.* Unpublished manuscript, University of California, Berkeley, CA.

Guszak, F. J. (1967). Teacher questioning and reading. *The Reading Teacher, 21,* 227–234.

Hancock, M. (1992). Literature Response Journals: Insights beyond the printed page. *Language Arts, 69,* 36–42.

Huck, S. C. (1976). *Children's literature in the elementary school* (3rd ed.). New York: Holt, Rinehart & Winston.

Hunt, L. C. (1971). Six steps to the individualized reading program (IRP). *Elementary English, 48,* 27–32.

Ingham, J. (1982). Middle school children's responses to E. Blyton in "The Bradford book flood experience." *Journal of Research in Reading, 5,* 43–56.

Jacobs, L. B. (1965). Telling stories to young children. In L. B. Jacobs (Ed.), *Using literature with young children* (pp. 15–20). New York: Teachers College Press.

Johnson, N. M., & Ebert, M. J. (1992). Time travel is possible: Historical fiction and biography—Passport to the past. *The Reading Teacher, 45,* 488–495.

Lalas, J. (1991). Infusing multicultural content into reading/language arts through children's books that portray ethnic minorities positively. *The California Reader, 24,* 8–11.

Landy, S. (1977). Why Johnny can read . . . but doesn't. *Canadian Library Journal, 34,* 379–387.

Langer, J. A., Applebee, A. N., Mussis, V. S., & Foertsch, M. A. (1990). *Learning to read in our nation's schools: Instruction and achievement in 1988 at grades 4, 8, and 12.* Princeton, NJ: Educational Testing Service.

Lynch-Brown, C. (1977). Procedures for determining children's book choices: Comparison and criticism. *Reading Horizons, 17,* 243–250.

McCracken, R. A. (1971). Initiating sustained silent reading. *Journal of Reading, 14,* 521–524, 582–583.

McCracken, R. A., & McCracken, M. J. (1978). Modeling is the key to sustained silent reading. *The Reading Teacher, 31,* 406–408.

Martinez, M. G., & Roser, N. L. (1991). Children's responses to literature. In J. Flood, J. M. Jensen, D. Lapp, & J. R. Squire (Eds.), *Handbook on research on teaching the English language arts* (pp. 643–654). New York: Macmillan.

Mathewson, G. (1976). The function of attitude in the reading process. In H. Singer & R. B. Ruddell (Eds.), *Theoretical models and processes of reading* (2nd ed.), (pp. 655–677). Newark, DE: International Reading Association.

Mathewson, G. (1985). Toward a comprehensive model of affect in the reading process. In H. Singer & R. B. Ruddell (Eds.), *Theoretical models and pro-*

cesses of reading (3rd ed.), (pp. 841–856). Newark, DE: International Reading Association.

Monson, D. L., & Sebesta, S. (1991). Reading preferences. In J. Flood, J. M. Jensen, D. Lapp, & J. R. Squire (Eds.), *Handbook of research on teaching the English language arts* (pp. 664–673). New York: Macmillan.

Morrow, L. M. (1991). Promoting voluntary reading. In J. Flood, J. M. Jensen, D. Lapp, & J. R. Squire (Eds.), *Handbook of research on teaching the English language arts* (pp. 681–690). New York: Macmillan.

Nelson, R. C. (1966). Children's poetry preferences. *Elementary English, 43,* 247–251.

Osborn, J. (1984). The purposes, uses and contents of workbooks, and some guidelines for publishers. In R. C. Anderson, J. Osborn, & R. J. Tierney (Eds.), *Learning to read in American schools.* (pp. 45–111). Hillsdale, NJ: Erlbaum.

Rasinski, T. V., & Padak, N. D. (1990). Multicultural learning through children's literature. *Language Arts, 67,* 576–580.

Rogers, C. (1961). *On becoming a person.* Boston: Houghton Mifflin.

Rosenblatt, L. M. (1985). The transactional theory of literary work: Implications for research. In C. R. Cooper (Ed.), *Researching response to literature and the teaching of literature: Points of departure* (pp. 33–53). Norwood, NJ: Ablex.

Rosenblatt, L. M. (1988). *Writing and reading: The transactional theory* (Report No. 13). University of California, Berkeley, CA: Center for the Study of Writing.

Rosenblatt, L. M. (1991). Literature—S.o.s.! *Language Arts, 68,* 444–448.

Routman, R. (1988). *Transitions: From literature to literacy.* Portsmouth, NH: Heinemann.

Routman, R. (1991). *Invitations.* Portsmouth, NH: Heinemann.

Row, B. H. (1968). *Reading interests of elementary school pupils in selected schools in Muscogee County, Georgia.* Unpublished doctoral dissertation, Auburn University, Montgomery, AL.

Ruddell, R. B. (1974). *Reading-language instruction: Innovative practices.* Englewood Cliffs, NJ: Prentice-Hall.

Ruddell, R. B. (1991, December). *A study of the effect of reader motivation and comprehension development on students' reading comprehension achievement in influential and noninfluential teachers' classrooms.* Paper presented at the National Reading Conference, Palm Springs, CA.

Ruddell, R. B. (1992). A whole language and literature perspective: Creating a meaning-making instructional environment. *Language Arts, 69,* 612–620.

Russell, D. H. (1970). Reading and mental health: Clinical approaches. In R. Ruddell (Ed.), *The dynamics of reading* (pp. 207–229). Waltham, MA: Ginn.

Scharer, P. L., & Detwiler, D. B. (1992). Changing as teachers: Perils and possibilities of literature-based language arts instruction. *Language Arts, 69,* 186–192.

Shannon, P. (1989). *Broken promises.* Granby, MA: Bergin & Gavey.

Shoop, M. (1986). InQuest: A listening and reading comprehension strategy. *The Reading Teacher, 39*, 670–674.

Shores, J. H. (1954). Reading interests and informational needs of children in grades four to eight. *Elementary English, 31*, 493–500.

Sloyer, S. (1982). *Readers Theatre: Story dramatization in the classroom.* Urbana, IL: National Council for Teachers of English.

Squire, R. J. (1989, May). *Research on reader response and the national literature initiative.* Paper presented at the International Reading Association Convention, Atlanta, GA.

Stevenson, J. (1990). *Transitions: Incorporating a new style of teaching and assessment into the elementary classroom.* Unpublished Master's thesis, University of California, Berkeley, CA.

Trelease, J. (1989). *The new read-aloud handbook.* New York: Penguin.

Vandergrift, K. (1965). Reading aloud to young children. In L. B. Jacobs (Ed.), *Using literature with young children* (pp. 11–14). New York: Teachers College Press.

Veatch, J. (1968). *How to teach reading with children's books.* New York: Citation Press.

Walker-Dalhouse, D. (1992). Using African-American literature to increase ethnic understanding. *The Reading Teacher, 45*, 416–422.

Wolfson, B. J., Manning, G., & Manning, M. (1984). Revisiting what children say their reading interests are. *Reading World, 24*, 4–10.

Zeman, N. (1991, September 9). Buzzwords. *Newsweek*, p. 6.

CHILDREN'S LITERATURE REFERENCES

Adams, A. (1980). *The great Valentine's Day balloon race.* New York: Macmillan.

Alexander, S. (1984). *Dear Phoebe.* Boston: Little, Brown.

Allard, H., & Marshall, J. (1977). *Miss Nelson is missing!* Boston: Houghton Mifflin.

Anno, M. (1974). *Anno's alphabet.* New York: Crowell.

Base, G. (1988). *The eleventh hour: A curious mystery.* New York: Harry N. Abrams.

Bay Area Kids (1991). *Books we love best.* San Francisco, CA: Foghorn Press.

Baylor, B. (1974). *Everybody needs a rock.* New York: Macmillan.

Berger, G. (1987). *Sharks.* New York: Doubleday.

Blume, J. (1971). *Then again, maybe I won't.* Scarsdale, NY: Bradbury.

Blume, J. (1972). *It's not the end of the world.* Scarsdale, NY: Bradbury.

Blume, J. (1972). *Tales of a fourth grade nothing.* New York: E. P. Dutton.

Brown, M. (1961). *Once a mouse: A fable cut in wood.* New York: Atheneum.

Burnett, F. H. (1911). *The secret garden.* Philadelphia: Lippincott.

Butler, F. (1989). *Skipping around the world.* New York: Ballantine.

Children's Book Council and International Reading Association (1992). *Kid's favorite books: Children's choices 1989–1991.* Newark, DE: International Reading Association.

Cleary, B. (1981). *Ramona Quimby, age 8.* New York: William Morrow.

Cleary, B. (1984). *Ramona forever.* New York: William Morrow.

Craighead, . (1972). *Julie of the Wolves.* New York: HarperCollins.

Dahl, R. (1973). *Charlie and the chocolate factory.* New York: Puffin.

Dahl, R. (1988). *Mathilda.* New York: Viking Kestral.

Dalgliesh, A. (1952). *The bears on Hemlock Mountain.* New York: Charles Scribner's Sons.

Eyerly, J. (1974). *Good-bye to Budapest.* New York: Berkley.

Feelings, M. (1974). *Jambo means hello: Swahili alphabet book.* New York: Dial.

Fitzhugh, L. (1964). *Harriet the spy.* New York: Harper & Row.

Frank, A. (1967). *Anne Frank: The diary of a young girl.* New York: Doubleday.

Freeman, D. (1968). *Corduroy.* New York: Puffin.

Fritz, J. (1973). *And then what happened, Paul Revere?* New York: Coward, McCann & Geoghegan.

Fritz, J. (1987). *Early thunder.* New York: Penguin.

Galdone, P. (1968). *Henny-Penny.* New York: Seabury Press.

Gibbons, G. (1985). *Dinosaurs.* New York: Holiday.

Gramatky, H. (1939). *Little toot.* New York: Putnam.

Hamilton, V. (1985) *The people could fly: American Black folktales.* New York: Alfred A. Knopf.

Hathorn, E. (1981). *The tram to Bondi beach.* Sydney, Australia: Methuen Australia Pty. Ltd.

Hoban, T. (1985). *Is it larger? Is it smaller?* New York: Greenwillow.

Hogrogian, N. (1971). *One fine day.* New York: Aladdin.

Holen, S. (1988). *Alaska wildlife: A coloring book.* Homer, AK: Paisley.

Houston, J. A. (1967). *The white archer: An Eskimo legend.* New York: Harcourt Brace Jovanovich.

Hutchins, P. (1968). *Rosie's walk.* New York: Macmillan.

Keats, E. J. (1970). *Hi, cat!* New York: Macmillan.

Konigsburg, E. L. (1967). *From the mixed-up files of Mrs. Basil E. Frankweiler.* New York: Dell.

Lee, J. M. (1982). *Legend of the milky way.* New York: Henry Holt.

Lewis, C. S. (1950). *The lion, the witch, and the wardrobe.* New York: Macmillan.

Lionni, L. (1964). *Tico and the golden wings*. New York: Pantheon Books.

Lionni, L. (1969). *Alexander and the wind-up mouse*. New York: Knopf.

McCloskey, R. (1941). *Make way for ducklings*. New York: Viking-Penguin.

McKissack, P. C. (1986). *Flossie & the fox*. New York: Dial.

MacLachlan, P. (1985). *Sarah, plain and tall*. New York: Harper and Row.

Martin, B. (1983). *Brown bear, brown bear, what do you see?* New York: Holt.

Matsunno, M. (1960). *A pair of red clogs*. Cleveland: William Collins & World.

Mayer, M. (1967). *A boy, a dog, and a frog*. New York: Dial.

Milne, A.A. (1927). *Now we are six*. New York: E.P. Dutton.

Milne, A. A. (1952). *When we were very young*. New York: E. P. Dutton

Morgan, W. (1988). *Navajo coyote tales*. Santa Fe, NM: Ancient City Press.

Munsch, R. (1984). *Millicent and the wind*. Willowdale, Ontario, Canada: Firefly Books.

Munsch, R. (1986). *Love you forever*. Willowdale, Ontario, Canada: Firefly Books.

Murphy, U. (1989). *The call of the wolves*. New York: Scholastic.

O'Dell, S. (1960). *Island of the blue dolphins*. New York: Dell.

Ormerod, J. (1981). *Sunshine*. New York: Lothrop, Lee & Shepard.

Paterson, A. B., & Macarthur-Onslow, A. (1981). *The man from snowy river*. Sydney, Australia: William Collins Pty. Ltd.

Perrault, C. (1954). *Cinderella*. New York: Aladdin.

Rawls, W. (1961). *Where the red fern grows*. New York: Bantam.

The Real Mother Goose (1916, 1944, ninety-fifth printing, 1993). New York: Checkerboard Press.

Rylant, C. (1982). *When I was young in the mountains*. New York: E. P. Dutton.

Sendak, M. (1963). *Where the wild things are*. New York: HarperCollins.

Shannon, G. (1989). *Stories to solve: Folktales from around the world*. New York: Greenwillow.

Silverstein, S. (1974). *Where the sidewalk ends*. New York: Harper & Row.

Steptoe, J. (1987). *Mufaro's beautiful daughters*. New York: Lothrop, Lee & Shepard.

Stevenson, R. L. (1985). *A child's garden of verses*. New York: Crown.

Taylor, M. (1966). *Henry the explorer*. New York: Atheneum.

Viorst, J. (1972). *Alexander and the terrible, horrible, no good, very bad day*. New York: Macmillan.

Viorst, J. (1978). *Alexander, who used to be rich last Sunday*. New York: Macmillan.

Vreeken, E. (1959). *The boy who would not say his name*. Chicago: Follett.

Wheatley, N., & Rawlins, D. (1987). *My place*. Melbourne, Australia: Collins Dove.

White, E. B. (1952). *Charlotte's web*. New York: Harper & Row.

Whitfield, P. (1990). *Why do volcanoes erupt?* New York: Viking.

Wilder, L. I. (1935). *Little house on the prairie.* New York: Harper & Brothers.

Wilder, L. I. (1937). *On the banks of Plum Creek.* New York: Harper & Brothers.

Wildlife Education (1989). *Zoo books: Wolves. 6-4.* San Diego, CA: Wildlife Education Ltd.

Wildsmith, B. (1965). *Brian Wildsmith's 1, 2, 3.* New York: Franklin Watts.

CHAPTER 6	READING ALOUD	STORYTELLING	RESPONSE JOURNALS	SHARING BOOKS
FOCUS ON	Enjoyment	Enjoyment	Recording responses to literature	Enjoyment
GUIDES STUDENTS	During reading		After reading; during writing	After reading
USE TO PLAN	Lessons, units, yearly activities	Lessons, units, yearly activities	Lessons, units, yearly activities	Units, yearly activities
MAY BE USED	Whole class, small groups	Whole class, small groups	Whole class, small groups, cooperative groups, partnerships	Whole class, small groups, partnerships
MAY BE COMBINED WITH (KNOWN STRATEGIES)	DL-TA	PReP, GMA, Semantic Maps	DL-TA, DR-TA, ReQuest, Reading Aloud, Storytelling	
MATERIALS PREPARATION	Light	Light	Light to moderate	Moderate to extensive
OTHER PREPARATION	Moderate	Extensive	Light	Light to extensive
OUTSIDE RESOURCES	Not needed	Necessary	Not needed	Necessary
HOW TO DO		Page 281		

Building Tables "grow" or build, successively from chapter to chapter. They tell you (1) the focus of each strategy introduced in a chapter; (2) how the strategy is best used; (3) what strategies from previous chapters combine well with new ones; (4) preparation requirements; (5) additional resources needed; and (6) the page on which a strategy's How-to-Do appears.

SSR	READERS THEATRE	INQUEST	THEMATIC UNITS
Practice reading	Story interpretation	Story analysis	Connecting concepts and literature
During reading	After reading	During, after reading, before writing	Before, during, and after reading and writing
Yearly activities	Lessons, units	Lessons, units	Lessons, units yearly activities
Whole class	Whole class, small groups	Whole class, small groups	Whole class, cooperative groups
	DR-TA, DRA	DR-TA, DRA	DR-TA, DRA, PReP, VSS, Concept Webs, Semantic Maps, SFA, Literature Response Journals, SSR, Readers Theatre InQuest
None	Moderate to extensive	Light	Moderate to extensive
None	Light	None	Moderate to extensive
Useful	Useful	Useful	Necessary
	Page 290		Page 297

GUIDING CHILDREN'S WRITING

Are you a writer? What do you like or not like about writing? Consider your history as a writer. Jot down memories and ideas about writing that come to mind.

INTRODUCTION

Children's writing has assumed growing importance in elementary classrooms over the past few years. Much of the reason for this may be traced to two generally concurrent influences: (1) widespread acceptance and application of instructional practices, developed largely by the National Writing Project and in the work of such people as Donald Graves, Lucy Calkins, and Nancie Atwell, that embed writing and writing activities naturally into curricula and classroom days; and (2) new understandings we all have from seminal research by Marie Clay (1975, 1991), Jerry Harste, Virginia Woodward, Carolyn Burke (1982, 1984), Anne Dyson (1983, 1986, 1990), Emilia Ferreiro and Ana Teberosky (1982), Elizabeth Sulzby (1989), Elizabeth Sulzby and Bill Teale (1985), and others about children's early written production, their progress from nonconventional to conventional writing practices, and their continuing development as writers. In addition, considerable research on children's early writing and writing development K–adult has been completed in the past decade by the Center for the Study of Writing at the University of California, Berkeley.

In this chapter, we will examine children's writing development (reviewing some of the discussion from Chapters 2 and 3), and look at instructional strategies and practices that promote writing growth. As one context for our discussion, take a moment now to reflect on your own writing development and yourself as a writer today.

What do you remember about your earliest writing?

What sort of writing went on in your home and community when you were a child?

How many *different* ways can you think of that you used writing in school (including passing notes to your best friend!)?

Have you ever kept a diary or a journal? Do you now?

Do you write poetry or stories? Accounts or letters to family and friends?

Have you ever kept a written account of a vacation trip?

How is your writing today different from the writing you did as a youngster or even five years ago?

How do you handle those times when ideas and words won't come? (In our house, we call it "listening to the computer hum"; each of us has our own ways of getting through those times—"keeping going," as Harste, Woodward, and Burke [1984] say.)

These reflections are important: They not only help us remember the overriding presence of writing in our lives but also cause us to stop a moment to consider the wonder of it all—the sheer magnificence of the writing act and of what we have accomplished and what we are watching children accomplish daily in our classrooms.

Keep in mind as we progress through this chapter that it is very difficult to separate reading and writing processes; they are, in fact, "different sides of the same coin" (M. R. Ruddell, 1993). Nor can we separate the reading and writing from other language and communicative acts. In their study of three-, four-, five-, and six-year-old-children's writing and reading, Jerry Harste and his associates (1984) documented the ways in which children move between various language media during writing:

> It is important to note the role which speech plays in...
> writing event[s]. Latrice's initial written response to
> our request, "Write your name and anything else you can
> write," was linear marking on paper. She then moved to art.
> Before she once again engaged in writing she announced,
> "Gonna write an i." (p. 37)

Harste et al. then state forcefully,

> *There has been a long, unfortunate history of separating reading from writing, speaking from writing, art from writing, and reading, writing, speaking, and listening from each other. One must… pause to ask, "Why?" Clearly the cause must be that, theoretically, researchers have seen these areas as distinct. Each has been assumed to have different origins, and their joint participation in language operations has been considered to be of no basic psychological import. Even when written language and speech are closely linked in one operation, as they are in reading and writing, they are reported as if one did not exist, or treated as if they are separable processes belonging to two completely different classes of phenomena. This is unfortunate, since language is a multimodal event. And so is language learning…*
>
> *Children gesture, act out, draw, and speak during the fulfillment of a request to write. Speech and the use of alternative communication systems arise spontaneously and seem to assist the child in planning. These activities do not lie outside the writing process, but are an intimate and integral part of that process. (p. 37)*

With that, let us now look at how children become and continue to grow as writers; later, we will discuss in detail instructional practices that foster writing growth.

BECOMING WRITERS

Children begin writing at very early ages, long before entry into school and the onset of reading and writing instruction (Ruddell & Ruddell, 1994). Granted, children's early writing may not look like conventional writing—it has for years been called "scribbling" or mistaken for drawing; nevertheless it is rule-governed, organized, and orderly in much the same way as conventional writing. In fact, today, rather than dismiss "scribbling" as random marks on paper, we use the term "scribble" or "scribble writing" (some people use "pretend writing") to designate the period of children's early writing when the written form itself has not yet taken on the appearance of standard English orthography (although "wavy scribble" does have a decidedly cursive look). Our understanding now is that scribble writing is, indeed, true writing that can be, and is, read by the children who wrote it; further, scribble writing will gradually yield to more and more conventional-like writing as children experiment with and discover conventional written language structures and rules.

We now actually know a great deal about how writers develop, and it is this body of information that serves increasingly as the foundation for classroom practice (Dyson & Freedman, 1991). In the following discussion, we present Leslie Morrow's (1993, pp. 234-237) summary statements of current understandings about children's writing development; we've added our own discussion and elaboration of Morrow's conclusions.

FAMILY AND COMMUNITY INFLUENCES

Children's early literacy experiences are embedded in the familiar situations and real-life experiences of family and community membership. Children begin writing at home from experiences they've had in their homes and social communities. In the past, we made great distinction between "language-rich" and "not-so-language-rich" homes and communities, and considered opportunities for writing and other language interactions to be substantially greater in the former than in the latter (Bernstein, 1961, 1964; Tough, 1977). We now acknowledge the wide variations that may comprise language- (and literacy-) richness in homes and communities (Heath, 1983; Heller, 1990; Moll, 1992); that is, we understand that homes and communities in all economic and social levels, lifestyles, cultures, and ethnicities are filled with language and literate actions, and that we cannot use these social categories to predict which students are more or less likely to become successful writers and readers (Harste et al., 1984; Sulzby, Teale, & Kamberelis, 1989). Rather, we acknowledge the diverse funds of language and literacy knowledge children bring with them to school, understand that school learning routines may or may not match language and learning routines from home and/or community social networks and may or may not build on the knowledge and abilities children already have (Au, 1993; Gallimore, Boggs, & Jordan, 1974; Heath, 1983; Moll, 1992), and seek ways to create closer links between children's home, community, and school experiences.

Luis Moll (1992) describes the intricate and varied language and literate behaviors found in working-class Latino homes and communities. He states, "These households are not socially or intellectually barren; they contain knowledge, people use reading and writing, they mobilize social relationships, and they teach and learn" (p. 225). He further challenges the prevailing belief that children from working-class homes suffer deficits in "funds of background knowledge" and suggests that the real deficit is a lack of extended social networks between homes and schools.

Consider for a moment the story shown in Figure 7-1 dictated by a homeless child, Angela (Van Hoorn, Nourot, Scales, & Alward, 1992, pp. 135-138); certainly, Angela could be thought to live in a lifestyle and community not language- or literacy-rich. Note, however, how manifestly literate Angela's dictated story is about life in a community of homeless people—how she uses

Once there was a
lady who lived
in a house and
didn't have anything
to eat.

Once there was a
woman dressed
in blue and
she wanted
to go

to the store
but she didn't
have any
money to buy
anything.

This is a lady who
was afraid to go
to the store because

Somebody might
kidnap her.

This woman has a
home and doesn't

have any soap, so she
had to buy some to wash
her dress.

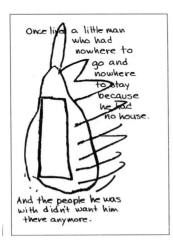

Once lived a little man
who had
nowhere to
go and
nowhere
to stay
because
he had
no house.

And the people he was
with didn't want him
there anymore.

Everything
was
stolen
and
there
was
nothing
left.

The End.

FIGURE 7-1

Angela's Dictated Story

conventional language markers to initiate events ("Once there was") and bring the story to a close ("The End"); then consider further how Angela's language, story, and life knowledge may or may not match learning routines and expectations in school.

EARLY WRITING PROGRESSION

As a process, early writing development is characterized by children's moving from playfully making marks on paper, through communicating messages on paper, to making texts as artifacts. One of the most striking characteristics of young writers is their ability to distinguish between art and writing (Harste et al., 1984). In Figures 7-2, 7-3, and 7-4, three-year-old Kenny and four-year-old Sarah and Ryan create art, drawing pictures about their trip to the local fire station, and then telling about their pictures when questioned by an adult. Kenny says of his picture (Figure 7-2):

> *These are the ladders. This is how big the fire truck is—that big—look at how all tall the ladder truck is. This [upper extreme left] is the fireman.*

Sarah (Figure 7-3):

> *Here is the fireman's truck. Here is a ladder; here is a ladder; here is a ladder . . . Nothing is happening in this story. [Sarah then points to another drawing she's done and tells a story about Big Bird. She returns to her first drawing.] Here is where I'm going to make a fireman on the ladder [middle of the page]. I forgot to make eyes for him. Here is the fireman and here is where he sprays the hose.*

Ryan (Figure 7-4):

> *There is all the firemen and this is the fireman on the ladder. This is the little ladder and the fireman again. [When asked about the horizontal lines in middle of page] That's the flag. This is all the guys putting out the fire with the hose.*

Clearly, these are works of art; nevertheless, they are very much an "intimate and integral part" of the children's writing development (recall Harste et al. from our earlier discussion). Each piece carries a story—Sarah's, explicitly— thus demonstrating the children's understanding that art itself is symbolic: Art is one option a writer has for representing meaning. Sarah clearly understands the symbolic value of her art; after initially listing objects ("Here's a ladder, here's a ladder") she comments, "There's nothing happening in this story." Later she returns to finish (and enliven) her work by adding human characters and action.

Whitney, at about the same age-range as Kenny, Ryan, and Sarah, had occasion to produce written messages (rather than stories). At the age of

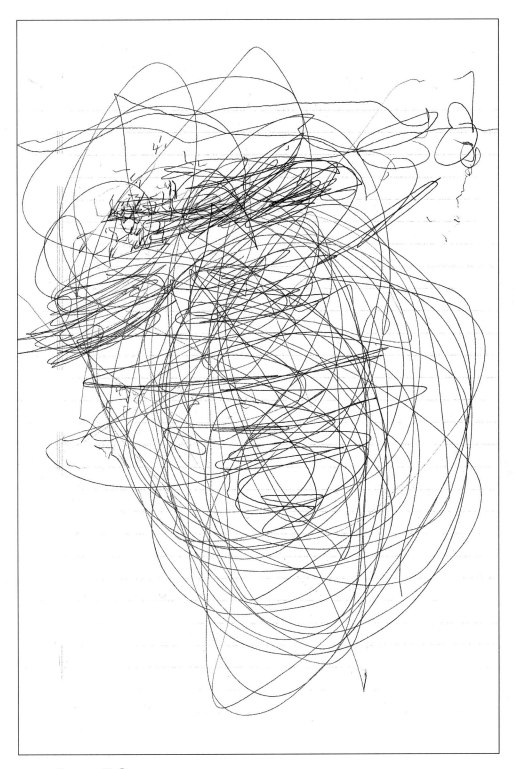

Figure 7-2

Kenny's Art

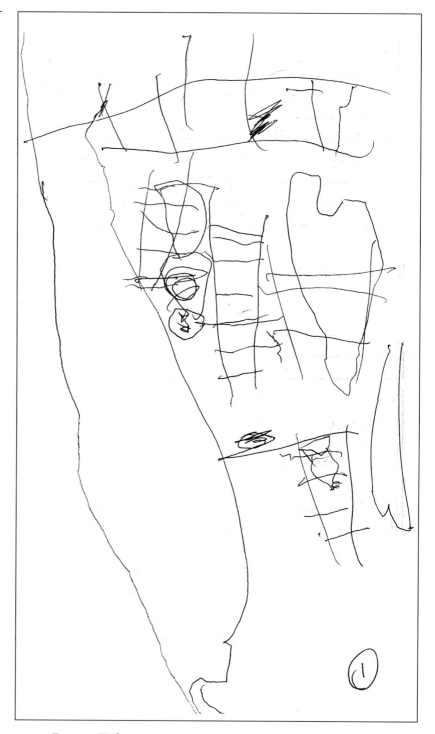

FIGURE 7-3

Sarah's Art

FIGURE 7-4

Ryan's Art

three, she signs her name to a birthday-present card (Figure 7-5), and later, at four, writes an Easter greeting (Figure 7-6). Notice the cursive "look" to Whitney's signature and to her Easter message. There is no mistaking the intent of these written messages.

FORM FOLLOWS FUNCTION

Children learn the uses of written language before they learn the forms. Whitney's birthday-gift card signature and Easter message (Figures 7-5 and 7-6) are evidence that form follows function in beginning writing. Ryan (see Figure 7-7), at seven years old, demonstrates his growing command of written language forms and, additionally, his understanding that story titles, capital letters, and punctuation have functions to serve in written text. Ryan uses his own, rather than conventional, rules of title presentation, capitalization, and punctuation in the story. After writing it, Ryan then read his story orally as follows (Ryan read the story flawlessly; the invented spellings in the story supported, rather than hindered, his oral reading):

Andrew and the Painted House

One day Andrew got paint and wanted to paint the house. He got messy. When he was done the house was messy too. But he liked it. His parents did not like it. "But least he learned how to paint," said Dad. But Mom said, "Not a very good job." But Andrew said, "But I like it. But least I painted it. Do you like it?"
The End

FIGURE 7-5

Whitney's Signature

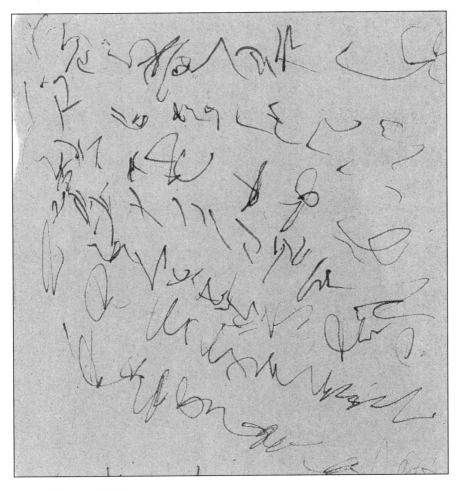

—— **FIGURE 7-6** ——————————————————

Whitney's Note

Harste and his associates (1984) illustrate further the ways in which children learn the use of written language before they learn the form. Four-year-old Alison wrote a story to record her own oral rendering of a wordless storybook (see Figure 7-8).

Alison chose to represent her story by writing repeated reconfigurations of the letters in her name: a-l-i-s-o-n. She then, over several months, faithfully read the following text for her story (with minor variations):

> One day Daddy came home and he said, "Hi Family, I'm home," and he's gonna take us to McDonald's. I'm gonna have a fun meal. (Harste et al., 1984, p. 10)

321

Andrew and the paydid house
One day Andrew giet paet
and. wiete to paet the house
he giet mise. wien he wes
dien. the house wes mise
to. but he Like it. his
paris dient tike it. but
Lest he Lrnd hiw to pate
sied Dad but Mom sied
not a vare god Jib but Andrew
sied but I Like it. but
Lest I paet it. do you Like
it.

FIGURE 7-7

Ryan's Story, "Andrew and the Painted House"

FIGURE 7-7 CONTINUED

INVENTION AND REINVENTION OF LANGUAGE FORMS

Children's writing develops through constant invention and reinvention of the forms of written language. Marie Clay (1975) identified a number of principles children discover about writing forms: the **recurring principle**—the idea that writing consists of recurring figures and moves (e.g., wavy, curved, straight, and rounded lines); the **generative principle**—the idea that, with a limited number of letters combined in different ways, one can generate an unlimited number of words; and the **flexibility principle**—

One day Daddy came home and he said, "Hi family, I'm home," and he's gonna take us to McDonald's. I'm gonna have a fun meal.

Story to Wordless Book
(Alison, Age 4.3)

—— **FIGURE 7-8** ——

Allison's Story

the idea that the same letters may be written in different ways (e.g., manuscript, cursive, upper- and lowercase, gothic, italic), but that there are limits as to the acceptability of letter reconfiguration and permutation (e.g., b, d, but not, ɔ).

Children discover these principles, and others, as they invent and reinvent written language forms; recall Alison's reconfigurations of a-l-i-s-o-n for an entire story (Figure 7-8) and Ryan's unconventional use of capitals and punctuation. Critical to understand here is that children move from nonconventional to conventional written forms *through the process of discovering* conventional forms of writing, i.e., inventing and reinventing written forms (Temple, Nathan, Temple, & Burris, 1993). Throughout this process, they construct theories and test hypotheses about the written language system (Ruddell & Ruddell, 1994).

Recent research has found further that, as children move from nonconventional to conventional written language, they individually and separately make essentially the same discoveries about written language in essentially the same order (Temple et al., 1993, p. 2). We thus are able to arrive at generalizations about children's written language development.

Sulzby, Barnhart, and Hieshima (1989) caution, however, that we should be wary of viewing children's progression toward conventional writing in terms of "developmental stages." They recommend, instead, that we focus on complex writing *patterns* that children use in individualistic ways while becoming conventional writers. Sulzby and her associates suggest further that, even though all children develop similarly, individual differences are to be expected. Writing patterns that a child uses at a given time reflect the specific hypothesis the child is testing about written language at that time; the pattern may or may not reflect other knowledge the child has about writing or her or his overall literacy development.

SELF-INITIATED AND SELF-DIRECTED WRITING

Children's involvement in written language, though typically embedded in social situations and interactions, is essentially self-initiated and self-directed. Morrow (1993) makes the important point that very young children and children not in school write when, and only when, they want to. Inducements and directives to write are usually ineffective. In *Living Between the Lines*, Lucy Calkins (1991) extends that idea by arguing forcefully that, in school, where inducements and directives to write generally *do* work, children churn out pages and pages of formulaic writing (i.e., writing that they think will please teachers) unless and until the writing they are engaged in grows from deeply felt events, experiences, and circumstances in their own lives. Much of Calkins's message is that, at every level—from the very youngest writers to the oldest students in school—we need instructional environments and practices that invite students to be "wide-awake" to their world and aware of those things that affect them deeply. Such "wide awakeness" and sensitivity, in turn, *compel* students to write both in and out of school, and establish life-long habits of self-initiated writing.

STORY MAKING

In writing, as in talking, story making is a primary impulse and activity. The human propensity is to create stories—stories that entertain, relay information, warn or caution, educate, and do many other things. Anne Dyson (1989, 1990) talks of the different worlds—imagination, fantasy, real or experienced, and social—that writers move within and between as they create not only stories, but the voices of characters and of themselves as well.

OBSERVING SKILLED WRITERS

Children learn about writing by observing more skilled others and by participating with them in literacy events. Vygotsky's (1986) notion of the *Zone of Proximal Development* assumes the presence of a "more skilled other" in learning, as we discussed in Chapter 2. Lucy Calkins (1986, 1991),

Nancie Atwell (1987), and Regie Routman (1991) state unambiguously that writing classrooms are ones in which *everyone* must write, and the teacher's role is to be a clear and dramatic model of a writer writing. Calkins and Atwell emphasize the value of children seeing not only how and what skilled writers produce, but that the teacher considers writing a serious and important part of his or her life. Atwell (1987) describes how she writes in her classroom:

> I sit down at an empty student desk—so kids can clearly see what I'm doing—with my favorite white paper and favorite Flair pen. I label my manuscript DRAFT #1, put my head down, and start writing one of the stories I'd considered in the mini-lesson. I don't look up. I'm not watching to see who's writing and who isn't. I'm busy, and I mean business, and my posture demonstrates that I'm expecting everyone else will become a writer and join me.
>
> And they do. After ten minutes or so, when I finally look up from my own writing, everyone is writing. Always. . . .
>
> As the year progresses I'll find pockets of time when no one needs me and when I trust that they don't. Then I can sit at an empty desk, pull the latest draft of a story or poem or article from my bookbag, and write among the writers. More often I'll bring to the workshop for student response something I've written from the night before—possibly an even more effective demonstration of my seriousness as a writer since it involves homework. (p. 84)

INDEPENDENT PRACTICE WITH WRITING FORMS AND FUNCTIONS

Children need to work independently on the functions and form of writing that they have experienced through interactions with literate others. Practice writing, like practice reading, is best done for purposes and in circumstances that are real. Children willingly practice writing when writing serves a true and useful purpose; watch them write up orders when playing restaurant or store, or write long (and sometimes impassioned) notes and letters to friends, or weave intricate written plots starring Teenage Mutant Ninja Turtles, Disney characters, Jurassic Park dinosaurs, or whatever the current rage happens to be. Sarah's letter to dad (Figure 7-9) when she was seven illustrates this clearly; it also illustrates Sarah's current writing penchant for chaining events together in her work with "and" ("and the goat took grandpas paper... and we got to run in the water . . . and we went to the ski show . . .").

An interesting aspect of independent work and practice writing is that such writing will display the nonconventional writing forms students use as

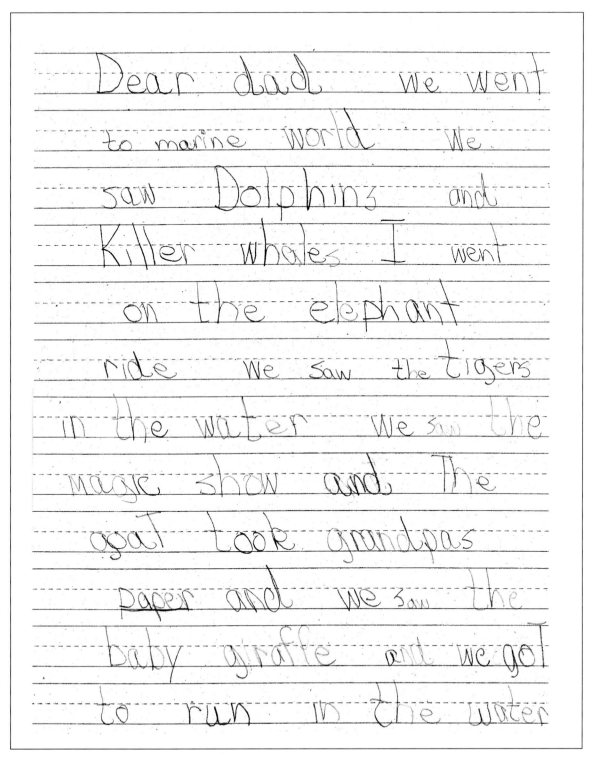

Dear dad we went
to marine world We
saw Dolphins and
Killer whales I went
on the elephant
ride We saw the tigers
in the water We saw the
magic show and The
ogat took grandpas
paper and we saw the
baby giraffe and we got
to run in the water

FIGURE 7-9

Sarah's Letter to Dad   327

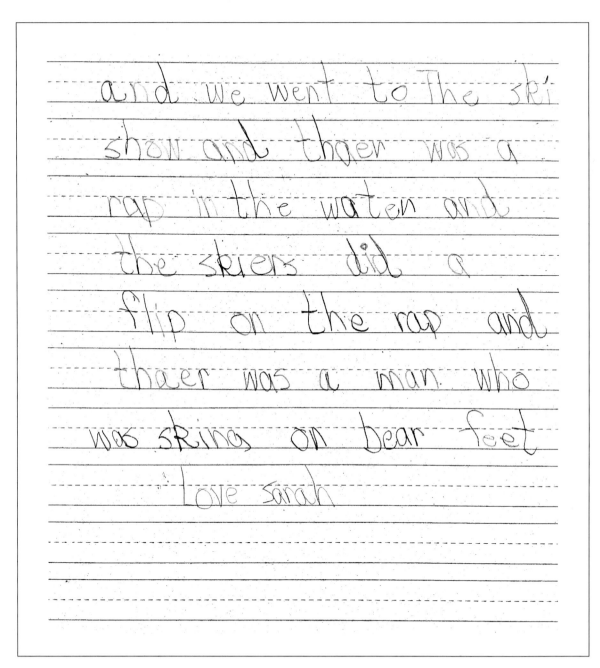

and we went to the ski
show and thaer was a
rap in the water and
the skiers did a
flip on the rap and
thaer was a man who
was sking on bear feet
Love Sarah

— **FIGURE 7-9** CONTINUED —

they progress toward conventional writing. This is not just with young writers, but with older, developing writers as well. Notice the nonconventional writing forms in John's letter to mother when he was almost eight (Figure 7-10): invented spellings ("Mather," "cold"), capital "M" used throughout, the "I have miss you" construction, and the comma-like mark

after his signature undoubtedly intended to serve as the period conventionally used after initials. Temple et al. (1993) emphasize the importance of
allowing students the freedom to explore and experiment with nonconventional forms without fearing that students will "overlearn" their own inventions and therefore never arrive at conventional form. Just as children discard nonconventional spoken language ("I runded" for "I ran"; "foots" for
"feet") through social interactions, so too will writers, as they interact with
other writers in their classrooms and communities and in the books they
read, move from their invented to conventional written forms.

Developing Students' Writing in Classrooms

Within the past decade, teaching practices to guide students' writing
have been revolutionized. Much of this great change has come about as the
result of teachers' participation in National Writing Project programs that
have, first and possibly foremost, turned teachers into writers. Concurrent
with programs run by the National Writing Project has been our changing
and deepening understanding of the interactive and transactive nature of all
language and literacy processes (see Chapter 2); thus, teachers' growing
awareness of their own power as writers, combined with a more fully integrated view of the reading and writing processes, has led to their implementation of Writing Project practices. Central to these is the writing workshop.
In the remainder of the chapter, we shall develop writing workshop practices in depth, discuss project-based writing and theme cycles, and consider
areas of teacher and parent concerns about children's writing.

The Writing Workshop

Writing workshop is the term currently used to describe writing
instruction in which a period of classroom time each day is set aside for
children to be immersed in writing (Atwell, 1987; Calkins, 1986, 1991;
Graves, 1983). Ideally, writing workshop begins with children's entry into
school and extends throughout the elementary grades and (hopefully) into
middle and secondary schools. In the writing workshop, the focus is, primarily, on *process*—engaging children in productive writing behaviors and
events that lead to ever-increasing writing fluency and sophistication—
rather than *product*, although many polished writing products emerge from
workshop activities. Focus is also on giving children considerable autonomy
in deciding their writing topics and styles and in making critical decisions
about such issues as editing choices, the final form a piece of writing will
take, how or whether a piece is to be submitted for grading, and other
aspects of written production. Nancie Atwell (1987) describes seven principles that undergird the writing workshop:

1. **Writers need regular chunks of time**—time to think, write, confer, read, change their minds, and write some more. Writers need time they can count on, so even when they aren't writing, they're anticipating the time they will be. Writers need time to write well.

2. **Writers need their own topics.** Right from the first day of kindergarten, students should use writing as a way to think about and give shape to their own ideas and concerns.

3. **Writers need response.** Helpful response comes during—not after—the composing. It comes from the writer's peers and from the teacher, who consistently models the kinds of restatements and questions that help writers reflect on the content of their writing.

4. **Writers learn mechanics in context,** from teachers who address errors as they occur within individual pieces of writing, where these rules and forms will have meaning.

5. **Children need to know adults who write.** We need to write, share our writing with students, and demonstrate what experienced writers do in the process of composing, letting our students see our own drafts in all their messiness and tentativeness.

6. **Writers need to read.** They need access to a wide-ranging variety of texts, prose and poetry, fiction and nonfiction.

7. **Writing teachers need to take responsibility for their knowledge and teaching.** We must seek out professional resources that reflect the far-reaching conclusions of recent research into children's writing. And we must become writers and researchers, observing and learning from our own and children's writing. (pp. 17-18)

Let us now look at how these principles are realized in writing workshop classrooms.

Time

Essential to the writing workshop classroom are daily, large chunks of time set aside for writing. The writing workshop works best when it happens every day, without fail, so that children can count on its regular occurrence (even on days when the normal schedule is interrupted) and when it covers a good portion of the morning or afternoon. At the very minimum, writing workshop needs to occur three days a week (Graves, 1983)—the *same* three days every week. Such a regular and dependable schedule is important for any number of reasons, not the least of which is the marvelous tendency of the human mind to anticipate writing that is to come—rehearsing at all manner of times and in all manner of places writing it knows it will be doing at 10:00 a.m. tomorrow (continuing from the work that began at 10:00 a.m. today). The payoff here is that children gather information, consider alternative ways of saying things, revise and rethink their writing and ideas outside of the writing workshop, and even when they are not in school. This anticipation and rehearsal for writing is how real writers write—how they polish and hone not only their writing but their thinking as well.

Time allocation within the writing workshop is equally important. Writing workshop needs to be sufficiently long enough each day for children to think, plan, discuss ideas, "noodle," revise, rethink, engage in "keep going" rituals; in short, to do all the myriad *things* that writers do. The

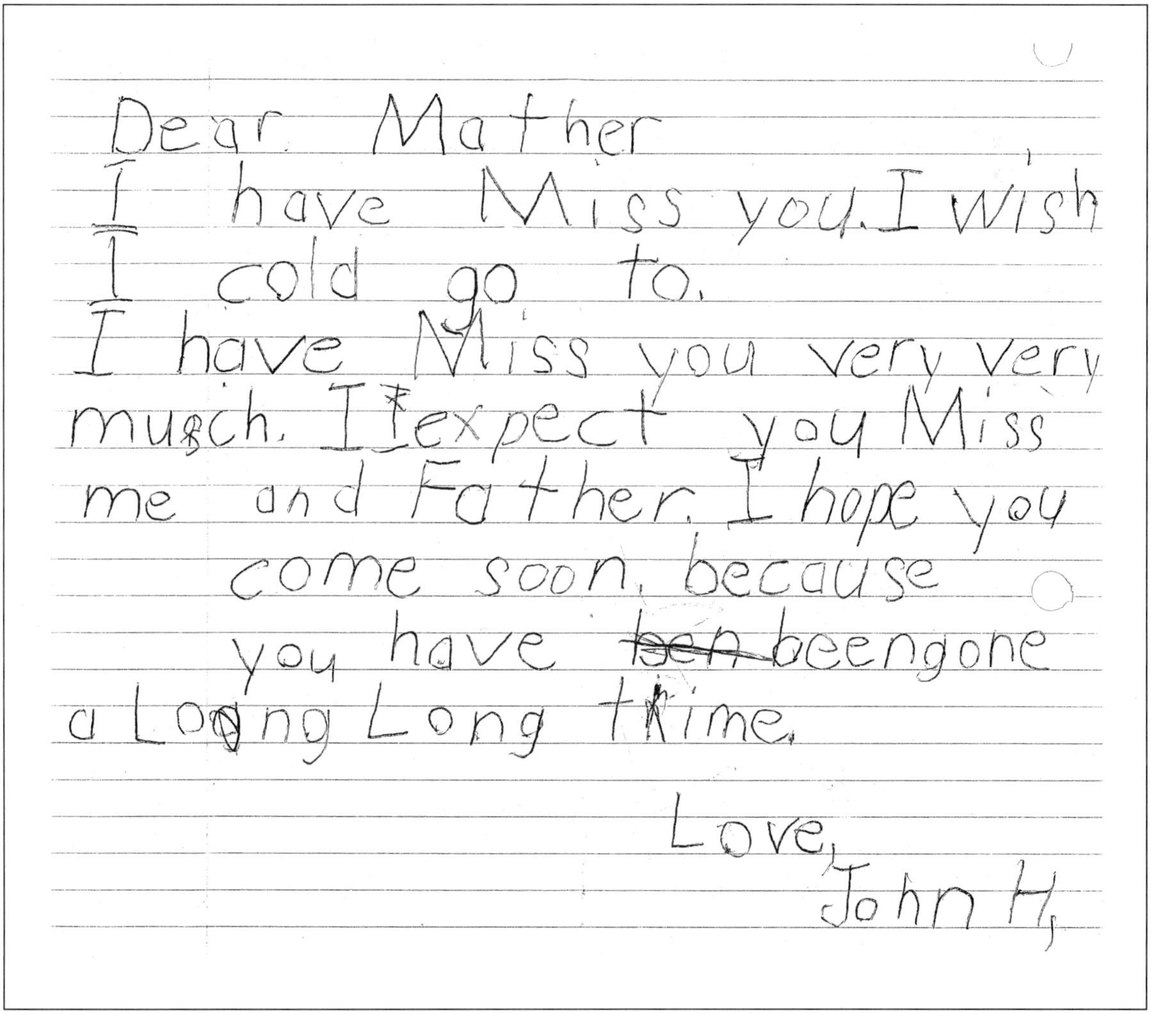

Dear Mather
I have Miss you. I wish
I cold go to.
I have Miss you very very
musch. I expect you Miss
me and Father. I hope you
come soon, because
you have been beengone
a loang Long time.
                    Love,
                      John H,

FIGURE 7-10

Children's Written Language Samples Illustrating Development Growth point, the fundamental reason for daily, large chunks of writing time, is to create the environment and conditions for young writers that professional, published writers create for themselves. As Nancie Atwell so aptly points out (1987), we have too many accounts of professional writers reflecting on their own writing process not to know that productive writing comes from writers' frequent, extended participation in their craft, the discipline they acquire from the daily act of getting words on paper, and their persistence in the face of days "listening to the computer hum."

Virtually every author's reflection on his or her own writing includes the message that to be a writer, one must "write every day" (Briggs, 1991). Writers claim to have no more talent or intelligence or inspiration than anyone else (Briggs, 1991; Vonnegut, 1981). Rather they extol the value of *time*—time to produce large amounts of text, to make mistakes, to rearrange and search for one perfect missing word, and time also to ride that gravy train when words are coming faster than they can be gotten on paper.

Time is forever at issue in schools; teachers never seem to have enough of it, and there's always a voice or group or authority out there telling them there's one more thing they must do. To find time for writing workshop, you may want to reconsider the use of time allocated in your class for reading, spelling, and language arts and choose to integrate all or most of this time and instruction into the writing workshop, or, if you will, the reading-writing workshop. Alternately, you may prefer to combine the writing workshop with project- or theme-based instruction that integrates other subject areas. (We'll discuss this in a later section of this chapter and in Chapter 9.) And, finally, you may find that careful analysis of the weekly schedule reveals slack time that may be creatively combined or clustered with other "found" time for a three- or five-day-a-week writing workshop schedule.

Environment and Room Organization

The writing workshop requires certain basic environmental and organizational structures if it is to be successful. Writing equipment and supplies, along with associated materials, must be available. You'll need to have on-hand rather generous supplies of lined and unlined paper of different sizes and shapes, and all manner of writing utensils. A key component here is variety. We've always had this strange affinity for absolute uniformity of writing materials and equipment in schools: We dispense wide-lined paper and fat pencils to every child in primary grades, and dictate "pen" or "pencil" even for first-draft writing in upper grades. Such uniformity is, quite simply, unnecessary; further, and, perhaps more important, it serves no useful educational purpose.

Children of all ages like to experiment with various writing media, especially bright marking pens, and very young children routinely write with standard #2 pencils at home; many young writers prefer using blank paper rather than lined; and most older students have their own preference for wide- or narrow-lined paper. In addition, children are developing keyboard skills at very early ages these days, and in classrooms where computers are available, may wish at times to bypass pencil and paper altogether. The point is that it's time for us to discard our old ways, to provide (or allow children to bring to school) widely varied writing supplies, and to encourage children to experiment with different writing media to find the ones that work best for them.

You'll also need folders or portfolios for filing drafts and works-in-progress and for displaying finished pieces. Writing workshop classrooms require systems for maintaining children's writing notes, writing drafts, works-in-progress, finished pieces, and works-abandoned-earlier-that-interest-me-now. File folders are generally central to these systems. You'll not only need file folders and portfolios, but also places and systems for storage. Journals and notebooks abound in writing workshop rooms as well; these are usually kept in children's desks or cubbies.

An environmental and organizational requirement for writing workshop rooms is that the room arrangement itself must be flexible and conducive to writing workshop activities. Using bookcases and/or tables already in the room, create a writing center that holds writing supplies (pens, pencils, paper, stapler, scissors, etc.), reference books, and other resources. You may want to incorporate an art center with paints, colored pens, chalks, paste, and other supplies into (or adjacent to) the writing center. Lee Galda, Bernice Cullinan, and Dorothy Strickland (1993) also recommend a separate "Do Not Disturb" table, where talking is not allowed, for children who want to write uninterrupted by peer or teacher conferences on a given day. In the absence of such an area or table, a "Do Not Disturb" sign displayed at one's desk signals the same intent.

Most classrooms now have movable desks and tables; make sure these are arranged to allow children to get quietly in and out of peer-editing group sessions and large group discussions, or place them in permanent clusters. Walking space is also important, not only so that you can move about the room to confer with children, but also so children may talk with one another, meet in informal working groups, use the pencil sharpener or stapler, and have easy access to the materials storage area (or writing/art center) and any other part of the room that writers may need to frequent, such as the "Do Not Disturb" table and special nooks or spaces set aside for partners and small groups to meet and share their writing.

Writing workshop rooms also need sufficient flexibility for furniture to be rearranged at the end of each workshop session so the entire class can gather to hear selected children share finished products or works-in-progress with the class each day (better yet, if at all possible, is permanent floor space set aside for informal class gatherings). The focal point of this space is the Author's Chair, where a child sits when he or she is sharing work with the class. The Author's Chair doesn't have to be fancy—a regulation table chair from the classroom or folding chair is fine—but a little something extra adds a certain pizazz. Instead of a standard classroom chair, you could use a director's chair with colored canvas seat and back; that would be an ideal (and inexpensive) Author's Chair, as would a webbed lawn chair, a molded plastic lawn/patio chair, or an easy chair you've de-cided you no longer need at home.

Writing Workshop Structure

Three major events comprise the writing workshop: (1) mini-lessons, (2) writing time and conferences, and (3) sharing time. Within each of these events, any number of activities occur, and, in the case of writing time and conferences, many different activities often occur simultaneously, so that writing workshop classrooms appear very busy, indeed. To the untrained eye, they might even seem chaotic—they certainly don't look like the "classroom writing" scene traditional to elementary school that many of us remember. An important aspect of the writing workshop to keep in mind is that it is based upon the assumption that we are establishing a *community of writers*, and that individuals in this community interact and transact with one another in the process of creating text. This interaction and transaction occurs throughout the three events of mini-lessons, writing time and conferences, and sharing-time meetings.

Mini-lessons. Mini-lessons are short, to-the-point instructional episodes in which one "something" is being taught. Mini-lessons occur at the beginning of each writing workshop session, rarely exceed five to ten minutes in length, and always end with a status report in which each child identifies his or her working goal for that day. Early in the year, during the time when you are introducing students to writing workshop, mini-lessons may focus more on workshop procedures and protocols than on writing issues per se. Nancie Atwell (1987) uses her very first mini-lesson to (1) model her own thinking process as she considers topics she'd like to write about and the thinking and rehearsal she does before actually beginning to write, (2) guide students in selecting their first writing topic for the year, and (3) establish workshop guidelines. Because of the introductory nature of this first mini-lesson, it frequently goes a little beyond the standard five to ten minutes.

The three elements of Atwell's first mini-lesson are designed to move children immediately into writing workshop behaviors and to set the tone for how the workshop will proceed throughout the year. In preparing to teach your first mini-lesson, spend some time thinking about your own topic-selection process when you write, and consider a piece of writing that you'd like to do right now. Introduce your mini-lesson by telling your students about your own thinking and prewriting processes, even if you rely mainly on academic writing you've done (course papers, for example). You might begin by saying, "When I am writing a research report, I usually begin by . . . " or something similar. If you do this, also remember to include your current consideration of a nonacademic topic. (It helps to do the kind of reflection on your own writing that we suggested early in this chapter to remind you of the many ways you use writing and how you select topics when you do.)

Following your revelations about your own topic selection process, ask the children to begin thinking about possible topics they'd like to write about right now—events, experiences, feelings, etc. Have them jot their ideas down and spend a few minutes considering how they might begin developing each. Then have the children share their ideas with a partner and begin narrowing their ideas down for today's writing. Encourage partners to give suggestions and borrow ideas from one another. After a few minutes, ask the children to decide on their topic; call each child's name and ask, "What topic are you writing on today?" Announce the writing guidelines, and have students begin writing. Paraphrased below are the writing guide-lines Nancie Atwell uses (1987, pp. 83-84):

1. **No erasing.** Save a record of your thinking and how it's changed. When you change your mind, draw a line through.

2. **Write on one side of the paper only.** Writers cut and paste to rearrange ideas. That's hard to do when writing on both sides of the paper.

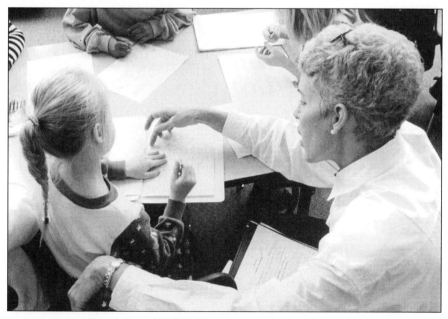

Writing Workshop Conference

3. **Save everything.** You're creating a history of your writing. Not only that, you may want at some time to go back to ideas you've worked on earlier.

4. **Date and label everything.** Mark it "Draft #1," or "Draft #2," or "Notes" if that's appropriate.

5. **Speak in quiet voices only.** Everyone needs quiet to think and write; I'll speak quietly and expect you to do so, also. There are places you can go to share your work with a friend.

6. **Work really hard.**

These guidelines are a useful starting place for developing your own classroom writing workshop "rules of the road." They will require some adjustment in classes where children use a computer to draft and revise their writing. Do understand that *procedural structure is important to the success of the entire writing workshop venture.* Writing workshop is *not* about anything-goes, out-of-control classrooms; it *is* about focused, energetic writers writing, conferring, sharing their work, and working productively. "What are you doing today?" signals the focused nature of what everyone is doing. It becomes the status-of-the-class roll-call report asked of everyone at the end of each mini-lesson and just before writing time each day.

After the first few days, workshop mini-lessons are determined by observations the teacher makes of children's writing and participation in the workshop. As we mentioned earlier, mini-lessons tend to be more procedural during the period immediately after writing workshop is initiated and more content-focused as children become accustomed to workshop procedures and protocols. Following are some topics that might be useful early mini-lessons:

1. How to decide what you're doing today, e.g., drafting, self-editing, revising, conferencing, peer-editing, polishing, etc. (This is Nancie Atwell's second mini-lesson.)

2. Rules and procedures for moving around the room during writing and conferences time.

3. How, when, and where to get needed supplies.

4. Options for working with peers.

5. How to get my attention when I'm working with others or doing my own writing.

6. Conferencing procedures and rules.

7. How to do peer conferences and peer editing.

8. Sharing-time meeting procedures.

9. What to do with notes, drafts, pieces ready for editing, and finished pieces.

10. Options for using special nooks and spaces during writing time.

Undoubtedly, other ideas for procedural mini-lessons will occur to you as the class launches writing workshop; just as undoubtedly, you'll soon find your mini-lesson topics shifting to address various content, design, and mechanics of writing issues.

Writing Time and Conferences. Writing time and conferences comprise the bulk of the writing workshop; writing time (including conferences) should be at least thirty minutes each day—longer, if possible and if appropriate for your students. Mini-lessons end and writing time begins with the status-of-the-class roll-call report ("What are you doing today?"). Nancie Atwell calls this the "status-of-the-class conference" and asserts that three minutes spent polling children to find out what each is doing that day, thus creating immediate focus for each child's work and writing, is three minutes very well spent (1987, p. 89). She recommends teaching students "writer language" (*draft, revise, abandon, conference, edit*) so they can be precise about their actions. She then records each student's response each day. Figure 7-11 suggests an appropriate form for status-of-the-class roll-call and some abbreviations for recording.

Writing time is for the business of writing. In kindergarten and first grade, children are invited to draw and to write "as best they can" (Calkins, 1987). In the primary-grade writing workshop, you can expect some children to be drawing, some to be drawing and writing, others to be writing and illustrating, and many not using conventional written forms. In upper grades, the issues are different; instead of children who are not yet writing conventionally, we have children who are writing the same cartoon-character story over and over. And in all classrooms, children learning English as a second language may create combination first-language-and-English text or use many graphics and drawings to support, or in place of, written text. ESL and other students with language or learning differences may be reluctant to produce written text at all.

What is important here is that children begin putting their thoughts on paper, in whatever the form—even if their stories and accounts are repetitive or seemingly mundane. You then respond by honoring what children are doing, giving them many opportunities to write and to read their work, surrounding them with written language, and encouraging their risk-taking and experimentation. In short, your response corresponds with the conditions for literacy learning developed by Cambourne and Turbill (discussed in Chapter 3). During writing time, and other times as well, your major role is to guide children in seeing the various ways they can change, develop, and improve their writing. One important way this can happen is during conferences.

Conferences occur throughout the writing workshop and may take many different shapes and forms. In the seven principles cited earlier that undergird the writing workshop, principles 3 and 4 state that "Writers need response" and "Writers learn mechanics in context." Response and learning in context are the central focus of the writing conference. Early on, the most frequent conference is between teacher and child, and is held in short exchanges as the teacher circulates around the room, pausing to talk with individual children as they write. We could call these "honeybee" conferences, because the goal here is for the teacher to stop at many children's desks or writing areas (just as bees flit from flower to flower) and conduct short, to-the-point conversations that assist and guide the children in continuing their writing. Guidelines for these conferences include:

1. Keep it short—one to two minutes.
2. See as many writers each day as possible.

STATUS-OF-THE-CLASS

Name	Monday	Tuesday	Wednesday	Thursday	Friday

D1= first draft; D2= second draft; A.B.= abandon; S.E.= self-editing; P.E.= peer editing; S.C.= self-conference; P.C.= peer conference; T.C.= teacher conference.

FIGURE 7-11

Status-of-the-Class Record Form

3. Go to your students, rather than having them come to you, so you can control the length of the conference.

4. Make eye contact with the writer by kneeling or sitting alongside his or her desk.

5. Don't tell writers what should be in their writing or, worse, write on their piece.

6. Build on what writers know and have done.

7. Resist making judgments (positive or negative) about the writing and avoid contrived praise.

8. Ask about things that really interest you in children's writing (Atwell, 1987, pp. 94–95).

Other, more elaborated conferences between teacher and child occur as the teacher circulates in the room or when students request a teacher conference. Lucy Calkins calls these "longer, slower conferences" (1991) and suggests that teachers engage in a few longer, slower conferences each day, both in response to student need and as the result of planned attention to each child. She further emphasizes how important it is to remember that "We are teaching the writer, not the writing" (1986, p. 120) in all conferences. By that she means that we must cede autonomy and authority to children, letting them tell us how they are doing and what help they need, rather than looking for opportunities to teach writing technique. Neither do we need to dazzle children with brilliant repartee. Rather, she recommends that the opening question of a conference should be "How's it going?" or "Where are you with this?" (1986, p. 119). Atwell (1987, pp. 95–96) suggests follow-up questions that are useful in helping children solve their own writing problems; these are shown in Figure 7-12.

Peer conferences are a central feature of the writing workshop. Peer conferences involve partners or small groups of children sharing their writing with one another and receiving assistance and ideas for moving their writing forward. Peer editing often accompanies peer conferences. Children require some preparation and practice in peer conferencing and editing. The very first component of that preparation is for them to have many opportunities to observe as you guide individual conferences and editing sessions. Your role as model is critical here. In addition, you need to conduct mini-lessons, and perhaps a simulation or two, about peer conferencing and editing in which you demonstrate peer conferencing procedures. You may even wish to provide some simple guidelines for peer conferees; the following, for example:

1. When listening to or editing someone else's writing, the very first thing you should say or write is one or more things you found interesting about the piece.

2. Ask questions that allow the writer to solve problems and improve the work. Questions should begin "How could you . . . ?" "How might you . . . ?" "What do you want . . . ?" and so forth.

QUESTIONS THAT CAN HELP

SITUATION	CONFERENCE APPROACHES
The piece is unfocused: it covers several or many different days, events, ideas, etc.	• Do you have more than one story here? • What's the most important thing you're trying to say? • What's your favorite part? How can you build on it?
There isn't enough information in the piece.	• I don't understand. • Please tell me more about it. • What else do you know about your topic? • How could you find out more about your topic?
There's too much information in the piece.	• Is all this information important to your reader? What parts don't you need?
The piece is a list of events and includes little of the writer's reflections.	• How did you feel when this happened? • What do you think about this? • Why is this significant to you?
The lead holds the reader at arm's length, going on about contextual details rather than introducing the writer's thesis.	• Does this lead bring your reader right into the piece? • Where does your piece really begin? Can you delete other information and begin there instead?
The conclusion is either too sudden or drags on and on.	• What do you want your reader to know or feel at the end of your piece? Does this conclusion do it? • Where does your piece really end?
There are no or few direct quotes in a piece in which people talk.	• What can you do to show how these people spoke, so your reader can hear their voices?
You want to bring closure to the conference and understand what the student is taking away from the conference situation.	• What do you think you'll do next?

FIGURE 7-12

Questions That Can Help Children Solve Writing Problems

The mechanics of editing practices and procedures need also to be taught, e.g., how to identify and signal spelling and punctuation errors, how to suggest sentence or paragraph reconstruction, or how to discuss editing recommendations with authors. A great simple source for young writers' checklists on editing (for both primary and intermediate grades) is *Writing Yellow Pages: For Students and Teachers* (1988). You may need to return to peer conferencing and editing in mini-lessons as you observe and monitor students' interactions with one another.

Self-conferences also are an important part of writing workshop procedures. Self-conferences occur when children spend time consciously viewing their own writing metacognitively and metalinguistically; that is, children step outside their own personal attachment to their writing, look at their work objectively, and begin to ask questions to guide their own writing development. Lucy Calkins suggests the following questions for structuring self-conferences (1986, p. 19):

What have I said so far? What am I trying to say here?

How do I like it? What's good here that I can build on? What's not so good that I can fix?

How does it sound? How does it look?

How else could I have done this?

What will my reader think as he or she reads this? What questions will they ask? What will they notice? Feel? Think?

What am I going to do next?

We recommend that you keep this list permanently posted in your classroom. You may also use it, with a few changes, as the basis for a mini-lesson, teaching students how to conduct peer conferences and self-conferences.

Sharing Time. After writing time and conferences each day, the writing workshop is brought to an end in a sharing-time meeting. This is the meeting in which one, two, or three students elect to sit in the Author's Chair and read a finished piece or work-in-progress to the entire class. One or more mini-lessons should be taught on sharing-time meeting procedures and rules before the first such meeting occurs. The point of sharing time is both to make real to young writers the notion of "audience," by providing daily a living, breathing audience response, and also to encourage and celebrate daily the natural human desire to share our stories with one another.

Even though sharing-time meetings should have some general procedures and direction, they are not intended to be highly ritualized or rigid. When planning mini-lessons about sharing-time procedures, determine the boundaries of peer response to Author's Chair readers that seem appropriate to you, and communicate that to students. For example, authors presenting works-in-progress may want class assistance and suggestions for further revision; one sharing-time meeting procedure might be that, when seeking assistance, the author should tell the class what it is he or she wants in advance of the reading. Another useful guideline might be that responses to finished work focus on interesting ideas and uses of language (rather than suggestions for improvement) or on personal responses to the author's work.

Sustaining the Writing Workshop

Throughout the literature on writing workshop and process writing in general, six steps in the writing process are identified: prewriting, drafting, revising, editing, sharing, and publishing. These steps describe what writers do in their continuing development as writers. Thus, the steps describe much of the content of the daily activity that sustains the writing workshop itself. We shall discuss them separately here. However, in reality, the steps tend to blend and blur into one another.

Prewriting. Prewriting is the period during which writers select a topic, consider content, decide what form or design their writing might take, and anticipate and mentally rehearse the writing that is to come. In the writing workshop, children's working folders contain lists of topic possibilities, notes, random ideas, "story starters," schematics, abandoned works-in-progress, and other written artifacts that may be reviewed periodically as children consider writing topics (remember, they save everything). During the prewriting time, children may brainstorm, diagram, or create maps and outlines to guide them in the development of their writing. Rehearsal occurs, often without the children's conscious knowledge, as they try out the opening words of a poem or story, consider various ways to order events or ideas, and envision alternative endings.

Drafting. Drafting is the time when writers are getting words on paper. The single most important point for children to understand about drafting, especially when writing first drafts, is that drafts are just that—drafts, not finished pieces. Drafts are messy, with mark-outs and margin notes and arrows, and cut-and-paste sections. It is highly likely that, after procedural matters are all in place, mini-lessons will predominantly focus on drafting issues: idea development, design/genre options (e.g., poetry, prose, fiction, nonfiction), language precision, idea elaboration, and so forth. Rehearsal is part of drafting every bit as much as it is of prewriting. Drafting rehearsal often occurs between writing times as authors continue to consider content and design possibilities of their work in anticipation of the next writing period.

Revising. Drafting and revising are particularly difficult to separate because many writers revise as they draft (although not all do), and all writers revise and redraft after first writing. In the writing workshop, revision is the central issue of many conferences and mini-lessons, and so is highlighted as a significant part of the writing process. One goal of the writing workshop is to make revision a natural and reasonable part of the writing process itself. All work is not revised, however; some texts are abandoned when they fail to develop (we abandon writing in much the same way and for many of the same reasons we abandon reading when it doesn't satisfy), and other text drafts may require only minimal adjustments and editing.

Editing. Editing is the final revision stage in which pieces are generally being prepared for publication. Editing includes content changes (wording, idea elaboration, etc.) as well as final attention to mechanics (spelling, punctuation, etc.) and is the point in the writing process that reference texts—dictionaries, thesauruses, grammar books, and so forth—are most relied upon. It is during the editing process also that mechanics are most easily learned. Mini-lessons on editing frequently teach a specific mechanics skill, e.g., use of quotation marks in dialogue, capitalization, spelling demons, uses for italics, using semicolons, and so forth.

Sharing. Sharing occurs in the writing workshop from the moment children call out their writing topic in status-of-the-class conferences, and continues as children confer with teachers and peers during writing time, go to a special nook and read their work to a friend, pin work on the bulletin board, share from the Author's Chair, and take work home for family and friends to see. This notion of sharing is critical to the writing process; it's the only way writers have to know what's *coming through* (Graves, 1990)—what the audience understands and remembers about their work.

Publishing. Publishing is the formal act of sharing. In writing workshop classrooms, publishing may begin with stapled-together pages and progress to cloth-bound books written, illustrated, and bound by the children (see Chapter 3 for suggestions) or comb-bound books finished at a local print or duplicating shop with a comb binder (or at school if you have a binding machine). Computer availability opens desktop publishing opportunities and provides "real print" final text; hypercard and advanced computer software add to the possibilities for inclusion of graphics, illustrations merged from reference texts, and even combined video disc and written displays. But publishing doesn't have to be high-tech or gee-whiz. It may be, and most often likely is, children's carefully copied, final-draft, polished written pieces displayed everywhere in the classroom; class-assembled books of children's poems, stories, and accounts; and selected final-draft pieces included in children's portfolios.

RECORD KEEPING AND EVALUATION IN THE WRITING WORKSHOP

Record keeping and evaluation procedures in the writing workshop do not need to be particularly elaborate, but they do need to be accurate and consistently maintained. Because the writing workshop is so unlike traditional instruction, where everyone is doing essentially the same thing in essentially the same way, the very first goal of record keeping in the writing workshop must be documentation. To avoid hopeless confusion, the teacher must at all times have an accurate, written record of what every child is doing and accomplishing on a daily, weekly, monthly, and yearly basis. A second goal is for the teacher to monitor every child's writing progress, including progress in specific writing skills. And, finally, evaluation procedures must be established that allow teachers to provide productive feedback to every child and her or his parents about that child's writing development.

Keeping Records of What Children Are Doing and Accomplishing. The Status-of-the Classroom record form (shown in Figure 7-11, p. 338) is the easiest and most reasonable way for you to maintain records of what children are doing during writing workshop. It's therefore important that you not skip status-of-the-classroom roll-call, and that you spend the very short amount of time needed daily to record children's responses. Make sufficient copies of the form to last the school year and keep each week's completed form in a permanent record book.

Probably the best way to maintain records of what children have accomplished is to have them do it themselves. Have the children prepare sheets of notebook or tablet paper with the following headings and staple them onto an inside cover of their daily folder:

Date	Work Planned for Today	Work Accomplished Today

Each day at the end of writing time, just before sharing time, take a minute or two for children to log the work they accomplished. Entries need not be lengthy, but they should be precise and accurate, e.g., "revised 4 pp." "drafted poem" "P.C. with Kim, began revision." Completed sheets may be collected at grading period intervals and filed with your stored status-of-the-class records. A set of notebook paper sheets should be stapled on the other inside cover of students' daily folder titled, "Titles and Dates of Finished Pieces" (Atwell, 1987). On these sheets, students chronicle finished work they've developed throughout the year.

For very young children, much of this record keeping will likely be yours, rather than theirs, to do. We recommend, however, that even in kindergarten, children participate in recording what they've accomplished. You may want to use a roll-call, "What did you do today?" at the end of writing time and record responses. At the earliest possible moment, however, invite students to maintain this record themselves.

Monitoring Children's Writing Progress. Two kinds of record keeping are useful for monitoring children's writing progress. First are written notes you keep of your conferences with children. Prepare a notebook (the loose-leaf notebook allows you to add and move pages easily), so that you have five or six pages allotted for each of your students. Write each student's name at the top of first page you've allotted for her or him. This is your "conference log." Every time you confer with a child, or assist the child in editing, or read a finished piece, write a dated entry in your conference log. Be specific in your entries, noting pertinent details about what that child's work demonstrates he or she *knows* (rather than doesn't know), what skills you taught or developed, and what progress you have seen since the last conference.

Nancie Atwell (1987) heads her conference record sheets as follows (p. 108):

Title of Piece & Date (comments)	Skills Used Correctly	Skills Taught (no more than 2)

You may wish to develop your own headings. Critical here is that you record *every day*; again, your entries don't have to be elaborate, but they do need to be accurate. You may find a pad of self-stick notes helpful when you're doing "honeybee" conferences so that you can remember what you need to record later. After longer, slower conferences, take the few necessary moments and record them.

In your conference log, you may wish to have a separate section titled "skills log." Here you keep records of your students' accomplishments in relation to writing skills that you consider important and/or that your district or state requires you to teach. Prepare a summary sheet with skills listed across the top and children's names down the left side. Behind the summary sheet, have some blank sheets for notes.

Survey the list of skills prior to the beginning of school and refresh your memory often. Then take every opportunity to see if your children are already doing whatever the skill is, e.g., using end-of-sentence punctuation marks correctly. If they are already using end-of-sentence punctuation marks correctly, then you do not need to teach that skill; simply document their accomplishment in your skills log. If they are not using end-of-sentence punctuation marks correctly, teach the skill *when it is appropriate to do so* in individual conferences or mini-lessons; document your teaching, and then document again when children have acquired the behavior.

Evaluation Procedures. At regular intervals during the school year (report card time), you will need to do formal evaluation of your students' writing development. This certainly is not the *only* evaluation you do, but this is the evaluation that gets the most attention. Some form of portfolio assessment seems most reasonable to use for evaluating children's writing workshop work (see Chapter 11 for further discussion of portfolios). Linda Rief (1990, 1992) describes an approach to portfolio assessment of students' writing in which she, the teacher, decided the *external* criteria for what students' were to do:

> *Each student's two best [written] pieces chosen during a six-week period from his or her working folder, trimester self-evaluations of process and product, and, at year's end, a reading/writing project (1990, p. 24).*

Here are the questions Rief used to guide students' self-evaluations (1990, p. 28):

> *What makes this your best piece?*
> *How did you go about writing it?*
> *What problems did you encounter?*
> *How did you solve them?*
> *What makes your most effective piece different from your least effective piece?*
> *What goals did you set for yourself?*
> *How well did you accomplish them?*
> *What are your goals for the next twelve weeks?*

These questions are clearly intended for older students, but are readily adaptable to all grade levels. Rief also suggests that children evaluate their own work by arranging their finished pieces from the grading period in order from "most effective" to "least effective" and write a rationale for their choices.

Following submission of children's writing portfolios and self-evaluations, you will need to write your response back to each child. These responses become very personal—intimate, actually—as you engage in substantive discourse with your students about their accomplishment in your classroom. Then you use the entire process—not just children's written products, but notes from your conference log and skills log, status-of-the-classroom records, children's self-evaluations and your responses—to make decisions about children's overall writing progress. These decisions and evaluations are then transmitted via report cards, parent conferences, and student conferences.

A FEW FINAL WORDS ABOUT WRITING WORKSHOP

In her most recent reflections on the writing workshop (1991), Lucy Calkins suggests structural changes in which workshop participants (children and teacher) would use notebooks, kept with them at school *and* home, to record moments of their lives, reflections, words and phrases that have a special sound, family stories, ideas, and other such. The content of these notebooks would then become the focus of much of the writing workshop: In mini-lessons and conferences, teachers would invite children to read and reflect on notebook entries so that the substance of writing early in the workshop would be concentrated in the notebook itself. Authors would continue for some time adding phrases, words, and drafts of ideas to their notebooks, with little pressure to redraft, revise, edit, and publish. After gathering this mosaic of many different kinds of writing, children would then develop their own rather substantive writing projects growing from their notebook work. In time, whole classes would launch research projects that would serve as the nucleus for writing workshop activities.

At first glance, Calkins's new vision of the writing workshop is a bit disquieting, suggesting as it does that much of the day-to-day structure of the workshop should be considerably different from currently accepted practice. On reflection, however, her new vision is actually comforting, and maybe just a little bit exciting. What she is saying is that the writing workshop is evolving, just as the teachers and children who participate in writing workshops themselves grow and change. This evolution of the writing workshop is the direct result of experienced writing workshop teachers observing and evaluating their own and their students' progress, and of the willingness of these teachers to listen to and trust their own reservoirs of knowledge about children and learning and the point of writing in school. Calkins illustrates what happens when we *don't* listen to and trust our own knowledge base:

> *Mary Ellen Giacobbe, a former teacher from Atkinson, New Hampshire, who now consults in school districts around the country, tells of being met at the airport by a group of teachers who confided immediately, and with great desperation, "We're so glad you're here. We've been waiting three months for your advice." "What's the problem?" Mary Ellen asked. "The kids are writing about farts," they answered. "We told them they could choose their own topics, and all over the school, they're writing about farts. What do we do?" "Tell them not to," Mary Ellen said, matter-of-factly. Surprised, the teachers responded, "We can do that?"*
>
> *We laugh and think, "How silly." But it's not silly. It's sad. The problem is not that the kids are writing about farts but that some of us have lost confidence in our ability to think for ourselves . . . (1991, p. 228)*

The writing workshop is a way of learning and teaching that requires students *and* teachers to think for themselves, and much of that thinking will, necessarily, bring change. Change is the essence of the seventh principle of the writing workshop itself: "Writing teachers need to take responsibility for their knowledge and teaching." When teachers seek out professional sources and remain current with emerging knowledge in their fields, and when they gain deeper understanding of learners and themselves as teachers, change is inevitable. New visions of and new structures in the writing workshop are therefore to be expected, and they will happen predictably in whatever rendition of the workshop you create

HOW TO DO . . . .

WRITING WORKSHOP

The writing workshop requires some thought, planning, and preparation before you begin. Central to this planning is that you assist yourself in making the big decisions: How much time each day or week do we have for writing workshop? What materials and resources do I need? How can I arrange my room to accommodate workshop activities? What special areas do I want to designate and where shall they be? What record keeping and evaluation procedures will I use?

After making these big decisions, the following steps should help you launch the writing workshop:

1. Establish the writing workshop schedule—days and times.

2. Gather and store paper, pens, pencils, folders, journal notebooks, and other writing workshop materials.

3. Decide how materials, supplies, and equipment will be dispensed or used.

4. Arrange the room to accommodate writing areas, centers, meeting areas, and so forth.

5. Make any signs you wish to post, e.g., self-conferencing questions, procedural guidelines, or work-area labels.

6. Develop and prepare all record keeping and evaluation forms and materials. Write the evaluation procedures.

7. Decide what signals you want to use—how you'll get everyone's attention during writing time, how you'll signal end of writing time, etc.

8. Prepare your first mini-lesson. Reflect on how you choose topics for writing, choose two or three examples of very different kinds of writing you have done, and be prepared to explain to your students how you arrived at those topics.

9. Plan your next two mini-lessons.

10. Set up the permanent record book and/or conference and skills log. Fill in children's names on log pages and status-of-the-classroom forms.

11. Initiate the workshop.

in your classroom. Chances are, you'll not approach writing workshop exactly as it is described here, or by Nancie Atwell, or by Lucy Calkins, nor will your approach be the same each year (or possibly, each month!). That's fine. The writing workshop will flourish in the face of many differences and changes as long as you understand what writing and learning are all about, pay attention to your writers, and act on what you know to be important.

PROJECT-BASED WRITING AND THEME CYCLES

Project-based writing and theme cycles are extensions, or perhaps logical progressions, of the writing workshop. They are actually part of the "reading and writing across the curriculum," or "teaching reading and writing in the content areas" approaches that we will discuss further in Chapter 9. It is important, however, to spend some time talking about project-based writing and theme cycles in this chapter because of the significant and substantive role writing plays in each.

Project Investigation

Project-Based Writing

Project-based writing, as its title suggests, centers around a major project that a class of children decides to undertake. The project may be ongoing throughout an entire school year—publishing a newspaper or magazine, for example—or it may be more short term, such as cleaning up an area park or developing an extended genealogical history of the class "family."

Jerry Harste (1994) emphasizes the importance of inquiry as the foundation for project-based writing. He is not talking about inquiry as a methodology here, but rather inquiry as a deeply felt, inner need to know. He states, "Viewing curriculum as inquiry means that I envision classrooms as sites of inquiry, or as communities of learners. Inquiry is not a technical skill to be applied at will, but rather a philosophical stance that permeates the kinds of lives we choose to live" (1994, pp. 1230–1231). Inquiry becomes the starting point and sustaining element that propels a classroom project itself, and thus the driving force of project-based writing.

Harste and Short (1988) use the "authoring cycle" (see Figure 7-13) to describe project-based writing. The authoring cycle should not look terribly unfamiliar to you, given its clear similarity with the writing process and procedures we've already discussed in the context of the writing workshop. In fact, Harste and Short's discussion of the authoring cycle (1988) captures much of the essence of the writing workshop (without calling it that) regarding how writing should proceed daily in the classroom. We include the authoring cycle here because, first, the schematic alone (Figure 7-13) is a dramatic illustration of the writing process and how children in school should participate in writing.

Second, we find the notion of inquiry, as Harste envisions it, to be powerful and important. Essentially, he is saying that children and teachers should examine what they know, look around their world, and decide what it is they want to know. *Then all writing and learning should grow from class exploration of questions generated in determining what the group wants to know.* The idea that deeply felt needs should guide curriculum choices in classrooms, that questions children and teachers ask and then energetically seek to answer are more important than state- or district-mandated curriculum guides, and that intensely focused writing stemming from the inquiry topic may be more legitimate than learning how to write formal and informal letters is revolutionary—and worth our attention.

And finally, we like the idea of projects as a focal point and center for writing. We have all seen children play, or create fantasy dramas and worlds, or go after an idea or object with absolute concentration and determination. *That's* what projects based on true inquiry capture. Consider for a moment how much more engaging it might be for a classroom of children to write logs, analyses, newspaper accounts, poems, and scientific essays based on experiments they conducted during a visit to an amusement park (e.g., wind resistance during roller coaster rides; heart rate and pulse studies on various rides; speed of the roller coaster in contrast to the speed of the Ferris wheel, the carousel, the bumper cars, etc.) than it is for them to learn the parts of these same kinds of writing (logs, analyses, newspaper accounts, poems, scientific essays) by studying texts and doing simulated writing.

To institute project-based writing in your class, begin by leading a class discussion about "Things We Know." Let children work in pairs or groups to list what they know; give them plenty of time and expect ideas to range considerably. Share these in whole class discussion. Then let them go back to their partner or group and list "Things We Don't Know" and later "Things We Want to Know." This may cover several days and may require that you "prime the pump" a bit; children are wholly unused to being asked what they'd like to learn in school. Finally, begin shaping the project idea with the class and considering as you go what writing seems reasonable within the context of this project. Offer children the possibility of publishing a project-related newspaper, newsletter, magazine, or book. Develop procedures and record-keeping systems *before you begin the project* so they are ready to go

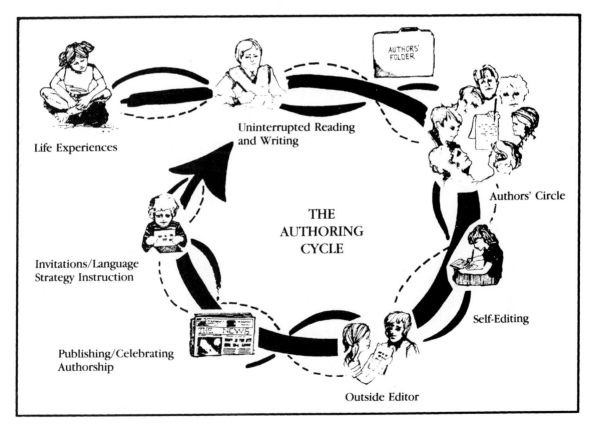

Figure 7-13

The Authoring Cycle

from the start. It wouldn't be a bad idea at all to have a status-of-the-class roll-call each day and the three-minute logging of daily accomplishments as part of your plan.

Theme Cycles

Theme cycles are highly similar to inquiry projects, and different in significant ways from the thematic and topical units we discussed in Chapter 6. **Theme cycles** are described by Bess Altwerger and Barbara Flores (1991) as cycles of study in which children negotiate the theme for instruction through class discussion and deliberation. Unlike thematic and topical units, the teacher doesn't predetermine the unit topic, gather and prepare materials and equipment, and generally coordinate the progression of the unit. In theme cycles (as in inquiry projects), children do most of the planning and carrying out of theme activities, including practical writing (e.g., letters inviting guest speakers) as well as other writing, as appropriate.

Lois Bird (personal communication, 1991) tells of an intermediate-grade class in a school adjoining a very large, and locally infamous, low-income housing project. In a class discussion one day, the children began talking about the many ways their neighborhood was blighted: unkempt yards and streets; clearly visible drug dealers and drug dealing; lack of physical safety on sidewalks and streets; virtually no police presence; a run-down, weed- and vermin-infested park where children could no longer play, and on and on. As the discussion continued, the children grew convinced that *they* should clean up the neighborhood. This became their class theme, and to carry out their work they wrote letters to the mayor and other city officials informing them of the many neighborhood problems, invited the chief of police to come talk to the class about ways the community and local police station could work together to improve the area (he came), and instigated a community coalition of adults, children, businesses, police, and the school for removing the presence of drug dealers from and increasing the safety of the neighborhood.

One can easily see how writing was integral to this theme project, not only with regard to the practical writing that needed to be done, but also the many possibilities for children to write about the work they were doing in their classroom and neighborhood. As with the inquiry project we discussed earlier, theme cycle planning requires that you lead students toward shaping the theme itself. The theme may grow naturally from the kind of discussion that led to a "clean up the neighborhood" campaign; it could be related to an experience children had, or local and world events. It will undoubtedly come from your sensitivity to "teachable moments." Whatever its source or impetus, use all the knowledge you have about the writing process and children's writing development to guide in planning writing opportunities to accompany the theme cycle. Encourage children to write, to develop and clarify their thinking through writing, and to share and publish their writing.

AREAS OF SPECIFIC CONCERN TEACHERS AND PARENTS HAVE ABOUT WRITING

Issues regarding spelling and handwriting arise in any discussion of children's writing development and writing instructional practices in schools. Spelling and handwriting are both topics that seem to invite public criticism and frequent calls for schools to return to the kind of instruction we had in the "good old days." The public perception is that writers in the "good old days" were all good spellers who wrote with flowing, textbook-perfect script; further, the perception is that schools don't teach spelling and handwriting today. Both perceptions are incorrect. We know of no substantive research to validate claims that people were generally better spellers or handwriters in past generations; we do know that literacy standards were lower during past generations than they are today (that is, people didn't have to be able to do as much as they have to do today to be considered "literate"), and we know that literacy rates among the adult population were lower in past generations than they are today (in other words, a lower percentage of adults could read and write at the level required to be considered "literate") (R. B. Ruddell, 1993). From this evidence, we strongly suspect that the "good old days" when everyone achieved perfect spelling and impeccable script are nice golden memories, but probably false. Nevertheless, perceptions remain. We know that spelling and handwriting are being taught in schools today; let us now look at ways spelling and handwriting may be taught productively in your classroom.

SPELLING

We have already discussed at some length in Chapter 2 the patterns or cycles of spelling development children move through on their way to conventional spelling. Included in these cycles are the patterns of (1) prephonemic, (2) phonemic, (3) letter-name, (4) transitional, and (5) derivational spelling. Children's use of these spelling patterns is indicative of their current theory(ies) about the spelling system; in addition, children discover the rules of conventional spelling primarily by their experimentation with many nonconventional spelling forms (Fitzsimmons, 1990; Gill, 1992; Gill, 1989; Henderson & Beers, 1980). Although wide variation can and does occur, most children are rapidly moving into conventional spelling practices by about first grade.

Conventional spelling has long been taught in U.S. schools using basal spelling texts that cluster and order words according to some set of generalizations or characteristics. Spelling text words are most usually clustered according to spelling pattern elements (e.g., *ar* words, final *z* words, compound words, homonyms, etc.), and weekly lessons focus on that pattern. Over the years, spelling instructions has shifted from rote learning in which children memorize spelling patterns and specific word spellings by writing words repeatedly to more contextualized learning that is intended to focus on word meanings. Unfortunately, publishers still group words by spelling patterns and not by meaning; consequently, teachers' attempts to contextualize have led to instructional products bordering on the bizarre.

One of us recently spent one day a week in a fifth grade classroom for a semester in which a weekly spelling exercise was for the children to write stories using their spelling words (Ruddell, 1991). The children were encouraged to use that week's list of challenge words or review words in addition to the twenty unit words for the week. Below are some sentences taken from the stories the children wrote:

1. Unit words were spellings of the vowel sound heard in the words "work" and "lurk"; review words were spellings of the vowel sound heard in "far."

   All *turtles* are always *tardy* to go to the *hardware* store.

   It *disturbs* me when people *depart* from their houses to *worship darkness*. They make the *worst* racket ever.

   Everyone would *starve* if we wouldn't have *artists* to make houses in the *world*.

   Some people *regard* that I am *worthy* to *charge* people *further* more money than they can afford.

2. Unit words were spellings of the vowel sound heard in the word "form"; challenge words were spellings for the plural of words ending in "o."

   Once upon a time a *volcano* erupted out of a *kangaroo* eating *potatoes* and *tomatoes*.

   I can't believe people would *reform* the *forest* into a place where there are *unicorns* and *kangaroos*.

3. Unit words were words ending with the sound of /s/ written "ce."

   Force had a *chance* to have a *dance* for *Prince police*man but they had to *replace* a man, so they *pounced* right on it and they found him.

These meaningless spelling-word "stories" are a clear demonstration that children will, indeed, churn out the kind of formulaic writing that Lucy Calkins decries (1991), and we are sure that this is not the only classroom where spelling-word stories are standard routine. Our concern about this practice is twofold: First, the stories are nonsense—they certainly do not grow from deeply felt events, experiences, and circumstances in children's lives; second, and just as important, we suspect that, in doing these stories, children neither learn the spelling pattern intended to be taught nor learn to spell the specific words in the spelling word list.

Recent understandings developed about children's need to discover the rules of the conventional spelling system are causing some schools and teachers to change traditional spelling instructional practices. In many classrooms, especially those in which writing workshop is well established, spelling lessons are embedded in the writing process itself rather than taught as a separate subject. Words drawn from the writing children produce form the list of words to be taught and are organized or clustered by spelling patterns only when it makes sense to do so. In such classrooms, teachers place spelling in the context of editing, and thus resist children's requests for spelling assistance during drafting. Teachers' response to "How do you spell _____ ?" during drafting is "Spell _____ as best you can," or "Spell _____ the way you think it should be spelled." Children are told to concentrate on their ideas and on getting words on paper; spelling will be attended to later. Then, during revising and, most particularly, editing, appropriate attention is given to conventional spelling patterns. In writing workshop classes, teachers teach spelling rules and generalizations in individual editing conferences and in small and large group mini-lessons.

Traditional spelling instruction and the writing workshop approach to spelling instruction are vastly different, and it is this difference that may explain why some people think spelling is not being taught in schools today. Others misunderstand completely the reason teachers emphasize ideas and writing fluency, rather than spelling, in drafting writing stages. A recent feature article in *The Kansas City Star* (Scott, 1993) typifies this misunderstanding:

> *Other parents, however, say students aren't learning to read or spell at all. Bad spelling isn't even corrected under whole language, they say. (p. A-10)*

You will undoubtedly have to make some decisions about spelling instruction in your classroom, even if a specific published spelling program is mandated for weekly instruction. One choice you can make is to allow your students to decide what the list of spelling words will be each week in much the same way they choose words using the Vocabulary Self-Collection Strategy described in Chapter 5. If you are using a published program, let the children survey the book and select words from the many lists there to constitute a weekly list. If you are not required to use a published program, let them nominate words for the weekly list from their own reading and writing, words they've worked on in editing conferences, or words they've heard. Or you may wish to use a combination of forced-choice (spelling book) and open-choice (students' own reading and writing) selections to constitute a weekly spelling list. After a list is determined for the week, you then develop and assign activities students do to help them learn word spellings.

Of very real importance here is that whatever choices you make about spelling instruction, *communicate to parents what and how spelling is to be taught in your classroom.* Spend some time clarifying what you're doing and why so you can tell parents, in a note home (see Chapter 3 for a sample) and on back-to-school night, in clear, crisp language what the spelling program is. Consider also the full effect that your choices have. Think through and prepare record-keeping systems. Estimate your time commitment. Decide what you'll do next when children conditioned to having adults spell words for them become frustrated by your response to, "Spell it the way you think it should be spelled." (Recall from Chapter 3: *Lead* them toward trying to spell it on their own by asking "How do you think that word starts?") And, finally, check to make sure that the spelling instruction you're planning is consonant with your understanding of how children's language and literacy develop and consistent with other aspects of literacy instruction in your classroom.

HANDWRITING

Handwriting instruction is still very much a part of the elementary classroom. In most schools, children use *manuscript* form (circles and sticks) through second grade, making a transition from manuscript to *cursive* in late second or early third grade (see Figure 7-14). In some schools, children start with a cursivelike system called D'Nealian form (see Figure 7-15). Whatever the formal system, children need practice writing to arrive at their own handwriting style.

Let us agree right now that the goal of handwriting instruction and practice is *not* that every child's handwriting should or will look just like the handwriting chart (and acknowledge that very few grown-up people's do—even from back in the "good old days"). The goals are *legibility* and *consistency*; that is, children's handwriting needs to be readable by someone other than the one who produced it, and handwriting needs to have a certain consistency—tall letters about the same height, short letters about the same height and width, letters and words evenly slanted, *l* 's consistently loopy, *t* 's consistently unloopy, etc. The way to reach these goals is first to provide instruction and very short doses of rote practice (it really doesn't hurt anybody to do a few minutes of letter *b* every so often). Then give children lots of real writing time (as in the writing workshop), discuss and model handwriting during conferences and mini-lessons that focus on publishing finished pieces. Encourage children's experimentation with handwriting just as you encourage their experimentation with other language forms; girls, especially, love to "heart" or "circle" rather than dot their *i*'s, and most children at one time or another play with different letter slants or handwriting "looks." Notice and comment when children's handwriting improves. Work on and improve your *own* handwriting—and let children know you're doing it. Guide children in self-analyzing their handwriting; Cathy Collins Block (1993) suggests the rating scale found in Figure 7-16. And finally, don't sweat the small stuff: Back-slanted handwriting can be just as readable and attractive as "correctly" slanted handwriting; put your efforts into legibility and consistency rather than some abstract ideal of handwriting perfection.

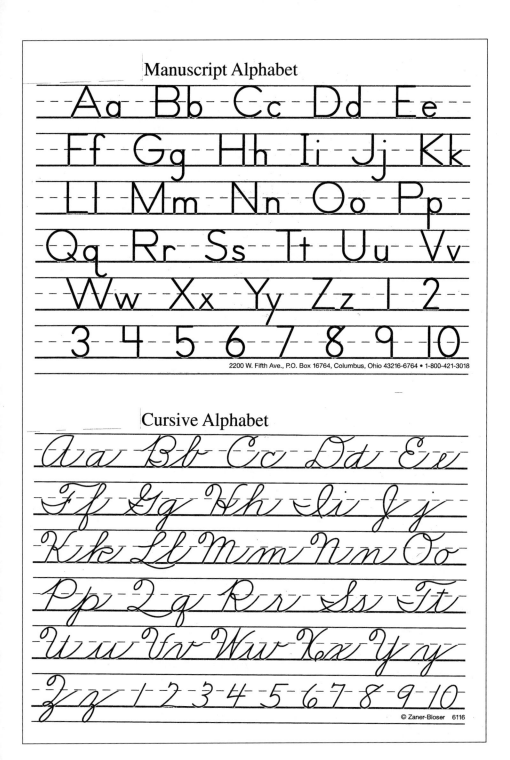

Manuscript Alphabet

Aa Bb Cc Dd Ee
Ff Gg Hh Ii Jj Kk
Ll Mm Nn Oo Pp
Qq Rr Ss Tt Uu Vv
Ww Xx Yy Zz 1 2
3 4 5 6 7 8 9 10

2200 W. Fifth Ave., P.O. Box 16764, Columbus, Ohio 43216-6764 • 1-800-421-3018

Cursive Alphabet

Aa Bb Cc Dd Ee
Ff Gg Hh Ii Jj
Kk Ll Mm Nn Oo
Pp Qq Rr Ss Tt
Uu Vv Ww Xx Yy
Zz 1 2 3 4 5 6 7 8 9 10

© Zaner-Bloser 6116

FIGURE 7-14

Manuscript and Cursive Alphabets

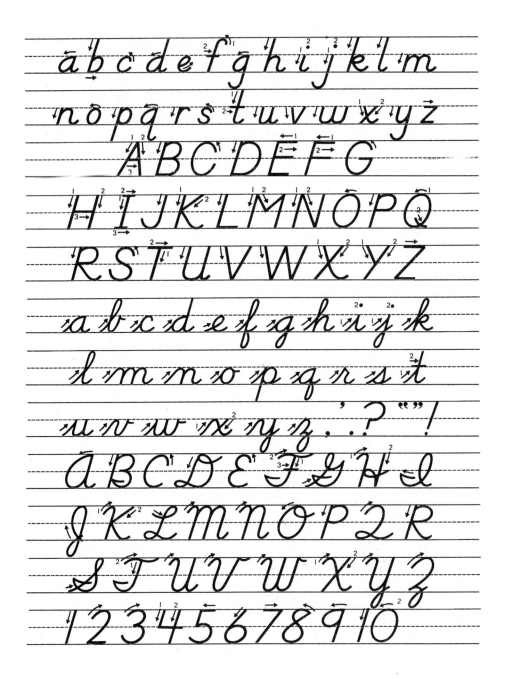

I. RATE THE QUALITY OF YOUR HANDWRITING
Excellent (1), Good (2), Average (3), Fair (4), Poor (5)

____ Neatness

____ Arrangement (margins, indentations)

____ Legibility

II. LOCATE THE TROUBLE SPOTS IN YOUR HANDWRITING
Check (✓) one or two areas in which you need special practice:

____ Slant (Do all your letters lean the same way; are your down strokes really straight?)

____ Space (Are the spaces between letters and words even?)

____ Size (Are your tall letters, i.e., *l, h, k, b,* and *f,* about three times as tall as the small letters; the middle-sized letters, i.e., *t, d, p,* twice the height of small letters; and the lower loop letters one-half space below the writing line?)

____ Alignment (Are all tall letters evenly tall; all small letters evenly small; and are all letters resting on the line?)

____ Line Quality (Is the thickness of letters about the same throughout the page?)

____ Ending Strokes (Are the endings without fancy swinging strokes; and are they long enough to guide the spacing between words?)

____ Letter Formation   (Are the loops open and equal in size?
Are the hump letters *m,n,h,u* rounded?
Are the letters *o,d,a,g,p,q* closed?
Have you made long retraces in *t, d, p*?
Are your capital letters well formed?)

____ Number Formation   (Do you use the correct form?
Do you use the correct slant?
Are the symbols well aligned?)

___ **FIGURE 7-16** _____

Rating Scale for Handwriting. (Reproduced with permission from Block, 1993, p. 300.

Guiding Children's Writing
A Summary

In this chapter, we have explored children's writing development from their very early writing experiences through writing experiences in elementary school. Significant to that development is children's discovery of the characteristics and rules of the writing system; this they do through a process of theory building and hypothesis testing as they invent and reinvent written language forms. Children refine their knowledge and become increasingly sophisticated users of the written language system as they continue through school.

Writing workshop is the form of instruction currently recommended for school writing instruction from kindergarten and through grade six. Writing workshop is focused on writing process rather than product and is based upon the notion that significant time will be set aside for children to write in classrooms every day. Writing workshop is structured around the three major activities of mini-lessons, writing time and conferences, and sharing time that shape the writing processes of prewriting, drafting, revising, editing, sharing, and publishing.

Project-based writing and theme cycles are natural extensions of the writing workshop. Both project-based writing and theme cycles grow from children's expressed desire to learn (or do) something, and are planned and carried out collaboratively by the children and the teacher. Project-based writing and theme cycles are not at all unlike Lucy Calkins's new vision of the writing workshop with the emphasis on exploration of the ideas that are important to children. Writing in school, as envisioned by the instructional approaches we've discussed here, is a natural continuation of children's early writing development: purposeful, uncontrived, gimmick-free, and pertinent to individual children's lives.

Concerns that schools are no longer teaching spelling and handwriting appear to be misplaced. Schools are teaching both spelling and handwriting, but instruction in today's classroom, especially in writing workshop classes, may be considerably different from traditional instruction. Both spelling and handwriting may be learned and practiced naturally within the context of writing workshop, project-based, and theme cycle classrooms.

DOUBLE ENTRY JOURNAL

If you are going to use the writing workshop in your classroom, what of your own writing will you develop and share with your students? What issues do you have to address and decisions do you have to make before you implement the writing workshop?

Supporting Activities

1. At the beginning of this chapter (starting with the section entitled Family and Community Influences) we discussed eight critical factors that influence children's early writing development. Develop an observational sheet by placing each of these factors in the left margin of a sheet of paper with space for observational notes to the right of each. Arrange to visit a kindergarten or first-grade classroom during reading and language arts instruction. Observe only one child during this visit. Use your observational form to identify examples to illustrate as many of these factors as possible during instruction and during the child's independent work activities. Encourage the child to interpret any artwork, drawings, or written work made during your observation. After completing your observations focus on the child's writing development and discuss how he or she uses any form of writing or drawing to communicate ideas and construct meaning. What role does the child's social interaction with other children, with the teacher, and with you play in this meaning construction and communication process?

2. In the discussion of the writing workshop, we suggested a wide variety of mini-lessons (see Mini-Lessons Section, above) that can be developed in the context of children's real writing about real topics that are relevant to them. Assume that Ryan has just presented the story shown in Figure 7-7

("Andrew and the Painted House") to you. Create one mini-lesson that you believe would be valuable for use in your conference with Ryan. Discuss your ideas with a class partner.

3. Return to Ryan's story in Figure 7-7. Assume you are conferencing with Ryan. What probes would you use to assist Ryan in planning for his "next draft"? You may find the conference approaches and questions suggested in Figure 7-12 of help. Briefly describe your suggestions and share them with a class partner.

4. Briefly discuss the differences and similarities between project-based writing and theme cycles. Which approach do you feel most comfortable with? Why? Discuss your ideas with a class partner.

5. Based on your reading of this chapter and your own insights, what role do you believe spelling instruction plays in the writing workshop? Briefly set out your plan for incorporating spelling instruction in your teaching.

Altwerger, B., & Flores, B. (1991). Theme cycles: An overview. In K. S. Goodman, L. B. Bird, & Y. M. Goodman (Eds.), *The whole language catalog*. New York: Macmillan.

Atwell, N. (1987). *In the middle*. Portsmouth, NH: Heinemann.

Au, K. H. (1993). *Literacy instruction in multicultural settings*. New York: Harcourt Brace Jovanovich.

Bernstein, B. (1961). Social structure, language, and learning. *Educational Research, 3,* 163–176.

Bernstein, B. (1964). Elaborated and restricted codes: Their social origins and some consequences. *American Anthropologist, 66,* 55–69.

Block, C. C. (1993). *Teaching the language arts*. Boston: Allyn & Bacon.

Briggs, J. B. (1991, June 9). Writers do it daily. *This World*, p. 4.

Calkins, L. M. (1986). *The art of teaching writing*. Portsmouth, NH: Heinemann.

Calkins, L. M. (1991). *Living between the lines*. Portsmouth, NH: Heinemann.

Clay, M. M. (1975). *What did I write?* Auckland, New Zealand: Heinemann.

Clay, M. M. (1991). *Becoming literate: The construction of inner control*. Portsmouth, NH: Heinemann.

Dyson, A. H. (1983). The role of oral language in early writing processes. *Research in the Teaching of English, 17,* 1–30.

Dyson, A. H. (1989). *Multiple worlds of child writers: Friends learning to write*. New York: Teachers College Press.

Dyson, A. H. (1990). *The word and the world: Reconceptualizing written language development or do rainbows mean a lot to little girls?* (Tech. Rep. No. 42). Berkeley, CA: University of California, Center for the Study of Writing.

Dyson, A. H., & Freedman, S. W. (1991). Writing. In J. Flood, J. M. Jensen, D. Lapp, & J. R. Squire (Eds.), *Handbook of research on teaching the English language arts* (pp. 754–774). New York: Macmillan.

Ferreiro, E., & Teberosky, A. (1982). *Literacy before schooling*. Exeter, NH: Heinemann.

Fitzsimmons, P. (1990). *Spellbound*. Unpublished Master's thesis, University of Wollongong, Wollongong, Australia.

Galda, L., Cullinan, B. E., & Strickland, D. S. (1993). *Language, literacy and the child*. New York: Harcourt Brace Jovanovich.

Gallimore, R., Boggs, J. W., & Jordan, C. (1974). *Culture, behavior and education: A study of Hawaiian-Americans*. Beverly Hills, CA: Sage.

Gill, C. T. (1992). Focus on research: Development of word knowledge as it relates to reading, spelling, and instruction. *Language Arts, 69,* 444–453.

Gill, J. (1989). The relationship between word recognition and spelling in the primary grades. *Reading Psychology, 10,* 11–135.

Graves, D. H. (1983). *Writing: Teachers & children at work*. Portsmouth, NH: Heinemann.

363

Graves, D. H. (1990). *Discovering your own literacy*. Portsmouth, NH: Heinemann.

Harste, J. C. (1994). Literacy as curricular conversations about knowledge, inquiry, and morality. In R. B. Ruddell, M. R. Ruddell, & H. Singer (Eds.), *Theoretical models and processes of reading* (4th ed.) (pp. 1220–1242). Newark, DE: International Reading Association.

Harste, J. C., Burke, C. L., & Woodward, V. A. (1982). Children's language and world: Initial encounters with print. In. J. A. Langer & M. T. Smith-Burke (Eds.), *Reader meets author/Bridging the gap* (pp. 105–131). Newark, DE: International Reading Association.

Harste, J. C., & Short, K. G. (1988). *Creating classrooms for authors*. Portsmouth, NH: Heinemann.

Harste, J. C., Woodward, V. A., & Burke, C. L. (1984). *Language stories & literacy lessons*. Portsmouth, NH: Heinemann.

Heath, S. B. (1983). *Ways with words*. New York: Cambridge University Press.

Heller, C. (1990). *Women writers of the Tenderloin*. (Tech. Rep.) Berkeley, CA: University of California, Center for the Study of Writing.

Henderson, E. H., & Beers, J. W. (1980). *Developmental and cognitive aspects of learning to spell*. Newark, DE: International Reading Association.

Moll, L. C. (1992). Literacy research in community and classrooms: A sociocultural approach. In R. Beach, J. L. Green, M. L. Kamil, & T. Shanahan (Eds.), *Multidisciplinary perspectives on literacy research* (pp. 211–144). Urbana, IL: National Council of Teachers of English.

Morrow, L. M. (1993). *Literacy development in the early years*. Boston: Allyn & Bacon.

Rief, L. (1990). Finding the value in evaluation: Self-assessment in a middle school classroom. *Educational Leadership, 47,* 24–29.

Rief, L. (1992). *Seeking diversity*. Portsmouth, NH: Heinemann.

Routman, R. (1991). *Invitations*. Portsmouth, NH: Heinemann.

Ruddell, M. R. (1991). Students' metacognitive response to ambiguous literacy tasks. *Reading Research and Instruction, 31,* 1–11.

Ruddell, M. R. (1993). *Teaching content reading and writing*. Boston: Allyn & Bacon.

Ruddell, R. B. (1993, June). *Motivating literacy: Influential teachers' approaches to developing comprehension and reader response*. Paper presented at the annual Indiana University Literacy Conference, Bloomington, IN.

Ruddell, R. B., & Ruddell, M. R. (1994). Language acquisition and literacy processes. In R. B. Ruddell, M. R. Ruddell, & H. Singer (Eds.), *Theoretical models and processes of reading* (4th ed.) (pp. 83–103). Newark, DE: International Reading Association.

Scott, L. J. (1993, June 1). Now it's 'foniks,' not phonics, in many schools. *The Kansas City Star,* pp. A-1, A-10.

Sulzby, E. (1986). Writing and reading: Signs of oral and written language organization in the young child. In W. H. Teale & E. Sulzby (Eds.), *Emergent literacy: Writing and reading* (pp. 50–89). Norwood, NH: Ablex.

Sulzby, E., Barnhart, J., & Hieshima, J. A. (1989). Forms of writing and rereading from writing. In J. M. Mason (Ed.), *Reading and writing connections* (pp. 31–50). Newark, DE: International Reading Association.

Sulzby, E., & Teale, W. H. (1985). Writing development in early childhood. *Educational Horizons, 64,* 8–12.

Sulzby, E., Teale, W. H., & Kamberelis, G. (1989). Emergent writing in the classroom: Home and school connections. In D. S. Strickland & L. M. Morrow (Eds.), *Emerging literacy: Young children learn to read and write* (pp. 63–79). Newark, DE: International Reading Association.

Temple, C., Nathan, R., Temple, F., & Burris, N. A. (1993). *The beginnings of writing* (3rd ed.). Boston: Allyn & Bacon.

Tough, J. (1977). *The development of meaning.* New York: John Wiley.

Van Hoorn, J., Nourot, P., Scales, B., & Alward, K. (1992). *Play at the center of the curriculum.* New York: Macmillan.

Vonnegut, K. (1981). *Palm Sunday.* New York: Dell.

Vygotsky, L. (1986). *Thought and language* (A. Kozulin, Trans. & Ed.). Cambridge, MA: MIT Press.

Writing yellow pages: For students and teachers (1988). Nashville, TN: Incentive.

CHAPTER 7	WRITING WORKSHOP	PROJECT-BASED WRITING	THEME CYCLES
FOCUS ON	Developing writing fluency and ability	In-depth inquiry and exploration of topics	Development of self-selected topic for study and action
GUIDES STUDENTS	Before, during, and after writing	Before, during, and after reading and writing	Before, during, and after reading and writing
USE TO PLAN	Units, yearly activities	Units, yearly activities	Units, yearly activities
MAY BE USED	Whole class, small groups, individuals	Whole class, cooperative groups	Whole class, cooperative groups
MAY BE COMBINED WITH (KNOWN STRATEGIES)		GMA, VSS Concept Webs, Semantic Maps, SFA, Reading Aloud, Story-Telling, Response Journals, Readers Theatre, Writing Workshop	GMA, VSS Concept Webs, Semantic Maps, SFA, Reading Aloud, Story-Telling, Response Journals, Readers Theatre, Writing Workshop
MATERIALS PREPARATION	Moderate to extensive	Moderate to extensive	Moderate to extensive
OTHER PREPARATION	Moderate to extensive	Moderate to extensive	Moderate to extensive
OUTSIDE RESOURCES	Necessary	Necessary	Necessary
HOW TO DO	Page 348		

Building Tables "grow" or build, successively from chapter to chapter. They tell you (1) the focus of each strategy introduced in a chapter; (2) how the strategy is best used; (3) what strategies from previous chapters combine well with new ones; (4) preparation requirements; (5) additional resources needed; and (6) the page on which a strategy's How-to-Do appears.

CHAPTER 8

USING WORD ANALYSIS STRATEGIES TO DEVELOP READER INDEPENDENCE: TRANSFORMING PRINT TO MEANING

INTRODUCTION

Word analysis skills are critical to your students' reading success. These skills hold the key to transforming printed text to meaning. Very simply, effective word analysis skills enable readers to understand the relationship between printed or written letters, letter patterns, and contextual clues and their already-familiar oral language counterparts and meanings. Your major instructional goal is to assist children in the development of these skills so that use becomes automatic, thus freeing their mental energy to focus on the primary purpose of reading—to construct meaning and develop personal interpretation

This chapter is designed to help you understand how to develop word analysis skills in your teaching regardless of the instructional approach that you use. As noted in Chapters 2 and 3, for many children word analysis skill development has already begun upon entry to school, as reflected in children's understanding of environmental print, book and print awareness concepts, and the use of invented spellings. However, this development will be very limited for children who have had little or no experience with print and books. Regardless of children's developmental progress in word analysis, however, it is important that you be familiar with the key processing strategies that need to be taught and refined under your direction. Your instructional role is critical. It will require your clear understanding of these skills and how to develop them so that students acquire the ability to read independently.

THE EXPERT READER

You have become an expert reader over the years and respond to print in a way markedly different from the kindergarten and first-grade student. Your expertise can be easily demonstrated by reflection on the way in which you are processing and understanding this very text. This process can be understood by quickly referring to Figure 2-3, the Meaning Construction Process (see Chapter 2). Your **learner objective** is to read and understand this text with the expected outcome of learning to teach word analysis skills effectively. We can assume that your **background knowledge** provides **concept clusters or schemata** that you will draw on in recognizing highly familiar letters, letter patterns, and words. You have developed highly refined **learning process strategies** as you set comprehension expectations and as your eyes skim rapidly over the letters and words in a near-automatic fashion. Your use of the sentence and intersentence contexts that contribute to understanding of word meanings assist in this process.

Most of this processing is automatic in nature. It is possible that a word like *schemata,* introduced in Chapter 2, will need to be pronounced orally, using a conscious word analysis procedure, and pondered on for a moment for comprehension, but probably not. Your **attitudes and values** toward the text are assumed to be positive, given that you are using this text because you wish to become an influential literacy teacher. Your **expected outcome** is **comprehension of the text related to word analysis skill development** as you process the text using your background knowledge to comprehend the text. Your rapid application of word analysis and comprehension skills in reading and comprehending this text is a truly amazing and mysterious feat.

Consider for a moment your encounter with a text using an unknown alphabet, as is the case with many kindergarten and first-grade children. Examine the cartoon caption in Figure 8-1 and use the new alphabet to comprehend the full meaning of Hank Ketcham's cartoon. As you use this new alphabet, reflect on the word-recognition and meaning-making strategies you are using. Before starting, glance at your watch, and make a quick note

FIGURE 8-1

Using a New Alphabet in Word Analysis—Becoming a First Grader Again. What word-analysis strategies did you use in reading the story caption? (Reproduced with permission of King Features.)

of the time. After finishing, also note the time to see how long it takes to use the new alphabet and make meaning of the cartoon caption. Start now.

Calculate the time it took you to use the new alphabet. Think introspectively for a moment and decide which of the following strategies you used to assist you in reading the caption as you applied the new alphabet.

- **Picture interpretation**—use of familiar schema, e.g., "bedtime storytime schema"

- **Cartoon schema**—use of title, familiar cartoonist, familiar characters, expectation of humor

- **Letter-sound relationships** as you transform and use the new alphabet (e.g., ⌐ = *I*; ⊤ ⌐ = *t o*) or recognition of frequent letter symbol for sound, e.g., ∟ = *e*, as in H*e*'s, asl*ee*p, com*e*s

- **Letter pattern–sound pattern relationship**—e.g., *s-ee* (consonant, vowel), *th-i-s* (consonant, vowel, consonant)

- **Rhyming ending**—familiar letter pattern, e.g., asl*eep*

- **Sentence context**—context clues from word sequence, e.g., "…how this *story* comes out"

- **Rapid recognition of word** after having completed part of word in sentence context—e.g., "I *just want* to see…"

In all probability, you used several of these strategies in rapid succession. Assuming this is the case, you made meaning of the cartoon caption in about 60 seconds. This word analysis approach is very **interactive** in nature, as you worked from "part to whole" and "whole to part," inferring missing information by holding a general bedtime story schema in mind and using bits of information to complete the meaning.

On the other hand, it is possible that you relied heavily on only one strategy, such as letter-sound relationships, that required one-to-one matching of the new alphabet with the old alphabet to construct each letter in each word throughout the caption. This construction produces a word-by-word meaning construction. This approach is a constant part-to-whole effort and is referred to as ***bottom-up*** in construction. It is also possible that you relied heavily on the picture interpretation and cartoon schema after initiating the new alphabet, even to the extent that you were guessing incorrectly about the text. This is a ***top-down*** approach. Heavy reliance on either of these approaches required approximately three minutes (or more) for meaning construction.

You may have shifted your approach from a bottom-up or top-down to *interactive*. This strategy shift may have included the use of several different strategies after you constructed part of the meaning, e.g., "He's asleep . . . I just want to see how this . . ." Assuming this is the case, you required approximately two minutes to complete the word analysis and meaning-construction process.

Whatever your approach, you have demonstrated the use of a meaning-construction and word-recognition process that operates at a very sophisticated level. You are highly effective in applying word analysis processing strategies from your already-familiar background knowledge as you use the new alphabet to form meaningful text even if you found yourself in the three-minute time zone.

You can further demonstrate that one additional word analysis strategy is under your control as you attempt to pronounce the following polysyllabic words representing different fields of study:

- *Choreography* (dancing, composing ballets)
- *Dermatology* (human skin)
- *Epidemiology* (incidence and risk of disease)
- *Uranography* (mapping of stars and galaxies)

You have developed an understanding of syllabication generalizations that enable you to identify visually pronounceable units, pronounce these, and blend them together in pronouncing the word. For example, you are aware that initial letter sequences such as *chor, der, ep,* and *ur* consistently represent strings of speech sounds that are pronounceable syllables in English; that some medial vowel letters stand for syllables, e.g., chor*e*ography, dermatol*o*gy, epidemiol*o*gy, and ur*a*nography; and that middle- and final-letter clusters such as *og, ra, phy, ma, tol, gy, de, mo, ol, gy, nog,* and *phy* also represent highly predictable pronounceable units. And, finally, you possess the ability to blend these units together to form the pronunciation of these multisyllabic words.

It is important to remember that you are an expert reader, and the issue in this chapter is how we help the novice reader develop such word analysis skills at a level of automatic processing. Some children will have their word analysis skills well under way upon entrance to school. Others, however, will have had minimal experience with pictures, print, and books. These children will depend on school, and your instruction, to acquire the word analysis skills so critical for developing reading independence, meaning construction, and school success.

WORD ANALYSIS AND PHONICS: A HISTORY OF CONTROVERSY

The instructional approach used in teaching word analysis skills has become one of the most controversial educational topics in this century (Adams, 1990a, 1990b; Chall, 1967, 1983; Flesch, 1955). Heated debate has centered and still centers around the issue of phonics versus whole word instruction. A brief historical overview will illuminate and familiarize you with the nature of the debate and move to our present context of the 1990s.

READING READINESS

During the 1920s and 1930s, reading instruction emphasized "reading readiness" and "language growth." This emphasis ranged from teacher-pupil-derived experience charts that drew heavily on children's background knowledge and experiences to publisher-produced reading programs. Publishers' programs introduced the preprimer, with the intent of providing an initial whole-word recognition vocabulary for children. Phonics instruction, with emphasis on sound-letter relationships, was introduced gradually over several grade levels in the context of the basal reader vocabulary. Teacher's Guides contained detailed suggestions for the gradual development of word analysis and comprehension skills based on the content of the reader.

The concept of "language growth" had emerged from a child-centered curriculum emphasis enhanced by the efforts of John Dewey and his followers. The central idea was to provide "enriched and direct experiences" through oral dramatization and creative writing in a content-oriented unit, which often related to the child's own experiences. Instruction in "correct usage" was still viewed as an important part of the curriculum. Spelling words were often derived from the unit activities, although a spelling text was commonly used in classrooms.

REMEDIAL READING INSTRUCTION

During the 1940s, World War II induction testing indicated that new armed forces personnel were unable to read and follow detailed verbal instructions in oral and written forms. Charges followed that both instruction and the literacy level of America's youth were inadequate. The armed services proceeded to offer literacy courses to raise performance levels of new inductees. In the late 1940s, public schools across the country began to provide remedial reading instruction on a wide-scale basis.

Basal reading programs during this period placed substantial emphasis on immediate word recognition and context clues with the gradual introduction of phonics and other word analysis skills. Initial instruction, however, still emphasized the development of a sight vocabulary (the whole-word emphasis) through frequent repetition of words in the basal reader. However, these readers made provision for a broader range of literary selections than was the case in the early part of the century.

PROTEST MOVEMENT AND CALL FOR PHONICS

By the 1950s, the stage was set for an angry protest movement. This movement was triggered largely by critic Rudolph Flesch and his widely-read book *Why Johnny Can't Read* (1955). Flesch's highly emotional and simplified argument called for phonics instruction that would teach children the names of letters and the sounds letters represent. This argument was not new, but his appeal captured a political connection between phonics and democracy in statements such as "Equal opportunity for all is one of the inalienable rights, and the word method interferes with that right." This work, in all probability, produced some positive effects by causing professional educators and publishers to reexamine and tighten the rationale underlying word analysis instruction.

Closely following the publicaiton on Flesch's book, Russia launched Earth's first satellite, *Sputnik*, thus refocusing and increasing the public's attention on American education. Into the early 1960s, charges were leveled at ineffective science and mathematics instruction and teaching of reading in U.S. schools. Such criticism was clearly evident in Arthur Trace's *What Ivan Knows That Johnny Doesn't* (1961), which included both faulty assumptions about and little understanding of reading instruction.

The effect of Flesch's book, and the writing of other critics such as Trace, was that the general public developed an oversimplified view of reading instruction in which they perceived a dichotomy between "whole word" and "phonics" instruction. Examination of reading programs during this time reveals that such a dichotomy did not exist in reality. In actuality, neither whole-word nor phonics instruction occurred as the sole means of word analysis instruction in any major basal reading series; rather, the difference centered on what was taught *first* (and therefore initially emphasized): letter sounds (phonics) or words (whole word). The *true* issue was not phonics versus whole word; the true issue was the degree of emphasis phonics and whole-word instruction received in programs and the sequence of introduction of each. The either-or viewpoint of the phonics versus whole word "debate," however, still lasts in the minds of many parents and some educators.

DECADE OF DEBATE AND RESEARCH

The 1960s produced a more rational decade in considering word analysis instruction. Notable during this period was Jeanne Chall's work *Learning to Read: The Great Debate* (1967). Chall's analysis of early reading instruction included the study of publisher-produced programs, observations in primary-grade classrooms, and the review of a wide range of reading research from that and earlier periods. She concluded that systematic phonics instruction used with connected and meaningful reading resulted in higher reading achievement for some children.

During the mid-1960s, a nationwide, federally funded cooperative research program, generally known as "The First Grade Studies" (Bond & Dykstra, 1967) was launched to examine various approaches to beginning reading instruction. This research involved twenty-seven research centers that used identical achievement tests and measures to study the question of what is the best method of early reading instruction. Conclusions of the first-grade studies revealed that combined approaches that used *both* systematic phonics *and* emphasis on connected reading and meaning produced superior results.

High and low achievement variation was noted, however, for children, regardless of the programs used in each of the studies; that is, for every instructional approach, some children achieved well and some did not. The most effective predictor of reading success was the students' ability to recognize and name upper- and lowercase letters of the alphabet at the beginning of first grade. This finding supports the importance of understanding print awareness and the relationships between letters and sounds. The finding, however, also reinforces the impact of literacy development at home on developing print awareness and letter-name and sound knowledge in the classroom (Dykstra, 1968).

Seven of these twenty-seven projects, including the project that one of us directed, continued through the second and third grades. At the end of third grade, few differences were found favoring any of the approaches, combined or otherwise. In this project (Ruddell, 1969), initial first-grade reading achievement gains were present for children's achievement in meaning-emphasis and systematic-phonic-emphasis programs, but these did not produce significant differences in children's achievement by the end of grade three. These findings may be explained in part by two factors. First, word analysis skills were developed in all programs studied by the end of grade three. Second, extensive reading of children's literature was emphasized during grades two and three with students in all programs studied. In effect, critical word analysis skills were taught in all programs by grade three and reinforced through application in reading children's literature.

Although it not a specific question studied in most of the cooperative research studies, we found that greater variation occurred in children's achievement levels between different teachers' classrooms than between the kinds of reading programs used. This finding supports the importance of effective teaching, regardless of the instructional emphasis present in a given reading program. The clear implication based on these findings is that *both* quality teaching and instructional programs that combine word analysis *and* connected reading and meaning contribute to children's reading achievement.

FOLLOW-THROUGH PROGRAM: IMPLEMENTATION AND STUDY

The 1970s saw the implementation of the federally supported "Follow-Through Program." This program not only served to implement new curricula but also to study children's achievement gains in the primary grades. Twenty-two instructional approaches were studied. All emphasized one of three areas: basic academic skills, cognitive and conceptual development, and child-centered activities focusing on effective development. Like The First Grade Studies cooperative research programs described above, the Follow-Through Programs emphasizing basic academic skills through highly structured word analysis produced the greatest gains for grades one and two. Few differences were found by grade three, and almost no differences in grade four (Adams, 1990b). Interestingly enough, however, the follow-up study of these students revealed that, by grades five and six, the students in the direct-instruction basic academic skills group achieved higher than students who were not in the Follow-Through Program (Becker & Gersten, 1982). An in-depth analysis of one of the schools in the Follow-Through Program revealed that the students were involved not only in a more structured program using word analysis but also in reading and interpreting stories from the beginning of the first grade. Again, the findings support the importance of integrated instruction that emphasizes not only word analysis but also interpretation of meaningfully connected reading (Chall, 1983).

WORD ANALYSIS AND PHONICS TODAY: CONTINUED DEBATE

The phonics and meaning controversy has not yet settled. In the 1980s, as the result of numerous reports on education and literacy education specifically (Anderson, Hiebert, Scott, & Wilkinson, 1985), legislation was sponsored by the late Senator Edward Zorinsky of Nebraska to commission a major study and report on phonics instruction. This resulted in *Beginning to Read* by Marilyn Adams (1990b). This extensive text covers educational, psychological, and sociolinguistic research since the early 1970s. Although the work may be criticized for its conceptualization of beginning reading using a skilled-reader model, it is both comprehensive and rational in nature. Nonetheless, it has generated major controversy, with phonics advocates feeling it is too meaning-based, and natural-language advocates concerned that it will overemphasize teaching print-sound knowledge systematically and too early.

Adams's conclusions support several of the key conclusions reached in previous decades and incorporate the most recent research findings. She calls for the development of print-awareness knowledge, use of invented spelling in word analysis instruction, systematic instruction in word analysis, instruction using meaning-based text, and opportunity for children to develop near-automatic word analysis skills through wide reading. As she notes in her conclusion to the book:

> Written text has both method and purpose. It is time for us to stop bickering about which is more important. To read, children must master both, and we must help them. In the interest of developing not just their reading skills but their own personal intellectual and productive potential, we must further encourage them to read frequently, broadly, and thoughtfully. (Adams, 1990b, p. 424)

During the decades of the 1960s, 1970s, 1980s, and early 1990s, publishers continued to produce reading programs with detailed Teacher's Guides and support materials such as workbooks. However, a noted shift in emphasis has occurred over this period, with word analysis skills being introduced in the earlier grades and in a more concentrated way. These are often, but not always, developed in the context of meaningful text.

During these same four decades, the "language-experience approach," the "whole language approach," and the "literature-based approach" to reading instruction have come into prominence in various parts of the country. In these approaches, emphasis is placed on the use of children's personalized stories and meaningful text, frequently children's literature. But instruction in word analysis skills is not neglected and is often taught in a more natural language context.

The "great debate" about word analysis will undoubtedly continue for years to come, fueled by the writing of lay critics, sensational newspaper articles, and nationwide advertising, as exemplified by *Hooked on Phonics*, that claims to have *the* method for teaching reading. It is important for you to realize that this controversy makes headlines and causes the public and some educators to choose sides; however, engaging in such debate fails to teach children to read. The critical point in this discussion is not whether we should use "phonics" or "whole-word" instruction, but instead that any teaching of word analysis skills must occur in a meaning-based context.

DEVELOPMENTAL STAGES OF WORD ANALYSIS

Recent research suggests that children progress through developmental stages in acquiring word-recognition ability (Ehri, 1991; Frith, 1985; Mason, Herman, & Au, 1991). Children's rate of progress through these stages depends heavily on their experiences with print and books at home and in the early grades. Linnea Ehri's extensive research review supports four such stages. These are:

1. **Logographic.** In this stage, children use cues relying on visual contextual or graphic features to read words. This may take the form of reading a word by remembering a letter or logo such as the golden arches and the word "McDonald's," reading a word with the help of a remembered visual cue such as *elephant* accompanied by a smudged thumbprint that happens to appear next to it on a flashcard, or reading a word such as *monkey* by remembering the "tail" on the word. This stage depends on a visual context and specific semantic connections to letter shapes, or other cues, in order to prompt memory. In this stage, some functional knowledge about print may be developed. However, word reading relies on visual and nonphonological (nonsound) clues. Kindergarten and entering first-graders frequently rely on a logographic system in reading environmental print and a limited number of "sight" words. Children's understanding of the alphabetic nature of printed language is only beginning to develop at this stage.

2. **Transition from logographic to beginning alphabetic.** In this stage, children begin to read words by shifting from visual context and a specific letter association to using the alphabetic principle. At this point, they begin to associate some letters seen in the spelling with sounds in the pronunciation of words. For example, the initial sound /d/ in the word dog is associated with the letter *d,* or the "two sticks" in the middle of the word *yellow* become associated with the "el" sound in the word. This transition stage starts to connect the printed letters to sounds and pronunciations. While these readers are able to use letter-identification

knowledge and beginning associations with sounds, they are still largely limited to reading "sight" words because the alphabetic principle is only beginning to develop. Many kindergarten and beginning first-grade children are at this rudimentary alphabetic stage of transition.

3. **Alphabetic.** This stage is characterized by the ability to read words by using letter-sound, or grapheme-phoneme, relationships. During this stage, children move from rather slow sounding-out and blending sounds in reading words to a rapid application of alphabetic principles. Their oral reading responses will range from processing time hesitancy to word substitutions to rapid reading, as they attempt to read new words. Some entering first-graders will have the alphabetic stage well developed, while others will not have entered this stage. You will find that some children, even in the second and third grades, will function at the beginning levels of this stage.

4. **Orthographic.** Here the student uses alphabetic principles but makes efficient use of predictable letter patterns and groups that are larger than letter-sound, or grapheme-phoneme, correspondences. These patterns and groups are established in memory, just as the letter-sound units are during the alphabetic stage (Ehri, 1991). These larger letter units help in analyzing multisyllabic words, reduce the number of units needed in memory, and speed up the process of reading words (Juel, 1983; Venezky & Massaro, 1979). These units become highly functional in "orthographic neighborhoods" for words that share letter sequences and stand for consistent pronunciations, e.g., *made, wade, fade,* or inconsistent pronunciations, e.g., st*eak*-cr*eak*, w*ave*-h*ave*, m*ost*-c*ost* (Glushko, 1979, 1981). Sensitivity to consistent patterns starts to emerge in first grade, while awareness of understanding of inconsistent patterns appears to occur about second grade. These units appear to possess a psychological reality for readers because of their predictable and rule-governed nature. We will discuss predictable patterning in greater detail later in this chapter. This orthographic stage begins to emerge after the alphabetic stage as children grasp the alphabetic principle and understanding of rhyme-based patterns.

At the end of this stage, children develop the ability to use analogy to read new words, e.g., they generalize from the *-ain* in r*ain* to read the new word tr*ain*. Orthographic-stage readers appear to divide the letter strings of multisyllabic words into root words and affixes or into syllables. They then convert these to pronunciations and blend them into known and recognizable words (Ehri, 1991). This phase may not become fully functional for some children until fourth or fifth grade, or even later. The use of context becomes an important meaning-based pronunciation check in this effort. The orthographic stage thus extends from late first and second grades through the intermediate grades for many children; however, great variation will be found across individual youngsters.

These stages provide a developmental backdrop for your word analysis program. Regardless of the methodology used in teaching word analysis skills, children appear to progress through these stages in acquiring independence in reading words. It is important to keep in mind, whether you are using a publisher-developed reading program or are crafting your own (as will be case in a language-experience or whole language program), that wide developmental differences will be present across individual students in your classroom. The sequence will be the same, but the time required for students to move from one stage into the next will vary widely.

GOALS AND OBJECTIVES OF WORD ANALYSIS INSTRUCTION

Your two goals in teaching word analysis are: *first*, to assist those children who depend on school for word analysis and literacy skill development to learn to read and comprehend printed text; and *second*, to enable them to enter a story or expository text and construct their own meaning. The purpose of this chapter, as stated earlier, is to help you understand the nature of word analysis instruction in a meaning-based context. This includes knowledge of the nature of print and sound relationships and acquisition of strategies that can be useful in your teaching. Specific word analysis objectives that are critical for your instructional program include the following:

1. Emphasizing word analysis instruction in the context of meaning construction.

2. Developing print awareness and letter-recognition knowledge to assist children in the transition from the logographic to the alphabetic stage of word analysis development.

3. Developing **phonemic awareness** (awareness of separate sounds in words) and **phonemic segmentation** (how sounds are separated and come together in words) as an important step in grasping the relationship between sounds and letters.

4. Building an understanding of letter-sound relationships and blending, as children develop key principles in the alphabetic stage and read words independently.

5. Developing an understanding of letter patterns and rhyming endings, as children enter the orthographic stage of word analysis.

6. Developing an understanding of syllable identification, using word- and letter-pattern clues to read multisyllabic words in meaning context at the orthographic stage.

7. Developing context clues, used in coordination with previously developed word analysis skills, to read and confirm meaning.

8. Providing opportunity to develop automatic recognition of high-frequency words.

Instruction in word analysis should lead to children's automatic and near automatic use of these various word analysis skills. You will find that some children, through wide reading of both narrative and expository texts, arrive at their own word analysis system with minimal guidance. Others, however, will depend heavily on your instruction and guidance to learn to read. In both cases it is important for children to read often and widely as they reinforce, apply, and practice the word analysis skills developed in your classroom.

General Learning Order and Placement of Word Analysis Skills

As we have seen, you will find wide variation in children's acquisition of word analysis skills at a given grade level. Our knowledge base, however, strongly supports the idea that children do move through the logographic, transitional, alphabetic, and orthographic stages. The word analysis skills that will be developed in the following discussion are placed in the context of these developmental growth stages.

The general learning order and placement of word analysis skills across the grades are indicated in Table 8-1. This table shows where you can expect key skills to be initiated, developed, and learned through major emphasis (***); where continued development and reinforcement will occur through minor emphasis (**); and where maintenance will occur through wide reading (*).

It is important to remember that Table 8-1 provides a *general* order and placement of skills. The skill placement should not be interpreted in any absolute sense because of the wide variation of word analysis skill development in a given grade. For example, at the intermediate-grade levels you can fully expect that you will have some children who will need major emphasis on letter-sound relationships and, particularly, letter-pattern, and syllable identification.

Word Analysis Skill Development in the Classroom

Again, keep in mind that instruction in word analysis skills will take place not only in the early grades but in grades four, five, and six, as well. This is

WORD-ANALYSIS SKILL	GRADE LEVEL						
	K	1	2	3	4	5	6
Print Awareness							
Print Organization	***	**	*				
Page Organization	***	**	*				
Book Organization	***	**	*				
Letter Names	***	**	*				
Letter Recognition	***	***	*				
Phonemic Awareness	***	***	**	*			
Phonemic Segmentation	***	***	**	*			
Letter-Sound Relationships							
Consonants	***	***	***	**	*	*	*
Vowels	***	***	***	**	*	*	*
Letter Patterns and Rhyme		***	***	**	*	*	*
Syllable Identification							
Compound Words		***	***	***	***	**	*
Prefixes, Suffixes, Roots			***	***	***	***	***
Consonant Groups and Digraphs			***	***	***	**	*
Context Clues	***	***	***	***	***	***	***
Rapid-Recognition Vocabulary		***	***	***	***	**	**
Skill Application Through Wide Reading		***	***	***	***	***	***

Key: *** *Major Emphasis—high probability of learning and development*
   ** *Minor Emphasis—continued development*
   * *Maintenance—reinforcement through wide reading*

TABLE 8-1

General Learning Order and Placement of Word Analysis Skills evident from the discussion above on developmental stages. Some children who enter kindergarten and first grade will be well along in their understanding of how print works and are at the beginning of the alphabetic phase. Others will in fact have already developed the ability to read text with some degree of fluency. These youngsters clearly understand that reading is a meaning-construction process prompted by printed text and illustrations. Still other youngsters will have had limited experience with print and books and may be at the logographic stage or in the logographic-alphabetic transitional stage. These children will need to develop key beginning-level print-awareness concepts and the connection between print and sounds and familiar meanings.

Unless children have developed a sound foundation in word-recognition skills and meaning construction by the end of third grade, they will encounter great difficulty in grade four and even greater difficulty in grades five and six (Ruddell & Williams, 1972). You can be reasonably sure that you will find a number of these children in your classroom at the intermediate-grade level. They have difficulty in using letter-sound relationships, blending, predictable letter patterns, visual identification of syllables, and context clues, and have a limited high speed recognition of frequently used vocabulary. More important, these children do not understand that reading is a meaning-construction process; quite simply, they do not enter text with the expectation of making sense. This may be due to poor instruction, prior teachers' inappropriate assumptions about children's learning ability, developmental learning difficulties, or other reasons. These children, however, depend on you and school literacy instruction to learn to read. Thus, it becomes critical that you understand and can apply specific word analysis instructional strategies and activities to help children develop needed word analysis skills in a meaning-based context. We emphasize here that word 93 analysis skills should *never* be taught in isolation from meaning construction, nor should word analysis instruction so predominate that little time is left for reading meaningful text.

The instructional approach recommended here is analytic in nature. That is, word analysis skills will be taught by using words as recognizable and meaningful wholes, followed by the use of these words to teach the letter-sound and letter-pattern-sound-pattern relationships. This contrasts with a synthetic approach that teaches letter-sound relationships in isolation followed by blending of these sounds to form words. The following discussion is designed to assist you in this instruction.

DEVELOPING WORD ANALYSIS IN THE CONTEXT OF MEANING CONSTRUCTION

In Chapter 3, "Understanding the Beginning Steps: Early Reading and Writing Development," we presented several key instructional principles that are critical to successful word analysis instruction. A brief review of these ideas suggests that you keep in mind that *children are active theory builders and hypothesis testers;* that *the driving force behind their questions and explorations is to make meaning;* that their *language performance and social interaction is directly connected to the classroom learning environment* that you create; and that their *oral and written language development is directly connected to their reading acquisition.* These principles translate to four instructional conditions that will greatly enhance word analysis instruction. Effective word analysis instruction needs to

1. be developed through activities and strategies that have meaning for children;
2. use children's own curiosity, interests, and background knowledge;
3. let children know that you expect them to be successful in the instructional activity; and
4. provide positive response and feedback, based on your observations, as children participate in instructional activities.

Word analysis instruction should thus be developed from the earliest levels using pronounceable, meaningful language units in the context of words, sentences, and extended text. Children's interests must be engaged—their active learning participation is critical. Your learning expectations, observations, and positive encouragement and feedback provide added motivation and instructional guidance. This approach enables children to discover the way in which letters, spelling patterns, and words represent oral language and to arrive at implicit generalizations about the nature of the print-sound relationship. To reach the goal of reader independence in transforming print to meaning, you will need to help students develop word analysis skills to an automatic level for most print; in addition, children must acquire procedures and analysis strategies for independent processing of unknown words when text is difficult.

Let us acknowledge at this point that word analysis instruction occurs in all classrooms—whole language and literature-based as well as more traditional, basal reading classrooms. The major differences center around the following:

1. **Sequence of instruction.** In basal reading classrooms, sequence of word analysis instruction is predetermined, while in whole-language- and literature-based programs word analysis skills are taught as needed.
2. **Materials for instruction.** Basal programs provide workbooks, blackline masters, and other materials with word analysis exercises built into them, while whole language and literature-based instruction embeds word analysis development in materials teachers create from children's writing, word banks, vocabulary journals, and/or from the books children are reading.

3. **Frequency and scope of instruction.** Basal reading programs identify a set of word analysis skills to be taught over the course of the program and include daily instruction or practice of word analysis skills, while whole language and literature-based instruction teach and/or reinforce those word analysis skills children do not acquire on their own when student performance suggests a need to do so.

4. **Planning and record keeping.** Basal programs provide built-in planning for word analysis instruction along with procedures/materials for documenting children's progress, while whole language and literature based instruction require that teachers develop these systems themselves.

In the remainder of this chapter, as we discuss instructional strategies for developing word analysis skills, you will need to consider carefully how you will implement such instruction in your classroom. That is, you will have to decide how the sequence, materials, frequency and scope, and planning/record keeping for word analysis instruction will occur within the context of your reading program. All of the instructional practices we suggest can be adapted for use in basal reading, whole language, or literature-based classrooms.

DEVELOPING PRINT AWARENESS AND LETTER-RECOGNITION KNOWLEDGE

In Chapter 3, we discussed specific concepts essential to building print awareness in early literacy instruction. A brief review of these important concepts will place them in the context of word analysis instruction for the discussion that follows. Print awareness includes knowledge of the following:

- Letters have names.
- Letters represent sounds.
- Words are made up of letters.
- Print is organized by words and the blank spaces between them.
- Lines of print are read from left-to- right and from top-to-bottom on the page.
- Special punctuation marks are used to indicate such information as beginning and end of sentences (.), to ask questions (?), to provide special emphasis (!), and to show that someone is talking (" ").
- Print is organized on pages that have top and bottom positions, and, when two pages are side by side, the left page is read first.
- Pages are organized in the form of books that have fronts and backs; pages are organized from left to right; and pictures and print can be used to tell a story or explain new ideas.

Print Awareness

A wide variety of instructional activities and strategies were introduced in Chapter 3 for the development of these print-awareness concepts. These included:

- Concepts About Print, p. 91.
- Developing Picture and Print-Awareness Concepts, p.91.
- Connecting Picture Awareness to Meaning, p. 92.
- Language-Experience Charts, pp. 92.
- Big Books, pp. 93.
- Oral Story-Reading, p. 94.
- Alphabet Books, pp. 94.
- Rhyming Books, pp. 95.

A section of Chapter 3, Developing a Sense of Observing and Writing, includes a range of activities that record oral language through print. These activities help children acquire print awareness and understand the nature of the alphabetic principle through writing. Chapter 3 should be reviewed carefully to refresh your memory on specific activities and strategies useful in developing print awareness knowledge for children at the logographic, transitional, and alphabetic stages of word analysis. This knowledge, particularly letter recognition, phonemic awareness, understanding of rhyming endings, and phonemic segmentation provides the foundation for word analysis skill development. These topics will be developed more fully in the discussion sections that follow.

Letter Recognition

Many children have learned to recognize and name the letters of the alphabet before entering school. In all probability, however, they will have learned only the uppercase, or capital, letters (Nurss, 1979; Ehri, 1988). Many parents teach their children to name the letters and write the alphabet, usually in capital forms. Programs such as "Sesame Street," "Reading Rainbow," and "Mister Rogers' Neighborhood" also provide valuable letter-recognition exposure.

It is, of course, necessary to learn both uppercase and lowercase letters in learning to read. This is not an easy task. Letters are abstract and require a specific orientation. A ball is a ball and a book is a book, regardless of how the objects are turned. Not so with letters. Each of the twenty-six letters must be recognizable in uppercase and lowercase manuscript print requiring a specific visual orientation. In later grades, two more letter sets are added as children learn cursive writing.

Research indicates that letters are not recognized by remembering their holistic patterns. Rather, we identify each letter through the analysis of its individual features such as orientation, line segments, and linecurves. This information is then stored in memory and used in the scanning and recognition process (Gibson, Gibson, Pick, & Osser, 1962; Pick, 1965). Visual discrimination of letters must be developed to a refined level in order to account for the following different features:

Left-right orientation, e.g., b-d, p-q

Top-bottom orientation, e.g., n-w, n-u, m-w

Direction of line extension, e.g., b-p, d-g, d-q

Presence of extension, e.g., i-j, q-a, d-a, n-h

Line-curve presence, e.g., U-V, P-F, u-v

Pick's research (1965) indicates that the presentation of these letter pairs in contrasting order, as shown above, may prove useful in instruction. We make one instructional caution, however, in teaching these letter pairs. It is important that the first letter in the pair, e.g., b, be thoroughly developed before teaching the second letter in the pair, in this case, d (Beck & McCaslin, 1978). The value of teaching pairs in this manner is to help children recognize the relevant contrasting features. It is important to note that letter reversals, commonly observed in first, second, and even third grades, reflect children's idiosyncratic knowledge of letter forms (recall children's ever-evolving language theory) and are not to be interpreted as a neurological problem for most children (Liberman, Shankweiler, Orlando, Harris, & Berti, 1971). Letter reversals by young children are simply one other representation, as are invented spellings, of children's understanding of how print works.

Children will come to recognize letters and to distinguish rapidly between them. Many of the suggestions found in the above section, summarizing and identifying strategies and activities from Chapter 3, will assist in developing letter-name and letter-recognition knowledge. Adams (1990a) makes three useful instructional recommendations in developing letter-recognition knowledge.

1. Teach the letter names first, so that children will have a "conceptual peg" to which they can attach their perceptions and observations.

2. Use highly motivating activities, which include rhyme, rhythm, and song in teaching the letter names. Teaching the "alphabet song" illustrates this type of instruction. Instruction in recognizing letters and connecting each name and letter should then follow.

3. In order to avoid confusing letter names and sounds, teach the letter-sound relationships after solid familiarity with letter names has been developed.

Letter-name knowledge will also be greatly facilitated as children combine writing with word analysis instruction (illustrated in Figure 8-2) and as children explore symbol systems. Recall from Chapter 7 Latrice's announcement, "Gonna write an *i*" as she moved from drawing to writing (Harste et al., 1984). The activities discussed in Chapter 3, specifically the section on Developing a Sense of Observing and Writing, will also be of value in placing manuscript printing and letter name recognition in a meaning-based context.

Your instruction will be greatly facilitated by displaying the alphabet in a classroom location that children can easily see. In primary classrooms letters may be accompanied by a picture representing each letter and several printed words containing the highlighted letter, e.g., letters *d* and *D*, accompanied by picture of a *dog*, and the words *dog, Dog; deer, Deer; door, Door*. This provides a mnemonic device to learn the letter name and to begin to associate the name with the letter sound in word context, and it provides an easy printing-writing reference for children. Alphabet cards of this type can be purchased at school-supply stores, and many basal reading programs provide an alphabet package with the program. Or you can easily make these for your classroom.

As you develop letter-name knowledge, be sure to use alphabet books such as *Dr. Seuss's ABC* (Seuss, 1963), *Animal Alphabet* (Kitchen, 1984), and

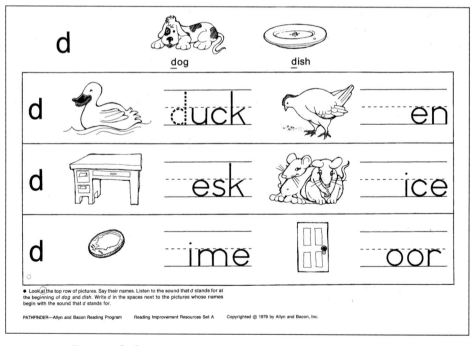

• Look at the top row of pictures. Say their names. Listen to the sound that *d* stands for at the beginning of *dog* and *dish*. Write *d* in the spaces next to the pictures whose names begin with the sound that *d* stands for.

PATHFINDER—Allyn and Bacon Reading Program   Reading Improvement Resources Set A   Copyrighted © 1979 by Allyn and Bacon, Inc.

FIGURE 8-2

Using Manuscript Printing to Reinforce the Development of Letter-Name Knowledge. (Reproduced with permission from Ruddell, 1979, #7A.)

A *Farmer's Alphabet* (Azarian, 1981). A more complete set of references is listed at the end of Chapter 3. These books provide wonderful illustrations and meaning contexts, often humorous, that have great appeal for children.

DEVELOPING PHONEMIC AWARENESS AND PHONEMIC SEGMENTATION

Phonemic awareness and phonemic segmentation are critical to the development of the alphabetic principle, as children learn to connect letter-sound, or grapheme-phoneme, relationships. As we discussed in Chapter 2, children acquire most of the phonemes, or sounds, of our language by age three or four. Having mastered these, their main focus shifts to understanding and using language in social settings as they communicate with siblings, peers, parents, and other caretakers. This communication shift directs attention to words and meanings of words in spoken discourse. Instruction in phonemic awareness and phonemic segmentation is designed to refocus attention on the sounds that compose words and in turn connect these to their written counterparts.

Phonemic Awareness

Phonemic awareness essentially involves understanding that spoken words are composed of sounds. Many children are not aware of this concept at kindergarten and beginning first-grade levels. They appear to move through several stages in developing phonemic awareness. Initially, they tend to think of the smallest unit of language as the word, e.g., *cat, kitten, neighborhood*. Next, children become aware of syllable breaks in words. Syllable breaks are apparent when we tap out the number of sound units in a word, e.g., *cat* (one tap), *kit-ten* (two taps), *neigh-bor-hood* (three taps). Then they become aware that syllables often have a beginning sound and a rhyming ending, e.g., *c-at, k-it t-en, n-eigh b-or h-ood*. The beginning and ending of the syllable have special labels used by linguists and psycholinguists. The beginning part is known as the **onset**, e.g., *c-*at and the ending, which includes a vowel and consonant ending, is known as the **rime**, e.g., c-*at*. (We will use the terms rime and rhyming ending interchangeably in the following discussion. These terms are discussed in more detail on pages 405–407) The recognition of onset and rime appears to develop before children can identify individual sounds or phonemes (Trieman, 1985). It is helpful to keep these stages in mind as you observe and develop children's phonemic awareness.

An excellent way to develop phonemic awareness is by reading familiar nursery rhymes and poetry to children. *Mother Goose* rhymes have special appeal for kindergarten and first-grade children, in part, because many children are already familiar with them. For example, "Little Boy Blue" or "Tom, Tom, the Piper's Son" provide wonderful opportunities to use familiar, meaningful text to teach and reinforce beginning sounds, or onset, and rime. By focusing attention on the rimes in *horn* and *corn*, *sheep* and *asleep*, and *eat* and *beat*, for example, you assist children in understanding how rhyming words are alike and different. After reading and reciting the familiar children's rhymes, you can place these words on the chalkboard and discuss them. Draw attention to the different beginning sounds (the onset) and the similar rhyming endings (the rime).

Children's books such as Dr. Seuss's *The Cat in the Hat* (1957) or *Hop on Pop* (1963) and Bill Martin's *Brown Bear, Brown Bear, What Do You See?* (1983) include rhymes and recurring word patterns that provide wonderful opportunities to develop phonemic awareness by focusing attention on the sounds of language. Poetry collections for this purpose include *Poems for Young Children* (Royds, 1986), *Catch Me & Kiss Me & Say It Again* (Watson, 1978), and *When the Dark Comes Dancing, A Bedtime Poetry Book* (Larrick, 1983).

By sharing poetry and rhyming books with children several times a day, every day, and by focusing attention on beginning and endings of rhyming words, you develop an essential foundation for building sound-letter relationships. As children listen to familiar rhymes and attend to how rhyming words are similar and different, they begin to incorporate phonemic awareness knowledge into their language theory. Thus, they are able to develop generalizations and apply and test hypotheses about that aspect of language and print.

Phonemic Segmentation

Phonemic segmentation involves the ability to direct and focus attention on the separate sounds in a word. This ability becomes important as children begin to establish the connection between sounds and letters using the alphabetic features of our writing system. Phonemic segmentation may be demonstrated by asking children to tap out the number of sounds they hear in a word, as described above, e.g., d-o-g (three taps). A second demonstration of this ability is to ask children to tell what word or sound sequence remains after a sound is removed from a word, e.g., "*cat* without the /k/" or "*mill* without the /m/." Another task is to ask children to blend sounds, e.g., "*m + at, c + at, r + at.* The ability to segment and blend individual sounds indicates that children are aware of, and can direct their attention to, the component sounds in words, and reflects their understanding of the nature of the sound system. The objective then is to build relationships between these sounds and the letters that stand for or represent them.

The following procedure will be useful in developing phonemic segmentation with those children who appear to have difficulty on the tasks described above.

Prepare five or six 3-by-3-inch square pieces of cardboard, and outline the borders using a black marker. Also have ready counters, such as buttons or small circles cut from construction paper.

Count the number of blank squares needed to represent each sound in each word used. For example, for the word *dog* three squares will be needed, the word *book* would also require three squares for each of the three sounds. Place these blank squares together, side by side, in front of the child.

1. Provide the child with a picture of a familiar object or animal, e.g., picture of a dog.
2. Pronounce the word slowly, taking care not to exaggerate sounds unnecessarily or distort pronunciation.
3. Ask the child to pronounce the word just as you have done.
4. Next, pronounce the word slowly and place a counter in each of the three squares as each sound in the word is articulated.

5. Remove your markers. Ask the child to repeat the word, pronouncing it slowly. As each sound is articulated, the child should place a marker in each square to correspond to the sound.
6. Ask the child to use the word in a sentence, and then practice the procedure once more.
7. Provide another picture, and follow the same modeling procedure and child's response as described in steps 1 through 6.

Sound-Letter Associations

A similar procedure can be used to develop a beginning understanding of sound-letter associations. Steps 1 through 3 model pronunciation of the word, as in the phonemic segmentation activity. Steps 4 through 6 shift to the use of letters to stand for or represent the sounds pronounced.

Plastic letters, purchased at a toy store, work well for this purpose. You can also simply use a marker to draw the number of squares needed for the sounds in a given word. You will need to fill in the letter(s) for each sound as you pronounce the word, and then quickly draw new squares for the child's response. In either case, after showing the child the picture, ask, "What letters do you think will go in each of the squares for this word?" Then place or write the letters in each square. Finally, ask the child to use the word in a sentence.

The phonemic segmentation procedure is also used in the Reading Recovery Program developed by Marie Clay. She suggests that the child's understanding of phonemic segmentation can be enhanced by asking the

Invented Spelling and Sound-Letter Associations

child, "What do you hear in the beginning?" "In the middle?" "At the end?" "What else do you hear?" (Clay, 1979).

Invented Spelling

In Chapter 2 we discussed the several patterns of children's invented spelling. We saw that children progress from pre- and early phonemic to letter-name and transitional spelling. At the early phonemic stage, letters and letterlike forms are used in short consonant strings, indicating the discovery of the alphabetic principle. In the letter-name spelling stage, letters are used to stand for sounds (except for silent letters), clearly reflecting the use of the alphabetic principle. In the transitional stage, letters are used to represent all sounds, including short and long vowel sounds.

The early phonemic and the letter-name spelling stages require skills that are very similar to those used in the development of phonemic awareness and phonemic segmentation. We might therefore expect that children who have used invented spellings in their classrooms will benefit, from their self-discovery of the alphabetic system, in learning to read words. Clarke's research (1988) contrasted the spelling and word-recognition achievement of children taught traditionally (in which "misspellings" were corrected) and those encouraged to use invented spellings. The findings indicate that, for children defined as "low-readiness students," the invented spelling group did indeed perform at a significantly higher achievement level on spelling and word-recognition tests. No differences, however, were found for children described as "high-readiness students" in both groups. This can be interpreted to mean that encouraging invented spelling is beneficial to students who most need assistance in literacy acquisition (e.g., "low-readiness" children), and is just as effective as traditional instruction for others. Another study by Mann, Tobin, and Wilson (1987) suggested that children's ability to represent sounds in their invented spellings was an excellent predictor of their success in learning to read words. While the connection between invented spelling and word analysis success needs further study, early indications suggests a close, positive relationship.

PRINCIPLES OF LETTER-SOUND RELATIONSHIPS

English is based on an alphabetic system, and the alphabet principle suggests that there is a one-to-one relationship between letters and sounds. This, of course, is not the case. There is, however, much regularity present. It thus becomes important, for instructional purposes, to understand the nature of this regularity both for letter-sound relationships and for highly predictable letter patterns. A quick summary of key principles follow:

1. **Single consonants**, are highly regular in the initial positions of words, e.g., b as in *bat*. As noted in Table 8-2, there are a few exceptions, such as c as in *can* (/k/) and *city* (/s/), g as in *get* (/g/) and *gym* (/j/), and s as in *sit* (/s/) and *sure* (/sh/). Note, however, that there are only two variations for each of these exceptions.

2. **Consonant digraphs**, two letters that stand for one sound, are also highly regular, as is evident in Table 8-3, e.g., *ch* as in *chip*, *kn* as in *knit*.

3. **Consonant blends**, two letters representing different sounds but blended together, likewise are very regular, as noted in Table 8-3, e.g., *bl* as in *blue*, *tr* as in *tree*.

4. **Short vowel sounds**, represented by the letters *a*, *e*, *i*, *o*, and *u* have a much lower level of predictability when considered in isolation, e.g., *a* as in *bat* and *talk*.

5. **Short vowel sounds**, however, have a relatively high level of predictability in the letter-pattern context of consonant-vowel-consonant (C-VC), as shown in Table 8-4, e.g., *a* is highly consistent in the patterns, -*ad* as in *d-ad*. The same is true of the consonant-vowel-consonant-consonant pattern (C-VCC), e.g., as in *s-and* and *b-ank*.

6. **Long vowel sounds**, represented either singly or in some combination of *a*, *e*, *i*, *o*, *u*, *y*, and *w*, have a lower level of predictability in isolation, e.g., *a* as in *said, aisle, Paul, law*.

393

7. **Long vowel sounds**, however, have a much higher predictability in letter pattern context of consonant-vowel-consonant-final *e* (C-VCe). This is evident by creating words based on the long vowel pattern *-ake* , as shown in Table 8-4, e.g., *b-ake, m-ake,* and *t-ake.* The same is true for the consonant-vowel-vowel pattern (C-VV), e.g., *-ay* as in *b-ay* and *h-ay,* and the consonant-vowel-vowel-consonant pattern (C-VVC), e.g., *-ain* as in *r-ain* and *p-ain.*

8. **Other vowels, or diphthongs**, which are complex vowel sounds formed by shifting from one vowel sound to another, are regular within the patterns noted in Table 8-5. For example, in the consonant-vowel-vowel pattern (C-VV), e.g., *-aw* as in *l-aw* or *p-aw,* or the consonant-vowel-vowel-consonant pattern (C-VVC), e.g., *-oi* as in *b-oil* and *s-oil.*

9. *R*-**controlled vowels**, noted in Table 8-5, are highly predictable in the consonant-vowel-*r* pattern (C-Vr) as illustrated in the words *c-ar* and *f-ar,* or the consonant-vowel-*r*-consonant pattern (C-VrC) as found in the words *b-ark,* and *h-arm.*

This brief summary suggests that the alphabetic system functions in a highly predictable way for single consonant letters, consonant digraphs, and consonant blends. The predictability for single vowels and vowel-consonant combinations increases dramatically when viewed in predictable letter-pattern contexts. The patterns noted for vowel letters that stand for diphthongs and *r*-controlled vowels also hold a high level of predictability. The use of such patterns will attain a near automatic level as children progress through the orthographic stage of word analysis described above.

You will note that the symbols used throughout this chapter (and throughout the book)—to show pronunciation of consonants, consonant digraphs, consonant blends, short vowels, long vowels, vowel diphthongs, and *r*-controlled vowels—follow those used in dictionaries rather than the phonemic symbols used by linguists. Our reason in doing this is that you already have some familiarity with the dictionary symbols.

BUILDING AND UNDERSTANDING OF LETTER-SOUND RELATIONSHIPS

The information contained in Tables 8-2 through 8-5 represents the key letter-sound and letter-pattern relationships that literate English speakers understand. Instruction will facilitate children's development of these understandings of both the alphabetic and the orthographic stages of word analysis. We now turn to the instructional approaches, strategies, and activities that will enable you to develop these concepts in your classroom. The following teaching guidelines will be helpful in teaching letter-sound relationships.

1. Develop letter-sound relationships in a meaning-based context.
2. Use discussions, activities, and reading material that will actively involve and interest children.

CONSONANTS		EXAMPLE OF MAJOR PATTERN USE	VARIED PATTERN USE
b	/b/	bat	tuba, cab
c	/k/	can	
	/s/	city	racer
d	/d/	doll	soda, mad
f	/f/	fit	heifer, life
g	/g/	get	tiger, rag
	/j/	gym	margarine
h	/h/	hat	ahead
j	/j/	jaw	pajama, rajah
	/w/	Juan	
k	/k/	kitten	baker, break
l	/l/	lake	sailor, metal
m	/m/	man	tamer, ham
n	/n/	nut	finer, hen
p	/p/	picnic	piper, drip
q	/k/	queen	liquor, opaque
r	/r/	run	bearer, car
s	/s/	sit	pets, pastel
	/sh/	sure	passion
	/z/	has, cars	
t	/t/	time	meter, hit
v	/v/	voice	mover, wave
w	/w/	work	shower, row
x	/ks/	box	
	/z/	xylophone	
y	/y/	yard	Sawyer
z	/z/	zoo	blazer, jazz
	/zh/	azure	

TABLE 8-2

Consonant Patterns: Letter-Sound Relationships

DIGRAPHS (TWO LETTERS STAND FOR ONE SOUND)		EXAMPLE OF MAJOR PATTERN USE
ch	/ch/	chip, porch
	/k/	chasm, archangel
gh	/g/	ghost
	/f/	tough
ph	/f/	photo
ck	/k/	bucket, rack
kn	/n/	knit
wh	/h/	who
sh	/sh/	ship
th	/th/	thin
th	/th/	then
wr	/r/	wreck

BLENDS (TWO LETTERS STAND FOR TWO BLENDED SOUNDS)		EXAMPLE OF MAJOR PATTERN USE
bl	/bl/	blue
cl	/kl/	close
fl	/fl/	fly
gl	/gl/	glass
pl	/pl/	please
sl	/sl/	slow
br	/br/	brick
cr	/kr/	crawl
dr	/dr/	draw
fr	/fr/	fry
gr	/gr/	great
pr	/pr/	pretty
tr	/tr/	tree
st	/st/	start
str	/str/	string
sk	/sk/	skate

TABLE 8-3

Digraph and Blend Patterns

VOWELS	PATTERNS AND EXAMPLES OF MAJOR USE		
SHORT VOWELS	PATTERN —	C-VC	C-VCC
		e.g., d-ad	s-and
a /ă/	-ab, -ack, -am, -amp, -ang, -ank, -ask, -at	-ad, -an, -ap,	-ag, -and, -ash,
e /ĕ/	-eck, -ed, -end, -ent, -et	-ell, -ess,	-en, -est,
i /ĭ/	-ick, -id, -im, -in, -ip, -ish,	-ig, -ing, -it	-ill, -ink,
o /ŏ/	-ob, -ock, -ot	-og,	-op,
u /ŭ/	-ub, -uck, -um, -ump, -unk, -ut	-uff, -un,	-ug, -ung,

LONG VOWELS	PATTERN —	C-VCe,	
	e.g.,	b-ake	
a-e /ā/	-ace, -ade, -ame, -ane,	-ake, -ate	-ale,
e-e /ē/	-ese		
i-e /ī/	-ice, -ide, -ine, -ive	-ike,	-ime,
o-e /ō/	-oke, -one,	-ope	
u-e /ū/	-use		

LONG VOWELS	PATTERN —	C-VV OR C-VVC	
	e.g.,	d-ay	p-ain
ay /ā/ ai	-ay (hay) -ain (rain)		
ea /ē/ ee	-ea (reach) -eep (peep)	-eet (beet)	
ie /ī/	-ie (pie)		
oa /ō/	-oat (boat)	-oast (boast)	

── **TABLE 8-4** ──

Short and Long Vowels in Major Letter Patterns

OTHER VOWELS OR DIPHTONGS	PATTERN— e.g.,	C-VV OR C-VVC l-aw, b-oil	
oi oy	/oi/	-oi (boil) -oy (boy)	
oo	/o͝o/	-ook (book)	
oo	/o͞o/	-oo (too), -oom (boom)	
ow ou	/ou/	-ow (cow) -ound (sound), -ouse (mouse)	
R-CONTROLLED VOWELS	**PATTERN—** e.g.,	**C-Vr OR C-VrC** c-ar, b-ark	
ar	/är/	-ar (far), -ark (bark), -arm (harm), -art (part)	
air are ear	/âr/	-air (fair) -are (dare) -ear (bear)	
eer	/ĭr/	-eer (sneer)	
ore orn	/ōr/	-ore (core) -orn (born)	

TABLE 8-5

Diphthongs and *R*-Controlled Vowels

3. Help children understand that "letters and letter patterns stand for sounds and sound patterns," not that "letters make sounds," which leads to confusion.

4. Use the following instructional sequence in your teaching:

■ introduce the new letter-sound relationship, or concept, in known vocabulary context;

■ develop visual association with the new letter or letter-pattern in the context of the written word;

■ provide a range of word examples using the new letter-sound concept in the same position and direct attention to the new concept in these examples;

- contrast the new letter-sound concept with a different letter-sound concept substituted in the same position to form a new word or words;

- encourage children to identify the name of the letter that stands for the sound at the beginning (or middle or end) of the words developed in the discussion; and

- use the word examples in a meaningful sentence context.

Introducing and Developing Consonants

The instructional sequence described above can be illustrated using the introduction and development of consonants. The new letter-sound relationship to be developed is the initial consonant *b*, /b/. This concept is selected because it is used frequently in a class story or language-experience chart.

A word card and a picture card (or a picture from a magazine) for the word *ball* is displayed to a small group of children. The picture shows a large inflatable ball with red and green stripes. The word is read, if necessary with your assistance, and used in discussion, as the children explore their experience with this type of ball. Picture cards or magazine pictures representing objects whose names have the initial consonant *b* are then displayed. The children are asked to identify each object and to listen for the initial sound in each picture word—for example, *boy, boat, book*. As the words are given, write each one on the board, or on chart paper that can be saved for later use. Direct the children's attention to the letter *b*, by pointing as you pronounce each word. Ask the children to identify the name of the first letter, then point out that the letter *b* stands for the first sound in each word. Encourage the children to think of other words that begin with the same consonant sound, e.g., *bat, beet, bought*, and add these to the list. Then ask each child in the group to come to the board, select a word, and draw a line under the initial consonant *b* in the word. Ask the child to pronounce the word, providing assistance as needed, and then to use it in a sentence.

This lesson may then be extended by pronouncing each word in the list and again directing the children's attention to the initial consonant *b* for each word. Select one or two of the words that can be easily varied by substituting another initial consonant. For example, the words *bat* and *book* may be changed using the initial consonant *h*. Write the word *bat*, beside the original word list on the board or chart paper. Write the letter *h* under the letter *b* in *bat*, and ask the children to create a new word by using the initial consonant *h*. Then ask what letters need to be added to form the new word *hat*. Contrast the two words and the initial consonants by focusing attention on letters *b* and *h*. Follow the same procedure using *book* and *hook*.

Conclude the lesson by quickly printing the words from the original wordlist, *ball, boy, boat, book* on blank tagboard cards using a felt-tip marker. Have the children pronounce the words, providing assistance as needed. Direct the children's attention to the initial consonant in each word as it is read, using your finger or by underlining the letter *b*. Ask the children to identify the letter that stands for the sound at the beginning of each word. This activity can easily be transferred to teaching other initial consonants, vowels, and final consonants.

Two commercially published reinforcement activities for the initial consonant *f* are illustrated in Figure 8-3. Note that the second activity (see bottom example) using the initial consonant *f* builds and reinforces this understanding through printing of the letter in word context. Teacher-designed activities are just as useful for reinforcing consonants. For example, after instruction or discussion of a target consonant (e.g., *b*) have children go through their word banks or vocabulary journals and find all the words that begin with *b* (this assumes that the word banks or journals are not organized alphabetically). Alternately, have the children look for words that have *b* in the middle or that end in *b*. This same exercise can occur using children's individual writing, class-generated language-experience charts, or a book or story the children just read.

Using Consonant Substitution in Context. The use of consonant substitution prompted by context is a more advanced word analysis skill and requires children to generalize word-ending sounds from one word to another. This is illustrated in the following activity.

Prepare a series of sentences each of which uses a word that contains one of the consonants that you wish to emphasize. Create a new word for each sentence by substituting another consonant at the beginning of the original word. The original word and the new word are then identified in parentheses at the end of each sentence. Place a blank space in each sentence for the original word. These sentences may be taken from language-experience stories and/or other writing that children have done. The children are asked to read each sentence, and identify the correct word to complete the sentence using the sentence context. For example:

1. The _____ was eating the foot-long hotdog. (toy, boy)
2. The girls had fun playing _____ (tag, bag)
3. The clown has a big red _____ (mall, ball)
4. The paper was very _____ . (thin, shin)

The use of word analysis analogy and context is also illustrated in Figure 8-3 (five, fish).

Introducing and Developing Vowels. The procedure for introducing letter-sound relationships for vowels follows that outlined at the beginning of this discussion. You should introduce the vowel using known vocabulary in context, focus attention on the visual association with the new letter-sound relationship, use the new vowel in a variety of meaningful word examples, contrast the new vowel concept with a different vowel substitut-

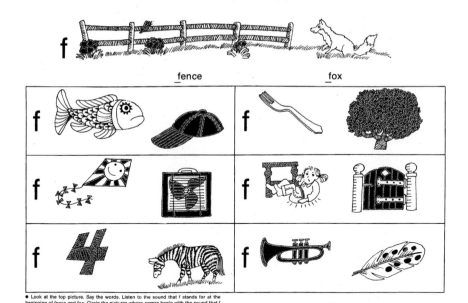

f   _fence   _fox

● Look at the top picture. Say the words. Listen to the sound that f stands for at the beginning of fence and fox. Circle the pictures whose names begin with the sound that f stands for.

PATHFINDER—Allyn and Bacon Reading Program   Reading Improvement Resources Set A   Copyrighted © 1979 by Allyn and Bacon, Inc.

f   _five   _fish

f fan   en
f eet   ire
f ox   ox

● Look at the top row of pictures. Say their names. Listen to the sound that f stands for at the beginning of five and fish. Write f in the spaces next to the pictures whose names begin with the sound that f stands for.

PATHFINDER—Allyn and Bacon Reading Program   Reading Improvement Resources Set A   Copyrighted © 1979 by Allyn and Bacon, Inc.

FIGURE 8-3

Developing Initial Consonants f and d Through Meaning Context and Printing. (Reproduced with permission from Ruddell, 1979, #9A.)

ed in the same position, refocus attention on the name of the key vowel letter used in words from the discussion and use the word examples in sentence context.

For example, to introduce the letter *a*, which stands for the short /ă/ vowel sound, display a word card and a picture card, or a picture from a magazine, of the word *hat*. Interest will be increased by having several types of hat pictures. Read the word, with assistance if needed. Encourage the children to share their experiences with a hat, e.g., their own hat, or where they have seen different kinds of hats worn. Write the word *hat* on the board or chart paper. Show other pictures for words that have the short *a* vowel, such as *mat* and *bat*. Ask the children to name these objects and briefly discuss them. Write *mat* and *bat* on the board under *hat*. Ask the children to identify the name of the middle letter *a*. As you pronounce each word, point to the letter *a* to emphasize the letter-sound relationship. Point out that the letter *a* stands for the short /ă/ vowel sound.

Encourage the children to think of as many words as they can that have the short /ă/ sound. Words such as *cat*, *pat*, and *sat* should then be added to the list of words. Ask each of the children to come to the board, select a word, and underline the letter *a*. Have the word pronounced, using assistance if needed, and have it used in a sentence.

Extend the lesson by quickly reviewing the words on the board, again pointing to the letter *a*. Select one of the words, such as *hat* or *sat*, which can be used to create a new word by substituting the letter *i*, which stands for the short vowel /ĭ/. Write *hat* beside the list of words. Under the letter *a* in *hat*, write the letter *i*. Ask the children if they can create a new word using the first letter *h* and last letter *t* in *hat*. Then complete the letters to form the word *hit*. Read the word *hit* and contrast it with the word *hat*, noting that different vowels are used. Point to the short *a* vowel as you pronounce *hat*, and the short *i* vowel as your pronounce *hit*. Ask the children to think of as many words as they can using the short /ĭ/ vowel. List words such as *sit*, *bit*, and *kit* on the board. Pronounce the words containing the letter *a* and point to the vowel letter as this is done. Follow the same procedure for the words containing the letter *i*, focusing attention on the letter *i*.

Conclude the lesson by quickly writing the words *hat*, *mat*, *pat*, and *sat* on blank tagboard cards. Have the children pronounce the words, with assistance if needed, and direct their attention to the short *a* letter as the words are read. Ask the children to identify the name of the letter that stands for the short /ă/ sound.

Figure 8-4 shows two commercially published reinforcement activities for the letter *a* standing for the short /ă/ sound. Again, note that the second activity (bottom of page) uses printing to reinforce the relationship between letter and sound. Consider also the many possible reinforcement activities available using vocabulary logs or journals, word banks, and language-experience charts.

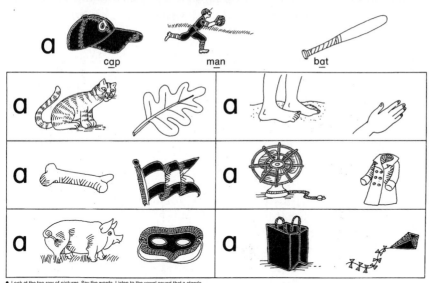

● Look at the top row of pictures. Say the words. Listen to the vowel sound that *a* stands
for in the words *cap*, *man*, and *bat*. Circle the pictures whose names have the same vowel
sound as *cap*.

PATHFINDER—Allyn and Bacon Reading Program   Reading Improvement Resources Set A   Copyrighted © 1979 by Allyn and Bacon, Inc.

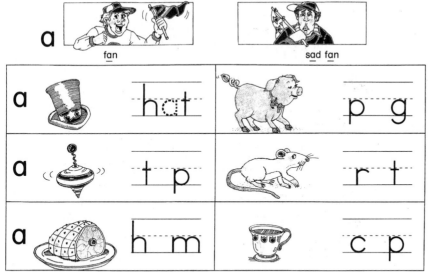

● Look at the top row of pictures. Say the words. Listen to the vowel sound that *a* stands
for in the words *fan* and *sad*. Write *a* in the spaces next to the pictures whose names have
the same vowel sound as *fan*.

PATHFINDER—Allyn and Bacon Reading Program   Reading Improvement Resources Set A   Copyrighted © 1979 by Allyn and Bacon, Inc.

FIGURE 8-4

Developing Letter-Sound Relationships for the Vowel Letter *a* That Stands for
the Short *a* Vowel. (Reproduced with permission from Ruddell, 1979, #43A.)

Long vowel letter-sound relationships are developed following the same instructional sequence described and illustrated above.

Suggestions for Instructional Sequence: Consonants. If you are using a published basal reading program, the sequence of word analysis skills is already specified. If you create your own program sequence, however, the following discussion may assist in your decision making. As you have seen, letter-sound relationships for consonants are highly predictable. Some consonants, however, are especially good candidates for early introduction. These consonants are known as **continuants**, because they are produced with a continuous flow of air. As a result, they can be easily pronounced without distorting the sound when you slowly pronounce a word containing them. This can be illustrated by pronouncing the words *mat* and *bat*. Note that you can prolong the /m/ in *mat* without distorting the sound. By contrast, if you try to prolong the /b/ in *bat*, you will find that you are really saying "buh" in the initial position. The continuants are /f/, /l/, /m/, /n/, /r/, /s/, /v/, and /z/. Because these consonants can be prolonged, they work well in helping you to establish the idea that letters stand for sounds in our alphabetic system.

An added value of introducing these particular consonants early is their use in teaching *blending* of sound units. As children learn letter-sound relationships and begin to apply this knowledge independently, they have to learn how to blend sounds together. For example, in reading the word *mother* in the sentence "My *mother* baked a cake for my birthday" the initial consonant sound /m/ can be prolonged to blend with the vowel to pronounce the first syllable in *mo*-ther or to blend with the rhyme ending in m-*other* to pronounce the word. Using the continuants to teach the blending process helps students avoid distorting sound values, which can lead to confusion.

Sequencing Vowels. The sequencing of vowel letter-sound concepts depends largely on the personal discretion of the textbook author or editor or of the teacher. In some publisher-developed programs the short vowels are taught before long vowels, while the reverse is true for others. There is some evidence that teaching children to expect one-to-one letter-sound consistency for vowels may inhibit their ability to transfer word analysis knowledge to new words, particularly those in which vowel letters do not fit the expected pattern (Levin, 1963). This finding suggests that children should be introduced to variable but predictable letter patterns in order to build a "set for diversity." This will encourage children to try varied pronunciations when they encounter different vowel letter patterns. For sequencing purposes, this means that you would first introduce children to a vowel concept, such as the short /ĭ/ in *bit* and *kit*, and teach this thoroughly. Next, you would introduce the corresponding letter for the long vowel concept, as in *bite* and *kite*. You would then contrast the short *i* and the long *i* letter sound relationships, emphasizing the letter patterns in *bit, -it,* and *bite, -ite* to develop the understanding that the letter pattern influences short and long vowels. In this way, you teach a "set for diversity" as children begin to anticipate optional and predictable letter-sound relationships for vowel letters used in specific letter patterns.

Developing Letter Patterns Using Rhyming Endings

As previously discussed, short and long vowels are highly predictable and stable within the letter patterns presented in Table 8-4. These letter patterns stand for rhyming endings for words, or for syllables in multisyllabic words, e.g., *-at* as in *bat* and *mat* or *-at* as in *bat-ter* and *bat-tery*. Rapid recognition of these letter patterns, or perceptual units, is essential to increase rapid word analysis, as children move into the orthographic stage of word recognition (see pages 379–380). The term **rime** or **rime pattern**, also referred to as rhyming ending, phonogram, and graphemic base, is helpful here. Essentially, when we use *rime*, we are talking about a "word family" that shares the same letter pattern that stands for the same vowel and ending-sound sequence. The use of the rime pattern is of great value to the reader because of the predictability of vowels in the rime letter-pattern context and the ease with which children learn them. The following letter sequences define four key rime patterns:

1. Vowel letter(s) + consonant, e.g., *-at* as in *bat, pat, catalogue.*
2. Vowel letter(s) + consonant group, e.g., *-and* as in *sand,* *-ound* as in *pound.*
3. Vowel letter(s) + consonant or consonant group + final *e*, e.g., *-ate* as in *mate,* *-edge* as in *ledge.*
4. Vowel letter(s) + consonant or group + final *y*, e.g., *-oggy,* as in *foggy,* *-unny* as in *funny.*

In short, rimes have high utility in teaching word analysis skills and greatly facilitate children's word analysis ability and their rapid recognition of new words.

Initial consonants, consonant digraphs, and blends, which represent the **onset**, or beginning, of a word, can be substituted in the same rime to make a variety of different words, e.g., *b-at, m-at* (initial consonants), *th-at, ch-at* (digraphs), and *fl-at, sl-at* (blends).

The development of letter patterns using rime is illustrated in the following instructional sequence. The selection of words used should be related to a story or expository text used in your class. Identify words that use a common letter-pattern rime, e.g., *-ite*, as in *kite, bite,* and *site.* Write these words in a column on the board, or chart paper, by letter-pattern grouping:

kite

bite

site

Ask the children to read the words, provide assistance as needed and briefly discuss the meaning of the words to ensure that they are in the children's working vocabulary.

405

Ask the children to examine the first group of words carefully to note similarities in the sequence of letters. The obvious similarities are that all the words end in *-ite* and rhyme. Ask the children to pronounce each word. As they do this point to the letter *i*, noting that each of the three words contains the *long i* vowel sound /ī/ represented in the letter pattern *-ite*. Ask the children to think of other words which end in the same letter pattern and stand for the *long i* vowel sound, e.g., *mite, write.* Conclude the discussion by pronouncing the words and focusing attention on the rhyming letter pattern *-ite* which contains and represents the *long i* vowel sound, /ī/.

The same procedure can be used several days later with the *-ate* rhyming pattern in the *mate, rate,* and *hate,* representing the long a vowel sound, /ā/. Next, write the long *a* patterned words beside of the long i pattern words on the board.

kite	mate
bite	rate
site	hate

Conclude the discussion by emphasizing that the first rhyming letter pattern contains the *long i* vowel sound and the second contains the *long a* vowel sound. Draw attention to the similar pattern in both word groups by noting that the letter patterns *-ite* and *-ate* have a **vowel letter**, a **consonant letter**, and a **final *e*,** and that in this letter pattern the first vowel letter stands for a long vowel sound.

After you have taught several vowel patterns, e.g., *-ite* and *-ate* and short vowel patterns, e.g., *-it* and *-at*, design a follow-up lesson to extend the idea of patterns. For example, write the words from the activity above, using the *-ite* and *-ate* patterns on the board or chart paper. Add words using the *-it* and *-at* pattern, representing the short vowels /ĭ/ and /ă/, as illustrated below.

-ite	*-it*	*-ate*	*-at*
kite	kit	mate	mat
bite	bit	rate	rat
site	sit	hate	hat

Have the children read the words using the *-ite* and *-it* patterns, providing assistance as needed. Ask them how these two groups of words differ in letter pattern and in pronunciation. Focusing attention on the *-ite* and the *-it* pattern makes the *final e* difference immediately obvious. The connection of the *-ite* letter pattern to the *long i* sound and the *-it* letter pattern to the *short i* sound is also readily apparent. Follow the same procedure in focusing on the *-ate* letter pattern, containing the *long a* sound, and the *-at* pattern, containing the *short a* sound.

Finally, ask individual members of the group to select a word from the list that uses a letter pattern that stands for the *long i* sound and underline that letter pattern. Do the same for the words using the letter pattern that stands for the *short i* sound. Contrast this letter pattern with the letter pattern found in the *long i* words noting the *final e*. Follow the same procedure for the *long a* and the *short a* word patterns, noting the *final e*. Conclude the discussion by emphasizing that the *-ite* and *-ate* rhyming patterns stand for endings that have long vowel sounds, i.e., *long i* and *long a*, while the *-it* and *-at* rhyming patterns stand for endings that have short vowel sounds, i.e., *short i* and *short a*. The key purpose of this discussion is to help children understand that there are regular letter patterns that stand for long and short vowel sounds and that can be helpful in pronouncing new words.

It is important to provide opportunity to reinforce the various letter patterns in meaningful context. While much of this reinforcement will occur through actual reading of children's literature and expository material in your classroom, you will find specific reinforcement activities helpful. Figure 8-5 illustrates a commercially published lesson for development of the *-ad* and *-at* letter patterns, representing the *short a* sound, and Figure 8-6 develops the *-ive* and *-ipe* patterns, which stand for the *long i* sound. Word bank and vocabulary journal searches for specific letter patterns are just as useful as searches for individual letters. Because letter patterns create rhymes, having children read and write charts and poems is also good reinforcement.

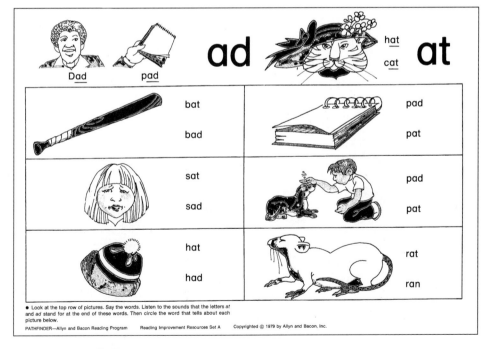

- Look at the top row of pictures. Say the words. Listen to the sounds that the letters *at* and *ad* stand for at the end of these words. Then circle the word that tells about each picture below.

PATHFINDER—Allyn and Bacon Reading Program   Reading Improvement Resources Set A   Copyrighted © 1979 by Allyn and Bacon, Inc.

FIGURE 8-5

Developing the *-ad* and *-at* Letter Pattern Rime That Represents the Short *a* Vowel Sound. (Reproduced with permission from Ruddell, 1978, #75A.)

DEVELOPING SYLLABLE IDENTIFICATION USING WORD- AND LETTER-PATTERN CLUES

A critical word analysis skill is that of syllabication. This consists of learning to break multisyllabic words into syllables that can be pronounced and blended to identify the unknown word. This does not call for learning complex generalizations about syllabication, but instead is based on developing an awareness of and sensitivity to pronounceable spelling patterns and units in words. The goal is to identify the pronounceable units, to pronounce these units and blend them into the word, and to check the meaning of the word based on background knowledge and the context of the sentence (Nagy, Winsor, Osborn, & O'Flahavan, in press; Shuy, 1973). The above discussion on spelling patterns and rhyme will contribute greatly to the identification of pronounceable units in long words.

The following four guidelines are simple but generally effective in identifying syllable breaks and pronounceable units in words.

1. **See if the word is a compound word made up of two or more words that you know.** If so, pronounce each word, blend the words together, and check the meaning of that word in the sentence, e.g., *playmate = play + mate*.

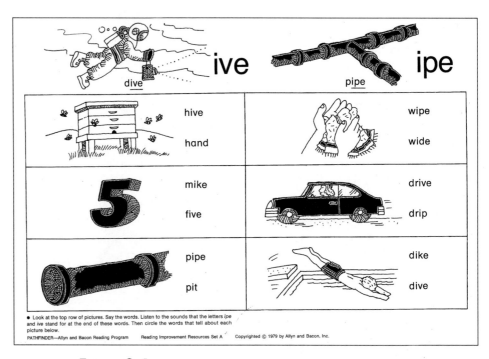

● Look at the top row of pictures. Say the words. Listen to the sounds that the letters *ipe* and *ive* stand for at the end of these words. Then circle the words that tell about each picture below.
PATHFINDER—Allyn and Bacon Reading Program   Reading Improvement Resources Set A   Copyrighted © 1979 by Allyn and Bacon, Inc.

FIGURE 8-6

Developing the *-ive* and *-ipe* Letter Pattern Rime That Represents the Long *i* Vowel Sound

2. **Look for prefixes (or word beginnings), root word parts, and suffixes (or word endings),** e.g., *defense, de-* and *-fense; slowly, slow-* and *-ly*. Look for other word parts you can pronounce, e.g., *-ceps* as in *biceps*. When you find these parts, divide the word by removing that part and pronounce the rest of the word. Blend the parts together to form the word and check the meaning of the word in the sentence.

3. **Look in the middle of the word for consonant pairs. If the consonants are the same letters,** divide the word between the consonants, pronounce each part of the word, and blend the two parts together, e.g., *bellow, bel-low*. **If the consonant letters are different and each has a separate sound,** also divide the word between the consonants, pronounce each part, and blend the parts together, e.g., *basket, bas-ket*. **If the consonant letters are different but stand for one sound** (consonant digraph), divide the word after the consonants, pronounce each part, and blend the parts, e.g., *bushel, bush-el*. Check the meaning in the context of the sentence in each case. It is important to note that the goal here is to identify pronounceable units that can be blended to form the word. You should avoid confusing this process with the precise syllable breaks found in dictionaries. It does not matter whether children break the word *basket* into *bas-ket* or *bask-et* as long as pronounceable units can be identified and blended to form the word in the sentence context.

4. **If there are no consonant groups (blends or digraphs) in the middle of the word, look for parts of the word you can pronounce.** First, divide the word after a vowel and consonant, pronounce the parts, blend, and check the meaning, e.g., *lizard, liz-ard*. Second, divide the word after the first vowel letter, or the second vowel letter, pronounce the parts, blend, and check the meaning, e.g.,*tiger, ti-ger; raisin, rai-sin*.

Keep in mind that while these guidelines are *generally* effective, they are not always useful. Children searching for "two words you already know" (guideline #1) have been known to arrive at "fat-her" for "father." Always, always, always the end-product pronunciation must be checked to see if the word, once pronounced and recognized, makes sense in the context in which it appears.

Teaching Compound Words

The recognition of compound words will rely heavily on vocabulary your children already know. For example, words such as *classroom, sidewalk,* and *airplane*, words containing familiar words, can be placed on the board or chart paper. The search for component words that comprise the compound word can then be conducted to identify recognizable words and syllable breaks to assist pronunciation, e.g., *class-room, side-walk,* and *air-plane*. Your discussion of these words should lead to the conclusion that there are two known words in each of the words. You must emphasize that each word contributes to the *meaning* of the compound word in highly specific ways and point out (or let children figure out) how they do, e.g., a "classroom" is a room where one has a class. Show children how to separate an unknown compound word into its component word parts, pronounce each, blend the parts back into a whole, and then check for meaning in context.

To form compound words, use the following activity using words from the children's reading material. The list below is from *Ramona the Pest* (Cleary, 1968):

rain	place
play	one
any	room
no	coat
class	ground
fire	body

Place these two columns of words on the chalkboard. Have the children match a word in the first column with a word (or words) in the second column to form a new word. Draw a line between the two words. Then ask the children to pronounce each word, blend the two words to form a compound word, and use the new word in a sentence. Spend time talking about the relationship of the component words to the meaning of the compound word. Write the new words on the board as they are given.

As you encourage children to search for known words in compound words, you must be very careful not to characterize this activity as "looking for little words in big words." If you do, children will begin searching for non-meaning-based "little words" that are common sound units in larger words. For example, in the words *anyone* and *somewhere* the identification of the "little words" *an, on,* and *me* provides inappropriate meaning and pronunciation clues. This will become evident in the attempt to pronounce these words and requires a shift to the search for larger word units and other pronounceable units, e.g., *any-one* and *some-where*. The key to avoiding this problem is to focus consistently and repeatedly on meaning and the contribution of the component words to the overall meaning of the compound word.

The following interchange demonstrates instruction in compound words in a third-grade class. The teacher and students are working on compound words using a game board designed by the teacher. Word cards have been prepared with a compound word on each card. The "deck" of word cards is placed with words facing down in the middle of the board. Each child draws a word card from the top and attempts to pronounce it. Each compound word has been rated in difficulty as reflected by a number placed in the bottom left corner of the card. Easy words are worth one move, with graduated difficulty to the hard words, which are worth five moves on the board.

      (James [S1] has just drawn a word card.)

T: Let's see what James has.

      (James looks at the word card in his hand.)

S1:   Summertime.

T: Wow! You are getting better and better every minute. OK.

S1:   Summer and time.

T: OK.

S1:   Wowie! I even pass here (pointing to a "return to square #3" space on game board).

T: (laughing) You were lucky to miss that one, you'd have had to go all the way back to three.

S2:   Now make a one and you'll be to the castle.

T: Maybe. All right, let's see what Mike's going to get. James, it's Mike's turn. OK.

      (Mike picks up the word *skyscraper.*)

S2:   Sky.

T: That's really a tough one. That might even have been a five. (The word's rating is three, i.e., worth three moves.)

S3:   I know it.

T: Don't tell. Would you like a hint (to Mike)?

S2:   That's "er." (Mike points to the end of the word.)

T: Yes it is. You found the ending.

S2:   And . . .

T: Now you have a problem. Would you like a hint? James, can you think of a hint that you can give without telling what the word is? So far Michael has the beginning and he has the ending, but he has a problem in the middle. Show him your card, Mike, so he can see where your problem is.

S3:   I know what it says.

S2:   Sky . . . scroap . . . scraper.

T: Good you have the right "sc" sound. What are the two words?

S2.: Sky . . . scraper.

S2:   But there are three kinds—sky . . . scrape . . . er.

T: All right, sky and scraper, but—and scrape is a word but if you use scrape as a word, then is "er" a word by itself at the end?

S2:   No.

T: So we have to call it that. OK?

S2: Scraper . . . skyscraper.

T: Great, Mike! Now can you use it in a sentence to tell us what it means?

S2: A skyscraper is a big, tall building with offices and stuff in it.

T: Yeah. The tops of the big tall buildings look like they "scrape," or touch, the sky. That's good, Mike!

Notice how the teacher encourages, observes, and provides support throughout the lesson. Mike continues to persist in his analysis of the word, pronounces the word, and then monitors his process by noting that there were three parts to the word in his original attempt to pronounce it. The teacher assists in guiding the monitoring process as Mike concludes that there are two words, "sky" and "scraper." This interchange provides an excellent example of information you can obtain by carefully observing your children's analysis process in working with compound words. This information can then be used in guiding the learning process as illustrated above.

Teaching Prefix, Suffix, and Root Identification

The basic idea in teaching affixes—prefixes and suffixes—and root words is to help children develop the strategy of identifying syllable breaks in order to locate pronounceable units. Instruction is developed by focusing attention on these parts, pronouncing the parts, blending, and testing the meaning of the word. For example, the words *delay* and *renew* contain prefixes that can be separated, e.g., *de-lay* and *re-new* to identify the pronounceable units in the words. This instruction may also be extended to develop the meanings associated with commonly used prefixes. For example, *de-* can mean *away from* or *off*, as in *delay* or *deport*. This can easily be contrasted with *re-*, meaning *back* or *again*, as in *return* or *repay*.

Awareness of prefixes can be developed by using exercises such as the following. Ask the children to add *de-* or *re-* to each word part below, then read each word, and identify the meaning.

de-	*re-*
_____ lay	_____ turn
_____ frost	_____ pair
_____ cay	_____ new

The children then use the words to complete the following sentences:

1. Words beginning with *de-*:
   a. To remove the frost _____
   b. To rot _____
   c. To put off _____

2. Words beginning with *re-*

    a. To mend _____

    b. To go and come back _____

    c. To begin again _____

You can also design word wheels to reinforce understanding and rapid identification of prefixes, suffixes, and roots. Simply fasten tagboard circles of different sizes together with a paper rivet. To develop suffixes, for example, print the root words such as *jump* and *open*, on the edge of the inner circle. Print appropriate suffixes, such as *s, ed, ing*, on the outer circle. Two children can then play this suffix game. The first spins the top circle and reads the word that is formed; the other uses this word in a sentence. This same activity can be prepared for prefixes, e.g., *a-bout, a-bove, a-lone.*

Prefixes, suffixes, and Latin roots that occur with high frequency and that should be developed in activities such as those discussed above are found in Table 8-6.

Using Consonant Clusters to Identify Pronounceable Units

The value in teaching consonant clusters, which occur in the middle of words, is to help children quickly identify word breaks for pronounceable units. These consonant clusters will consist of **consonant groups**, which stand for two different sounds, such as *-sp-* and *-nt-* in *whisper* and *centered*; and **consonant digraphs**, which stand for one sound, illustrated by *-th-* and *-ck-* as in *brother* and *bucket*.

The key point is to develop rapid recognition of these consonant groups and digraphs in the middle of the word. Your instruction teaching letter-sound relationships will have already placed emphasis on individual consonants that form the consonant groups and the consonant digraphs. The individual consonants composing the consonant groups were presented in Table 8-2, and the consonant digraphs were presented in Table 8-3. The location of these consonant groups in the middle of words, however, requires a shift of focus to the medial positions to assist children in their rapid identification and use in locating pronounceable word parts.

The following strategy will be of assistance in this instruction. This strategy assumes that you have developed a basic understanding of consonants and consonant digraphs with your children.

1. Look at the word and find the consonants in the middle of the word, e.g., *whisper* or *centered*. If the consonants stand for **two different sounds**, divide the word between the two consonants, *whis-per* and *cen-tered*. Pronounce each part to yourself. Put the two parts together and read the whole word. Check the word for meaning in the sentence.

2. Look at the word and find the consonants in the middle, e.g., *brother* or *bucket*. If the consonants stand for **one sound**, divide the word

PREFIX	EXAMPLE	MEANING
a-	aboard, ashore, ablaze	in, into, on, in the act of
be-	beset, bewitch, befriend	around, make, affect by
de-	depart, decline, depress	away from, off, down
ex-	expel, exempt, exert	from, out of
in-, im-	infer, invade, impale incapable, impeach	in, into, not
pre-, pro-	prewar, precede, prophet	before in time, in front of
post-	postgraduate, postpaid	after in time, later, behind
re-	repay, react, retell	back, again
sub-	submarine, subgroup	under, below, division into smaller parts
super-	supervisor, superimpose superhuman	over, above, on top of
trans-	transcontinental, transcend	across, over, beyond
un-	unknown, unemployed, unhappy	not, lack of, opposite of

SUFFIX	EXAMPLE	MEANING
-able	debatable	capable of being
-al	educational	pertaining to
-er, -ian,	grader, musician	performer of
-ist, -or	pianist, tailor	performer of
-ful	playful, thankful	full of
-ly, -y	slowly, funny	in the manner of
-sion, -tion	provision, redemption	act of

ROOT	EXAMPLE	MEANING
fac, fact	factory	to make or do
fer	refer, transfer	to bear or carry
mot, mov	motion, movement	to move
port	report, transport	to carry
sta, stat	stable, statue	to stand
tend, tens	extend, extension, tension	to stretch
ven, vent	convene, convention, prevent	to come
vid, vis	video, television, revision	to see

— **TABLE 8-6** —————————————————

Common Prefixes, Suffixes, and Roots Useful for Rapid Word
Pronunciation and Meaning

after the consonants, *broth-er* and *buck-et*. Pronounce each part to
yourself. Put the two parts together and read the whole word. Check
the word for meaning.

Discussions and independent activities can be developed using words drawn from the reading material used in the regular classroom reading period. Children can be asked to underline *consonant groups* in words like *napkin, cactus, candle* and *summer, bottle, middle,* and then to divide the word, pronounce the parts, blend the parts, and pronounce the word. The same procedure is followed for words containing *consonant digraphs,* such as *bucket, pickle, jacket* and *fashion, cushion, bushel.* After underlining the consonant digraphs, the children should divide the word after the digraph, pronounce the two parts, blend the parts to pronounce the word, and conduct the meaning check.

USING CONTEXT CLUES IN WORD IDENTIFICATION

Context clues provide an important word analysis resource from two perspectives: *first,* as a meaning check after pronouncing the new word in the context of the sentence or story; *second,* as a source of information that children can use in combination with other word analysis skills. Your instruction should emphasize the importance of several key questions that your children need to keep in mind.

- Does the pronounced word make sense in the context of the sentence?

- Does the word fit the meaning of the story?

- Does the word seem appropriate to the context of the story illustrations?

These questions will confirm or reject the tentative pronunciation of the word.

A simple but effective procedure for developing context clues is the planned deletion of certain words in the sentence. This is a modified form of the Cloze procedure (discussed in Chapter 5). This modified Cloze procedure can take a variety of forms:

1. Context with initial consonant clue.

   Lad, the d_____, wagged his tail.

   The boy threw the ball h_____ into the air.

   Magic dribbled the ball down the floor and ran into.

   another player. The r_____ blew his whistle.

2. Context designed with varied meaning possibilities.

   The little _____ ran into the barn.

   The _____ sank one of our ships.

3. Context with narrowed meaning intent.

   The little _____ , which was three days old, ran into the barn to find the mother cow.

   The deep-running _____ sank one of our ships.

Other activities illustrating the development of context clues include the following:

415

1. Select several sentences from the reading material used in your classroom that can be separated into meaning-bearing units. Place the sentence parts in two columns. Have the students use the sentence context to form the original sentence by drawing a line to connect the two parts.

Mike plays	a dog house.
Amy likes to ride	with his pet squirrel.
Rob built	her new bicycle.

2. Select a group of sentences from your reading material and delete several letters in key meaning-bearing words. Ask the children to identify the missing words, using sentence context.

The p _____ drew their covered wagons into a large cir _____ for protection at night.

Both astro _____ stepped onto the moon's _____ face.

The huge tractor rig crashed th _____ the divider wall and sm _____ into the building.

The s _____ caught the wind and the crew cheered as the b _____ sped _____ y toward the finish line.

3. Create a sentence using vocabulary from the children's reading material. Delete a key word in the sentence and leave a blank space. Provide the key word with another word to form a multiple-choice-type sentence. The children are asked to circle the appropriate word based on the sentence context.

John's_____ is to clean out the garage.
     respectability
     responsibility

Maria slipped and fell _____into the water.
       backward
       upward

The _____ helped the boys find the racing book.
    politician
    librarian

Many activities using context can be found throughout the reading and literacy activities of the day. We encourage lots of paired, small group, and whole class discussion and interaction when using Cloze activities (as we recommended in Chapter 5), so that children have access to each other's thinking during the process. This allows the logic of context use to become explicit and therefore available to all (e.g., "It has to be the name of something because 'the' is right before it" or "It's gotta be 'calf' because it's only three days old and it's looking for the mother cow"). By combining this meaning aspect of word analysis with other word analysis skills, children can become highly effective in self-monitoring tentative pronunciation—and understanding—of new words.

Developing Rapid Recognition of Frequently Used Words

A comparatively small number of words occur with very high frequency in reading material. For example, the word the occurs about every tenth word in children's text. A number of word lists have been constructed, based on frequency counts of "running words" in various types of reading material (Durr, 1973; Kucera & Francis, 1967; Walker, 1979). Many of the high-frequency words play a basic role in uniting vocabulary into the highly regular and predictable sentence structures of English. Others are nouns, verbs, and adjectives that occur so often that we recognize and use them automatically. A central objective in your instruction, then, is to develop high-speed and automatic recognition of these words that occur over and over again in printed text. This "automaticity" enables your children to focus their attention on meaning construction of text, which is, after all, the primary goal of reading.

Ed Fry (1977) developed a highly functional list of high-frequency words. This list of "Instant Words" gives approximate grade-level recommendations for their use. Our observations suggest that word placement must be based on your observations and knowledge of individual students. Some children will develop an extensive rapid-recognition vocabulary early in the primary grades, while others will need assistance into the intermediate grades. The "Instant Words" list, however, will be helpful in providing a core of words that need to be developed at a high-speed recognition level

High-Interest Reading and Automatic Word Recognition

and will be useful for implementing the activities discussed below. The list is found in Table 8-7.

Activities for developing rapid-recognition vocabulary should account for meaning through a picture context, written sentence or story context, or oral language context. These activities should involve active thinking involvement of your children in individual, partner pair, or small group settings. Such activities include the following:

1. Cut from magazines pictures that represent high-frequency vocabulary. These will include nouns, e.g., *mother, father, girl, boy, house, book, people, tree, eyes,* and *water;* verbs, e.g., *jump, fly, ride, eat, drink,* and *wash;* and adjectives, e.g., *red, blue, yellow, little,* and *funny.* Such words will appear again and again in reading material and in the children's language-experience stories. Many of these will be found in the "Instant Words" list in Table 8-7. Paste the pictures in a large circle on tagboard. Attach a tagboard pointer in the center of the circle with a paper rivet. Prepare a set of tagboard word cards with the words representing the pictures. These materials may be used by individual children, partner pairs, or small groups. Each child spins the pointer and notes the word represented by the picture. He or she then quickly sorts through the word cards, locates the word that matches the picture, and uses the word in a sentence. When partner pairs play, the score can be kept of the number of correct words identified. A stopwatch or minute sand-timer adds higher motivation for this rapid word-recognition activity.

2. Use illustrations or large cut-out magazine pictures that represent a variety of high-frequency words. Prepare sentences on tagboard to match the action in the pictures. For example,

   The boy threw the ball to his friend.
   It smashed the big picture window.
   The angry man is talking to the boys.

   This activity may be varied by cutting the tagboard sentences apart for each sentence, e.g.,

boy	the	ball		.	friend	his	threw	The	to

   Clip the words for each sentence together. Each child then builds a sentence to represent the action. Again, partner pairs work well for this type of activity.

3. A variation of this activity will use the illustration, or picture, and the first two sentences from the above activity. After examining the illustration and reading these two sentences, individual children, or

418

partner pairs, are asked to complete the ending to the episode. In advance, write the following words on tagboard word cards and clip the word cards for each column of words together, e.g., The, An, That; angry, sad, mad.

The	angry	man	is	talking	to	the	little	boys.
An	sad	woman	was	shouting	at	those	big	kids.
That	mad	girl	was	pointing	at	the	scared	friend.

The ending is to be completed using a word from each group. The advantage of this activity stems from the reinforcement recognition of a wide variety of high-frequency words used in a meaningful context.

4. Prepare a set of word cards by printing your high-frequency words on 5-by-8-inch tagboard cards. Paste a small picture clue to the word identification and meaning on the back of the card. Expose each word card for a few seconds to individual children or partner pairs and have students name the word. Complete a meaning check by using the picture on the reverse side. This activity may be varied by having individual or partner pairs use the cards, referring first to the picture clue and the meaning and pronunciation of the word, and then tracing the word with the index and middle fingers. This adds a tactile-kinesthetic reinforcement for the high-frequency words.

5. Prepare this activity by writing the rapid-recognition words on tagboard strips. On the reverse side of the strip, use the word in a sentence context, or add a picture meaning clue. Place a paper clip on each and place the cards in a small bowl or box. Partner pairs are each provided with a short stick with a string and magnet attached. They are now ready to go "fishing." Each child "fishes" a word card out of the container, places the card "word side up" on the desk and attempts to reads it in a few seconds. If the child has difficulty reading the word, the card is turned over and the picture clue is used, but the "fish" must be thrown back. A new word card is drawn from the container until the child is successful. Each correctly pronounced word scores one point. The game may again be played using a sand- or clock-timer for a set period of time to increase motivation.

In Chapters 3 and 5, we discussed many ideas that can be of value in developing rapid-recognition vocabulary. These ranged from developing language-experience stories and vocabulary boxes using individual word collections to creating vocabulary logs and journals. You may wish to look back at these discussions now to add additional ideas to your rapid-recognition vocabulary repertoire.

The development of automatic recognition of frequently used vocabulary requires time and opportunity to read. This is best accomplished in

Fry's List of "Instant Words"

First Hundred Words
(approximately first grade)

Group 1a	Group 1b	Group 1c	Group 1d
the	he	go	who
a	I	see	an
is	they	then	their
you	one	us	she
to	good	no	new
and	me	him	said
we	about	by	did
that	had	was	boy
in	if	come	three
not	some	get	down
for	up	or	work
at	her	two	put
with	do	man	were
it	when	little	before
on	so	has	just
can	my	them	long
will	very	how	here
are	all	like	other
of	would	our	old
this	any	what	take
your	been	know	cat
as	out	make	again
but	there	which	give
be	from	much	after
have	day	his	many

Second Hundred Words
(approximately second grade)

Group 2a	Group 2b	Group 2c	Group 2d
saw	big	may	fan
home	where	let	five
soon	am	use	read
stand	ball	these	over
box	morning	right	such
upon	live	present	way
first	four	tell	too
came	last	next	shall
girl	color	please	own
house	away	leave	most
find	red	hand	sure
because	friend	more	thing
made	pretty	why	only
could	eat	better	near
book	want	under	than
look	year	while	open
mother	white	should	kind
run	got	never	must
school	play	each	high
people	found	best	far
night	left	another	both
into	men	seem	end
say	bring	tree	also
think	wish	name	until
back	black	dear	call

Third Hundred Words
(approximately third grade)

Group 3a	Group 3b	Group 3c	Group 3d
ask	hat	off	fire
small	car	sister	ten
yellow	write	happy	order
show	try	once	part
goes	myself	didn't	early
clean	longer	set	fat
buy	those	round	third
thank	hold	dress	same
sleep	full	tell	love
letter	carry	wash	hear
jump	eight	start	yesterday
help	sing	always	eyes
fly	warm	anything	door
don't	sit	around	clothes
fast	dog	close	through
cold	ride	walk	o'clock
today	hot	money	second
does	grow	turn	water
face	cut	might	town
green	seven	hard	took
every	woman	along	pair
brown	funny	bed	now
coat	yes	fine	keep
six	ate	sat	head
gave	stop	hope	food

420

THE SECOND 300 WORDS (APPROXIMATELY FOURTH GRADE)

GROUP 4a	GROUP 4b	GROUP 4c	GROUP 4d	GROUP 4e	GROUP 4f	GROUP 4g	GROUP 4h	GROUP 4i	GROUP 4j	GROUP 4k	GROUP 4l
told	time	word	wear	hour	grade	egg	spell	become	herself	demand	aunt
Miss	yet	almost	Mr.	glad	brother	ground	beautiful	body	idea	however	system
father	true	thought	side	follow	remain	afternoon	sick	chance	drop	figure	line
children	above	send	poor	company	milk	feed	became	act	river	case	cause
land	still	receive	lost	believe	several	boat	cry	die	smile	increase	marry
interest	meet	pay	outside	begin	war	plan	finish	real	son	enjoy	possible
government	since	nothing	wind	mind	able	question	catch	speak	bat	rather	supply
feet	number	need	Mrs.	pass	charge	fish	floor	already	fact	sound	thousand
garden	state	mean	learn	reach	either	return	stick	doctor	sort	eleven	pen
done	matter	late	held	month	less	sir	great	step	king	music	condition
country	line	half	front	point	train	fell	guess	itself	dark	human	perhaps
different	remember	fight	built	rest	cost	hill	bridge	nine	themselves	court	produce
bad	large	enough	family	sent	evening	wood	church	baby	whose	force	twelve
across	few	feet	began	talk	note	add	lady	minute	study	plant	rode
yard	hit	during	air	went	past	ice	tomorrow	ring	fear	suppose	uncle
winter	cover	gone	young	bank	room	chair	snow	wrote	move	law	labor
table	window	hundred	ago	ship	flew	watch	whom	happen	stood	husband	public
story	even	week	world	business	office	alone	women	appear	himself	moment	consider
sometimes	city	between	airplane	whole	cow	low	among	heart	strong	person	thus
I'm	together	change	without	short	visit	arm	road	swim	knew	result	least
tried	sun	being	kill	certain	wait	dinner	farm	felt	often	continue	power
horse	life	care	ready	fair	teacher	hair	cousin	fourth	toward	price	mark
something	street	answer	stay	reason	spring	service	bread	I'll	wonder	serve	president
brought	party	course	won't	summer	picture	class	wrong	kept	twenty	national	voice
shoes	suit	against	paper	fill	bird	quite	age	well	important	wife	whether

TABLE 8-7

A List of Frequently Used Words for Automatic Recognition

Source: From Elementary Reading Instruction *(p. 73) by Edward Fry. Copyright © 1977. Used with permission of the author.*

three ways: *first,* use activities such as those described above to target key words for high-speed recognition; *second,* provide a wide range of high-interest reading material that is just below each student's instructional level; *third,* provide many writing opportunities. Encourage your children to read, read, read! The books in your classroom literature and reading center and those in your school library will provide an invaluable resource for this purpose. A quick review of the section in Chapter 6 entitled "Selecting Literature and Organizing Classroom Resources" will assist you in this effort. Automatic recognition of high-frequency words will provide major benefits in the form of interest in reading and freedom to focus on the construction of meaning leading to higher comprehension of text.

Word Analysis Strategies and Reader Independence

A Summary

At the beginning of this chapter, we emphasized the importance of word analysis strategies as the key to transforming print to familiar language counterparts and meaning. As we demonstrated, you, as an expert reader, have developed a high degree of fluency and automatic processing as you use your own word analysis strategies to transform printed text to meaning.

Our summary of the controversy that surrounds word analysis and phonics revealed that the "whole word" versus "phonics" debate sheds more heat than light on the issue of reading instruction. While it is important for you to understand the nature of this conflict, it is of paramount importance that you be sensitive to teaching word analysis skills in a meaning-based context. Many children do depend on school and your instructional expertise to develop reading and literacy skills.

The research on children's developmental stages of word analysis reveals that they first use a logographic system that relies on visual contextual or graphic features to read words. They then move through a transition stage from logographic to the beginning use of the alphabetic system, as they use initial letters that stand for sounds to recognize words. The alphabetic stage follows as children develop the ability to use letter-sound relationships to unlock and read words. The most advanced orthographic stage enables children to take full advantage of the alphabetic principle and predictable letter-pattern sequences. This stage relies on "word families" and "orthographic neighborhoods" that share common letter sequences, as children rapidly read words in meaningful context. At this stage, children begin to use word analogies as they incorporate prior orthographic knowledge in reading new words. As we have discussed, you should expect wide developmental stage differences across individual students in your classroom. This means that you shoulder an important responsibility in teaching word analysis skills not only in the primary grades but throughout the intermediate grades as well.

The discussion of specific word analysis skill development included strategies and activities for the following special areas: word analysis teaching in a meaning-based context; the development of print-awareness knowledge, letter recognition, phonemic awareness, and phonemic segmentation; building letter-sound relationships; developing letter patterns using rhyming endings; identification of syllable units using word- and letter-pattern clues; using context clues; and developing rapid recognition of high-frequency vocabulary. Your knowledge of these strategies and how to implement them in the classroom becomes critical to your success in developing independent readers.

So, in summary, we may ask, "What do we tell children to do when they meet a new word they don't know?" The best answer to this question is the functional system of word recognition that we discussed in Chapter 5, Context-Structure-Sound-Reference (CSSR). You should review that system now (see pages 221–223). We remind you that all of the activities and separate skills we discussed in this chapter do children no good whatsoever if they are not incorporated into this functional system.

We have stressed the importance of teaching word-recognition skills in a meaningful context throughout this chapter. It is of critical importance that children have the opportunity to apply their word analysis skills in real reading situations. The best opportunity to practice these skills and to intuit their own generalizations about reading comes through wide reading of children's literature and of high-interest expository material. Many of us have recollections of a key turning point in the primary grades when we read our first "chapter book," or our first "real book." At this point, many of the reading skills had become almost automatic. We no longer struggled to "figure out" words, and we possessed the ability to "cross over and enter the story" directly. Our dual goals, then, in teaching word analysis skills are quite simple and straightforward: first, to develop reader independence, which will enable children to transform print to meaning; and second, to enable them to enter the story or the expository text and construct their own meaning.

DOUBLE ENTRY JOURNAL

Go back to the ideas you jotted down before reading this chapter. Rearrange your ideas under the headings Information Useful for Teaching Reading *and* Information Not Useful for Teaching Reading. *Add any new ideas. After categorizing, look at your "useful" list and begin formulating your philosophy and approach for teaching word analysis in your classroom.*

Outline a note to parents or the talk you'll give on Back to School Night to explain your approach to parents.

Supporting Activities

1. What do you do when you encounter a word that you are unfamiliar with in pronunciation or meaning? (For example, the words *epidemiology* and *uranography* were used earlier in the chapter, but not developed.) What word analysis skills did you use to decipher those words? Briefly make notes on the mental processes you used in pronouncing and understanding these two words. Now read slight variations of the words in the following sentence contexts:

The *epidemiologist* worked to identify the location and plot the frequency of occurrence of the new measles outbreak.

The *uranographologist* used the giant telescope to identify and map the stars in the new galaxy.

What additional skills did you use in reading and understanding these words? Did your motivation change as you encountered the words in context? What implications for your teaching can you derive from your self-analysis of the reading process? Share your ideas with a class partner.

2. How would you respond to a parent who makes the statement, "Phonics isn't being taught, especially like it was years ago, and that's

why kids can't read today"? Why do you think such a viewpoint is often held by the news media and some educational critics?

3. Arrange for an observation of a kindergarten or first-grade classroom during reading instruction. Before visiting the class, review our discussion of the characteristics of the four stages of word analysis development (logographic, transitional, alphabetic, orthographic). During your visit, observe a single student or a small group of students. Attempt to identify the developmental level of the student or different development levels in the small group of students. Briefly describe examples that support your conclusion.

4. Identify one word analysis skill (e.g., letter recognition, phonemic segmentation, letter-sound relationships, letter patterns, syllable identification, context clues, rapid word recognition) that you believe is very important in teaching at the grade level of your choice (reader maturity level). Explain why this skill is an important one for this level. Briefly illustrate how you would teach this skill by developing an instructional example.

5. Assume for the moment that a computer software company has asked you to develop sample materials for a first-grade reading program. They have asked you to submit the following information in your proposal:

a. Identify the first six letters you would use and briefly explain your rationale for selecting these.

b. Create a beginning vocabulary using these letters.

c. Write a brief story using this vocabulary, adding simple illustrations if necessary.

d. Indicate what word analysis skills you would teach from the story. Develop your proposal and share your ideas with a class partner.

REFERENCES

Adams, M. J. (1990a). *Beginning to read: Thinking and learning about print.* Cambridge, MA: MIT Press.

Adams, M. J. (1990b). *Beginning to read: Thinking and learning about print: A summary.* Urbana-Champaign: University of Illinois, Center for the Study of Reading.

Anderson, R. C., Hiebert, E. H., Scott, J. A., & Wilkinson, I. A. G. (1985). *Becoming a nation of readers: The report of the Commission on Reading.* Washington, DC: National Institute of Education.

Beck, I. L., & McCaslin, E. S. (1978). *An analysis of dimensions that affect the development of code-breaking ability in eight beginning reading programs* (LRDC

425

Report No. 1978/6). Pittsburgh, PA: University of Pittsburgh Learning Research and Development Center.

Becker, W. C., & Gersten, R. (1982). A follow-up of Follow-Through: The later effects of the direct instruction model on children in fifth and sixth grades. *American Educational Research Journal, 19,* 75–92.

Bond, G. I., & Dykstra, R. (1967, summer). The cooperative research program in first-grade reading instruction. *Reading Research Quarterly, 2*(4), 5–142.

Chall, J. S. (1967). *Learning to read: The great debate.* New York: McGraw-Hill.

Chall, J. S. (1983). *Learning to read: The great debate* (rev. ed.). New York: McGraw-Hill.

Clarke, L. K. (1988). Invented versus traditional spelling in first graders' writing: Effects on learning to spell and read. *Research in the Teaching of English, 22,* 281–309.

Clay, M. M. (1979). *Reading: The patterning of complex behavior* (2nd ed.). Auckland, New Zealand: Heinemann.

Durr, W. (1973). Computer study of high frequency words in popular trade juveniles. *The Reading Teacher, 27,* 37–42.

Dykstra, R. (1968). Summary of the second-grade phase of the Cooperative Research Program in Primary Reading Instruction. *Reading Research Quarterly, 4,* 49–71.

Ehri, L. C. (1987). Learning to read and spell words. *Journal of Reading Behavior, 19,* 5–31.

Ehri, L. C. (1988). Movement into word reading and spelling: How spelling contributes to reading. In J. Mason (Ed.), *Reading and writing connections* (pp. 65–81). Boston: Allyn & Bacon.

Ehri, L. C. (1991). Development of the ability to read words. In R. Barr, M. L. Kamil, P. Mosenthal, & P. D. Pearson (Eds.). *Handbook of reading research: Volume II* (pp. 383–417). New York: Longman.

Flesch, R. (1955). *Why Johnny can't read.* New York: Harper & Row.

Frith, U. (1985). Beneath the surface of developmental dyslexia. In K. E. Patterson, J. C. Marshall, & M. Coltheart (Eds.), *Surface dyslexia* (pp. 301–330). London: Erlbaum.

Fry, E. (1977). *Elementary reading instruction.* New York: McGraw-Hill.

Gibson, E. J., Gibson, J. J., Pick, A. D., & Osser, H. A. (1962). A developmental study of the discrimination of letter-like forms. *Journal of Comparative and Psychological Psychology, 55,* 897–906.

Glushko, R. J. (1979). The organization and activation of orthographic knowledge in reading aloud. *Journal of Experimental Psychology: Human Perception and Performance, 5,* 674–691.

Glushko, R. J. (1981). Principles for pronouncing print: The psychology of phonography. In A. M. Lesgold & C. A. Perfetti (Eds.), *Interactive processes in reading* (pp. 61–84). Hillsdale, NJ: Erlbaum.

Juel, C. (1983). The development and use of mediated word identification. *Reading Research Quarterly, 18,* 306–327.

Kucera, H. & Francis, W. N. (1967). *Computational analysis of present-day American English.* Providence, RI: Brown University Press.

Levin, H. (1963). *A basic research program on reading.* (Cooperative Research Project No. 639). Ithaca, NY: Cornell University.

Liberman, I. Y., Shankweiler, D., Orlando, C., Harris, K. S., & Berti, F. B. (1971). Letter confusions and reversals of sequence in the beginning reader: Implications for Orton's theory of developmental dyslexia. *Cortex, 7,* 127–142.

Mann, V. A., Tobin, P., & Wilson, R. (1987). Measuring phonological awareness through the invented spelling of kindergartners. *Merrill-Palmer Quarterly, 33,* 365–391.

Mason, J. M., Herman, P. A., & Au, K. H. (1991). Children's developing knowledge of words. In J. Flood, J. M. Jensen, D. Lapp, & J. R. Squire (Eds.), *Handbook of research on teaching the English language arts* (pp. 721–731). New York: Macmillan.

Nagy, W. E., Winsor, P., Osborn, J., & O'Flahavan, J. (in press). The role of structural analysis in reading. In J. Osborn & F. Lerehr (Eds.), *Finding a balance: Reading instruction for the 21st century.* Hillsdale, NJ: Erlbaum.

Nurss, J. R. (1979). Assessment of readiness. In G. E. MacKinnon & T. G. Waller (Eds.), *Reading research: Advances in theory and practice* (Vol. 12) (pp. 31–62). New York: Academic Press.

Pick, A. D. (1965). Improvement of visual and tactual form discrimination. *Journal of Experimental Psychology, 69,* 331–39.

Ruddell, R. B. (1969). A longitudinal study of four programs of reading instruction extended into third grade. In J. A. Figurel (Ed.), *Reading and realism* (pp. 605–615). Newark, DE: International Reading Association.

Ruddell, R. B. (1974). *Reading-language instruction: Innovative practices.* Englewood Cliffs, NJ: Prentice-Hall.

Ruddell, R. B. (1979). *Reading improvement resources.* Boston: Allyn and Bacon.

Ruddell, R. B., & Williams, A. (1972). *A research investigation of a literacy teaching model: Project DELTA* (Project No. 005262). Washington, DC: Department of Health, Education and Welfare, Office of Education, EPDA.

Shuy, R. W. (1973). Some relationships of linguistics to the reading process. In T. Clymer & R. B. Ruddell (Eds.), *Teachers edition of how it is nowadays* (pp. 22–24). Boston: Ginn.

Trace, A. (1961). *What Ivan knows that Johnny doesn't.* New York: Random House.

Trieman, R. (1985). Onsets and rimes as units of spoken syllables: Evidence from children. *Journal of Experimental Psychology, 39,* 161–181.

Venezky, R. L., & Massaro, D. W. (1979). The role of orthographic regularity in word recognition. In L. Resnick & P. Weaver (Eds.), *Theory and practice of early reading* (pp. 85–107). Hillsdale, NJ: Erlbaum.

Walker, C. M. (1979). High frequency word list for grades 3 through 9. *The Reading Teacher, 32,* 802–812.

Azarian, M. (1981). *A farmer's alphabet.* Boston: Godine.

Cleary, B. (1968). *Ramona the pest.* New York: William Morrow.

Kitchen, B. (1984). *Animal alphabet.* New York: Dial.

Larrick, N. (1983). *When dark comes dancing: A bedtime poetry book.* New York: Philomel/Putman.

Martin, B. (1983). *Brown bear, brown bear, what do you see?* New York: Holt.

Royds, C. (1986). *Poems for young children.* New York: Doubleday.

Seuss, Dr. (1957). *The cat in the hat.* New York: Beginner Books.

Seuss, Dr. (1963). *Dr. Seuss's ABC.* New York: Random House.

Seuss, Dr. (1963). *Hop on Pop.* New York: Random House.

Watson, C. (1978). *Catch me & kiss me & say it again.* New York: Philomel.

CHAPTER 9

DEVELOPING CHILDREN'S LITERACY
ABILITIES IN CONTENT AREAS

INTRODUCTION

"Reading and writing across the curriculum" and "content area reading and writing" are the current phrases and language we use in the field of reading and language development to describe the fundamental importance of reading and writing in subject area learning. Significant here is that the language itself signals a newly complex conception of the relationships among reading, writing, and subject area learning. Where once we viewed reading and writing as important but essentially technical adjuncts to learning—that is, learning "tools" or "study skills," as things learners *do* or *use* in the course of acquiring knowledge—we now understand that reading and writing are integral parts of the learning process itself.

For over fifty years, reading has been viewed as a study skill of major importance in learning. This study-skills perspective is based on the belief that certain reading behaviors—e.g., identifying main ideas, separating main ideas from significant details, using graphs and charts—contribute significantly to study-type reading ability and thus to learning from subject area texts. The causal relationship is thought to be that the greater the reading/study skills, the more one is able to read and learn from text.

The study-skills perspective of literacy and subject area learning, however, does not, in and of itself, account for the full complexity of reader-text interactions. It is not sufficient for understanding (or promoting) efficient, expert reading of subject area text. Certainly, having the right "tools" or "skills" for reading subject area texts is important, but current theories of reading and learning suggest that learners do far more than apply reading/study skills to text. Rather, readers construct (or create) meaning *in the very act of reading*—extending their prior knowledge base, arriving at insights, integrating new information, and constructing new subject area knowledge. These constructions of meaning, both during and after reading, are influenced not only by application of reading/study "skills," but, more important, by the myriad interactions and transactions that occur in reading events: transactions involving readers' prior knowledge base, reader intent or stance, social interactions, reading and learning goals, instructional decisions, and so forth (Ruddell, 1993; Ruddell & Unrau, 1994). Thus it is that meanings children construct during and after reading, while certainly influenced by reading/study skills, are fundamentally shaped by the complex interactions and transactions that characterize the comprehension process itself, and these constructions of knowledge form the basis for subject area learning.

In the past decade, our understanding of the relationships between writing and learning has changed and broadened in a manner similar to the way changes have occurred in our understanding of the reading-learning relationship. Much of this change is due to the work of the National Writing Project and research and theory development from the Center for the Study of Writing (see Chapter 7). The traditional role of writing in subject area learning has always been to record and document learning, rather than to exert influence on the learning process itself; hence the dominant and continuing presence in classrooms of written book and informational reports, essay tests, term papers, and the like.

Beginning with their first informational report copied from an available encyclopedia, children have long understood that the purpose of writing in subject area learning was to "show what you know," even when, in the showing, they used others' words rather than their own (whether they understood those words or not). Up until the early 1980s, virtually all discussion of writing in subject areas focused on some form of report-type writing (informational reports, lab reports, research papers, essays, creative writing, term papers), the writing/study skills necessary for report writing, and an emphasis on mechanics (paragraph construction, punctuation, outlining, etc.). Much of this discussion fell under the rubric of "composition" rather than "writing."

Today, we view writing-learning relationships from new vantage points: We now understand that writing is considerably more than a way to record and demonstrate knowledge. Writing is, most important, a *way of knowing*, a way of working through confusion and fuzzy ideas and moving toward clarification and articulation of knowledge. Writers literally achieve insight *in the act of writing*; new ideas come as we write and from what we write (Ruddell, 1993, p. 29). All of us have had the experience of writing something and realizing that we didn't know that we knew what we'd written until it came off the end of our pencil (or appeared on our monitor screen, as the case may be). Such experiences illustrate how it is we achieve insight and create new thoughts as we write. Writing thus becomes a means for working through new ideas and constructing new knowledge rather than simply a tool for recording what was previously learned (Langer & Applebee, 1987; Ruddell, 1993).

SUBJECT AREA LITERACY IN PERSPECTIVE

The central and critical roles of reading and writing in subject area learning compel us, then, to reexamine how we view subject area literacy and what we do in classrooms under the aegis of "teaching reading and writing in the content areas." It simply is not enough for us to teach reading and writing study skills, important though these may be, because such skills do not begin to address the full extent of the relationships among reading, writing, and learning. Nor is it enough for us to assume that children's general reading and writing abilities will transfer automatically to subject area learning. They will not. Rather, what we must understand is that subject area instruction must guide children's reading and writing to produce the kind of literacy interactions and transactions that yield rich, full learning opportunities. Such instruction not only assists children in learning the content itself, but teaches them how to become increasingly independent, fluent readers and writers in subject areas.

The purpose of this chapter is to suggest ways for you to guide your students' reading and writing in subject areas in order to (1) provide maximum opportunity for children to interact and transact with text, with their own prior knowledge base, and with each other for the purpose of learning; and (2) guide children's reading and writing in subject area learning so that they become increasingly fluent subject area readers and writers. The chapter is predicated on the notion that *telling* children to engage in literacy events associated with subject area learning (e.g., "Read Chapter 10"; "Write a summary of our trip to the Miwok Adobe") does not stimulate rich reader-text or other learning transactions, nor does it *teach learners how to do what it is we want them to do* (Ruddell, 1993). For children to learn *how* to become highly effective subject area readers and writers, they must experience rich literacy interactions and transactions repeatedly as they learn content, and this requires teacher guidance and instruction.

A further assumption here is that subject area literacy instruction is not something set off and apart from general reading and writing instruction or subject area learning itself; rather, it is a natural extension of both. Thus, what goes on in the writing workshop or during "reading instruction" becomes part and parcel of subject area literacy learning, and vice versa.

And finally, in this chapter we assume that teachers have considerable responsibility for developing children's literacy abilities in content areas; this responsibility is just as strong and just as compelling as is teachers' responsibility for any other instructional aspect of elementary school life. Instruction and guidance children receive in their elementary school years become the foundation for their continued growth and increasing independence in subject area reading and writing in later years.

LEARNING FROM TEXT

READING

A summary of research conducted during the 1980s (Pearson, Roehler, Dole, & Duffy, 1990) provides a profile of the text comprehension strategies that highly effective readers use. Pearson and his associates label such readers "expert" or "thoughtful" readers and draw from many different research studies to arrive at the following expert reader characteristics. Thoughtful readers

- constantly search for connections between what they know and what they encounter as new information in the text is read;

- constantly monitor the adequacy of the models of text meaning they build;

- take steps to repair faulty comprehension once they realize that they have failed to understand something;

- learn very early to distinguish important from less important ideas in the text they read;

- are especially adept at synthesizing information within and across texts and reading experiences;

- make inferences during and after reading to achieve a full, integrated understanding of what they read;

- sometimes consciously, almost always unconsciously, ask questions of themselves, the authors they encounter, and the texts they read.

Pearson and his associates suggest also that these seven complex reader characteristics ". . . can be the goals that constitute the infrastructure of what we teach in the name of comprehension instruction" (1990, p. 13). We concur and recommend further that these same reader characteristics should be the objective of content reading instruction as well, whether that instruction occurs in self-contained or specialized classrooms. That is, we believe that as you teach science and mathematics and social studies, you need also to be guiding children's reading of science, mathematics, and social studies texts so that the children become increasingly able to (1) develop connections between what they already know and new information in texts, (2) monitor the adequacy of the meanings they construct, (3) repair faulty comprehension when it does occur, (4) distinguish important from less important information in text, (5) synthesize information within and across texts, (6) draw inferences during and after reading, and (7) ask questions of themselves and the texts they read. In short, we believe that children need to be taught to be strategic readers of subject area texts.

In all too many elementary classrooms, however, little (if any) attention is given to developing children's strategic reading abilities with subject area text. When content reading instruction does occur, the study skills approach generally predominates (as we suggested earlier), so that instruction and attention are focused primarily on identifying main ideas, using graphs and charts, locating details, and so forth, rather than on making connections, monitoring reading progress, repairing faulty comprehension, synthesizing information within and across texts, and all the other reading strategies thoughtful readers use. In some classrooms, teachers do nothing to guide children's content reading, or, when they do, the "guidance" of choice is having children read the passage or chapter orally, taking turns up and down the rows or around the circle, in unrehearsed, Round-Robin Oral Reading.

Let us take a moment here to state emphatically that unrehearsed oral reading has only one educationally valid use in a classroom, and that is when teachers administer an Informal Reading Inventory individually to children, as described in Chapter 11. Otherwise, unrehearsed oral reading *has no place in your classroom*. It does *not* help the poorer readers or limited-English-speaking students understand and learn content or become better readers (they're too terrified of having to read to be able to learn anything). It does nothing to challenge or engage the thinking of better readers; it certainly doesn't promote any of the characteristics of "thoughtful readers" we discussed earlier; and it is a dreadfully boring—sometimes agonizing—experience to endure the tortured performances of children who do not read well.

Round-robin oral reading aside, the point here is that not enough attention is given in elementary classrooms to guiding children's reading of subject area texts and developing their abilities to read science, mathematics, and social studies. We believe that much of the reason for this comes from the very heavy emphasis placed on general reading instruction in elementary classrooms, and teachers' (possibly unconscious) assumption that if they can teach children to be good *readers*, then this general reading ability will transfer somewhat automatically to subject area reading. Unfortunately, that assumption doesn't hold. The fact is, children who can read well, can read well in *some* subject areas (generally those for which they have high interest/aptitude) and need instruction and guidance in others; children who can't read well need instruction and guidance in all subject area reading. Much of the time, that instruction is not forthcoming.

To test the validity of this premise, reconsider for a moment your own literacy history in content areas (from the Double Entry Journal at the beginning of the chapter). Rate your general reading abilities on the following scale, using your remembered learning experiences and the characteristics of "thoughtful readers" listed above to guide your analysis:

5—I am now, and have always been, one of the best readers in the room, if not *the* best.

4—I'm definitely a superior reader; I rarely encounter problems and almost always get high grades and high reading scores.

3—I'm a good reader; I feel comfortable and confident in my literacy abilities and my capability for doing whatever reading I want or need to do.

2—I'm just a so-so reader; I manage to do the reading I need to do. While I can read certain things fairly well, I find most study reading somewhat difficult.

1—I'm really not a very good reader; I get along in academic and work settings by paying close attention to discussions and other information. I generally avoid reading whenever possible.

After rating your general reading ability, think for a moment about the academic subject area or areas in which you were/are *least* able; you can be very general in your categories (e.g., mathematics, science, social studies), or as specific as you wish (algebra, chemistry, English, history, general mathematics, geometry, physics, foreign language, biology, literature, geography, philosophy, anthropology, psychology, calculus, etc.). Go back to the scale and rate your reading ability *in that (or those) subject area(s)*. Now do the same rating for the subject area(s) in which you're *most* able. Finally, think back on the subject area instruction you experienced: Do you remember teachers guiding your reading in mathematics books, poetry books, or science and social studies texts, or was reading simply assigned? Do you remember exciting, exuberant discussions about subject area text, doing class and small group projects, and really getting "into" a topic or project? How often do you remember doing round-robin oral reading in subject area texts (and what do you remember about this activity)?

We suspect that most of you got about the same results as we did when we reflected on our own subject area learning experiences: Some degree of discrepancy (maybe even great difference) between your general reading ability and the subject area(s) in which you're least able; considerable congruence between your general reading ability and reading ability in the subject area(s) in which you're most able; little or no guidance in reading mathematics books, poetry books, or science and social studies texts; mostly question-and-answer "discussions" instead of class and small group projects, and rather a *lot* of round-robin oral reading. This profile is fairly common and is a clear reflection of the tradition of subject area instruction in U.S. schools.

WRITING

Very nearly everything we've just said about expert reading, content reading instruction, and children's experiences with subject area reading can also be said about writing; only the details differ. Research examining the uses of writing in the subject areas has traditionally focused on secondary, rather than elementary, classrooms (Applebee, 1981; Martin, D'Arcy, Newton, & Parker, 1976), in all likelihood because the subject areas are so clearly distinct in secondary schools (although that may be changing soon). However, there can be little doubt that, at the elementary level, subject area writing has always been dominated by the informational report—the traditional "staple" of elementary classrooms as Beach (1983) suggests. (Beach also comments that the headaches that accompany informational reports, for students and teachers alike, are just as traditional as the assignment itself!)

The informational report is, in our minds, clearly parallel to round-robin oral reading: a ritualistic classroom event that children learn to do that only touches the surface of the text of whatever is to be learned, and in which children's real attention and interest are not engaged. Some children become very, very good at both round-robin oral reading and informational report writing; others do not. Whichever the case, there is little inherent in either task that invites engagement, avid attention, or learning. One of Nancie Atwell's stories (1990) captures poignantly the real essence and effect of report writing in elementary schools and makes Beach's point as well:

> *My unhappiest memory of elementary school involves*
> *report writing. I think the assignment was typical: pick a*

country and write a report about it. Describe its history, system of government, geography, population, major occupations, and natural resources. Include a topographical map, a bibliography, and an illustrated cover. At least twelve pages long. Due in one month, as homework.

Full of Anglophilia and sixth-grade arrogance I put in a bid for Great Britain, which the teacher okayed. This meant I would have to come up with four versions of all the above, one each for England, Ireland, Scotland, and Wales. Never mind that to do even one of the subtopics justice would require at least a book.

Now add a new variable: I am a world-class procrastinator. I think I have finally learned to judge just how long I can stall in the face of a deadline. I have also learned to write on my feet, to mentally rehearse my writing in the midst of doing something else, so that these days, when I do confront a blank page, my mind generally isn't. In sixth grade I had no idea of how to budget my time for a major writing project. If I thought about the report at all, it was to assure myself that I could pull off my usual something at the last minute. I didn't rehearse the report mentally because I was not a writer; thinking about writing, the compulsion that Don Graves (1983) calls "offstage rehearsal," only happens to children who write regularly.

In addition to lacking a writer's habits of mind, I had nothing to think about Great Britain, or at least nothing to think about the topics outlined in the assignment. From my English grandmother, also named Nancie Atwell, I knew about English cooking, gardens, pubs, games, slang, and country life. But what I could teach others or what I wanted to

learn were not considerations in the assignment, apart from two essential skills: I was expert in the subtle art of plagiarizing The World Book, *and I could trace maps.*

The weekend before the report was due I finally adjourned to my bedroom and began. By Sunday afternoon I knew I was in deep trouble. I stayed up as late as my mother would allow that night, hardly slept, and went to school empty-handed the next morning. While my classmates bustled around me putting the finishing touches on their illustrated covers, I pretended to be fascinated with the inside of my desk. When the reports were passed up the rows to the front of the room, I held my breath. And the teacher…

Never mentioned the missing report. Not that day, not ever. For the remaining three months of the school year I lived, alternately, in dread and anticipation of the moment when she would take me aside and end the torture, a word I don't use lightly. I thought about the report all the time but had no idea what to do about it now that the deadline was past.

On the last day of sixth grade, in the flurry of cleaning up the room and saying our good-byes, my teacher handed back the social studies reports. I escaped to the girls' room when I saw her come around from behind her desk with a stack of illustrated covers in her arms, and that was that— except for the gnawing at my conscience that has never eased in all these years.

What I realized in writing about this memory is that my sixth-grade teacher did not discover until the last day of school that I hadn't submitted the report. For the same reason that I had postponed writing it she had postponed grading it: sheer boredom. The reports, as tedious to read as they were to write,

PEANUTS *Charles Schulz*

*informed and entertained no one. I can't blame the teacher.
The sixth-grade curriculum required a report on a country,
and she had obliged. (Atwell, 1990, pp. xi–xii)*

We think Nancie Atwell's story is an important one, a vivid example of how well-intended, but not well-thought-out, instructional practices can cause learning events to go awry. In sixth grade Nancie Atwell had a lot to say about Great Britain, considerable prior knowledge (English cooking, gardens, pubs, games, slang, and country life), and real interest in the topic (Anglophilia); unfortunately, nothing that happened in the classroom or in the assignment allowed her to validate and build on what she already knew and supported or encouraged her to learn more. No connection was made between her world and the world of information to be learned, no opportunity was available for her to talk over her ideas and plan her project, and no attempt was made to connect the informational report project to anything going on in the classroom itself. Atwell's story is not unique; you surely remember doing those reports, and even though you may not have suffered the humiliation and torture she felt (or failed to turn one in), the essential fact remains: Informational reports, long a tradition in elementary classrooms, are exercises in plagiarism, tracing, and tedium.

INSTRUCTION FOR GUIDING CHILDREN'S READING AND WRITING IN SUBJECT AREAS

The goal of subject area reading and writing instruction is to create thoughtful readers and writers in mathematics, science, and social studies and to give children the deeply satisfying experience of *really learning* in school. Think for a moment about a time in your life when you *really learned*—it may have been a project, a moment, an entire year, or an even longer period in or out of school. Remember how you felt and what you did during that learning time. In all likelihood, your memories include all or some of the following: visceral response to learning (excitement, exhilaration, "having fun"); learning that was "easy" and self-propelled or self-perpetuating; lots of talking about learning topics with interested others; solid, clear connections between what you were learning and what you already knew; avid reading and writing as natural, integral parts of the learning process; curiosity and intense interest; feeling "time fly" during learning events.

This kind of eager learning response is the hallmark of *real learning*, and if we are to create a learning environment in schools that encourages such response, we must be willing to look honestly at traditional instructional practices and eliminate those that are not rich, complex, and full. We simply cannot tolerate classroom events and assignments that are exercises in tedium. Further, we must guide children's reading and writing in subject area texts so that avid reading and writing become a natural part of all learning. That is what the rest of this chapter is about. Here, as elsewhere (Chapter 7), we are separating reading- and writing-based subject area instruction in what we know to be an artificial separation. We do this for ease of discussion and for you to see the essential focus of each instructional practice. As in Chapter 7, we bring reading and writing together in the last section on theme cycles and project-based instruction.

Figures 9-1, "What Students Need to Do When Learning from Text," and 9-2, "What Teachers Need to Do to Guide Students' Learning from Text" (Ruddell, 1993, pp. 132–133) serve as the basis for the discussion of instructional strategies for developing subject area literacy. If you look carefully at **what students need to do** when learning from text, you'll note the discussion

---

Students need to:

1. *Recall prior knowledge and previous experience*—Identify what they know; raise questions about what they do not know; and predict what text will be about.

2. *Organize information while reading*—Predict what information will be found; conform/adjust predictions; and relate new information to prior knowledge.

3. *Organize information after reading*—Respond to text in some important way; identify major concepts and ideas; perceive relationships between concepts and ideas; perceive relationships with prior knowledge; and understand relative importance of ideas.

4. *Synthesize and articulate new learning*—Arrive at new understanding and insights; integrate new understands into prior knowledge base; find out how much was learned; and establish base for further learning.

5. *Learn vocabulary that labels important concepts, elements, and relationships*—Identify new words and terms; identify known words and terms in new contexts; use new words and terms in meaningful ways; and relate new vocabulary to prior knowledge base.

6. *Produce or create something new and apply new information*—Work through new ideas in writing; build, make, create something new, or perform.

FIGURE 9-1

What Students Need to Do When Learning from Text

441

Teachers need to:

1. *Determine students' prior knowledge and previous experience concerning the topic at hand*—Provide means for students to articulate their prior knowledge base; find out what students already know; and determine the magnitude of difference between what students know and what is to be learned.

2. *Provide means for students to organize information while reading*—Focus students' attention; engage students in the cycle of predicting/reading/adjusting predictions/reading some more; and develop linkages between prior knowledge and new information.

3. *Provide means for students to organize information while reading*—Establish various means for students to respond to text; engage students in elaborative discussion and follow-up activities; and encourage and teach various organizational structures for recording information.

4. *Provide means for students to synthesize and articulate new learning*—Allow opportunity for students to talk and write about what they have learned; further develop linkages between prior knowledge and new information; and identify linkages between new information and what is yet to come.

5. *Identify and teach vocabulary that labels important concepts, elements, and relationships*—Allow students to identify words and terms they need to know; find out what words and terms students already know; develop linkages between new words and terms and prior knowledge base; and develop activities for students to use new words and terms in meaningful ways.

6. *Provide opportunity for students to produce or create something new*—Promote elaborative projects and activities; find out what students learned; and evaluate degree of teaching/learning success.

—— **FIGURE 9-2** ——————————————————

What Teachers Need to Do to Guide Students' Learning from Text

includes many of the characteristics of *really learning* that we discussed before: many opportunities to connect prior knowledge with new learning, reading and writing that are natural and integral parts of the learning processes and lots and lots of talking about learning topics with others. Much of **what teachers need to do** includes creating an environment and learning conditions that make "time fly" and encouraging student excitement, exhilaration, intense interest, and curiosity in learning.

GUIDING CHILDREN'S READING IN SUBJECT AREA INSTRUCTION

Content Directed Reading-Thinking Activity (DR-TA), Group Mapping Activity (GMA) (Study Maps), and Vocabulary Self-Collection Strategy (VSS)

One of the easiest, and most natural, ways to guide children's reading of subject area text is to adapt, combine, and apply to content reading instructional strategies we've already discussed in other chapters of the text. Some adaptations and combinations that are particularly effective are the content DR-TA, GMA, and VSS. Following our presentation of the combined DR-TA, GMA, and VSS, we will introduce other instructional strategies.

Content DR-TA. The content DR-TA is one way to adapt the Directed Reading-Thinking Activity (DR-TA) to subject area texts (Haggard, 1985, 1989; Ruddell, 1993). Content DR-TA begins with the children gathered in two- or three-person teams. Each team has paper, pencil, and the text to be read (or the text is nearby and ready to be handed out when it is time to read). Student teams are first asked to jot down everything they know about a *general topic* within which the lesson topic fits. For example, the teacher might say, "Jot down everything you know about sharks" for a lesson about the different varieties of sharks, or "Jot down everything you know about addition" as the class moves into three-place numeral adding, or "Jot down everything you know about the Mississippi River" before reading about recent flooding on the Mississippi River. The children in their teams work together to compile their list, with one member of the team recording ideas. The teams have seven to eight minutes to work; the teacher observes to hear what information is being exchanged (recall from Figure 9-2 that the teacher needs to find out what students already know) and to assist if teams have trouble getting or staying on task. The noise level is likely to reduce at some point well before the end of eight minutes as children "dig around" in their memories for more information. That's fine. Give them the time necessary to do some memory searching. With very young children, or with some topics, the working time should probably be reduced to five or six minutes.

After ideas are jotted down, the teacher then announces the *specific topic* of the lesson and gives directions to focus the children's attention on that topic: "Today we're going to read a section in our text called 'Meet the Sharks' (or 'Adding with Three-Place Numerals,' etc.). Go back to your list and put a checkmark (✓) beside anything on the list that you think you'll find in our reading. Add any new ideas that occur to you." Student teams have two to three minutes for this, after which the teacher initiates the reading by saying "Now read 'Meet the Sharks' " and distributes or directs

443

students' attention to the text to be read. The teacher then directs, "As you read, circle (or put an asterisk beside) any idea on your list that you find in your reading."

The children read the assignment individually; however, you can expect a considerable "buzz" of working discussion while they read. Since the student teams have generated their lists cooperatively, there's a tendency for children to notify each other when something on their list appears in the text, and a certain amount of "claiming" of ideas that individuals contributed to the list. Children will read to each other, chat about information found in text, and discuss what items on their list should or should not be circled or asterisked.

After the reading, the teacher leads a short discussion that focuses primarily on what information the children already knew and what information was learned in reading. This discussion might be directed by the question "What are some things you already knew about varieties of sharks (or adding three-place numerals, or lessons of the Mississippi)?" followed by "What are some things you learned?" Discussion here is not prolonged, so that the class can move immediately into GMA. The goal here is to give the children opportunity to begin the process of organizing the knowledge they've constructed during the learning event.

Group Mapping Activity (GMA) (Study Maps). GMA (Davidson, 1982), as we discussed in Chapter 4, helps children integrate and synthesize information from text. As a study aid, maps are particularly useful in guiding children's learning and developing their ability to understand and remember information. Maps give children the "big picture" of topics that grow over a period of days or weeks; they also capture and hold important details.

Instructions for creating Study Maps are slightly more structured than the mapping instructions presented in Chapter 4. First, Study Maps focus explicitly on the topic of study (e.g., varieties of sharks, adding three-place numerals, lessons of the Mississippi) instead of leaving the decision of focus up to each child; second, they are explicitly identified as Study Maps for recording and keeping information throughout a given time period or unit of study. Instructions for developing Study Maps should be something like the following (we are assuming here that children already have done some mapping):

> *Without looking back at the book or talking to anyone,*
> *map your understanding of the important ideas in the reading*
> *we just did on varieties of sharks. You are going to use this map*
> *to record information as we go through our unit on sharks;*
> *later, the map will help you as you develop your own shark*
> *project. Be sure to include on your map all the information you*
> *think is important. (Ruddell, 1993)*

As the children create their maps, the teacher observes, offering help to those who need it. Some children may be concerned that they cannot look back at the text; assure them that you'll let them do so a little later and repeat your request that they not do so right now (we've found that if allowed to use the text at this point, children get bogged down trying to get *every* detail on the map and frequently lose sight of the big picture in so doing).

When maps are complete, student teams share their maps with one another; children are directed to identify for their partner or team *what* they considered important in the reading, *how* they chose to organize their map, and *why* they organized it as they did. The other team member(s) respond by asking questions to draw information out of the person who is sharing (e.g., "Why did you organize you map that way?" or "What made you choose these lines here?"). After all team members have shared, the teacher then instructs the teams to make sure everyone's map has all the important information on it. Emphasize here that *the maps do not have to look alike;* however, they do need to be as complete as possible. Encourage the children to look back in their text at this time, and ask partners or team members to assist each other in completing the maps.

You can expect that the maps will reflect children's individual prior knowledge base and will vary considerably in appearance and emphasis. Don't worry about this difference, particularly if the endpoint is for children to create their own individual or group projects to pursue. The maps will help them organize their knowledge and give them support in that effort. If the endpoint is a test and you have specific information or knowledge goals that will be covered by the test, make sure students have every opportunity to know what those goals are. If you do see maps that suggest confusion or misunderstanding, work individually with children to clarify meanings and remove misunderstandings. Maps often change and grow when used throughout a unit; invite children to make changes, or start over if they wish, as they use their study maps.

Vocabulary Self-Collection Strategy (VSS). VSS (Haggard, 1985, 1989; Ruddell, 1993) may be used in subject area learning exactly as described in Chapter 5: Children in pairs or teams are asked to nominate one or two words or terms that they believe the class should learn or know more about; the teacher also nominates one or two words. The major difference here is that children will tend to focus on topic-specific words and terms, although no direction is given for them to do so (and children will forever nominate enticingly interesting words and terms that may or may not be topic-related: "cavernous maw" *always* is chosen for one passage about humpbacked whales). After all words are nominated, the class narrows the list down to a manageable number (probably no more than five or six words), clarifies agreed-upon definitions, and records the words and definitions.

One very important aspect of VSS used for subject area learning is that the words and terms chosen by the class must be recorded in such a way that they are contextually situated (Ruddell, 1993). After the final list is determined, have students enter their VSS words on their maps "where they make sense" and mark the words in some manner to identify them as vocabulary words (circle, underline, color-code, etc.). Then, throughout the unit of study, give special attention to VSS words and use them in a variety of activities (see Chapter 5), including Semantic Maps, Semantic Feature Analysis exercises, word sleuthing, and so forth.

Value of Content DR-TA, GMA (Study Maps), VSS. You will find that this particular combination of instructional strategies has many advantages. Probably the greatest value of the content DR-TA, GMA, VSS combination is the degree to which children direct and guide their own learning. Certainly, you are directing the *lesson*, but it is the *children's* prior knowledge that opens the team discussions and, later, whole-class discussion. It is the *children's* constructions of knowledge that form their study maps and guide map-sharing discussions and team efforts to assist in completing each other's maps. And it the *children's* choices that comprise the list of words to be learned.

Second in importance is the way in which reading and writing are such natural (and important) parts of learning. Children are jotting down ideas, looking for their own ideas in text, checking and circling information from their prior knowledge that they find in text, using all manner of symbolic and written text representations in their maps, reading and rereading text purposefully, and recording words and definitions that they've deemed important to the topic of study. These are all behaviors used by strategic readers and writers, and their continued use integrates into children's working repertoires all of the characteristics of thoughtful readers and writers. (Note how really difficult it is to separate reading in content areas from writing; while this discussion is about guiding children's reading in subject area instruction, writing is certainly an integral and important part of the instructional event.)

And finally, this combination of instructional strategies allows the kind of *real learning* we discussed earlier. There's lots of talking and exchanging of information, from the initial activity in the lesson right through to the final one. The lesson begins with what children know and ends with what children want to learn. There are many opportunities for children to negotiate meaning collaboratively—during team and whole-class discussions, as maps are shared and discussed, while seeking words to nominate and choosing the final list. And children repeatedly consult their prior knowledge base and the text itself for real purposes. A wonderful phenomenon that occurs with the content DR-TA, GMA, VSS combination is that children willingly read, and reread text as the lesson progresses; this is a "wonderful phenomenon" because, so often, children do not want to read content text more than once. They want, most of the time, to read the text once and then never set eyes on it again, behavior that is learned from the traditional instructional pattern of once-over reading, followed by question-answer sessions, and then on to the next topic. With the content DR-TA, GMA, VSS combination, children learn that returning to text is useful, productive, and a natural part of learning. One of the greatest values of the combined content DR-TA, GMA, VSS for the *teacher* is how easily these strategies may be used with just about any subject area materials. In fact, you can just as easily use this combination with media other than written text (e.g., videotapes, movies, demonstrations, simulations, etc.) as you can with written text. Whatever the medium, you need do no great alterations of text or major preparations to use the content DR-TA, GMA, VSS combination.

HOW TO DO . . . .
THE CONTENT DR-TA, GMA (STUDY MAP), VSS COMBINATION

CONTENT DR-TA

1. Ask student teams to list everything they know about a *general topic* (e.g., sharks, addition, the Mississippi River).

2. Announce the *specific topic* (e.g., varieties of sharks, adding three-place numerals, lessons of the Mississippi).

3. Ask students to predict what information they have on their lists will appear in the text (✓); add any new ideas to their lists.

4. Have students read the assignment and note how well they predicted (circle or *).

5. Lead a short discussion about what students knew before they read and what new information they found ("How well did you predict?" or "What were some of the things you knew before we read? What are some new things you found?").

GMA (STUDY MAPS)

6. Ask students to map what they believe to be the important information from the text without talking to anybody or looking back at the text. Remind the children that the maps will be used throughout the unit and should include all the information they consider to be important.

7. Have children share their maps with their partner or team. Remind them to tell each other *what* they chose to include, *how* they chose to map, and *why* they made the choices they did.

8. Have partners or teams work collaboratively to finish the maps. Encourage children to refer to the text at this time.

continued…

HOW TO DO CONTINUED. . . . .

VSS

9. Ask student teams to choose one or two words or terms that they think the class should learn or know more about. Teams should be prepared to tell *where* they found the word, *what* they think the word means, and *why* they think it's important (you also nominate one or two words).

10. Lead a discussion as words are nominated and defined; write nominated words on the board.

11. Allow the class to choose the five or six words it wishes to designate for the class list. Review and refine the definitions for the class list words.

12. Have students enter their VSS words on their maps where the words make sense; mark the VSS words in some manner.

13. Develop opportunities for children to use and apply VSS words meaningfully.

14. Provide opportunity for children to elaborate on what they have learned (projects, etc.).

K-W-L Plus

K-W-L Plus (Carr & Ogle, 1987) is highly similar to the content DR-TA and GMA combination. *K* stands for what students already *know; W* represents what they *want to know;* and *L* is what they *learned.* The "Plus" refers to mapping. K-W-L Plus begins with children listing everything they *know* about a topic under the *K* on a K-W-L worksheet (see Figure 9-3). The children then brainstorm what they *want* to know about the topic and list those items under *W* on the worksheet. Students then read the passage and summarize what they've *learned* under the *L* on the worksheet. Note in Figure 9-3 that information in column *L* is categorized and given category designations. These designations become the starting point for developing maps (see Figure 9-4).

K-W-L Plus is just as suited to partnership and student-team work as the content DR-TA and GMA. It has the added flash of the K-W-L worksheet (that children generally like), and can easily have VSS added in the final stage of discussion. K-W-L Plus has all of the advantages and values of the content DR-TA, GMA, VSS combination and can be used as the format for a major project-search discussion of "what we know," "what we don't know," and "what we'd like to know," as described in Chapter 7. Use your computer

K (KNOW)	W (WANT TO KNOW)	L (LEARNED)
They live in oceans They are vicious. They eat each other. They are mammals.	Why do they attack people? How fast can they swim? What kind of fish do they eat? What is their description? How long do they live? How do they breathe?	D—They are the biggest member of the dolphin family. D—They weigh 10,000 pounds and get 30 feet long. F—They eat squids, seals, and other dolphins. A—They have good vision underwater. F—They are carnivorous (meat eaters). A—They are the second-smartest animal on earth. D—They breathe through blow holes. A—They do not attack unless they are hungry. D—They are warm -blooded. A—They have echo-location (sonar). L—They are found in the oceans.
Description Food Location		

Final category designations developed for column L, information learned about killer whales: A = abilities, D = description, F = food, L = location.

FIGURE 9-3

K-W-L Worksheet on Killer Whales. (Reproduced with permission from Carr & Ogle, 1987.)

or one the school has available to make a really snazzy K-W-L worksheet form. Make lots of copies and have them available for the learning you direct in class and for students to use when pursuing independent research and study. Completed K-W-L worksheets and follow-up maps and other writing are useful additions to portfolios (see Chapter 11).

The Directed Inquiry Activity (DIA)

The DIA is an instructional strategy that Keith Thomas (1986) developed to apply the Directed Reading-Thinking Activity to subject area instruction. The DIA is a bit more structured than the content DR-TA or the

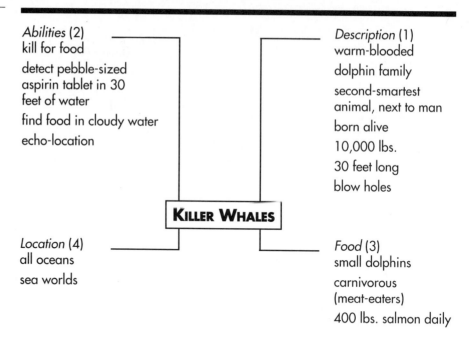

Abilities (2)
kill for food

detect pebble-sized
aspirin tablet in 30
feet of water

find food in cloudy water

echo-location

Description (1)
warm-blooded

dolphin family

second-smartest
animal, next to man

born alive

10,000 lbs.

30 feet long

blow holes

KILLER WHALES

Location (4)
all oceans

sea worlds

Food (3)
small dolphins

carnivorous
(meat-eaters)

400 lbs. salmon daily

(1) *through* (4) *indicate the order of categories the student chose later for writing a summary.*

FIGURE 9-4

Map Generated from a K-W-L Worksheet. (Reproduced with permission from Carr & Ogle, 1987.)

K-W-L Plus, but still retains the important characteristic of using children's prior knowledge and having them predict the content of the text. The DIA also relies rather heavily on the kind of follow-up response probes that are characteristic of the DR-TA.

In preparation for the DIA, the teacher develops five or six inquiry questions from the material to be read. (See Chapter 4 for discussion of interpretive, applicative, and transactional questions.) These questions should focus on important ideas and issues raised by the lesson text and are used initially for children to make some predictions about what the text will contain. The questions may be written on the board with lots of space for predictions or they may be printed on individual worksheets for the children to use (again, with lots of space for predictions). The teacher asks students to preview the reading assignment and shows them how to page through the text, glancing at chapter and topic headings, reading bits and pieces of text, looking at charts and graphs, and so forth. Then, after previewing, children use their background knowledge and any information they picked up while previewing to predict responses to the inquiry questions. Children's predictions are

HOW TO DO . . . .
K-W-L PLUS

1. Have children brainstorm what they know about the lesson topic (you may want to use partnerships or teams).

2. Direct them to organize what they know and make a list of their knowledge in the *K* column of the K-W-L worksheet.

3. Have children then list what they want to know about the topic in question under the *W* column; they should anticipate what they're going to read as much as they can.

4. Direct children to read the assignment; they may add questions to their *W* list as they read, if they wish.

5. Have children list what they learned under the *L* column and then categorize learned information and label the categories.

6. Ask children to develop their own maps using the categories and information learned.

7. Lead a discussion as children display and explain their maps.

8. Develop appropriate follow-up activities.

recorded on the board or on worksheets; the teacher probes student responses to find out how they arrived at their predictions. "What makes you say that?" and "How did you arrive at that idea (or prediction)?" are highly useful questions in this process.

Following the discussion of student predictions, the children read the passage to confirm or adjust their predictions, and then generate additional responses to the inquiry questions. During this discussion, the students and teacher have further opportunity to analyze earlier predictions, make connections between children's prior knowledge and the new information in the text, and refine understandings of the material.

The DIA has a stronger emphasis on teacher-direction than do some other instructional strategies and is particularly useful for focusing student attention on specific learning objectives. The kinds of inquiry questions you develop clearly influence the direction of discussions and what children learn. These questions should be broad-based, they should be important, and they should lead to further inquiry and investigation.

The DIA is quite amenable to partnership and student-team work. Allow children to work in pairs or teams to do the initial previewing of text and predicting. Then lead a discussion in which pairs/teams share their predictions

HOW TO DO . . . .

THE DIA

1. Determine lesson objectives and write five or six inquiry questions that reflect these objectives.

2. Decide what portions of the text the children are to preview and note specific text features they should consult (e.g., chapter headings, marginal notes, charts and graphs, etc.).

3. Write the inquiry questions on the board or on a worksheet to be reproduced and distributed to students. Leave room for predictions and other responses.

4. Ask the children to preview the reading assignment and make predictions about the inquiry question responses.

5. Lead discussion for children to share their predictions; be sure to probe responses for logic and reasoning.

6. Have students read the assignment.

7. Lead discussion to reexamine inquiry question responses and refine knowledge in light of new information. As a group, develop ideas and questions for further inquiry.

8. Lead or assign any follow-up activities (GMA and VSS would both be appropriate).

and in which you ask questions that probe the reasoning and logic that led to the predictions. After reading, allow the pairs/teams to arrive at collaborative responses to the inquiry questions and then share these responses in whole-class discussion.

Reading Response Groups

Reading response groups are just as useful for subject area learning as they are for literature response (see Chapters 6 and 12). The main difference here is that, for subject area learning, prompts to guide response group discussion focus more explicitly on the text content than might literature prompts, and they may not be as wide-ranging as literature prompts (Farnan, 1992). John O'Flahavan (1989) recommends that the teacher use three questions with response groups that focus on the following areas: (1) background knowledge—what the children already know about the text topic; (2) ideas derived from the text—what meaning children construct;

Reading and Writing Mathematics

and (3) ideas that go beyond the text—how children interpret or react to the text. In a social studies unit on "community," the following three reading response prompts might be used (the labels in parentheses are solely for the purpose of identifying the category of each prompt; they shouldn't appear on the prompts given to children):

1. In your own words, describe our neighborhood community. What do you think are the most important parts of a community? (background knowledge)

2. Based upon what you read, what new ideas would you add to your definition of "community"? Why are you adding those ideas? (ideas derived from text)

3. What would you like to add to or change about our community? What would you do first? Why? (ideas that go beyond text)

Children working in reading response groups might be given some time to work through the prompts individually, and then enter into group discussion. After the groups have had plenty of time for discussion, the class then shares the results of these discussions in a large group. Response groups should have clear instructions regarding what they are responsible for producing during their discussion time and what they are to bring and/or contribute to the whole class discussion.

Occasionally, reading response groups have difficulty doing what it is they're supposed to do (Eeds & Wells, 1989; Raines, 1991). Reading response group instruction is relatively unstructured in comparison to teacher-led discussions and activities, and is thus vulnerable to "bird-walking" (getting

453

off the subject) and other forms of off-task behavior. When reading response groups do work well, the key to success appears to be well-constructed and well-communicated task goals (Raines, 1991) that clearly define what children are to do. It helps also for children to find some inherent interest in the topic of study (yet another reason to connect with what they already know) and for them to be seasoned cooperative or collaborative group workers (we'll discuss more about this in Chapter 13). One way to make subject area reading response groups more effective is to spend the time necessary to hone and refine the writing prompts you develop for the groups to use. Prompts should focus on important ideas rather than niggling details; they should invite children to "think big" and well beyond the limits of the text; and they should make children curious and eager to learn more.

Reading response groups may be used on a small scale, as you convene groups occasionally for a one- or two-day group response; or response groups can be brought together for an entire unit of study in which groups propose, design, and develop a major group project. Most teachers keep things on a small scale until children have become seasoned response group participants; then they begin extending response group tasks.

Strategy Review

We said earlier that a reasonable and natural approach for guiding children's reading of subject area text is to adapt and combine instructional

HOW TO DO . . . .

READING RESPONSE GROUPS

1. Determine lesson or unit objectives.

2. Establish reading response groups (four to five children in each).

3. Spend whatever time necessary to make sure children know how to work in reading response groups; develop and communicate guidelines for group work (see Chapter 13).

4. Prepare response group prompts and write them on the board, or prepare a handout for each group.

5. Observe children working in their reading response groups; troubleshoot when and if necessary; monitor group progress.

6. Lead whole-class discussion of groups' responses to prompts; spend some time having students reflect on the response group process.

strategies we've discussed throughout this text. We wish to reiterate that here and remind you that DL-TAs (Chapter 3) are appropriate for subject area instruction (you can very productively read to children—even older children—text that they may not be able to read for themselves), as are DR-TAs, and such strategies as QAR, PReP, and ReQuest (all found in Chapter 4). These strategies need only minor adjustments to guide children's learning in subject areas; equally important, the strategies all promote full, rich interactions with text and guide children toward the strategic behaviors that thoughtful readers use.

GUIDING CHILDREN'S WRITING IN SUBJECT AREA INSTRUCTION

Writing Workshop in Subject Areas

We begin our discussion of guiding children's writing in subject area instruction with a short review and subject area application of the writing workshop, because it is difficult to address any aspect of subject area writing instruction without first acknowledging the writing workshop (see Chapter 7). The writing workshop is rather easily incorporated into subject area learning; teachers have only to remember that basic to the writing workshop philosophy is that children (all of us, actually) write best what they know. So it is important that many rich learning experiences and opportunities for children to explore new ideas occur before subject area writing workshops begin.

Patricia Collins (1990) describes her experience extending the writing workshop in her sixth-grade class to include students' study of the Middle Ages. She introduced the unit by bringing many materials and resources to class, showing videotapes and reading books to the children, and alerting students three weeks in advance that they would be choosing individual projects for which they would write research papers. Collins encouraged students to begin browsing in resource materials and the library and considering project topics early; in the meantime, she continued her presentations so that children could see many different possible topics they might wish to pursue.

Then, after many presentations and much preparation, the writing workshop began: mini-lessons, daily status-of-the-class roll calls, honeybee conferences, longer conferences, planning, drafting, revising, editing, and publishing final papers. In mini-lessons, Collins gave children ideas for the many forms their final work could take—ranging from picture books, to poetry, to imaginary conversations between historical figures, to shadow boxes and dioramas, to annotated family trees, to formal research paper writing—and allowed each student to choose his or her own genre. She used the following evaluation standards for the final projects (Collins, 1990, p. 30):

1. Carefully thought out research questions.
2. Used class time well.
3. Took careful notes.

4. Showed a willingness to revise and improve drafts.
5. Edited the piece carefully before submitting it for editing.
6. Submitted all work with the final draft.
7. Showed creativity and careful thought.
8. Correctly completed bibliography.
9. Completed work on time.
10. Project format enhanced the research.

Other activities and instructional practices, many of which are often incorporated into the writing workshop, may be used to guide children's subject area writing.

Journal Writing

Journal writing has become an accepted component of subject area learning at all educational levels (Ruddell, 1993; Zinsser, 1988) and is especially popular in elementary classrooms. Journals are most generally kept in the classroom in a special place and are used for private written conversations between teacher and child. Often journal writing is completely freeform, so that children write on topics of their own choosing and in any forms and formats they desire. Journals used for guiding children's subject area writing are more frequently structured in some manner. For example, many teachers like to use prompts for subject area journal writing:

"Write everything you can remember about what you learned about long division today."

"Based upon our observations and records from the past week, what conclusions do you draw about our current weather pattern?"

"What was the hardest thing about completing last night's language arts homework? What was the easiest?"

Others like to use approximately the same prompt every day; writing in mathematics often is focused on what was learned today or what was hardest/easiest. Many teachers like to use a "letter to the teacher" format that allows the conversation between teacher and child to be very personal (Graves, 1990; Thompson, 1990). Donald Graves (1990) comments that letters from children to teachers progress from accounts written in a "to whom it may concern" tone to highly personal, intimate exchanges between teacher and child. And finally, one highly popular journal-writing format is the Quick Write, in which children at various times during the day or a lesson respond to their learning in a three- or four-minute quick write. All journal entries are dated.

Journal writing is adaptable to many different teaching/learning environments and virtually all ages; you will therefore find it quite easy to adapt journal writing to meet the learning needs of your own students. To the extent possible, journal writing (like the writing workshop) should happen on a predictable, scheduled routine; children benefit from writing in their journals at a given time every day for precisely the same reason they benefit from having writing workshop happen every day: They soon begin planning and rehearsing for the journal writing they know is to come.

Because journal writing involves written conversations between teachers and individual children, you must read what children write and respond in writing to them. You needn't respond to *everything* children write in their journals, but you do need to read journals frequently and regularly, and write responses. An important consideration here is that journal reading and response *must be done overnight or over the weekend* so that journals are back in students' hands the following school day. A reasonable schedule, if children are writing in their journals every day, is for you to read each child's journal about once a week. Given that, reading one-fifth of the class's journals each night seems equally reasonable (one-fifth of 30 journals is only 6 journals a night).

As you consider using journals as part of subject area instruction, you need to answer some important questions and make decisions based upon your answers: (1) What is your purpose for instituting journal writing with subject area instruction? (2) How often do you want children to write? Daily? Various times during the day? All subject areas? (3) How shall writing be focused? Will you let children write anything they want in free-form style? Do you want to use prompts? If so, what kinds of prompts? (4) Where will journals be housed? Will you let children take them home overnight? What will you do if a journal is lost? (5) What other rules or standards do you wish to accompany journal writing?

One of the greatest advantages that journals offer is the opportunity for children to wonder, ruminate, work through difficult ideas, record their thinking, and confide in you their important thoughts and big ideas; of equal importance, children's thinking, writing, and notetaking are preserved, so that entries may be revisited and possibly used at a time well after they were originally written. Journals are private and personal, and therefore highly confidential; no one should feel free to share journal excerpts without the express permission from the person or persons involved in the journal entry.

Learning Logs

Learning logs are a special kind of journal (Blake, 1990; Chard, 1990). They are more specifically focused on subject area learning than journals are, and may or may not be used in the conversational manner that journals assume. Learning logs are perfect places for children to record brainstorming they do for content DR-TAs or K-W-L Plus and to keep maps. Much learning log writing comes from prompts that teachers provide before, during, and after learning events; prompts may be both content-specific ("What is a

457

habitat?") or procedural ("What was the most successful part of your group's work today?"). As with journals, each learning log entry is dated.

A key to the success of learning logs is that teachers' writing prompts are generative and contribute to rich learning experiences. Very frequently, learning log prompts ask children to think about what they already know about a topic and serve as the starting point for discussion and reading, e.g., "List everything you know about fractions." "Jot down everything you think of when I say 'geography.'" "Describe why you think it's warmer in the summer and cooler in the winter." Other learning log prompts focus on children's learning goals: "What would you like to learn about Native Americans?" "What do you want to know about electricity?" "What are some questions you have about the solar system?" "What do you feel you still need to learn about solving equations?" And yet others are more expressive: "Pretend you are a delegate to the Constitutional Convention of 1787. Write a letter home describing your experiences and participation at the convention." "Write a letter to our mayor describing what you think are the greatest strengths and weaknesses of our community." "Write an account of how your family celebrates holidays or other special events." Learning log prompts may take many different forms and are limited only by topic scope and teachers' imaginations.

Double Entry Journals (DEJs)

Double Entry Journals (DEJs) (Vaughn, 1990) are yet another special kind of journal (and by now you are probably experienced DEJ writers). DEJs require spiral or loose-leaf notebooks that allow children to begin with their journal open to two facing pages. The left page is for children's initial response to writing prompts, e.g., "List or draw everything you know about trees." Children are encouraged to draw, doodle, create maps, make notes, or any other kind of notetaking or writing they wish to do on the left page. The right page is for "cooking" the ideas jotted or drawn on the left page (Vaughn, 1990) and arriving at new insights and ideas. Between left-page brainstorming and right-page consolidation of knowledge, a learning event of some sort—reading, demonstrations, simulations, discussions, etc—takes place that encourages construction of new knowledge from the combination of prior knowledge and the learning event itself. Many times, teachers provide writing prompts for both left-page and right-page writing, and these prompts may be both content-specific and procedural (as with learning log prompts). In fact, any type of learning log prompt is just as appropriate for a DEJ.

One of the great advantages of Double Entry Journals is that they quickly become useful guides for children's subject area reading. The teacher develops a prompt for a DEJ left-page entry prior to the reading, and another prompt for a DEJ right-page entry after reading. To do this, teachers have to sort out what it is they want children to know or be able to do after the reading (i.e., the lesson objectives) in order to develop prompts that focus children in that direction. DEJs are also very effective for showing children how to get from notes jotted down during brainstorming (left page) to written analyses and accounts based upon those notes (right page). DEJs thus become a means for teaching children how to develop and organize their thinking and learning.

Beginning Researchers

Donna Maxim (1990) describes a project she once launched to move her third-grade students away from the traditional informational report-writing mode (plagiarism, tracing, and tedium) and teach them how to become real researchers. Maxim developed three phases of the program: first, she taught students how to take notes and develop research ideas from listening; second, she developed their ability to read without notetaking and, subsequently, to develop notes; and third, she taught students how to initiate and carry through a research plan by actually implementing it.

Phase One: Taking Notes and Developing Research Ideas from Listening. The program begins by teaching children how to take notes without copying ("reading and writing at the same time," as Maxim calls it) through the simple expedient of teaching notetaking by reading to students rather than having them do the reading themselves. The teacher reads a book or book section to the class. The book may be nonfiction or fiction, but should have sufficient informational content for notetaking to be relatively easy. After the reading, the children are asked to record in their logs (1) facts and information they recall from the reading, followed by (2) questions and speculations these facts and information generate. (The first time you use this, it might be a good idea to go through the process in a whole-class discussion using chart paper to recall facts and write questions so that children can see how the notetaking is done). After each listening-notetaking experience, children share their individual notes and questions with the class, and the teacher leads discussion in which children speculate as to what research projects might grow out of the information and questions they've collected.

Any number of books are appropriate for this exercise. You may find that nonfiction informational books are particularly good for initiating notetaking. Such books as Ruth Heller's *The Reason for a Flower* (1983) and *Plants That Never Bloom* (1986) are perfect for younger children. *Sharks* (Berger, 1987), *Anne Frank: The Diary of a Young Girl* (Frank, 1967), *Farewell to Manzanar* (Houston & Houston, 1973), and biographies of various kinds are appropriate for older children. Don't limit the reading to non-fiction, however; any number of fiction books have social and/or scientific import and are highly useful for stimulating research projects. McCloskey's *Make Way for Ducklings* (1941), Byrd Baylor's *Everybody Needs a Rock*

(1974), Winter's *Follow the Drinking Gourd* (1988), O'Dell's *Island of the Blue Dolphins* (1960), and Jean Craighead George's *Julie of the Wolves* (1972) and *My Side of the Mountain* (1959) are certainly all reasonable choices. Many, many other books are available. We recommend that you gather lots of books related to the area of study you're targeting the research projects for, and that you read daily from this pool and have students do the note-taking and question generation at the end of each reading.

Phase Two: Reading and Taking Notes. After children become quite good at listening and taking notes, they're ready to learn reading and note-taking skills. This phase begins by distributing informational magazines to the children. (Maxim used back issues of *Zoobook*, published by Wildlife Education Ltd.; any number of other excellent informational magazines are quite likely available in schools.) The children are told not to open their magazine but to look at the cover and generate questions they think they'll find answers to inside. Questions are recorded in students' logs. Then, the children are asked to leave their desks and their lists and pencils, and go sit someplace else in the room to read their magazines for ten minutes. At the end of ten minutes, they *leave their magazines at the place where they were reading*, return to their desks, and write out any answers they found to their list of questions.

Maxim reports that the children found this exercise very difficult; they wanted to be able to look back at their reading and do the kind of copy-notetaking they'd become so used to. We feel sure that you're likely to encounter some resistance to the activity as well, and we further predict that, the older your students and more entrenched their encyclopedia-copying habits are, the stronger the resistance will be. We encourage you to stand firm in this. It will take several repetitions of the exercise for children to realize that they can, indeed, take notes without copying. Keep the source material well within a range of reasonable difficulty (a good reason for using magazines) and repeat the activity frequently.

Phase Three: Initiating and Carrying Out Research. As we suggested earlier, it is useful for the class to be engaged in a unit of study throughout the period that the children are learning about notetaking from listening and reading. It is also important that the students see how their newly learned notetaking skills might be applied to a project in that unit of study. As many resources as possible should be made available if they are appropriate within the context of the unit—slide shows, speakers from educational organizations and governmental offices (e.g., Department of Forestry), field trips, movies and documentaries on videotape, library resources both at school and in the community, and so forth.

In the course of this study, and as children become acquainted with various materials and resources, they should begin recording in their logs ideas and question(s) that they deem worthy of further investigation. Through large class discussion and individual conferences, help children frame their research question(s), consider and list possible resources, and decide on their plan for the research itself. The children then launch their projects and carry them out. Implementing the subject area writing workshop (as we discussed earlier in this chapter) is highly appropriate at this point.

Donna Maxim's approach for teaching children how to become researchers is, we think, a particularly sound practice. Essentially, it provides guided, sheltered simulation of a productive research process for children to engage in concurrent with a unit of study for which they will subsequently do research. Implementing this approach is not difficult, but it does require planning and thought.

Guided Writing

Guided writing (Prenn & Honeychurch, 1990) is an activity for developing children's ability to think about subject area topics through expressive writing. **Expressive writing** is "thinking aloud on paper," writing in which personal thoughts and feelings about topics and ideas are explored (Britton, Burgess, Martin, McLeod, & Rosen, 1975; Prenn & Honeychurch, 1990). The goal of expressive writing in subject area learning is to give children the opportunity to connect with learning topics by voicing their own internal thoughts, experiences, and opinions. Expressive writing is also valuable as the basis for subsequent study and more formal writing.

Doing Research

Guided writing is particularly useful at the beginning of a unit of study; however, it may be used periodically throughout. Writing journals or learning logs are useful places for children to do the actual writing. In guided writing, the teacher reads a series of related writing prompts that ask students to assume roles and imagine scenes in a topic-related mini-drama. Questions within the prompt guide children in exploration of their knowledge base and experiences, their feelings and beliefs, and view of themselves in relationship to the topic. Below is a series of guided writing prompts that might be used in an intermediate grade unit on space; the prompts are designed to be used sequentially in one writing session.

Prompt 1: You have decided to apply for the U.S. astronaut training program. A college graduate and highly trained scientist, you've decided that the astronaut training program is perfect for you. What are your reasons for making this decision? What do you expect the program and astronaut career will bring for you? What do you want to achieve as an astronaut?

Prompt 2: You have recently completed your astronaut training and are ready for your first extended trip into space. Your mission is a scientific one, and you are responsible for many experiments. What do you expect the experience of extended space travel to be like? What studies and work will you do? What will you say to your family and friends before leaving on this trip?

Prompt 3: You are now in space, and have been for several days. Earlier today, you and two other astronauts did a "space walk" and performed experiments outside your ship. What do you see and feel? Describe the Earth as you see it now. What was your space walk like? How are your experiments going?

Prompt 4: You have returned from your mission and are going through the routine debriefing session with other scientists and officials at the space study center. What will you tell them about your experiences? What results did you get in your experiments? What did you learn on your space walk?

Prompt 5: You, the highly trained astronaut, are standing in your backyard. It is a clear, starry night. What do you see and feel? What do you know about the great space above you? How do you describe it now? What are your next plans for your career as an astronaut?

Prenn and Honeychurch recommend three guidelines for guided writing lessons:

1. Tell the children that the writing they're doing here is not going to be graded.
2. Instruct children to write immediately after the prompt is read, and reread the prompt questions a few times as the children write; keep the pace moving and let children know you're going to move to the next prompt when approximately two-thirds of the class have finished writing.
3. Have children share their writing with the class.

HOW TO DO . . . .

BEGINNING RESEARCH

1. Decide unit of study topic and learning objectives.

2. Collect many and diverse resources for the unit. Make arrangements for visiting speakers, field trips, and so forth.

3. Collect many books, nonfiction and fiction, that relate to the unit.

4. Mark the reading passages in the books and determine at least the beginning order in which you wish to read books.

5. Arrange for children to all be supplied with learning logs.

PHASE I: LISTENING AND NOTETAKING

6. Begin the listening and notetaking phase. You may want to first demonstrate the process by having children contribute notes aloud, record them on chart paper, and then generate questions as a group. Remember:

   a. All learning log entries are dated.

   b. Children take notes of facts and information they got from the reading *after* the reading is finished. All notes are recorded in learning logs.

   c. Notes are followed by questions and ideas for further research.

7. Continue reading to children each day from a variety of the books you've collected. Have them listen, take notes, and generate questions each day.

PHASE II: READING AND NOTETAKING

8. Find sufficient copies of an informational magazine for each child to have a copy.

9. Distribute magazines asking children *not* to open them.

10. Have children look at the front of their magazines and generate questions that they think will be answered by an article inside. Questions are recorded in learning logs.

11. Have children leave their desks, logs, and pencils and find another place in the room to read their magazines. Let children read for ten minutes.

12. Have children *leave their magazines where they read*, return to their desks, and take notes from memory about the answers they got to the questions they'd generated.

13. Lead a discussion in which children share the notes they took.

14. Repeat the exercise using other magazines and moving to textbook text when it seems appropriate.

PHASE III: INITIATING AND CARRYING OUT RESEARCH

15. Concurrent with Phases I and II, involve students in a number of experiences and events related to the unit of study. Tell children that they will be doing research later in the unit.

16. Introduce children to resources in the school and community libraries.

17. Toward the end of Phase II, when children have become confident of their ability to take notes without copying and are well acquainted with materials and unit research possibilities, work with individual children in developing their own research projects.

Prenn and Honeychurch also note that guided writing prompts do not always have to be written by the teacher; vivid written accounts of historical events or adventures (e.g., a biography of Harriet Tubman or Louis Pasteur) may serve as prompts for expressive writing as well.

Advantages and Values of Guiding Children's Subject Area Writing

One of the greatest strengths of the instructional approaches we've discussed here is the ease with which all may be implemented. None requires much in the way of equipment, materials, or resources beyond those needed for a subject area unit of study. Every instructional approach in this section could be easily incorporated into the writing workshop; in fact, much of it grew from writing workshop practices.

Guiding children's writing in subject areas is really quite important. First and foremost, you need to convince yourself how educationally valuable it is for children to write in *every subject area*; they need to write about the process they experience when working through their mathematics problems just as surely as they need to write science lab reports. We haven't emphasized nonacademic subject areas, but children really should have the opportunity to write about their own experiences with physical movement, music, and art. Children who are immersed in writing, children who write about what they're learning every day, and children who become increasingly fluent writers will succeed in subject area learning far better than children who do not.

GUIDING CHILDREN'S READING AND WRITING WITH THEME CYCLES AND PROJECT-BASED INSTRUCTION IN SUBJECT AREAS

We have already discussed at some length in Chapter 7 the rationale and structure of theme cycles and project-based learning. One of the most well-known curriculum approaches that embodies the notion of theme cycles and project-based learning is Foxfire, a way of teaching and learning developed by Elliott Wiggenton in 1966 (Payne, 1992).

> *Foxfire is an inconspicuous fungus that grows on decaying matter along the dark floors of the Appalachian forest. Inconspicuous, that is, until it encounters a chance beam of light. Being phosphorescent, it beams back a wispy blue-green light of its own, turning the forest floor into a seeming reflection of the summer night sky.*
>
> *Foxfire is also an approach to teaching that sprang up in the wooded hills of Appalachia. . . . [I]t is also inconspicuous, requiring neither shiny new buildings nor high tech equipment. But look into a Foxfire student's eyes, and you are likely to see a sparkle equaled only by a midsummer night sky in the country. (Payne, 1992, p. 4)*

The Foxfire approach is founded on the notion that learning is most productive in an environment marked by child-generated projects and energetic inquiry into the world around us. Wiggenton started Foxfire when he was faced with recalcitrant, difficult students who literally would not sit still for his traditional teaching approach. Wiggenton immersed his students into a broad-based, year-long study of the "old ways" of Rabun Gap, Georgia, that included hours of interviews with parents, grandparents, and community members; visits to watch soap being made and furniture constructed; days of planning, interview transcription, and writing about what they had learned. Foxfire is built on the Eleven Core Practices (Payne, 1992):

1. All work must flow from student desire.
2. Teacher acts as collaborator and guide.
3. The academic integrity of the work is clear.
4. All work is characterized by student action.
5. There is teamwork and peer teaching.
6. There is a tie to the community.
7. There is an audience (someone who really wants the product).
8. Work spirals naturally from the known to the unknown.
9. There is an aesthetic component to the work.
10. There is time for reflection.
11. There is a thorough evaluation of the work, the skills acquired, and the changes in student attitude.

465

Sinatra, Beaudry, Stahl-Gemake, and Guastello (1990) describe an urban sort of Foxfire project they developed with middle-school children in which the children were placed in pairs with the task of exploring various aspects of their neighborhood. The students were to begin their project by planning and taking snapshots of the parts of the neighborhood they wished to investigate. (The teacher in this project had cameras donated by a camera manufacturer; disposable cameras are readily available, relatively cheap, and are now being recycled.)

To carry out this project, children work with their partner to plan the photo shots they want to take and then go out into the community to do the photography. Upon receiving the developed photos, the partners are responsible for organizing and producing a storyboard to tell the story they have planned about the neighborhood; the storyboard then serves as the outline for a written essay the partners produce to accompany the storyboard itself. Sinatra et al. call this a "visual literacy" approach because of the prominence of the photographs and the way in which the visual aspect of the project supports literacy. They comment specifically regarding the value of the visual elements of the project for ESL students (1991, p. 613).

Theme cycles, project-based learning, and visual literacy approaches are complex learning events that are not at all unlike Foxfire. What is important here is to understand that such learning experiences increase the content children learn, as well as increasing the development of literacy abilities in content areas. This is truly what we're talking about in education when we discuss the "integrated curriculum." The integrated curriculum is *not* about simply combining different subject area instruction so that one subject occurs in the presence of others; rather, the truly integrated curriculum embodies the kind of inquiry we discussed in Chapter 7 (Harste, 1994) and the kind of complex learning experiences we've just been discussing. Regie Routman (1991) recommends that, when planning for this kind of integrated learning experiences, teachers need to ask and answer a number of important questions about the project they're getting ready to launch:

- What important concepts do I want students to learn?
- Why should students learn these concepts? Are they intellectually rich and important?
- What learning experiences will help develop these conceptual understandings?
- What skills and strategies am I helping develop?
- Am I setting up a climate that encourages inquiry and choice?
- Am I putting in place alternative evaluation procedures?
- What student attitudes am I fostering?

We like Routman's questions because they help teachers sort out and specify what it is they're doing and why they're doing it. Clarity of purpose is very important when planning complex learning experiences.

We hope you will do some form of project-based learning in your classroom each year. You may want to start on a small scale and enlarge or build your scope as you experience success. That's fine. The key here is letting children decide what it is they want to learn, guiding them as they plan their own learning, and guiding literacy events and processes along the way. When this happens, you provide the opportunity for students to *really learn*—to be engaged, eager, active learners determined to find the answers to the questions they've raised.

STUDY SKILLS AND SUBJECT AREA READING AND WRITING

Because we made such a point earlier that the study skills approach to subject area learning was not sufficient, we thought it important to talk for a moment about the rightful place of study skills in subject area learning and the most effective instructional practices for teaching study skills. First, we acknowledge that there are definable study skills, for example:

1. Understanding and using book parts (tables of contents, indices, marginalia, glossaries, etc.).
2. Alphabetizing, using head notes and pronunciation guides, understanding abbreviations in reference sources (dictionaries, encyclopedias, atlases, etc.).
3. Using other references (telephone directories, newspapers, etc.).
4. Using the library (card files, data bases, Dewey Decimal System, etc.).
5. Adjusting reading to purpose (skimming, scanning, intensive reading).
6. Reading graphs, charts, maps, globes, and other pictorial information.
7. Notetaking.
8. Finding main ideas, separating main ideas from important details.
9. Outlining.
10. Summarizing.
11. Report writing.

All of these study skills are important and useful abilities for children to develop. Our view is that the instructional strategies we've discussed in this chapter have these study skills (and others) embedded in them in such a way that the skills themselves become a natural and useful part of the learning process. We do not believe that isolated instruction and drill on study skills is very effective; we *do* believe it is far better to build skill instruction and practice directly into purposeful learning, as Donna Maxim (1990) did in

467

her approach to beginning research. Content DR-TAs, writing workshop, DIAs, journal writing, project-based learning, and all the other instructional strategies we've discussed here provide many opportunities for teachers to observe children, noting whether and how they're using study strategies, and teach those that need to be taught as students need them.

To teach study skills in an embedded rather than isolated manner, you need, first, to be aware of which study skills are appropriate for your students and for the ongoing work of class or individual projects. Any number of lists are available in curriculum guides, published language arts materials, and books such as this (all told, our list is relatively comprehensive). Second, you need to discover what study skills children already have and make decisions about what skills need to be taught. This is most easily done using the format described in Chapter 7 for evaluating children's writing skills. Draw a grid with the children's names down the left margin and targeted study skills listed across the top. Observe children as they read, write, and do research; look to see what study skills they have and document those. Look also to determine which ones they need to learn; teach these in mini-lessons or individual conferences as children need them.

Embedding study-skills instruction in the instruction intended to create thoughtful readers and writers ensures that study skills assume their rightful place as necessary and important *parts* of reading and writing processes, but that they do not become instructional goals in and of themselves. Study skills help thoughtful readers and writers read and write, but attention to them in the classroom must be contextually situated—that is, study skills must be taught and learned in the context of their immediate use. If we isolate study skills and teach them without apparent context, and if we make study skills the central focus of what we do to teach subject area reading and writing, we are likely to forget about or obscure the many other transactions and interactions with text that are necessary for children to construct full, rich meaning in subject areas.

Subject Area Literacy
A Summary

In this chapter, we have looked at ways for teachers to guide children's reading and writing in subject areas. Central to the rationale here is that children construct meaning in the act of reading and writing; instruction must therefore promote rich reading and writing experiences.

The content DR-TA, GMA, and VSS combination, along with K-W-L Plus, the Directed Inquiry Activity (DIA), and reading response groups are all useful strategies for guiding children's subject area reading. All of them have the advantage of promoting deep, rich understanding of text by helping children make connections between their prior knowledge base, information in the text, and information they gain from one another.

The writing workshop and many of its elements—journals, learning logs, Double Entry Journals (DEJs), research skills, and guided writing—are recommended for developing children's writing in subject areas and as alternatives to the traditional informational report that has dominated subject area instruction in elementary classrooms. Important here is the understanding that writing is far more than simply a means for recording what was learned; rather, learners learn by writing. Writing, therefore, needs to permeate subject area instruction.

Theme cycles, project-based learning, the Foxfire approach, and visual literacy projects are all ways to bring reading, writing, and subject area learning into an integrated whole. Each of these approaches assumes that children should make important decisions about what is to be learned, and that real learning grows from the complex events of research and project completion.

Study skills are necessary, but not sufficient, components of learning processes. Study skills are most efficiently learned as children need them to carry out self-determined projects. Rather than isolated instruction and drill, study skills instruction may be embedded in full, rich instructional approaches that guide children toward the end of becoming expert, thoughtful readers and writers in subject areas.

DOUBLE ENTRY JOURNAL

Consider ways you can guide children's literacy learning in content areas to make their experiences reading and writing in content areas rich and full. What specific strategies seem suited to your style and to your beliefs about literacy acquisition and development? How are the experiences these strategies create different from your own experience in school? What strategies or activities can you use to eliminate round-robin oral reading and report writing from your classroom?

Supporting Activities

1. Return to the "personal reading history and profile" rating scale in content area reading that you responded to earlier in this chapter (see "thoughtful readers" discussion). Reflect for a moment on your reading ability in your *least* able and *most* able areas. Now, recall your best teachers in content areas from elementary grades through high school. What teaching characteristics sets these teachers apart from your worst teachers? What match do you find between the characteristics that distinguish your best teachers and those features found in Figure 9-2, which describes what teachers need to do to guide students' learning from text? Discuss your responses with a class partner.

2. Briefly reread Nancie Atwell's report writing experience, which parallels an experience many of us have had, presented earlier in this chapter. Identify the key instructional and learning problems that this type of instruction illustrates. How does this teacher's report writing approach differ from our recommendations on instruction for beginning researchers? Quickly jot down your ideas and discuss them with a class partner.

3. Locate a high-interest content article or a chapter from a social studies or science text on a topic appropriate for the grade level of most interest to you. Quickly review our discussion of the integrated content DR-TA, GMA (Study Map), and VSS. Now develop an instructional plan to use these combined strategies to teach the content area material you have selected. What value do you see in combining these approaches in instruction? What limitations? Share your plan and ideas with a class partner.

4. You have become familiar with the use of the Double Entry Journal (DEJ) from your experience with chapters in this text. Obtain a copy of a social studies or science textbook at the grade level that is of most interest to you. Carefully read the first two chapters of this book and identify what it is that you want your children to know and be able to do after reading. Now design your DEJ by using these objectives as the basis to create your "prior reading prompts" and "after-reading prompts" to focus the readers' purpose. Discuss and refine your prompts with a class partner.

5. Reflect on your specialized content knowledge to identify topics in which you have both expertise and high interest. This knowledge and your interest areas may have been developed from travel, special skill and talent areas, and your academic preparation. Select one topic that is of high interest to you and that you believe would hold interest for students at your favorite grade level. Reexamine our discussion on theme cycles and project-based instruction that develops ideas from the highly successful Foxfire approach. Sketch out a possible unit of instruction using the launch questions proposed in this discussion by Regie Routman. Share your ideas with a class partner and make refinements based on your discussion.

Applebee, A. N. (1981). *Writing in the secondary school.* Urbana, IL: National Council of Teacher of English.

Atwell, N. (1987). *In the middle.* Portsmouth, NH: Heinemann.

Atwell, N. (Ed.). (1990). *Coming to know: Writing to learn in the intermediate grades.* Portsmouth, NH: Heinemann.

Beach, J. D. (1983). Teaching students to write informational reports. *Elementary School Journal, 84,* 213–220.

Blake, M. (1990). Learning logs in the upper elementary grades. In N. Atwell (Ed.), *Coming to know: Writing to learn in the intermediate grades* (pp. 53–60). Portsmouth, NH: Heinemann.

Britton, J., Burgess, T., Martin, N., McLeod, A., & Rosen, H. (1975). *The development of writing abilities.* London: Macmillan Education.

Carr, E., & Ogle, D. (1987). K-W-L Plus: A strategy for comprehension and summarization. *Journal of Reading, 30,* 626–631.

Chard, N. (1990). How learning logs change teaching. In N. Atwell (Ed.), *Coming to know: Writing to learn in the intermediate grades* (pp. 61–68). Portsmouth, NH: Heinemann.

Collins, P. J. (1990). Bridging the gap. In N. Atwell (Ed.), *Coming to know: Writing to learn in the intermediate grades* (pp. 17–31). Portsmouth, NH: Heinemann.

Davidson, J. L. (1982). The group mapping activity for instruction in reading and thinking. *Journal of Reading, 26,* 52–56.

Eeds, M., & Wells, D. (1989). Grand conversations: An exploration of meaning construction in literature study groups. *Research in the Teaching of English, 23,* 4–29.

Farnan, N. (1992). Promoting connections between reader and text: A reader response approach. *The California Reader, 25,* 6–8.

Graves, D. H. (1983). *Writing: Teachers and children at work.* Portsmouth, NH: Heinemann.

Graves, D. H. (1990). *Discover your own literacy.* Portsmouth, NH: Heinemann.

Haggard, M. R. (1985). An interactive strategies approach to content reading. *Journal of Reading, 29,* 204–210.

Haggard, M. R. (1989). Instructional strategies for developing student interest in content area subjects. In D. Lapp, J. Flood, & N. Farnan (Eds.), *Content area reading/learning: Instructional strategies* (pp. 70–80). Englewood Cliffs, NJ: Prentice-Hall.

Harste, J. C. (1994). Literacy as curricular conversations about knowledge, inquiry, and morality. In R. B. Ruddell, M. R. Ruddell, & H. Singer (Eds.), *Theoretical models and processes of reading* (4th ed.) (pp. 1220–1242). Newark, DE: International Reading Association.

Langer, J. A., & Applebee, A. N. (1987). *How writing shapes thinking* (NCTE Research Report No. 22). Urbana, IL: National Council of Teachers of English.

Martin, N., D'Arcy, P., Newton, B., & Parker, R. (1976). *Writing and learning across the curriculum.* London: Ward Lock Educational.

Maxim, D. (1990). Beginning researchers. In N. Atwell (Ed.), *Coming to know: Writing to learn in the intermediate grades* (pp. 3–16). Portsmouth, NH: Heinemann.

O'Flahavan, J. (1989). *An exploration of the effects of participant structure upon literacy development in reading group discussion* (Doctoral dissertation, University of Illinois at Urbana-Champaign).

Payne, A. C. (Fall, 1992). Mountainfire Foxfire. *West Virginia University Alumni Magazine, 15,* 4–6.

Pearson, P. D., Roehler, L. R., Dole, J. A., & Duffy, G. G. (1990). *Developing expertise in reading comprehension: What should be taught? How should it be taught?* (Tech. Rep. No. 512) Champaign, IL: University of Illinois at Urbana-Champaign, Center for the Study of Reading.

Prenn, M. C., & Honeychurch, J. C. (1990). Enhancing content area learning through expressive writing. In N. L. Cecil (Ed.), *Literacy in the '90s* (pp. 114–121). Dubuque, IA: Kendall/Hunt.

Raines, B. (1991). *Response and collaboration in literature discussion groups: A two-year study of an intermediate grade classroom* (Master's thesis, Sonoma State University, Rohnert Park, CA).

Routman, R. (1991). *Invitations.* Portsmouth, NH: Heinemann.

Ruddell, M. R. (1993). *Teaching content reading and writing.* Boston: Allyn & Bacon.

Ruddell, R. B., & Unrau, N. (1994). Reading as a meaning construction process: The reader, the text, and the teacher. In R. B. Ruddell, M. R. Ruddell, & H. Singer (Eds.), *Theoretical models and processes of reading* (4th ed.) (pp. 996–1056). Newark, DE: International Reading Association.

Sinatra, R., Beaudry, J. S., Stahl-Gemake, J., & Guastello, E. F. (1990). Combining visual literacy, text understanding, and writing for culturally diverse students. *Journal of Reading, 33,* 612–617.

Thomas, K. J. (1986). The Directed Inquiry Activity: An instructional procedure for content reading. In E. K. Dishner, T. W. Bean, J. E. Readence, & D. W. Moore (Eds.), *Reading in the content areas* (2nd ed.) (pp. 278–281). Dubuque, IA: Kendall/Hunt.

Thompson, A. (1990). Thinking and writing in learning logs. In N. Atwell (Ed.), *Coming to know: Writing to learn in the intermediate grades.* Portsmouth, NH: Heinemann.

Vaughn, C. L. (1990). Knitting writing: The Double-Entry Journal. In N. Atwell (Ed.), *Coming to know: Writing to learn in the intermediate grades.* Portsmouth, NH: Heinemann.

Zinsser, W. (1988). *Writing to learn.* New York: Harper & Row.

Baylor, B. (1974). *Everybody needs a rock.* New York: Macmillan.

Berger, G. (1987). *Sharks.* New York: Doubleday.

Frank, A. (1967). *Anne Frank: The diary of a young girl.* New York: Doubleday.

George, J. C. (1959). *My side of the mountain.* New York: E. P. Dutton.

George, J. C. (1972). *Julie of the wolves.* New York: Harper & Row.

Heller, R. (1983). *The reason for a flower.* New York: Grosset & Dunlap.

Heller, R. (1986). *Plants that never bloom.* New York: Grossett & Dunlap.

Houston, J. W., & Houston, J. D. (1973). *Farewell to Manzanar.* New York: Houghton Mifflin.

McCloskey, R. (1941). *Make way for ducklings.* New York: Viking-Penguin.

O'Dell, S. (1960). *Island of the blue dolphins.* New York: Dell.

Winter, J. (1988). *Follow the drinking gourd.* New York: Knopf.

CHAPTER 9	CONTENT DR-TA, GMA, AND VSS	K-W-L PLUS	DIA
FOCUS ON	Content reading, writing, and learning	Content reading, writing, and learning	Content reading, writing, and learning
GUIDES STUDENTS	Before, during, and after reading; before writing	Before, during, and after reading; before writing	Before and during reading; before writing
USE TO PLAN	Lessons, units	Lessons, units	Lessons, units
MAY BE USED	Whole class, small groups	Whole class, small groups	Whole class, small groups
MAY BE COMBINED WITH (KNOWN STRATEGIES)	Thematic units, writing workshop, project-based units, theme cycles	Thematic units, writing workshop project-based units, theme cycles	Thematic units, writing workshop
MATERIALS PREPARATION	Light to moderate	Moderate	Moderate
OTHER PREPARATION	Light	Light	Moderate
OUTSIDE RESOURCES	Useful	Useful	Necessary
HOW TO DO	Pages 447–448	Page 451	Page 452

Building Tables "grow" or build, successively from chapter to chapter. They tell you (1) the focus of each strategy introduced in a chapter; (2) how the strategy is best used; (3) what strategies from previous chapters combine well with new ones; (4) preparation requirements; (5) additional resources needed; and (6) the page on which a strategy's How-to-Do appears.

READING RESPONSE GROUPS	JOURNAL WRITING	LEARNING LOGS	DEJ	BEGINNING RESEARCH
Content reading, writing, and learning	Response to reading and learning	Recording and summarizing learning	Connecting ideas and concepts	Developing research abilities
During and after reading; before writing	After reading and learning event	After reading and learning event	Before and after reading and learning event	Before, during, and after reading and writing
Lessons, units, yearly activities	Lessons, units, yearly activities	Lessons, units, yearly activities	Lessons, units, yearly activities	Units and yearly activities
Whole class, cooperative groups	Whole class, small groups	Whole class, small groups	Whole class, small groups	Whole class, small groups
DR-TA, DRA, response journals, Content DR-TA GMA VSS, K-W-L Plus, project-based units, theme cycles	DR-TA, DRA, GMA, VSS, InQuest, thematic units, K-W-L Plus, theme cycles	DR-TA, DRA, GMA, VSS, thematic units, K-W-L Plus	DR-TA, DRA, GMA, VSS, thematic units, K-W-L Plus	Thematic units, project-based units, theme cycles
Light to moderate	None	None	None	Light
Light to moderate	None	Moderate	Moderate	Moderate
Useful	Not needed	Useful	Useful	Necessary
Page 454				Pages 463–464

CHAPTER 10

UNDERSTANDING LANGUAGE, CULTURAL, AND ACHIEVEMENT DIVERSITY IN THE CLASSROOM

INTRODUCTION

The student population in our schools today has greater diversity in language, culture, and achievement than at any previous time in the history of our country. In 1992, for example, over one million new immigrants arrived in the United States. Of this number, approximately 800,000 were documented and at least 200,000 are thought to have settled undocumented (Kershner, 1993). According to the Immigration and Naturalization Service, some 8.9 million people have immigrated to this country legally over the past decade. It is estimated, however, that an additional 3 million have entered the country undocumented (Mydnas, 1993). While immigration prior to the middle of this century was primarily from Europe, most recent immigrants are from Latin America, Asia, the former Soviet Union, Iran, and India. Like the earlier immigrants, they come in search of jobs, political freedom, and economic security. Many settle in large urban areas such as New York, Miami, Houston, Los Angeles, San Francisco, and Honolulu, while others settle in rural agricultural areas. Future immigrants can certainly be expected from politically disrupted Eastern European and other countries.

Our most recent census indicates that 15 percent of our total population has a non-English-speaking background. Over 3 million minority-language speakers are found in California, New York, and Texas alone, and over one million are located in Illinois, Florida, New Jersey, Pennsylvania, and Massachusetts (Kershner, 1993; Rotbert, 1982; Waggoner, 1984). It is projected that by the year 2000, there will be approximately forty million people in the United States whose language background is not English. Further, and of great significance to your teaching, 3.4 million of these will be school-age children between five and fourteen years of age. Projections indicate that 1.7 million of this number will live in California, New York, and Texas, with the remaining 1.7 million distributed throughout urban and rural regions of the country (Ramirez, 1985).

IMPACT ON THE CLASSROOM

This recent immigrant diversity will undoubtedly have an impact on your classroom regardless of what grade level you teach. You can expect students who speak a dialect different from your own, students who are bilingual, and students who speak little or no English. You can also expect these children, along with many children born in the United States, to represent different cultures that hold varied and different expectations for your role as teacher and for students' school experiences.

In addition to the rich cultural and language diversity in schools, you should anticipate finding students of all cultures and language backgrounds who range from those with specific learning disabilities to those identified as gifted. Not unexpectedly, you will find substantial achievement diversity across your classroom. All these factors affect students' learning needs. Your task is to create a supportive instructional environment that will make provisions for diverse learning needs. The purpose of this chapter is to assist you in this effort. In this chapter, we will explore the following four areas:

1. Understanding the nature of the language and cultural diversity.
2. Learning and acquiring instructional strategies that can be used effectively in teaching students with language and cultural differences.
3. Recognizing and understanding the learning diversity of students with physical, developmental, emotional, and other learning differences, including giftedness.
4. Creating a multicultural environment conducive to the reading and writing development of the diverse range of children in your classroom.

Understanding the Nature of Language and Cultural Diversity

It is important to examine your own attitudes and feelings toward the language and cultural diversity of your students. Each of us possesses values that influence our attitudes and beliefs about language use, languages, and cultural groups different from our own. Consider, for example, the following interchange described by Piestrup (1973). This first-grade teacher has prepared sentences on strips of tagboard from a story, and the children are asked to read each sentence. The teacher has asked Lionel (C1), an African-American child, to read the first sentence. The text being read aloud is identified by italics.

T: This one, Lionel. This way, Lionel. Come on, you're right here. Hurry up.

C1: *Dey—*

T: Get your finger out of your mouth.

C1: *Call—*

T: Start again.

C1: *Dey call, "What i' it? What is it?"*

T: What's this word?

C2: *Dey.*

C1: *Dat.*

T: What is it?

C2: *Dat.*

C3: *Dey.*

C4: (Laughs)

C1: *Dey.*

T: Look at my tongue. *They.*

C1: *They.*

T: *They.* Look at my tongue. (between her teeth)

C1: *They.*

T: That's right. Say it again.

C1: *They.*

T: *They.* OK. Pretty good. OK, Lionel.

(Piestrup, 1973, pp. 54–55)

What reaction do you have to this interchange? What understanding of Black English is reflected in the teacher's response to Lionel? What attitude toward Lionel's language diversity is reflected in the teacher's response? What effect will this type of interaction have on Lionel's comprehension? On his attitude toward group participation?

479

Contrast the instructional episode above with the following story discussion episode from a second-grade classroom as reported by Au (1980). The children are native speakers of Hawaiian Creole English. The central character in the story line is concerned about the outcome of using the frog he has found for bait. The teacher is identified by T and the students are identified as A, V, L, and S. The bracket marks show the children's overlapping speech.

T: If you're gonna use it for bait, what do you have to do with that frog? You just throw it in the water?

V: Uh-uh. (negative)

A: Put it on a hook.

T: Oh n-o-o-o! He's gonna have to stick it on a hook. (Gestures hooking something with hands, glances at S, then back to A)

L: And den go like dat, an den dat. (Gestures casting a line)

T: And throw it in the water,

    [and (also makes gesture of casting)

A: [En den, en mi [ght (?)

S: [The

    fish

    [might come and eat it.

A: [Da fish might come

    and eat it.

    (Au, 1980, pp. 104–105)

What reaction do you have to this discussion? What attitude is reflected toward the children's language diversity? What effect will this type of interaction have on the children's comprehension and their desire to participate in group discussion?

The first episode, with Lionel, clearly demonstrates that the teacher has little understanding of the systematic and rule-governed nature of Black English. The focus on the child's language use and constant interruption to "correct" pronunciation completely disrupts the reading and meaning-construction process. Just as devastating is the teacher's rejection of the child's home language in this interchange. By contrast, the teacher in the second episode provides a supportive language environment in which she encourages the children's responses, paraphrases their statements ("He's gonna have to stick it on a hook"), and represents their gestures through language ("And throw it in the water"). Attention is focused on the children's thoughts and communication intent, not on their pronunciation (Au, 1993). Your understanding and appreciation of language and cultural diversity will be critical to your teaching success. We will return to this important issue after a brief survey of legislation that has supported diversity in our schools during the last three decades.

A Brief Overview of Legislation on Diversity

As our school population has become more diverse, especially over the last three decades, educators have assumed increased responsibilities in attempting to meet the instructional needs of students. Long before this, of course, teachers have ideally carried a sense of social justice and fairness into their classrooms. However, increased sensitivity to student diversity developed from the desegregation legislation in the 1950s, the civil rights movement of the 1960s, and the language diversity, gender, and physical disabilities legislation of the 1970s and 1980s.

The educational reform movement began with African-American protests against racial segregation in the schools. The 1954 landmark decision in *Brown v. Topeka Board of Education* ruled that segregation of educational facilities was illegal. The "separate but equal" rationale used in segregating students in classrooms across the country was declared unconstitutional on the basis of the Fourteenth Amendment (Grant & Sleeter, 1993). This reform movement was greatly assisted by the *Civil Rights Act* of 1964, which prohibited public institutions from receiving federal support that segregated students on the basis of their race, color, religion, or national origin. The *Economic Opportunity Act*, passed in the same year, provided for initiation of the Head Start, Follow-Through, and Upward Bound programs. During this period much of our society became highly sensitized to major social injustices and civil rights infringements in schools and in employment, housing, and public accommodations.

In 1965, the *Elementary and Secondary Education Act* (ESEA) was passed. Title I provided extensive funding for compensatory education to enhance educational opportunities for African-American, Hispanic, Appalachian, and low-income students. This act also provided for school library resources, textbooks, other instructional materials, and supplementary education centers and services. The *Bilingual Education Act* (Title VII of ESEA) was passed in 1967. It is interesting to note that in draft form this act contained specific provision for Hispanic students. Reference, however, to Hispanics was dropped before executive approval (Stein, 1986). The broader wording provided the first legislation that provided federal funds for minority groups who were non-English-language speaking (Wilson, 1993).

National Origin, Gender, Disabilities

The *Civil Rights Act*, as noted in the above discussion, prohibited segregation not only on the basis of race but also on the basis of national origin (Title VI). Even so, the major enforcement of this act emphasized African-American issues in the immediate years following its passage. In 1969, however, the Office of Civil Rights initiated vigorous efforts to identify discrimination against "national origin minority group children" (Weinberg, 1977). As a result, the concept of minority discrimination was expanded to include not only racial but also national origin minorities. School districts were advised in 1970 that to comply with Title VI of the act, they must take steps to provide equal access to their instructional programs for students of national origin minorities who spoke a different language. This interpretation thus accounted not only for "equal opportunity" but also "equal access" for students. In 1974, the *Lau v. Nichols* decision, initiated by Chinese-American public school students in San Francisco, ruled that schools must provide for students' language needs in order to provide equal educational opportunity (Allen, 1991).

Concern for gender with respect to equal opportunity and access is reflected in Title IX of the 1972 *Educational Amendments*. This section of the 1972 act prohibits sex discrimination in treatment of students including counseling, testing, financial aid, and educational activities. The intent is clearly to eliminate gender discrimination in schools (Banks & Banks, 1989).

Concern for children with special needs culminated in *Public Law 94-142*, passed in 1975, and amended in 1986 (PL 99-457) and 1990 (PL 101-476). A key provision of this legislation was that of "mainstreaming," or the placement of children with disabilities in the least restrictive instructional environment. This in effect called for the integration of these students into regular classrooms for some or all of their day, rather than segregating them into special schools or classrooms. This legislation clearly reflects the importance of providing opportunity for children with special needs to interact with and succeed with other youngsters in the regular classroom setting (Smith & Luckasson, 1992).

Dropout Rates

This brief survey of legislative response to diversity gives clear indication of the national commitment to meet the needs of the diverse population of students in our classrooms. Even so, however, recent statistics (Snyder & Hoffman, 1991, p. 110, Table 97) indicate that great disparity exists between the high school dropout rate of Caucasian (12.4 percent) and African-American (13.8 percent) students and students of Hispanic Origin (33 percent). Our need to understand differences and diversity and create instructional environments for children from varied language and cultural backgrounds and to make provision for gender, academic, and physical differences is clear.

We now turn to important instructional goals and guidelines that will assist you in teaching students with language and cultural differences.

GOALS AND GUIDELINES FOR TEACHING LINGUISTICALLY AND CULTURALLY DIFFERENT STUDENTS

The beliefs and attitudes you hold toward children will strongly influence your teaching. Many student-related variables must be understood and accounted for in successful instruction. These range from general background factors such as race/ethnicity and social class to individual features such as self-esteem and preference for working individually or cooperatively in groups. Each of these variables influences student interaction, participation, and achievement. Your students' race/ethnicity and language proficiency in English may directly influence their language interaction styles, their ability to work individually or in groups, and in turn their academic success and self-esteem. For example, as Gallimore, Boggs, and Jordan (1974) found, Hawaiian Creole-speaking children were "manifestly competent" in home and community, where information-giving and concept development are transmitted during group conversation or verbal play, but not at school, where information-sharing rules are distinctly different. Your awareness and understanding of these variables will strongly influence instructional planning and children's success in the classroom. Given the range of possible variables, however, you need to identify key instructional principles, which will assist in focusing your instructional efforts.

Instructional Principles

The seven instructional principles that follow are designed to increase your awareness of the specific learning needs of children and your responsibility to create active learning environments for linguistically and culturally different students (Allen, 1991; Au, 1993; Hernandez, 1989; Moll, 1988; Ruddell & Ruddell, 1994). To be effective teacher in a diverse environment you will need:

First, to understand that students do not arrive from inferior cultures, nor do they suffer from language deficits; instead they possess *culture, dialect, and language differences* that vary from your own.

Second, to understand that children's acquisition of language and literacy abilities is meaning based and best facilitated by interactive meaning-construction activities.

Third, to understand the importance of learning as much as possible about your students' homes, communities, languages, and cultural backgrounds in order to incorporate this knowledge into instructional content and language and literacy interactions in the classroom.

Fourth, to understand the importance of creating a context-rich, interactive, and supportive classroom environment for language exploration and use, which will lead to language and literacy development.

Fifth, not only to help children develop those social language skills that facilitate language and literacy interactions both in and out of school, *but also* to understand the importance of helping them develop academic and content-based language and literacy skills.

Sixth, to provide instructional opportunities in language and literacy use that will encourage risk-taking and will develop the understanding that we learn from our mistakes as we acquire a new language.

And seventh, to help children build a positive self-concept as language and literacy users by providing frequent academic and social interactive opportunities for meaning-based language use.

Instructional Guidelines

As you work toward achieving personal and professional understanding of language and cultural diversity, you should realize that previous chapter discussions, including many instructional strategies, have strong relevance for instruction designed for diversity. For example, as we discussed in Chapter 3, children of all languages and cultures are active theory builders and hypothesis testers. The driving force behind their theories, hypotheses, questions, and explorations is their need to make meaning—to make sense of their world. Their language acquisition is greatly enhanced through active participation in this meaning-construction process as they begin to acquire and use the language in their new environment. The opportunity for meaningful interaction using the new language is also greatly facilitated through interaction with their peers, teachers, and other individuals in their school and community environment.

This perspective is strongly supported by Allen's (1991) five conclusions based on her extensive review of research on teaching bilingual children and those who are learning English as a second language. She concludes that instruction should provide opportunity for children to:

1. acquire the language naturally, using the language for real purposes;
2. receive linguistic input that is made comprehensible by a strong and supportive context;
3. experiment with, hypothesize about, and try out language in low-anxiety settings;
4. work with English-speaking peers on meaningful tasks that create opportunities and real reasons to talk, write, and read together; and
5. use language for a broad variety of functions, both social and academic.

The importance of creating a low-anxiety language-learning setting (noted in the third conclusion above) is also emphasized in Krashen's (1987) discussion of the "affective filter" hypothesis. He observes that a key requisite for language acquisition is a low-risk and low-anxiety learning environment that keeps the "affective filter" low. Further, instruction should provide meaningful high-interest content that focuses the student's mental energies on meaning construction. Krashen states that for optimal success instruction must:

- be comprehensible,
- be interesting/relevant,
- not be grammatically sequenced,

- provide for quantity of language use,

- have a low affective filter, and

- provide tools for conversational management.
  (Krashen, 1987, p. 127)

Children's Language-Acquisition Strategies

Lily Wong Fillmore provides insight into strategies used by five- to seven-year-old children acquiring a second language (1976). She notes that children use chunks of language such as "Gimme," "What's that?" and "My turn" that enable them to communicate before they began to manipulate structures in the language. The following five strategies are identified as those that children use as they begin to acquire English:

1. They assume that what people are saying is related to the context of the ongoing situation.
2. They learn a few stock expressions and use these in their interactions.
3. They look for recurring patterns in the language.
4. They use the language forms they have acquired and make the most of these.
5. Their major effort is spent in getting meaning across with minimal concern for refinements.

Goodman and Goodman (1978) highlight the importance of children's background knowledge in acquiring literacy in a second language. Their study of children from four different language groups (Arabic, Navaho, Samoan, and Spanish) revealed that background knowledge was one of the most critical factors in successful reading and retelling of stories. In effect, the more the children knew about the story content, the more effective they were in reading and understanding the story. Implications based on these findings emphasize the importance of your awareness of the background knowledge that second-language students bring to the classroom, and the need to build on and develop this knowledge.

It is easy to assume that the development of social language opportunities and skills with your children is the major instructional approach to acquiring English. While this is important, the academic and content-based language and literacy skills are also critical. Saville-Troike (1984) studied the English language development of students in an English as a Second Language (ESL) class. Seven different languages were spoken by these newcomers to the United States. While the children were able to share meaning with their peers through language formulas, gestures, and mime in social settings, this ability did not assist them in effective communication within the classroom setting. This may be explained in part because of the context-embedded language used in social settings, such as a play corner of the classroom, and may be in distinct contrast to the context-reduced discussion in a social studies lesson (Cummins, 1981, 1986). Providing a rich context in the development of new concepts and meaning-construction strategies is thus essential to successful instruction.

Native Language as a Basis for Second-Language Learning

Cummins (1989) proposes a language-learning framework that supports the use of the children's native language in learning English (or a new second language). His perception of language development identifies an underlying base of language proficiency in the native language that can be drawn on in learning English. This underlying cognitive base includes an understanding of areas such as literacy concepts, logic, abstract thinking, comprehension, analysis, application, synthesis, evaluation, inference, notions, and **metalanguage** (awareness of the use of language in comprehending and understanding). He proposes that, while the surface aspects of the child's native language and English (pronunciation, grammar, vocabulary) are different, the underlying cognitive and conceptual aspects of thinking are similar. Cummins thus believes that the child can transfer these underlying thinking processes and literacy-related skills used in the native language to the acquisition of English (or any second language). His view of this transfer process, however, is qualified by noting that the child

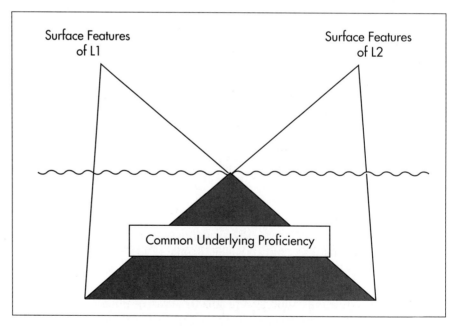

FIGURE 10-1

The Linguistic Interdependance Model. (Reproduced with permission from Cummins, 1989, p. 23.)

must have developed a minimal level of competence in language and literacy in his or her native language before transfer can occur.

In explaining this theory Cummins uses the "iceberg" metaphor shown in Figure 10-1. The tips of the two superimposed icebergs represent the surface aspects of language competence (pronunciation, vocabulary, grammar) used in the child's first language (L1) and the language to be learned (L2). These tips constitute the Basic Interpersonal Communication Skills (BICS) used by the child in each language.

The submerged body that connects the two icebergs represents the child's underlying language proficiency (literacy concepts, synthesis, inference, metalanguage) which is used in the native language and can be transferred to English. The submerged part of the iceberg is known as the child's Cognitive/Academic Language Proficiency (CALP). In short, this viewpoint holds that language and literacy competency in the child's native language should provide support and a distinct advantage to the child in becoming proficient in English (or any second language), assuming there is competence in the native language. By contrast, such an advantage in learning English would not be expected if there is a very low level of language and literacy development in the native language.

Children's Hypotheses About Language

The development of children's metalanguage and metalinguistic awareness is also important in acquiring a second language. Selinker (1972) identifies this process as the student's "interlanguage," which enables children to create informal theories and hypotheses about how the new language works and to test out these hypotheses by using them in communication with peers and adults. As these language hypotheses are tested, errors will in all likelihood be made. Errors thus provide an indication of children's language acquisition and growth. It is of critical importance that the classroom be considered a psychologically safe environment for language exploration, and that language exploration errors be valued, rather than discouraged through overcorrection and peer ridicule. Children's self-concepts can be very fragile in this language-testing and exploration stage.

Clearly, opportunity to use the new language in social and academic contexts is an important factor that will influence children's English acquisition process. The period of time required for them to become proficient users of English is an important consideration as you create instructional expectations. The length of this period will depend on a variety of factors, such as exposure to English both in and out of the school setting, attitude toward learning, opportunity to use the language, and language and literacy proficiency in the first language. The time required from initial acquisition to competent use of English will extend from approximately two to six years (Valdés, 1991; Wong Fillmore, 1986). As noted above, many personal and instructional factors will influence this acquisition process.

UNDERSTANDING LANGUAGE AND CULTURAL DIFFERENCES

Our language is defined by a unique group of sounds, grammatical rules, and lexical elements acquired in a culture that enables us to communicate effectively with each other. These features have developed through experiences strongly influenced by the language used in home, community, and school environments.

As discussed in Chapter 2, children also acquire understanding of a variety of language functions, in effect, a "wardrobe" of different oral and written language forms that are appropriate for different social and academic settings. These range from informal discussions and hurried notes to friends to formal presentations and papers. Children quickly become aware of what language forms are appropriate for different social settings and occasions. Their language knowledge is thus closely intertwined with their culture. However, children who have experienced a culture different from the "mainstream" culture may not have developed language functions that are critical to effective participation in the school environment, even when the children are Native English speakers. For example, Heath's (1982, 1983) study of children from three different communities revealed distinctly different home language routines and attitudes toward written language. The language and literacy development of children from the communities of Roadville (a community of white mill workers and their families) and Tracton (a community of black mill workers and their families), while extensive, did not as closely match the classroom language and literacy routines and expectations as did the children of Townspeople (black and white families from the mainstream community). Heath concluded that the children of Townspeople entered school not only familiar with book-reading routines, but with well developed comprehension strategies as well. It is important to understand the close connection between language and culture as you provide for the instructional needs of children from different languages and cultures.

Standard English Dialects

We can think of language and cultural differences as ranging along a continuum from our own language and culture to those languages and cultures that are distinctly different and of which we have little understanding. As you consider this idea for a moment, think of your own language. We will assume for now that this is English (although English may not be your first language). Your speech contains pronunciation, grammatical, and lexical (vocabulary) markers that define your dialect of English. (We often think that only other people have dialects as we listen to English speakers from various regions of the United States or from other countries such as England or Australia, and we fail to realize that our own speech is also a dialect.)

The early English settlements in the United States along the eastern seaboard transported variations in spoken English to the colonies. These early dialects have grown less distinct over time as the early settlements grew, the western expansion developed and, more recently, as modern transportation, communication, and media have provided greater interaction among people. Nevertheless, regional dialects are still marked in the United States. We only need to listen to excerpts from speeches of presidents of the United States, ranging from John F. Kennedy, Lyndon B. Johnson, and Jimmy Carter to Ronald Reagan, George Bush, and Bill Clinton to realize that regional dialects still exist.

Three broad dialect areas have been identified across the United States. These include the Northern region (imagine the area north of a line drawn across the Northern edges of Pennsylvania, Ohio, Indiana, Illinois, Iowa, and north through the middle parts of the Dakotas), the Southern region (roughly a line starting in northern Virginia that follows the Appalachian mountain range through the western part of Virginia, North Carolina, South Carolina, and northern Georgia, then westward through the midsections of Alabama, Mississippi, and Arkansas to Texas) and the Midland region (the area between the northern and southern regions).

Vocabulary, grammatical, and pronunciation differences are present across these three regions. For example, in the Northern and Midland areas the animal with a stripe down its back and at times of a putrid odor is known as *skunk*, while in the Southern and parts of the Midland regions it is known as *polecat*. In the Northern areas the utensil used to carry water or milk is known as a *pail*, but it is a *bucket* in the Midland and Southern areas. Grammatical variation is evident in the use of the past tense for the word *dive*. In the Northern area the word commonly used is *dove*, while in the Midland and South it is *dived*. Pronunciation varieties are evident in the word *greasy*, which is pronounced as grea*s*y in the north and sections of the north Midland, but as grea*z*y in the Southern region. The words *Mary* (female name), marry (to wed), and *merry* (happy) are pronounced with distinct differences in the northeastern part of the Northern region, but no distinction is made in the Midland and in parts of the Southern areas. The region west of Nebraska and Kansas and into the far west (Arizona, California, Oregon, Washington) represent much more of an amalgam of dialects as regional groups mingled in the settlement of the western United States.

The critical point in this discussion is that you do speak a dialect of English, which is defined by key features of pronunciation, grammatical structure, and vocabulary. This dialect, however, in all probability will be considered a Standard English form. That is, it is a dialect form that uses features thought of as mainstream, "news broadcast"-type English, used in business and education. Many of the children you teach will also speak Standard English, but many will use a nonmainstream dialect that is different from your own. It is important to understand that your children's language and culture are closely intertwined. Again, remember that nonmainstream language forms represent language and cultural differences.

These forms do not represent a language or cultural deficit nor an inferior language form.

We now turn to nonmainstream dialects that children may use and that differ in distinct ways from your own Standard English forms. Later in the chapter we will examine the language features of bilingual students, and then develop instructional strategies that will help you in your teaching.

Nonmainstream Dialects

As Au (1993) emphasizes, in school literacy development we may consider the eventual use of Standard English a goal, but it is not a prerequisite to the development of literacy learning. Standard English should not be viewed as a replacement of children's nonmainstream dialect but as an alternate dialect form that can be used in school and work when appropriate and necessary. William Labov (1967), a sociolinguist, notes that an individual using nonmainstream forms 20 to 30 percent of the time will be heard as using the forms all of the time.

Children who speak nonmainstream dialects such as Black English (also known as Black English Vernacular), Hawaiian Creole English, and Appalachian English can communicate effectively in their communities and in the context of the classroom. You will, however, observe key pronunciation and grammatical variations in their language and in their oral reading. Some variations between Standard English and Black English are illustrated in Tables 10-1 and 10-2.

Many of these nonmainstream forms, such as redundant pattern elements (e.g., "Where you at?") noted in Table 10-2, will not interfere with children's comprehension. Other forms, however, such as the omission of past-tense markers, may have some effect on comprehension (Labov, 1967). For example, in the sentence, "When I passed by, I read the posters," the past tense signaled in *passed* cues the pronunciation of the word *read* to reflect the past tense. The absence of possessive forms, future- and past-tense markers, or alternative placement of adverbs may produce some comprehension inter-ference when children first encounter these Standard English forms.

The key point in considering nonmainstream dialects is to understand that the language forms your children use represent their predictable and regular speech patterns. The major instructional emphasis should be placed on comprehension and understanding rather than on pronunciation and speech patterns, as was the case with the teacher working with the African-American children in the example used at the beginning of this chapter.

Children who speak a nonmainstream dialect are able learners, as is the case with other children in your classroom, and will encounter minimal communication interference because of their dialect. Their dialect, noted primarily because of the pronunciation and grammar surface features, represents only the tip of the Cummins "iceberg" discussed earlier. Our more basic instructional concern is found in the submerged part of the "iceberg,"

STANDARD ENGLISH FORM	BLACK ENGLISH EQUIVALENT	THE DIALECT-SPEAKING CHILD MAY PRONOUNCE _____ AS _____.	
INITIAL POSITION			
/th/ becomes /d/		this	dis
		that	dat
/thr/ becomes /tr/		three	tree
		thrust	trust
/str/ becomes /scr/		stream	scream
		strap	scrap
FINAL POSITION			
/th/ becomes /f/		Ruth	roof
/nt/ becomes /n/		meant	men
		bent	Ben
/ng/ becomes /n/		sing	sin
/skt/ becomes /ks/		asked	axed
/sts/ becomes /s/		fists	fis
/l/ is not sounded		tool	too
		help	hep
/r/ is not sounded		four	foe
		guard	God
/d/ is not sounded		road	row

FINAL POSITION			GRAMMATICAL CONSEQUENCE
/ft/ becomes /f/	laughed	laugh	Past tense not signaled
/md/ becomes /d/	aimed	aim	Past tense not signaled
/dz/ becomes /d/	loads	load	Agreement not signaled
/lz/ becomes /l/	holes	hole	Agreement not signaled
/ts/ becomes /t/	hits	hit	Agreement not signaled
/ks/ becomes /k/	knocks	knock	Agreement not signaled

TABLE 10-1

Examples of Pronunciation and Grammatical Differences in Standard English and Black English

DESCRIPTION	EXAMPLE
Copula (or linking verb) omitted, as in	He tired. You playing here.
Use of **be** in place of other verb forms, as in	They always **be** messing around. Most of the time he **be** in the house.
Absence of regular verb ending -ed, as in	He pick me. He turn around.
Use of **ain't** to signal past tense of verbs not changed in past tense, as in	**Ain't** he finished? **Ain't** nobody see it.
Plural overgeneralization, as in	mens, peoples, teeths, mices
Absence of plural form cued by context, as in	two dog, several cat
Substitution of **they** for **their**, **you** for **your**, as in	**They** eyes are brown. You brought it on **you** own self.
Use of **more** with adjectives in comparative form, as in	He is **more** taller than you.
Alternate placement of adverbs such as **mostly**, as in	That's what **mostly** we call 'em. This is a crazy world we **absolutely** livin' in.

SENTENCE PATTERNS:

Omission of **do** forms in questions, as in	How he fix that? How it taste?
Redundant pattern elements such as **at** in "where" questions, as in	Where you at? Where he work at?
Double negatives used with each indefinite pronoun or adverb, as in	Nobody don't know. I ain't never had no trouble wit' none of them.
Doubling of forms, as in	My brother he going. I didn't play with only but Wayne and Tyrone.

TABLE 10-2

Examples of Grammatical Differences in Standard English and Black English which deals with the development of language and literacy competencies. We have discussed these in previous chapters and will further develop them later in this chapter.

As a speaker of a Standard English dialect, you should carefully examine your own attitude toward nonmainstream language forms, remembering that these forms are surface language differences. As you provide a wide range of opportunities for the meaningful use of language and literacy and develop understanding and use of varied language functions with your students, you will observe their consistent language growth and development. Some nonmainstream-dialect-speaking students will become completely bidialectal, able to shift easily between nonmainstream and mainstream English, while others will retain their predominant nonmainstream dialect-features. The degree to which this occurs relates to a variety of factors, such as attitude toward each of the dialect forms, peer and community pressures, family attitude, and academic and economic opportunities.

Bilingual Learners

In all probability, you will find a number of bilingual learners in your classroom and will assume the major instructional responsibility for their literacy development. As discussed earlier in this chapter, an enormous number of immigrant families have arrived in the United States over the last three decades, and particularly in recent years. Children in immigrant families and of immigrant parents comprise the majority of the bilingual population in schools; however, keep in mind that substantial numbers of bilingual students are in the United States, often as members of well-established cultures within the country—the Navaho, Eskimo-Aleut, other Native Americans, and the Louisiana French, for example (Ovando, 1988; Portes & Rumbaut, 1990). Still others speak Creole or other nonmainstream varieties of English as their first language—e.g., Native Hawaiians, Sea Islanders from the Carolinas, and African-Americans—either exclusively or in addition to mainstream English (Ovando, 1988).

Bilingual children come to school with varying degrees of proficiency in English, and may or may not be fluent and literate in their native language. The following terminology is commonly used in schools to characterize bilingual students.

1. **Non-English speakers** communicate very little, if at all, in English and use their native language (first language or L1) as their primary means of communication.

2. **Limited English Proficient** (LEP) students are able to demonstrate some degree of oral language fluency in English. This fluency is insufficient for independent learning in classrooms where English is the main language of instruction. LEP students rely primarily on their native language for

communication with peers, family, and community and use familiar "chunks of language" (English), mime, and gesture to function in the classroom.

3. **Fluent English Proficient** (FEP) students can participate fluently in conversations and have sufficient independent control of English and literacy to participate in the predominantly English-speaking classroom.

Several types of programs are offered throughout the United States to meet the needs of these students. These include English as a Second Language (ESL), bilingual education, and transition-type programs.

English as a Second Language programs rely heavily on an immersion approach for students who have varying degrees of competency in English. The children are "immersed" in an English-speaking classroom, and the teacher often speaks only English. The content is focused primarily on acquiring English language skills.

Bilingual education provides instruction in students' primary language, focusing on the content areas, while providing instruction in English during part of the school day (Ruddell, 1993). Many schools situate their bilingual programs at the primary level (grades K–3), with the intent of bringing children into the program as early as possible so that the children are able to make a successful transition into English-only classrooms by late second or early third grade. Still other schools or districts have two-way bilingual education programs in which English-only children acquire fluency and literacy in the predominant other language in the school. Bilingual programs do exist at the intermediate level to accommodate older students with minimal English fluency; however, ESL programs predominate at the higher grade levels. Bilingual education programs require that everyone in the class have the same primary language, and so are found only in schools with large concentrations of non-English-speaking or bilingual students who share a common native language. They also require teachers who are fluently bilingual and bilingually literate (Ruddell, 1993).

Transitional language programs are designed to assist students in making transition from ESL and bilingual classes to the regular English-speaking classroom. Some transition classes use **sheltered English** as the primary instructional approach. Sheltered English is characterized by adjusted language demands in subject content, use of a familiar lesson format, presentation of new content in known contexts, and provision for rich small-group interaction (Ruddell, 1993).

The instructional reality for many bilingual learners is that they are placed in classrooms where the teacher does not speak their native language, may or may not have much knowledge about the children's language *or* culture, and has had limited experience in teaching English as a second language. This creates a major dilemma for all parties involved. Many states are currently encouraging teachers to increase their knowledge of second-language learning and to gain understanding of the cultures represented by students in their schools. The clear intent is

- to provide a context-rich language and literacy-learning environment for ESL students,
- develop concepts and language useful for their participation in the school environment,
- build on their experiences and background,
- teach learning strategies useful for constructing meaning,
- develop their ability to participate in small group interactions,
- adjust literacy task demands.

You will recognize that many of these ideas have already been discussed in this text with respect to English-speaking students. We will further discuss ways to meet these needs later in this chapter. We will now briefly develop key points of difference between the language of LEP students and English-speaking students.

LANGUAGE DIFFERENCES FOR LIMITED ENGLISH PROFICIENCY (LEP) CHILDREN

Major urban centers such as Los Angeles, San Francisco, New York, Chicago, and Miami have large percentages of language minority children. In addition, some rural areas, particularly in the west and southwest, have settlements of recent immigrant families. Many of these children have to some extent acquired their native language, but are limited in their English language and literacy proficiency. As ESL children begin to acquire English, there are several immediate needs. First, they will need to understand how the native language differs from English in pronunciation and grammatical forms, which may have an impact on meaning. Second, students will need to acquire vocabulary, new concepts, and background knowledge related to the subject area content. And third, they need to learn classroom conversational routines, classroom language concepts, and meaning-construction strategies in English. We will first examine selected pronunciation and grammatical form differences for two languages and then turn our discussion to instructional strategies.

Spanish and Chinese languages comprise a significant percentage of ESL children in the United States. You can develop some idea of pronunciation and grammatical form differences between English and Spanish by examining Table 10-3, and between English and Chinese in Table 10-4. Again, these are consistent and predictable variations.

ENGLISH FORM	SPANISH EQUIVALENT	THE HISPANIC-AMERICAN CHILD MAY PRONOUNCE _____ AS _____.	
/ă/	/ĕ/ or /ŏ/	bat	bet
		hat	hot
/ĭ/	/ē/	bit	beet
/ŭ/	/ĕ/	but	bet
/ā/	/ĕ/	late	let
/ŏŏ/	/ōō/	full	fool
/b/	/p/	bar	par
/v/	/v/	vote	boat
/g/	/k/	goat	coat
/j/	/ch/	jump	chump
/th/	/s/t/or/ f/	thank	sank
/z/	/s/	zoo	sue

GRAMMATICAL DIFFERENCES	ENGLISH FORM	SPANISH-ENGLISH SPEAKER
Agreement	The car runs.	The car run.
Tense	Joe said that he was ready.	Joe said that he is ready.
Use of **be**	I am five years old.	I have five years.
Negative	Joe isn't here.	Joe is no here.
	Don't come.	No come.
Pronoun	Is he a farmer?	Is farmer?
Omission	Is he ready?	Is ready?
Adjective use:	The red cap is pretty.	The cap red is pretty.
Order	It is bigger.	It more big.
Comparison	It is the biggest.	It most big.

TABLE 10-3

Language Differences Between Standard English and Spanish

It is important to keep in mind that children's motivation for acquiring English as their second language may be somewhat different from that of nonmainstream-dialect children for acquiring Standard English forms. Most nonmainstream-dialect speakers are already somewhat bidialectal in the sense that they can comprehend Standard English forms and thus successfully communicate with their teachers and other children. This is not the case with LEP children whose native language is not English. They are frequently highly motivated to acquire proficiency in English for peer and classroom communication purposes.

ENGLISH FORM	CHINESE EQUIVALENT	THE CHINESE-AMERICAN CHILD MAY PRONOUNCE _____ AS _____.	
/ā/	/ĕ/ or /ă/	bait	bet or bat
	/ŭ/	came	come
/ē/	/ĭ/	beat	bit
/o͞o/	/o͝o/	Luke	look
/b/	/p/	rib	rip
/g/	/k/	rig	rik
/d/	/t/	rid	rit
/z/	/s/	zoo	sue
/v/	/f/	have	half
/zh/	/s/	leisure	leaser
/th/	/d/	that	dat
/sh/	/s/	she	see
/n/	/l/	need	lead
/r/	/l/	rice	lice
		read	lead
/w/	/v/	will	vill

GRAMMATICAL DIFFERENCES	ENGLISH SPEAKER	CHINESE-ENGLISH SPEAKER
Agreement	He lives in San Francisco.	He live in San Francisco.
Tense	I am working.	I right at work.
	I had just finished watering the lawn.	I just water finish lawn.
Use of **be**	He is sick.	He sick.
Be substituted	I was here yesterday.	I at here yesterday.
Negative	I cannot go.	I no can go.
Plural	Many houses are beautiful.	Many house beautiful.
Pronoun	You have known him a long time.	You know he long time.
Preposition omitted	I live in San Francisco.	I live San Francisco.
Conjunction omitted	You and I are alike.	You I alike.
Question form	Are you going home?	You go home?
Word order	Will you come to my house for dinner?	You tonight come I of home dinner?

TABLE 10-4

Language Differences Between Standard English and Chinese

STRATEGIES FOR TEACHING BILINGUAL LEARNERS

The instructional strategies effective for teaching bilingual students are remarkably similar to the most effective strategies for teaching English monolingual students. The strategy selection process is best guided by the conditions, or principles, for optimal language instruction discussed early in Chapter 3. You will recall that these include:

1. Children are immersed in language with emphasis on the communication of meaning and meaning construction.
2. Meaningful demonstrations of language in action are provided with the active involvement of children.
3. Language is used for real-life purposes that provide opportunity for using and developing literacy for personal, social, and academic needs.
4. Children are encouraged to assume responsibility for their own learning as they develop independence and self-direction in language and literacy use.
5. Approximation, not perfection, of the targeted language skill is encouraged through a supportive, meaning-based, and psychologically safe classroom environment.
6. Feedback and support is provided to the children as a consistent and ongoing process.
7. Instructional expectations hold that all children will learn and acquire language and literacy.

These principles are supported by Moll's (1988) study of Spanish-English bilingual and English monolingual classrooms. He concluded that the essence of literacy development for students in both groups of classrooms was found in the belief that "both comprehension and expression are built and developed collaboratively by students and teachers through functional, relevant, and meaningful language use. Thus, a major goal of teaching is to make classrooms highly literate environments in which many language experiences can take place and different types of 'literacies' can be practiced, understood, and learned" (p. 466). He notes further that this goal emphasizes the development of instruction that encourages children to use and manipulate language as they construct meaning and assume control of oral and written literacy skills.

DETERMINING INSTRUCTIONAL NEEDS

Even though the instructional strategies used for bilingual and English-speaking students may be similar, it is important to discover as much as possible about the language background of your bilingual students in order to use these strategies effectively to meet literacy needs. Gunderson (1991) has developed a "decision heuristic" or chart based on his classroom teaching

	NON-ENGLISH	VERY LIMITED	LIMITED	LIMITED FLUENCY
LI LITERACY NONE				
1-2 YEARS				
3+ YEARS				

───── **FIGURE 10-2** ─────

The Elementary ESL Decision Heuristic. (Reproduced with permission from Gunderson, 1991, p. 23.)

and research to assist teachers in determining ESL instructional levels. The heuristic accounts for two important areas: first, English oral-language proficiency; and second, level of L1 literacy instruction (the number of years students have received literacy instruction in their native or primary language). These two areas are shown in Figure 10-2.

The heuristic is straightforward to apply. The child's English oral-language proficiency (L2) can be roughly determined using the following descriptions based on your classroom observations (Gunderson, 1991, p. 26):

Zero-Level English

Cannot answer even yes/no questions.

Is unable to identify and name any objects.

Understands no English.

Often appears withdrawn and afraid.

Very Limited English

Responds to simple questions with mostly yes/no or one-word responses.

Speaks in one- or two-word phrases.

Attempts no extended conversations.

Seldom, if ever, initiates conversations.

Limited English (Limited English Proficient—LEP)

Responds easily to simple questions.

Produces simple sentences.

Has difficulty elaborating when asked.

Occasionally initiates conversations.

Limited Fluency (Fluent English Proficient—FEP)

Speaks with ease.

Initiates conversations.

May make phonological or grammatical errors, which can then become fossilized.

Makes errors in more syntactically complex utterances.

Freely and easily switches codes.

Teachers must obtain information related to the child's L1 literacy history (native or primary language) from parents, a relative, an older sibling, or the student. It may be necessary to use an interpreter as you attempt to find out as much as possible about the child's literacy instruction in L1 (primary language). This information is related to our earlier discussion of the importance of the child's underlying language competency, which may assist in acquiring English (Cummins, 1989). You can expect, for example, that one to two years of L1 literacy instruction will have developed an understanding of the relationship between print and language (Gunderson, 1991).

Your assessment of ESL students' English oral-language proficiency and L1 instructional history will assist you in deciding what instruction will be most helpful for them. For example, students with Zero-Level English proficiency and no L1 literacy instruction will greatly benefit from a bilingual education program. If such a program is not available, you will need to introduce new concepts and vocabulary in a language-rich and supportive social and instructional context. This initial instruction will focus heavily on pantomime accompanied by oral language to help your students acquire Limited English Proficiency (LEP), which will serve as the basis for initial reading instruction. You will find the ideas discussed in the remainder of this chapter of value in teaching these youngsters.

By contrast, you can expect that students who are Limited English Proficient (LEP) and who have had one or more years of L1 instruction will function well in your classroom. These students and those who are Fluent English Proficient (FEP) possess sufficient English fluency and L1 literacy understanding to enable them to benefit immediately from English language and literacy instruction.

INSTRUCTIONAL APPROACHES AND STRATEGIES

As you identify the degree of English fluency and L1 instruction your children possess, you can proceed to adjust your instructional program to meet their learning needs. The following discussion will focus on three instructional areas that deserve special attention for ESL students who are Limited English Proficient (LEP) and Fluent English Proficient (FEP). These are:

first, developing background and conceptual knowledge;

second, encouraging meaning construction and meaning monitoring;

and third, motivating group and individual responses.

You will find that you have already developed an understanding of many strategies that will prove useful in teaching your ESL students based on our previous discussions. It is important, however, to keep uppermost in mind the seven language-learning conditions we reviewed earlier as you use these strategies with ESL students. Communication of meaning and active meaning construction for real-life purposes will add greatly to children's motivation to acquire and use language and literacy skills. It is also very important to create a low-anxiety classroom to reduce children's "affective filter" (Krashen, 1987) by using rich contextual support in a psychologically safe environment. Approximation, not perfection, and increased risk-taking in using English are key concepts leading to successful instruction.

Becoming Bilingual

Developing Background and Conceptual Knowledge

The development of background and conceptual knowledge is critical to children's meaning construction. The use of Sheltered English is one strategy that has proven useful for ESL students. In addition the Vocabulary Self-Collection Strategy, learning logs and journals will prove to be of value. We emphasize at this point that we do not recommend these strategies from a "remedial" perspective at all; rather, we view them as being applicable for all students and particularly appropriate for ESL because of the language-rich interactions they promote.

Sheltered English. The purpose of Sheltered English is to increase the accessibility of content for ESL students who have not achieved full fluency in English (LEP and FEP students). Watson, Northcutt, and Rydell (1989) recommend the following principles to assist in adapting instruction through Sheltered English.

1. Adjust the language demands of the lesson by modifying speech rate and tone, using context clues extensively, and relating the discussion to students' personal experiences through analogy.

2. Build students' background knowledge by teaching (a) the vocabulary of instruction and (b) the vocabulary necessary to understand lesson content.

3. Develop an understanding of a set lesson format (at least initially) that will enable students to focus on the content rather than on how you are presenting the new information.

4. Use visuals and manipulatives that clearly and powerfully illustrate the new content.

5. Use small group cooperative-learning activities that actively involve your students in meaning construction and minimize lecture time.

6. Increase wait-time to enable students to construct meaning and formulate their response in discussions.

7. Emphasize predictable questions that lead to greater involvement with content and higher-level thinking.

As you examine these principles, you will find they closely parallel those in our discussion of comprehension (Chapter 4) and vocabulary development (Chapter 5).

Watson, Northcutt, and Rydell (1989) outline a seven-step plan for Sheltered English instruction. The How to Do we feature next was adapted from their plan.

We emphasize that Sheltered English instruction is, fundamentally, *good teaching*, similar in many ways to the instruction that you should provide for all students—fluent English speakers as well as ESL students. The primary instructional differences are found in provision for the introduction

HOW TO DO . . . .

SHELTERED ENGLISH LESSONS

1. **Plan the year by developing themes.**

   Decide what the students need to master.

   Organize units of study around themes.

2. **Think of ways to bring lessons to life.**

   Develop objectives for thematic content and language development.

   Identify visuals and manipulatives.

   Identify concrete models to illustrate ideas.

3. **Set the stage.**

   Present a broad overview of the unit or lesson content.

   Initiate each lesson with a brief review of what was learned yesterday
     and/or predictions about what will happen today.

4. **Preteach two vocabulary sets.**

   Teach words necessary for understanding the lesson or unit content.

   Teach words that will be used in the lesson to explain or elaborate ideas.

5. **Guide initial learning.**

   Use consistent lesson formats and plans, at least initially.

   Find ways to animate instruction with role playing,

     realia, experiments, and activities.

6. **Guide practice.**

   Provide examples and tryouts.

   Demonstrate explicitly how practice activities relate to initial learning.

7. **Guide independent practice.**

   Maximize student interactions (partner pairs, groups, cooperative
     learning).

   Evaluate students using student-developed products and tests.

of new concepts—both instructional and content based—in an enriched
supportive context and in the need for longer response time. These developmental differences will disappear over time as your ESL students gain
opportunity to grasp new concepts, use them in meaning construction, and
increase fluency in English.

Vocabulary Self-Collection Strategy (VSS). While VSS (Haggard [now M. Ruddell], 1982) was discussed in detail in Chapter 5 (see pp. 223–227), it is important to consider this strategy for ESL students. You will recall that VSS is designed to develop personal interest in vocabulary learning by inviting students to learn words they need and want to know. ESL students have *many* new words they need and want to know and soon respond avidly to this invitation. VSS has the added advantage of increasing children's sensitivity to the words in their environment, a quality that can work only to the benefit of children acquiring a new language. And finally, VSS makes words and language primary topics of conversation in the classroom—and when *everybody's* talking about new words and *everybody's* looking for new words to learn, then the language acquisition tasks of the second-language learner don't stand in such stark contrast to the rest of the class.

Vocabulary Logs and Journals. Vocabulary Logs and Journals fit VSS in a very natural and logical way and enables ESL students to record and review their self-collected vocabulary. At the initial stage, you should encourage students to use the new vocabulary in sentence context and illustrate the words (when possible) using magazine and newspaper pictures. As they become more proficient in English, formal definitions of each word may be constructed and checked using the dictionary. An added bonus derived from vocabulary logs is their availability as a personal dictionary reference source for spelling and writing. We encourage you to reexamine the vocabulary development strategies discussed in Chapter 5, including Teaching Vocabulary in Context strategy (TVC, pp. 217–220), concept webs (pp. 230–231), semantic maps (pp. 232–237), semantic feature analysis (pp. 237–240), and word sleuthing (pp. 242–245).

Meaning Construction and Meaning Monitoring

Many of your ESL students will have had little opportunity to develop meaning-construction and meaning-monitoring strategies. This will be especially true of children who have had little or no instruction in L1 (their native or primary language) and are LEP. The following strategies, a number of which have been introduced in earlier chapters, will prove to be of special value in your instruction.

Directed Listening-Thinking Activity (DL-TA). You will recall from Chapter 3 (p. 114–114) that the DL-TA (Stauffer, 1976) is presented orally to the students. This provides a distinct advantage for ESL students, because it does not require fluent reading. It is also important to use high-interest material that contains clear illustrations that provide a context to assist LEP students in meaning construction. Big books, which provide enlarged reproductions of illustrations, are valuable in this effort (see Chapter 3); and big books that use repetitive language and predictable story lines are especially valuable by providing a rich context through illustrations and language. Big books such as *Brown Bear, Brown Bear, What Do You See?*

(Martin, 1983) and *Hattie & the Fox* (Fox, 1987) are good examples that provide such context. The children's literature list found at the end of Chapter 3 will also provide a valuable starter resource for you.

You should review Chapter 3 for details in using the DL-TA; however, a quick review of key instructional points follows:

1. The key purpose of the DL-TA is to develop prediction and inference comprehension skills through rich language interaction and to build high student motivation.

2. The DL-TA can be used with small or large groups of children as you present the story orally.

3. Identify key stop-points that you will use for establishing predictions and inferences; these will include the title, two to four other stops at key points in the story, and a final stop-point just before the story ending.

4. The questioning patterns for the stop-points consist of: title ("With a title like that, what do you think this story will be about? Why do you think so?"); within story ("What do you think will happen now? Why do you think so?"); final point ("How do you think the story will end? Why?").

5. It is important to accept student predictions and inferences as long as there is some logical justification for the prediction.

Keep in mind that wait-time is important for the ESL student as meaning construction takes place. It is also important to establish a risk-taking environment with respect for the responses of ESL students who may use varied pronunciation and grammatical forms as they gain control and fluency in English. Monitoring of meaning will begin to occur as students compare their individual responses with those provided by other students.

Directed Reading-Thinking Activity (DR-TA). As you will recall from Chapter 4 (p. 153–159), the DR-TA (Stauffer, 1969, 1976) follows the same questioning pattern as the DL-TA. This strategy holds the same potential for developing predictions and inferences using high-level thinking. Remember, however, that this strategy will have greatest application as ESL students become fluent readers. The DR-TA can be used in the early stages with predictable books such as *One Fine Day* (Hogrogian, 1971), *The Gingerbread Boy* (Galdone, 1975), and *Are You My Mother?* (Eastman, 1960).

Question-Answer Relationships (QAR). The value of QAR (Raphael, 1982, 1986) for ESL students is that this strategy promotes understanding of the thinking demands of questions and how to use information sources. As discussed in Chapter 4 (p. 174–181), four types of information sources are developed. In quick review, these are:

1. **Right There**—the information is explicitly stated in the text requiring recall and the factual level of thinking.

2. **Think and Search**—the information source is text-based but requires inference at the interpretive level of thinking.

3. **Author and You**—the information is based on the author's text but requires use of the students' background knowledge and the interpretive, applicative, or transactive level of thinking.

4. **On My Own**—the information involves the author's text but relies heavily on the student's background knowledge, using the applicative and transactive levels of thinking.

QAR is especially valuable in providing the thinking tools for meaning construction and monitoring. The strategy provides immediate feedback to students, moves from short text passages to more involved text, develops thinking skills from the factual level to the interpretive, applicative, and transactive levels, and provides a rich verbal context and group support that will lead to student independence. Keep in mind that QARs can also be used with your students in oral story presentations. The four-day plan discussed in detail in Chapter 4 (pp. 174–180) can readily be applied to instruction with ESL students.

Reciprocal Questioning (ReQuest). This strategy is designed to model thinking processes in creating questions, establishing reading purpose, and building comprehension and self-monitoring responses. It can be used with individual students or small groups. As we discussed in Chapter 4 (pp. 181–184), ReQuest (Manzo, 1969; Manzo & Manzo, 1990) is initiated with students asking questions of you related to the initial part of the text; you then ask questions that serve as a model for your students' questions. This process continues through the first few paragraphs of the text, at which point the reading purpose is established through a predicting question in which students speculate regarding story resolution, e.g., "How will Pa get through the blizzard?" After students complete the reading, a follow-up discussion returns to the students' individual predictions. This part of the discussion may involve pairs or small groups of students. ReQuest provides valuable insight into the background knowledge and reasoning processes of individual students and teaches them how to ask questions that enhance meaning construction. This feature is especially valuable in teaching your ESL students.

Reciprocal Teaching. You will recall that this strategy (Palincsar & Brown, 1986) is somewhat similar to ReQuest in that teacher modeling is used to help students develop questions and predictions. Reciprocal Teaching provides a "scaffolding" for the ESL student by giving temporary instructional support in developing the following four skill processes:

1. **Predicting**—speculating on what the author will discuss next in the text.

2. **Question Generation**—creating questions based on the text and the student's background knowledge.

3. **Clarifying**—focusing on meaning-construction problems and taking steps to restore meaning.

4. **Summarizing**—identifying the key idea in a paragraph or a specified section of the text.

The teacher's role in directing discussion is gradually decreased. As individual students in turn assume the teacher's role in using the four skill processes, self-monitoring and student responsibility for learning are developed. A quick review of our discussion of Reciprocal Teaching in Chapter 4 (pp. 184–189) will refresh your memory of this seven-step strategy.

Group Mapping Activity (GMA). The GMA (Davison, 1978, 1982) builds comprehension as students integrate and synthesize story ideas and concepts. A special value of GMA for ESL students is the creation of their own graphic representations of a story. This provides for personal interpretation of story relationships among characters, key events, and plot. These visual representations reflect students' understandings and thinking processes and reduce language fluency demands. But, as we discussed in Chapter 4 (p. 189–196), the activity also provides a close integration of the graphic representation and use of language as students explain their representations. The four steps consist of:

1. After reading or listening to a literature or content selection, students are asked to create their "map" or diagram of what the story is about. (Remember this is a free, unstructured map, which is very different from that produced in concept webs.)

2. Have each student hold up his or her map so that the group can see what he or she has drawn.

3. Invite individual students to share their maps with the rest of the group and provide reasons for developing them. Encourage students to explore relationships among characters, events, and story plot.

4. Continue sharing with peer partners, as students explain why they constructed their map as they did.

5. Conclude the GMA by emphasizing that each map helps us understand the story characters and events, and how these are connected to the story plot. Recognize and positively reinforce children's thinking and mapping efforts.

The GMA helps children reflect on their own thinking as they share their maps with other students. This instructional strategy will also provide important insights into the thinking processes of your ESL students and will be helpful in understanding their language growth.

Motivating Individual and Group Response to Literature

Many ESL students will find your classroom a strange and foreign setting. They are encountering a new language, new interaction patterns, strange classroom rules, and new faces and personalities. These factors have a strong impact on children's self-concept as individuals and as learners. A major responsibility that you carry is to help ESL students understand that they are in a psychologically safe environment, and that their participation is not only welcome but encouraged. Your classroom can provide a stable social and academic environment for their language and literacy development. A significant key to this development is found in instruction that motivates individual and group responses.

It is important to explore the special interests of your children based on your classroom observations. This information will help you to identify literature and informational books that can be used to develop high-interest, motivation, and individual and group response. (Suggested selections are found at the end of this section.) You will find the following strategies valuable in encouraging ESL students' motivation and response to literature.

Read-Aloud Strategy. The read-aloud strategy, discussed in Chapter 6 (pp. 272–279), provides a high degree of instructional flexibility and multiple opportunities for ESL student response. Selections may range from high-interest poetry to predictable books to chapter books.

Try to provide a specific time each day for reading aloud. It is especially important for ESL students that books you select to read are filled with illustrations that support the plot development or informational content of the reading. You may also supplement the illustrations with visual props (a mouse, a monster mask, a model shark, a toy dinosaur), which can be used to enhance story interest. Selections may range from thematic poetry collections, such as *Mice Are Nice* (Larrick, 1990), to high-interest fiction, such as *Where the Wild Things Are* (Sendak, 1963). Informational content books, such as *Sharks* (Berger, 1987), and chapter books, such as *Dinotopia* (Gurney, 1992), can also be used effectively.

Specific suggestions for implementing the read-aloud strategy include the following:

1. Identify the literature, poetry, or information selection. Use a predominately aesthetic instructional stance that will emphasize identification with key characters and will elicit feelings and positive attitudes toward the content. After you become aware of the children's interests, involve them in selecting books. The objective is to encourage motivation, high interest, and response.

2. Familiarize yourself with the story, identify the moods and feeling tones you wish to create in reading the story, and complete a practice reading of at least part of it.

3. Think of the background knowledge and new concepts that may need to be developed in presenting the story to your ESL students by asking yourself, "What new concepts or ideas are central to the story and need to be briefly explained to my students?" Also consider the nature of individual and group response you wish to develop during and after the story. This may range from individual participation, such as creating special animal

sounds during the story, to predicting story outcomes for various parts of the story you have identified (following the DL-TA pattern).

4. Establish an atmosphere for story-reading time by following a ritual such as ringing a special story-reading bell. Make sure your children are seated comfortably and can easily see the illustrations in the book.

5. Present the story-reading using voice intonation (and possible visual aids) that help create story characters, setting, mood, and plot development. Be sure to use a reading pace that matches the visualization of the story, a feature that is very important for ESL students. Let your enthusiasm for the story be evident.

6. Decide on the nature of reader response you wish to use at the conclusion of the story. This may range from the use of the Group Mapping Activity followed by discussion between partner pairs to a group discussion that creates a new ending for the story. Be sensitive to the comfort level of ESL students and encourage their participation through partner pair discussions, small peer-group discussions, and questions that capture the gist of the story rather than specific details. Make sure that you provide sufficient wait-time for responses.

7. Read many books that come from and/or are representative of ESL students' cultures (sources for such books are listed at the end of this section). When possible, use books written in two languages, reading the text to the class in both languages if your fluency in other languages permits. If your ESL students are literate in their primary language, consider inviting one or more of them to co-read a dual-language book with you: Page by page you read the English, the student(s) reads the other language. One cautionary note: We've found some books purporting to be representative of a given culture in which stereotypical illustrations or misrepresentational illustrations belie the fact. Preview books carefully, checking for quality and cultural validity.

Keep your students' attention span in mind to ensure that the read-aloud time is appropriate. The use of literature response journals, discussed below, is a natural follow-up to the Read-Aloud Strategy.

Literature Response Journals. Response journals provide a way for children to express their innermost thoughts, ideas, and feelings related to their literature encounters, including personal responses on topics ranging from peer friendships and school to parents and home. The detailed discussion of literature response journals in Chapter 6 (p. 282–284) provides specific steps for initiating this activity. You will find the ten question prompts in that discussion of particular value in working with ESL students. These range, for example, from "Who was your favorite character? Why?" to "What does this story remind you of in your life?" We recommend also that you allow, and even invite, ESL students to use graphic as well as written response in their journals.

The key point in developing response journals is to encourage ESL students to construct meaning based on their personal interaction and transaction with the text. Your written response to children's journal responses subsequently motivates children and encourages them to continue to express their ideas and communicate with you. Remember that the basic purpose of the journal response is to promote real exchange of ideas about literature and to increase children's transactions with text and with you. It is *not* to provide an opportunity for you to correct spelling and grammar—particularly with ESL students. You may also wish to encourage individual children to exchange journals with a partner and to discuss responses to literature that has been read.

Investigative Questioning Procedure (InQuest). This strategy also holds excellent potential for motivating group and individual responses from ESL students. You will recall from Chapter 6 (pp. 290–292) that InQuest (Shoop, 1986) encourages children to play one of two roles, that of the central story character, or that of an "investigative reporter" who interviews the central story character about key story events. This strategy is designed to help children develop an understanding of how to form questions and how to use them. The "news conference" setting adds realism to the question-and-answer interchange. By directing a follow-up discussion of the news conference, you can have students examine examples of interview questions and responses to determine their effectiveness. These will include "why?" questions to elicit additional information as well as reflection-, evaluation-, and prediction- type questions. InQuest can also serve to develop a higher comfort level for children as they understand the nature of question-and-response interactions.

Multicultural/Multiethnic Literature. The use of multicultural and multiethnic literature holds at least four distinct values for ESL, ethnic minority, and mainstream children. These are (Au, 1993):

1. Students of diverse backgrounds feel pride in their own identity and heritage.
2. Both mainstream students and students of diverse backgrounds learn about the diversity and complexity of American society.
3. All students gain more complete and balanced views of the historical forces that have shaped American society.
4. All students can explore issues of social justice.

In addition, multicultural and multiethnic literature can be used to greatly facilitate children's motivation to read, write, and respond to literature by enhancing their identification, catharsis, and insight as discussed in Chapter 6 (pp. 259–260).

A central instructional goal is to encourage reader response through identification with story characters and personal interpretation, and especially through establishing connections to children's personal life experiences. This instructional stance is predominately aesthetic in nature (see Chapter 6, p. 261) and is designed to encourage children to step through the "magic curtain" and enter into the "journey" of the story or text (Rosenblatt, 1985, 1988). By contrast, the efferent instructional stance may be more predominant in guiding reading to develop knowledge and information to be retained after reading (Rosenblatt, 1988, 1991). Thus, you will be using both the aesthetic and efferent stances to some degree, whether the students are reading fiction or informational material.

The following "starter" list of books has been selected using criteria based on the four values of multicultural/multiethnic literature identified above. Note that an *approximate* age range (4–6, 6–8, 7–9, 8–10, 9–12, 12–young adult) is provided for each book. Remember that the approximate age is just that. You will find that some selections can be used above and below the indicated age, depending on the maturity and interests of your children. While this list primarily contains fiction, you will also find some references to poetry, folktale anthologies, and informational-type books. We have focused our selection on four cultural/ethnic groups. These are Asian-American, found in Table 10-5, African-American, in Table 10-6, Hispanic-American, in Table 10-7, and Native American, in Table 10-8.

There are a number of reference resource books that are helpful in identifying children's books and providing additional ideas on teaching multicultural/multiethnic literature. Some of these include:

Bernice E. Cullinan (Ed.). (1993). *Fact and Fiction: Literature Across the Curriculum.* Newark, DE: International Reading Association.

Vilot J. Harris (Ed). (1992). *Teaching Multicultural Literature in Grades K–8.* Norwood, MA: Christopher-Gordon Publishers, Inc.

Ginny Moore Kruse and Kathleen T. Horning (1991). *Multicultural Literature for Children and Young Adults: A Selected Listing of Books 1980–1990 by and About People of Color.* Madison, WI: Cooperative Children's Book Center, University of WisconsinMadison, Wisconsin Department of Public Instruction.

Mirri V. Lindgren (Ed.). (1991). *The Multicolored Mirror: Cultural Substance in Literature for Children and Young Adults.* Fort Atkinson, WI: Cooperative Children's Book Center, Highsmith Press.

Carol Lynch-Brown and Carl M. Tomlinson (1993). *Essentials of Children's Literature.* Boston: Allyn & Bacon.

Betty Ansin Smallwood (1991). *The Literature Connection: A Read Aloud Guide for Multicultural Classrooms.* Reading, MA: Addison-Wesley.

Multicultural/multiethnic literature will play an important role in your instructional program, not only for your culturally and ethnically diverse students but for your mainstream students as well. We strongly encourage you to review the many ideas for developing literature experiences in your classroom presented in Chapter 6. You will find the discussion on planning and organizing thematic units (pp. 292–296) of particular value in developing your multicultural/multiethnic literature program.

Rhona Blumberg (1985). *Commodore Perry in the Land of the Shogun.* New York: Lothrop. Ages 9–12.

Tricia Brown (1991). *Lee Ann: The Story of a Vietnamese-American Girl.* New York: Putnam. Ages 6–8.

Sook Nyul Choi (1991). *Year of Impossible Goodbyes.* Boston: Houghton Mifflin. Ages 9–12.

Ann Nolan Clark (1978). *To Stand Against the Wind.* New York: Viking. Ages 9–12.

Momoko Ishii (1987). *The Tongue-Cut Sparrow.* New York: Dutton. Ages 7–9.

Ellen Levin (1989). *I Hate English!* New York: Scholastic. Ages 7–9.

Betty Bao Lord (1984). *In the Year of the Boar and Jackie Robinson.* New York: Harper. Ages 7–9.

A. Louie (1982). *Yeh Shen: A Cinderella Story from China.* New York: Philomel.

Junko Morimoto (1990). *My Hiroshima.* New York: Viking. Ages 8–10.

Huynh Quang Nhuong (1982). *The Land I Lost: Adventures of a Boy in Vietnam.* New York: Harper. Ages 9–12.

Nina Pelligrini (1991). *Families Are Different.* New York: Holiday. Ages 6–8.

Dianne Snyder (1988). *The Boy of the Three-Year Nap.* Boston: Houghton Mifflin. Ages 7–9.

Yoshiko Uchida (1971). *Journey to Topaz.* New York: Scribner's. Ages 9–12.

Yoshiko Uchida (1978). *Journey Home.* New York: Atheneum. Ages 9–12.

Ian Wallacez (1984). *Chin Chiang and the Dragon's Dance.* New York: Atheneum. Ages 7–9.

Blia Xiong (1989). *Nine-in-One, Grr! Grr!* New York: Children's Book Press. Ages 6–8.

Paul Yee (1990). *Tales from Gold Mountain: Stories of the Chinese in the New World.* New York: Macmillan. Ages 8–10.

Laurence Yep (1975). *Dragonwings.* New York: Harper. Ages 9–12.

Laurence Yep (1977). *Child of the Owl.* New York: Harper. Ages 12–young adult.

Laurence Yep (1991). *Tongues of Jade.* New York: HarperCollins. Ages 8–12.

TABLE 10-5

Asian-American Literature and Resource Books

Verna Aardema (1975). *Why Mosquitoes Buzz in People's Ears.* New York: Dial. Ages 5–7.

Verna Aardema (1981). *Bringing the Rain to Kapiti Plain: A Nandi Tale.* New York: Dial. Ages 7–9.

Arnold Adoff (1973). *Black Is Brown Is Tan.* New York: Harper. Ages 8–10.

William H. Armstrong (1969). *Sounder.* New York: Harper. Ages 9–12.

Jan Carew (1980). *Children of the Sun.* New York: Little, Brown. Ages 6–8.

Lucille Clifton (1988). *Everett Anderson's Good-bye.* New York: Holt. Ages 5–7.

James Collier & Christopher Collier (1981). *Jump Ship to Freedom.* New York:

Delacorte.

Ossie Davis (1982). *Langston: A Play*. New York: Delacorte. Ages 8–10.

Veronica Freeman Ellis (1981). *Afro-Bets First Book About Africa*. New York: Just Us Books. Ages 4–6.

Muriel Feelings (1974). *Jambo Means Hello: Swahili Alphabet Book*. New York: Dial. Ages 6–8.

Valeri Flournoy (1985). *The Patchwork Quilt*. New York: Dial. Ages 5–7.

Paula Fox (1973). *The Slave Dancer*. New York: Bradbury. Ages 9–12.

Eloise Greenfield (1988). *Under the Sunday Tree*. New York: Harper. Ages 6–10.

Eloise Greenfield (1989). *Nathaniel Talking*. New York: Black Butterfly. Ages 6–10.

Virginia Hamilton (1974). *M.C. Higgins, the Great*. New York: Macmillan. Ages 9–12.

Virginia Hamilton (1984). *The People Could Fly: American Black Folktales*.

Virginia Hamilton (1990). *Cousins*. New York: Philomel. Ages 9–12.

Virginia Hamilton (1991). *The All Jahdu Storybook*. New York: Harcourt.Ages 7–9. New York: Knopf. Ages 7–9.

Mary Hoffman (1991). *Amazing Grace*. New York: Dial. Ages 6–8.

Belinda Hurmence (1982). *A Girl Called Boy*. New York: Clarion. Ages 9–12.

Lynn Joseph (1991). *A Wave in Her Pocket: Stories from Trinidad*. New York: Clarion. Ages 7–9.

Julius Lester (1968). *To Be a Slave*. New York: Dial. Ages 9–young adult.

Julius Lester (1987). *The Tales of Uncle Remus: The Adventures of Brer Rabbit*. New York: Dial. Ages 7–9.

Sharon Bell Mathis (1975). *The Hundred Penny Box*. New York: Viking. Ages 7–9.

Gerald McDermott (1972). *Anansi the Spider: A Tale from the Ashanti*. New York: Holt. Ages 7–9.

Patricia McKissack & Frederick McKissack (1989). *A Long Hard Journey: The Story of the Pullman Porter*. New York: Walker. Ages 8–10.

Milton Meltzer (1984). *The Black Americans: A History in Their Own Words: 1619–1983*. New York: Crowell. Ages 12–young adult.

F. N. Monjo (1970). *The Drinking Gourd*. New York: Harper. Ages 6–8.

Walter Dean Myers (1991). *Now Is Your Time: The African-American Struggle for Freedom*. New York: Harper. Ages 9–12.

Lillie Patterson (1989). *Martin Luther King, Jr. and the Freedom Movement*. New York: A Maker of American Books, Facts on File. Ages 11–young adult.

Leontyne Price (1990) *Aida*. New York: Harcourt. Ages 8–10.

Faith Ringgold (1991). *Tar Beach*. New York: Crown. Ages 6–8.

John Steptoe (1987). *Mufaro's Beautiful Daughters*. New York: Lothrop. Ages 7–9.

Mildred Taylor (1976). *Roll of Thunder, Hear My Cry*. New York: Dial. Ages 9–12.

Glennette Tilley Turner (1989). *Take a Walk in Their Shoes*. New York: Cobblehill. Ages 9–12.

Mary Hays Weik (1966). *The Jazz Man*. New York: Atheneum. Ages 6–8.

Camilla Yarbrough (1979). *Cornrows*. New York: Coward-McCann. Ages 6–8.

TABLE 10-6

African-American Literature and Resource Books

Verna Aardema (1991). *Borreguita and the Coyote*. New York: Knopf. Ages 6–8.
Pura Belpre (1973). *Once in Puerto Rico*. New York: Warne. Ages 8–10.
Lori M. Carlson & Cynthia L. Ventura (Eds.) (1990). *Where Angels Glide at Dawn: New Stories from Latin America*. New York: Lippincott. Ages 12–young adult.
Omar S. Castaneda (1991). *Among the Volcanoes*. New York: Lodestar. Ages 12–young adult.
Ann Nolan Clark (1952). *Secret of the Andes*. New York: Viking. Ages 9–12.
Lulu Delacre (1989). *Arroz con Leche: Popular Songs and Rhymes from Latin America*. New York: Scholastic. Ages 6–10.
Maria Hall Ets & Aurora Labastida (1959). *Nine Days to Christmas: A Story of Mexico*. New York: Viking. Ages 6–8.
Dennis Haseley (1991). *Ghost Catcher*. New York: Harper. Ages 6–8.
Francisco Hinojosa (1984). *The Old Lady Who Ate People*. Boston: Little, Brown. Ages 6–8.
M. A. Jagendorf & R. S. Boggs (1960). *The King of the Mountains: A Treasury of Latin American Folk Stories*. New York: Vanguard. Ages 7–9.
Joseph Krumgold (1953). *And Now Miguel*. New York: Crowell. Ages 8–10.
Marcos Kurtyca & Ana Garcia Kobeh (1984). *Tigers and Opossums: Animal Legends*. Boston: Little, Brown. Ages 7–9.
David Mangurian (1979). *Children of the Incas*. New York: Macmillan. Ages 8–10.
Carolyn Meyer & Charles Gallenkamp (1985). *The Mystery of the Ancient Maya*. New York: Atheneum. Ages 8–10.
Scott O'Dell (1981). *Carlota*. Boston: Houghton Mifflin. Ages 9–12.
Leo Politi (1949). *Song of the Swallows*. New York: Scribner's. Ages 6–9.
Harriet Rohmer (1989). *Uncle Nacho's Hat*. New York: Children's Book Press. Ages 6–8. (English-Spanish)
Gary Soto (1990). *Baseball in April and Other Stories*. New York: Harcourt. Ages 9–12.
Jonah Winter (1991). *Diego*. New York: Knopf. Ages 7–9. (English-Spanish)
Rosalma Zubizarreta, Harriet Rohmer, & David Schecter (1991). *The Woman Who Outshone the Sun*. New York: Children's Book Press. Ages 6–8. (English-Spanish)

TABLE 10-7

Hispanic-American Literature and Resource Books

LEARNING DIVERSITY: STUDENTS WITH SPECIAL NEEDS

In all probability, you will find a range of students with special needs in your classroom. To facilitate our discussion, these students are defined by the following four descriptors and types of classroom responses:

1. **Physical diversity**—responses indicate unusual differences in hearing, vision, speech, neurological response, and physical maturation.

Aliki (1976). *Corn Is Maize: The Gift of the Indians.* New York: Crowell. Ages 6–8.

Laura Adams Armer (1931). *Waterless Mountain.* New York: Longman. Ages 9–12.

Brent Ashabranner (1984). *To Live in Two Worlds: American Indian Youth Today.* New York: Dodd. Ages 9–12.

Olaf Baker (1981). *Where the Buffaloes Begin.* New York: Warne. Ages 7–9.

Byrd Baylor (1975). *The Desert Is Theirs.* New York: Scribner's. Ages 7–9.

Byrd Baylor (1976). *Hawk, I'm Your Brother.* New York: Scribner's. Ages 8–10.

Byrd Baylor (1981). *A God on Every Mountain Top: Stories of Southwest Indian Mountains.* New York: Scribner's. Ages 8–10.

Alex Bealer (1972). *Only the Names Remain: The Cherokees and the Trail of Tears.* New York: Little, Brown. Ages 9–12.

Nathaniel Benchley (1972). *Only Earth and Sky Last Forever.* New York: Harper. Ages 11–young adult.

John Bierhorst (1987). *Doctor Coyote: A Native American Aesop's Fables.* New York: Macmillan. Ages 7–9.

John Bierhorst (Ed.). (1982). *The Whistling Skeleton: American Indian Tales of the Supernatural.* New York: Four Winds. Ages 7–9.

Caron Lee Cohen (1988). *The Mud Pony.* New York: Scholastic. Ages 6–8.

Tomie dePaola (1983). *The Legend of the Bluebonnet.* New York: Putnam. Age 6–8.

Normie Ekoomiak (1990). *Arctic Memories.* New York: Holt. Ages 9–12. (English-Inuktitut)

Russell Freedman (1988). *Buffalo Hunt.* New York: Holiday. Ages 9–12.

Jean Craighead George (1972). *Julie of the Wolves.* New York: Harper. Ages 9–12.

Paul Goble (1978). *The Girl Who Loved Wild Horses.* New York: Bradbury. Ages 6–8.

Paul Goble (1989). *Beyond the Ridge.* New York: Bradbury. Ages 8–10.

Paul Goble (1991). *Iktomi and the Buffalo Skull.* New York: Orchard. Ages 7–9.

Jamake Highwater (1977). *Anpao: An American Indian Odyssey.* New York: Lippincott. Ages 9–12.

Jamake Highwater (1986). *I Wear the Morning Star.* New York: Harper. Ages 9–12.

Marcia Keegan (1991). *Pueblo Boy: Growing Up in Two Worlds.* New York: Cobblehill. Ages 7–9.

Albert Marrin (1990). *War Clouds in the West: Indians and Cavalrymen 1860– 1890.* New York: Atheneum. Ages 7–9.

Bill Martin and John Archambault (1987). *Knots on a Counting Rope.* Boston: Little, Brown. Ages 6–8.

Miska Miles (1971). *Annie and the Old One.* Boston: Little, Brown. Ages 7–9.

Scott O'Dell (1960). *Island of the Blue Dolphins.* Boston: Houghton Mifflin. Ages 9–12.

Scott O'Dell (1988). *Black Star, Bright Dawn.* Boston: Houghton Mifflin. Ages 9–12.

Gail Robinson (1982). *Raven the Trickster: Legends of the North American Indians.* New York: Atheneum. Ages 8–10.

Chief Seattle (1991). *Brother Eagle, Sister Sky.* New York: Dial. Ages 6–10.

Virginia Driving Hawk Sneve (1989). *Dancing Tepees: Poems of American Indian Youth.* New York: Holiday. Ages 9–12.

Elizabeth George Speare (1983). *The Sign of the Beaver.* Boston: Houghton Mifflin. Ages 8–10.

John Steptoe (1984). *The Story of Jumping Mouse.* New York: Lothrop. Ages 7–9.

William Toye (1977). *The Loon's Necklace.* New York: Oxford. Ages 7–9.

TABLE 10-8

Native American Literature and Resource Books

2. **Developmental Learning Diversity**—responses reflect a gap between expected achievement and actual achievement performance or responses may indicate delayed language development, difficulty in integrating and retaining information, and understanding abstract ideas.

3. **Emotional Diversity**—responses range from withdrawn to high levels of activity and aggression.

4. **Giftedness**—responses reflect high creativity, verbal ability, motivation, curiosity, and ability to quickly integrate relationships and ideas.

Children with these special characteristics and differences constitute about 15 percent of school-age students (Lerner, 1985). You will recall from our earlier summary of legislation on diversity that the mainstreaming legislation of 1975 (Public Law 94-142) and the amendments in 1986 and 1990 require the placement of children with indentified disabilities in the "least restrictive instructional environment." This integration of youngsters who had previoulsy been taught in special classrooms into regular classrooms is designed to provide learning opportunities that will enable them to interact with and succeed with mainstream students. The discussion that follows is concerned not only with students defined by the mainstreaming legislation but also with a broader group of children who exhibit characteristics identified by the four descriptors above.

The purpose of this discussion is to assist you in identifying children with special needs in your classroom and in becoming sensitized to their

The Mainstreamed Classroom

learning needs. Some students, such as those with correctable vision and hearing problems or with physical limitations, may be fully mainstreamed in your classroom. Others, such as those with speech differences, will be in your classroom most of the day but will receive special instruction from the speech therapist for part of the school day. Still other students will be in your class along with an American Sign Language (ASL) interpreter, an instructional aide, or guide dog. Some students with severe intellectual or emotional disabilities will receive instruction in public or private separate school or residential facilities.

INSTRUCTIONAL GUIDELINES

The following five guidelines will be helpful in identifying and adjusting instruction to the learning needs of special-needs children:

1. Carefully observe your students' responses to identify behavior suggesting special learning needs. For example, when a child asks to have questions repeated or is consistently unable to follow oral directions, there may be a hearing problem.

2. Understand the school district procedure for referring children to obtain follow-up help and support in identifying the specific nature of the problem. For example, children with speech-correction needs can be identified early in the school year and should be referred at the earliest possible time for special assistance.

3. Involve parents and discuss the special school support planned or the need for outside medical support to assist in diagnosing and correcting the child's suspected problem. Many vision, hearing, and speech problems can be greatly improved and corrected when identified early enough in the child's school experience.

4. Attempt to understand the nature of the learning diversity of children in your classroom through discussions with special education, reading, and other support teachers and staff. Pursue readings suggested to you by them.

5. Use effective learning principles that you have found successful in your teaching. You will find that praise and encouragement, acceptance of approximation rather that insisting on perfection, positive feedback on success, supportive help with learning difficulties, and encouragement of active learning and enthusiasm, are effective principles in teaching special-needs students (just as they are with *all* students).

6. Adjust and adapt your instructional program to meet whatever special learning needs are present in your classroom. Remember that your personal observations, instructional knowledge, insight, and patience will be your most valuable resources in meeting these needs.

The instructional strategies discussed in this and previous chapters can be used with great effectiveness to enhance the learning experiences of special-needs youngsters. The following discussion will be helpful in increasing your identification and understanding of and sensitivity to these students.

PHYSICAL DIVERSITY

Although many physical problems will have been identified and corrected by the time children enter school, you should be alert to "obvious" vision, hearing, speech, and physical maturation problems that may interfere with learning.

A near-vision problem is evident if children hold reading material very close or far away in the attempt to focus vision. The child who squints at writing on the chalkboard, rubs his or her eyes, and has a short attention span may have distance-vision difficulty. The commonly used Snellen vision test will help identify students who have difficulty with distance vision, but not those who have difficulty with close vision, nor will it detect eye fusion problems. Strabismus, the muscular imbalance of one or both eyes, may result in fusion difficulty. Rapid eye fatigue, frequent rubbing of the eyes, headaches, and a limited attention span in dealing with symbols at close range can be symptoms of vision-related problems and may prompt you to refer a child to an ophthalmologist or optometrist for a detailed visual examination. Special care should be given to seating the child whose visual correction does not restore full acuity closer to the center of instructional activities.

A hearing loss can be a serious impediment to language development and can affect literacy acquisition in various ways. Constant requests for repetition of simple directions and inability to respond to questions or comments when the speaker is out of a child's visual field are symptomatic of a hearing loss. These symptoms suggest the need for referral to an audiologist. Hearing loss, particularly of sounds in the high-frequency range, can make it difficult to perceive sound differences and establish sound-letter relationships. For example, the consonants sounds *c, b, k, p, s, th*, and *v* are produced with a relatively high frequency and may present a special problem when such hearing loss is present. Facing these children during instruction and when giving directions and locating their seats close to you can be of great assistance to their learning.

You should be alert for speech difficulties, particularly in the early grades. Be careful not to confuse a speech problem with the highly regular nature of nonmainstream-dialect language forms discussed earlier in this chapter nor with wide ranges of normal language development or temporary conditions (e. g., missing teeth). However, approximately 10 percent of children have a speech problem that will interfere to some degree with communication. Approximately one-half of these youngsters have problems with simple sound substitution, such as *f* for *th*, or *th* for *s*. Many minor special problems can be corrected in the classroom with help and suggestions from your school-district speech therapist, but problems of a more serious nature will require specific therapy or medical attention. For example cleft palate, in which the roof of the mouth has failed to fuse before birth, can be corrected by surgery. If this is not completed early in the child's language development, it is more difficult for the child to develop clear enunciation after correction. The special therapy for later correction will require assistance by the speech therapist.

You should also be sensitive to differences in physical maturation of your children. For many children the hand-eye motor coordination necessary for writing presents a formidable task. Handwriting involves small-muscle coordination and control that takes time to develop in the early grades. Individual variation in muscular control must be expected. Manuscript printing, for example, requires less muscular coordination than does cursive writing, and some children should be encouraged to continue to use manuscript forms, with a gradual transition to cursive writing.

DEVELOPMENTAL LEARNING DIVERSITY

Intellectual development in children varies, and it is important to take this into account in your language and literacy instruction. A child whose learning rate is very fast may be completely frustrated in a classroom that provides only for traditional "three group" instruction. By contrast, a child with a slower learning rate will be constantly discouraged and soon experience motivation and achievement difficulties if provision is not made for his or her learning rate.

Among children of average intellectual ability, it is not unusual to find children who do not perform at their level of ability. In the early grades, a disproportionately large number of such children will be boys. The reason for this gender difference is not completely understood, but a probable cause in this country is cultural expectation, which differs for boys and girls. Girls are encouraged to engage in social activities and games that are more verbally oriented, but boys are expected to be "rough and tumble" and more physically oriented. Another factor contributing to this difference is found in the more rapid physiological development of girls in fine-motor control.

It is possible that you will encounter a child in your classroom who experiences difficulty in achieving independence in word-analysis skills and independent reading, but is able to listen to and comprehend language normally. The term *dyslexia* is often used to describe this learning difficulty. Great care must be exercised, however, in using this label. The word dyslexia derives from the Latin root "dys," meaning *bad* or *difficult*, and the Greek root "lexia" meaning *word*. Dyslexia has become a catch-all term used by some educators and psychologists to describe inability to read, regardless of reason.

The term dyslexia was introduced in the late 1800s by Berlin, a German ophthalmologist, to "describe a special group of patients who experienced great difficulty in reading because of cerebral disease" (Lindholm, 1993; Richardson, 1989). This definition of dyslexia, and others such as "cognitive word blindness" are very misleading, and can serve to label children in a most negative way.

Recent work on the study of the phenomenon labeled as dyslexia allows us to be more specific in our meaning. Kamhi (1992) defines dyslexia as a developmental language disorder that involves difficulty in processing phonological (speech sound) information. This involves difficulty in processing letters (and print) through the neurological system and connecting them with a phonological representation in memory. Children who experience this problem often have difficulty in developing phonological awareness and oral reading. You will recall from our discussion in Chapter 8 that phonemic (or phonological) awareness, the understanding that spoken words are composed of sounds, is a critical concept essential to developing children's understanding of sound-letter relationships in the reading process.

The value of this recent definition is that it describes dyslexia in a specific way using descriptors that enable us to distinguish between students with these characteristics and students who may be experiencing difficulty because of negative attitude, poor instruction, and a variety of other reasons. If you find a child who is having great difficulty in developing phonemic awareness, phonemic segmentation, and the development of letter-sound relationships (see Chapter 8), pay close attention to that child for possible referral for additional evaluation. Before referral, however, work with the child to develop these areas. Many of the instructional strategies discussed in Chapter 8 under the topic "Developing Phonemic Awareness and Phonemic Segmentation" (pp. 389–392) will be of value in working with children who exhibit this type of problem. In addition, the comprehension strategies developed in Chapter 4 can be applied to comprehension development in both listening and early reading.

Some children may experience substantial general learning difficulty in their educational experience. These youngsters may have delayed language development, exhibit a very short attention span, and have difficulty in grasping, integrating, and retaining new information. These characteristics may be indicative of a developmental learning disability known as mild mental retardation. Some developmental learning disabled students may be mainstreamed in your classroom for part of the day, but in most cases will receive additional instruction from special education teachers. The educational goals for these students will in most ways be very similar, if not identical, to those for your regular students. The following suggestions will be helpful in working with learning disabled students (Smith & Luckasson, 1992, p. 146):

1. Make you sure you have the student's attention as you introduce new concepts and initiate instruction.

2. Select learning goals and objectives that incorporate the student's background knowledge and interests.

3. Use rich contextual support in your instruction and relate the new ideas to the student's background knowledge and experience.

4. Use concrete materials and manipulatives (rather than symbols or representations) in introducing new skills and concepts.

5. Provide for the child's active participation and involvement as you introduce and develop the new idea or concept.

6. Provide opportunity for practicing and applying the new information in active learning situations over a period of time.

As you account for developmental learning diversity in your classroom, it is important to keep three points in mind: First, children do vary in individual learning rate; second, because of learning rate, their language and literacy achievement variation across your classroom will increase as the year progresses; and third, your instruction needs to account for this developmental learning diversity.

EMOTIONAL DIVERSITY

It is often difficult to determine whether a child's emotional adjustment is the source of difficulty in his or her literacy progress or if the literacy difficulty has contributed to the emotional state. The features presented in Table 10-9 describe children who are having emotional adjustment difficulty (Smith & Luckasson, 1992, p. 316).

Few or no friends
Problems with family relations
Problems with relationships with teachers
Hyperactive behavior, indicated by excessive movement
Aggression toward self and others
Impulsivity
Immature social skills
Feelings of depression and unhappiness
Withdrawal into self
Anxiety or fearfulness
Ideas of suicide expressed
Distractibility or inability to pay attention for
  a length of time comparable to peers

TABLE 10-9

Possible Signs of Emotional Adjustment Difficulty in School
Source: Reproduced with permission from Smith & Luckasson, 1992, p. 316.

521

Some children with emotional problems read without difficulty and even use reading as an escape from their problems. By contrast, there are children who show no sign of emotional difficulty outside the instructional environment but demonstrate significant adjustment problems when confronted with reading and other literacy tasks. Frequently these children have come to school eager to learn, but repeated failure in the classroom and inadequate provision for instructional needs have produced high-level frustration and anxiety.

Although negative parental attitudes toward school can contribute to a child's learning difficulty, such attitudes are seldom the sole causal factor in literacy development. Nevertheless, it is important to be alert to evidence suggesting that the child may be experiencing excessive pressure from home to achieve, continuous home conflict between parents, overprotection, or other emotionally disturbing home influences. Such home environments can contribute significantly to a child's anxieties and uncertainties and interfere with a positive concept of self. Should such evidence be present, it is important to arrange a conference or some other communication with the child's parents or caretaker.

Additional factors, such as a child's social adjustment or a personality conflict between you and the child, can interfere with the child's emotional stability and literacy achievement. Some children use classroom failure as a way of obtaining special attention from the teacher, which may reflect lack of emotional support at home, at school, or both. If a child has emotional adjustment problems, it is important to provide a sympathetic and supporting classroom environment *and* to clearly identify the nature of classroom interaction and social boundaries. The following suggestions will be of value in teaching emotionally diverse students (Smith & Luckasson, 1992, p. 322):

1. Establish clear rules for the class.
2. Role play and practice the rules with the students.
3. Reinforce individual students when they follow a rule.
4. Provide fair and realistic consequences for following and not following rules.
5. Foster cooperation and friendship by using cooperative learning techniques to teach students how to work in small groups.
6. Communicate regularly with the students' parents or caretakers.
7. Teach students to negotiate and mediate conflict.
8. Keep up-to-date records on behavior changes, especially during changes in medication.
9. Find at least one opportunity each day to praise the child.
10. Learn to carefully observe and listen to the child.

The importance of consistent communication with the child and with adults at home cannot be overemphasized in your work with emotionally diverse students.

GIFTEDNESS

GIFTEDNESS

Students identified as "gifted" possess learning characteristics that allow rapid acquisition of literacy skills. These students frequently have a cluster of intellectual abilities such as exceptional verbal reasoning, curiosity, creativity, motivation, and ability to apply background knowledge rapidly and integrate new relationships and ideas. These students are often high achievers and appear to learn and retain knowledge easily. They are often self-critical, socially mature, persistent, individualistic, and leaders.

Given this description, we often think of gifted children as those individuals who sail through school with no problems. In fact, gifted students do have difficulties in school. Tuttle (1991) identifies gifted characteristics and potential problems in school as shown in Table 10-10. These potential problem areas deserve careful consideration as you plan your instruction. Chief among these is the need to adjust your attitude toward their creative and individualistic

CHARACTERISTICS	SAMPLE POTENTIAL
Curiosity	Continually raises questions that sometime interfere with the teacher's lesson; needs access to a variety of materials.
Persistence	Focuses on areas of personal interest, sometimes at the expense of work in other areas often required by the teacher; is viewed as stubborn.
Critical Thinking	Is reluctant to submit work that is not perfect; may not even begin a project because of feeling that it may not reach own excessively high standards; criticizes peers and teachers, causing negative reactions and feelings.
Abtract Thinking	Neglects details once generalizations are mastered; jumps to conclusions about specific steps or details in a procedure; becomes frustrated by others' inability to understand general concepts quickly; designs own procedures that may be in conflict with those taught by the teacher.
High Verbal Ability	Dominates class and informal discussions; is sarcastic of others; argues for the sake of argument, detracting from the progress of the lesson; uses humor not always understood or accepted by others.

—— **TABLE 10-10** ——

Characteristics Associated with Giftedness
Source: Reproduced with permission from Tuttle, 1991, p. 373. See also Ruddell, 1993, p.335, Figure 10.5.

responses, the need to involve them in cooperative activities and develop their tolerance to responses from others, and the need for them to challenge and broaden their literacy and intellectual growth beyond the planned curriculum.

Many of the strategies discussed in previous chapters hold excellent potential for challenging gifted students. The following suggestions will also be helpful in designing literacy instruction for them (Smith & Luckasson, 1992):

1. Encourage your students to become independent learners who pursue topics of high personal interest.
2. Initiate small group cooperative-learning activities to develop social interchange skills and tolerance for the thinking of others.
3. Enrich units of study with guest speakers, field trips, demonstrations, and interest centers.
4. Watch for signs of boredom and provide intellectual stimulation through cooperative learning problem-solving discussions involving interpretative, applicative, and transactive thinking.
5. Create a psychologically safe classroom environment where novel ideas can be discussed and accepted.
6. Develop instructional interactions and activities that use questions to generate application of higher-level thinking skills.
7. Teach and foster the use of independent library and research skills.

It is important to note that many of these suggestions are readily applied to mixed-ability groups as well. By creating a stimulating and active learning environment, you not only provide for your gifted students but for all children in your classroom.

SPECIAL-NEEDS STUDENTS AND CHILDREN'S LITERATURE

Table 10-11 contains a "starter list" of children's literature that you will find helpful for your special-needs students. You will find that many of these books are appropriate for most children in your classroom depending on their interest and background knowledge. This literature is probably best used by encouraging students to explore and read at their leisure. A central point for children in this reading is to gain understanding of self and to build a positive self-concept. Keep in mind Gentile and McMillan's (1987) recommendation, however, that children should not be *required* to read materials that parallel specific conditions or traumatic events in their lives.

1. PHYSICAL DIVERSITY
SPEECH, VISION, OR HEARING
Edna S. Levine (1974). *Lisa and Her Soundless World.* New York: Human
  Sciences. Ages 6–8.
Jean Little (1972). *From Anna.* New York: Harper. Ages 9–12.
Patricia MacLachlan (1949). *Through Grandpa's Eyes.* New York: Harper & Row.
  Ages 8–10.
J. W. Peterson (1984). *I Have a Sister. My Sister Is Deaf.* New York: Harper
  & Row. Ages 8–12.
Ellen Raskin (1968). *Spectacles.* New York: Atheneum. Ages 6–9.
E. B. White (1970). *The Trumpet of the Swan.* New York: Harper & Row. Ages 10–12.
Jane Yolen (1977). *The Seeing Stick.* New York: Crowell. Ages 1–12.

PHYSICAL
Frances Hodgson Burnett (1912). *The Secret Garden.* New York: Lippincott.
  Ages 10–young adult.
Tricia Brown (1984). *Someone Special, Just Like You.* New York: Holt. Ages 6–8.
Eloise Greenfield & Alesia Revia (1981). *Alesia.* New York: Philomel. Ages
  12–young adult.
Joe Lasker (1980). *Nick Joins in.* New York: Whitman. Ages 5–8.
Mary L. Riskin (1981). *Apple Is My Sign.* Boston: Houghton Mifflin. Ages
  10–young adult.
Harriette Gillem Robinet (1980). *Ride the Red Cycle.* Boston: Houghton
  Mifflin. Ages 7–11.
Ron Roy (1985). *Move Over, Wheelchairs Coming Through!* Boston:
  Houghton Mifflin. Ages 6–12.

2. DEVELOPMENTAL LEARNING DIVERSITY
Betsy Byars (1970). *Summer of the Swans.* New York: Viking. Ages 10–12.
Lucille Clifton (1980). *My Friend Jacob.* New York: E. P. Dutton. Ages 5–7.
Jamie Gilson (1980). *Do Bananas Chew Gum?* New York: Lothrop, Lee &
  Shepard. Ages 9–11.
Patricia Hermes (1983). *Who Will Take Care of Me?* New York: Harcourt
  Brace & Jovanovich. Ages 6–10.
Janet Kamien (1979). *What If You Couldn't …? A Book About Special
  Needs.* New York: Scribner's. Ages 8–12.
Joe Lasker (1974). *He's My Brother.* Chicago: Whitman. Ages 5–8.
Jean Little (1968). *Take Wing.* Boston: Little, Brown. Ages 8–12.
Maureen Crane Wartski (1979). *My Brother Is Special.* New York:
  Westminster. Ages 10–12.

3. EMOTIONAL DIVERSITY
Byrd Baylor (1974). *Everybody Needs a Rock.* New York: Aladdin. Ages 6–8.
Rose Blue (1980). *Wishful Lying.* New York: Human Science Press. Ages 6–9.
Miriam Cohen (1967). *Will I Have a Friend?* New York: Collier-Macmillan. Ages 6–8.
Aylette Jonness (1990). *Families: A Celebration of Diversity, Commitment,
  and Love.* Boston: Houghton Mifflin. Ages 6-12.
Steven Kroll (1981). *Friday the 13th.* New York: Holiday House. Ages 5–7.
Judith Viorst (1972). *Alexander and the Terrible, Horrible, No Good, Very
  Bad Day.* New York: Aladdin. Ages 6–10.
Eiveen Wimann (1982). *It Takes Brains.* New York: Atheneum. Ages 10–12.

TABLE 10-11

Children's Literature for Special Needs Students

4. GIFTEDNESS

Graeme Base (1988). *The Eleventh Hour: A Curious Mystery*. New York: Abrams. Ages 10–12.

John D. Fitzgerald (1967). *The Great Brain*. New York: Dell. Ages 8–12.

Louis Fitzhugh (1964). *Harriet the Spy*. New York: Dell. Ages 8–12.

C. S. Lewis (1950). *The Lion, the Witch, and the Wardrobe*. New York: Collier. Ages 10–young adult.

Lois Lowry (1979). *Anastasia Krupnik*. New York: Bantam. Ages 8–12.

Marilyn Sadler (1992). *Alistair's Time Machine*. New York: Simon & Schuster. Ages 5–8.

Sandra Warren (1987). *Being Gifted: Because You're Special from the Rest*. New York: Trillium. Ages 4–7.

TABLE 10-11 CONTINUED

Creating a Multicultural Environment for Diversity

A Summary

Our discussion has emphasized the great language, cultural, and achievement diversity found in our schools today. We have described the nature of this diversity that you can, in all probability, expect to find in your classroom. A variety of instructional strategies have been presented and reviewed from earlier chapters to assist you in meeting the instructional needs of your diverse group of children.

In addition to these ideas and strategies, it is important for you to consider the overall philosophy and commitment you hold toward creating a multicultural teaching environment for children. Banks (1989, 1993) has proposed a way of thinking about our commitment to multicultural education. He proposes four approaches that reflect different levels of commitment to the integration of ethnic content. Banks' approaches are shown in Figure 10-3 and explained here.

Level 1, the Contributions Approach, is the traditional approach that most of us have experienced in our schooling. The major focus is on cultural heroes and holidays and specific aspects of a given culture such as customs we believe to be unique to that culture. This, for example, may involve reading Lillie Patterson's *Martin Luther King, Jr. and the Freedom Movement*, celebrating this national holiday and examining Martin Luther King, Jr.'s role in the civil rights movement. This multicultural approach is the most convenient and easiest to use and may fit well into a given time of the year. We are not suggesting that you abandon this aspect

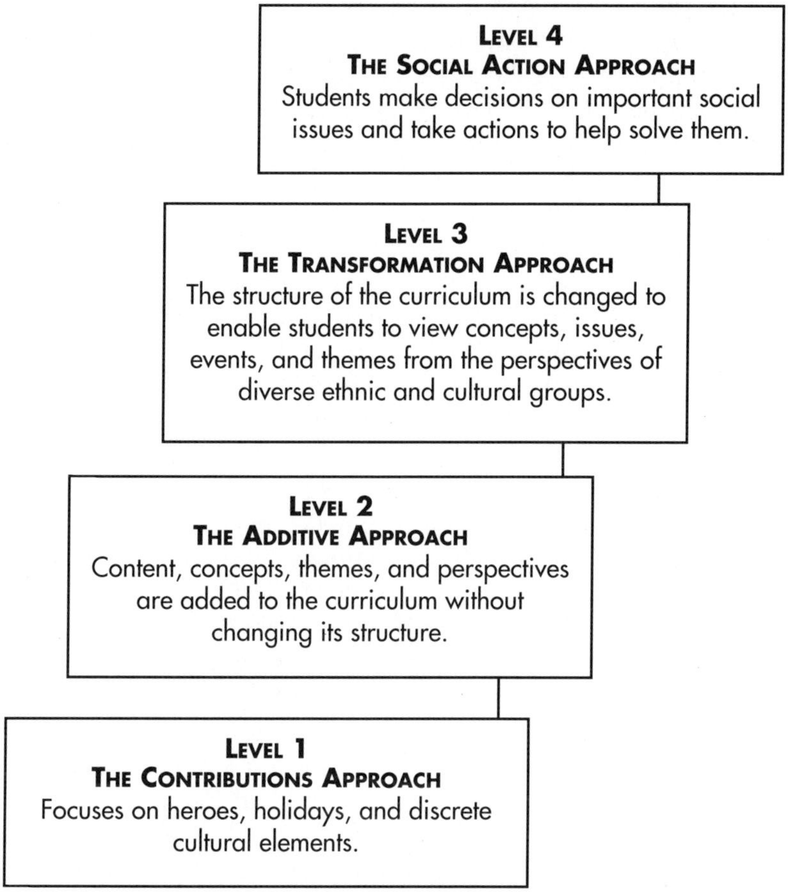

```
┌─────────────────────────────────────┐
│              LEVEL 4                 │
│      THE SOCIAL ACTION APPROACH      │
│   Students make decisions on important social │
│   issues and take actions to help solve them. │
└─────────────────────────────────────┘

┌─────────────────────────────────────┐
│              LEVEL 3                 │
│     THE TRANSFORMATION APPROACH      │
│   The structure of the curriculum is changed to │
│     enable students to view concepts, issues,   │
│      events, and themes from the perspectives of │
│        diverse ethnic and cultural groups.       │
└─────────────────────────────────────┘

┌─────────────────────────────────────┐
│              LEVEL 2                 │
│        THE ADDITIVE APPROACH         │
│   Content, concepts, themes, and perspectives │
│      are added to the curriculum without      │
│           changing its structure.             │
└─────────────────────────────────────┘

┌─────────────────────────────────────┐
│              LEVEL 1                 │
│      THE CONTRIBUTIONS APPROACH      │
│   Focuses on heroes, holidays, and discrete │
│              cultural elements.             │
└─────────────────────────────────────┘
```

FIGURE 10-3

Levels of Multicultural Education. (Reproduced with permission from Banks, 1994, p. 25.)

of your curriculum but that you recognize that, when used alone, it frequently fails to identify underlying cultural values and the historical and cultural contexts.

Level 2, the Additive Approach, essentially adds content and concepts in the form of thematic units of study. For example, the thematic unit may be developed around folktales using the Cinderella theme (Au, 1993). The addition of Steptoe's *Mufaro's Beautiful Daughters* (see Table 10-5) and Louie's *Yeh Shen: A Cinderella Story from China* (see Table 10-6) provides other versions of this theme in representations of different cultures. While this approach at least exposes children to literature of diverse groups, it presents little opportunity to consider the underlying relationships between cultures.

In Level 3, the Transformational Approach, the relationship between cultures is examined and students are enabled to consider concepts, issues, and events from the perspective of diverse ethnic and cultural groups. An example of this approach is found in the use of *Julie of the Wolves* by Jean Craighead George as a focal book to foster consideration of similarities and differences between another culture (that of the Eskimos or Inuits) and the cultures of your children, and of the changes and conflicts that occur in a society over time (see Chapter 6, p. 294). The Transformational Approach offers opportunity to understand how our society has been changed through contributions of diverse cultures and provides opportunity for students to develop pride in their own culture as they recognize these contributions. This approach requires greater time and energy to become familiar with new content and resources and meld these into your transformed instructional program. The value of this approach, however, is the integration of ethnic and cultural content much more effectively into the curriculum.

Level 4, the Social Action Approach, is designed to assist students in identifying and gathering information related to important social issues and problems, examining values and assumptions underlying these, and taking action by proposing solutions to solve them. For example, key social issues confronted by African-Americans may be found in literature such as Faith Ringgold's *Tar Beach* at the primary grade level and Mildred Taylor's *Roll of Thunder, Hear My Cry* at the intermediate grade levels. The importance of equal rights, the absence of discrimination in the community and at work, and the need for change in attitudes and perceptions toward different ethnic and cultural groups are key issues and problems for consideration. Such discussion enables students to clarify their own thinking, search for new information related to these issues, and consider possible actions and solutions. This approach calls for your willingness to plan more extensively as you locate resources, examine possible issues to be developed, incorporate cooperative discussion groups, and become prepared to raise controversial issues and assist in resolving them. The great value, however, is in communicating the contributions and importance of cultural and ethnic diversity to our society. Theme cycles and project-based learning fit the social action approach nicely.

Our discussion in this chapter presents a major challenge to you as you assume the instructional leadership for your classroom—that of providing a multicultural/multiethnic environment that will provide for the diverse learning needs of all of your students. The approach recommended is consistent with previous chapters by viewing language and literacy development from a constructivist perspective that calls for meaning construction and active learning as the centerpieces of your teaching.

DOUBLE ENTRY JOURNAL

Go back to the map you created before reading the chapter. Add to it, make changes, or create a new map of diversity *based upon your new ideas, impressions, and understandings. Share both your maps with a partner and explain the differences.*

Supporting Activities

1. Reread the two transcripts featuring Lionel and the children using Hawaiian Creole English found at the beginning of this chapter. What effect does teacher sensitivity and understanding of language and cultural diversity have on children's motivation to learn? How is Krashen's "affective filter" and instructional requirements for optimal success (see Instructional Approaches and Strategies) related to this motivation issue? Discuss these questions with a class partner.

2. Review our brief overview of legislation on diversity. What impact do you believe the legislation enacted over the past half-century has had on classroom instruction? What effect does it have on your teaching? Why do you believe the change process designed to meet instructional needs for children from diverse ethnic and language groups takes so long to implement in the classroom? Capture your thoughts through notes and share your ideas with a class partner.

3. Arrange for an observation of an elementary classroom where nonmainstream English and/or bilingual children are represented. Identify one child to observe during reading and writing instruction. Briefly describe the child's dialect and/or proficiency in English. How does the child respond and communicate with the teacher? With other children? How does the teacher communicate with the child? How would you describe

the child's attitude toward learning and classroom instruction? How would you describe the teacher's attitude toward the child and her or his progress? Discuss your observations with a class partner.

4. Briefly review our discussion and guidelines on using the Sheltered English strategy. Identify a high-interest story appropriate for the grade level (and developmental reading level) of greatest interest to you. Use your story and outline an instructional plan for ESL students of Limited English Proficiency using the Sheltered English guidelines. Be sure to account for vocabulary that is important in understanding the content of the story and vocabulary that will be used in your lesson to explain the content. Discuss your outline and ideas with a class partner.

5. Identify and review two children's literature books that represent two cultures different from your own (see Multicultural/Multiethnic Literature discussion). Use one of these books and develop a brief lesson plan using the read-aloud strategy. Arrange for a classroom visitation to present your literature selection to a small group of children. What insights did you derive from the children's responses? How would you change your presentation plan for a second presentation?

6. Review our discussion on Learning Diversity: Students with Special Needs. Select the area of student diversity that is of greatest interest to you. Formulate a series of interview questions related to classroom instruction and special learning needs for these children. Arrange to interview a classroom teacher and the school principal using your questions. Share your findings with a class partner.

REFERENCES

Allen, V.G. (1991). Teaching bilingual and ESL children. In J. Flood, J. M. Jensen, D. Lapp, & J. R. Squire (Eds.), *Handbook of research on teaching the English language arts* (pp. 356–364). New York: Macmillan.

Au, K. H. (1980). Participation structures in a reading lesson with Hawaiian children: Analysis of a culturally appropriate instructional event. *Anthropology and Educational Quarterly, 11(2)*, 91–115.

Au, K.H. (1993). *Literacy instruction in multicultural settings.* New York: Harcourt Brace Jovanovich.

Banks, J. A. (1993). Approaches to multicultural curriculum reform. In J. A. Banks & C. A. M. Banks (Eds.), *Multicultural education: Issues and perspectives* (2nd ed.) (pp. 195–214). Boston: Allyn & Bacon.

Banks, J.A. (1994). *An Introduction to multicultural education.* Boston: Allyn & Bacon.

Banks, J. A., & Banks, C. A. M. (1989). *Multicultural education.* Boston: Allyn & Bacon.

Cummins, J. (1981). Four misconceptions about language proficiency in bilingual education. *NABE Journal, 5,* 31–45.

Cummins, J. (1986). Empowering minority students: A framework for intervention. *Harvard Educational Review, 56,* 18–36.

Cummins, J. (1989). Language and literacy acquisition in bilingual contexts. *Journal of Multilingual and Multicultural Development, 10*(1), 17–31.

Davidson, J. L. (1978, April). *Mapping: A dynamic extension of the DR-TA.* Paper presented at the meeting of the IRA Language-Experience Special Interest Group, San Antonio, TX.

Davidson, J. L. (1982). The group mapping activity for instruction in reading and thinking. *Journal of Reading, 26,* 52–56.

Gallimore, R., Boggs, J. W., & Jordan, C. (1974). *Culture, behavior and education: A study of Hawaiian-Americans.* Beverly Hills, CA: Sage Publications.

Gentile, L. M., & McMillan, M. M. (1987). *Stress and reading difficulties: Research, assessment and intervention.* Newark, DE: International Reading Association.

Goodman, K., & Goodman, Y. (1978). *Reading of American children whose language is a stable rural dialect of English or a language other than English* (NIE-C-00-3-0087). Washington, DC: U.S. Department of Health, Education and Welfare.

Grant, C. A., & Sleeter, C. E. (1993). Race, class, gender, and disability in the classroom. In J. A. Banks & C. A. M. Banks (Eds.), *Multicultural education: Issues and perspectives* (pp. 48–68). Boston: Allyn & Bacon.

Gunderson, L. (1991). *ESL literacy instruction: A guidebook to theory and practice.* Englewood Cliffs, NJ: Prentice-Hall.

Haggard, M. R. (1982). The vocabulary self-collection strategy: An active approach to word learning. *Journal of Reading, 26,* 203–207.

Heath, S. B. (1982). What no bedtime story means: Narrative skills at home and school. *Language and Society, 2,* 49–76.

Heath, S. B. (1983). *Ways with words: Language, life, and work in communities and classrooms.* Cambridge, UK: Cambridge University Press.

Hernandez, H. (1989). *Multicultural education: A teacher's guide to content and process.* Columbus, OH: Merrill.

Kamhi, A. B. (1992). Response to historical perspective: A developmental language perspective. *Journal of Learning Disabilities, 25,* 48–52.

Kershner, V. (1993, June 21). Why immigration laws are so hard to change. *San Francisco Chronicle,* p. A7.

Krashen, S. D. (1987). *Principles and practice in second language acquisition.* Englewood Cliffs, NJ: Prentice-Hall.

Labov, W. (1967). Some sources of reading problems for Negro speakers of nonstandard English. In Alexander Frazier (Ed.), *New Directions in Elementary English* (pp. 143–153). Champaign, IL: National Council of Teachers of English.

Lerner, J. (1985). *Learning disabilities: Theories, diagnosis, and teaching strategies* (4th ed.). Boston: Houghton Mifflin.

Lindholm, K. A. (1993). *The dyslexic child: Suggestions to meet the need of the student in the classroom.* Unpublished Master's thesis, University of California, Berkeley, CA.

Manzo, A. V. (1969). The ReQuest procedure. *Journal of Reading, 13,* 123–126.

Manzo, A.V., & Manzo, U. (1990). *Content area reading: A heuristic approach.* Columbus, OH: Merrill.

Moll, L. C. (1988). Some key issues in teaching Latino students. *Language Arts, 65*(5), 465–472.

Mydnas, S. (1993, June 24). Immigration opposition grows. *San Francisco Chronicle,* p. A3.

Ovando, C. J. (1988). Language diversity and education. In J. A. Banks & C. A. M. Banks (Eds.), *Multicultural education: Issues and perspectives* (pp. 208–227). Boston: Allyn & Bacon.

Palincsar, A. S., & Brown, A. L. (1986). Interactive teaching to promote independent learning from text. *The Reading Teacher, 39,* 771–777.

Piestrup, A. M. (1973). *Black dialect interference and accommodation of reading instruction in first grade* (Monographs of the Language-Behavior Research Laboratory, No. 4). Berkeley: University of California.

Portes, A., & Rumbaut, R. G. (1990). *Immigrant America: A portrait.* Berkeley: University of California Press.

Ramirez, A. G. (1985). *Bilingualism through schooling: Cross-cultural education for minority and majority students.* Albany, NY: State University of New York Press.

Raphael, T. E. (1982). Question-answering strategies for children. *The Reading Teacher, 36,* 186–190.

Raphael, T. E. (1986). Teaching question-answer relationships, revisited. *The Reading Teacher, 36,* 516–523.

Richardson, S. O. (1989). Specific developmental dyslexia: Retrospective and prospective views. *Annals of Dyslexia, 39,* 3–23.

Rosenblatt, L. M. (1985). The transactional theory of literary work: Implications for research. In C. R. Cooper (Ed.), *Researching response to literature and the teaching of literature: Points of departure* (pp. 33–53). Norwood, NJ: Ablex.

Rosenblatt, L. M. (1988). *Writing and reading: The transactional theory* (Report No. 13). Berkeley: University of California, Center for the Study of Writing.

Rosenblatt, L. M. (1991). Literature—S.o.s.! *Language Arts, 68,* 444–448.

Rotberg, I. C. (1982). Some legal and research considerations in establishing federal policy in bilingual education. *Harvard Educational Review, 52*(2), 149–168.

Ruddell, M. R. (1993). *Teaching content reading and writing.* Boston: Allyn & Bacon.

Ruddell, R. B., & Ruddell, M. R. (1994). Language acquisition and literacy processes. In R. B. Ruddell, M. R. Ruddell, & H. Singer (Eds.), *Theoretical models and processes of reading* (4th ed.)(pp. 83–103). Newark, DE: International Reading Association.

Saville-Troike, M. (1984). What *really* matters in second language learning for academic achievement. *TESOL Quarterly, 18*, 199–220.

Selinker, L. (1972). Interlanguage. *International Review of Applied Linguistics, 10*, 209–231.

Shoop, M. (1986). InQuest: A listening and reading comprehension strategy. *The Reading Teacher, 39*, 660–674.

Smith, D. D, & Luckasson, R. (1992). *Introduction to special education: Teaching in an age of challenge.* Boston: Allyn & Bacon.

Snyder, T., & Hoffman, C. M. (1991). *Digest of educational statistics, 1990.* Washington, DC: National Center for Educational Statistics.

Stauffer, R. G. (1969). *Directing reading maturity as a cognitive process.* New York: Harper & Row.

Stauffer, R. G. (1976). *Teaching reading as a thinking process.* New York: Harper & Row.

Stein, C. B., Jr. (1986). *Sink or swim: The politics of bilingual education.* New York: Praeger.

Tuttle, F. B., Jr. (1991). Teaching the gifted. In J. Flood, J. M. Jenson, D. Lapp, & J. R. Squire (Eds.), *Handbook of research on teaching English and the language arts* (pp. 372–379). New York: Macmillan.

Valdés, G. (1991). *Bilingual minorities and language issues in writing: Toward profession-wide responses to a new challenge* (Tech. Rep. No. 54). Berkeley: University of California Center for the Study of Writing.

Waggoner, D. (1984). The need for bilingual education: Estimates from the 1980 census. *NABE Journal, 8*(2), 1–34.

Watson, D. L., Northcutt, L., & Rydell, L. (1989). Teaching bilingual students successfully. *Educational Leadership, 46*, 59–61.

Weinberg, M. (1977). *A chance to learn: The history of race and education in the United States.* Cambridge, MA: Harvard University Press.

Wilson, C. (1993). *The relative influence of language versus minority status on the educational achievement of language minority students: A review of the literature.* Unpublished manuscript, University of California, Division of Language and Literacy, Berkeley.

Wong Fillmore, L. (1976). *The second time around: Cognitive and social strategies in second language acquisition.* Unpublished doctoral dissertation, Stanford University, CA.

Wong Fillmore, L., & Valadez, C. (1986). Teaching bilingual learners. In M. C. Wittrock (Ed.), *Handbook of research on teaching* (pp. 648–685). New York: Macmillan.

Asian-American literature and resource books—see Table 10-5, p. 512

African-American literature and resource books—see Table 10-6, pp. 512–513.

Hispanic-American literature and resource books—see Table 10-7, p. 514

Native American literature and resource books—see Table 10-8, p.p. 515.

Children's literature for special needs students—see Table 10-11, pp. 525–526.

General Children's Literature References

Berger, G. (1987). *Sharks.* New York: Doubleday.

Eastman, P. D. (1960). *Are you my mother?* New York: Random House.

Fox, M. (1987). *Hattie and the fox.* Scarsdale, New York: Bradbury.

Galdone, P. (1975). *The gingerbread boy.* New York: Clarion.

Gurney, J. (1992). *Dinotopia.* Atlanta: Turner Publishing.

Hogrogian, N. (1971). *One fine day.* New York: Aladdin.

Larrick, N. (1990). *Mice are nice.* New York: Philomel Books.

Martin, B. (1983). *Brown bear, brown bear, what do you see?* New York: Holt.

Sendak, M. (1963). *Where the wild things are.* New York: HarperCollins.

General Multicultural/Multiethnic Literature References

Cullinan, B. E. (Ed.). (1993). *Fact and fiction: Literature across the curriculum.* Newark, DE: International Reading Association.

Harris, V. J. (Ed.). (1992). *Teaching multicultural literature in grades K–8.* Norwood, MA: Christopher-Gordon.

Kruse, G. M., & Horning, K. T. (1991). *Multicultural literature for children and young adults: A selected listing of books 1980–1990 by and about people of color.* Madison, WI: Cooperative Children's Book Center, University of Wisconsin-Madison, Wisconsin Department of Public Instruction.

Lindgren, M. V. (Ed.). (1991). *The multicolored mirror: Cultural substance in literature for children and young adults.* Fort Atkinson, WI: Cooperative Children's Book Center, Highsmith Press.

Lynch-Brown, C., & Tomlinson, C. M. (1993). *Essentials of children's literature.* Boston: Allyn & Bacon.

Smallwood, B. A. (1991). *The literature connection: A read aloud guide for multicultural classrooms.* Reading, MA: Addison-Wesley.

CHAPTER 10	SHELTERED ENGLISH
FOCUS ON	Guiding ESL students' reading, writing, and learning
GUIDES STUDENTS	Before, during, and after reading, writing, and learning
USE TO PLAN	Units, yearly activities
MAY BE USED	Whole class, small group, individuals
MAY BE COMBINED WITH (KNOWN STRATEGIES)	DL-TA, DR-TA, DRA, PReP, QAR, ReQuest, GMA, TVC, CSSR, VSS, Concept Webs, Semantic Maps, SFA, Reading Aloud, storytelling, response journals, SSR, Readers Theater, InQuest, thematic units, writing workshop, project-based units, theme cycles, Content DR-TA– GMA– VSS, K-W-L Plus, DIA, reading response groups, journal writing, learning logs, DEJ, beginning research
MATERIALS PREPARATION	Moderate to extensive
OTHER PREPARATION	Moderate to extensive
OUTSIDE RESOURCES	Necessary
HOW TO DO	Page 503

Building Tables "grow" or build, successively from chapter to chapter. They tell you (1) the focus of each strategy introduced in a chapter; (2) how the strategy is best used; (3) what strategies from previous chapters combine well with new ones; (4) preparation requirements; (5) additional resources needed; and (6) the page on which a strategy's How-To-Do appears.

CHAPTER 11

EVALUATING CHILDREN'S PROGRESS IN READING AND WRITING

INTRODUCTION

Evaluation of students' progress is integrally bound to your teaching. Opportunities abound throughout the school day to observe your students as they learn and apply meaning-construction processes. These will range from your interactions with children as you use a Directed Reading-Thinking Activity (DR-TA) with high-interest fiction and note their use of predictions and higher-level thinking, to their selection of literature during free-reading time, which reflects growing and expanding reading interests. These observations are essential in developing insights that are vital to understanding children's literacy growth and to planning instruction for individual students and for small and large groups.

Your teaching role will also involve helping students develop self-evaluation skills as they increase responsibility for self-monitoring. In addition, you will need to develop effective communication with classroom parents regarding their children's progress as you build cooperation between school and home. Your overall evaluation goal will be to understand children's meaning construction processes better, to support their learning through instruction designed to enhance their reading and writing growth, and to enlist parental cooperation in this process.

Evaluation has other purposes as well, however, purposes that relate not only to your classroom but also to the information demands of your school, school district, state department of education, and federally supported programs. Because of these various demands you will, in all probability, be involved in administering standardized achievement tests. This evaluation will frequently be related to the following agencies and purposes:

- **Local school district**—to assess student progress for purposes of assisting district-wide curriculum and policy decisions.

- **State department of education**—to determine achievement progress of children in your school and the overall progress of your school district relative to other districts in your state for resource allocation purposes.

- **State or federal programs**—to determine your children's achievement growth and project effectiveness related to continued funding support.

You will receive test-score information from such testing and will need to be able to interpret these results. This will require that you be aware of both the values and the distinct limitations of standardized testing. For example, large-scale testing programs may be designed to measure progress of your entire school by grade level. These results often do not provide information on individual children, but only on each entire grade level in your school, as is the case with some state assessment programs. On the other hand, when testing is initiated by your local school district to estimate children's achievement growth, you will often receive test scores for individual students. Again, your understanding and interpretation of these achievement test scores become important as you attempt to gain insight into children's progress.

DISCUSSION PURPOSES

The perspective that we take in this discussion is that your observations and insightful evaluation are a critical part of literacy instruction. This process is interpretive in nature, as you observe students and interact with them in constructing meaning, gain insight into the nature of their processing, and plan supportive instruction based on your interpretations. This process should be enlightening both to you and to your students as you carefully reflect on their growth and achievement and plan instruction designed to enhance their reading and literacy development.

The purpose of our discussion is fourfold:

first, to identify seven principles of assessment that underlie instructional decision-making in your classroom;

second, to develop your understanding of informal observations, more structured observations and inventories, portfolio assessment, and the individual reading inventory that will assist you in gaining insight into children's meaning-construction processes and strategies, their interests and motivation, and their instructional needs;

third, to suggest means for you to (a) develop effective communication with students and their parents regarding student progress, including the use of report cards, and (b) encourage student self-assessment and home cooperation; and

fourth, to develop an understanding of formal achievement tests, including their values and limitations.

PRINCIPLES OF ASSESSMENT

Over the past two decades, our beliefs about and understanding of assessment has changed dramatically. We have moved from the behavioral objective and accountability era of the 1970s and early 1980s to a view of assessment that is situated in real, or authentic, classroom learning. In effect, our present view holds that classroom-based assessment must be weighed heavily by observations of children as they are engaged in real classroom literacy events. While confirming information may be derived from multiple-choice test items, this type of assessment is very limited in providing insight into children's meaning-construction processing and is far removed from authentic literacy tasks. Key differences in this new view of literacy assessment are summarized in Table 11-1 (Valencia & Pearson, 1987).

The following principles of assessment thus derive from an authentic assessment perspective.

1. **Assessment should be primarily based on observations of children engaging in authentic classroom reading and writing tasks.** Instructional goals such as developing higher-level thinking at the interpretive, applicative, and transactional levels and children's self-selection of high-quality literature and their proficiency in a variety of writing tasks can best be assessed through your observations of them in real learning settings. The use of standardized achievement tests may serve to confirm general achievement levels but holds limited instructional value.

2. **Assessment should focus on children's learning and the instructional goals of your curriculum.** This focus enables you to observe meaning-construction processes and to identify students' strengths and their instructional needs. It is important to remember that children's

NEW VIEWS OF THE READING PROCESS TELL US THAT...	YET WHEN WE ASSESS READING COMPREHENSION, WE...
Prior knowledge is an important determinant of reading comprehension.	Mask any relationship between prior knowledge and reading comprehension by using lots of short passages on lots of topics.
A complete story or text has structural and topical integrity.	Use short texts that seldom approximate the structural and topical integrity of an authentic text.
Inference is an essential part of the process of comprehending units as small as sentences.	Rely on literal comprehension test items.
The diversity in prior knowledge across individuals as well as the varied causal relations in human experiences invite many possible inferences to fit a text or question.	Use multiple-choice items with only one correct answer, even when many of the responses might, under certain conditions, be plausible.
The ability to vary reading strategies to fit the text and the situation is one hallmark of an expert reader.	Seldom assess how and when students vary the strategies they use during normal reading, studying, or when the going gets tough.
The ability to synthesize information from various parts of the text and different texts is hallmark of an expert reader.	Rarely go beyond finding the main idea of a paragraph or passage.
The ability to ask good questions of text, as well as to answer them, is hallmark of an expert reader.	Seldom ask students to create or select questions about a selection they may have just read.
All aspects of a reader's experience, including habits that arise from school and home, influence reading comprehension.	Rarely view information on reading habits and attitudes as being important information about performance.
Skilled readers are fluent; their word identification is sufficiently automatic to allow most cognitive resources to be used for comprehension.	Use tests that fragment reading into isolated skills and report on performance on each.
Reading involves the orchestration of many skills that complement one another in a variety of ways.	Rarely consider fluency as an index of skilled reading.
Learning from text involves the restructuring, application, and flexible use of knowledge in new situations.	Often ask readers to respond to the text's declarative knowledge rather than to apply it to near and far transfer tasks.

TABLE 11-1

A Set of Contrasts Between New Views of Reading and Current Practices in Assessing Reading

Source: Reproduced with permission from Valencia & Pearson, 1987, p. 731.

"approximation" to acquiring a new skill or concept is a positive, rather than a negative, event in the learning process. Your support and encouragement toward acquiring the instructional goals that you have set is critical in the cycle of teaching, learning, approximation, observation, supportive teaching based on learner needs, and learning acquisition.

3. **Assessment should be continuous, based on observations over a substantial period of time.** The acquisition of new concepts and literacy strategies requires not only a supportive classroom environment but time and opportunity to use the new concepts and strategies. It is thus important to note individual student progress and growth in various aspects of reading and writing, ranging from story and character interpretation to the use of imaginative language and imagery in story writing.

4. **Assessment should take into account the diversity of students' cultural, language, and special needs.** In short, your assessment must be equitable and avoid systematically biased evaluations of individuals or groups of children because of language, culture, gender, or physical or intellectual diversity. This will require sensitivity to student needs on your part and in some cases the use of special services for children's assessment.

5. **Assessment should be collaborative and include the active participation of children.** The ongoing nature of authentic assessment provides many opportunities for student participation. This ranges from students' use of literature response journals (and in turn your responses to them) to use of a collaboratively created self-evaluation checklist for their own writing. Students need to have a clear understanding of your instructional goals and what you value in instruction. You, in turn, need to understand clearly children's perceptions of these goals and values and what is important to them. A central objective in this assessment effort is to encourage your students to assume greater responsibility in their own assessment and learning. You will also find information derived from this assessment principle to be of great value in communicating with parents as you explain the reading and writing progress of their children and enlist their support.

6. **Assessment should recognize the importance of using a variety of observations rather than relying on one assessment approach.** This principle stresses the importance of your interpretive evaluation of student growth using observations from many sources. For example, children's interactions during a literature discussion using the DR-TA and GMA will provide rich information on their thinking processes and progress, just as will interactions during writing conferences. By contrast, the use of a standardized achievement test on reading comprehension and writing proficiency may contribute some information on "how much" but will provide little indication of the "why" of their progress.

541

7. Assessment must be knowledge-based and reflect our most current understanding of reading and writing processes. Your knowledge and beliefs about reading and writing processing will strongly influence your assessment of children's progress and, in turn, the way in which you provide for their instructional needs. These will range from decisions related to the use of higher-level thinking strategies such as the DR-TA, GMA, and reciprocal teaching to the use of "wait time" for individual children's responses during discussions and the mini-lessons taught during writing workshop.

These assessment principles form the foundation for the discussion that follows. Our intent is to provide assessment strategies that will assist you in observing, recording, and interpreting children's reading and writing growth, and in planning for effective needs-based instruction in your classroom.

CLASSROOM OBSERVATIONS

We have developed a wide variety of instructional strategies for reading and writing development in earlier chapters. Each of these strategies provides opportunity to observe and assess children's growth, ranging from the shared-book experience and the DR-TA lessons discussed in early chapters to the writing workshop and Sheltered English lessons developed in later chapters. The common denominator for these various strategies is found in the opportunity to observe children as they construct meaning using their background knowledge, thinking strategies, and interactions during discussion with you and their peers.

The key to successful authentic assessment is the application of the knowledge and experience you already possess (and which you will continue to develop through your professional growth and experience), to make observations, inferences, and interpretations. For example, examine Marlene's illustration in Figure 11-1 (Avery, 1991, p. 61) and ask yourself, "What observations can I make that will provide some clues to this first-grader's literacy progress?" Briefly reexamine the Early Reading and Writing Assessment Checklist found in Table 3-3 (pp. 123–124) to assist you in your observations, interpretations, and instructional planning.

Now, read the following description of Marlene's writing conference with her first-grade teacher, Carol A., and ask, "What additional information is evident regarding Marlene's progress?"

> *Carol A. is having a writing conference with Marlene, one of her first-graders. Carol describes her responses: I asked Marlene to read her writing to me. "I am outside, under a rainbow and beside a tree," she read as she moved her finger under the letters in a very precise, deliberate fashion.*

FIGURE 11-1

Marlene's Story. (Reproduced with permission from Goodman, 1991, p. 503.)

"Tell me about these O's," I responded. Marlene looked at me and giggled that I didn't see what was so obvious.

"Those aren't O's," she said. "They're circles."

"Circles?" Now I was puzzled. "Well, why did you decide to put circles in the middle of your writing?"

"Because. See, I couldn't tell what letters make those sounds so I just put circles for what goes there because something goes there only I don't know what. I can't tell what letter makes that sound, so I just put circles."

Marlene read and pointed her way through the line again. "I am—oops, I forget to write I." Her finger lands under the first circle as she says am. She continues on, and I can see that Marlene has correctly written S for side, RB for rainbow, BS for beside, and T for tree. The sounds she was unable to identify are vowel sounds, but Marlene was able to develop a strategy to deal with this.

When I looked again at Marlene's writing and listened to her explanation, I understood that she could distinguish vowel sounds in words but could not identify them with a corresponding letter. (Avery, 1991, pp. 61–62)

As you combine your initial interpretation of Marlene's illustration with her teacher's observations from the writing conference, you begin to develop a mental profile of her literacy progress. Our checklist from Chapter 3 (Table 3-3) assists in concluding that Marlene is well along in her development. She clearly understands many of the features related to the "Language of Instruction," based on her explanation of her writing and illustration; she has a fine-tuned sense of "Picture and Print-Awareness Knowledge," as evidenced by her understanding of print order and use in representing ideas; she is still working on letter-sound relationships but has a strong self-awareness of this knowledge need as she notes "I can't tell what letter makes that sound, so I just put circles." She "Knows How to Use Observing, Recording and Writing Knowledge," as reflected in her picture and one-line story; her "Sense of Story and Narrative" is developing nicely, with Marlene as the key character and the rainbow and tree the setting as shown in her illustration; and she shows a "Positive Attitude Toward Reading and Literacy Activities," as is evident in her enthusiasm in explaining and sharing her illustration and story.

From this relatively short interaction with Marlene, we learn an extraordinary amount about her literacy progress. What is most valuable here is that we have a complete literacy event—Marlene's full story and illustrations and the teacher's interaction with her—as the basis of the evaluation; this is one way we do "authentic assessment." Notice also that the teacher's interaction with Marlene is not a long, drawn-out affair; it is short, sweet, and to the point, an interaction easily done in the context of a real-life classroom in which Marlene is just one of thirty or more children. This is assessment that is authentic, highly productive, and do-able.

It is important to remember that the assessment observations of your students should take place over time. This may range from several weeks to several months, depending on your instructional objectives and goals. The following strategies will be of value to you in this assessment process and will help you develop a systematic way of recording and examining students' learning processes and their products. You will need to decide what observations and samples of children's work you wish to collect at the beginning of the school year in order to provide a baseline for noting growth. This collection may include the following types of information:

- Brief notes reflecting immediate learning observations for individual children.
- Developmental observations over a longer time period.
- Interest inventory observations.
- Literature response journal entries.
- Drawings, illustrations, and related writing.
- Selected writing samples and reports.
- Student self-assessment information.
- Letters and notes to and from parents.
- Informal reading inventory information for selected individual students.

In addition, it is wise to project, at the start of the school year, the evaluation time intervals during which you will record observations and collect samples of children's work. These may or may not coincide with the normal six-week report card period in your school district. Your evaluation plan should include children's involvement in deciding what work they would like to have included in the collection. You will find many specific ideas of value in developing your observations for interpretive evaluation in the following discussion. Portfolio assessment, discussed below, will be of particular value to you in your process and product evaluation effort.

QUICK OBSERVATION NOTES

You will frequently find that many insights about children's learning will occur to you during actual instruction; however, demands required in directing instruction for your entire classroom of children often prohibit capturing these ideas. A very simple procedure that can be of great value involves the use of "stick-on Post-It notes" for quick observation notes to yourself. Each

545

note will include the date, the child's name, and one or two words quickly jotted down—enough information to remind you of the observation or insight. Simply spread several of the small self-stick notes on a clipboard and have this ready for your brief observations. For example, as you interact with children during a DR-TA, you may observe that Janet has consistent difficulty in forming story predictions. Your note may simply read, "9/15/94—Janet—story predict. prob." Remember to include observations of children's successes as well, such as, "9/22/94—Janet—great story insight."

Your self-stick note observations can be briefly elaborated later in the day to include the story being read and other brief bits of information that will assist you in your evaluation over several days and in your instructional planning. These observations can then be quickly placed in a folder that you have previously created for each child.

THE DEVELOPMENTAL INVENTORY

The Developmental Inventory (Ruddell, 1991, 1993) provides a systematic way to record your observations based on routine classroom literacy activities and interactions. This inventory can be used to evaluate reading/listening and writing/speaking and is easily used during instruction involving strategies that we have previously discussed, such as the DR-TA, Content DR-TA, VSS, GMA, and writing workshop.

The inventory consists of two separate, but parallel, sets of literacy skills and knowledge for listening/reading (see Figure 11-2) and speaking/writing (see Figure 11-3). Within each set four areas are emphasized. These are:

1. Guides Self (or Audience) Through Text.
2. Knows How Text Works.
3. Understands Social Aspects of Meaning Construction.
4. Uses Range of Strategies While Listening/Reading
   (or Speaking/Writing).

Four Categories of the Inventory

The inventory provides a place to start your observations of children's literacy progress. As you use and become familiar with the inventory, you may feel the need to add categories or to revise descriptions based on your specific needs. A brief description of the major categories follows.

1. **Guides Self (or Audience) Through Text.** This category is designed to indicate how a student progresses through text. When listening or reading, does the student make predictions about what will happen in a story or what information may come next? Are the predictions supported by explanations using prior or text-based knowledge? The key issue here is not *complete accuracy* but evidence of reasoning that is *reasonable* and *appropriate*. Responses that indicate the student is

STUDENT NAME _____ GRADE ___ DATE _____

OBSERVATION AND EVALUATION OF:

LISTENING   READING

(circle one)

Instructions: Circle the appropriate letter to describe how each statement fits this student during your most recent period(s) of observation.

U=Usually   O=Occasionally   R=Rarely

GUIDES SELF THROUGH TEXT
1. Makes predictions.   U O R
2. Supports predictions with logical explanations.   U O R
3. Uses both prior knowledge and text information to support predictions.   U O R
4. Changes and refines predictions as reading/discussion proceeds.   U O R

KNOWS HOW TEXT WORKS
5. Demonstrates knowledge of common text elements and patterns.   U O R
6. Draws inferences from spoken and written text.   U O R
7. Understands how to use various source materials and events appropriate to age/grade level.   U O R
8. Demonstrates fluency and confidence when engaged with text.   U O R

UNDERSTANDS SOCIAL ASPECTS OF MEANING CONSTRUCTION
9. Is aware and tolerant of others' interpretation of spoken language and written text.   U O R
10. Supports and maintains own position in face of opposition.   U O R
11. Participates in interactions to negotiate meaning construction.   U O R

USES RANGE OF STRATEGIES WHILE LISTENING/READING
12. Raises questions about unknown information.   U O R
13. Uses illustrations and/or other graphic information to construct meaning.   U O R
14. Relocates and uses specific information to support predictions, inferences, and conclusions.   U O R
15. Revises meaning as new information is revealed.   U O R
16. Uses a functional system to gain meaning for unknown words (e.g., context-structure-sound-reference).   U O R

This developmental inventory may be reproduced for classroom use.

--- **FIGURE 11-2** ---

Developmental Inventory—Listening/Reading. (Reproduced with permission from Ruddell, 1993, p. 212.)

STUDENT NAME _____ **GRADE** ___ **DATE** _____

OBSERVATION AND EVALUATION OF:

SPEAKING   WRITING

(circle one)

Instructions: Circle the appropriate letter to describe how each statement fits this student during your most recent period(s) of observation.

U=Usually   O=Occasionally   R=Rarely

GUIDES AUDIENCE THROUGH TEXT

1. Uses language markers to identify the beginning, middle, and end of spoken or written accounts.   U O R
2. Develops and elaborates ideas.   U O R
3. Uses descriptive names for objects and events.   U O R
4. Provides adequate information for audience understanding of events, ideas, arguments, and accounts.   U O R

KNOWS HOW TEXT WORKS

5. Demonstrates knowledge of common text elements and patterns.   U O R
6. Relates information in a logical sequence.   U O R
7. Uses language and sentence structures appropriate to text type and age/grade level.   U O R
8. Demonstrates fluency and confidence while speaking and writing.   U O R

UNDERSTANDS SOCIAL ASPECTS OF MEANING CONSTRUCTION

9. Understands and appreciates various speech and writing styles.   U O R
10. Adjusts language to clarify ideas (spontaneously or over time).   U O R
11. Participates in interactions to negotiate meaning construction and develop elements of text and style.   U O R

USES RANGE OF STRATEGIES WHILE SPEAKING/WRITING

12. Uses ideas and language effectively to show sequence of events, cause-effect relationships, and to support main ideas.   U O R
13. Revises extemporaneous speech or first-draft writing to arrive at a more polished product.   U O R
14. Develops cohesion through idea organization and language use.   U O R
15. Explores topics with some degree of breadth and depth.   U O R
16. Develops graphic, spoken, and written text that illuminates meaning.   U O R

This developmental inventory may be reproduced for classroom use.

FIGURE 11-3

Developmental Inventory—Speaking/Writing. (Reproduced with permission from Ruddell, 1993, p. 212.)

growing in ability to change, extend, and refine predictions as new information is revealed are important. Awareness of audience (speaking, writing) as reflected in the development of events, ideas, and arguments shows a growing maturity in language control. Many of the strategies that we have discussed (DR-TA, DRA, ReQuest, and VSS) provide rich language interactions that offer opportunities to evaluate this aspect of listening and reading.

2. **Knows How Text Works.** Progress in knowing how text works is marked by your children's growing awareness of common story elements and patterns. In the early primary grades, this may take the form of understanding the beginning-middle-end progression of text events, whether the text is spoken or written. Does the child perceive this progression while listening to or reading a text? Is he or she able to tell or write a story that reflects this progression? You will notice an overlap here with the category "Guides Audience Through Text." Many of the language markers that serve as guides are also reflective of beginning, middle, and ending story elements. Your goal is to make inferences about the student's understanding of story elements and allowable sequences that comprise a conventional story. As students progress, your insight into their understanding and use of different text forms such as narrative and expository becomes important. From knowledge of text structure, is he or she able to draw inferences from spoken and written text? Does his or her spoken and written language reflect growing awareness of the similarities and differences between spoken and written text and narrative and expository texts?

3. **Understands Social Aspects of Meaning Construction.** The social nature of meaning construction and literacy development has been emphasized in our earlier discussions. Students engage in numerous interactions with peers, parents, and teachers in their effort to construct meaning about written text and spoken language. They must come to understand how to create and shape ideas, make modifications, and listen to other viewpoints as they negotiate through personal interactions with others. To become skilled at this shared meaning construction process, each student needs to develop a tolerance for different interpretations of text and different writing and speaking styles. At the same time, the student must be able to maintain and support his or her own position, even when it is not the popular one.

Helpful questions related to social aspects of meaning construction include the following:

Does the student listen to other points of view?

Is his or her response thoughtful and does it demonstrate awareness and tolerance of other ideas?

Is he or she willing to achieve a balance between maintaining position of self and negotiation with the position of peers?

Does the student understand, appreciate, and use various writing and speaking styles?

4. **Uses Range of Strategies While Listening/Reading (or Speaking/ Writing).** It is very important that students understand various coping, revision, and "fix up" strategies if they are to become effective language users, readers, and writers. The ability to raise questions and make predictions is central to purpose setting in reading. The ability to locate and use helpful information, illustrations, and graphics, and quickly relocate ideas and information related to purpose all serve as the reader's tools in information gathering and are focused by the reader's purpose. And finally, the ability to deal independently and strategically with unknown words in text is critical to the meaning construction process.

These strategies are just as important in speaking and writing. Here, as with other parts of the inventory, note that we distinguish between first draft and polished efforts. Initially, however, we encourage you to examine how well students are able to marshal thoughts and language to construct meaning. As the school year progresses, you will need to observe and evaluate the children's progress in writing revision as they begin to refine idea organization and language use to convey intent and meaning.

Useful questions for evaluating effectiveness of strategy use are:

Does the student raise questions? Are the questions useful for arriving at new understandings?

Are topics explored and discussed with some breadth and depth?

Is the student able to shift topics, attitudes, and speaking/writing styles appropriate to her/his age and grade level?

Has the student shown progress in understanding the importance of revising and drafting in speaking and writing, and does she/he demonstrate intent in revision efforts?

Is the student able to revise meaning, or revise her or his own speaking and writing, in light of new information, or with the intent to refine and polish text?

Using the Developmental Inventory

You will find the inventory helpful in your assessment of individual student progress, as a "map" to guide instruction, and in individual discussions with your students and parents. Suggestions for using the inventory are as follows:

1. Make copies of the inventory, one for each student, and keep them on your desk or in a convenient place in the room.

2. Organize your thinking and observations around the four areas of the inventory. As you become familiar with these key areas, you will find that the items under each area serve to define that area in an easily understood way.

3. Start slowly. Select three or four students for observation over several days' time. By focusing on a small number of students, you will become familiar with the four areas as you note those students' literacy progress. Set an initial plan that calls for a complete set of observations for all of your children during the first four to six weeks of school. Thereafter, attempt to set a personal goal to complete observations for all of your children every six weeks of school.

4. Note each child's progress by circling the appropriate letter on the checklist. First, note success areas; then identify areas that require special attention. It will also be helpful to make a brief note indicating the nature of the instructional activity the child was participating in during your observation.

5. Sensitize yourself to the importance of making regular observations to identify the children's progress and to use this information in designing and shaping your instructional program.

6. Use the Developmental Inventory not only in instructional planning, but also in conferences with your students and with their parents.

EARLY READING AND WRITING ASSESSMENT CHECKLIST

This checklist, discussed in detail in Chapter 3 (Table 3-3, pp. 123–124) is designed to assess beginning reading and literacy development. The checklist accounts for five areas critical to early reading and literacy success. These are:

1. Understands Language of Instruction and Group Participation.
2. Understands Picture and Print-Awareness Knowledge.
3. Knows How to Use Observing, Recording, and Writing Knowledge.
4. Demonstrates Sense of Story and Narrative.
5. Demonstrates Positive Attitude Toward Reading and Writing Activities.

The use of the checklist closely parallels that of the Developmental Inventory. You will find the checklist of particular value for kindergarten and first-grade levels, and we encourage you to briefly reexamine it.

INTEREST INVENTORY OBSERVATIONS

Information related to children's interests becomes very important as you plan instruction that incorporates their personal motivation. You have many opportunities throughout the school day to observe children's special interests. This will range from their selection of children's literature to individual activity choices made during free time. Your interactions with children during classroom instruction will also give valuable information providing insight into special interest and knowledge areas. Conversations with children on the playground and during lunch time will often reveal an entirely different range of interests and motivations that would otherwise be unknown to you.

The interest inventory (Figure 11-4) is another excellent way of identifying important information to help you better understand your children's in- and out-of-school interests and motivations. You will need to use the inventory on an individual basis for most children in the early primary grades because of limited writing development. Upper primary- and intermediate-grade children, however, can complete the inventory independently, but even at these levels you will obtain much more direct information if you can administer the inventory orally to individual children.

Note that questions 1 through 5 are focused on school activities, while 6 through 10 are oriented toward home and out-of-school interests. Children's responses to this inventory will provide important leads for selecting children's literature, creating and sharing language-experience stories and books, and involving children in instructional activities related to their special in- and out-of-school interests.

WRITING WORKSHOP EVALUATION

Observation and evaluation of children's writing progress are a critical part of the writing workshop. As you will recall from our discussion in Chapter 7, this process involves documentation, monitoring of progress toward specific writing skills, and evaluation and interpretation that gives productive feedback to individual children. Our previous suggestions on teacher evaluation and children's self-evaluation will provide helpful guidelines and suggestions in writing evaluation. We encourage you to briefly review these ideas in Chapter 7 (pp. 344–346).

PORTFOLIO ASSESSMENT

A **portfolio** is a representative collection of a child's in-progress or completed literacy work during the school year. It parallels the portfolio used by artists in the sense that it forms a collection that documents the child's work and serves as the basis for evaluating work-in-progress or work completed over a period of time. The portfolio approach to assessment offers strong appeal for three reasons (Valencia, 1990):

1. It makes provision for capturing and capitalizing on the best work that each child has to offer.
2. It encourages you to use many different ways to evaluate learning and literacy growth.
3. It provides for the evaluation of children's authentic literacy tasks that cannot be found in formal achievement testing.

NAME _____ **AGE** _____

GRADE _____ **DATE** _____

1. What do you like to do at school when you can do anything you want to?

_____

_____

2. Do you like to read? _____ If you do, what are your favorite books?

_____

_____

3. Do you have any books of your own? _____ If you do, what is your favorite? _____

4. What do you like most about reading?_____

_____

5. How do you know if someone is a good reader?

_____

6. Check the activities that you like best.
a) Reading books _____
b) Listening to stories _____
c) Going to the library _____
d) Watching TV _____
e) Going to the movies _____
f) Going to the zoo _____
g) Playing outside _____
h) Playing with my friends _____
i) Playing with my brother or sister _____
j) Helping my mother or father at home _____

7. What do you like to do when you go home from school? _____

_____

8. Of all your toys and other things at home, what do you like best?

_____

_____

Why?_____

9. What are your special interests outside of school?_____

_____

10. If you could have three wishes what would they be?
a) _____
b) _____
c) _____

This inventory may be reproduced for classroom use.

— **FIGURE 11-4** —

In- and Out-of-School Interest Inventory

Portfolio Conference

The development of the portfolio requires a collaborative selection of samples of work based on your instructional purposes and goals. For example, after reading a piece of high-interest fiction using a DR-TA, the child's story map (GMA), and an accompanying Reading Response Log entry may represent and document your goal of developing story integration and synthesis and fostering personal response to literature. Your evaluation of these samples not only provides insight into the child's success in achieving this goal but also supplies clues enabling you to plan effectively for that child's instructional needs. Your instructional purposes and goals are very important to provide focus for the selection of samples to be included in each child's portfolio. The children's portfolios should be kept in a location in your classroom that is easily accessible to you and your students.

Physically, a portfolio takes the form of a designated folder (the accordion-type folder works well) that is used to hold a representative sample of the child's work over the school year. The folder can easily be personalized by stapling a photograph of the child (use a picture from home or take one with a Polaroid camera), or a self-drawn portrait, and adding his or her name on the front cover. The contents of the folder will cover a wide range of in-progress and completed literacy samples. These samples will reflect a range of instructional goals and purposes and will include such items as writing and illustrations based on children's literature, Reader Response Log or Literature Response Journal entries, mapping and accompanying story summaries, "showcase" written work that has been polished and selected by the individual child, self-evaluation checklists, and progress notes from conferencing. The portfolio folder houses samples of the child's literacy work that demonstrates her or his literacy growth, both from process and product standpoints, over time.

ESTABLISHING INSTRUCTIONAL PURPOSES

As you begin to use portfolio assessment, you will need to focus on the purposes of your instruction and how these may be reflected in children's portfolios. The following potential purposes, based on the California Assessment Program Portfolio Project (1989), are helpful in stimulating ideas in this initial step:

1. To examine students' reading and writing progress over a given time period.
2. To identify instructional strengths and areas needing special attention.
3. To assist students and teachers in setting goals.
4. To involve students in a process of self-evaluation.
5. To provide student ownership, motivation, sense of accomplishment, and participation.
6. To serve as a vehicle for publication.
7. To demonstrate to students their own progress and growth.
8. To serve as a means for reporting student progress to parents and the public.
9. To serve as the basis for parent conferences.
10. To supplement or substitute for state-mandated testing.
11. Other _____

Note that these purposes account for your assessment, goal setting and instructional planning (items 1–3); student-centered purposes (items 3–7); and communication with parents, the public, and other educators (items 8–10). You will, in all probability, add other purposes as you initiate portfolio assessment in your classroom.

INITIATING AND MANAGING PORTFOLIOS

As you initiate portfolio assessment in your classroom, you will need to consider three basic questions (Murphy & Smith, 1991). These are:

1. What should be included in the portfolios?
2. How do I involve my students cooperatively in deciding what to enter into their portfolios?
3. How do I evaluate my students' portfolios?

What Should Be Included

Your purposes and goals of instruction will in large part provide the answer to the first question. Essentially, you need to ask "What meaning-construction processes and products are my students involved in that can be used to reflect their growth in literacy development?" Your answer to this question will provide a rich assortment for portfolio contents. The following list suggests what to include in portfolio contents (Ruddell, 1993):

1. *Samples of child's writing*, including idea development (brainstorming notes), first drafts, revision and rewrite drafts, and final pieces. Writing samples should reflect work over time.
2. *Story Maps* from a variety of literary sources. Writing growing from the mapping experience should also be included.
3. *Reading Response Log*, based on pleasure reading and/or in response to class projects, topics, and issues.
4. *Vocabulary Journal or Log* that shows words the student has collected and the definitions he or she developed for them. Written vocabulary activity work may also accompany the journal.
5. *Artwork, illustrations, photographs, project papers*, and other products of completed work.
6. *Daily journal* or student's personal thoughts, reflections, and ideas.
7. *Showcase selections*, identified for inclusion by the child. These selections have moved through the cycle of prewriting, drafting, revising, editing, sharing, and publishing (see "The Writing Workshop" in Chapter 7). Again, these selections should reflect work over time.
8. *Letters* exchanged with pen pals, children's book authors, classroom visitors, and others in the school and community.
9. *Self-assessment responses* collected over a period of time.
10. *Observation and observational assessment results*, including your informal self-stick notes and more structured observations such as the Early Reading and Writing Assessment Checklist (early primary grades; see Table 3-3), the Developmental Inventory (all grades; see Tables 11-2 and 11-3), and the In- and Out-of-School Interest Inventory (all grades; see Table 11-4).

You will add a variety of additional children's samples and observations as you consider your instructional goals and ways to reflect these in the portfolios.

Involving Your Students

In response to the second question, you will find that as you clearly communicate your instructional intent and expectations to children, they will become actively involved in building their portfolio collections. They need to understand that their portfolios should contain samples of their work that reflect different aspects of their reading and writing growth. There will be at least two types of work included. The first is "in-progress and ongoing" work, which, for example, may range from their idea notes and first writing drafts to Reading Response Logs and Vocabulary Journals; the second is "showcase" work that they have refined and polished over a period of time to reflect their best quality effort.

Conferencing with your students using writing workshop questions, as discussed in Chapter 7, will greatly assist them in developing self-evaluation processes and increase their interest in their portfolio collection. Questions such as "What makes this your best piece?" "What makes your most effective piece different from your least effective piece?" "What goals did you set for yourself?" "Did you accomplish them?" and "Now, what are your goals for the next several weeks?" lead to personal insights and active involvement in self-assessment. Children should be encouraged to use these questions to guide their written self-evaluation.

Children's explanations of their showcase pieces can increase interest, involvement, and self-analysis. The student response map, "My Portfolio and Me," from a second-grade ACOT (Apple Classrooms of Tomorrow) classroom (Denver & Leedham, 1992), shown in Figure 11-5, can be used to facilitate showcase explanations.

Evaluating Student Portfolios

Your evaluation of students' portfolios will take two forms. The first consists of using the portfolio during individual student conferencing. For

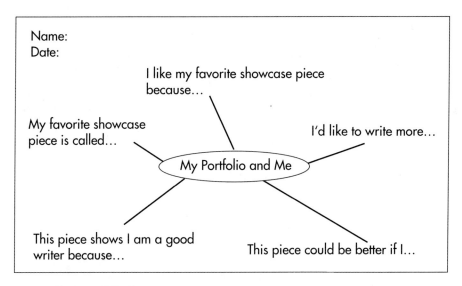

FIGURE 11-5

My Portfolio and Me. (Reproduced with permission of Stevens Creek Elementary School.)

example, you may be focused on a child's current piece of writing and wish to examine the child's progress on it, in relationship to the work previously collected in the student's portfolio. The collection of an individual student's work will also be of value should you, for example, detect ongoing interest and motivation problems in reading. A quick overview of the entries in the child's Reading Response Log or the In- and Out-of-School Interest Inventory will provide important clues leading to an understanding of the problem the child is encountering.

The second form is overall portfolio evaluation at periodic intervals in the school year to assess each student's reading and writing progress. You may decide to complete this evaluation to coincide with your preparation of report cards and parent conferences. The criteria you use in this evaluation will relate directly to your instructional goals and purposes.

Three examples of criteria for portfolio analysis are presented below. You will need to examine the criteria included in each to determine how closely they match your instructional purposes and goals. The first example, in Table 11-2, identifies evaluation criteria on the left of the page with room for comments under three general categories: Overall, Reading Strengths/Needs, and Writing Strengths/Needs (Tierney, Carter, & Desai, 1991). The second example, in Table 11-3 (Tierney, Carter, & Desai, 1991) consists of seven important process and product categories for reading and writing development. The third example, the Portfolio Assessment Guide, in Table 11-4 (Tierney, Carter, & Desai, 1991), uses three levels of overall analysis—Beginning, Intermediate, and Advanced—with detailed literacy criteria for each. The intended purpose of these guides is to identify strengths and areas of instructional need for individual students and *not* for ranking students in literacy progress. These three overall portfolio evaluation examples will assist you as you tailor your own portfolio evaluation criteria.

SUMMARY OF PORTFOLIO ASSESSMENT

Portfolio assessment does require time and commitment on your part. You will find, however, that this form of authentic assessment provides greater insight into children's progress and their instructional needs than most forms of assessment. The following points will be of value as you launch this exciting effort (Ruddell, 1993; Tierney, Carter, & Desai, 1991; Valencia, 1990):

1. Start your portfolios by identifying specific instructional goals and then select one or possibly two projects that you and your children find of special interest to develop these goals. Good starter examples include progressive writing samples, based on writing workshop, mapping and written story summaries, and Reading Response Logs.

2. Discuss your goals and expectations in building portfolios with your children. Consider what projects you will start with and how each child will select items to go into his or her portfolio. Use the chalkboard or chart paper to record key selection ideas and criteria.

PORTFOLIO ANALYSIS

NAME: _____

DATE: _____

TYPES OF READING/WRITING

- Projects
- Genres
- Selection

Process
- Goal Setting
- Problem Solving
- Engagement
- Use of Resources
- Troubleshooting

Self-Evaluation
- Analysis
- Ongoing Goals

Improvement, Effort, Motivation
Other:

TYPES OF READING

Process
- Planning
- Comprehension Strastegies
- Engagement
- Decoding and Troubleshooting
- Versatility

Reading-Writing Relationship

Reflection and Reconsideration

Self-Evaluation
- Analysis
- Ongoing Goals
- Motivation

Other:

TYPES OF WRITING

Process
- Planning
- Problem Solving and Troubleshooting
- Revision
- Use of Resources (Peers, Books)

Reflection and Reconsideration

Self-evaluation
- Analysis
- Ongoing Goals
- Motivation

Other:

OVERALL

Well organized—3 pieces of writing: 2 expository: 1 personal narrative. Table of contents for reading and writing sides.

Variety of books read—7 total.

Self-evaluation—brief but specific to each piece. Sets goals.

Highly interested in developing her portfolio.

READING STRENGTHS/NEEDS

Responses-Mostly retelling. Includes primary characters and major events. Good supporting details. Reading a lot! Good personal reflection. Interest high. Could take a more personal stance in journal.

WRITING STRENGTHS/NEEDS

3 pieces—all include personal evaluation.

- Wants help with paragraphing.

Writing has beginning/middle/end. Strong voice.

Sentence-level errors.

Informational piece—includes use of variety of sources. Good details.

TABLE 11-2

Portfolio Analysis

Source: Reproduced with permission from Tierney, Carter, & Desai, 1991, p. 129.

STRONG PERFORMANCE		NEEDS IMPROVEMENT
VERSATILITY		
Wide variety of reading and writing across genre.	Some variety.	Little or no variety. Collection shows little breadth or depth.
PROCESS		
Samples reveal discoveries or pivotal learning experiences.	Process illustrated in inflexible or mechanistic ways.	Minimal use of process to reflect on achievements.
RESPONSE		
Engaged with story. Discusses key issues. Evidence of critical questioning.	Personal reflection, but focus is narrow.	Brief retelling of isolated events.
SELF-EVALUATIONS		
Multidimensional. Wide variety of observations.	Developing insights. Some specifics noted.	Single focus, global in nature.
Establishing meaningful goals.	Limited goal setting.	Goal setting too broad or nonexistent.
Notes improvement.	Vague idea of improvement.	
INDIVIDUAL PIECES		
Strong control of a variety of elements: organization, cohesion, surface features, etc.	Growing command evidenced. Some flaws but major ideas are clear.	Needs to improve: sophistication of ideas, text features, and surface features.
PROBLEM SOLVING		
Wrestles with problems using various resources. Enjoys problem solving and learning new ways	Uses limited resources. Wants quick fix.	Seems helpless. Frustrated by problems.
PURPOSEFULNESS/USES		
Uses reading and writing to satisfy various goals, including sharing with others.	Uses reading and writing to meet others' goals.	Apathetic, resistant.

TABLE 11-3

Descriptors for Portfolio Assessment in the Reading-Writing Classroom.
Source: Reproduced with permission from Tierney, Carter, & Desai, 1991, p. 134.

Beginning

Students may appear to be at the beginning stages for a number of different reasons: they may be emerging learners or learners who are only partially engaged with the classroom community in this activity. They have yet to realize their full potential: they may not be aware of or engage with their potential. These portfolios exhibit:

- Some or very little versatility, little risk taking in trying out new forms, a preference for routine tasks over exploration.
- Detachment from the portfolio process.
- Unidimensional self-evaluations: either global statements or focusing on one aspect of the work.
- Individual pieces reflect inexperience with written organization, Standard English conventions, and/or written development of ideas. Their message may be distorted due to surface-feature errors.
- Responses include brief restatement of an incident and little evidence of personal stance or involvement.
- Limited interest in or use of reading and writing beyond classroom requirements.
- Ongoing goals and goal-setting processes are either global or sketchy.
- Improvement: few shifts apparent.
- Problem-solving processes reflect few resources, disengagement, lack of confidence, and/or lack of motivation.
- Limited use of resources such as sharing or peer input.

Intermediate

Developing learner exhibits strengths and independence in selected areas and potential yet to be realized in others. These portfolios exhibit:

- Expanding versatility.
- A reasonable effort to complete the portfolio with some attention to detail, organization, and overall aesthetics.
- Self-evaluations that may be multidimensional but lack specific details and/or breadth.
- Individual pieces that falter on more than one feature. For example, papers may meander from the topic at times or there may be significant spelling or punctuation errors. The pieces in the portfolio falter in development, structure, and/or sophistication of ideas without distorting the central message.
- Responses include comments about important incidents, but their focus is narrow and has little development.
- Some interest in using reading and writing beyond assignments in classroom.
- Goal setting occurs, but is restricted or does not grow or shift across time.
- Depends on repetitive use of strategies for problem solving.
- May use resources and support in a rote fashion.

CONTINUED...

--- **Table 11-4** ---

Portfolio Analysis Guide

Source: Reproduced with permission from Tierney, Carter, & Desai, 1991, p. 133.

ADVANCED

More fully engaged, independent learner. These portfolios exhibit:

- Versatility in the variety of forms chosen.
- Clear organization of contents.
- Multidimensional self-evaluations that include reflections about a wide variety of observed traits: process, text features, surface features, voice, word choice, audience awareness, perspective, and purpose.
- Individual pieces that have a strong voice, stay on topic, are well organized, have well-formed sentences, and demonstrate effective word choice.
- Responses represent strong engagement and understanding of story elements: key issues are discussed.
- Uses reading and writing for many different reasons. Motivated to go beyond class assignments.
- Goal setting is expansive and shifts in relevant ways across time.
- Problem solving involves using various resources in expansive and meaningful ways.
- Flexible use of resources and support.

───── **TABLE 11-4 CONTINUED** ─────

3. Provide folders (preferably accordion-type with rubber bands around them) and have each child personalize the portfolio with her or his name, and if possible, a photograph or self-portrait.

4. Decide on the first portfolio items to be included, and initiate this work through group discussion and individual conferencing.

5. Discuss showcase items and determine how these are to be developed. A good starting point here is with written work that has progressed through the writing workshop stages of prewriting, drafting, revising, editing, sharing, and publishing.

6. Encourage your students to share their portfolios with peers and with their parents at open house.

7. Review each child's portfolio at regular intervals and provide an overall evaluation of his or her progress. Use the three sample guides shown in Tables 11-2, 11-3, and 11-4 to assist you in the design of your own overall evaluation form. Consider doing this at the regular intervals that coincide with report cards. Conference with each child on his or her progress and identify those areas of success and those that need work. Establish collaborative goals based on your evaluation and discussion.

8. Update the portfolios at regular intervals by encouraging children to decide on what work is to be retained and what work might be added to illustrate their progress over the next several weeks.

9. Use your portfolios during parent conferences to demonstrate children's progress and special instructional needs.

INFORMAL READING INVENTORY (IRI) AND MISCUE ANALYSIS

The Informal Reading Inventory (IRI) is an informal observational evaluation of children's unrehearsed oral reading. (Doing an IRI and miscue analysis is the *only* legitimate reason for unrehearsed oral reading in your classroom.) The IRI can serve at least three purposes:

1. To help you understand how a student constructs meaning and applies word analysis strategies, especially a student you believe is encountering special reading problems.
2. To provide a rough indication of reading placement level for a student.
3. To gain insight into a student's comprehension and word analysis strategies by applying IRI interpretations as he or she reads aloud and interacts during small group instruction.

The Informal Reading Inventory (IRI) is administered individually to a student using prepared reading passages that have approximate grade-level indications. You may wish to construct your own IRI using reading passages representing various grade levels if you are using a basal reader or have one available. (We will discuss this process later in the chapter.) IRIs are also available commercially and include reading passages, graded word lists, observation forms, and specific scoring instructions. More recent publisher-produced inventories, such as the *Classroom Reading Inventory* (Silvaroli, 1994), now include a literature-type format to evaluate children's ability to make predictions, analyze characters, perceive problems, and anticipate outcomes. Many basal reading programs have an IRI provided in the Teacher's Guide and contain selected passages and related questions representing different grade levels in the program.

Before you use the IRI, it is important that you:

1. understand the concept of *reading miscue* as children attempt to construct meaning;
2. become familiar with the administration of the IRI and the notational system used to record the children's responses;
3. consider how to interpret reading miscues and other student responses as clues to the word analysis and comprehension strategies used by the children; and
4. determine how to use the IRI to help you identify children's reading strengths and instructional needs as an aid in planning instruction.

563

READING MISCUES

The term *miscue* was introduced by Yetta and Kenneth Goodman (Goodman, 1972; Goodman, Watson, & Burke, 1987; Goodman, 1991; Goodman, Hood, & Goodman, 1991; Goodman & Goodman, 1994) to describe a child's response to written text when the response differs from the printed text. *Miscue* was introduced to replace the term *error*, which, prior to that time, was the most generally used label for reader deviations from text. The prevailing attitude had been that any deviation from written text during oral reading was wrong—an error made by the reader. Through their observations of many oral reading episodes, the Goodmans and their colleagues noted that not all deviations from text *were* wrong—that is, the deviations in no way disturbed or distorted text meaning, and oftentimes served as a means for self-correction. Further, they realized that by analyzing these deviations, we could gain considerable information about readers' expectations for print, their background knowledge, how they approach new words in text, how they process text, and much, much more. *Miscue*, then, was introduced to remove the stigma of error and the accompanying assumptions of pathology (something is "wrong") when readers deviate from written text in oral reading. Miscue conveys an assumption of neutrality and encourages us to look beyond the *fact* of the deviation from text and examine the information about text processing the miscue reveals. We agree with this viewpoint and will use the term *miscue* in our discussion of reader responses and explanations of these.

Oral reading miscues are important indications of the reader's thinking processes and the comprehension and word analysis strategies he or she uses. Miscue analysis allows us to examine the *qualitative* nature of a child's reading. In other words, we search for possible explanations as we examine the quality of responses. The *quantitative* approach simply counts the number of errors. While a large number of miscues certainly indicate that a child may be experiencing difficulty, little light is shed on the nature of the difficulty without additional analysis. Yetta Goodman (1972) provides three questions that are valuable in understanding a child's oral reading:

1. Why do readers make miscues?
2. What categories or patterns do the miscues make?
3. What is the significance of the miscue pattern?

Miscues can occur at any point as the child reads written text. The type of miscue may suggest the nature of the child's text processing and why the miscue was made. Even miscues that do not interfere with meaning yield important information about a child's language/text knowledge and processing. For example, as you examine the child's response to the text below, what is your interpretation of the miscue?

Text: The girls are drawing a picture.
Response: The girls is drawing a picture.

Text: Every day the boy is going fishing.

Response: Every day the boy be going fishing.

The nature of these responses clearly suggests that the child is a nonmainstream speaker and is highly efficient in using her familiar dialect to translate the printed text in oral reading.

Some miscue responses, however, suggest a meaning interference problem, which may reflect limited background knowledge, word analysis skills, and comprehension strategies. This is the case in the following example:

Text: By four weeks a puppy can bark.

Response: By four weeks a puppy can walk.

This response suggests that the child is very effective in using sentence context to construct meaning, probably has some prior knowledge about puppies, and expects print to make sense (*bark* and *walk* are parallel forms, both syntactically and semantically). Notice how similar *bark* and *walk* are structurally—each is four letters, second letter "*a*," and end in "*k*." This is an easy miscue to make, particularly in light of the fact that readers use the least amount of text information necessary to construct meaning. In all probability, the child saw the "*k*," knew that puppies must learn to walk after birth, and created that meaning. Critical to analysis of this miscue is what follows it, because if the text elaborates on barking and the child goes back and self-corrects it says one thing (the child wasn't attending to the "*b*" but soon realized the miscue and corrected it appropriately); if, on the other hand, the child doesn't self-correct, it says another (the child not only didn't attend to the "*b*," he or she isn't making meaningful connections between the sentence and the subsequent text).

Table 11-5 presents a number of questions (Goodman, Watson, & Burke, 1987) that are helpful in the search for miscue patterns and interpretation of children's responses. Our explanation of the significance of each miscue is noted in the right-hand column of the table. These questions and their possible interpretations provide important clues as we attempt to understand the nature of children's oral reading miscues. This qualitative analysis of miscues suggest that they are closely connected to the oral language, background knowledge, word analysis strategies, and comprehension strategies used by the child. Miscues *are significant* when they:

1. alter the meaning and interpretation of the text;
2. reflect consistent word analysis patterns suggesting overreliance on one cueing system, e.g., graphic, phonemic, etc.;
3. interfere with comprehension and construction of meaningful relationships in text;
4. affect reading fluency that in turn may (or may not) influence comprehension and meaning construction.

QUESTION	SIGNIFICANCE
1. Is a dialect variation involved in the miscue?	A "yes" answer indicates that the child is constructing meaning using the language that sounds right to him or her. Dialect miscues that do not change meaning *according to the rules of that dialect* are not considered significant.
2. How much does the miscue look like what was expected?	A high degree of similarity indicates that the child was attending to graphic features as well as context to construct meaning.
3. How much does the miscue sound like what was expected?	A high degree of similarity may indicate dialect involvement that the child was attending to phonological cues more than to context or meaning cues.
4. Is the grammatical function of the miscued word the same as the word in the text (e.g., noun substituted for a noun)?	A "yes" answer suggests that the child understands the syntax of English and expects to find appropriate parts of speech in their appropriate places in text.
5. Is the miscue corrected?	Self-corrections indicate that the child has realized his or her miscue and is correcting to achieve consistency in meaning construction. Self-corrections are not considered significant.
6. Does the miscue occur in a context that is semantically acceptable?	A "yes" indicates that the child understands meaning relationships and is constructing meaningful text. Semantic miscues may substitute word meanings without changing the meaning of the text (e.g., "blanket" and "cover").
7. Does the miscue result in a change of meaning?	A "yes" indicates that the meaning the child was constructing is different from the expected meaning.

TABLE 11-5

Questions and Significance of Miscues

Source: Questions from Goodman, Watson, & Burke, 1987.

Miscues are *not significant* when:

1. they are self-corrected by the child during reading;
2. they do not alter the meaning and interpretation of the text;
3. they are dialect-related and do not change the meaning of the text.

RECORDING MISCUES

As you administer the IRI, you need a quick and efficient system to record a child's miscues. You will need a copy of the text being read by the child for your notations. Your preselected passages for reading (from a basal reader or children's literature) can easily be photocopied for this purpose. It is highly desirable in administering an IRI to use a tape recorder to capture the child's oral reading, especially when you are learning to use the notational system. This will enable you to replay certain sections of the child's reading to check the accuracy of the miscues in your original written notation. With very little practice, you will find the following notational system easy to use to record miscues for interpretation.

Of the seven miscue notations described below, the first four (1, 2, 3, 4) are for *meaning influence miscues*, those that most frequently influence and alter children's comprehension.

The last three miscue notations (5, 6, 7) provide insight into a child's fluent processing of text. These are *fluency influence miscues*, and may (or may not) influence reading comprehension.

1. **Omission of a word, part of a word, or punctuation as reflected in oral reading intonation.** Circle the word, word ending, or punctuation. Omissions may or may not be significant, depending on whether they interfere with meaning. Omission of word endings may be dialect-related. Frequent omissions will usually interfere with meaning.

   Example: She had wanted to take…
   …and they moved like water.

2. **Substitution of a word.** Draw a light line through the word and write the substituted word above it. This miscue is significant if it interferes with meaning.

   Example: Angela was seven…
   Example: The women all were beautiful white…

3. **Insertion of a word, word ending, or words.** Place a caret (^) at the point of insertion and write the inserted word, word ending, or words above the line. This miscue frequently occurs as a child relies on his or her normal oral language pattern and expectations regarding the text. This is not significant unless the meaning is significantly changed.

   Example: … to take dancing lessons …

567

4. **Teacher provides word, after five-second pause, or when you recognize that teacher assistance is needed.** Place a *T* (for *Teacher*) over the word supplied. This miscue is usually significant; frequent need for the teacher to pronounce words suggests the reading material is too difficult and/or the need to develop background knowledge and word analysis skills.

Example: The women all wore beau$\overset{\text{T}}{\text{ti}}$ful white…

5. **Self-correction of miscue.** Record the initial miscue as it is made. After the self-correction, circle the word and place a *C* above the circle. This miscue indicates that the child is actively monitoring the meaning construction process and applying "fix up" strategies to derive meaning.

Example:…saw some dancers $\overset{\text{C}}{\overbrace{\boxed{\substack{\text{in}\\\text{on}}}}}$ TV.

6. **Repetition of a word.** Underline the word or words repeated using a reverse arrow. Word repetition is often a means children use to mark time in order to apply word analysis skills to the next word or group of words. This may indicate the need for reading material that is at a lower level of difficulty.

Example: Angela was seven years old.
$\overleftarrow{\text{…to take dancing lessons}}$…

7. **Word-by-word reading and hesitation between words.** Place a check mark between the words or where hesitation occurs. Hesitation suggests a fluency problem, especially if the words are those that occur with high frequency. This may indicate the need to encourage practice with high-interest material at a lower level of difficulty.

Example: Angela$^\checkmark$ is$^\checkmark$ seven$^\checkmark$ years$^\checkmark$ old.

Now, apply these miscue notations to the following transcript of Maria's reading. Record your notations using the text following the transcript.

The Transcript:

> Angela—Angela is (pause) seven (pause) years (pause) old. She wants to take some dancing (pause)—dancing lessons since she saw some dancers in (pause)—on TV. The women all were (pause)—wore—(pause—"I don't know that word." Teacher says "beautiful.") beautiful (pause) white (pause) dresses,—wore beautiful white dresses, and they move like water. Angela wants to dance just like them.

The Text for Your Transcript:

Angela was seven years old.

She had wanted to take dancing lessons ever since she saw some dancers on TV.

The women all wore beautiful white dresses, and they moved like water.

Angela wanted to dance just like them.

Now, check your notations with our analysis below.

Angela ~~was~~ seven years old. (with ✓is ✓ ✓ ✓ notations)

She (had) wanted to take some dancing lessons (ever) since she saw some dancers (on/in) TV.

The women all (wore/were) beautiful white dresses, and they moved like water.

Angela ~~wanted~~ wants to dance just like them.

We need to observe Maria's reading in greater depth to develop a full analysis. However, our interpretation of this brief sample of her reading suggests several things. First, she is monitoring her comprehension processing as noted in her two self-corrections (on/in; were/wore); second, she uses substitutions and insertions that follow a normal oral language pattern (Angela *is* seven years old;… take *some* dancing lessons… ; Angela *wants* to dance. . .); and third, her reading indicates the need to develop increased fluency using material that is a bit less difficult (word-by-word reading, substitution of high-frequency words such as *was* and *on* [self-corrected] and omission of high-frequency word *had* and ending *-ed* in moved).

APPLYING MISCUE ANALYSIS

The passage in Figure 11-6 reflects miscue notations for Rebecca's oral reading completed late in the second grade. Her teacher noted that Rebecca appeared to have difficulty in applying word analysis skills but her comprehension seemed at least average or above average. Rebecca's reading interests were very limited, and her spelling during writing activities suggested heavy reliance on letter-name spelling (letters used to stand for sounds with few silent letters represented, letter-sound relationships for vowels still developing—see Chapter 2). She was very verbal, however, and expressed high interest in illustrating her own stories. She was also very social in nature and had a brother who was two years younger. The teacher expressed the view that the following passage was representative of Rebecca's reading level. Rebecca's miscue transcript for her reading of the passage is found in Figure 11-6.

A Trip to the Store

Bill and Jimmy were on their way to the store.

They walked down the street.

Jimmy said, "That dog is looking out the ~~window~~.

"Yes," said ~~Bill~~. "He is the worst one in town. I am ~~glad~~

he is ~~inside~~ today."

The boys came to the store. They went ~~to the~~ IN door.

Swoosh!

The door opened all by itself!

"Wow," said Jimmy. "Look at that! A magic door!"

"You are silly!" said Bill. "~~The~~ new doors work by

electricity."

"What's electricity?" asked Jimmy.

"I'll tell you later," said Bill. "Come let's get the

bread."

The boy's mother needed bread for sandwiches.

Bill looked for a long time. The bread had been moved to a

new place in the store.

Then he ~~spotted~~ it.

But where was Jimmy?

FIGURE 11-6

Rebecca's Miscue Transcript

A summary of our analysis of Rebecca's (1) meaning influence miscues and (2) fluency influence miscues is presented in Table 11-6.

After reading the passage, the following questions were asked, with Rebecca's responses noted.

1. What did the boys' mother need from the store? (factual) — _some bread_

2. What made the door work? (factual) — _electric_

3. Why did Bill have trouble finding the bread? (factual) — _cause it moved to a new place_

4. Why did Bill think the dog was the worst one in town? (interpretive)

cause he might bite everybody that comes next to him

5. Do you think Bill was older or younger than Jimmy? (interpretive)

younger

6. Why do you think so? (interpretive)

I just think he's younger

7. Where would you have looked for Jimmy? (applicative)

Look all over the store and in the cereal toy place

8. What would you do if you did not find him there? (applicative)

I'd call the police and tell them all about the thing that happened, and tell them what he looks like and describe him. Then I'd drive in the police car and point out if I see him.

These responses indicate that Rebecca answered six of the eight questions (75 percent correct) with acceptable comprehension responses. Did this surprise you, given the miscues noted on the passage? We now turn to the analysis of *meaning influence* and *fluency influence* miscues in our search for insights into Rebecca's meaning construction and word analysis processing of text.

INTERPRETING MISCUES

Look briefly at Table 11-6. Rebecca had a total of 14 *Meaning Influence Miscues,* representing 11 percent of the words in the 134-word passage. However, only 5 miscues (4 percent) directly affect meaning construction in this passage. These are Substitution and Teacher-Provided miscue responses. The Substitution miscues (*something* for the unknown words *window* and *inside*) indicate that Rebecca has created a useful meaning construction strategy by simply saying "something" when she comes to a word she doesn't know, and then relies on context. The Teacher-Provided word (*magic*) could have presented a more serious problem had this word been critical to understanding the passage. As you examine the passage, you will see that the remaining Omission (electric*ity*, door*s*) and Insertion (Bill*y*, let's *go* get) miscues do not have direct impact on the meaning of this particular passage. In fact, the Insertion miscues reflect Rebecca's use of natural oral language patterns and her expectancy for the text.

Next, Rebecca experienced 16 *Fluency Influence Miscues* (12 percent) in the passage. These miscues are helpful in providing insight into her meaning

Miscue Type	Miscue Example	Frequency	Meaning Affected	

1. Meaning-Influence Miscues:

			Yes	No
1) Omission ("O")	-s, -ity, -s, I'll.	4	0	4
2) Substitution (–)	*something* for window, *Billy said* for "said Billy" *something* for "glad" &"inside" *I* for "I'll" *stopped* for "spotted"	7	4	3
3) Insertion (^)	Billy, let's go get.	2	0	2
4) Teacher Prov .(T)	magic T	1	1	0
	Total —	**14**	**5**	**9**

Passage length 134 words; % of miscues —— 11%   **4%**   **7%**

Meaning-Influence Miscue Summary

Miscues affecting meaning	= 4%
Miscues unrelated to meaning	= 7%
Total miscues	=11%

— **Table 11-6** —

A Summary of Rebecca's Reading Miscues

construction process. She is quite adept at using a Self-Correction strategy (*look* self-corrected to *looking*). The comparatively large number of miscues, however, demonstrates a need to develop greater fluency as illustrated in her Repetition miscues. When she encounters a new or unusual word (to the *IN* door) or a word group (moved *to a new place*) she needs additional processing time and follows the pattern of pause, "back up," reread the word(s) just read, and continue as she "links up" with the new word(s). This is also evident in her Word-by-Word miscues, which occur before individual words requiring word analysis and processing time (is – looking, the – window). These responses indicate the need to develop immediate and automatic recognition of high-frequency words and increased fluency.

Overall, our analysis of Rebecca's miscue patterns is that she is skilled in the construction of meaning. This is reflected in her adaptive strategy in substituting *something* when she encounters a word she cannot pronounce and using context to "fill in the blank." She demonstrates risk-taking in this strategy as she persists in continuing to read the passage. She also relies on oral language patterns as reflected in her insertions of the more familiar Bill*y* and "let's *go get*

MISCUE TYPE	MISCUE EXAMPLE	FREQUENCY	MEANING AFFECTED	
2. FLUENCY-INFLUENCE MISCUES:			YES	NO
5) Self-Correct (C)	*look* to *looking*, *worse* to *worst*, *shoo* to *swoosh*, *thuh* to *where*.	4	0	4
6) Repetition (◄—)	*to the* IN *door*, *The boy's mother needed*, *moved* to a new place.	3	0	3
7) Word-by-Word (✓)	is ✓ looking the ✓ window am ✓ glad is ✓ inside the ✓ IN door all ✓ by ✓ itself mother ✓ needed been ✓ moved place ✓ in the store	9	0	9
TOTAL —		16	0	16

PASSAGE LENGTH 134 WORDS; % OF MISCUES —— 12%   0%   12%

FLUENCY-INFLUENCE MISCUE SUMMARY:

Miscues affecting meaning	= 0%
Miscues unrelated to meaning	= 12%
Total miscues	= 12%

—— **TABLE 11-6 CONTINUED** ——————————————————

the bread." Rebecca needs additional word analysis processing time when she encounters longer and less familiar words such as *looking, window,* and *moved.*

Our major concern relates to the need to develop Rebecca's reading fluency. This analysis was completed late in the second grade, and word groups such as *is looking, out the window,* and *I am glad* should be read in a highly fluent and near automatic manner, especially in a story context. In addition, she should have developed word analysis skills enabling her to read words such as *window, glad, something,* and *magic.* These miscues suggest the need to encourage Rebecca to read high-interest children's literature at a lower difficulty level. Special attention should be given to developing an understanding of how to analyze words (visual breaks for syllabication and compound words) as she encounters words such as *window* and *something.*

Rebecca's comprehension responses indicate a clear factual understanding of the story events. She experienced some difficulty with two of the interpretive level questions, which may be related to her need to focus a great deal of her attention on text processing. Her correct responses to the one interpretive level question ("Cause he might bite everybody that comes next to him") and to the two applicative level questions demonstrate a rich background knowledge enabling her to go beyond the story. Her extensive answer to the question "What would you do if you did not find him there?" shows a clear problem-solving strategy and possible story empathy related to her younger brother.

Our conclusion is that Rebecca is equipped with well-developed coping strategies for reading. She clearly demonstrates understanding of the story at inferential and applicative levels. She thus has a solid base to become an excellent reader. Her teacher's observation that Rebecca expresses little interest in reading suggests that Rebecca is not doing a lot of independent reading and is thus not experiencing sufficient opportunity to acquire the fluency she needs.

Based on this brief analysis, we suggest three instructional goals that are important to Rebecca's reading growth. The *first* is to develop greater fluency in her reading by encouraging her to read high-interest children's literature at a lower reading level. Even though Rebecca's comprehension is at a 75 percent level (6 of 8 correct) the number of fluency-based miscues (16 miscues or 12 percent), combined with her significant meaning based miscues (5 miscues or 4 percent), suggest that she is experiencing some degree of difficulty reading this passage. Practice reading easier text will increase Rebecca's automatic processing of text and reduce word-by-word reading.

Second, her interest in drawing and illustrating her writing should be capitalized on by encouraging her to write frequently and by stimulating her interest in children's literature illustrations and the joy of reading. Useful books to encourage this are *Alexander and the Wind-up Mouse* (Lionni, 1969), using collage illustrations; *Where the Wild Things Are* (Sendak, 1963), with delightful and entertaining illustrations of Max's travels; *Tar Beach* (Ringgold, 1991), using illustrations based on a quilt painting depicting Cassie Louise Lightfoot's dreams; and *I Hate to Read* (Marshall, 1992), with entertaining and detailed drawings of Victor Dickens and his discovery that words in a book can take on a life of their own. High-interest and low-vocabulary books, such as *The Cat in the Hat* (Seuss, 1957), and predictable books, such as *Are You My Mother?* (Eastman, 1960), can be used to increase automatic word recognition and fluency (see Chapter 3).

And *third,* emphasis should be placed on the continued development of Rebecca's already considerable verbal and comprehension abilities through the use of DL-TA and DR-TA (see Chapter 4). The use of the Reading Response Log and the Vocabulary Self-Collection Strategy (VSS) is also highly appropriate in working toward these goals (see Chapters 4–6).

If Rebecca's pattern of oral miscues across passages gives evidence of problems with compound words and word endings, some attention should be given to word analysis in order to develop strategies that will enable her to address multisyllabic words. This instruction is most appropriately done within the context of a *system* of word recognition, e.g., Context-Structure-Sound-Reference (CSSR). (see Chapters 5 and 8).

ESTIMATING APPROXIMATE READING LEVELS

Independent, Instructional, and Frustration reading levels are descriptors we use to identify three rather distinct degrees of reading proficiency. The levels are based on estimated grade-level difficulty of texts (1–12) and are useful in reminding us that reading ability is multidimensional; that is, no one reads just at the first or fifth grade level, rather, we read differentially at various levels. The **Independent Reading Level** is the *highest* level at which the child can read with ease—reading is characterized by fluency, normal intonation, few miscues, and no physical signs of stress or tension. The **Instructional Reading Level** is the level at which the child can read comfortably *with teacher guidance*—reading is generally proficient with some miscues and some need for guidance. The instructional level is almost always a range (e.g., grades 4–6) rather than one specific grade level. The **Frustration Reading Level** is the lowest level at which all reading and learning break down—reading is halting, often in an unnatural intonation or monotone, and is accompanied by physical signs of stress.

Helpful guidelines to provide an approximate estimate of children's Independent, Instructional, and Frustration reading levels, based on placement level studies (Betts, 1946; Johnson, Kress, & Pikulski, 1987; Leu & Kinzer, 1991; Powell, 1970; Ruddell & Williams, 1972), are presented in Table 11-7. It is important to remember, however, that these levels are indeed approximate and your observations and instructional judgment are critical in appropriate placement.

CREATING YOUR OWN IRI

You may wish to make your own Individual Reading Inventory to assist you in obtaining an approximate indication of children's reading placement. Keep in mind that IRIs are *not* to be given to all the children in your class. IRIs are generally only given to children for whom there is reason to suspect a reading problem or where there is a need to find out more about how they process text. To make an IRI use the following steps:

1. Identify reading passages from your basal reader or from literature selections that are approximately one hundred to two hundred words long. These selections should, if at all possible, represent a self-contained part of a story, such as an introductory episode or one complete story event. A key objective in this process is to identify selections that represent different levels of difficulty from grades one through six. Use a basal reader, or various literature selections, and identify six or eight possible selections. Your own judgment of difficulty level becomes important here, because stories within a given grade level of a basal

575

READING LEVEL	OBSERVATIONS	MISCUE ACCURACY		COMPREHENSION ACCURACY
Independent	Reads fluently with few miscues; self-corrects and self-monitors; comprehends easily; shows high interest in selected material.	95% + (5 miscues per 100 words)	with	90% +
Instructional	Reads with fluency; some miscues are evident; some word-by-word reading to provide processing time; comprehension presents challenge but not to extent of discouragement; reading interest is expressed.	90% + (10 miscues per 100 words)	with	75% +
Frustration	Reads with hesitation and limited fluency; large number of miscues are in evidence; word-by-word reading frequent; comprehension limited; little interest and even avoidance of reading is in evidence.	85% (15 miscues per 100 words)	with	75% +
Listening Capacity (Estimate of Reading Potential)	Listens with interest; comprehends and discusses content.			75% +

— TABLE 11-7 —

Determining Approximate Reading Levels

reader can vary as much as one or even two grade levels in difficulty. To check your judgment on approximate grade level, you can use the Fry readability scale (1977) in Figure 11-7. Make up a title for each of your selections.

2. Photocopy the selected pages, some of which will contain illustrations, type the title on each, and mount them on tagboard. Insert your sample passages in a three-ring binder that will be easy to use with children.

3. Develop six or eight comprehension questions for each passage. Factual (two or three), interpretive (two), applicative (two) and transactive (one or two) questions should be created for each passage. Review our discussion in Chapter 4 to assist you in this process.

4. Retype the passages in double-spaced format, for your binder, for easy miscue coding during the student's oral reading. Write the number of words at the end of the passage to help you estimate the percent of miscues. Make several photocopies of your passages and your accompanying comprehension questions for future use (you will need one complete set of passages and comprehension questions for each administration of your IRI, so you will want to save your originals, too).

5. Before you administer your IRI, determine a reading level starting point (passage difficulty) for the student, based on your instructional observations. Use the passage *below this level* for the first passage to ensure reading ease. Remember, the use of a tape recorder will be of great value, especially at first, to assist you in checking and refining your coding.

Note: It is also possible to use your IRI to obtain a rough estimate of a child's comprehension potential by administering your IRI as a listening comprehension inventory. In this case, you will read the starting selection you have identified to the child and use the comprehension questions you have developed. Continue reading passages until the comprehension level decreases to 75 percent or lower.

6. Create as comfortable a setting as possible for the administration of the IRI. Explain to the child that you are interested in learning more about his or her reading. Then begin by asking the child to read the title of the selection and tell what he or she thinks this selection might be about.

7. As the child reads orally, use the miscue notation system discussed earlier, and ask the questions you have prepared. During the reading, carefully observe the child's interest and persistence in reading the passage. Have the child continue to read the IRI passages until comprehension drops to approximately the 75 percent level and/or you

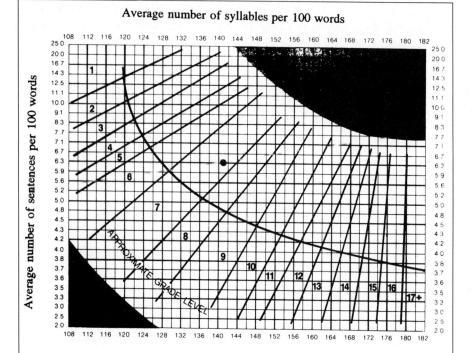

Average number of syllables per 100 words

1. Randomly select three (3) sample passages and count out exactly 100 words each, beginning with the beginning of a sentence. Do count proper nouns, initializations, and numerals.
2. Count the number of sentences in the hundred words, estimating length of the fraction of the last sentence to the nearest one-tenth.
3. Count the total number of syllables in the 100 word passage. If you don't have a hand counter available, an easy way is to simply put a mark above every syllable over one in each word, then when you get to the end of the passage, count the number of marks and add 100. Small calculators can also be used as counters by pushing numeral 1, then push the sign for each word or syllable when counting.
4. Enter graph with *average* sentence length and *average* number of syllables; plot dot where the two lines intersect. Area where dot is plotted will give you the approximate grade level.
5. If a great deal of variability is found in syllable count or sentence count, putting more samples into the average is desirable.
6. A word is defined as a group of symbols with a space on either side; thus, *Joe, IRA, 1945,* and & are each one word.
7. A syllable is defined as a phonetic syllable. Generally, there are as many syllables as vowel sounds. For example, *stopped* is one syllable, and *wanted* is two sylla bles. When counting syllables for numerals and initializations, count one syllable for each symbol. For example, *1945* is four syllables, *IRA* is three syllables, and & is one syllable.

FIGURE 11-7

The Fry Readability Scale. (Reproduced with permission from Fry, 1977.)

note about 15 significant miscues per hundred words (15 percent). At this point, you have reached the child's Frustration level (see Table 11-7).

8. Complete your analysis and interpretation by using a summary sheet similar to that in Table 11-6. Use the information in Table 11-7 to determine the child's approximate Instructional and Independent reading placement levels. You will find that administration and interpretation of your IRI will provide valuable insights into your student's meaning-construction and word analysis strategies. Incorporate your insights into your instructional planning and selection of reading experiences for the child.

COMMUNICATING WITH PARENTS

Your communication with parents provides a vital link between home and school. Parents depend on you to provide information on the progress of their child. You, in turn, depend on parents to provide the personal and academic home support that will enable children to achieve effectively in school. It is important that parents clearly understand the goals and purposes of your instructional program, your expectations for their child, your evaluation procedures, and their child's progress during the school year. It is just as important that you and parents collaboratively determine next-step goals for their child.

Parent-Teacher Conference

579

Parental involvement in your classroom will vary widely. Some parents will willingly contribute several hours each week under your direction, in tutoring or in story reading and discussion with small groups. Others will be supportive of their child's growth but be unable to participate due to work schedules or home responsibilities. Still others will need encouragement to demonstrate interest in their child's progress and provide home support. Whatever the level of parental interest and support, your role is very important in communicating to parents the nature of your instruction program and their child's progress throughout the school year.

One approach to parent involvement is found in sending children's work home periodically to highlight their reading and writing progress. For example, you and your children may select portfolio samples and showcase

---

STEVENS CREEK PORTFOLIO PROJECT
PARENT RESPONSE SHEET

Student's name _____

Date _____

Which writing sample was your <u>child's</u> favorite? _____

_____

_____

Why did he/she select it as the favorite? _____

_____

_____

What was <u>your</u> favorite writing sample? _____
Why? _____

_____

_____

Other comments _____

_____

FIGURE 11-8

Parent Response Sheet. (Reproduced with permission of Stevens Creek Elementary School.)

pieces, which are taken home to invite parent involvement and participation. The sample parent response sheet in Figure 11-8 (Denver & Leedham, 1992) provides questions useful in initiating this process. Many teachers send daily or weekly packets of student work samples home.

Open house provides a second important opportunity to present an overview of your program to parents. Children's work can be displayed in a variety of ways, ranging from bulletin-board displays to individual portfolios and showcase work. The time provided at most evening open house events will limit you to describing your program goals, briefly examining a few samples of children's work, and discussing broad program issues with parents.

A third, and one of the most effective ways to interpret your program and children's progress, is the parent-teacher conference. This one-on-one opportunity enables you to show, explain, and interpret children's work, and to enlist parents in a reciprocal relationship with the school. A child's portfolio provides an excellent way to demonstrate clearly her or his progress to a parent.

The following guidelines will be helpful in planning for and conducting a parent conference:

1. Prepare for the conference by reviewing the child's progress during this reporting period. Again, portfolios are extremely valuable in this effort. If you have not developed a portfolio collection, review your observations, notes, and available work completed by the child. Consider how you can communicate the child's progress through samples of work, obtain parental reaction and response, and enlist parental support.

2. Send a letter home specifying the time and location of the conference. Briefly explain your expectations for the conference, and encourage the parent(s) to think of issues important to your discussion. Your letter should contain a bottom "tear off" portion, also showing time and location, which can be returned with the child, confirming that the parent(s) can meet with you or asking the parent(s) to suggest an alternate meeting time if this is necessary.

3. Locate the conference in a comfortable setting in your room where the parent(s) can see displays of children's work. Arrange chairs for a side-by-side discussion designed to open communication as much as possible. If the parents' language is not English, you may need to arrange for an interpreter.

4. To initiate the conference, briefly explain the nature of your instructional goals and purposes, and connect these to specific samples of the child's work.

5. Describe and interpret the child's successful progress in your program (also see report card discussion on p. 584). In this discussion you may, for example, identify the child's reading comprehension development,

ORINDA UNION SCHOOL DISTRICT

Grades 1, 2, and 3 (Circle One)

Name _____

Teacher _____

School _____

	C			2			3			4		
	Demonstrates this skill	Making progress	Needs more time to develop	Demonstrates this skill	Making progress	Needs more time to develop	Demonstrates this skill	Making progress	Needs more time to develop	Demonstrates this skill	Making progress	Needs more time to develop

ENGLISH/LANGUAGE ARTS

READING   Effort
- Oral Reading
- Understanding what he/she reads
- Word-attack skills
- Independent reading

Written Work   Effort
- Letter/number formation
- Written expression
- Language mechanics
- Assigned spelling words
- Spells correctly in written work

Communication Skills   Effort
- Actively listens to others
- Oral expression

582

				THIRD PERIOD
MATHEMATICS Effort				
Learning math facts				
Understanding concepts				
Applies problem-solving skills				
HISTORY/SOCIAL SCIENCE Effort				
SCIENCE Effort				
PHYSICAL EDUCATION Effort				
Sportsmanship				
VISUAL & PERFORMING ARTS				
Art Effort				
Music Effort				
SOCIAL/PERSONAL DEVELOPMENT				
Follows directions				
Assumes responsibility				
Completes work on time				
Works independently				
Works cooperatively with group				
Uses time wisely				
Self-discipline/control				
Is considerate				
Positive attitude				
Next Year's Assignment				
Teacher's Signature				

FIGURE 11-9

Report Card for the Orinda Union School District. (Courtesy of Orinda
Union School District, Orinda, California, 1993.)

writing progress, ability to engage in class discussions, use of free activity time, and your perception of her or his special interests and motivations. This is also the time to identify specific instructional needs and special problems that you have identified. Encourage the parent(s) to provide insight into the child's success and need areas.

6. Summarize the conference and set out next-step goals for the child and collaboratively identify ways in which home and school will support the child's progress.

The report card is the fourth way student progress is communicated to parents. The reporting process in many school districts is often limited to a very narrow view of reading and writing development in the form of A, B, C, and D grades. The recent authentic assessment movement, however, has encouraged many teachers and curriculum coordinators to re-examine their report card approach. This has been most evident at the kindergarten and primary grade levels, where broader descriptions of children's progress are provided. Our observations suggest that fewer changes have been made in report cards at the intermediate grade levels, due in part to resistance from parents and some teachers who hold the belief that children "need to be graded" in preparation for middle or junior high school.

A recently revised school district report card for the primary grades is shown in Figure 11-9 (Orinda Union School District, 1993). The skill and content areas have broad descriptions under each (e.g., Reading: "Oral reading," "Understanding what he/she reads," "Word attack skills," and "Independent reading." One of three progress areas is checked to evaluate each description ("Demonstrates this skill," "Making progress," and "Needs more time to develop"). A special feature of this report card is found in the "Effort" description. The small circle for each general category is used to indicate an effort indicator for the child—O for outstanding, S for satisfactory, and N for needs to improve. Note that four reporting periods are reflected in the vertical column lines. The first (C) is for the initial fall parental conference, the second and third periods occur during the middle of the school year, and the fourth at the conclusion of the school year. Space is provided for teacher comments for the initial parent conference and for the second and third reporting periods.

Our discussion in this chapter, ranging from the developmental inventory to portfolio assessment, strongly supports a descriptive approach to report cards. This issue, however, is determined in large part by teachers and parents at the local school district level. Even if the report card used in your district has a narrow focus and uses only letter or numeric grades, you can supplement this report by providing descriptive categories and comments following the Developmental Inventory and portfolio assessment pattern. We encourage you to consider the following guidelines in developing and using report cards (Tierney, Carter, & Desai, 1991):

1. Keep report cards as open-ended and descriptive as possible.
2. Focus on the student's achievements and ongoing learning goals rather than on weaknesses.
3. Expand the descriptors of possible topics for discussion to include those that follow portfolio use and the Early Reading and Writing Assessment Checklist (kindergarten and early primary grades; see Table 3-3) and the Developmental Inventory (all grades; see Figures 11-2 and 11-3).
4. Involve students and parents in developing a collaborative report that describes and communicates progress.

FORMAL ASSESSMENT: PURPOSES AND CONCEPTS

Our major emphasis in this chapter has focused on informal assessment and observations of children that relate directly to your instructional program. In all probability, however, you will be required to administer a standardized achievement test of some type during the school year. It is thus important to understand the use of formal assessment and key concepts related to testing.

PURPOSE OF FORMAL ASSESSMENT

The major purpose of formal (standardized) achievement assessment is to obtain some indication of "how much" your students have learned. This is in contrast to our informal assessment and observations that focus on the "why" and "how" your students use reading and writing processes to construct meaning (Farr & Beck, 1991). Our previous discussion in this chapter, and particularly the contrasts in assessment viewpoints found in Table 11-1, has emphasized the importance of a process approach to assessment. Nevertheless, formal testing, as discussed earlier, is used by local school districts, the state department of education, and special state and federal programs to assess the "how much" of student progress in relation to curriculum innovation and resource allocation. This practice is widespread throughout the country and will undoubtedly continue in years to come.

FORMAL TESTING INSTRUMENTS

There are a variety of standardized achievement testing instruments that you will encounter in your teaching. These tests require enormous investments of time and money for development by the publisher. Such tests are **norm-referenced**, that is, they are administered to large numbers of students in order to develop norms. The *norms* essentially represent the average performance of a large number of students tested at a specific grade and age level. It very important for you to know the characteristics, including socioe-

585

conomic and cultural diversity, of the norming group. This information is provided in the test technical manual. In effect, when you administer an achievement test to your students, you are comparing their achievement to the achievement of the norming group used in developing the test.

A **survey test** or **achievement test** measures the general achievement of children in reading and literacy development (or in other areas such as mathematics or social studies) relative to the student group on which the test was normed. These results usually have several subtests such as comprehension, vocabulary, and word analysis, which are combined to provide a total reading score. Examples of survey tests include the Metropolitan Readiness Test, the Gates–MacGinitie Reading Tests, or reading subtests of the Comprehensive Test of Basic Skills, the California Achievement Test, or the Stanford Achievement Test. Remember, these test results are general in nature and provide very limited information for instruction. Such tests may be used to provide a general idea of your children's achievement and may (or may not) validate your observations of your children's progress.

A **test battery** is a group of several tests that have been normed on the same group of students. These generally include sections on reading, writing, language, mathematics, social studies, and science. Examples include the Comprehensive Test of Basic Skills, the Stanford Achievement Test, and the California Achievement Test.

A **diagnostic test** is designed to identify specific strengths and weaknesses. These tests differ from the survey and test battery subtests in that they measure more specific skills, e.g., reading comprehension, vocabulary, visual and auditory discrimination, structural analysis, and phonics. These tests provide both group and individual scores and a profile of scores. A diagnostic test may be designed for group administration, as is the case with the Stanford Diagnostic Reading Test, or for individual administration, as is the case with the Diagnostic Analysis of Reading Tasks and the Gates-McKillop-Horowitz Reading Diagnostic Test.

Criterion-referenced tests are designed to provide an indication of whether a student has met specific instructional goals or *criteria*. These tests differ from those discussed above in that they are not normed for comparison to other students. Such tests simply compare a student's level of performance on a set of test items to a predetermined criterion. The student is required to reach a minimum level of competency to pass. These tests are sometimes referred to as **minimal competency tests**. Examples of the Criterion Referenced tests are found in reading management systems such as Fountain Valley and end-of-unit tests in some basal readers.

IMPORTANT TESTING CONCEPTS

There are three essential test concepts that you need to be familiar with as you examine, administer, and interpret an achievement test (Farr & Beck, 1991).

The first concept is **test validity** and refers to what the test purports to measure. Your close examination of the test items will provide a strong indication of whether the test evaluates the skills and knowledge taught in your curriculum. You in effect examine the "face" of the test, or its *face* validity. Test authors and publishers also provide specific information showing how closely the test results are related to other established tests measuring the same thing. This is known as **concurrent** validity and is usually shown in the form of correlations that express the strength of the relationship between the two tests. Test manuals will also frequently discuss **construct** validity, which provides an indication of the theoretically based constructs that underlie the test items.

Reliability, the second concept, refers to the stability of the test scores. This concept is illustrated through your expectation that a scale at the grocery store will weigh a head of lettuce the same if you removed it from the scale and then replaced it. If so, the scale is reliable, if not, you talk to the grocery clerk regarding the reliability of the scale. Test scores that are reliable have accuracy, stability, and dependability. Your main concern centers on the degree of confidence you have that your students' scores are, in fact, measured reliably. Information in the technical manual will indicate how reliability was determined. Reliability is usually determined by testing and retesting, splitting the test in half by taking odd and even items to form two tests, or by designing two equivalent test forms and checking their relationship. Should the test and retest, split half tests, and equivalent test forms produce identical results, the test reliability would be perfect and show a correlation of 1.0. Most achievement tests, however, range from .9, acceptable for individual student interpretation, to .7, the minimum acceptable for group assessment.

It is important to note that validity and reliability are also important concerns in informal observation evaluation. As Valencia (1990) notes, there are several features in informal classroom observations that address these concerns.

1. Validity is accounted for as we establish common understanding of our goals and the criteria we will use to evaluate these goals with children.

2. Assessment is ongoing throughout the school year as we observe, collect, and evaluate using many indicators related to our children's reading and literacy achievement. This "why" and "how" information is quite different qualitatively from the "how much" information derived from a sixty-minute reading achievement test.

3. Our evaluations are based on observations of children's activities and product development and the use of more structured observations, such as the Early Reading and Writing Assessment Checklist (see Table 3-3) and the Developmental Inventory (Figures 11-2 and 11-3), discussed earlier in this chapter; all of these tend to ensure both validity and reliability.

The third concept, **standard error of measurement**, reflects an estimate of test error in a student's score. This is an important concept, because it tells you how secure you can be in interpreting a given test score. The standard error of measurement is usually identified as SEM with a $\pm$ notation before a number. For example, if SEM = + 4 for Lisa's reading comprehension test score of 34, this means that her true score is somewhere between 30 (-4) and 38 (+4). You can see that as the SEM increases, the greater the test error and the less reliance you can place on a given score. The important caution here is to understand that if Lisa's reading comprehension score is 34 in the fall of the year and 37 (or 31) in the spring testing, you *cannot interpret these results* as demonstrating an achievement gain (or loss) on the test. This is because you do not know how much of the "gain" (or "loss") is due to the error present in the test. For this reason, it is important to know the SEM for a specific test as you examine scores for individual students. If this is not available in the test manual, you should request it from the test coordinator in your school district.

INTERPRETING TEST RESULTS

As you score your students' tests or receive your test results back from the testing coordinator, you need to be aware of the following terms and the concepts they represent (Ruddell, 1993):

1. **Raw Score**. The *raw score* is the number of correct responses on the test or, in some cases, the number of correct responses minus some percentage of incorrect responses (a guessing penalty).

2. **Mean Score/Median Score.** The *mean* score is obtained by totaling all scores and dividing by the number of scores—it is the arithmetic average. The *median* score is the middle score, when your children's scores (or any group of scores) are listed from highest to lowest. The median divides a set of scores into two equal parts. Mean and median scores are often the same for any one test.

3. **Mode Score.** The *mode* is the score that is obtained by the largest number of students; it is the score that occurs most frequently.

4. **Grade Equivalent (GE) Score.** The *grade equivalent* is obtained by converting raw scores to grade level estimates. GE scores are derived by statistical interpretation of norm group raw scores. A GE score of 2.9 is interpreted as second grade, ninth month. GE scores assume a ten-month school year. These scores are frequently used with parents who are anxious about their child's progress. It is important, however, to use caution in interpreting the GE score. First, remember that the GE score is converted from a raw score statistical interpolation. Second, a GE score of 2.9 doesn't tell us very much about a student in a real sense or relative to other students. A GE score of 2.9 must be interpreted relative to a student's grade level. A GE score of 5.4 for Amika, who is near the

end of second grade, does *not* mean that reading material at the fifth-grade level is appropriate for her.

5. **Percentile Ranks**. A *percentile rank* is also a converted score based on the student's raw score. This rank tells us the position of the raw score between the lst and the 99th percentile, using the norm group scores. (Remember the norm group scores were based on the original students used by the test publisher in "norming" the test.) For example, a 90th percentile means that Jaime scored equal to or above 90 percent of the students in the original norm group (and below 9 percent of these students). Percentile ranks have nothing to do with percent of correct responses, but are often erroneously confused with them. Percentile ranks are useful scores for understanding a student's relative achievement and may be helpful as one piece of information in student and parent discussions.

6. **Stanine Scores**. *Stanine scores* also compare a student's score with the norm group scores. Stanine scores are interpreted on a nine-point scale of standard scores ("standard nine") with the score of 5 representative of the mean (average) in the scale. Stanines correspond roughly to percentile ranks, e.g., a stanine score of 5 is approximately at the 50th percentile. Stanine scores are most useful for comparing student progress from fall to spring or from one year to the next.

It is important that you spend time examining the administration and technical manuals of the particular test you will be using, both to develop an understanding of the specific test features and potential results, and to assist you in your informed interpretation of your students' test scores.

FORMAL ASSESSMENT CAUTIONS

As you approach formal assessment, it is important to ask and answer the following questions:

1. What is the purpose of the testing?
2. How does the formal assessment relate to my instructional program?
3. What information can I expect to obtain from the test?
4. How will this information be used at the classroom, school, and school-district level?

In response to these questions, it will be helpful to keep following six standardized test cautions in mind (Ruddell, 1970, 1973, 1978; Ruddell & Kinzer, 1982):

1. Standardized achievement tests are designed to measure highly generalized skills. They do not measure specific instructional objectives nor do they account for the "how" and "why" of your students' reading and writing processing.

589

2. Achievement tests should not be the only basis for planning or evaluating an instructional program, because only a few of the complex literacy skills can be sampled in any one measurement instrument.

3. Standardized achievement tests include tasks closely related to those used to measure intelligence, so they reflect factors other than the effectiveness of classroom instruction.

4. Because the "objective" scores for standardized literacy achievement tests are based on norm groups, these tests tell little about student achievement unless the students in the norm groups are completely and accurately defined and have characteristics similar to your students. Boards of education, the community, parents, the press, and even professional educators often misinterpret achievement test scores for this reason.

5. Pressure for high test scores can corrupt standardized tests. Each test can only sample specific areas of student achievement. Direct teaching of test-related items in these areas ("teaching to the test") can make test results an invalid measure of total student achievement.

6. Reliability measures for group achievement tests, provided they are not corrupted by such special preparation, are used to provide some assurance of the comparability of results. This assumes that the tests are administered in the same manner and at the same time in the school year, and that your students have the same characteristics as the students in the norm group. Even so, the test score of one individual student is subject to a significant error of measurement. Group tests can measure group achievement with some degree of accuracy, but not necessarily the achievement of an individual child. In spite of this important warning, group achievement tests are frequently used to assess and place individual students.

Our research (Ruddell & Kinzer, 1982) indicates that the majority of teachers believe that teacher evaluation and achievement testing have a strong impact on the curriculum. Not unexpectedly, teachers and principals use evaluative information that is most closely associated with individual students for instruction, placement, and indications of student growth. Local school-district office personnel, on the other hand, use test data to identify achievement trends for the school district and the state department of education, and to report on special state and federal projects. All school personnel, however, from teachers to district office administrators, express the view that the time spent in testing is too great and moves the teacher and students away from instruction. From an instructional perspective, achievement test results are best used as one piece of information that is combined with your authentic classroom observations and assessment as you interpret your children's progress and plan for their instructional needs.

Evaluating Reading and Literacy Processes

A Summary

Our viewpoints and understanding of reading and literacy evaluation have changed in striking ways over the past decade. The discussion in this chapter began with the identification of seven assessment principles that focused on your classroom goals and on authentic assessment based on your observations of your children's learning. We have detailed a variety of observation strategies, including the recording of immediate observations, the Developmental Inventory, the Early Reading and Writing Assessment Checklist, the In- and Out-of-School Interest Inventory, Writing Workshop Evaluation, Portfolio Assessment, and the Informal Reading Inventory. These observations provide rich assessment information that enables you not only to identify your children's instructional needs but to plan collaboratively with them for instruction.

Our discussion of report cards and communication with parents emphasizes the vital importance of the home and school connection. A descriptive approach to report cards was stressed, where you interpret your children's progress to parents and encourage their participation in their children's learning.

We briefly examined formal achievement testing and a number of concepts basic to understanding and interpreting these tests. A number of cautions regarding the limitations of achievement tests were set out in the hope that by understanding these you will more appropriately use such test results.

Our perspective, grounded in our teaching experience and extensive work with teachers, holds that evaluation of reading and literacy progress and instruction designed to meet your students' learning needs is best achieved through authentic assessment based on your classroom observations.

DOUBLE ENTRY JOURNAL

What are some ways the literacy assessment practices you recall from your elementary experience were and were not authentic? What specific authentic assessment practices do you now use or expect to use in your classroom? What benefits will this assessment provide? Share your ideas with a partner.

Supporting Activities

1. Arrange for a visit to an elementary classroom at a grade level of high interest to you. To prepare for this visit, photocopy the Developmental Inventory—Listening/Reading (see Figure 11-2) and the Developmental Inventory—Speaking/Writing (see Figure 11-3). With the help of the teacher, identify one child for observation during your visit. Use the major categories in each developmental inventory to focus your observations. What insights did you glean regarding the child's literacy development? What recommendations do you have for instruction? If time permits, share your observations and insights with the teacher and obtain her or his ideas on the child's progress.

2. Carefully review the In- and Out-of-School Interest Inventory (see Figure 11-4). Add additional items that you believe important in assessing children's interests. Arrange to interview a child at the grade level of interest to you. (If possible, interview the child you observed in #1 above.) Use the Interest Inventory as your interview guide with the child. Briefly describe your insights into the child's in- and out-of-school interests. What implications for instruction would you recommend based on your interview? Share your ideas with a class partner.

3. With the help of your professor, identify a teacher who uses some form of Portfolio Assessment. Review our discussion on Portfolio Assessment and develop a series of questions that you would like to pursue. Pay particular attention to the questions we propose under "Initiating and Managing Portfolios." Arrange for an interview with the teacher and use your questions as a guide. Summarize the information from your interview. Now briefly outline the critical features in your personal plan for developing a system of Portfolio Assessment.

4. Review our discussion on "Creating Your Own IRI." With the help of your professor or a classroom teacher, locate an appropriate basal reader or collection of books for sample material and follow the steps outlined in our discussion to create your own IRI. Share your completed IRI with a class partner and reexamine the reading passages with particular attention to the comprehension levels represented in your questions for each passage. Based on your discussion, make any changes that will improve your IRI.

5. Use your IRI constructed in #4 above, or, if this activity was not developed, use a publisher-produced IRI (e.g., see the Silvaroli *Classroom Reading Inventory* reference or an IRI recommended by your professor) and arrange to administer it to a child. Attempt to select a student from the second through the fourth grades in order to provide a reading response range covered by the IRI. Rely on the miscue coding system (see "Recording Miscues" discussion) for your personally constructed IRI, or on that provided in the manual of the publisher-produced IRI. Complete your analysis of the child's reading responses with particular attention to the *meaning-influenced miscues* and the *fluency-influenced miscues*. What instructional recommendations do you have for the student based on your interpretation of her or his responses?

6. Obtain a copy of a widely used standardized reading achievement test and the test manual from your professor, the library, a classroom teacher, or a nearby school-district office. Review our discussion of formal testing and formal assessment cautions (see Formal Assessment: Purposes and Concepts). Carefully review the test items and the test administration manual. Be sure to account for test validity, reliability, standard error of measurement, and test interpretation and use in your discussion. Share your findings with a class partner.

Avery, C. S. (1991). Organizing for whole language. In Y. M. Goodman, W. J. Hood, & K. S. Goodman (Eds.), *Organizing for whole language* (pp. 58–64). Portsmouth, NH: Heinemann.

Betts, E. A. (1946). *Foundations of reading instruction.* New York: American Book.

California Assessment Portfolio Project. (1989). Sacramento, CA: California Department of Education.

Denver, B., & Leedham, L. (1992, November). *Stevens Creek portfolio project: Apple Classrooms of Tomorrow.* Paper presented at the meeting of the California Reading Association, San Diego, CA.

Farr, R., & Beck, M. (1991). Evaluating language development: Formal methods of assessment. In J. Flood, J. M. Jensen, D. Lapp, & J. R. Squire (Eds.), *Handbook of research on teaching the English language arts* (pp. 489–501). New York: Macmillan.

Fry, E. (1977). Fry's readability graph: Clarification, validity, and extension to level 17. *Journal of Reading, 21,* 242–252.

Goodman, Y. M. (1972). Qualitative reading miscue analysis for tracher training. In R. E. Hodges & E. H. Rudorf (Eds.), *Language and learning to read: What teachers should know about language* (pp. 160–166). Boston: Houghton Mifflin.

Goodman, Y. M. (1991). Informal methods of evaluation. In J. Flood, J. M. Jensen, D. Lapp, & J. R. Squire (Eds.), *Handbook of research on teaching the English language arts* (pp. 502–509). New York: Macmillan.

Goodman, Y. M., & Goodman, K. S. (1994). To err is human: Learning about language processes by analyzing miscues. In R. B. Ruddell, M. R. Ruddell, & H. Singer (Eds.) *Theoretical models and processes of reading* (4th ed.) (pp. 104–123). Newark, DE: International Reading Association.

Goodman, Y. M., Hood, W. J., & Goodman, K. S. (1991). *Organizing for whole language.* Portsmouth, NH: Heinemann.

Goodman, Y. M., Watson, D. J., & Burke, C. L. (1987). *Reading miscue inventory.* New York: Richard C. Owen Publishers.

Johnson, M. S., Kress, R. A., & Pikulski, J. J. (1987). *Informal reading inventories* (2nd ed.). Newark, DE: International Reading Association.

Leu, D. J., & Kinzer, C. K. (1991). *Effective reading instruction. K–8.* New York: Macmillan.

Murphy, S., & Smith, M. A. (1991). *Writing portfolios: A bridge from teaching to assessment.* Markham, Ontario: Pippen Publishing.

Orinda Union School District. (1993). *Progress report—Orinda Union School District.* Orinda, California.

Powell, W. R. (1970). Reappraising the criteria for interpreting informal reading inventories. In J. DeBoer (Ed.), *Reading diagnosis and evaluation.* Newark, DE: International Reading Association.

Ruddell, M. R.-H. (1991). Authentic assessment: Focused Observation as a means for evaluating language and literacy development. *The California Reader, 24*(2), 2–7

Ruddell, M. R. (1993). *Teaching content reading and writing.* Boston: Allyn & Bacon.

Ruddell, R. B. (1970). *Reading achievement in California: Miracle or mirage?* White Paper for California Assembly Committee on Education. Sacramento, CA: California State Legislature.

Ruddell, R. B. (Ed.). (1973). *Accountability and reading instruction: Critical issues.* Urbana, IL: National Council of Teachers of English.

Ruddell, R. B. (1978). Minimal competency testing—for better or for worse? *California School Boards Journal, 37*, 28–31.

Ruddell, R. B., & Kinzer, C. H. (1982). Test preferences and competencies of field educators. In J. Niles & L. A. Harris (Eds.), *New inquires in reading research and instruction* (pp. 196–199). Clemson, SC: National Reading Conference.

Ruddell, R. B., & Williams, A. (1972). *A research investigation of a literacy teaching model: Project DELTA* (EPDA Project No. 005262). Department of Health, Education and Welfare, Office of Education.

Silvaroli, N. J. (1994). *Classroom reading inventory* (7th ed.) Dubuque, IA: Brown & Benchmark.

Tierney, R. J., Carter, M. A., & Desai, L. E. (1991). *Portfolio assessment in the reading-writing classroom.* Norwood, MA: Christopher-Gordon Publishers.

Valencia, S. (1990). A portfolio approach to classroom reading assessment: The whys, whats, and hows. *The Reading Teacher, 43*(4), 338–240.

Valencia, S., & Pearson, P. D. (1987). Reading assessment: Time for a change. *The Reading Teacher, 40*(8), 726–732.

CHILDREN'S LITERATURE REFERENCES

Eastman, P. D. (1960). *Are you my mother?* New York: Random House.

Lionni, L. (1969). *Alexander and the wind-up mouse.* New York: Knopf.

Marshall, R. (1992). *I hate to read.* Mankato, MI: Creative Editions.

Ringgold, F. (1991). *Tar beach.* New York: Crown Publishers.

Sendak, M. (1963). *Where the wild things are.* New York: HarperCollins.

Seuss, Dr. (1957). *The cat in the hat.* New York: Beginner Books.

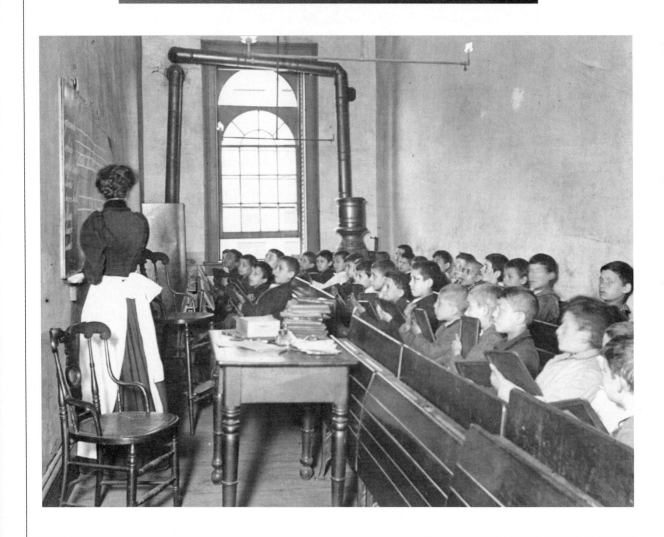

EXAMINING INSTRUCTIONAL APPROACHES: BASAL READER, LITERATURE-BASED, WHOLE LANGUAGE, AND SUPPLEMENTARY PROGRAMS

INTRODUCTION

As teachers approach the beginning of the school year, we always feel a level of excitement and some exhilaration that comes from anticipating the arrival of new students. We also experience a strong sense of responsibility as we prepare and plan instruction for the school year. Each year reality sets in and requires that we carefully examine the major premises upon which our instruction is based.

For elementary school teachers the focus of all this thought and concern is often on the instructional approach you will use to guide children's acquisition of reading and writing skills. It helps to remember that you have a broad range of background knowledge and understanding of children's reading and writing development to assist you in this process. You have also developed understanding of a wide variety of instructional strategies that can be used in your classroom regardless of the approach you elect to follow. A quick review of our major discussion topics in this text reveals the following areas of emphasis:

■ Understanding characteristics and features important to influential teaching (Chapter 1) and children's meaning construction processes (Chapter 2).

■ Developing reading and writing skills and thinking processes in kindergarten and grade one (Chapter 3).

■ Developing reading comprehension (Chapter 4) and vocabulary knowledge (Chapter 5) across the grades.

■ Using children's literature and reader response to boost reader interest and motivation (Chapter 6).

■ Guiding children's writing development (Chapter 7).

■ Developing word analysis strategies to provide for greater reader independence (Chapter 8).

■ Guiding children's reading and writing across the content areas (Chapter 9).

■ Understanding children's language, cultural, and achievement diversity (Chapter 10).

■ Using informal observations to evaluate children's reading and writing progress (Chapter 11).

You thus understand important literacy concepts and learning processes that will prove invaluable in your teaching.

The instructional approach that you use in your classroom will be influenced by a variety of factors. These will include:

1. Your knowledge and personal beliefs about the most effective way to develop reading and writing instruction.

2. Your personal experience in using a particular approach that tempers and refines your knowledge and beliefs.

3. Your willingness to devote the time and energy required to develop a particular approach and shape it to fit your own knowledge and belief system.

4. Your school district's philosophy regarding literacy instruction, which includes the textbook adoption process, flexibility and willingness to use a variety of instructional approaches, and financial support for the purchase of materials and supplies.

The first three factors are directly under your control. The fourth, however, will depend heavily on factors and individuals outside your control—your school principal, school board policies, the curriculum coordinator, curriculum practices in your school district, and, in some areas, on state or municipally mandated requirements.

The purpose of this chapter is to present and discuss the most widely used instructional approaches to reading and writing development and to consider the strengths and limitations of each. More specifically the following objectives will guide this discussion:

1. To develop a brief historical perspective of literacy instruction in the United States that identifies major influences and changes from colonial days to the present.
2. To examine three major instructional approaches (basal reader, literature-based, and whole language) for literacy learning and the strengths and limitations of each. (We will also briefly address supplementary programs that can be used in tandem with a major approach.)
3. To present criteria for materials selection to assist you in this process at the classroom and district-wide level.

A Brief Historical Perspective on Literacy Instruction in the United States

A brief overview of the past history of literacy instruction in the United States—spanning nearly four hundred years—enables us to gain perspective on the enormous progress that has been made in literacy instruction, materials, classroom facilities, and teacher preparation (Chall & Squire, 1991; Smith, 1974; Venezky, 1991), much of which occurred over the past half-century.

Table 12-1 presents a synthesis showing historical events, key influences, materials used and their content, instructional emphasis, and recommended teacher preparation for four different time periods: 1607–1840; 1840–1910; 1910–1960; 1960–1990s. You will find this table easiest to comprehend by starting with a time period and reading "down the table." Note, for example, in the 1607–1840 period, the impact of the religious and patriotic beliefs of a new nation on the materials used, instructional emphasis, and teacher qualifications. Similarly, the influence of the civil rights movement, federal support for education, and research and theory in education on materials, instruction, and teacher preparation is evident for the 1960–1990s time period. By reading "across the table" you can identify significant changes for each major category across time. For example, you will find that the instructional emphasis used in the 1600s and early 1700s for reading development is on letter-name knowledge, spelling, and elocution skills in contrast to the 1990s emphasis on word analysis and comprehension skills developed in story context.

	1607–1840	1840–1910	1910–1960	1960–1990s
1. HISTORICAL EVENTS	Jamestown, Declaration of Independence, War of 1812	Gold Rush, Western expansion, Industrial Revolution, Railroads, Civil War, Population 70% rural, Electric lights, telephone, radio, Urban movement begins	World War I, Great Depression, World War II, Television, Korean war, Technology, Launch of Sputnik, Jet air travel, Large urban populations	Civil rights movement, Vietnam war, Free Speech-movement, Moon landing, Federal support for education, Computers, Gulf War, close of Cold War, Poverty and health care key concerns
2. KEY INFLUENCES	Religious views, Patriotic views, New country	Expanding nation, Technology grows, Rural society, Schools needed and "school districts" formed, German-Pestalozzian influence, developmental view of children, Scientific movement in education begins	World view expands, Research in education, Child-centered curriculum (Dewey), Literacy awareness—World War II induction testing, Technology and communication, Lay critics (Flesch & Trace), Publisher impact on schools, Urban center needs	School integration, Federal funding for special programs, Minority group equality and justice, Research-theory in education, Technology, New immigration movement

TABLE 12-1

Historical Perspective on Reading and Literacy Instruction

	1607–1840	1840–1910	1910–1960	1960–1990s
3. Materials Used	Hornbook, Bible, New England Primer (speller, moral sayings, catechism), Webster's Blue Back Speller Content: religious and patriotic Classroom: benches, poor lighting and heating	McGuffey's Graded Readers, Materials become more available Illustrations are used more frequently Content: still moralistic but expands to include literary, history, and geography selections Classroom: desks are fastened to oil-treated floor, Beginning of grade levels based on age	Basal reading programs, Language programs, Teacher manuals developed to guide instruction Content: wide range reflects technology Classroom: rigid seating arrangement but becoming more flexible, Concern increased for better lighting and comfort	Basal reading programs, Children's literature, Whole language approach, Supplementary programs Content: great range of story content, incl. minority and var. gender roles Classroom: use of movable seating, high concern for lighting and comfort
4. Instruct. Emphasis	Letter-name knowledge, Pronounce Oral reading, "Spell Downs," Memorization of Bible; Letter-sound relationships, Art of elocution important to democratic government	Phonics and syllable work in isolation and context, Oral reading, Recitation of memorized passages, Handwriting emphasis, little composition, Beginning of achievement test use	Word analysis and comprehension emphasized, "Usage" main language emphasis, Reading groups by ability, increased use of testing, Concern for individual student	Word analysis and comprehension based on story context, Oral and written language are integrated, Formal testing used, Informal evaluation for instructional planning is emphasized, Increased teacher options and choices
5. Teacher Prep.	Able to read and write, Good moral character, Usually a male	One- and two-year normal schools, Women enter teaching in large numbers for first time	Four-year teacher colleges and universities, School-district in-service, Advanced specialist work encouraged	Five-year preparation programs, more in-service and advanced degree work available and encouraged

——— **Table 12-1 continued** ———

601

INSTRUCTIONAL MATERIALS, 1607–1840

The Hornbook (Figure 12-1), was used at the time of the Jamestown settlement and is one of the most widely used early reading materials of that time period. The primary reason for learning to read in the early colonies was to be able to read and understand biblical scriptures. This was made very clear in the "Old Deluder Satan Law" passed in Massachusetts in 1647 that pronounced the right of individuals to read the Scriptures for themselves (Smith, 1974). The Hornbook, the basic tool of literacy, was a paddle-shaped hardwood board covered by a thin sheet of transparent horn. As you examine Figure 12-1, you will see that it contained the alphabet and a few syllables, followed by the Lord's Prayer. This combined with the Bible constituted the major early teaching tools.

The *New England Primer* (Figure 12-2), the first schoolbook, was originally published about 1690 and reprinted in many editions over the next

FIGURE 12-1

The Hornbook (Early 1600s)

hundred or more years. The primer contained a speller, moralistic sayings of the time illustrated by woodcuts, and a catechism. Some three million copies of this short text were printed. The instructional emphasis in teaching reading and spelling consisted of developing letter-name knowledge and "spelling out" of a word, followed by pronunciation of the word. Oral reading, "spell downs," a form of today's spelling bee, and memorization of biblical selections consumed a significant portion of the school day.
The Hornbook (Early 1600s)

A BRIEF HISTORICAL PERSPECTIVE ON LITERACY INSTRUCTION IN THE UNITED STATES

INSTRUCTIONAL MATERIALS, 1840–1910

The *McGuffey Readers* (McGuffey, 1837/1930), mark the beginning of the 1840–1910 period. McGuffey was a professor at Miami University in Ohio. His home (and collection of readers) is preserved as a small museum on that campus today. These readers were the first widely used set of materials that organized reading selections according to different reading levels, gradually increasing the difficulty across the grades. The *McGuffey Readers*

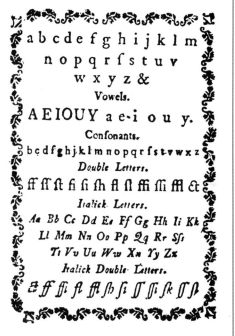

--- **FIGURE 12-2** ---

Sample Pages from the *New England Primer* (1690)

LESSON XXVII

said	their	school	fa'ther	ev'er-y
roar	great	li'ons	slow'ly	look'ed
cross	chain	ca'ges	a-fraid	pleas'ed
James	beasts	ma'ny	dan'ger	show'man
George	struck	te'gers	wald'ed	play'mates

THE WILD BEASTS

1. James and Gearge had been good boys at school, all the week.

2. They had been very kind and mild to their play-mates. So their father said he would take them to the show.

3. They saw at the show a great many wild beasts in cages.

4. Some of the beasts had a chain round one leg, made fast to a post.

5. There were lions, tigers, and a great many other beasts.

6. The boys walked round slowly, and looked at ev-er-y thing.

7. They felt a little afraid of some of the beasts.

8. But they were very much pleased with most that they saw.

9. The show-man went into the cage with the lion. The boys were then afraid.

10. But a man, who sat near them, told them there was no danger.

11. The show-man struck the lion with a large whip.

12. This made him roar very loud, and look cross, but he did not hurt the man.

13. James said, "I wish the man would come out. I do not like to see him there.

14. "The big lion might eat him up, and then I should be sorry."

15. James was a good boy, and did not like to see any one hurt.

Exercises-Where did the father of James and George take them? Why? Ought not boys to be always kind? What is a show? Tell what the boys saw.

FIGURE 12-3

Sample pages from *McGuffey's Second Eclectic Reader* (1837)

held sway in U.S. education for well over forty years, and continued to be reissued and revived from time to time (and are probably in use somewhere in the country today). For many Americans in the early to mid-twentieth century, the *McGuffey Readers* were their only access to literature (Smith, 1974).

The sample from *McGuffey's Second Eclectic Reader* (Figure 12-3) is typical of the series. The illustration of "The Wild Beasts" depicts the circus setting to establish context and is followed by vocabulary and word analysis instruction. The story about James's and George's experiences at the "show" reflects the moralistic emphasis of the materials. The program emphasized phonic elements and syllables in isolation but also in the reading context. Repetition of new words was used to develop a recognition vocabulary. Note the emphasis on factual level comprehension and moral development in the concluding "Exercises." Upper-grade materials included literary selections and social science selections, emphasizing areas such as history and geography.

The German-Pestalozzian movement (named after Swiss educational reformer Johann Heinrich Pestalozzi) strongly influenced the development of graded materials that appeared in several reading programs of the 1800s.

Proponents of the movement called for the development of mind through graded exercises "and inclusion of material dealing with objects and experiences familiar to children" (Smith, 1974).

INSTRUCTIONAL MATERIALS, 1910–1960

The 1910–1960 period included a new emphasis on "reading readiness," silent reading, the introduction of the preprimer by the publishing industry, and phonics instruction that developed sound-letter relationships in context. The concept of "language growth" emerged from a child-centered curriculum emphasis that was enhanced by the early efforts of John Dewey (Crosby, 1964). This viewpoint emphasized "enriched and direct experiences" that

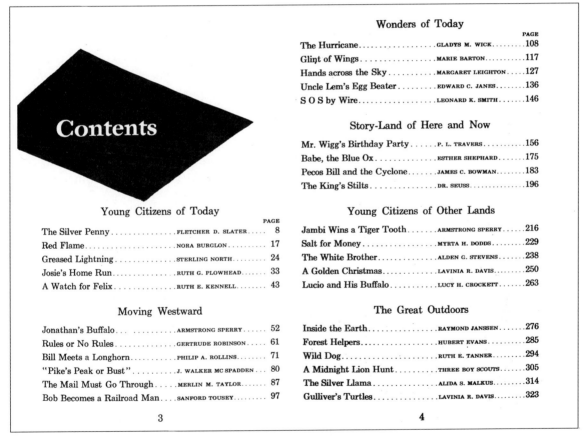

Contents

3

4

FIGURE 12-4

Table of Contents from Days and Deeds, Fifth-Grade Reader (1947). (Reproduced with permission from Gray & Arbuthnot, 1947, pp. 3 and 4.)

would draw on the child's personal knowledge and background. Oral dramatization, creative writing, and spelling were encouraged and often based on unit study intended to integrate content areas.

The sample of material found in Figure 12-4 consists of the table of contents from *Days and Deeds*, a fifth-grade reader from the *Curriculum Foundation Series* published in 1947 (Gray & Arbuthnot). This series of readers, commonly known as the "Dick and Jane Readers," was used widely across the United States. It is thought that Gray's two children served as the models for Dick and Jane, the fictional story characters found in the primary-grade books of the program. A quick overview of these two pages, reveals the impact of new communication ("The Mail Must Go Through" and "SOS by Wire"), transportation ("Bob Becomes a Railroad Man"), and technology ("Glint of Wings"). The content of reading material broadened significantly during this period and included stories from other countries, folktales, biography selections, and poetry. Teacher Guides and workbooks were introduced for the first time during this period and were used extensively.

INSTRUCTIONAL MATERIALS, 1960–1990S

The 1960–1990s period encompassed major changes in our society, ranging from the civil rights movement in the early 1960s to major concern for poverty and health care in the 1990s. The period is characterized by increased awareness of social injustice in the nation, resulting in nationwide school integration efforts and special emphasis on implementing educational programs to meet the needs of nonmainstream students more effectively through federally supported programs (see discussion in Chapter 10). For the first time, minority characters were represented in basal readers, gender roles began to vary in illustrations and stories (Hamlin, 1982), and characters with various physical differences were included in publisher-produced stories. Instructional materials were also affected by the impact of a variety of academic disciplines, such as sociolinguistics, psycholinguistics, and cognitive psychology, all of which contributed to an improved understanding of children's meaning construction processes. Teacher preparation programs began to shift to five-year programs to provide additional time and greater focus on theory and classroom practice.

The sample of material in Figure 12-5 represents this period. This page is from the teacher edition of *Castles in the Sand* (Pearson, Johnson, Clymer, Indrisano, Venezky, Baumann, Hiebert, & Toth, 1989), recommended for the beginning part of third grade. This annotated page for the story *Mufaro's Beautiful Daughters* (Steptoe, 1987) contains "Guided Reading" questions and suggestions for "Highlighting Literature." Detailed suggestions are provided earlier in the lesson for vocabulary development, building the students' background, and developing a purpose for reading. Follow-up suggestions are also presented to encourage the integration of language arts, word analysis, and other skill areas. This strategy follows that of the DRA (Directed Reading Activity) strategy discussed in Chapter 4. The lesson concludes by making connections to other curriculum areas such as art, mathematics, and social studies. The program also has accompanying skillbooks and a variety of other supplementary materials for teaching. The children's reader is in full color, as is the original literature selection, and contains follow-up questions and activities related to the story.

The 1960–1990s period is characterized by a wide array of materials available for teaching. These range from basal readers, such as the one described above, to excellent children's literature selections. A great deal of children's literature is available in low-cost paperback books that enable teachers to use multiple copies of the same book in designing their own literature- and language-based instructional program. Stronger emphasis is

A young woman expresses kindness to everyone she meets. Even the king learns of her goodness— in a most surprising way.

CALDECOTT HONOR 1988

MUFARO'S *Beautiful* DAUGHTERS
AN AFRICAN TALE

written and illustrated by John Steptoe

A long time ago, in a certain place in Africa, a small village lay across a river and half a day's journey from a city where a great king lived. A man named Mufaro (əm fä' rō) lived in this village with his two daughters, who were called Manyara (män yä' ra) and Nyasha (nyä' sha). Everyone agreed that Manyara and Nyasha were very beautiful.

P 296   MUFARO'S BEAUTIFUL DAUGHTERS   P 297

GUIDED READING

Page 297   Where and when does the story take place? (a long time ago in a small village in Africa) RECALL: SETTING

★ **Page 297   How are Mufaro's two daughters alike?** (They are both beautiful.)   ANALYZE: COMPARISON

HIGHLIGHTING LITERATURE

Page 297   Point out to students that they can tell this story will be a fairy tale. There is a clue in the first sentence — the words *A long time ago*. Also explain to students that many times in fairy tales kings, queens, princes, and princesses are main characters.

FIGURE 12-5

Teacher Manual Page from a Modern Reader (1989). (Reproduced with permission from Pearson et al., 1989, p. 583.)

placed on process writing and integrating reading and writing instruction. Instructional supplies for writing and other classroom activities are readily available and at least one computer with limited software is available in most classrooms. This period has also encouraged the use of informal observations of children during instruction to evaluate instructional needs more effectively and provide for these in instruction. More teacher options and choices enable teachers to select and design instruction for children with a wide range of achievement to a greater degree than has been true in any previous time period.

Literacy progress over the years can be measured in part by the degree of literacy achieved by citizens. At the time of the signing of the Declaration of Independence in 1776, only 15 percent of the population was literate. This figure moves upward to a 45 percent level at the time of World War I and approximately 65 percent by World War II. Today, approximately 85 to 95 percent of our population possess literacy skills sufficient to enable them to function effectively in society. While part of this dramatic increase in literacy may be attributed to new materials, new instructional programs, greater availability of literature, wider variety of reading material, and the proliferation of the mass media, a significant part of the increase is directly related to the efforts of teachers, who have been instrumental in teaching countless millions of students to read and write.

This historical perspective of reading and literacy development can be summarized in seven ideas:

1. Historical events and political influences in our society contribute to and shape the content of materials used for literacy learning, the instructional approaches, and the preparation of teachers.

2. A shift in emphasis has occurred across the years in our conception of the way in which children develop reading and writing skills from the early isolated skill-and-drill approach to the present view of children's literacy development as an integrated active process of meaning construction.

3. Instructional materials of the 1990s differ dramatically from the early materials of the 1600s, 1700s, 1800s, and early 1900s in availability, appropriateness, interest, and breadth of content.

4. Teacher choice in identifying both materials and instructional approaches is much greater and distinctly different from earlier periods.

5. Greater concern than ever before is present in identifying children's instructional needs through informal observation and meeting these needs through instruction.

6. Heightened sensitivity to children's language, cultural, and achievement diversity has developed in recent years and represents a major step in meeting their instructional needs.

7. Professional programs of teacher preparation are more theory and strategy driven and provide a broader range of teaching experiences

than ever before. Teachers are encouraged to continue to pursue their professional development through in-service in school districts and through advanced degree work.

We now turn to the major instructional approaches that you will encounter and use in your teaching.

Instructional Approaches for Literacy Development

While there are a variety of instructional approaches for reading and language development, three approaches are currently relied on most heavily. The basal reader, literature-based, and whole language approaches are used in at least 95 percent of classrooms across the nation (Chall & Squire, 1991). We will examine each approach to develop an understanding of its:

1. background and philosophy,
2. instructional features and strategies,
3. strengths and limitations, and
4. adaptability to the classroom.

The first two features, in effect, define an instructional approach. The philosophy and conceptual base of an approach guides the teacher and/or author-publisher in selecting the predominant strategies used for instruction and for student evaluation. This belief system also strongly influences the selection of the reading content, skills development, and the use of supporting materials and instructional activities.

The third feature relates to the implementation of the approaches in your classroom. Each approach has distinct strengths and limitations, and it is important to understand these and the way in which they will affect your teaching. The fourth feature—adaptability—is connected to your own philosophy of teaching and ease of modifying the approach to fit this philosophy in your teaching. Our discussion in Chapter 13 will be devoted to classroom organization and management, emphasizing each of these approaches.

It is helpful to think of these instructional approaches extending along the continuum shown in Figure 12-6. This continuum reflects the teacher's or author-publisher's instructional philosophy about literacy development and extends from the "Bottom Up" skills orientation on the left of the figure to the "Top Down" whole literacy orientation on the right. The Bottom Up philosophy places a major emphasis on initiating instruction by teaching a predetermined scope and sequence of skills in such areas as word analysis and comprehension. The Top Down belief stresses situating all literacy instruction within the context of natural, whole literacy events in which attention to skills occurs as needs arise.

```
                    Continuum of Beliefs
                  for Instructional Approaches

Bottom Up    Phonics      Basal       Literature-  Whole      Top Down
(Skills      Program      Reader      Based        Language   (Whole literacy
orientation)                                                  orientation)

              <<<<Teacher Decision–Making>>>>
```

—— **FIGURE 12-6** ————————————————————

An Instructional Continuum of Beliefs About Reading and Literacy
Development

A skill-based phonics program and the three major instructional
approaches are placed on the continuum relative to their Bottom Up or Top
Down emphasis. The supplementary skill-based phonics program is placed
very close to the Bottom Up end of the continuum. The basal reader
approach is placed at near midpoint but toward the Bottom Up side of the
continuum because of the emphasis on a predetermined sequence for skill
development, even though meaning construction is a recognized goal. The
literature-based approach is also found at midpoint but toward the Top
Down side of the continuum, reflecting its heavy reliance on full-length literature selections, although it also recognizes the need for skill development
and comprehension instruction. The whole language approach is located
near the Top Down side, reflecting emphasis on literacy development within
the context of whole literacy events and attention to skills as needs arise.

Note that "Teacher Decision–Making" extends across the bottom of the
continuum to highlight the important role of the teacher in determining
what instructional emphasis should be placed on skills development and
meaning construction. Teacher decision–making enables the teacher to
override a given approach and shift instructional focus. This feature of the
continuum becomes very important, for example, if one of the three major
instructional approaches is adopted in your school district, which may
require decision–making on your part to modify it to meet the instructional
needs of your students. Keep this continuum in mind as we examine each of
the three approaches to reading and literacy instruction.

THE BASAL READER APPROACH

Background and Philosophy

The basal reader is the most widely used instructional approach for literacy
development in the United States. Current estimates are that basal readers are
the chief instructional tool in 75 to 85 percent of elementary classrooms.
During the 1970s and early 1980s, some fifteen publishers produced basal

readers. Over the past ten years, however, this number has been reduced to six (Harcourt Brace, D. C. Heath, Houghton Mifflin, Open Court, Scott Foresman, and Silver Burdett & Ginn) due to corporate consolidation, acquisitions, and mergers. The total investment to produce a complete basal reading program has been estimated to range from $20 million to $50 million. These costs include editorial and author costs, permission fees (paid to reprint published stories), product research and field testing, promotion and sales training, printing and binding, and distribution and warehousing of the initial printing runs.

While basal reading programs differ in degree, the underlying philosophy for many basals is similar. This philosophy holds the view that children can best be taught to read by teaching a systematic, predetermined sequence of skills, using selections in the student reader, guided by recommendations in the teacher guide, and reinforced through practice activities provided in the student workbook. This philosophy also recognizes the need to go beyond these materials to provide for reading full-length literature selections and for integration of skills instruction with other areas of the curriculum, such as social studies, mathematics, and science.

Developing a Basal Reader

A basal reader is conceptualized and designed by the author team members composed of respected individuals in literacy education and publishing house editors. After these teams have set out the initial philosophy and plan for development, the literature and content area selections are identified for the student text, based on general themes ranging from "families" and "friendship" in the early grades to "memories" and "machines" in the intermediate grades. Selections in the student reader are often analyzed by a readability check to ensure consistent difficulty level of material at each grade level. The selection process and readability checks may be completed by editorial and author members or may be "jobbed out" to an independent company specializing in this part of the program development. Stories and content area selections for the beginning levels of the program are often custom-written to follow a predetermined skills sequence, vocabulary, and thematic unit plan.

Permissions are then obtained for the literature excerpts, full-length stories, and content area pieces. The corporate editorial team, almost all former teachers, and in some cases members of the author team, write lesson plans for the teacher's guide. Each selection follows a carefully prescribed skill sequence related to such program strands as word analysis, vocabulary, comprehension, and literature. The student workbook and supplementary materials are developed in a similar fashion. These parts of the program may also be "jobbed out" for development by a specialty company. The student text, teacher guides, workbooks, and supplementary material are carefully edited and revised "in-house," based on the predetermined skill sequence and prescribed strands, and prepared for manufacturing.

The various program parts are then manufactured and readied for distribution. In the meantime, sales representatives for the company are introduced to the program and its unique features as they prepare for marketing. Consultants are also trained to do program presentations and in-service work with teachers to "install" the new program in classrooms for school districts that adopt it. This entire process requires from three to five years and, as noted above, represents an enormous financial investment.

Instructional Features and Strategies

The following predominant features and instructional strategies characterize the basal reader approach:

1. The program is designed to develop literacy skills that follow a *predetermined skill sequence* that relies on selections in the student text and is supported by a *lesson plan* that develops specific guidelines and suggestions for each selection from the *teacher's guide.*

2. Skills development is directed by the *teacher's guide* and is organized around specific *instructional strands* including word analysis (Chapter 8), comprehension (Chapter 4), vocabulary (Chapter 5), language (Chapters 3 and 7), literature (Chapter 6), content area reading and study skills (Chapter 9), and thinking strategies (Chapter 4).

3. The *predominant instructional strategy* used in teaching selections using the teacher's guide is the Directed Reading Activity (DRA). As you will recall from Chapter 4, the DRA follows the steps of developing readiness to read as the selection is introduced, vocabulary introduction, guided silent reading, end-of-story comprehension check and discussion, possible rereading the parts of the selection based on comprehension check, and follow-up activities to reinforce and extend skill development. We suggest that you quickly review this pattern illustrated in the basal reader selection "Slipstream" discussed in Chapter 4 (pp. 161–167).

4. Stories and other reading material in the *student text* are organized in *unit themes* by identifying a *common theme* that serves to weave the selections together. The theme is based in part on the students' assumed developmental interests at a particular grade level.

5. The *reading difficulty is adjusted* to approximate grade level during the selection process and is based on perceived difficulty established through children's book review recommendations, authors' and editors' teaching experience, and, frequently, the use of readability formulas.

6. The *student workbook* is designed to support the skills taught and provide opportunities for practice and reinforcement. The *teacher's edition of the workbook* contains answers to skill activities in the student workbook. Other instructional aids are frequently provided, including picture and word cards, sentence strips, pocket charts, and "big books," particularly at the beginning levels.

7. *Evaluation of student progress* is frequently determined by *end-of-unit tests* (in the form of criterion-referenced tests in the student skillbook) that assess skills taught in that particular unit and/or check of maintenance skills taught earlier in the program. Informal teacher observation is also encouraged in understanding student progress.

We now turn to the instructional components used in teaching and evaluation.

The Teacher's Guide. The teacher's guide is a critical part of the basal approach and is designed to assist the teacher in the teaching process. A planning guide for a unit theme from the third-grade teacher's guide for *Castles in the Sand* (Pearson et al., 1989) is illustrated in Table 12-2. This group of stories and one poem are placed in Unit 4, called "Get the Message," and cluster around the theme of verbal and nonverbal communication and miscommunication. As shown in Table 12-2, each story is identified in the left column by title with accompanying unit skills, integrated language arts, and cross-curriculum connections. The skill strands emphasized (under Unit Skills) include word analysis, comprehension, and vocabulary. In addition there are three specific skills lessons in the unit: World of Reading, telling about various words and other language-based means of communicating; Comprehension, discussing how we express comparisons; and Vocabulary, dealing with the fact that some words have more than one meaning, depending on how they are used. The unit introduction (not shown here) provides a brief overview of the unit theme and a very brief synopsis of each story to orient the teacher to the unit. For example, the synopsis for *Mufaro's Beautiful Daughters* by John Steptoe states, "This African tale explores goodness and greed. Winner of a *Boston Globe Award* and a *Caldecott Honor Award*."

Lesson Plan and Annotated Student Text. The teacher's guide plan for each selection in the student text contains a detailed story summary, an overview of the lesson, and specific suggestions for each part of the lesson, following a DRA strategy. Most teacher's guides are annotated and contain not only teaching suggestions but also reproduce the student text, instructional charts, and the workbook pages connected to the specific lesson, in reduced size. The first step of the DRA (activating prior knowledge, and introducing new vocabulary and concepts) is shown for *Mufaro's Beautiful Daughters* in Table 12-3. Note the use of the semantic mapping strategy in this lesson, building the understanding of *good mood* and *bad mood* (key character traits for Mufaro's daughters, Nyasha and Manyara). The conclusion of the story, showing the annotated form of the student text, is shown in Table 12-4. Two options are suggested to the teacher in the form of "Guided Reading" and "Highlighting Literature."

The Student Workbook. The workbook provides practice and reinforcing activities for the skills taught. An example of a workbook page (Pearson et al., 1989) designed to develop vocabulary based on *Mufaro's Beautiful Daughters* is found in Table 12-5. This page is from the teacher's edition of

UNIT 4 PLANNING GUIDE

TITLE	UNIT SKILLS	INTEGRATED LANGUAGE ARTS	CROSS-CURRICULUM
Listening Lessons: Heidi	• Homographs	Attentive Listening Speaking: Description Using Detail	
Forecast	• Character* • Long Word Decoding* • Suffixes: *ion, tion* (Maintain)	Speaking: Weather Information; Acting Out Story Scenes; Weather Superstitions; Weather Broadcasts Writing: Weather Collage; Weather Poems; Animal Fantasy; Funny Weather Stories	Science: Weather Charts; Weather Instrument Book Art: Cloud Formation Pictures
"Secret Talk" (poem)		Listening: A Poem's Message Speaking: Picture Comparisons	
Words in Our Hands	• Main idea (Maintained) • Multiple Meanings* • Signs Symbols (Maintained)	Speaking: Sign Language; Welcoming Committee Presentation: Finger Spelling	Health and Safety: Posters on Hearing Safety Social Studies: People with Physical Disabilities Science: Devices for the Deaf
	World of Reading: Words and Other Codes		
Sports Signals	• Referents* • Prefixes: *de, dis* • Homophones (Maintain)	Speaking: Television Sports Interviews; Sports Teams Writing: Illustrated Baseball Glossary; Comic Strips: Newspaper Article: Story Map	Social Studies: Research— Names of Sports Teams Science: Pitching Speed Research Geography: Sports Teams, Locations Careers: Sports Stars

Comprehension: Comparisons

The Horse Who Lived Upstairs	• Story Elements (Maintained) • Suffix: *ment* (Maintained)	Writing: Travel Brochures; Postcard; Fantasy Speaking: Improvisation Listening: Story Themes	Social Studies: Farm Crops of New York Science: Horses Art: Farms
Mufaro's Beautiful Daughters	• Compare/Contrast (Maintained) • Making Inferences (Maintained)	Speaking: Fairy-Tale Improvisation; African Tales Writing: Modern Cinderella Story; Character Clusters	Art: African Masks Social Studies: Maps—African Countries Mathematics: Word Problems

Vocabulary: Multiple Meanings

The Boy Who Cried Wolf	• Predicting Outcomes (Maintained) • Compare/Contrast (Maintained) • Classification (Maintained)	Speaking: Story Mapping, Dramatization Writing: Character Clusters; Play Dialogue	Art: Story Character Puppets Social Studies: Sheep Farms Music: Songs for Story Characters
Reading Corner: In Which Piglet Meets a Heffalump		Writing: Draw and Name Creatures; Paragraph; Illustrations	

*Tested skill in this unit

TABLE 12-2

Teacher's Manual—Planning Guide for Unit 4, "Get the Message." (Reproduced with permission from Pearson et al., 1989, p. 469.)

Vocabulary Strategies

Developing Concepts

Use brainstorming to tap prior knowledge about being in good moods and bad moods.

Discuss the expressions *good mood* and *bad mood* as a starting point for teaching vocabulary. Encourage students to describe how they feel and what they do when they are in good and bad moods. *(good mood: laugh, play, enjoy being with others; bad mood: do not feel like being with others, are sad or angry, seldom laugh)* Ask students to brainstorm words that describe someone in each mood. Then list their responses on the chalkboard.

Teaching Vocabulary

Discuss meanings of Story Critical words.

Read each context sentence on the Teaching Chart and identify the new word. Then use the questions below to help students understand each word. When necessary, provide a definition.

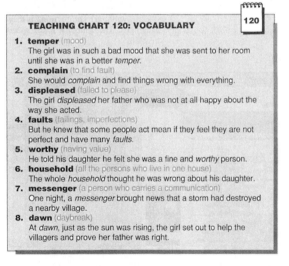

TEACHING CHART 120: VOCABULARY 120

1. **temper** (mood)
   The girl was in such a bad mood that she was sent to her room until she was in a better *temper*.
2. **complain** (to find fault)
   She would *complain* and find things wrong with everything.
3. **displeased** (failed to please)
   The girl *displeased* her father who was not at all happy about the way she acted.
4. **faults** (failings, imperfections)
   But he knew that some people act mean if they feel they are not perfect and have many *faults*.
5. **worthy** (having value)
   He told his daughter he felt she was a fine and *worthy* person.
6. **household** (all the persons who live in one house)
   The whole *household* thought he was wrong about his daughter.
7. **messenger** (a person who carries a communication)
   One night, a *messenger* brought news that a storm had destroyed a nearby village.
8. **dawn** (daybreak)
   At *dawn*, just as the sun was rising, the girl set out to help the villagers and prove her father was right.

temper **1. What other words or phrases mean about the same as *temper*?** (mood, state of mind, feeling) STRATEGY: SYNONYMS

TABLE 12-3

Teacher's Manual—Developing Vocabulary Strategies for *Mufaro's Beautiful Daughters.* (Reproduced with permission from Pearson et al., 1989, p. 580.)

"Do not go to the king, my sister. Oh, please, Father, do not let her go!" she cried hysterically. "There's a great monster there, a snake with five heads! He said that he knew all my <u>faults</u> and that I <u>displeased</u> him. He would have swallowed me alive if I had not run. Oh, my sister, please do not go inside that place."

It frightened Nyasha to see her sister so upset. But, leaving her father to comfort Manyara, she bravely made her way to the chamber and opened the door.

On the seat of the great chief's stool lay the little garden snake. Nyasha laughed with relief and joy.

"My little friend," she exclaimed. "It's such a pleasure to see you, but why are you here?"

"I am the king," Nyoka replied.

And there, before Nyasha's eyes, the garden snake changed shape.

"I am the king. I am also the hungry boy with whom you shared a yam in the forest and the old woman to whom you made a gift of sunflower seeds. But you know me best as Nyoka. Because I have been all of these, I know you to be the Most Worthy and Most Beautiful Daughter in the Land. It would make me very happy if you would be my wife."

| P 306 | MUFARO'S BEAUTIFUL DAUGHTERS | P 307 |

GUIDED READING

Page 306   How close was your prediction about why Manyara was screaming? Tell why it did or did not match what happened. (Allow students to discuss their predictions and evaluate them.)   EVALUATE: PREDICTING OUTCOMES

★ **Page 306   How is Manyara's behavior different from the way she behaved toward Nyasha at the beginning of the story?** (Instead of being cruel to Nyasha, she tries to warn her away from danger.) ANALYZE: COMPARISON

Page 306   Who had the king been before? (the garden snake, the hungry boy, and the old woman) RECALL: DETAILS

HIGHLIGHTING LITERATURE

Page 306   Have students point out the events on this page that show it is a fairy tale. (They will probably mention the king's ability to change shape, most likely by use of magic. They may also mention the idea of testing good and bad characters through disguises, a common theme in fairy tales.) Encourage them to mention other fairy tales in which a character changes shape and in which good and bad characters are tested. (Answers may include "Cinderella", in which a pumpkin is changed into a coach, mice into footman, and Cinderella herself transformed into a beautiful princess.)

TABLE 12-4

Teacher's Manual—Conclusion of Guided Reading for *Mufaro's Beautiful Daughters. (Reproduced with permission from Pearson et al.,* 1989, p. 588.)

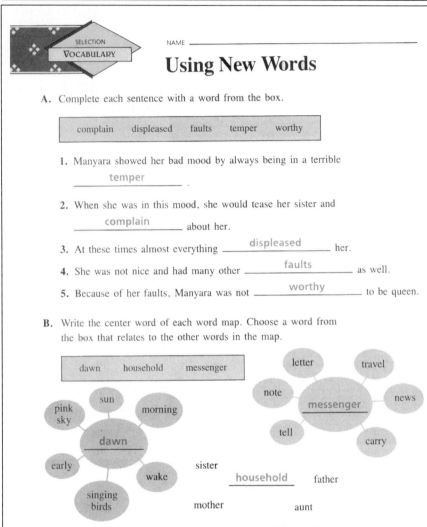

NAME _____

Using New Words

A. Complete each sentence with a word from the box.

| complain | displeased | faults | temper | worthy |

1. Manyara showed her bad mood by always being in a terrible
   _____ temper _____ .

2. When she was in this mood, she would tease her sister and
   _____ complain _____ about her.

3. At these times almost everything _____ displeased _____ her.

4. She was not nice and had many other _____ faults _____ as well.

5. Because of her faults, Manyara was not _____ worthy _____ to be queen.

B. Write the center word of each word map. Choose a word from
the box that relates to the other words in the map.

| dawn | household | messenger |

pink sky · sun · morning · **dawn** · early · wake · singing birds

letter · travel · note · **messenger** · news · tell · carry

sister · **household** · father · mother · aunt

C. On separate paper, make your own word map. Write a story
word from Part A in the middle of the map. Then around it
write other words that are related to it. See Teacher Notes.

150 "Mufaro's Beautiful Daughters"   Selection Vocabulary

TABLE 12-5

Student's Workbook Page for Vocabulary Development to Be Used with
Mufaro's Beautiful Daughters. (Reproduced with permission from
Pearson et al., 1989, p. 150.)

the workbook and provides the desired answers to assist the teacher in evaluating students' responses. This page also appears in the teacher's guide in reduced size for quick reference.

Grade and Level Organization. From the time of the *McGuffey Readers* until the mid-1970s, publishers used grade designations for their readers, ranging from first grade (readiness, preprimers, primer [pronounced primer], and first reader) through sixth grade or eighth grade. This use of grade designations has shifted over the past two decades to level designations that are cross-referenced to grades. The idea behind the level identification is to place a student at the reading level, rather than the grade level, most appropriate for instruction. The success of the idea, however, depends directly on two factors: first, the classroom teacher's understanding of the appropriate levels for different children in his or her classroom; and second, the willingness of the central office personnel in the local school district to order materials from publishers based on the teacher's recommendation. The cross-referencing of grade-level difficulty of a text and title to instructional level in the program is illustrated for series of two different publishers, Silver Burdett & Ginn (Pearson et al., 1989) and D. C. Heath (Alvermann, Bridge, Schmidt, Searfoss, Winograd, Paris, Bruce, Priestley-Romero, & Santeusanio, 1993), in Table 12-6.

The need to familiarize yourself thoroughly with the basal reading program adopted in your school is evident from this table. For example, the Silver Burdett & Ginn program, shown in the left of the table, designates the reader for early second grade (2-1), *Garden Gates*, as Level 6, while the D. C. Heath program, in the right side of the table designates the 2-1 grade level book, *Cats Sleep Anywhere*, as Level 2-1. Familiarity with the adopted program's level designations is essential as you check the availability of readers for your students' instructional levels and discuss the program with teachers immediately above and below your grade level.

Strengths and Limitations of the Basal Reader Approach

The basal reader approach offers the distinct advantage of an instructional program with preselected and developed skill strands already prepared for the classroom. This includes literature (usually excerpts from full-length stories) and expository selections in the student text. Extended suggestions for teaching the selection are provided in the teacher's guide and follow a Directed Reading Activity (DRA) instructional pattern. In addition, workbooks, including the teacher's edition, and various supplementary materials are available to support and reinforce the development of the preselected reading material and skill areas. This approach thus provides a significant savings in teacher time.

The basal approach, however, represents something of a two-edged sword for the teacher. One edge, as described above, provides the teacher with a time-saving preprepared program. The other edge limits the range of literature and

SILVER BURDETT & GINN			D. C. HEATH	
GRADE LEVEL	**TITLE**	**INST. LEVEL**	**TITLE**	**INST. LEVEL**
R	Clap Your Hands	R	Along Came a Fox	1-1
PP1	All Through the Town	1	(Use for R,	
PP2	Out Comes the Sun	2	PP1, PP2,	
PP3	Morning Bells	3	PP3)	
P	Make a Wish	4	Little Duck Dance	1-2
1st	A New Day	5	My Best Bear Hug	1-2
2-1	Garden Gates	6	Cats Sleep Anywhere	2-1
2-2	Going Places	7	Come Back Here, Crocodile	2-2
3-1	Castles of Sand	8	A Soft Pillow for an Armadillo	3-1
3-2	On the Horizon	9	Never a Worm This Long	3-2
4	Silver Secrets	10	Turtles Like to Sleep In	4
5	Dream Chasers	11	Rare as Hens' Teeth	5
6	Wind by the Seal	12	I Touched the Sun	6
7	Star Walk	13	Through the Starshine	7
8	Worlds Beyond	14	Roads Go Ever Ever On	8

TABLE 12-6

Grade Level, Book Title, and Instructional Level for Two Basal Reading Programs

Sources: Based on information in Pearson et al., 1989, and Welcome to Heath Reading: A Program Overview, D.C. Heath, 1993.

expository material children read for instruction if the basal approach is strictly adhered to in the classroom. Heavy reliance on the DRA strategy limits children's approach to reading and the way they think about reading as a process. The skill activities in the accompanying workbooks and supplementary materials often follow a set pattern of development and can become more busywork than useful activity if not used with great care.

Adapting and Using the Basal Reader Approach

The important key to using the basal reader approach effectively is adapting the program to meet the instructional needs of children rather than adhering strictly to the teacher's guide.

Preparing to Use Basal Readers. Begin by familiarizing yourself thoroughly with the program; carefully read the literature and expository selections in the student text. Constantly pose the questions "Will my children find this story of interest?" "How can I effectively introduce this selection?" "Is this selection taken from a full-length story? If so, can I find the full-length story in the school library to make it available for those children who would enjoy continuing it? Or would I rather teach the full-length story?" Your goal is to present and develop the literature and expository selections in the most effective way possible by taking full advantage of the instructional strategies that you know *and the knowledge of your students that only you possess.*

Examine the teacher's guide with care and be selective in identifying the activities you wish to use from the many found there. Remember that the teacher's guide activities are often written and/or edited by publishing editors who have been former teachers themselves. Guide writers write lesson plans for a specific story according to a prescribed skill sequence, and often do so with a great deal of creativity and perception. They write, however, under enormous time pressure and restricted space limitations and, no matter how perceptive they are, they cannot perceive your students' specific needs. For these reasons and others, some activities do not work well in actual teaching. The point is this: *You have not only the freedom but the responsibility to identify carefully those activities you believe will work, and to use, or adapt, these.* Discard those that do not seem fruitful to you. The program *assumes* that you will pick and choose activities; in fact, if you used every activity found in a single lesson plan, you could easily spend two weeks or more in teaching just one story, an unfortunate event that is deadly dull for children. Be selective.

Examine the student workbook and supplementary program activities likewise. You have full control over the use of these activities with your students. The activities should go beyond busywork and time fillers for children and provide development and reinforcement of important lesson concepts. Use *only* activities that support your instructional goals and students' needs, and eliminate those that do not.

Using Basal Readers. Alter the instructional strategy used with the basal reader stories to make it your own and fit the needs of your children. For example, you may wish to use a Directed Reading-Thinking Activity (DR-TA) with some story selections in place of the DRA to build prediction and problem-solving thinking skills (see Chapter 4). This requires your familiarity both with the story and the DR-TA strategy. Recall the conversion of a DRA to a

621

DR-TA in Chapter 4, using the "Slipstream" story found there. Consider following the DR-TA with the Group Mapping Activity (GMA) that we explored in Chapter 4 to build story summary and story synthesis skills. You may also wish to hold the introduction of vocabulary in a given lesson, and instead substitute the Vocabulary Self-Collection Strategy (VSS) discussed in Chapter 5, or use both the vocabulary introduction before reading and VSS after. Do remember that the editorial preselection of vocabulary for your students (unseen by and unknown to those who did the selecting) constitutes a big leap of faith. If you use the preselected vocabulary, think carefully about your children and words that you believe they are already familiar with as well as those words in the preselected list (and other words in the story) that they may not know.

Consider ways to engage children actively as you use stories in the student text. For example, a story like *Mufaro's Beautiful Daughters* (Steptoe, 1987) is perfectly suited for Reader's Theatre, as discussed in Chapter 6. Literature response journals can also be used effectively with many story selections in the student text. Expand children's opportunities and experiences to explore full-length literature stories and expository books beyond the basal reading program. Authors and editors of basal reading programs are fully aware of the limitations found in story excerpts. For this reason you will often find suggestions for extended reading in the teacher's guide. Go beyond these suggestions, however, and immerse children in literature by developing your own literature and reading center as outlined in our discussion in Chapters 3, 6, and 13.

Use informal observations recorded in your quick observation notes, the Early Reading and Writing Assessment Checklist (Chapter 3, Table 3-3), and the developmental inventory (Chapter 11, Figures 11-2 and 11-3) to assist in student assessment. The information from these observations can then be combined with end-of-unit tests to assess student progress and plan for meeting your students' instructional needs. Remember that you have the knowledge, ability, and control to adapt the basal reading program to fit your own philosophy in meeting the instructional needs of your children.

THE LITERATURE-BASED APPROACH

Background and Philosophy

The literature-based approach has gained in popularity during the past decade and is part of the school reform movement spearheaded by a number of school districts and state departments of education across the country. This approach grew in part from the belief that children were not receiving adequate exposure to and opportunity to read full-length quality literature. The essence of this view is found in Robert Hutchins's observation,

> *We have been so preoccupied with trying to find out how*
> *to teach everybody to read anything that we have forgotten*
> *the importance of what is read. Yet it is obvious that if we*
> *succeeded in teaching everybody to read, and everybody read*

Using Basal Readers

nothing but pulp magazines, obscene literature, and Mein Kampf, *the last state of the nation would be worse than the first. Literacy is not enough. (1943, pp. 14–15)*

The advent of the literature-based approach has prompted and motivated publishers, more than ever before, to include high-quality literature excerpts and full-length story selections in basal reader programs. At least one publisher has marketed a literature-based program for schools, and others have added full-length books to their programs as recommended, but optional, supplements.

The general goals of the literature-based approach include not only the development of literacy skills but also developing children's intellectual and aesthetic growth, developing a sense of citizenship, building a sense of rootedness in our society, and developing ethical responsibility (California State Department of Education, 1987). These goals are not new to American education, and in fact most teachers would express the viewpoint that these are shared goals in their instruction regardless of the instructional approach used. A literature-based approach, however, offers a unique opportunity to develop these goals, based on the literature selections used.

A literature-based program uses literature in at least three ways in the classroom. The *first* way, and a defining characteristic of this approach, employs a core set of books that provide shared literary experiences for children at each grade. The *second* extends the use of literature selections by supplementing and enriching the curriculum in areas such as social studies and science. And the *third* way involves the use of literature primarily based on individual student interest and motivation. The second and third uses of literature are already found in many classrooms today; however, the use of a common core of literature selections is not. This approach requires a strong commitment and knowledge base on the part of the teacher in both literacy and literature teaching (California State Department of Education, 1987; Ruddell, 1992; Walmseley, 1992).

Instructional Features of the Literature-Based Approach

Literature-based programs tend to be highly individualistic; teachers, schools, and districts design and implement programs that are often so different that the *only* shared characteristic between them is the use of the core set of books. Some literature-based programs use *classroom* sets of core literature books so that all children are reading the same book at any given time. Our choice for a literature-based program is one in which teachers use a number of core sets of books and allow children to work in small groups to read and respond to the books.

We call the small group arrangement in literature-based programs *reading response groups* (other people may use other names—literature response groups, for example). In reading response groups, four or five children form an independent working group to read and respond to literature. The teacher allows children to self-select themselves into reading response groups based on their choice of book to read. The teacher then guides the reading response groups by providing reading or discussion prompts (O'Flahavan, 1989) for them to use in the course of their discussions. Prompts should access (1) children's background knowledge (how their experiences relate to the text); (2) ideas derived from text (how students constructed meaning); and (3) ideas that go beyond the text (how students interpret or react to text) (O'Flahavan, 1989). The following prompts are useful with reading response groups:

1. Tell about a time when you had an experience or problem like Ira's (*Ira Sleeps Over*). How did you solve your problem?

2. How do you interpret Dicey's situation (*Dicey's Song*)? What advice would you give her at this point?

3. If you were going to interpret this part of *Farewell to Manzanar* as art, music, or dance, what would it look, feel, or sound like? What would be the most effective way to present your interpretation?

Children maintain individual response logs or journals throughout the reading response group experience. End-of-book activities typically involve productions—plays, puppet shows, murals, reports, Reader's Theatre, dance—in which reading response groups interpret the literature they have read in the manner they choose.

Identifying Core Readings. Core literature selections are generally identified by a teacher committee representing various grade levels. (In some schools you may be able to choose your own.) A core selection is a full-length children's book deemed to be of exceptional quality and identified as meeting a literature-based instructional goal. The teacher committee may be at the school site level or the school district level and should include at least one elementary school librarian. Reaching a consensus on the core selections is the first important step in launching the literature-based approach.

The process of identifying core selections is guided by the teachers' and librarians' experiences in using literature with children at various grade levels to account for developmental interest and motivation. It is important that *major literary genre* such as fiction (realism and fantasy), nonfiction (biography, autobiography, and informational), and poetry be represented in the core selections (see Chapter 6). This selection process also needs to account for a *balance* across the old favorites, such as folktales and fables, children's classics that have stood the test of time, and the most recent modern fiction for children. Care must be taken to include varied cultural and ethnic representations and representations of many kinds of diversity in the core collection (see Chapter 10). It is also important to have a balanced representation of males and females as strong central characters and representation of both sexes in nonstereotypical activities. A range of difficulty levels must be provided for each grade to account for individual student reading needs. This is particularly important at the upper primary and intermediate grades, where a wider achievement range is to be expected.

The core books selected are reserved for instruction at the grade levels specified; although, we hope that you will not go to the extreme of barring a child's individual choice of a book to read because that book is on the core list for the next grade level. This extreme has, indeed, happened ("No, you can't read that book. You read it next year."). There should be a minimum of eight to ten separate titles per grade level. Teachers are free to use any literature titles they wish outside of the core books.

Multiple copies of each core book for each grade level need to be purchased. We find that six to ten copies of each title can provide for the type of reading response group instruction we described earlier. If you assume, for example, that ten separate titles have been identified for fourth-grade level and you desire to have ten multiple copies of each title, you will need to purchase one hundred books for that grade. The cost of this purchase can be greatly reduced by acquiring paperback copies of the core selections, assuming they are available.

Implementing the Literature-Based Approach. An important step in using the literature-based approach is to identify, very early in the process, the major instructional goals and objectives of the program. These should include the six literature objectives discussed at the beginning of Chapter 6, which range from fostering high motivation toward reading and development of new concepts to understanding the power of language to convey human experiences and to reinforce the development of reading skills and strategies.

It is also important to consider the instructional stance that will be used with the core selections. Some pieces will be most effectively used with a predominantly aesthetic stance to develop identification with story characters, personal interpretation, and transaction with the story. Other selections may require a predominantly efferent stance as you build new ideas and concepts. Our sample discussion questions for each stance in Chapter 6 will be of great value in implementing a predominantly aesthetic or efferent stance, depending on the core selection being used.

Instructional strategies to be used with the core selections deserve careful consideration. We highly recommend the reading response group approach with teacher-designed prompts to guide individual group discussion. If you prefer to lead the discussion yourself, DR-TA and other open-ended approaches are fine. A major problem in school districts that have previously used a basal reader approach is that teachers often simply transfer basal practices (the DRA strategy) to the reading of literature; in effect, they "basalize" the literature selections. The story is introduced, vocabulary is developed, directed guided reading is conducted throughout the selection, follow-up questions are asked, rereading takes place to substantiate or locate answers, and a teacher-designed worksheet is used for skill development or reinforcement. It is important to consider the many options and strategies available to you in addition to the DRA, as you use the core literature selections. The use of the DR-TA, QARs (Question Answer Relationships), and the GMA (Group Mapping Activity) can play an important role in the literature program (see Chapter 4).

Other instructional strategies that hold high potential for use in the literature-based approach include reading aloud (story and poetry sharing), storytelling, literature response journals, Reader's Theatre, InQuest, and the development of topical and conceptual thematic units—all discussed in detail in Chapter 6. A key goal in your literature program is to develop high reading motivation and encourage children to enjoy the aesthetic pleasure that derives from experiencing literature. Two examples of a "planning web" for a literature-based lesson are found in Figures 12-7 and 12-8. These examples illustrate key literary elements to be developed, connections across content areas, and reading and language skills to be emphasized. The first example (California Association of County Superintendents of Schools, 1989), based on *Ira Sleeps Over* (Waber, 1972), is designed for the primary grades (Figure 12-7), and the second example (California Association of County Superintendents of Schools, 1989), using *The Velveteen Rabbit* (Williams, 1958), is for the intermediate grades (Figure 12-8).

The reading center in your classroom is an essential part of a literature-based approach. This will serve as the central location for the core books selected and your collection of high-interest enrichment literature. The center conveys the idea that reading and enjoying literature is an important goal, and it provides an inviting place to browse and explore books. Our discussions that outline suggestions on how to develop this center (see Chapters 3, 6, and 13), including children's and teachers' favorite books, will assist in this process.

Evaluation of the literature-based approach will depend heavily on informal observations of children as they respond to literature and construct meaning. Your evaluation will be based on a variety of observations including:

- your observation and evaluation of reading response groups (more about this in Chapter 13),

- your quick observation notes from instruction,

- your responses to students' literature response journals,

- individual and group writing samples related to literature selections and literature projects,

- student progress notes, kept by you or the children, that show the title of the book, title of chapter, date read, and a brief response to the chapter, and

- your observations and impressions based on individual conferences and small-group discussions.

You will find portfolios (Chapter 11) of great help in literature-based assessment. In addition, you will find our focusing questions related to evaluating children's response to literature of value (Chapter 6).

Strengths and Limitations of the Literature-Based Approach

The literature-based approach provides the widest possible freedom for the teacher in the literature selection process. An excellent range of high-interest and high-quality children's literature is available, much of which is in inexpensive paperback form. The freedom you have to select instructional strategies for carrying out instructional goals of the program is another great advantage. The literature and reading center becomes a resource reservoir for instruction and provides opportunity for children to develop both reading interests and reading skills.

Just as literature-based instruction offers great teacher freedom in book selection and instructional design, so also does it carry with it significant responsibility. The development of a literature-based approach requires a high level of teacher commitment. The time and energy required to establish instructional goals, identify appropriate literature selections, select and create instructional strategies, and implement the program with twenty-five to thirty-five children is substantial. If such an effort is to be successful, the teacher must possess an in-depth knowledge of children's literature, children's interests and motivation, instructional stances and strategies, and the ability to build bridges between children and books. This approach also assumes that instruction in word analysis and other skills will be developed either through the literature itself or through a supplementary program of some type. Finally, the implementation of a literature-based approach requires curriculum and financial support from the local school principal

SAMPLE PLANNING WEB FOR AN INTEGRATED LITERATURE-BASED LESSON: PRIMARY

Note: The selection of literature determines the literary elements, interdisciplinary content, and language arts skills to be taught.

• Using the selected planning web, write the book title in the center of the web.
• Record possible activities designed to address the instruction of the relevant elements.
• Identify Into (I), Through (T), and Beyond (B) Activities.

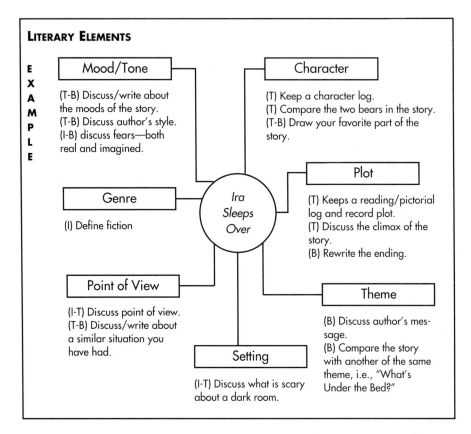

LITERARY ELEMENTS

EXAMPLE

Mood/Tone
(T-B) Discuss/write about the moods of the story.
(T-B) Discuss author's style.
(I-B) discuss fears—both real and imagined.

Character
(T) Keep a character log.
(T) Compare the two bears in the story.
(T-B) Draw your favorite part of the story.

Genre
(I) Define fiction

Ira Sleeps Over

Plot
(T) Keeps a reading/pictorial log and record plot.
(T) Discuss the climax of the story.
(B) Rewrite the ending.

Point of View
(I-T) Discuss point of view.
(T-B) Discuss/write about a similar situation you have had.

Theme
(B) Discuss author's message.
(B) Compare the story with another of the same theme, i.e., "What's Under the Bed?"

Setting
(I-T) Discuss what is scary about a dark room.

FIGURE 12-7

Ira Sleeps Over: Sample Planning Web for an Integrated Literature-Based Lesson—Primary Grades. (Reproduced with permission from California Association of County Superintendents of Schools, 1989, p. v–13.)

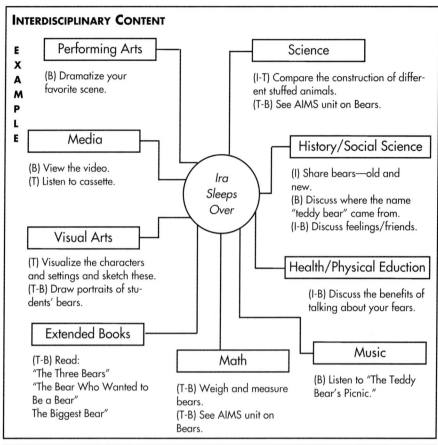

INTERDISCIPLINARY CONTENT

E
X
A
M
P
L
E

Performing Arts

(B) Dramatize your favorite scene.

Science

(I-T) Compare the construction of different stuffed animals.
(T-B) See AIMS unit on Bears.

Media

(B) View the video.
(T) Listen to cassette.

History/Social Science

(I) Share bears—old and new.
(B) Discuss where the name "teddy bear" came from.
(I-B) Discuss feelings/friends.

Ira Sleeps Over

Visual Arts

(T) Visualize the characters and settings and sketch these.
(T-B) Draw portraits of students' bears.

Health/Physical Eduction

(I-B) Discuss the benefits of talking about your fears.

Extended Books

(T-B) Read:
"The Three Bears"
"The Bear Who Wanted to Be a Bear"
The Biggest Bear"

Math

(T-B) Weigh and measure bears.
(T-B) See AIMS unit on Bears.

Music

(B) Listen to "The Teddy Bear's Picnic."

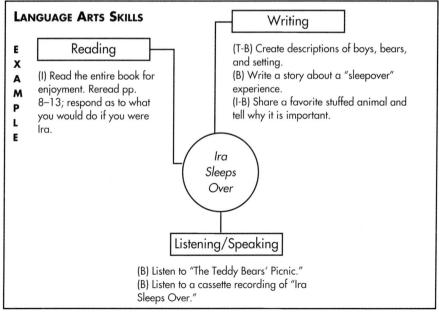

LANGUAGE ARTS SKILLS

E
X
A
M
P
L
E

Reading

(I) Read the entire book for enjoyment. Reread pp. 8–13; respond as to what you would do if you were Ira.

Writing

(T-B) Create descriptions of boys, bears, and setting.
(B) Write a story about a "sleepover" experience.
(I-B) Share a favorite stuffed animal and tell why it is important.

Ira Sleeps Over

Listening/Speaking

(B) Listen to "The Teddy Bears' Picnic."
(B) Listen to a cassette recording of "Ira Sleeps Over."

FIGURE 12-7 CONTINUED

SAMPLE PLANNING WEB FOR AN INTEGRATED LITERATURE-BASED LESSON: INTERMEDIATE

Note: The selection of literature determines the literary elements, interdisciplinary content, and language arts skills to be taught.

- Using the selected planning web, write the book title in the center of the web.
- Record possible activities designed to address the instruction of the relevant elements.
- Identify Into (I), Through (T), and Beyond (B) Activities.

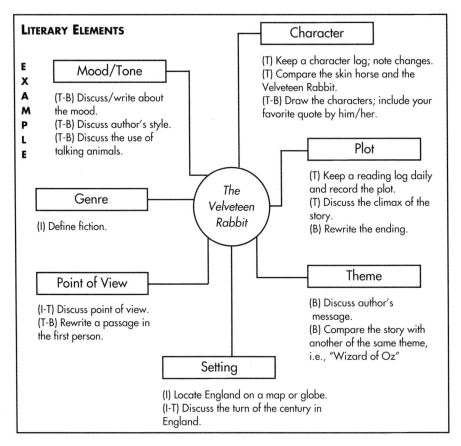

LITERARY ELEMENTS

E X A M P L E

Mood/Tone

(T-B) Discuss/write about the mood.
(T-B) Discuss author's style.
(T-B) Discuss the use of talking animals.

Genre

(I) Define fiction.

Point of View

(I-T) Discuss point of view.
(T-B) Rewrite a passage in the first person.

Character

(T) Keep a character log; note changes.
(T) Compare the skin horse and the Velveteen Rabbit.
(T-B) Draw the characters; include your favorite quote by him/her.

Plot

(T) Keep a reading log daily and record the plot.
(T) Discuss the climax of the story.
(B) Rewrite the ending.

Theme

(B) Discuss author's message.
(B) Compare the story with another of the same theme, i.e., "Wizard of Oz"

Setting

(I) Locate England on a map or globe.
(I-T) Discuss the turn of the century in England.

The Velveteen Rabbit

─── **FIGURE 12-8** ───

The Velveteen Rabbit: Sample Planning Web for an Integrated Literature-Based Lesson—Intermediate Grades. (Reproduced with permission from California Association of County Superintendents of Schools, 1989, p. v–14.)

INTERDISCIPLINARY CONTENT

E X A M P L E

Performing Arts

(B) Dramatize your favorite scene.

Science

(I-T) Discuss different uses and construction of fabric.
(I-T) Study real rabbits and their habits. See video "Real Rabbits."
(T) Share pet rabbits.

Media

(B) View the video.
(T) Listen to cassette.

History/Social Science

(T) Discuss "putting on airs" and false pretenses. Explore relationships and friendships.
(I) Discuss historical period.
(I) Share antique toys.

Visual Arts

(T) Visualize the characters and settings and sketch these.
(T-B) Make fabric collages of toys.

The Velveteen Rabbit

Health/Physical Education

(T) Reenact the scene where the Velveteen Rabbit becomes real.
(T) Discuss scarlet fever, communicable diseases, and quarantine.

Extended Books

(T-B) Read "Wizard of Oz."

Music

(B) Listen and respond to "Nutcracker Suite."

Math

LANGUAGE ARTS SKILLS

E X A M P L E

Reading

(I) After hearing Chapter 3, read Chapter 4 with a partner.

Writing

(B) Create descriptions of rabbit, skin horse, settings.
(I-B) Write an adventure story.
(B) Share a stuffed animal; write about its importance.

The Velveteen Rabbit

Listening/Speaking

(B) Listen to "Nutcracker Suite."
(B) Listen to a cassette recording of story.
(I) Vocabulary: Use sentences from the story containing words such as "scarlet fever," "nursery," "nanny," "putting on airs," "bracken," "real," to check for understanding in context.

FIGURE 12-8 CONTINUED

and the school district. Teachers must be careful that their approach does not "basalize" literature (as we previously discussed) or become diluted by lack of focus or clarity regarding instructional goals and responsibilities. The literature-based approach can prove to be an exciting way to stimulate in children the joy of reading while developing language and literacy abilities. It does require teacher commitment, time, and support.

Adapting the Literature-Based Approach

Many teachers are unable to expend the commitment, energy, and time required to implement a full-fledged literature-based approach and/or do not have sufficient school or district support to do so. Others wish to work gradually toward the literature-based approach by modifying their current teaching practices. Various aspects of the approach may be adapted to meet these needs. The following ideas are derived from the literature-based approach and are highly effective and relatively easy and inexpensive to implement in your classroom.

Build a collection of children's literature based on the excerpts used in your basal reading program. For example, if an excerpt is used from a chapter in *Julie of the Wolves* (George, 1972), locate or purchase a paperback copy of the book for your reading center. Explain that the story in the basal reader is taken from *Julie of the Wolves* and encourage your children to peruse the full-length book. You will find that many stories in the basal reading program are excerpted from full-length books; this approach enables children to encounter the actual book and explore characters and plot in depth.

Social Interactions in the Literature-Based Approach

Extend your discussion of content area topics in social studies to include children's literature. Make it possible for your children to explore the American Revolution through the eyes of Johnny Tremain (*Johnny Tremain*, Forbes, 1943), live with Jeanne Wakatsuki in the Manzanar internment camp during World War II (*Farewell to Manzanar*, Houston & Houston, 1973), experience the hopes and fears of Anne Frank (*Anne Frank: The Diary of a Young Girl*, Frank, 1967), or enjoy the dreams of Cassie Louise Lightfoot, a young African-American girl living in New York City (*Tar Beach*, Ringgold, 1991). Many opportunities are present to explore scientific concepts through beautifully illustrated books such as *Why Do Volcanoes Erupt?* (Whitfield, 1990) and *Plants That Never Bloom* (Heller, 1984) or to learn more about dinosaurs by traveling with Professor Denison and Will on their shipwrecked adventure to the lost island of Dinotopia (Gurney, 1992).

Build collections in your reading center that focus on each of the six key internal reading motivations (Ruddell, 1992) of your students (see Chapter 6). These include:

1. Problem Resolution, e.g., *Charlotte's Web*; *Island of the Blue Dolphins*;
2. Prestige, e.g., *Henry the Explorer*; *The Man from Snowy River*;
3. Aesthetic, e.g., *When I Was Young in the Mountains*; *Sarah, Plain and Tall*;
4. Escape, e.g., *Where the Wild Things Are*; *The Lion, the Witch, and the Wardrobe*;
5. Intellectual Curiosity, e.g., *The Eleventh Hour: A Curious Mystery*; *Navajo Coyote Tales*;
6. Understanding Self, e.g., *Alexander and the Terrible, Horrible, No Good, Very Bad Day*; *The Secret Garden*.

Use these potential motivations to "hook" your children on books as you encourage them to enter into and transact with literature.

THE WHOLE LANGUAGE APPROACH

Background and Philosophy

The whole language approach is grounded in the belief that reading and literacy skills can be developed most effectively by providing children with "rich, authentic, developmentally appropriate school experiences" (Goodman, 1991, p. 4). This approach is based on a philosophy of language acquisition and literacy processing that calls for highly integrated learning experiences in the classroom.

It is important to understand the key ideas that underlie the whole language philosophy in order to understand the instructional goals and instructional features and strategies for this approach. The whole language approach acknowledges the following characteristics of language and literacy development (Ruddell & Ruddell, 1994):

1. Children are active participants in their own language and literacy development; they build theories and test hypotheses as they construct meaning about their world.

2. Children's perceptions of print and their productions of oral and written language follow rule-governed, coherent behavior that reflects their current understanding of how print and language work.

3. Children enter school with a high degree of language competence; their reading and writing development progress throughout the elementary grades in a parallel and interactive manner.

4. Children's reading and writing acquisition are influenced by their language and world knowledge, social interactions, and literacy environment, including available language models (family, teacher, peer group), language and literacy routines, and opportunities to use language in meaningful interactions.

5. Children's home and community language and literacy environments, interactions, and routines strongly influence their reading and writing development; close home-school linkage is important to their language and literacy growth.

The whole language approach shares with the basal reading and the literature-based approaches the common goal of developing children's reading and literacy skills to their highest potential. Whole language, however, is more closely related, in instructional approach and strategies used, to the literature-based approach by its emphasis on using full-length literature selections and focus on naturalistic response to literature. Further, the whole language approach explicitly integrates reading and writing development.

The whole language approach considers reading and writing skills to be highly interrelated and developed in the social context of the classroom. The overall goal of developing children's active meaning construction in both reading and writing is a high priority. This is illustrated in Atwell's (1987) guiding questions that demonstrate the close connection between writing and reading as process, noted in Table 12-7.

More specific instructional goals focus on skill development in areas such as word analysis, comprehension, vocabulary, language, written expression, literature, study skills, and thinking processes. The approach to developing these skills, however, differs significantly from the preselected skill development found in the basal reader approach. The teacher is viewed as an instructional decision-maker who creates the instructional goals and objectives, the learning environment and instructional plans that will foster reading and writing skills in the problem-solving, risk-taking, and collaborative social context of the classroom.

Instructional Features and Strategies

The predominant instructional features of a whole language approach are the seven conditions for optimal instruction (Cambourne & Turbill, 1987;

WRITING AND READING AS PROCESS

WRITERS AND READERS **REHEARSE,** PLANNING AND PREDICTING:

- What will I write?
- What will it be like?
- How will it be shaped by my prior experiences as a writer?

- What will I read?
- What will it be like?
- How will it be shaped by my prior experiences as a reader?

WRITERS AND READERS **DRAFT,** DISCOVERING MEANING:

- Where will these words I am writing take me?
- What surprises, disappointments, problems, questions, and insights will I encounter along the way?

- Where will these words I am reading take me?

WRITERS AND READERS **REVISE,** RESEEING AND RESEEKING MEANING:

- Is this what I expected, what I hoped for?
- What do I think of the words on the page?
- What new thoughts do I think because of the words on the page?
- What makes sense? What needs to be changed so sense can be made?

—— **TABLE 12-7** ——————————————

Writing and Reading as Process. (Reproduced with permission from Atwell, 1987, p. 155.

Ruddell, 1992) that we discussed in Chapter 3. These features, in effect, serve as instructional guidelines for implementing whole language instruction and evaluating student progress. Briefly summarized, these are:

1. Children are immersed in language—from print to personal sharing of home and school events.

2. Children are actively involved in meaningful demonstrations of language in action—from predicting to discussing.

3. Language and literacy are used for real life purposes—from writing pen pals to stories based on a field trip.

4. Children assume responsibility for their own learning—from self-selecting books to deciding on use of free time.

5. Teachers and parents hold expectations that all children will learn—from understanding developmental learning differences to goal setting and conferencing.

6. Approximation to the targeted reading and literacy skill is encouraged—from story predictions to writing revisions.

7. Evaluation and learner feedback are ongoing processes—from informal observations during story discussions to periodic portfolio assessment.

Instructional strategies that are compatible with these features must account for student background knowledge and active meaning construction using relevant literacy events in the social context of the classroom. These strategies are meaning-process-driven rather than content-driven.

The content used in the whole language approach, however, is important from the standpoint of relevance to the background knowledge, conceptual development, age, and interests of children. Children's literature and informational books become a most valuable resource in providing high-interest and relevant content appropriate for a wide range of age and maturity levels. The creation of the reading center (Chapters 3, 6, and 13) is a must to provide single and multiple copies of high-interest books that children can read, discuss, listen to, write about, and enjoy. As is the case with the literature-based approach, you will undoubtedly plan instruction around specific pieces of literature. Multiple copies of core literature selections will be of great value for peer reading and discussion in reading response groups, and for stimulating reader response writing. In addition, the philosophy of the approach extends instruction to other content areas through theme cycles or project-based instruction (see Chapters 7 and 9).

Classroom events of all kinds hold potential opportunity for reading and writing in the whole language approach. These will range from pen pal writing opportunities to planning and summarizing field trip events, to developing a monthly classroom newspaper or designing posters to advertise the school bake sale fundraiser, and to interviewing community members on special interest topics such as air pollution or completing a research project on causes of pollution in our community. Any event relevant to the lives of children holds potential for reading, writing, and developing language and literacy abilities.

It is important to realize, however, that whole-language instruction is not *laissez faire*. A great deal of planning is required to identify instructional goals and specific reading and literacy objectives, to locate children's literature and informational materials to carry out the instruction, to plan events such as field trips, and to identify the instructional strategies and activities best suited to achieve your goals (see Chapter 13). One of the great values of this approach is the involvement of children in various aspects of the planning process.

As you assume responsibility for designing instruction using the whole language approach, your knowledge and understanding of a wide range of instructional strategies, activities, and evaluation techniques are of vital importance. These become your "conceptual tools" for guiding children's progress. We have developed many of these in our discussions in Chapters 3 through 11. The following strategies, activities, and evaluation approaches are grouped by area of emphasis and are keyed to our discussions in earlier chapters. You have these at your fingertips and will find that they can be used effectively in guiding and implementing the whole language approach:

1. **Early reading and writing development** (Chapter 3):
   Developing picture and print awareness
   Language experience charts

Using big books
Oral story reading
Using alphabet and rhyming books
Vocabulary development and the "mystery box"
Shared book experience
Using predictable books
DL-TA (Directed Listening-Thinking Activity)
Developing a reading center and book selection.

2. **Comprehension development** (Chapter 4):
   Questioning and discussion strategies
   Group reading approaches:
     DRA (Directed Reading Activity)
     DR-TA (Directed Reading-Thinking Activity)
     PReP (Prereading Plan)
     QARs (Question Answer Relationships)
     ReQuest (Reciprocal Questioning)
     Reciprocal Teaching
     GMA (Group Mapping Activity).

3. **Vocabulary development** (Chapter 5):
   TVC (Teaching Vocabulary in Context)
   CSSR (Context-Structure-Sound-Reference)
   VSS (Vocabulary Self-Collection Strategy)
   Interactive cloze
   Concept webs
   Semantic maps
   (SFA) Semantic Feature Analysis
   Vocabulary logs and journals
   Word sleuthing.

4. **Literature and reader response** (Chapter 6):
   Internal reader motivation
   External reader motivation
   Types of children's literature
   Organizing the reading center
   Favorite children's books
   Designing a book checkout system
   Reading aloud strategy
   Storytelling
   Reader response and literature response journals
   Book reports or sharing responses about books
   SSR (Sustained Silent Reading)
   Reader's Theatre
   InQuest (Investigative Questioning Procedure)
   Creating thematic units:
     Topical units
     Conceptual units.

5. **Writing development** (Chapter 7):
   Self-initiated and self-directed writing
   Story-making
   Writing workshop
   Project-based writing
   Theme cycles
   Spelling
   Handwriting.

6. **Word analysis and reader independence** (Chapter 8):
   Print awareness and letter recognition
   Phonemic awareness and phonemic segmentation
   Letter-sound relationships—consonants, vowels
   Letter patterns and rhyming endings
   Syllable identification:
      Compound words
      Prefix, suffix, and root identification
      Consonant clusters
      Pronounceable units
   Using context clues.

7. **Reading and writing across content areas** (Chapter 9):
   Content DR-TA (Directed Reading-Thinking Activity)
   VSS (Vocabulary Self-Collection Strategy)
   K-W-L Plus (Know–Want-to-know–Learned Plus)
   DIA (Directed Inquiry Activity)
   Writing Workshop
   Journal writing
   Learning logs
   DEJ (Double Entry Journal)
   The developing researcher
   Guided writing
   Theme cycles
   Project-based learning
   Foxfire ideas.

8. **Language, cultural, and achievement diversity** (Chapter 10):
   Sheltered English
   VSS (Vocabulary Self-Collection Strategy)
   DL-TA (Directed Listening-Thinking Activity)
   DR-TA (Directed Reading-Thinking Activity)
   QAR (Question-Answer Relationship)
   ReQuest (Reciprocal Question)
   Reciprocal teaching
   GMA (Group Mapping Activity)
   Reading aloud strategy
   Literature response journals

InQuest (Investigative Questioning Procedure)
Multicultural/multiethnic literature.

9. **Evaluation approaches** (Chapter 11):
   Quick observational notes
   Early Reading and Literacy Assessment Checklist
   Developmental Inventory
   Evaluating responses to children's literature
   Interest Inventory observations
   Writing Workshop evaluation
   Portfolio assessment
   Informal Reading Inventory and Miscue Analysis
   Communicating with parents
   Formal assessment.

Your understanding and control over these strategies, activities, and evaluation techniques allow you to create and implement a whole language approach classroom.

Strengths and Limitations of the Whole Language Approach

Like the literature-based approach, the whole language approach provides broad instructional freedom and options for teachers. Over the past ten to fifteen years, the whole language movement has gained a growing support group of teachers and professionals to help explore instructional concepts, strategies, and activities that work effectively with this approach—TAWL (Teachers Applying Whole Language). The availability of children's literature in paperback form has greatly reduced the cost of books, and more new and experienced teachers encounter whole language approaches in university-based teacher education and master's programs. The philosophy underlying the approach also has strong theoretical support in the knowledge base of language and literacy.

The greatest limitation of the whole language approach is one of its greatest strengths: the teacher commitment required to create and implement this approach in the classroom. Time, energy, teaching experience, and a thorough knowledge of language and literacy development are critical to creating and implementing a successful whole language program. Such a commitment, indeed, has already developed among a significant number of teachers across the country.

Our discussions with teachers who use the whole language approach suggest to us that teachers are excited and enthusiastic about their teaching and the way in which their students' language and literacy abilities are developing. Some teachers do express concern about their ability to teach word analysis skills, due in part to their reliance in the past on the presequenced skill program found in the basal reader approach. We suggest that this issue can be addressed by careful examination of our discussion in Chapter 8 and the targeting of specific skills to be emphasized as they are needed. Skills development needs to occur in the context of children's reading and writing activities as the skills become germane to the reading and writing itself. While some children will develop word analysis strategies and generalizations almost independently, our observations suggest that this will not be the case for others. Careful observation and record keeping are required if teachers are to know which children need what in the way of skills instruction. In general, however, whole language provides an exciting approach to the development of children's reading and writing skills and interests by placing active meaning construction at the heart of instruction.

Adapting the Whole Language Approach

The whole language approach, as discussed above, is based on a view of the interrelated nature of reading, writing, speaking, and listening. The role of background knowledge and experiences, social interactions, and reader-writer transactions with text are critical aspects of the whole language philosophy. These ideas hold strong appeal to most of us as teachers. It is possible, however, that your commitment to creating and implementing a whole language approach classroom is limited because of time and instructional preparation constraints, administrative support, and a variety of other reasons. These limitations need not hinder you from using the meaning construction philosophy of the whole language approach in your teaching.

Regardless of the instructional approach you are using, the five instructional principles for language and literacy development and the seven instructional features discussed above can be applied to increase the meaning-centered nature of your instruction. These principles and features fit the whole language approach well because of the great freedom and flexibility afforded the teacher in program design and implementation, but they are not limited solely to whole language. Let us assume for a moment that you are using a basal reader approach but are interested in incorporating aspects of a whole language approach. You have the option of retaining, decreasing, or even eliminating parts of the basal instructional program as you see fit. For example, you may wish to use the reading selections in the basal student reader but increase the whole language emphasis of instruction by forming children into reading response groups and allowing each group to construct its own themed unit by choosing the selections they wish to read from the basal text. These experiences may then be connected to writing development using the reading response logs or a full-blown implementation of the writing workshop.

We find that many teachers use the underlying philosophy of the whole language approach and strategies based on it in their instruction, even when they rely on the skills structure provided by other approaches. You have the opportunity to alter and shape the instructional experiences and to emphasize or deemphasize various aspects of skill development that you use in your classroom. We encourage you to consider ways to adapt the parts of the basal reader, literature-based, and whole language approaches to meet your students' needs. In the final analysis, you are the individual who holds the key to effective instruction in your classroom.

USING SUPPLEMENTARY PROGRAMS

Many programs are published each year to supplement reading instruction. Such programs are usually narrow in focus and are designed to meet three types of perceived special needs. The *first* type is usually in a discrete skill area such as phonics, study skills, or comprehension. The *second* is designed for enrichment, exemplified by activities based on specific children's literature selections. The *third* is designed for areas such as bilingual, gifted, or special education classrooms. These supplementary programs usually follow a workbook format with a brief teacher's guide. Some programs, however, are in kit form and use audiotape and videotape materials to accompany the student activities.

Criteria for Selecting Supplementary Materials

You must exercise great care in selecting a supplementary program. Programs vary greatly in the quality of activities produced—from excellent to inappropriate for classroom use. The key questions you need to ask in this selection process are:

1. Do the instructional objectives of the program meet my students' needs? The answer to this question should be based not only on the advertising material and the salesperson's discussion but on your actual examination of the student materials.

2. Are the activities presented in an attractive and appealing format that teaches, reinforces skills, and requires meaning construction on the part of my students? If activities are developed in a near formulaic style that requires very little thinking, they will produce very little, if any, positive student growth.

3. Can the program be integrated with ease into the main instructional approach that I am currently using?

4. How does the cost of the program compare to the cost of other instructional materials that would be of value in my classroom? For example, should I spend the money on this supplementary program or buy more paperback literature selections? Is the program cost-effective enough to warrant sacrificing some of these?

You will find that a number of supplementary programs can indeed enhance special areas of your reading program. This is best determined, however, by your own firsthand examination of these materials as you pose the above four questions.

Computers and Selection of Software

Computers are available to classrooms in ever increasing numbers. You will in all probability have at least one computer in your classroom that can serve to supplement your reading and writing instruction. Computer-aided instruction (CAI) can serve two important functions: *first,* as a patient and unflappable tutor in special areas such as word analysis, vocabulary and comprehension development; and *second,* as an instructional tool to assist in such activities as story writing, research reports, project development, book publishing, classroom newspaper publishing, and the like.

A major issue that you will encounter is the selection of software to use with your computer. The key questions discussed above for the selection of

CRITERIA	RATING (1–.5–0)	CHARACTERISTICS
Age appropriate		Realistic presentation of concepts
Child control		Actors not reactors; children set pace; can escape
Clear instructions		Verbal instructions; simple and precise directions; picture choices
Expanding complexity		Low entry, high ceiling; learning sequence is clear; teaches powerful ideas
Independence		Adult supervision not needed after initial exposure
Process orientation		Process engages, product secondary; discovery learning, not skill drilling; intrinsic motivation
Real-world model		Simple, reliable model; concrete representations, objects function
Technical features		Colorful; uncluttered realistic graphics; animation; loads and runs quickly; corresponding sound effects or music; study disks
Trial and error		Children test alternative responses
Transformations		Objects and situations change; process highlighter

TABLE 12-8

Developmental Scale for Rating Computer Software

supplementary programs also apply to the selection of computer software. In addition, however, there are features that are unique to software selection. These range from compatibility with your classroom computer and required memory capacity for software, to difficulty of keyboard use and command requirements (level of "user-friendliness").

The checklist in Table 12-8 suggests important questions that you should consider in the software selection process (Haughlan & Shade, 1990, p. 21). To rate software, assign each of the ten criteria with a point rating in the following way:

1.0 = The software reflects all the characteristics described.

0.5 = The software reflects at least half of the features described.

0 = The software reflects less than half of the features described.

The total score in the evaluation process is obtained by adding the points given. Haughlan and Shade recommend that when a total score of 7.0 or above is obtained (out of possible total rating score of 10.0) the software is considered developmentally appropriate. A major value in using this rating process is making explicit in your mind the strengths and weaknesses of any given software program.

Using Computers and Classroom Technology

Evaluating and Selecting Instructional Programs

The evaluation and selection of instructional materials can have a major impact on your teaching. This is evident in our discussion of the three major instructional approaches to literacy development. Most instructional programs today are selected by teacher committees who hold the power to choose materials and make adoption recommendations. Imagine yourself in this role and ask "What do I look for in evaluating publisher-produced programs being considered for adoption in my school or school district?" It is important for you to identify key criteria that can be used in this process.

The textbook adoption process varies from state to state and district to district across the nation. In general, however, about one-half of our states, including California and Texas, use State Department of Education criteria and adopt new textbooks on a cycle of every five to six years. The remaining states, including Ohio and Illinois, known as "open territory" states, may provide general recommendations, but leave the adoption process and the adoption cycle to the local school districts. Publishers are closely attuned to this process and often encourage school districts to pilot their instructional programs at various grade levels shortly in advance of the adoption cycle. Teachers, curriculum coordinators, administrators, and state department of education personnel are lobbied both formally and informally by publishers in this process.

The following questions represent criteria and starting points for you as you examine instructional programs. These are also developed in abbreviated form in the Instructional Program Evaluation Checklist found in Table 12-9.

1. Do the philosophy of the program and the instructional materials integrate reading and writing processes with meaning-centered strategies and activities that encourage active meaning construction on the part of children?

2. Does the program reflect the latest literacy development theory and research?

3. Do the objectives of the program account for important areas of literacy development including: beginning reading and writing, comprehension, vocabulary, literature and reader response, word analysis, writing, and reading and writing across content areas?

4. Are the objectives of the program clearly developed through instructional strategies and activities that are appropriate and suitable for the range of children's needs and interests?

5. Does the program include high-quality children's literature and informational material that will appeal to children? Is the literature altered to provide for a lower readability level or is it original? Are there any full-length original stories and illustrations presented in the material? Do the

Evaluator _____ Date _____

Name of Program _____

Title of Level(s) _____

Recommended Grade-Level Use _____

Specific Materials Examined: teacher manual _____ , student text _____ ,

workbook _____ , other material _____

Criteria	**Rating**				
	Poor			Outstanding	
	1	2	3	4	5
1. Informed philosophy (meaning-based?)	1	2	3	4	5
2. Research and theory base evident	1	2	3	4	5
3. Range of objectives (beginning literacy, comprehension, vocabulary, literature and reader response, word analysis, writing, reading and writing across content)	1	2	3	4	5
4. Instructional strategies and activities provide for range of needs and interests	1	2	3	4	5
5. Quality literature and informational selections; cultural and ethnic diversity; varied gender role models; other forms of diversity	1	2	3	4	5
6. Materials and activities hold high potential for developing learning motivation and interest	1	2	3	4	5
7. Teacher's guide—quality and ease of use	1	2	3	4	5
8. Recognition of importance of informal observations and ongoing evaluation	1	2	3	4	5
9. Adaptability of program relative to instructional philosophy	1	2	3	4	5
10. Belief that program can be be used effectively	1	2	3	4	5

Total ratings for program _____

Summary observations:

___ **TABLE 12-9** ___

Instructional Program Evaluation Checklist

literature selections account for cultural and ethnic diversity? Varied gender role models? Various kinds of diversity?

6. Do the materials and instructional activities hold potential for developing children's learning motivation and interest?

7. Are the teacher guides written clearly and developed in a format that can be used with ease? Do they contain annotated pages of the student text? the workbook?

8. Does the program recognize the importance of informal observations and ongoing evaluation of individual students? Are parts of the program adaptable to portfolio assessment?

9. Is the program organized in such a way that you can adapt it to your own instructional philosophy by selecting units or unit portions instead of having to follow the program lesson by lesson and unit by unit to the end as prescribed by the publisher?

10. Do you believe you can use the program effectively and integrate it into your own instructional approach?

Remember that you possess the knowledge and understanding of literacy instruction that forms the basis for careful evaluation of instructional programs. Your active involvement in this process, when the opportunity presents itself, can make a vitally important contribution to your classroom, school, and school district.

Examining Major Instructional Approaches

A Summary

In our early discussion, we examined major instructional changes in reading and literacy development from the time of the Hornbook and *New England Primer*, in the 1600s and 1700s, to the advent of the meaning-centered instructional approaches of the 1990s. The influence of key historical events, ranging from the birth of a nation to the recent influx of new immigrant populations, were noted. Clear and pronounced changes have occurred in instructional materials, reading content, classroom environment, instructional emphasis, and teacher preparation over the past three centuries.

We have discussed three major instructional approaches and the philosophy, features and strategies, strengths and limitations, and classroom adaptation for each. You should now have a much better conceptual and applied understanding of differences and similarities among the basal reader approach, the literature-based approach, and the whole language approach. We identified a number of cautions in your selection of more narrowly focused supplementary materials and computer software for use with your major instructional approach.

The materials selection discussion offered ten "starter criteria" and an instructional program evaluation checklist for you to use in the adoption of a new reading and writing program. This adoption process is critical as you select an instructional program that fits your instructional philosophy and that of your fellow teachers. We encourage you to participate actively in the textbook selection process and to expand your literature and reading collection as you plan and implement instruction to meet the literacy needs of your children.

DOUBLE ENTRY JOURNAL

Go back to your list of elements and aspects of an ideal program for teaching reading and writing. Place your program where you think it belongs on the Bottom Up/Top Down continuum. Decide which approach—basal reader, literature-based, whole language—best characterizes your program. What new ideas would you add to your program now?

Supporting Activities

1. Think about the changes that have occurred during the last century in reading instruction. Locate a basal reader published between 1910 and 1960 in your library. Select a reader, if at all possible, at the grade level that is of greatest interest to you. Now, locate a reader at the same grade level for a program published within the last ten years. Briefly contrast these two readers with particular attention to story content, story inter-

est, cultural and gender diversity, and skill emphasis. Discuss the influence of a changing and developing nation on the differences you find (see Table 12-1). Given a choice, which of these readers would you prefer to use in classroom instruction? Why?

2. Examine the instructional continuum found in Figure 12.6 and review the related discussion. Where would you place your own personal instructional belief system on this continuum? Why? Briefly discuss your ideas with a class partner.

3. Obtain a copy of a recently published basal reader, teacher guide, and workbook for the grade level of highest interest to you. Select one story that you believe children at this grade level would enjoy. Read the story and carefully examine the teaching recommendations found in the teacher guide and the activities in the accompanying workbook. Identify those recommendations and activities that you believe are most appropriate for instruction. Now, create a brief lesson plan using the Directed Reading-Thinking Activity (DR-TA) and Group Mapping Activity (GMA) to introduce and develop the story (see Chapter 4). Share your plan and ideas with a class partner.

4. Review our discussion of the literature-based approach. Identify one high-interest children's literature selection appropriate for a grade level of special interest to you. Review the sample planning webs in Figures 12-7 and 12-8. Create a planning web and integrated literature-based lesson plan for your literature selection. Share your plan with a class partner.

5. Arrange for a classroom visit with a teacher who relies heavily on the whole language approach in her or his literacy instruction. Before your visit, review our discussion on the whole language approach. Design a brief checklist of instructional features and strategies that you expect to find during your observation. Pay particular attention to the way in which reading and writing are integrated in the social context of the classroom. If at all possible, find a few minutes to interview the teacher to explore his or her views on the advantages and limitations of this approach. After completing your observation, summarize your ideas. Were your expectations realized? Why or why not? Discuss your findings with a class partner.

6. You will at some time in your teaching career be involved in the selection of textbooks for your school or school district. Review our discussion on "Evaluating and Selecting Instructional Programs." Carefully examine the Instructional Program Evaluation Checklist (see Table 12-9). Obtain a copy of a basal reader, teacher's manual, workbook, and other support material at the grade level of highest interest to you. Use the evaluation checklist to assist you in evaluating these materials and identifying strengths and limitations. Write a brief summary of your evaluation and recommendations for or against adoption. Share your ideas with a class partner.

Alvermann, D., Bridge, C. A., Schmidt, B. A., Searfoss, L. W., Winograd, P., Paris, S. G., Bruce, B., Priestley-Romero, M., & Santeusanio, R. P. (1993). *Cats sleep anywhere: Teacher's edition.* Lexington, MA: D.C. Heath.

Atwell, N. (1987). *In the middle: Writing, reading, and learning with adolescents.* Portsmouth, NH: Heinemann.

California Association of County Superintendents of Schools (1989). *Cooperative county course of study: English-language arts supplement, 1989–1994.* Sacramento, CA.

California State Department of Education. (1987). *Handbook for planning an effective literature program.* Sacramento, CA.

Cambourne, B., & Turbill, J. (1987). *Coping with chaos.* Portsmouth, NH: Heinemann.

Chall, J. S., & Squire, J. R. (1991). The publishing industry and textbooks. In R. Barr, M. L. Kamil, P. Mosenthal, & P.D. Pearson (Eds.), *Handbook of reading research: Volume II* (pp. 120–146). New York: Longman.

Crosby, M. (1964). *Curriculum development for elementary schools in a changing society.* Boston: D. C. Heath.

Ginn & Company (1963). *The New England primer: Twentieth Century reprint.* Boston, MA: Ginn. (Originally published in Boston in 1690.)

Goodman, Y. M. (1991). What is whole language? In K. S. Goodman, L. B. Bird, & Y. M. Goodman (Eds.), *The whole language catalog* (pp. 4–5). Santa Rosa, CA: American School Publishers.

Gray, W. S., & Arbuthnot, M. A. (1947). *Days and deeds.* Chicago, IL: Scott, Foresman.

Hamlin, T. (1982). American reading materials: A selective reflector. In E. M. Sheridan (Ed.), *Sex stereotypes and reading: Research and strategies* (pp. 49–63). Newark, DE: International Reading Association.

Haughlan, S. W., & Shade, D. D. (1990). *Developmental evaluations of software for young children.* Albany, NY: Delmar.

Hutchins, R. M. (1943). *Education for freedom.* Baton Rouge, LA: Louisiana State University Press.

McGuffey, W. H. (1930). *McGuffey's second eclectic reader.* New York: American Book Company. (First edition published in 1837.)

O'Flahavan, J. (1989). *An exploration of the effects of participant structure upon literacy development in reading group discussion.* Doctoral dissertation, University of Illinois-Champaign.

Pearson, P. D., Johnson, D. D., Clymer, T., Indrisano, R., Baumann, J. F., Hiebert, E., & Toth, M. (1989). *Castles of sand: Teacher edition.* Needham, MA: Silver Burdett & Ginn.

Pearson, P. D., Johnson, D. D., Clymer, T., Indrisano, R., Venezky, R., Baumann, J. F., Hiebert, E., & Toth, M. (1989). *Castles of sand: Workbook, teacher edition.* Needham, MA: Silver Burdett & Ginn.

649

Ruddell, R. B., & Ruddell, M. R. (1992). A whole language and literature perspective: Creating a meaning-making instructional environment. *Language Arts, 69,* 612–620.

Ruddell, R. B., & Ruddell, M. R. (1994). Language acquisition and literacy processes. In R. B. Ruddell, M. R. Ruddell, & H. Singer (Eds.), *Theoretical models and processes of reading* (4th ed.) (pp. 83–103). Newark, DE: International Reading Association.

Smith, N. B. (1974). *American reading instruction.* Newark, DE: International Reading Association.

Venezky, R. L. (1991). The development of literacy in the industrialized nations of the West. In R. Barr, M. L. Kamil, P. Mosenthal, & P. D. Pearson (Eds.), *Handbook of reading research: Volume II* (pp. 46–67). New York: Longman.

Walmsley, S. A. (1992). Reflections on the state of elementary literature instruction. *Language Arts, 69,* 508–514.

CHILDREN'S LITERATURE REFERENCES

Base, G. (1988). *The eleventh hour: A curious mystery.* New York: Harry N. Abrams.

Burnett, F. H. (1911). *The secret garden.* Philadelphia: Lippincott.

Forbes, E. (1943). *Johnny Tremain.* Boston: Houghton Mifflin.

Frank, A. (1967). *Anne Frank: The diary of a young girl.* New York: Doubleday.

George, J. C. (1972). *Julie of the wolves.* New York: HarperCollins.

Gurney, J. (1992). *Dinotopia.* Atlanta: Turner Publishing.

Heller, R. (1984). *Plants that never bloom.* New York: Grosset & Dunlap.

Houston, J. W., & Houston, J. D. (1973). *Farewell to Manzanar.* New York: Bantam.

Lewis, C. S. (1950). *The lion, the witch, and the wardrobe.* New York: Macmillan.

MacLachlan, P. (1985). *Sarah, plain and tall.* New York: Harper & Row.

Morgan, W. (1988). *Navajo coyote tales.* Sante Fe, NM: Ancient City Press.

O'Dell, S. (1960). *Island of the blue dolphins.* New York: Dell.

Paterson, A. B., & Macarthur-Onslow (1977). *The man from Snowy River.* Sydney, Australia: William Collins Pty, Ltd.

Ringgold, F. (1991). *Tar beach.* New York: Crown.

Rylant, C. (1982). *When I was young in the mountains.* New York: E. P. Dutton.

Sendak, M. (1963). *Where the wild things are.* New York: HarperCollins.

Steptoe, J. (1987). *Mufaro's beautiful daughters.* New York: Lothrop, Lee & Shepard.

Taylor, M. (1966). *Henry the explorer.* New York: Atheneum.

Viorst, J. (1972). *Alexander and the terrible, horrible, no good, very bad day.* New York: Macmillan.

Voight, C. (1983). *Dicey's song.* New York: Atheneum.

Waber, B. (1972). *Ira sleeps over.* Boston: Houghton Mifflin.

White, E. B. (1952). *Charlotte's web.* New York: Harper & Row.

Whitfield, P. (1990). *Why do volcanoes erupt?* New York: Viking.

Williams, M. B. (1958). *The velveteen rabbit; Or, how toys became real.* New York: Doubleday.

ORGANIZING AND MANAGING CLASSROOMS FOR LITERACY LEARNING

Consider all the things you associate with orga-
nizing and managing classrooms. Make a list.
Speculate as to which of these will be addressed in
this chapter. Put a check mark beside every item
on your list that you think will be discussed in
this chapter.

INTRODUCTION

L et us begin our discussion on organizing and managing classrooms for literacy learning by making explicit the premise underlying this entire chapter: *Teachers' beliefs and assumptions about how children learn, and teachers' choices about how they teach, influence and guide physical organization of the classroom, organization of the classroom day, and efficient management of classroom activities.* You, as teacher, exert enormous influence on the learning environment in your classroom—by virtue of:

- the beliefs you have and assumptions you make about how children acquire literacy and continue to develop as literate beings,
- the decisions you make about using (or not using) certain instructional strategies and practices, and
- the subsequent organizational and management structures that follow logically from your beliefs, assumptions, and decisions.

The extraordinary influence teachers exert on learning environments is often overlooked. It should not be. Teachers have always been a primary source of, and influence on, classroom environments, just as you already are, or will be, in your classroom.

We've asked you a number of times in this text to reflect on your own literacy development and elementary schooling experience. We'd like you to do so once again. Consider your years in elementary school, starting at kindergarten or first grade, and list what you remember about (1) how classrooms were physically organized; (2) how literacy instruction was organized and managed; (3) how classroom days, months, and years proceeded; and (4) how classroom events were managed, especially with regard to maintenance of order, student behavior, materials distribution and collection, student movement in the room, and so forth. After you've completed your list, look "behind" the items on it and ask yourself, "What beliefs and assumptions about literacy learning and what instructional practices created the organization, structure, and management of the classrooms I experienced?" We expect that you will be able to list the beliefs and assumptions prevailing in your school about how children become literate and continue their literacy development, along with the perceived relationships between literacy and subject area learning. We expect, also, that you're able to remember rather well the instructional decisions resulting from those beliefs and assumptions that created the organizational plans and management of literacy instruction and classroom days.

John Goodlad (1984), in his seminal study of the structure and content of U.S. classrooms, describes the patterns of organization and instruction he and his research team found in their in-depth study and visitation in more than one thousand K through 12 classrooms. His findings reflect the tradition of U.S. schooling for at least the last fifty years. Goodlad describes what the research teams found (Goodlad, 1984, pp. 123–124):

> First, the dominant pattern of classroom organization is a group to which the teacher most frequently relates as a whole. Much of what goes on is conditioned by the need to maintain orderly relationships among from 20 to 30 or more persons in relatively small space. Demands for such order are conveyed to students early, and their socialization into it is rather thoroughly achieved before the end of the early elementary grades.
>
> Second, each student essentially works and achieves alone within a group setting…
>
> Third, the teacher is the central figure in determining activities, as well as the tone, of the classroom. The teacher is virtually autonomous with respect to classroom decisions—

selecting materials, determining class organization, choosing instructional procedures, and so on.

Fourth, the domination of the teacher is obvious in the conduct of instruction. Most of the time the teacher is engaged in either frontal teaching [standing in front of the class lecturing or explaining], monitoring students' seat-work, or conducting quizzes....

Fifth, there is a paucity of praise and correction of students' performance, as well as of teacher guidance in how to do better next time.... And our impression is that classes generally tend not to be strongly positive or strongly negative places to be. Enthusiasm and joy and anger are kept under control.

Sixth, students generally engage in a rather narrow range of classroom activities—listening to teachers, writing answers to questions, and taking tests and quizzes. Strikingly similar "schooling activities" transcend teachers, grade levels, and subjects....

Seventh, the patterns summarized above describe early elementary classes less well than they do classes in higher grades. They are quite commonly descriptive of upper elementary grades....

Eighth, large percentages of the students we surveyed appeared to be passively content with classroom life. In general, they felt positive about both peers and teachers. They expressed considerable liking for all subjects and classroom activities—even the repetitive listening to teachers' talk....

Ninth, even in the early elementary years there was strong evidence of students not having time to finish their lessons or not understanding what the teacher wanted them to do....

We suspect that Goodlad's description of classroom life is not unlike your own recollections; it is certainly congruent with ours. Important here is that traditional literacy instruction was very much like the rest of the school day; that is, what Goodlad describes as characteristic of elementary classrooms as a whole is similarly characteristic of the reading and writing instruction most of us received: children working alone in group settings; teacher as the central figure, telling, explaining, quizzing; activity routines repeated over and over (read story, discuss, learn skill, practice skill in workbook, check workbook, read new story, discuss...); students passively content with the routine.

Life in elementary classrooms is changing, however, in part due to a general environment of reform and restructuring in the educational community, but also due to our most recent understandings about language and literacy processes, literacy learning, and effective instructional practices in elementary schools. (We have discussed these at some length in preceding chapters.) Central to our new knowledge is increased insight into (1) complexities associated with literacy processes themselves (Applebee, 1991; Rosenblatt, 1994; Tway, 1991); (2) how children learn language and acquire and develop literacy (Calkins, 1991; Cambourne & Turbill, 1987; Dyson, 1990; Harste, Woodward, & Burke, 1984; Sulzby, 1985); (3) social and language transactions in classrooms (Ruddell & Unrau, 1994; the Santa Barbara Classroom Discourse Group, 1992; Vygotsky, 1986); and (4) interrelationships between literacy processes and subject-area learning (Atwell, 1986; Ruddell, 1993). These new understandings are thus creating the need for new classroom organization and management structures.

CHAPTER PURPOSE

The purpose of this chapter is to examine various classroom organization and management structures for literacy instruction. Our goal here is to give you a number of ideas for arranging your classroom and classroom day in a such a way that the environment you create supports the beliefs you have, the assumptions you make about how children learn, and the decisions you've made about instruction. We have already addressed many issues of organization and management throughout this text as we focused on learning and teaching (describing specific instructional approaches, summarizing instructional strategies in How To Do, and integrating strategies in Building Tables). In this chapter, we focus primarily on organization and management issues; along the way, we may, of necessity, touch upon or repeat some of what we've said before.

We *first* address general issues associated with classroom organization and management. *Second,* we examine classroom organization and management structures for early and beginning readers and writers (instruction described in Chapters 3 and 7). And *third,* we address organization and management structures appropriate for basal reader, literature-based, and whole language instructional approaches (instruction described in Chapters 6, 7, and 12). In each of these discussions, we will review beliefs and assumptions underlying instruction (these are discussed in detail in the chapters cited above) and address physical organization of the classroom, organization of the classroom day, and management issues associated with each.

ORGANIZING AND MANAGING LITERACY INSTRUCTION

CLASSROOM ORGANIZATION

"Classroom organization" is often thought to be only the physical arrangement of furniture and materials in a room. It is, however, much more than that (Tway, 1991). Along with furniture and materials arrangement, classroom organization involves classroom schedules and events as well, and these schedules and events must be orchestrated on a moment-to-moment, daily, monthly, and yearly basis. Both the room arrangements and schedule of events are complexly tied to the content and form of instruction itself. In other words, *what* we teach and *how* we teach it are connected with how the room is arranged and how days and weeks in the classroom progress. Added to these complex interactions is the fact that teachers have influence over part, but not all, of classroom organizational structures.

Teachers are *assigned* to classrooms, and classrooms come in all manner of sizes, shapes, and conditions. Below are listed less-than-ideal classroom conditions that the two of us have experienced in our teaching careers; numbers 1 and 2 occurred when we were first-year teachers *(these are not made up)*:

1. A one-room school, grades K through 6, complete with rows of desks bolted to the floor and a coal-burning stove. (The teacher arrived early enough to get the stove going on cold winter mornings.)

2. A school in which the new kindergarten and sixth-grade wing being added to the school was still under construction until October 1 (the result of a construction strike over the summer). All three sixth-grade classes met in the multipurpose room in which portable bulletin board dividers created three separate "classrooms." Daily sounds of construction, including jackhammers, added to the sounds of two other teachers teaching (and sixty other sixth-graders learning).

3. A very, very small classroom in the old, wood-floor section of a school, underneath the second-floor gymnasium, and right next to the band room where the band met daily. An added attraction was the arrival of the hydraulic lift garbage truck right outside the classroom windows every day at 1:35 p.m.

4. An inner "pod" (i.e., room) of a "modular building" in which inner pods had no windows in an un-air-conditioned building in a climate where both the temperature and the humidity hovered in the upper 90s during the first four weeks of school.

While it is unlikely that you will teach in a one-room school (although a few still exist today) or face rows of desks bolted to the floor or even have to endure squeaking clarinets next door and hydraulic-lifts or jackhammers outside your window, other possibilities exist for less-than-ideal classroom assignment (portable and "temporary" classrooms, for example). The fact is that teachers generally have to take what they get in the way of the raw material of the classroom. Then they improvise: They bring carpet remnants, posters, plants, easy chairs, and various other accoutrements to school; they arrange and rearrange tables, desks, chairs, bookcases, and storage bins to get the most out of the space they have; and they learn (and teach children) how to work around or accommodate themselves to whatever limitations the room has.

Orchestration of the classroom day and week are also aspects of classroom organization over which teachers have only partial influence. In most schools, daily and weekly schedules are determined at the district level. In some schools, district mandates are limited to starting time, dismissal, lunch and recess schedules, bus schedules, and the like. In others, daily schedules are more micromanaged. For example, some schools have flexible primary-grade schedules in which half the class arrives one-half hour or forty-five minutes "early" for reading instruction and are then dismissed one-half hour or forty-five minutes before the other half of the class who stay "late" for reading instruction. In some schools, children may change classrooms at certain times during the day for reading and/or language arts (sometimes mathematics as well), and in some, while class exchanges don't take place, teachers are expected to adhere to block schedules for specific content instruction. Some (lucky) schools still have periodic schedules for art, music, and physical education teachers to teach their specialty, and generally all schools have one type or another of special scheduling for reading, learning disability, special education, gifted, and instrumental music programs.

The point here is that teacher decision-making is not fully autonomous; rather, it occurs in relationship to assigned classrooms and to district- and school-mandated daily and weekly classroom schedules. This discussion may leave you feeling that there is not much room for teacher choice. In reality, however, there is, even in schools where schedules are more micromanaged. At the very least, there are relatively large blocks of time in the classroom day during which your decision-making determines the structure, content, and form of learning. As you undoubtedly perceive, much of this structure, content, and form is linked closely to what you believe and understand about learning processes, how you choose to organize the room physically, and what materials and approaches you choose for instruction.

CLASSROOM MANAGEMENT

Classroom management is just as complex and multifaceted as is classroom organization. And, just as classroom organization often is thought of only as room arrangement, classroom management is frequently equated solely with class discipline. Certainly, classroom management does include issues of child deportment and discipline, classroom rules, and teacher response to inappropriate behaviors. It is, however, more than *just* these things. It involves, rather more importantly, time allocation and use, establishment of routines and procedures to support whatever organizational decisions have been made, productive utilization of materials and equipment, provision for ongoing and useful assessment of children's progress and of the curriculum, and a myriad of other events and decisions. In short, classroom management is the *system* you use to implement or realize the instructional decisions and organizational plans you've made. It requires thoughtfulness, planning, understanding of the Big Picture in combination with attention to details, ability to foresee (and minimize) possible problems, and skill in thinking on your feet. Without effective management, Grand Plans fall apart, complex learning opportunities and organizational structures collapse, and, all too often, chaos reigns (or teachers resort to sit-at-your-desk-and-fill-out-your-workbook-and-no-talking classroom days). It is when management fails that class discipline becomes an issue, and we can say categorically that no "discipline system" ever devised will overcome poor management.

What is critical here is that you get a sense of the management implications your instructional decisions have. With respect to literacy instruction in your classroom, whatever instructional approach you use (or are required to use)—be it whole language, basal reader, writing workshop, theme cycles, literature-based instruction, or some combination—from the moment of decision-making, you must begin consideration of how that instruction will be managed. What materials are appropriate? Where will they be housed? How will materials be distributed and collected? What do the children need to know in order to do what I want them to do? What about the current room arrangement does and doesn't work for what I want to do? How will I get the children's attention when the room is loud with working noise? What "house rules" will work best here? How can I store leftover papier-mâché paste? How many groups can work in the space I have? What do I need to prepare and how long will it take me to do it? How many kids do I want around my desk at one time? What should children do when they're stuck and I'm busy with another child or group? Who's going to oversee the paint table? What can the children do when they've finished? And on, and on, and on. It's called thinking ahead. It's called planning and forethought. It's called classroom management, and it must be done if classrooms and children are to be successful.

ORGANIZATION AND MANAGEMENT OF LITERACY INSTRUCTION FOR EARLY AND BEGINNING READERS AND WRITERS

Kindergarten and first-grade classrooms house most early and beginning readers and writers in schools. Since many children now are well on their way toward fluent literacy when they enter first grade, we're going to concentrate our discussion here on kindergarten classrooms (and we're well aware that some children enter *kindergarten* well on their way to fluent literacy). Pertinent to our discussion is that kindergarten classrooms enjoy a unique characteristic, which is that, even though instructional approaches for developing children's literacy abilities vary from school to school (e.g., basal reader, literature-based, whole language), the essential organization and management structures for kindergarten are relatively similar. This is because the three instructional approaches share many assumptions about the foundations of literacy and the form that early and beginning instruction should take. We are therefore able to discuss organization and management of literacy instruction for early and beginning readers without distinguishing between specific instructional approaches. We do point out that much of what we discuss is directly applicable in first grade and other classrooms.

UNDERLYING BELIEFS AND ASSUMPTIONS ABOUT LITERACY LEARNING: EARLY AND BEGINNING READERS AND WRITERS

Our current understanding of how children continue their development into fluent literacy during kindergarten includes the following beliefs and assumptions (these are synthesized from discussions in Chapters 2, 3, and 7):

1. Children learn the language of written text by hearing and seeing written text and by experimenting with written text themselves.
2. Children acquire and develop picture and print concepts, a sense of story structure, and theories about how written language works as they invent and reinvent oral and written text forms, test current language hypotheses, and successfully negotiate meanings in transactions with text.
3. Children's language and literacy learning are mediated by social interactions and transactions with peers and with literate others.

The foregoing beliefs and assumptions, in turn, suggest certain experiences and events that need to be present in kindergarten classrooms to promote children's language and literacy development. These events and experiences are as follows:

1. Early and beginning readers and writers need lots of time and space for drawing, reading, writing, and illustrating their own written work;
2. Early and beginning readers and writers need time for rich language interactions as, and after, they play and work—time for sharing experiences, elaborating ideas, and exploring and making sense of new experiences and events;
3. Early and beginning readers and writers need to be in a literate environment where they experience many different kinds and forms of written text in many different circumstances;
4. Early and beginning readers need many opportunities to read and write together;
5. Early and beginning readers and writers need to be read to every day.

So, we see that kindergarten classrooms need space for play and work. They need the materials of literacy—books, paper, pencils, pens, magazines, crayons, paints, and so forth. They need written text everywhere. They need blocks of time for exploring, talking, reading, and writing. They do not need to be, and in fact should not be, "pin-drop" quiet. They need adults who demonstrate literate behaviors in many different ways.

PHYSICAL ORGANIZATION OF THE CLASSROOM: EARLY AND BEGINNING READERS AND WRITERS

Kindergarten classrooms should be large to accommodate a number of defined areas in the room. Our experience has been that kindergarten classes usually are assigned the larger rooms in a building and may even have facilities that no other classrooms have (bathrooms, for example). Within the room, evidence of literacy should be everywhere: signs, books, posters, paper, writing utensils, magazines, labels, lists, displays of children's writing, and all manner of written messages. Certain areas are designated and stocked with materials for specific purposes, with clearly defined boundaries and pathways (Nourot, in press). Defined areas include the circle area for class gathering, book corner, writing center, art center, science and math centers, play area, children's desks or home tables, coat and backpack storage area, and general storage area. One such organizational plan is shown in Figure 13-1.

Circle Area

The circle area is a multipurpose area where the class gathers for large group discussions. Children generally sit on the floor and the teacher sits in a low chair. The circle area hosts many and varied discussions: opening and closing routines each day, Author's Chair and sharing time for the writing workshop, the teacher or other adults reading to the children, big book readings, guest speakers and presenters in the classroom, and so forth.

To define the circle area and make the floor a little more comfortable, bring (or ask the school to provide) a carpet or large carpet remnant for the floor. This has the advantage of making it easier for small bottoms to accommodate to a hard, cold surface; it has the disadvantage of making spills and other sorts of accidents a little more difficult to clean up. Most teachers feel the advantage outweighs the disadvantage. The area (or rug) should be large enough so that the children can sit comfortably without crowding. Since opening and closing routines are usually done in the circle area, it's wise to locate the area next to a bulletin board and chalkboard so that these may be used as needed. Bordering one side of the circle area, arrange storage shelves to hold materials children commonly carry away from circle discussions (e.g., writing paper), and, if possible, locate children's individual cubbies or baskets there as well. Having the cubbies near the circle area allows you then to put into them any papers or materials you're distributing or returning for

661

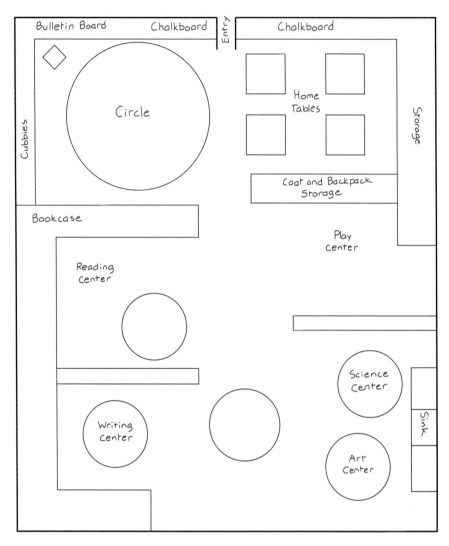

FIGURE 13-1

Physical Organization of the Classroom: Early and Beginning Readers

children to pick up as they leave the room after end-of-day closing exercises in circle. The chair, or chairs, that you place at the front of the circle should be low rather than of standard height so that you, and children or others invited to be featured speakers, don't tower over those sitting on the floor.

Reading Center

The book corner, or reading center (see Chapter 3), is where children go to browse, choose new books to read, and spend some time reading for pleasure.

Stock the book corner with all manner of reading materials—books on loan from the school library, paperback books, big books, books children have written and made, magazines, comic books, maps, charts, newspapers, and any other reading materials your children might enjoy. Comfortable chairs are a nice touch for book corners; after all, very few of us do our pleasure reading sitting at a table or desk. You might want to bring an outcast easy chair or sofa from home, or purchase some beanbag chairs, oversized pillows, or child-sized patio chairs. You might also want to put a rug in the book corner. Locating the book corner adjacent to the circle area allows you to let children use the circle rug for comfortable free reading as well.

Writing Center

The writing center should be located right next to the book corner if at all possible. This location is explicit acknowledgment of the close relationship between reading and writing, and it further allows writers easy access to reading material (access that writers often need during drafting and revising stages). It also allows readers access to writing materials (something readers often need). As we described in Chapter 7, the writing center should be stocked with many different writing media (pens, pencils, markers, etc.), different paper types and sizes, one or more computers or word processors and a printer (if at all possible), dictionaries and other aids, book-making and binding materials, and other writing supplies—scissors, staplers, paper clips, etc. You may wish to include a table with chairs for a designated number of children to work in the writing center, and provide beanbag lap desks for pleasure writing. Here, again, the circle rug becomes a probable place where children could take a lap desk to do free writing. Children's writing folders or journals may be stored on shelves or bins in the writing center, or you may prefer to store them individually in the children's cubbies. If possible, you may wish to have a bulletin board in or near the writing center for displaying children's writing.

Art Center

The art center is where children draw, paint, and use chalks and other media to create works of art, illustrate their writing, or explore art media for the fun of it. Art centers are frequently not open for "free" activity in the same way as book corners and writing centers are for free reading and writing. That's because creating art is often messy, and because spills and mishaps are more likely to happen in art centers than elsewhere. If possible, you should locate the art center close to a water source and cleanup materials; also, keep the art center away from rugs, cubbies, and open materials storage areas. Stock the art center with easels, paints, brushes, colored chalks, colored markers, crayons, scissors, glue, papers of many colors and textures, popsicle sticks (for mixing, stirring, etc.), and any other materials for producing art— fabrics, sequins, string, glitter, ribbon—the list is almost endless. Designate an area in or near the art center for displaying children's work.

Collaborative Play and Literacy Development

Other Centers

Two or more other centers in the room provide areas for designated subject-area materials and displays or for creating center activities as part of ongoing thematic units. For example, you may wish to have a permanent science center that houses the weather-charting materials, leaf collections and displays, beans sprouting in paper cups, an incubator with warm eggs inside, and other materials and equipment for children to experiment with and explore their physical world. Nearby, you may have a math center stocked with Cuisenaire rods, blocks of various sizes, activity cards, an abacus, and various other manipulatives. Or you may simply establish center areas and set up specific equipment, materials, and activities as needed to accompany instructional plans. Whatever arrangement you prefer, include writing materials—pencils, pens, paper, journals—at subject-specific centers for children to record, illustrate, and reflect on their experiences there.

Play Area

The play area is a place where children engage in collaborative play. Both spontaneous and guided play develop language and provide a motivating context for literate behaviors (Van Hoorn, Nourot, Scales, & Alward, 1993). Play areas may be subject-specific—social studies, for example—or they may be more general. In rooms that already have subject-area centers, play areas are either provisioned for many different kinds of play or designated in other ways, and often change as children's interests and attention change. Grocery-store play areas are common, as are restaurants and playhouses.

Stock play areas with widely various tools and accessories. For example, in a restaurant play area include a wok and other Asian cookware and a tortilla press as part of the standard kitchenware (Nourot, in press). Be sure also to provide plenty of paper and writing tools in play areas for children both to use in their play and to record and reflect on it. If play areas are not specifically designated for a particular theme, you may wish to keep "prop boxes" (Nourot, in press) filled with costumes, accessories, tools, and other materials for dramatic play that children can use to create whatever themes they wish. Puppet theaters are nice to have in play areas with handy supplies for creating puppets, writing scripts, and producing puppet plays.

Table or Desk Clusters

Most kindergarten classrooms have an area where children's "home" tables and desks are clustered. Tables are generally preferable to separate desks, and desks are usually clustered into tablelike arrangements when they must be used. Sometimes tables have storage capacity for keeping personal writing materials, books, and other items. Children are free to pursue solitary activities at the home table or engage in a variety of reading and writing activities that they wish to do outside the writing or reading centers. In some classrooms, the chairs at home tables are the only place children have to hang sweaters and coats.

Home tables should not be where young children spend most of their days in kindergarten. In fact, Pat Nourot states emphatically,

> An environment that gives children cues for sedentary and passive behavior such as listening to the teacher talk for long periods of time or restricting movement in assigned seats is at odds with the biological need of young children for physical activity and active engagement. An environment that provides space for both active play and quiet or solitary activity meets children's physical needs and goes a long way towards fostering feelings of safety and security. (in press, p. 5)

Home tables provide a place in the room where each child has his or her own space for "settling in" and returning to. Home tables may be used as part of the center rotation, so that, while some children are working or playing in the art, writing, reading, science, and play centers, one group of children may be working individually or in groups at the home table. Thus, the home table cluster provides an additional center area in the classroom.

ORGANIZATION OF THE CLASSROOM DAY: EARLY AND BEGINNING READERS AND WRITERS

Most kindergarten classroom days are approximately one-half the regular school day. Some kindergarten days are shortened full school days. Whatever the length, kindergarten days include most or all of the following activities:

665

1. Play and work centers (science, reading, writing, mathematics, art, etc.).
2. Group projects (dramatic play, puppet shows, science experiments, etc.).
3. Class meetings, opening and closing routines, sharing time.
4. Reading time when an adult or peer reads to the class.
5. Motor play and movement.
6. Music and drama.
7. Snack and recess.

It is a good idea to plan the day so that you have two or three large blocks of time for extended activities in centers and working on projects that alternate with motor activity and whole-class meetings for sharing and discussion. Table 13-1 presents a typical half-day kindergarten schedule. Table 13-2 suggests a whole-day kindergarten schedule.

As you can see from these two schedules, many and varied activities comprise the classroom day for early and beginning readers. In each of these activities, opportunity abounds for developing children's language and literacy abilities through language interactions and literate acts.

8:30 – 9:00	***Centers***—art, reading, writing, science, play, mathematics. Children choose center and stay in that center for full half-hour. Circle rug available for reading center children to use.
9:00 – 9:15	***Clean up/settle down***—necessary cleanup is done, children go to their home table as cleanup is completed.
9:15 – 9:35	***Circle***—attendance, morning song, daily helpers appointed, calendar, weather chart, sharing, story/poetry.
9:35 – 10:05	***Snack and recess.***
10:10 – 10:40	***Group projects***—dramatic play, construction blocks, puppet theater, literature discussion circles, writing workshop.
10:45 – 11:10	***Music and movement/art projects/seasonal projects***—alternate singing, instrumental music, dance, music interpretation, papier-mâché projects, murals, finger painting, holiday plays and projects.
11:10 – 11:25	***Clean up/settle down.***
11:25 – 11:35	***Circle***—Reflections on the day, story/poetry.
11:35	***Dismiss.***

TABLE 13-1

Organization of the Kindergarten Day: Half-Day

8:15 – 8:30	**Settle in**—put folders in cubbies, store snacks and lunches, go to home tables.
8:30 – 8:45	**Journal writing and special words**—children share special words to go into their word banks. Everyone writes in her/his journal.
8:45 – 9:15	**Circle**—calendar, weather, attendance, sharing, story/poetry.
9:15 – 10:00	**Language arts**—story dictation, literature circles, story illustration, journal writing.
10:00 – 10:15	**Morning snack and recess.**
10:15 – 11:00	**Math, science, and social studies projects**—six tables with manipulatives and experiments/projects. Children choose tables and stay in one center for the forty-five-minute time block.
11:00 – 11:30	**Music.** (Music teacher three days a week.)
11:30 – 11:45	**Clean up/settle down.**
11:45 – 12:30	**Lunch and recess.**
12:30 – 1:30	**Quiet time**—free reading, writing, and art or nap; quiet sharing of books, writing or art with a partner.
1:30 – 2:00	**Physical education/Spanish/8th-grade buddies**—physical education, Monday and Wednesday; Spanish, Tuesday and Friday; 8th-grade buddies, Thursday. (Physical education and Spanish teachers)
2:00 – 2:30	**Free play**—dramatic play, construction blocks, puppet theater, play centers.
2:30—2:45	**Circle**—reflections on the day, story/poetry.

—— **TABLE 13-2** ————————————————————————

Organization of the Kindergarten Day: Whole Day

MANAGEMENT ISSUES: EARLY AND BEGINNING READERS AND WRITERS

A major aspect of the kindergarten year is for children to learn how to "do" school (Dyson, 1984). In kindergarten, children come to understand school routines and expectations, language and literacy tasks, group membership roles, the language and materials of learning, interpersonal relationships, cultural and language backgrounds of other children, and myriad other facets of the culture and ecology of classrooms and schools. Management issues in kindergarten classrooms begin with "doing school," and one of your biggest

667

challenges as a kindergarten teacher is realizing the wide range of experience and knowledge about doing school that children bring to your classroom. Then you must plan to accommodate those differences.

You can expect some children to arrive in kindergarten fresh out of two or more years of organized day care; these children probably already know a great deal about many school routines and expectations. On the other hand, you may have children who have had no day care experience, but who have played hours of "school" with older siblings and friends and thus also have considerable knowledge about school. Yet other children may be (1) those with no day care experience and little or no knowledge about schools, (2) singleton ("only") children whose main social contacts have been with adults rather than other children, and (3) immigrant children suddenly immersed in a country, culture, and language different from their own. The range of backgrounds young children bring to school is wide, and we have not exhausted the list of possibilities here. Your planning with regard to classroom management must take this wide range of experience and background knowledge into consideration. There are any number of steps you can take to manage kindergarten classroom successfully.

Organizing the Environment and Yourself

One of the first things you can do to simplify classroom management is to organize the environment toward the ends of efficiency and order. As you are deciding physical arrangement of the room, keep in mind how and when materials and equipment are to be used, distributed, and stored. Plan pathways and work/play areas to avoid situations where children crowd one another or bump into each other in the course of their work or play, and make sure that cleanup pathways for spillables are short and uncluttered. Look for simple ways to streamline materials distribution, cleanup, and other chores: Keep paper and writing supplies near the writing center; arrange science and art centers near the water supply and cleanup equipment; store playground equipment in one container near the door from which children exit for recess. Find, buy, or build sufficient storage bins and shelves to accommodate the full range of materials, equipment, props, and supplies you use and make sure these are placed so that you have quick, efficient access to them (this is the "A place for everything and everything in its place" rule).

Just as important as planning for the physical environment is planning for your own organization. Think ahead to identify all the materials, equipment, and supplies you'll need for an entire day, and have them at your fingertips (or in place) for use. Consider how materials may be most efficiently distributed and decide distribution plans *before* you are in the middle of an activity with twenty-five or thirty five-year-old children. Check equipment in advance to make sure it works as you expect it to. The planning we're suggesting here sounds pretty self-evident, but lack of this kind of planning accounts for a considerable number of management problems. We can assure you that many lessons have been lost and many discipline problems created while teachers were getting a videoplayer cord from the AV room, rummaging in the closet for construction paper, or trying to make the overhead projector light bulb illuminate. Lack of planning loses lessons and creates problems just as surely when thirty children rush to get valentine-making supplies all at once. It bears repeating: When teachers are not well organized and activities are not well thought out in advance, discipline problems are *created*.

Rules and Routines

In order for classrooms to be safe and orderly places, children must come to understand and abide by certain rules. Pat Nourot makes the important point that children in kindergarten are just beginning to understand that rules have meaning, and reminds us that "endless negotiation about roles and themes, dialogs and plot lines characterize the play of preschool and kindergarten children" (in press, p. 8). She notes further that, when conflict occurs, young children step in and out of fantasy worlds or play events to negotiate rules to allow the event to continue. Because children's understanding of how rules work is still developing in kindergarten, it is important that we deal with classroom rule-setting explicitly and reinforce rules by frequent gentle reminders.

On the first day of class in a kindergarten room, you should begin discussion of rules, roles, and conduct and continue this discussion throughout the school year. You may wish to begin by identifying one or two rules you believe to be important and have the children add others. A very few rules of general deportment should be sufficient for your class, e.g., "Listen when others are talking," "Be considerate of others' belongings." "Treat books, materials, and toys with care." "Do not disturb others at work." Special rules are required for activities with high spill and slosh rates (painting, planting seeds, cooking) and/or potentially dangerous materials or equipment (scissors, thermometers, Cuisenaire rods, hot plates); these rules must be clearly defined and rigorously enforced. Post general classroom rules where they are easily seen by everyone in the room, and early in the year, make a point to remind children of the rules *before* the rules have been broken. Continue to discuss rules as the year progresses.

Routines are patterns of action teachers use consistently to manage movement and activity in the classroom. For example, the teacher may wish to establish a routine for dismissal in which the last event of every class day is a chant or song in circle followed by the teacher signaling each child's departure by handing out take-home folders. Another less elaborate routine is the teacher's signal for attention when the room is busy with working noise—a raised hand, tap of a bell, or tone sounded on a musical instrument. Routines reduce uncertainty about what children are supposed to do when, thus creating a sense of stability and order in the classroom. (For example, "When you come into the class each morning, put your take-home folder in your cubby, store your backpack in the coat area, then you may use the play center or reading center, or read, write, or talk quietly at your home table.") Routines decrease the need for lots of teacher rules; further, routines that reduce confusion and encourage orderly movement are particularly important in classrooms where the teacher wants to allow many opportunities for children to move about and work in various centers.

Classroom Helpers

Many kindergarten teachers find it helpful to have other adults working with them in the classroom. Such assistance allows close supervision of multiple activity and play centers in the room and provides children easy access to adult help when they need it. Paid classroom aides are available in some schools and districts; in others, volunteers and parents work in classrooms.

If paid or volunteer aides are not available, and even when they are, you should probably consider some plan for parent volunteers to work in your room. Parent involvement in classrooms has many advantages, not the least of which is that it opens up communication lines between home and school and gives everyone greater understanding of what goes on, both at home and in school. Make no mistake about it, however, having one or more other adults in your classroom creates some degree of additional work on your part; for such arrangements to work well, you will need to prepare aides and parents for their responsibilities and roles in your room. Such preparation includes (1) clarifying what your classroom and curriculum are about and why, (2) developing their understanding of your instructional approach, (3) making sure they understand classroom rules and routines, (4) assigning and coordinating their activities and duties, and (5) handling problems that do arise. Once aides or volunteers understand activities and routines, their supervisory and assistance work allows you considerably more freedom to work closely with specific groups or individual children for sustained periods of time. Don't forget also that aides and parents bring their own interests, abilities, and talents into the room; their expertise can be a rich resource for you and your classroom.

ORGANIZATION AND MANAGEMENT OF LITERACY INSTRUCTION FOR THE BASAL READER INSTRUCTIONAL APPROACH

As we stated in Chapter 12, the basal reader approach is used in 75 to 80 percent of classrooms today. How teachers actually use basals in their classrooms, however, varies widely from teacher to teacher. Further complicating the distinctions between the basal reader approach and other approaches is the fact that basals are often used in classrooms where some form of literature-based instruction and/or project-based subject area instruction is in place. Our discussion here will focus on "typical" organization of basal reader instruction, in which the basal is considered to be the primary source of reading and language arts learning. In addition, we will limit our discussion to self-contained classrooms, although we recognize that other organizational plans exist.

UNDERLYING BELIEFS AND ASSUMPTIONS ABOUT LITERACY LEARNING: BASAL READING INSTRUCTION

The basal reader approach for developing children's literacy includes the following beliefs and assumptions (these are synthesized from Chapter 12):

1. Children's acquisition and development of fluent literacy is best accomplished by their progression through a systematic, predetermined sequence of skills that are taught in conjunction with carefully selected short narrative and expository texts.

2. Children acquire and develop fluent literacy as they become increasingly proficient in the areas of word analysis, vocabulary, comprehension, language knowledge, content area reading, and independent reading.

3. Materials for developing children's literacy need to be selected from literature of high quality and presented in an ordered sequence of difficulty to support children's growing literacy competence.

4. Lessons for fostering children's literacy development need to include the following elements: (a) development of background information and vocabulary knowledge, (b) guided silent reading, (c) comprehension development, (d) skill development and application, and (e) extension and skill practice.

5. Children acquire and develop fluent literacy best by learning in small groups that are organized according to proficiency and matched to reading materials of comparable difficulty.

PHYSICAL ORGANIZATION OF THE CLASSROOM: BASAL READER APPROACH

Grouping by proficiency or ability levels is a major component of basal reading instruction; most basal reader classrooms have three or four reading groups, each group using a different text, or working in different parts of the same text, in the basal series. Instruction for groups is teacher-led. Organization of the classroom must therefore provide an area where the teacher is able to work with a small group of children while the rest of the class works independently. The small-group working area needs to contain materials and equipment for reading instruction, and physical arrangements must allow groups of children to move easily to and from the reading group

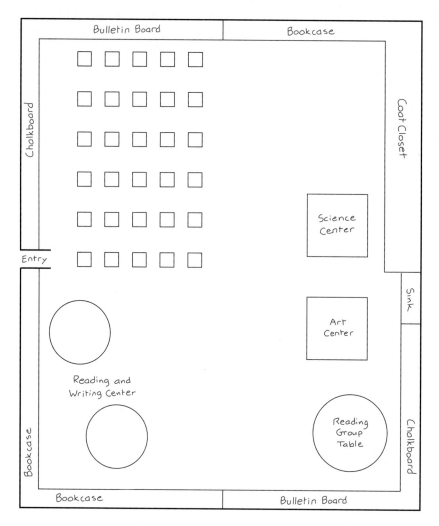

Bulletin Board

Bookcase

Chalkboard

Coat Closet

Science Center

Entry

Sink

Art Center

Reading and Writing Center

Reading Group Table

Chalkboard

Bookcase

Bookcase

Bulletin Board

FIGURE 13-2

Physical Organization of the Classroom: Basal Reader Approach

instructional area and their assigned seats and other areas for independent work. These are the only special physical arrangements that need to be made for basal reading instruction. Figure 13-2 shows a classroom arrangement for basal reading instruction.

Reading Group Instructional Area

The reading group instructional area should be located somewhere at the room periphery as far removed from other work areas as possible.

Corners are particularly nice. The table where you and the reading group children sit should be large enough so everyone can fit comfortably with books and writing materials without crowding. Carpet in this area helps absorb sound so that discussion here doesn't travel to the rest of the room.

First on the list of important things to do in this area is to arrange the table so that the children sit with their backs to the rest of the room and you sit *facing* the rest of the room (see Figure 13-2). A number of considerations make this important. By having the children face away from where the rest of the class is working independently, you direct the reading group children's voices away from other children, thus reducing noise for the class and increasing the feeling of intimacy between you and the small group you're teaching. It serves also to reduce the reading group children's feeling that they're "in a spotlight" with everything they're saying heard throughout the room. By facing the room yourself, you have plenty of opportunity to scan the room to ascertain that all is progressing well with the children working independently and to handle small problems before they become large ones. If you reverse this arrangement, you can expect the hijinks that happen when children you can't see behind you gesture, make faces, giggle, and do whatever they can do to get and hold the attention of children in your small group.

A second consideration for your basal reading instruction area is to locate it near a chalkboard if possible so that you have the board available when you need it; a chalkboard is particularly useful for teaching vocabulary and various aspects of word analysis. If you can't locate next to a chalkboard, get a portable or lap-sized one to use. You simply do not want to disrupt the class by going across the room to a chalkboard and talking across the rest of the class in order to illustrate an idea or discuss vocabulary with your reading group. In primary classrooms, a pocket chart easel is also useful in or near the reading group area.

The final major arrangement needed for the reading group area is a bookcase and/or storage closet or bin to house any and all materials you need for reading instruction. We recommend that the basal readers themselves are stored here; you can then distribute them as needed, and when children take the basals to their desks for further reading, provision can be made for the books to be returned when the area is not in use. Basals kept in children's desks suffer considerable wear and tear, so storing in a central location generally preserves them. Just as important, basal instruction involves questioning routines that ask children to make predictions and speculations about the text to be read (e.g., DR-TA and DRA discussed in Chapter 4), and, if children have basals at their desks and have already read the stories, the lesson is diluted, to say the least.

Other materials should be stored with the basal readers. Have supplies of paper and writing utensils for mapping and other writing activities. You will also want to keep your teacher's guide here, visuals, a selection of full-length books from which basal selections were drawn, related literature, and perhaps some puppets or other dramatic props.

8:20 – 8:40	**Morning warm-up**—attendance, current events, sharing, weather, story/poetry
8:45 – 9:10	**Spelling**—self-collected spelling words
9:15 – 10:30	**Language arts**—three basal reading groups
10:30 – 10:45	**Snack, recess.**
10:50 – 11:30	**Math.**
11:30 – 12:15	**Social studies.**
12:15 – 12:50	**Lunch, recess.**
12:50 – 1:10	**Story.**
1:10 – 1:45	**Science.**
1:45 – 2:15	**Physical education** (M,W). **Music** (T). **Art** (Th).
2:15 – 3:00	**Group projects** (M–Th)—children working on self-selected projects stemming from interests developed from science, math, social studies, music, physical education, and art. **Library** (F).
3:00 – 3:15	**Sustained silent reading or writing.**
3:15 – 3:30	**Reflect on day, story/poetry, dismiss.**

TABLE 13-3

Organization of the Classroom Day—Basal Reader Instruction

ORGANIZATION OF THE CLASSROOM DAY: BASAL READER INSTRUCTION

Most basal reading instruction occurs at a designated time during the class day, usually in the morning. The length of time allotted to reading instruction and the time of day may both be determined at the school or district level or by teachers themselves. Reading instruction may be part of a larger language arts block, or it may be separated from spelling and writing instruction. Table 13-3 presents a class schedule for basal reading instruction.

MANAGEMENT ISSUES: BASAL READER INSTRUCTION

Much of what we've already discussed about management in kindergarten classes—organization of the environment and yourself, rules and routines, and classroom helpers—applies equally to management of basal reader instruction. Three additional issues are important here: scheduling basal reading groups, rules and routines for reading instruction, and the effects of grouping.

Scheduling Reading Groups

Once your time block for basal reading instruction is established and your groups decided upon, further decisions need to be made about how you will schedule your groups into the time block. One assumption some teachers make is that they must meet with each group every day; they therefore simply divide the allotted time by the number of groups they have to arrive at meeting time length for each group. In our example (9:15–10:30), we have seventy-five minutes for reading instruction and three groups; this figures out to twenty-five minutes per group. Twenty-five minutes per group allows only minimal time for everything to be accomplished—introducing the story and its vocabulary, guiding children as they read silently, discussing the story, and developing and extending reading skills. Although it is a rather common practice, scheduling short reading group meetings (thirty minutes or less) usually has one of two effects: Either substantive parts of the lesson get left out (and, unfortunately, the omitted part is usually in-depth discussion of the story) or the lesson is extended over a number of days or a full week, in which case children often lose interest and attention.

A far better arrangement is to assume that it is *not* necessary to meet with each group every day. Then look to see how you can best arrange the schedule so that you have one or more extended periods with each group every *week*. Table 13-4 shows how we might schedule reading groups. The key to this schedule is that you start Monday off with a different group each week so that you have two forty-five-minute meetings with two groups each week and one forty-five-minute period with one. Note that in the week shown in Table 13-4 we have two forty-five-minute periods with Groups A

	Monday	Tuesday	Wednesday	Thursday	Friday
9:15–10:00	Grp. A	Grp. C	Grp. B	Grp. A	Grp. C
10:00–10:30	Grp. B	Grp. A	Grp. C	Grp. B	Journals

TABLE 13-4

Scheduling Basal Reading Groups—Week 1

and C and one with Group B. On Monday of the next week we'll begin with Group B, and the following week with Group C. So for the next two weeks our schedule will look like that shown in Table 13-5. This is not a perfect arrangement—you'll probably spread some stories over two days for each group occasionally—but it does give you blocks of time with groups that are sufficiently long for extended and elaborated discussions and interactions. We think that is worth having. It does minimize what we call "freight train teaching" where you just run instruction past children like a train roaring down the track and never have time to enter into full, rich engagements. There are, of course, many other ways basal reading instructional blocks can be scheduled; use your imagination and make the schedule work for you and your instructional goals.

Routines and Rules for Basal Reading Groups

Routines and rules for basal reading instruction need to be established early in the year so that they are clearly defined, rehearsed, and well known to everyone. Later, they will become second nature and will require little monitoring on your part. The first important routine for reading groups is getting children to and from the small group with all their required materials and supplies. Determine what signal you wish to use for calling children to group: One easy way is to write the schedule on the board every morning (this is especially useful if your schedule changes from week to week) and then quietly announce at the appointed time, "Tarik's group" or "Alejandra's group." Spend some time clarifying the routine. Let children know what

	Monday	Tuesday	Wednesday	Thursday	Friday
Week 2 9:15 – 10:00	Grp. B	Grp. A	Grp. C	Grp. B	Grp. A
10:00 – 10:30	Grp. C	Grp. B	Grp. A	Grp. C	Journals
Week 3 9:15 – 10:00	Grp. C	Grp. B	Grp. A	Grp. C	Grp. B
10:00 – 10:30	Grp. A	Grp. C	Grp. B	Grp. A	Journals

TABLE 13-5

Scheduling Basal Reading Groups—Weeks 2 and 3

they are to bring to group, what deportment you expect, and what they are to do upon arrival at the group table. Then see to it that the routine is consistently followed.

During the time you're working with the small groups, you need to be free of interruptions from other children who have questions or want to tell you something. A good idea here is to establish the rule that you are not to be interrupted during meetings for any reasons other than emergencies; then, during changeovers, children may raise their hands for your attention or come to you to get help. It's wise to become skilled at eye control for handling small problems while you're in group discussion. Scan the room frequently, use small gestures and facial expression, smiles, or a silent "no" as needed, and try not to interrupt the interaction with your small group. Scanning also lets you see when a child *does* need your immediate attention; in such a case, leave the group and take care of whatever distress the child is experiencing.

The Effects of Grouping

You will find that ability grouping does have an effect on children and can serve to exacerbate status issues that may already be present in your class. No matter how seemingly neutral your group names are, and no matter how careful you are to give equal instruction to all groups, children will know early on who's in the "high" and who's in the "low" group; in fact, this is information they figured out about the second week of first grade when they were initially put in groups, and that knowledge will have traveled with them through the grades. In schools with large populations of immigrant children and children who speak English as a second language, an additional unfortunate effect is that ESL children are usually grouped together in the low reading group or isolated into a group by themselves. Whatever the circumstances, grouping will increase the impact of status issues in your classroom. It cannot be avoided.

One way to reduce status effects caused by grouping is to alternate basal reading instruction with literature-based instruction in which you use multiple copies of five full-length novels and allow children to group themselves into reading response groups according to which book they want to read, thus giving them opportunities to cross basal reading group lines. In this arrangement, you might progress through one basal reader unit, then spend a period of two or three weeks reading novels in self-selected groups, and then return to the basal. Another approach is to have project groups at another time during the day in which children group themselves according to interest or some criterion other than reading ability (as we show in the 2:15–3:00 period of our daily schedule example in Table 13-3). While self-selected literature groups and project groups do not remove status differences, they do soften these differences somewhat. You should understand, however, that it is not particularly easy to create cohesive cross-ability groups in classrooms and schools where ability grouping is entrenched; nevertheless, it is important to do so, so that children come to understand the many strengths other children have.

ORGANIZATION AND MANAGEMENT OF LITERACY INSTRUCTION FOR THE LITERATURE-BASED INSTRUCTIONAL APPROACH

Just as wide variation exists in how teachers use basal readers in classrooms, so too is there considerable variation in the form and day-to-day operation of literature-based programs. In some classes, literature-based instruction is predominantly "whole class," in which everyone reads the same literary work, discusses their reading in a large group led by teacher questions, and then completes follow-up activities. In other classrooms, literature-based instruction is part individualized and part small group. Children read a book by sections, fill out worksheets, and then meet in small groups for discussion of the story using the worksheets to guide the discussion. Still other classrooms have highly individualized literature-based programs in which children are all reading books of their own selection.

The focus we will take here is on literature based programs of the type we highlighted in Chapter 12, where four or five core books form the nucleus for reading response groups (also called literature response groups). The teacher selects multiple copies (five to ten) of each book and allows children to decide which book they wish to read and the group they wish to be in. With teacher guidance, groups read the books in designated sections and meet to discuss their reading and response. The teacher monitors individual and group progress through books and maintains records documenting each child's literacy development.

UNDERLYING BELIEFS AND ASSUMPTIONS ABOUT LITERACY LEARNING: LITERATURE-BASED INSTRUCTION

Literature-based instruction includes the following beliefs and assumptions (these are synthesized from our discussion in Chapter 12):

1. Children acquire and develop fluent literacy by reading and responding to complete literary works of high quality.
2. Children read and respond avidly to literature that interests them even when the difficulty of given literary works does not match their apparent ability level.
3. Children do not need to understand every word of any text in order to construct full, rich meaning for that text.
4. Children as active theory builders and hypothesis testers will acquire all the requisite language and literacy skills for competent reading and

writing in the course of their progression through many works of literature that interest them.

5. In the event that specific skills are needed for children's literacy development, these skills should be taught in the context of that immediate need.

PHYSICAL ORGANIZATION OF THE CLASSROOM: LITERATURE-BASED INSTRUCTION

Literature-based classrooms of the type we're focusing on in this chapter require only three critical physical organizational characteristics:

1. a reading and literature center for storing the many books and other reading matter that such a program needs;
2. flexible floor space for moving children in and out of reading response groups and for giving response groups plenty of room so that groups can converse without interference from other groups; and
3. working areas and materials and props for developing end-of-book productions.

Figure 13-3 suggests one possible arrangement for a literature-based classroom.

The Reading Center

As we mentioned in Chapter 12, the reading center is the heart of the literature-based classroom. Here is where you house the classroom library of many kinds of interesting and enjoyable literature. You should have children's classics here as well as lesser works, comic books, magazines, reference books, joke books, and anything else children like to read (see Chapter 6 for an extensive discussion). The reading center should be a large part of the classroom; it should make a clear statement of the value placed on books in your class and the enjoyment everyone expects to encounter with books. Sets of core books that children will read in their reading response groups may be stored in a closet, bin, or shelf in the reading center, but should not be available for individual checkout until after they've been used in the reading response groups. You may wish to acquire one or two copies of response group books separate from the class sets in order to allow individual checkout and to keep class sets intact and untattered.

Given the number of books you need for your reading center, you will undoubtedly rely rather heavily on paperback books. You can purchase many, many good paperback titles relatively cheaply through book clubs (*Scholastic*, for example) and use bonus book opportunities to add to your collection. You should also plan to have hardback books on loan from your school or district library, and make sure you have plenty of titles that complement the core book collection with regard to topic and authors. For example, if your reading response groups will be reading *Ira Sleeps Over* (Waber, 1972), make sure other books about children's fears, frustrations,

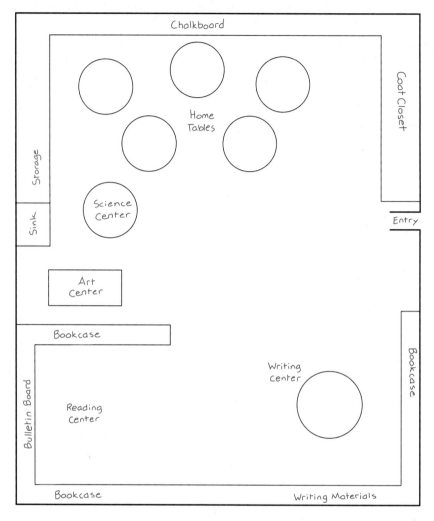

FIGURE 13-3

Physical Organization of the Classroom: Literature-Based Instruction

and security objects are in the reading and literature center—*Everybody Needs a Rock* (Baylor, 1974), *Frederick* (Lionni, 1967), *Goodnight Moon* (Brown, 1947). Or, if response groups are reading *The Lion, the Witch, and the Wardrobe* (Lewis, 1950), by all means stock the rest of the Narnia series in the reading center.

You may find that swivel paperback bookracks are useful for book storage in the reading and literature center along with standard bookshelves and bookcases. Magazines and comic books can be stacked or stored in hanging file boxes. Your center should also have comfortable chairs, pillows, or beanbag chairs for reading. You may wish to have a table and chairs in the center available for general use while children are browsing and then used for a reading response group discussion during that activity. Writing materials should also be available in the reading and literature center.

Flexible Floor Space

The literature-based classroom need lots of space and furniture and need to be rearrangeable to accommodate various activities. Decide how the reading response groups will be arranged during discussion times. One way is to have movable desks that children can arrange into reading response groups and rearrange back into "regular" formation for other class activities. Many desks are now designed so that four desks fit nicely into a table arrangement. Another alternative is to have tables and chairs with children assigned to tables according to their reading response groups; alternately, children may sit at tables according to some other criterion and then exchange places during reading response group discussion. Yet another possibility with tables and chairs is for children to move their chairs into small group circles scattered about the room; the disadvantage here is that they then don't have a good writing surface for any writing the group may want to do or that you ask them to do. And finally, you may have the luxury of having sufficient table centers in the room—at the reading center, listening center, or writing center—that you can have children leave their assigned seats and relocate in a center for reading response group discussion.

An important feature here is for you to find small-group discussion areas with as much room as possible between groups so that talking noise from groups doesn't disturb other working groups. Whatever you do, don't have reading response groups meet at tables or centers where work in progress is on the table or experiments or displays are set up. Response group areas should be fully conducive to attentive discussion and participation in the response group task.

Work Areas and Materials for Productions

Still more flexibility is needed for groups to carry out productions they decide to do as their final interpretation of a literary work. The art center, puppet stage and props, and writing center will be useful for productions; however, you may need to clear out corners or space for play productions, mural painting, space rocket constructions, and dance practice on occasion. The key here is to be alert for possible ways to accommodate these major activities and to be willing to consider various creative solutions to space needs.

Most materials for student productions are, in all probability, already in your classroom or school—in the various centers, prop boxes, and in storage bins and closets in the room. When they are brought from home, you'll need to find space for storing or maintaining materials so that such things do not interfere with other space needs.

ORGANIZATION OF THE CLASSROOM DAY: LITERATURE-BASED APPROACH

Many teachers who have chosen to use a literature-based approach simply use the designated time for reading or language arts as the time when reading response groups meet and other reading, writing, and language activities take place. So, for example, in the basal reader classroom day we illustrated earlier in Table 13-3, the time block from 9:15–10:30 would be used in a literature-based program, as shown in Table 13-6.

MANAGEMENT ISSUES: LITERATURE-BASED INSTRUCTION

Two major management issues are prominent in literature-based instruction as we are defining it here. The first is movement of children into and out of reading response groups in such a manner that wasted time and confusion are minimized. The second issue is ascertaining that children are engaged in truly rich, productive discussion in their response groups. Routines and rules are helpful in each case; collaborative learning strategies assist independent student discussion.

Routines and Rules in Literature-Based Instruction

Any time you have everyone in classroom moving at the same time, you create the possibility for disruptions and problems. Children *will* playfully

9:15 – 9:20	**_Focus, discussion prompts_**—teacher guides response group discussion by focusing attention ("Create a group map that shows the mood of your story") or with response prompts ("As a group, find a section of today's reading that everyone in the group really likes. Jot down some reasons why the group likes that section.").
9:20 – 9:50	**_Reading response group discussion_**—children follow focus or prompt as major topic of discussion.
9:50 – 10:15	**_Whole-class sharing_**—the essence of each group's discussion is shared with class.
10:15 – 10:30	**_Journal writing_**—children reflect and record responses to their reading and discussion.

TABLE 13-6

Organization of the Language Arts Period—Literature-Based Instruction push and shove, trip each other, punch and poke, and shoot "baskets" into the trashcan. Sometimes this escalates into rowdiness and out-of-control behavior. Poking, punching, tripping, and rowdy behavior make it necessary for you to use precious time for crowd control, thereby reducing the time children have for discussion in their response groups. Further, such behavior has potential for real injury or harm to students. Rules and routines are very helpful in preventing problems of this sort.

One routine that is especially useful is *not* to have everyone in the room moving at the same time. The routine is that you announce each reading response group, in turn, to move to their discussion area, and give groups time to settle before announcing another. So, you might say "Thy Friend, Obadiah (Turkle, 1969) group, go to your discussion area," allow those children to get to their group area, and announce, "Mufaro's Beautiful Daughters (Steptoe, 1987) group," then call "The Lion, the Witch, and the Wardrobe (Lewis, 1950) group," and so on. Early in the year, discuss with the children what materials they are to bring to their response group meetings and what your expectations are for their deportment en route. It's worth doing some "dry run" practice with very young children and those who are not used to moving in and out of small groups. You may choose to give focus instructions ("Create a map that shows the mood of your story") either before or after children are in their groups, but, however you do it, do it the same way every time. Focus instructions and prompts, then, become part of the routine itself. Practiced and monitored early in the year, getting to and from response groups will become an easy, effortless routine.

Plan also, and tell children about, how you will get their attention at the end of response group discussion time, or during their discussions if you should need it. Room noise does swell, even (or, perhaps, especially) when everybody is fully engaged in the response group discussion tasks. We mentioned earlier tapping a bell or sounding a tone on a musical instrument. Both signals work fine. Some teachers flick the lights or simply turn the room lights off. Here again, the choice is yours, and many options are available. Just make sure that your signal is easily noticed by children in the midst of working activity, is soothing and quieting rather than clanging or noisy, and works every time.

Assuring Quality in Response Group Discussions

Making sure that group discussions are of a high quality is probably the most bothersome management issue about literature-based instruction using reading/literature response groups. The reason is simple: Teachers give up "control" of the discussion when they put children in response groups and are concerned that discussions do not degenerate into idle talk, classroom gossip, silliness, or play. Teachers, rightfully, want some assurance that what the children are doing in reading response groups is educationally productive. Focus instructions and discussion prompts are highly useful for

Classroom Rules and Routines

increasing the quality of literature response groups. Bonnie Raines (1991), a teacher in a third-fourth grade class using a literature-based approach, found that clear discussion task directions were critical for stimulating high-quality literature discussions with her students.

Some teachers use discussion role assignments to assist in guiding and focusing discussion. You are probably familiar with a number of these. The following role assignments may be useful for literature response groups (Ruddell, 1993, p. 297):

Facilitator—responsible for leading the discussion, making sure everyone has a chance to participate, encouraging reticent members, helping talkative members curb their input, and making sure the task is completed.

Recorder—responsible for keeping notes on the discussion, ideas generated by the group, alternative solutions, explanations, and any other important information. The recorder is responsible for any final write-up, as needed.

Timer—responsible for allocating and monitoring time so that all parts of the task are completed as required. The timer notifies the group periodically about time considerations.

Worrier—responsible for whether the group is on- or off-topic, whether ideas being generated are on track with the task goal, and whether the "grand plan" (say, for productions) can be accomplished in the time available. The worrier begins most sentences with, "I'm worried that…"

Reporter—responsible for reporting progress during the meeting and/or final solutions in the whole-class wrap-up meeting. You may wish to use these or other role assignments in your reading response groups. You will need to prepare students a bit for their roles, and should rotate the roles within groups at frequent intervals. One caveat is important here: In her study of literature response groups (1991), Bonnie Raines found that, because of inexperience, facilitators sometimes asked questions that interrupted the flow of discussion and limited, rather than extended, elaboration of ideas. She abandoned group roles and concentrated on developing engaging discussion tasks.

An additional issue here is how you monitor small-group discussions so that you can evaluate individual and group growth and literacy development. One obvious way to do this is to spend response group discussion time "listening in" from a distance to group discussions. It's not hard to do with a little practice. Another way is to join each group for part of their discussion time each day; however, your very presence in the group will change the group dynamic, and may reduce children's spontaneity. If you have adult aides and/or volunteers in the classroom, they can also sit in with groups, but make sure they know how to do this without taking over the group. Bonnie Raines (1991) came up with an excellent solution: She purchased five audiotape recorders and distributed one to each group; after the initial flurry of children's self-consciousness at being recorded, the tape recorders quickly became unobtrusive elements in the small group settings. Raines then listened to the tapes on regular basis and was able to monitor the quality of discussions and comment to the children about the content of the discussions and their group process. She found the tape recorders to be important contributions to the quality of reading response group discussions.

A final issue here concerns your management and maintenance of records charting children's continuing language and literacy development. You will need to record what books children read in their response groups, what productions they participated in and the substance of their contributions, and your evaluation of their literacy progress. You will especially want to demonstrate that children in your class have acquired and are developing all the reading and writing skills identified by your school district as requisite for their grade level. Design a form similar to the one we suggested in Chapter 7 for the writing workshop in which you list children's names vertically and skills/abilities horizontally. As you observe children applying those skills, note that on your form. Maintaining portfolios of work children complete in their response group is equally useful, as are anecdotal records of your observations (see Chapter 11 for more on this topic). It *is* important to understand that because end-of-unit tests and other evaluation events are not built into the literature-based approach, evaluation procedures become a management issue. Your task here is to decide upon, develop, and maintain an evaluation system that yields productive information about children's literacy development.

ORGANIZATION AND MANAGEMENT OF LITERACY INSTRUCTION FOR THE WHOLE LANGUAGE INSTRUCTIONAL APPROACH

Whole language instruction requires considerable teacher-developed organization and structure by virtue of its own philosophical stance. There is no one "right way" to construct a whole language classroom; there are no instructional algorithms or pat answers, no scope and sequence charts, and no teacher guides. Thus, it is important to have a solid grasp of the instructional approach itself in order to develop the organization and management structures necessary for its implementation.

UNDERLYING BELIEFS AND ASSUMPTIONS ABOUT LITERACY LEARNING: WHOLE LANGUAGE APPROACH

The whole language approach includes the following beliefs and assumptions (synthesized from Chapter 12):

1. Children actively seek to extend their own language and literacy abilities as they interact with the physical and social environments.
2. Children's language and literacy development are socially mediated through ongoing interactions and transactions with other learners and proficient language and literacy models.
3. Children acquire and develop fluent literacy as they participate in and use literate behaviors in active, naturalistic learning events.
4. Children acquire and extend language and literacy abilities interactively with all other learning; language and literacy instruction must necessarily be integrated with all other instruction.
5. Children acquire and develop language, literacy, and learning skills as they participate in learning events that incorporate language and literacy abilities.
6. When specific language and literacy skills are needed for continuing development, these skills should be taught in the context of authentic learning events.

PHYSICAL ORGANIZATION OF THE CLASSROOM: WHOLE LANGUAGE APPROACH

Most whole language classrooms are filled with activity centers and/or project areas where children are engaged in the kind of projects or theme cycle activities we described in Chapters 7 and 9. Because every aspect of classroom life and learning in whole language classrooms is an opportunity for language and literacy learning as well, centers and project areas are all stocked with materials for literacy—books, magazines, paper, writing utensils, staplers, paper clips, paste, tape, and other reading and writing materials. Figure 13-4 suggests one physical organization plan for a whole language classroom.

It is an interesting fact that whole language classrooms look and feel considerably like classrooms for early and beginning readers—only details differ. This is true because the whole language classrooms require the same accommodations for movement and activity, exploration, and the hustle-bustle of productions, constructions, and project completion. So (to review), the layout

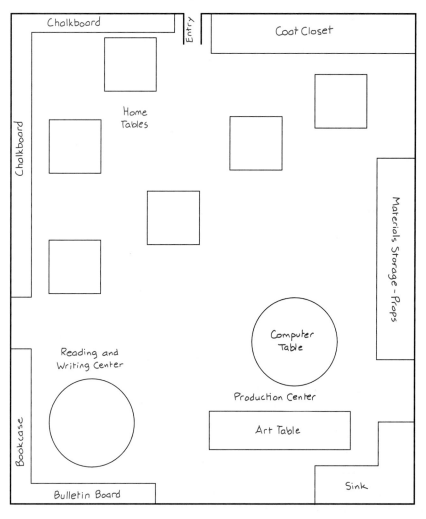

—— **FIGURE 13-4** ——

Physical Organization of the Classroom: Whole Language Approach of the room must account for clearly defined pathways, plenty of storage room at each center for equipment and supplies, a ready water supply (if possible), lots of working space where children can spread out and work without crowding one another, and readily available supplies that allow children to be literate in every activity they pursue. Centers provide working areas in the room where children work on projects and activities (see our discussion earlier in this chapter describing the characteristics of such centers). If possible, the room should have one or more computers and a printer for all of the in-depth research (hypercard, telecommunicating) and publishing children do.

ORGANIZATION OF THE CLASSROOM DAY: WHOLE LANGUAGE APPROACH

Activity- and project-based instruction requires large blocks of time for children to engage in extended exploration, research, and inquiry. In addition, frequent opportunity must be available for children to clarify their work goals, share their triumphs and frustrations with the rest of the class, and hear from others some sort of feedback about how work is progressing. Table 13-7 presents a daily class schedule for a whole language classroom.

Large Blocks of Working Time

As you can see from this schedule, whole language classroom days pivot around three large blocks of working time. In this class we've identified three major activities to comprise children's work during the blocks of time: (1) theme cycle projects (8:35–9:30), (2) writing workshop (10:30–11:30), and (3) activity time (12:50–1:50). There are any number of other important projects and activities for these blocks of time; critical here is that these time blocks have designated focus. When children are given forty-five minutes to an hour to work in groups or individually, the work must have definition, specific goals and plans, and accountability throughout. The times themselves are hefty—forty-five minutes to an hour—so that children have time to plan, negotiate ideas and working strategies, and do in-depth exploration and inquiry. Times will undoubtedly need to be adjusted for different age and grade levels, different activities, and even for different days. For example, in the stage where groups are bringing their projects to a close, when productions and reports are being completed, more than likely, time extension will be appropriate. Alternately, very young children may only be able to work effectively in independent groups for periods ranging between twenty and thirty minutes.

Reflection, Feedback, and Goal Setting

Surrounding the large blocks of working times should be short, to-the-point discussions of what groups are planning to accomplish and have

8:15 – 8:30	**Attendance, opening, poetry/song.**
8:30 – 8:35	**Status-of-the-groups roll call—Theme cycle units—**check with each group leader about plans for the day and what the group expects to accomplish.
8:35 – 9:30	**Theme cycle projects**—each group engaged in inquiry and research on the topic and issues selected regarding environment.
9:30 – 9:45	**Projects meeting–whole class**—groups discuss accomplishments of the day, assistance they need, and plans for tomorrow.
9:45 – 10:15	**Book clubs**—Small-group and partner gatherings to share good books. Special interest groups (e.g., comic book collectors, mystery buffs) encouraged.
10:15 – 10:30	**Snack, recess.**
10:30 – 10:45	**Writing workshop Mini-Lesson and Status-of-the-class roll call.**
10:45 – 11:30	**Writing time and conferences.**
11:30 – 11:50	**Sharing time and Author's Chair.**
11:50 – 12:30	**Lunch, recess.**
12:30 – 12:50	**Story time—Read to students.**
12:50 – 1:50	**M, T, Th, F – Activity Centers**—group problem solving—integrated math, science, social studies, art, language arts. Children work in two centers each day. **W – Library.**
1:50 – 2:15	**M, W – Music.** **T, Th, F – Physical education.**
2:15 – 2:45	**M, W – Recess 2:15–2:30; free activity 2:30–2:45.** **T, Th, F – Free activity**—children read, write in journals, share a book or some writing with a friend, do follow-up project work, listen to music, use art center.
2:45 – 3:10	**End-of-day reflections**—whole group, story/song.
3:10	**Dismiss.**

—— **TABLE 13-7** ——————————————————

Organization of the Classroom Day—Whole Language Approach

accomplished each day. These "status-of-the-group" or "status-of-the-class" roll calls are guided by the questions "What are you doing today?" and "What do you plan to accomplish?" Slightly longer reflection periods following group work give groups and individuals opportunity to monitor their own progress ("What did we accomplish today?") and share with other students and the teacher what they've found in their research and/or problems they're encountering. Analytical discussion of this kind increases children's ability to self-monitor their working progress and develops their planning and strategic inquiry skills. It also keeps you informed of the progress they're making and provides information for your record-keeping and evaluation procedures. Develop a form or other means for maintaining a careful record of individual and group responses to status-of-the-group roll call and after-work reflective questions.

Figure 13-5 illustrates one way to maintain records of group work planning and progress. Make a copy of the Project Work Management Sheet for each working group. Put the group's name or project topic at the top and list all group members in the space allotted. Each day at status-of-the-groups roll call, record (in abbreviated form) each group's outline of its plan for the day. Later, during reflection time ("What did you accomplish today? What do you need for continued progress?") record group accomplishments. Make note of any other pertinent information.

MANAGEMENT ISSUES: WHOLE LANGUAGE APPROACH

Management is probably the single most important concern associated with whole language instruction. Because there are no algorithms or teacher's guides, because whole language can take so many different forms, and because whole language classrooms really are centers of action and activity, good management is critical to its success. We have discussed at length in other sections of this chapter many management issues that have direct application to whole language classrooms—organizing the environment and yourself, developing classroom rules, provision for high-spill and potentially dangerous activities, rules and routines for gaining children's attention during periods of high activity and noise, routines for moving children into and out of activities, ways to increase the quality of children's small-group discussions, and maintenance of records for evaluating individual and group performance. Virtually all of that discussion applies to the whole language classroom as well. What is critical for you to understand is that you need to look at all of the management issues we've raised here, decide how you will address each, and make the plans necessary to do so. It's not really hard to do, but it takes some time, some thinking, and quite a bit of creative problem-solving on your part.

Creating the Environment for Learning

One of the great advantages of the whole language approach is that children's interests and self-determined inquiry questions and concerns are the

PROJECT WORK MANAGEMENT SHEET

GROUP: _____

MEMBERS: _____

Date	Work Planned	Work Accomplished

—— **FIGURE 13-5** ——

Project Work Management Sheet

central focus of what goes on in the classroom. Thus, children's natural curiosity and need to know help guide activity in the classroom in positive and productive ways. Keep in mind, however, that natural curiosity and inquiry will not overcome a capricious or chaotic environment; all of us require a certain amount of order and stability to function at our highest capacity. For children to work at their highest capacity they need freedom

691

from the distractions of capricious and chaotic classrooms; they need to know that they won't be disturbed by other students' acting-out behavior or constantly having to stop their work so the room can be brought back "into control." You are the person responsible for seeing to it that an orderly and stable environment exists in your classroom. You do this by careful planning, and by establishing and maintaining the rules and routines that allow lots of activity and action along with order.

You also create a stable environment through consistency (Ruddell, 1993). Consistency means that you respond to children today just as you did yesterday and will tomorrow; that whatever the rules and routines are, you follow them today as you did yesterday and will tomorrow; and whatever you *are*, you are today as you were yesterday and will be tomorrow. Consistency has to do with your classroom *style*, and we have ample evidence that children readily adapt to many varieties of teacher styles (structured, unstructured, informal, formal) as long as they can depend on its constancy. If you ignore acting-out behavior one day and come down hard on it the next, or if you're chipper and bright one day and morose the next, children have no alternative but to be just as unpredictable as you are (and they will be). Extreme behavior on your part encourages extreme behavior in children.

One of the greatest attributes you can bring to the classroom is having a short memory. In a whole language classroom where exploration and self-directed inquiry are paramount, children will make missteps and mistakes (actually, we all know that part of the human condition is making missteps and mistakes). Some problems will result from inappropriate decisions, others from inappropriate behavior. Whatever the situation, deal with it, bring it to closure, and then forget that it happened. In cases where you need to be stern and unyielding, be so, but don't continue to punish a child or group after an error has been corrected. Let it go so they can pick up the pieces and continue on. You need to be able immediately following the incident to address the child or group in your normal, cheerful, accepting manner.

Fostering Independence

In the whole language classroom, children need to become increasingly independent in planning and directing their own learning; group activities and projects *require* independent thought and action. The most powerful lessons in independence occur when children observe you as you use questioning and thinking modes for self-direction in status-of-the-group roll calls and reflection meetings that are built into the classroom day. When you say to students first thing every morning, "Community Clean-Up group, what are you doing today? What do you expect to have accomplished by 9:30?" you teach them that "What am I doing?" and "Where am I going with it?" are important questions to ask in the process of reaching one's goal. Just as important are conversations in reflection sessions in which you guide groups through problem solving—when you say, "Hmm. Now what are you going to do about that?" after a problem is presented and then lead children through a brainstorming session to seek possible solutions. The point here is that you guide children in planning their work rather than telling them what to do; you guide children through problem solving when snags occur rather than giving them solutions. Children rapidly adopt the problem-solution processes you model.

Organizing and Managing Classrooms

A Summary

In this chapter, we have examined issues of classroom organization and management and explored organization and management structures for guiding children's language and literacy development. Classroom organization involves physical arrangement of the room, materials and equipment in the room, as well as orchestration of classroom schedules and events. Classroom management has to do with time allocation and use, establishment of classroom rules and routines, productive use of materials and equipment, deportment, and development of useful assessment of children's progress and the curriculum. Classroom organization and management are closely linked to underlying beliefs teachers have and assumptions they make about how children learn.

Kindergarten classrooms, where most early and beginning readers are, require open space, many work and play centers, and well-organized materials and props for activities that develop language and literacy learning. Daily activities alternate work/play, motor activities, and whole class meetings for sharing and discussion. Management issues include organizing the environment, establishing rules and routines for activity in the classroom, and organizing and using the assistance of paid and volunteer classroom aides and parents.

The basal reader approach requires organization of the classroom for teacher-led small-group reading instruction that occurs as the rest of the class works independently. Reading groups may meet with the teacher every day or every other day to allow for more in-depth discussion and interaction. Rules and routines guide children in moving into and out of the reading group area and provide a means for children working independently to get help when they need it. Status effects caused by ability grouping may be reduced by cross-ability grouping for other activities.

The literature-based approach requires a well-stocked reading and literature center, flexible floor space for reading response groups to meet,

DOUBLE ENTRY JOURNAL

Go back to the list you made before reading the chapter. Put an asterisk by every item on your list that was discussed in the chapter. Add any important information from the chapter that is not on your list. Now look at your list and decide what areas of organization and management you think you need to work on a bit. Choose three areas to work on and circle those. Share your ideas with a friend.

and working areas and materials for end-of-book productions to be developed. Routines are useful for moving children into and out of reading response groups and getting their attention when groups are meeting. Developing clear discussion task goals and assigning group roles are ways to increase the quality of response group discussions.

The whole language approach centers around large blocks of time when children are engaged in projects and group activities. Language and literacy learning occur as a natural part of the projects and activities. Frequent opportunity for short goal-setting and reflection activities provide guidance for children in their exploration and inquiry projects. Rules and routines assist in creating a stable and orderly environment that gives children freedom to work and fosters children's increasingly independent action.

Supporting Activities

1. At the beginning of this chapter you were asked to reflect on your memories of classroom instruction. How did these memories of your instructional experiences compare to the findings of the John Goodlad study presented in this discussion? How were they similar? How different? Share your ideas with a class partner.

2. Think for a moment about key principles that you consider of highest priority in guiding your classroom management of twenty-five to thirty-five

students at the first-grade level. Identify your top five. Now, identify your top five principles for managing twenty-five to thirty-five students at the fifth-grade level. How are these two sets of principles similar? How are they different? Now use your principles and sketch a diagram of the physical organization of your classroom at the grade level of your choice. Be sure to identify your desk, your children's desks, centers and work areas, chalkboards, and work display areas. Discuss your principles and classroom sketch with a class partner.

3. Review our discussion on "Organization and Management of Literacy Instruction for Early and Beginning Readers and Writers." During the review process make notes on major ideas that you believe important for successful teaching at this level. Arrange for a visit to a kindergarten or first-grade classroom during language arts instruction and use your major ideas to guide your observation. Briefly summarize your observational notes. Did you find instructional practices that reflected your expectations based on the major ideas that you had identified? Similarities? Differences? Discuss your conclusions with a class partner.

4. Identify the instructional approach (basal reader, literature-based, whole language) or combination of approaches that has greatest appeal to you. Briefly explain your rationale for the approach at the grade level of your choice. Now use this rationale and create the following: (a) a daily time schedule with a brief description for each time "chunk" from 8:20 AM to 3:20 PM; (b) a sketch of the physical organization of your classroom; and (c) a brief description of the literacy materials and equipment in your classroom. Discuss your rationale, schedule, classroom organization plan, and description of materials with a class partner.

5. Arrange for an observational visit to one of the following types of classrooms that most closely reflects your personal preference: (a) basal reader; (b) literature-based; (c) whole language; (d) combination of approaches. During your visit to the classroom, pay particular attention to the following: the teacher's philosophy as reflected in her or his instruction and social interaction with the students; the instructional time blocks and physical room arrangement; and the literacy materials used and constructed by the teacher and students. Based on your observations, briefly describe these aspects of the instructional approach. Share your observations and conclusions with a class partner.

REFERENCES

Applebee, A. N. (1991). Environments for language teaching and learning: Contemporary issues and future directions. In J. Flood, J. M. Jensen, D. Lapp, & J. R. Squire (Eds.), *Handbook of research on teaching the English language arts* (pp. 549–556). New York: Macmillan.

Atwell, N. (1986). *In the middle.* Portsmouth, NH: Heinemann.

Calkins, L. M. (1991). *Living between the lines.* Portsmouth, NH: Heinemann.

Cambourne, B., & Turbill, J. (1987). *Coping with chaos.* Portsmouth, NH: Heinemann.

Dyson, A. H. (1984). Learning to write/learning to do school: Emergent writers' interpretations of school literacy tasks. *Research in the Teaching of English, 18*, 233–265.

Dyson, A. H. (1990). *The word and the world: Reconceptualzing written language development or do rainbows mean a lot to little girls?* (Technical Report No. 42). Berkeley, CA: University of California, Center for the Study of Writing.

Goodlad, J. I. (1984). *A place called school.* New York: McGraw-Hill.

Harste, J. C., Woodward, V. A., & Burke, C. L. (1984). *Language stories and literacy lessons.* Portsmouth, NH: Heinemann.

Nourot, P. M. (in press). *Curriculum guides for the California Department of Education early primary initiative.* Sacramento, CA: California State Department of Education.

Raines, B. (1991). *Response and collaboration in literature discussion groups: A two-year study of an intermediate grade classroom.* Master's thesis, Sonoma State University, Rohnert Park, CA.

Rosenblatt, L. M. (1994). The transactional theory of reading and writing. In R. B. Ruddell, M. R. Ruddell, & H. Singer (Eds.), *Theoretical models and processes of reading* (4th ed.) (pp. 1057–1092). Newark, DE: International Reading Association.

Ruddell, M. R. (1993). *Teaching content reading and writing.* Boston: Allyn & Bacon.

Ruddell, R. B., & Unrau, N. J. (1994). Reading as a meaning-construction process: The reader, the text, and the teacher. In R. B. Ruddell, M. R. Ruddell, & H. Singer (Eds.), *Theoretical models and processes of reading* (4th ed.) (pp. 996–1056). Newark, DE: International Reading Association.

The Santa Barbara Classroom Discourse Group. (1992). Constructing literacy in classrooms: Literate action as social accomplishment. In H. H. Marshall (Ed.), *Refining students' learning: Roots of educational change* (pp. 119–150). Norwood, NJ: Ablex.

Sulzby, E. (1985). Children's emergent reading of favorite storybooks: A developmental study. *Reading Research Quarterly, 20*, 458–481.

Tway, E. (1991). The elementary school classroom. In J. Flood, J. M. Jensen, D. Lapp, & J. R. Squire (Eds.), *Handbook of research on teaching the English language arts* (pp. 425–437). New York: Macmillan.

Van Hoorn, J., Nourot, P., Scales, B., & Alward, K. (1993). *Play at the center of the curriculum.* New York: Merrill.

Vygotsky, L. (1986). *Thought and language* (Trans., Rev., & Ed., A. Kozulin). Cambridge, MA: MIT Press.

CHILDREN'S LITERATURE REFERENCES

Baylor, B. (1974). *Everybody needs a rock.* New York: Macmillan.

Brown, M. W. (1947). *Goodnight moon.* New York: Harper & Row.

Lewis, C. S. (1950). *The lion, the witch, and the wardrobe.* New York: Macmillan.

Lionni, L. (1967). *Frederick.* New York: Pantheon.

Ringgold, F. (1991). *Tar beach.* New York: Crown.

Steptoe, J. (1987). *Mufaro's beautiful daughters.* New York: Lothrop, Lee & Shepard.

Turkle, B. (1969). *Thy friend, Obadiah.* New York: Viking Penguin.

Waber, B. (1972). *Ira sleeps over.* Boston: Houghton Mifflin.

CONTINUING PROFESSIONAL CHANGE AND GROWTH: REACHING THE INFLUENTIAL TEACHER GOAL

Consider for a moment the many and complex aspects of continuing professional change and growth for teachers. List some areas of professional change and growth that you think are, and will continue to be, important to you. What resources do you think are available to you in each area you listed? Jot these down.

INTRODUCTION

This concluding chapter presents a variety of ideas and suggestions that will be of value to you as you assume responsibility for your own classroom, continue your professional growth, and work toward the goal of becoming an influential literacy teacher.

The opening of the school year and meeting your children for the first time always produce simultaneous responses of excitement and anxiety. We can state with certainty that you will find these twin responses present on the first day of school, even after years of teaching experience. You will be asking yourself questions such as "What will my new children be like?" "Will I be prepared to teach them effectively?" "What help and support will there be to assist me in my teaching?" "What instructional materials will be available for my teaching?" "Will I find other teachers who I can share ideas with and confide?" and "Will my principal be supportive of me and my teaching ideas?" These questions are natural and normal and mark the beginning stage of your professional change and growth process in teaching.

Your brief reflection over discussions in our earlier chapters should provide reassurance of your knowledge and understanding of reading and writing instruction. These discussions have:

1. Introduced instructional principles critical to creating rich language and literacy environments for children from varied language and cultural backgrounds;

2. Explored the most recent thinking and ideas that support the view that the driving motivations underlying children's language and literacy development are social interaction and the search for meaning; and

3. Developed a wide range of instructional strategies and approaches that you can use in teaching and evaluating reading and writing skills to all children—mainstream as well as children with diverse language and cultural backgrounds.

You thus possess a solid knowledge base that will stand you in good stead in your classroom.

Of course, there is still much to learn from experience as you apply these principles, ideas, and strategies and approaches with children. You will also encounter many new ideas, strategies, and instructional approaches that will be crafted in years to come. As you strive toward the goal of becoming an influential literacy teacher, it is important to reflect constantly on your own teaching and your effectiveness with children, and to be open to new ideas, strategies, and approaches that can be adapted and implemented in your classroom.

Our discussion here will focus on five areas of importance that will be helpful in achieving the goal of becoming an influential teacher:

1. Understanding personal change and growth.

2. Examining the change process and teacher characteristics.

3. Finding support through school connections.

4. Changing and growing through professional connections.

5. Setting your personal influential teacher goals.

UNDERSTANDING PERSONAL CHANGE AND GROWTH

To meet the demanding challenges as well as the exciting opportunities that will confront you as a teacher, it will be helpful to think about the process of personal professional change and growth. Change is constant in most professional fields today, and this is especially true of reading and writing education. We have only to reflect on changes in recent immigration patterns in this country to understand this point. Current projections indicate that by the year 2000 one out of three youngsters in our classrooms will be from diverse language and cultural backgrounds. These children will represent a wide variety in previous educational experiences, home backgrounds and culture, and achievement. Your knowledge base must account for the instructional needs of these children, as well the needs of your mainstream students. To meet this challenge, you will need to possess knowledge and understanding of this wide range of students and of the instructional strategies and approaches that will be most useful in developing their reading and writing abilities. This challenge will require that you examine your own instructional beliefs and will involve readiness to change your ideas, instructional approaches, and strategies to meet the varied needs of your children.

Our own teaching experience and direct observations of teachers and their beliefs have led us to the conclusion that successful professional change is a necessary, constant, and ongoing process. The process of changing instructional beliefs, approaches, and strategies is often slow and frustrating, and it takes place over several years' time—but change can and does take place.

But what is the nature of this process from a personal perspective? Change is dynamic and requires personal involvement and interchange with new ideas. It can be summarized as a three-stage process (Ruddell & Sperling, 1988; Ruddell & Williams, 1972):

1. *Confronting* a new idea.
2. *Resisting but examining* the idea.
3. *Negotiating and adapting* the idea to your belief system.

You will experience this process in action as you enter your school for the first time and encounter a profusion of new ideas extending from pre-adopted textbooks to detailed guidelines for handling disciplinary problems, or as you attend your first in-service workshop and feel inundated by ideas and strategies that differ from your own instructional knowledge or belief system. At these times, you will struggle to understand, examine, and adapt ideas as you engage in the dynamics of the change process. Some new teachers are unable to adjust to the demands of change as they enter the profession. This problem contributes significantly to the departure of 30 percent of all new teachers from education after their first two years of teaching, and another 20 percent five to seven years later (California Commission on Teacher Credentialing, 1992).

The key to successful change, however, is to recognize the process of *confronting* new ideas, *resisting* but *examining,* and *negotiating* and *adapting* as a natural and normal process. This process essentially follows that of concept

701

and schema development that we discussed in Chapter 2. As we *confront* new ideas or information, we attempt to align and assimilate this new information using our background knowledge and prior beliefs. This is a difficult process for most of us, however, and often results in disequilibrium, a sort of mental unbalancing, as we attempt to manipulate and adjust the new information into our prior conceptions of instruction. This *resisting but examining* stage of the process motivates us to search for understanding and make sense of things from our own personal perspective. It is possible that the resistance based on our previous beliefs is so strong that the change process stops at this point. But, if our understanding process continues, we then work toward *negotiating and adapting* the new idea as we adjust and restructure our prior mental schema to accommodate the new information and, in effect, restore our equilibrium and mental balance.

This conception of change means that you may experience initial resistance as you confront teaching strategies or instructional approaches that are new and different from those you have previously encountered. We have observed a significant number of curriculum projects and potentially valuable innovations that have failed at the *resisting but examining* stage because of the lack of understanding of the dynamics of change. An important key to facilitating this process is collaborative efforts among teachers, principals, and curriculum personnel that make provision for voicing concerns and addressing these concerns to facilitate the negotiating and adapting stage of the process. Following such collaboration, there is need to provide implementation support for teachers in launching and using the ideas or innovation. Your awareness of these three stages in the personal dynamics of change will sustain you through the period of disequilibrium as you adjust to new ideas and innovations and will also provide a "change map" as you adjust to a new school, unfamiliar curriculum, and new children.

EXAMINING THE CHANGE PROCESS AND TEACHER CHARACTERISTICS

THE CHANGE PROCESS

Studies of the change process (Rogers, 1983; Ruddell & Sperling, 1988; Smith & Orlosky, 1974) provide strong evidence that new ideas are most quickly incorporated into practice when the teacher *perceives the change* in one or more of the following five ways:

1. It has a *distinct advantage* over the alternative instructional approach or strategy used by the teacher.
2. It is *compatible with the knowledge and beliefs* that the teacher knows and possesses.

3. It is *not too complex* and does not present too heavy a cognitive burden to be acted on.

4. It can *be tried out and/or observed* in practice to allow the teacher to make judgments and decisions about it.

5. *Opportunity is provided to commit* to or to reject the new ideas.

These five features constitute a "user-friendly" approach to change. These features explain why the publishers' basal reading approach has been widely accepted by teachers in many elementary schools. This approach provides preselected reading material, skillbooks and teacher guides with detailed instructional guidelines (#1); is often representative of how teachers themselves learned how to read and so is at least partly compatible with instructional beliefs (#2); often provides publisher- or district-sponsored in service workshops to explain the program during installation (#3); offers opportunity for pilot demonstration trials and observations in selected classrooms (#4); and encourages teacher involvement in the selection process (#5).

Awareness of these five factors that serve to enhance the change process can be of value to your personal understanding of change and innovation. For example, if you wish to incorporate the literature-based approach or the whole language approach, either partially or fully, into your classroom, you will need to understand the distinct advantages of the approach, your belief compatibility, and the instructional complexity of the approach (Ruddell, 1992). Our previous discussions will be of great value in developing your knowledge and understanding of these instructional approaches. Ideally, you will have the opportunity to observe the approach being used in other classrooms and to try it out before committing to it. If such observation is not possible, you may wish to incorporate various aspects of these approaches into the instructional program already in place in your school, using the range of ideas discussed in Chapters 12 and 13.

Instructional change, however, requires strong teacher desire and awareness of the need for change, supportive leadership by the principal, and a school administration that encourages change by accounting for these five change features. The experienced principal or curriculum coordinator will be cognizant of these features when new ideas and instructional approaches are introduced in your school.

TEACHER CHARACTERISTICS

Additional insight into the relationship between teacher characteristics and instructional change can be found in our research (Ruddell & Sperling, 1988; Ruddell & Williams, 1972). This work identifies four teaching styles that are predictive of willingness or unwillingness to explore new ideas and curriculum-change potential and is based on an eighteen-month on-site study of elementary school teachers. As in any other professional group, teachers differ widely, not only in attitudes and personalities, but also in their abilities to work effectively and productively in curriculum change. These teacher styles, characteristics, and acceptance and change potential are presented in Table 14-1. As you examine each style and the related characteristics, place a check mark beside those that most closely fit your perception of your self and then identify the teacher style that most closely represents you.

The first style descriptor is that of the **Supportive-Productive** teacher. These teachers use a *Communication System* that relies on open, two-way interactions, and they consistently seek clarification and resolution of issues discussed both with their students and their teacher peers. Their *Perception of Self* relative to their peers in cooperative planning is as an equal. They possess a *Management Style* that leads to cooperatively determined actions and group planning with both students and peers and creates high motivation. These teachers value student involvement and motivation. Their *Problem Solution Approach* toward learning exhibits a high level of intellectual curiosity based on their questions and responses to children, a high degree of self-confidence, and open consultation in problem solving.

Supportive-Productive teachers are "self-starters" with strong internal drive and direction defining their locus of control. And they hold a very positive attitude toward learning, along with high learning expectations for children. Our observations indicate that these teachers are highly supportive of group-established innovation and change and are highly productive in transferring innovation and change to their classroom teaching. They readily and willingly accept leadership responsibilities that may extend their time commitment beyond the normal school day. These teachers place their hearts, minds, and very souls into curriculum innovation and are highly productive in their classrooms.

The second descriptor is the **Supportive-Nonproductive** teacher. These teachers are supportive of the innovation, but at a "lip service" level. They experience great difficulty in transferring new ideas to their teaching and instructional program. This lack of productivity may result from a *Classroom Communication System* that is only partially open and frequently defensive. Their *Perception of Self* in relation to their peers is inferior, while their Management Style with their children relies heavily on assigned action with little use of cooperative involvement, some praise, and admonition. They do little to motivate children and exhibit low motivation themselves in curriculum-development participation. These teachers express little intellectual curiosity, and their locus of control is for the most part external, relying on directions and leadership from others. Their acceptance of new ideas is at a moderate level and they hold low potential for change.

The third teacher style is **Nonsupportive-Productive.** These teachers are also only partially open to new ideas. They are fiercely defensive of their current teaching approach and strategies and express little interest in ideas proposed by their peers. In the event that they have agreed to participate in the

TEACHER STYLE	CHARACTERISTICS				CHANGE PROCESS
	COMMUNICATION WITH STUDENTS AND TEACHER PEERS	PERCEPTION OF SELF IN RELATION TO PEERS	MANAGEMENT STYLE/ MOTIVATION	PROBLEM SOLUTION APPROACH	NEW IDEAS/ CHANGE POTENTIAL
1. Supportive-Productive	Open, two-way interaction, seeks clarification and resolution	Equal	Cooperatively determined action, praise/high motivation	Intellectually curious, confidence in self, open consultation, internal locus of control/positive, high expectations	High/ high
2. Supportive-Nonproductive	Partially open, defensive, self-deprecating, self-inadequate	Inferior	Assigned action, praise, admonition/moderate to low motivation	Little curiosity expressed, relies heavily on work and support from others, external locus of control/moderate/low expectations	Moderate/ low
3. Nonsupportive-Productive	Partially open, defensive of personal beliefs, little concern for ideas of others, verbally aggressive	Superior	Use of authority, admonition/moderate to low motivation	Little curiosity expressed, rejection of others' ideas and provocation of others, internal locus of control/moderate to negative, moderate expectations	Low/ low
4. Nonsupportive-Nonproductive	Closed, defensive, hostile, conflict	Inferior, rejected	Use of authority, reprimand/very low motivation	Little or no curiosity expressed, overwhelmed by problem, external locus of control, low expectations	Very low/ very low

—— **TABLE 14-1** ——

Teacher Styles, Characteristics, and the Change Process

Source: Based on Ruddell & Sperling, 1988, Table 2, p. 324.

innovation or new curriculum project, they continue involvement in the planning and early implementation stages. They appear, however, to remain convinced of the excellence of their own instructional program, and in fact they are often satisfactory teachers in their own right, and in this sense are productive. Their *Perception of Self* appears to be superior in relation to their peers. Their *Management Style* uses teacher authority and admonition, some praise, and rarely involves cooperatively determined instruction with their children or planning with their peers. The *Problem Solution Approach* used by these teachers is very limited, with little intellectual curiosity in evidence during their teaching. Their degree of acceptance of new ideas and innovation and their potential for change is relatively low.

The **Nonsupportive-Nonproductive** style presents a very bleak picture for new idea acceptance and change potential. These teachers often respond in one of two ways to change and innovation. Either they express the view that the new ideas presented and the innovation goals do not meet their needs or those of their students, or they express no viewpoint and become extremely quiet and almost withdrawn in peer planning discussions. Their *Communication System* is closed, defensive, and even hostile. Their Perception of Self is best characterized as inferior to their peers, and they believe that their ideas are often rejected. Their *Management Style* relies on teacher authority and reprimand, resulting in very low student motivation. They exhibit low-level *Problem Solution* interest or intellectual curiosity in their teaching. Their locus of control is for the most part external, requiring intensive support and leadership from others. They exhibit little creativity in their own ideas and almost no desire to consider alternatives to their own set, and frequently formal, approach to instruction. These teachers show little interest in new ideas, and their potential for change is very low.

Based on our discussion of these four teacher styles, it becomes clear that the Supportive-Productive teachers are the early innovators in school change. They are not only open to new ideas but are willing to work cooperatively and passionately toward new curriculum implementation. The Supportive-Nonproductive teachers hold moderate potential for change, although substantial support, creativity, and implementation energy must be provided by other teachers, the principal, and the curriculum innovator. Nonsupportive-Productive teachers hold low potential for change because of the strong belief in the superiority of their own instructional approach. They may, however, serve an important role in staff discussions by venting emotions, reducing tensions, and encouraging other teachers to carefully examine the reasoning behind the innovative practices being proposed. The Nonsupportive-Nonproductive teachers hold very low potential for change and for the most part are closed to new curriculum change ideas. Our curriculum implementation work with teachers over the years supports the view that change and innovation for the Nonsupportive-Productive and Nonsupportive-Nonproductive teachers is very slow but possible. This change is most effectively initiated by their observations of the innovation in action through peer demonstration teaching and enhanced by teacher peer pressure and principal support.

We now return to our earlier question: Were you successful in identifying the teacher style characteristics that most closely describe you? What other characteristics would you add to further define yourself under the major headings in Table 14-1?

FINDING SUPPORT THROUGH SCHOOL CONNECTIONS

During the early weeks of the school year, you will find yourself immersed in your classroom as you meet and come to know your students and your new reading and writing curriculum (as well as curricula in other areas), and as you stay a step ahead in instructional preparation. You will find four types of support of great value during this time period and during the school year. These consist of:

1. Personal knowledge and ingenuity,
2. Influential peer teachers,
3. The principal, and
4. Supportive parents.

YOUR PERSONAL KNOWLEDGE AND INGENUITY

Your first and immediate support resource is found within yourself. Your beliefs and convictions about education that have been shaped and influenced through years of schooling will represent an important resource. You will find that your professional preparation, ranging from theory and methods courses to field experience practice teaching, provides an important information base. This includes knowledge and understanding of abilities and interests of primary- and intermediate-grade students, reading and writing development approaches and strategies, and the culture of the school. This background will prove invaluable in your teaching. Should you have the good fortune to have classroom teaching experience on your own, you will draw heavily on this experience.

We asked you in the first chapter of this book to think of those influential teachers you have had in your own schooling from kindergarten through the college or university setting. Do so again. Carefully reflect on your memories of these teachers and visualize:

- their personal characteristics, including their energy, commitment, passion, flexibility, and expectations of self;
- their understanding of student potential and learner expectations and how they adjusted their instruction to meet their students' needs;

- their attitude toward content and skills instruction, exhibited in their enthusiasm and their ability to create intellectual excitement in their students;

- their concern for student life-adjustment through personal attention to academic progress and personal problems; and

- the way in which they organized and directed instruction by making content relevant to students, approached teaching from a strategy-oriented perspective, and engaged students in a process of intellectual discovery.

Your former influential teachers and their teaching characteristics will provide important role models as you assume full responsibility in your classroom. You will find yourself asking, "How would *(your influential teacher)* have presented this lesson (or handled this difficult situation)?" And more often than not, you will find a partial answer from the imaged role models of your influential teachers.

Your reflections should also include those teachers you considered to be absolutely dreadful in your educational experiences. Think for a moment about the reasons these teachers were not effective. These memories and reflections will highlight negative teaching features that you will guard against, at all costs, in your own teaching.

Approach language and literacy teaching, as well as other skill and content-area instruction, as a problem-solving process. This requires that you clearly identify your purpose and intent in your instruction, collect information, materials, and resources that you believe useful in developing the instruction, plan and design your instruction using the strategies and approaches discussed in earlier chapters to fulfill your purpose, and try out your plan with your children. Reflect on the "why" of the successes and difficulties you encountered and adjust your next instructional plan using this new knowledge.

You will find that you have a rich "hidden reservoir" of ideas from your past educational experiences, and that you are able to use this reservoir effectively in directing instruction. You will even find yourself returning to class notes, course projects, and texts used in your teacher preparation program. All of these will contribute to your successful problem-solving approach to teaching.

Remember the three central principles for maintaining a classroom environment discussed in Chapter 13 (see "Creating the Environment for Learning") that will enable you to come to know and engage your students in a positive way (Ruddell, 1993):

1. Establish clear, explicit expectations and make sure everyone knows them.

2. Be consistent.

3. Have a short memory.

These three ideas will help launch the first day of your new school year.

INFLUENTIAL PEER TEACHER

You should begin your search from the first day of school to identify the individual who can serve as your influential peer teacher (and friend). Potential influential peer teachers exist in every school. You will recognize them as friendly and outgoing, energetic and enthusiastic, intellectually curious, and open to consultation. They have developed a successful track record of teaching, and are very willing to share their ideas, resources, and wisdom, just for the asking.

Your initial search goal is to find a teacher who possesses an instructional belief system and philosophy compatible with your own. Contact with teachers at your school will occur just before the opening of the school year, during your room preparation and introductory teacher meetings. Take these opportunities to introduce yourself briefly and find out about peer teachers and their teaching beliefs and approaches to reading and writing instruction. Their room preparation will provide important clues to their sensitivity to individual student needs and learning expectations. For example, the use of bulletin boards to display the work of individual students, student desk arrangements to encourage interaction with teacher and peers, and the presence of an attractive and inviting reading and literature center will reveal important clues to a teacher's instructional belief system. Your conversations will include diverse topics such as the children that attend the school, the instructional programs and approaches used in the school, the reputation and supportive (or unsupportive) nature of the principal, and personal outside-of-school interests. All of this information will be of value as you work toward the identification of your influential peer teacher.

Influential Peer Teachers

Your influential peer teacher will play an important support role as your school year progresses. This teacher in effect becomes your in-house "consultant" who can provide valuable information on the operation and organization of the school, the nature of the curriculum, the expectations of the principal, and answers to a multitude of questions that will arise throughout your school year.

After you have established a comfortable level of trust with your influential peer teacher (by now your friend), you will be able to reveal successful instructional experiences as well as concerns about your teaching, your classroom, and the school. One great value that derives from this relationship is sharing ideas and searching for resolution to problems that you may be experiencing. Your influential peer teacher will prove to be a valuable asset, friend, and guard not only against isolation in your classroom but also against the depression that can sometimes occur with the heavy demands of teaching.

YOUR PRINCIPAL

The principal of your school assumes direct responsibility for instructional and administrative leadership and is empowered by the superintendent of schools to assume these key roles. The principal's effectiveness, however, will depend to a great extent on his or her stance toward instruction and administrative duties. There is strong evidence (Gallagher, Goudvis, & Pearson, 1988; McLaughlin & Marsh, 1978; Ruddell & Sperling, 1988) to support the view that the successful principal will exhibit many of the following characteristics:

1. Holds the belief and expectations that every child will achieve.
2. Demonstrates leadership that is consultative with teachers and involves them in open, process-oriented change and innovation in the school curriculum.
3. Participates actively in in-service workshops and project training sessions.
4. Legitimatizes and empowers teachers to work toward improved teaching effectiveness, innovation, and change.
5. Develops a positive school atmosphere that is orderly without being oppressive.
6. Exhibits enthusiasm and optimism toward the important role of the school in educating and changing the lives of children.

It is very important that you come to know the principal and his or her beliefs and philosophy toward language and literacy development and the curriculum in general. It is also important for you to convey your instructional beliefs and philosophy as demonstrated through your teaching. This will include your attitude toward teaching and children, the organization of your classroom, and the display of children's work reflecting their progress.

Your belief and philosophy of teaching can best be demonstrated through your teaching and your classroom environment. After you have your classroom "up and running," think of ways you can involve your principal in your classroom. This may take the form of invitations to visit your classroom to observe a Reader's Theatre presentation by your children, to examine a thematic literature unit you have developed using children's literature such as *Julie of the Wolves* (see Chapter 6), or to use his or her expertise on a special topic of study, ranging from ocean life to wilderness survival.

Remember that part of your principal's administrative and instructional duties consists of evaluating your teaching during your beginning years. This evaluation will be based on his or her knowledge of you as a teacher and will come from both informal and formal visits to your classroom. The ideas suggested above for informal visits will acquaint the principal with you and your teaching style, your classroom, and your children before the first formal evaluation visit. Formal observations will normally be agreed on with you beforehand. Even so, your anxiety level will increase substantially when this visit occurs. This level will be reduced by already acquainting the principal with your classroom through early invitations to visit and by careful instructional planning and preparation that will highlight your teaching effectiveness.

The principal also plays an important role in decision-making that will affect your classroom. This ranges from providing instructional supplies throughout the year to the use of "end-of-year" monies available for purchase of books and resource materials. As the school year progresses, start a "wish list" of items, such as children's literature you would like to add to your classroom reading and literacy center, educational software for your classroom computer(s), or even large budget items such as an overhead projector. Should such funds become available, you will have your "wish list" items prioritized with full information for purchase.

Most principals are also very supportive of in-service and continued education for their teachers. Again, your knowledge and understanding of the principal's educational beliefs and priorities will be of value. For example, you might wish to attend a reading or literacy conference held in your state to assist you in learning about and implementing new ideas such as cooperative learning strategies or a literature-based approach in your classroom. It will be important to discuss with the principal how this will be of value to you and to the school, what dates you will need to be released, and what costs are involved. The principal often influences the use of professional development days in his or her school and can serve as your advocate in support of your continued professional growth. We will say more about your professional development opportunities later in this chapter.

SUPPORTIVE PARENTS

Parents are important participants in their children's literacy development and can be of great value to you throughout the school year. It is important to develop communication and contact with parents early in the school year. Our discussion in Chapter 11 developed key ideas for communicating with parents, ranging from encouraging responses to children's work sent home and open house to parent-teacher conferences and report cards. A quick review of these ideas (pp. 579–585) will be helpful as you begin your school year.

But parents can also become partners in your classroom instructional program as we indicated in Chapter 13. In a time of tight school budgets, you will find fewer and fewer school-supported classroom teacher aides. Parents, however, are often willing to contribute volunteer time to their children's classrooms, if only a few hours each week. Direct parent participation in your classroom will provide four key values:

1. Interpretation of your instructional program and how this program develops literacy growth in the parent's child.
2. Participation through observing and leading instructional experiences involving the parent's own child and other children.
3. Development of the parent's understanding of ways to provide home educational support for his or her child.
4. Assistance to you in regular classroom instruction and during special school events such as day-long field trips.

You will find that parent desire, willingness, and opportunity to work with you in the classroom varies widely. Reasons for this include such concerns as anxiety toward visiting the school because of personal negative experiences in schooling, the belief that they are not welcome in the school environment, and work schedules of one- and two-parent families that prevent participation. Your contact with these parents will occur for the most part during scheduled parent-teacher conferences. These conferences should be designed (as discussed in Chapter 11) to reduce parents' anxiety toward the school, communicate your high interest in their child, and help parents understand that they are indeed welcome in your classroom as a partner in their child's educational development.

On the other hand, you will find that many parents hold a positive view of the school and feel welcome in the school environment. In addition, these parents have both the opportunity and desire to make time in their home responsibilities and work schedules to participate several hours each week in your classroom. These parents are often highly motivated to assist you in a variety of ways to enhance the learning opportunities of their children and other children as well.

You can initiate parent participation early in the school year by using a home letter designed to identify special interests and time commitments they may have and are willing to contribute to your classrooms. Parent time commitments can be adjusted to your special classroom needs, ranging from limited involvement in special events such as field trips to regular involvement in storytelling or tutoring. The parent involvement letter found in Figure 14-1 and the parent volunteer checklist in Table 14-2 can be used as models that you can tailor to your instructional program and your plans for parent involvement.

As your children return the parent volunteer checklist, you will need to examine each one carefully, noting what assistance has been offered and when parents are available for volunteer participation. You can then make a master scheduling list, noting the days of the week (across the top of a page) and the hours of the school day (down the left side of the page) to determine the most effective schedule. The volunteer response sheets should be three-hole punched and placed in a three-ring binder called "Parent Resources." This information will also be of value as you plan day-long field trip events to the zoo, aquarium, or historical sites, and special school fund-raising projects such as the school carnival or fiesta.

(Date)
(Your Name)
(Name of School
(Address)

Dear   (parent name),

    I am looking forward to working with   (child's name)   this year. As we begin our new school year, I would like to invite you to participate in my classroom as your time schedule provides. This will enable us to work together in our instructional program and in a variety of school activities. Your participation will also provide opportunity for you to see   (child's name)   learning in our classroom. To do this, I need to know any specific ways you are willing to work with me and when you will be available.

    I am aware that your home responsibilities and work schedule may present difficulty in finding school participation time. I will, however, greatly appreciate your response as you consider volunteer time that you might contribute. Please complete the following checklist and return it with your child. We need the help and assistance of all who enjoy and are willing to help in these kinds of activities. Grandparents and other relatives are welcome, as well as mothers and fathers.

                  Cordially,
                   (your name)

FIGURE 14-1

Model Letter Requesting Parent Involvement in Your Classroom

Name _____

My child ____(Fill in child's name)_____

Phone _____

I would like to help in _____'s classroom in the following ways:

1. Classroom learning, working directly with students
___ listening to children read
___ taking dictation of children's stories or poems
___ assisting children as they do assigned work
___ going on short school field-trip walks with children
___ going on day-long field trips

2. Assisting a small group or individual students with a special project such as:
___ arts or crafts
___ drama (plays, puppets)
___ creative writing
___ music
___ storytelling and children's literature
___ photography or film-making
___ special hobby _____
___ other_____

3. Assistance with large school projects
___ carnival, fiesta (or special event)
___ fund-raising
___ student council
___ school newspaper
___ other _____

4. Special school-wide tasks
___ library assistance
___ office assistance
___ make phone calls
___ other _____

I will be able to participate at school on the following days and times:
Day: M   T   W   Th   F   Any day
Time: Morning time _____   Afternoon time _____

I cannot participate in your classroom on a regular basis but would be available for special events. _____

_____
Signature

TABLE 14-2

Parent Volunteer Checklist Information

It is important in working with parent volunteers that you provide some initiation to your classroom, including your philosophy of teaching and your expectations of their role in assisting you. A brief one-page handout is useful in this regard. For example, the seven conditions of optimal instruction (ranging from immersing children in language and print to feedback to learners as an ongoing process) that we discussed in Chapter 3 (pp. 73–74) could represent a starting point in articulating your philosophy. It is important that parent volunteers clearly understand that you appreciate their cooperative participation; however, you must assume final responsibility for your children's instruction. You will find the following brief set of suggestions helpful in orienting parents to tutoring or leading instruction:

1. Be consistent.
2. Be alert to children's responses—respond to these and use them in your discussions.
3. Encourage active participation by working *with* the child.
4. Work toward approximation of a skill or concept—not perfection.
5. Give feedback and praise.
6. Don't pry or betray confidences.
7. Follow through on promises.

It is essential that you articulate the instructional objectives and plans for parent participation through clear directions and discussion. You should set out materials, children's literature, and whatever else is needed for them to participate in the activity they will be leading. While this will require planning on your part, you will find the time and preparation well invested through the return in children's learning and parent cooperation and support.

CHANGING AND GROWING THROUGH PROFESSIONAL CONNECTIONS

The continued development of your professional growth will occur primarily through three avenues. These are:

1. in-service and staff development experiences in your school district;
2. professional organizations that provide opportunity for local, state, and national meeting presentations;
3. continued education through a college or university in your area.

It is important that you be alert to opportunities available in each of these avenues as you work toward your goal of becoming an influential teacher.

IN-SERVICE AND STAFF DEVELOPMENT

You will find a variety of opportunities available for encountering new instructional ideas and approaches in your local school district. These opportunities usually take one of two forms: first, in-service sessions designed to present a specific set of ideas and to motivate you to use these in your classroom; second, ongoing staff development related to important instructional concerns in your school or school district that is conducted across the school year.

In-service sessions usually do not provide opportunity for follow-up with the speaker(s) but can still provide a valuable professional experience. For example, the "back-to-school" in-service day at the beginning of the school year may focus on a topic such as "Developing Comprehension and Higher Level Thinking Through the Literature Program." This will usually consist of a keynote speaker who introduces the topic and is followed by four or five speakers who develop related topics such as "Literature and Thinking Processes in the Primary Grades" or "Using Children's Literature to Enrich Social Studies and Science Teaching." You then have the opportunity to choose topics of the greatest interest to you. In most cases, the topic and speakers have been selected by a committee composed of teachers, principals, and central office personnel. The committee members select topics that they believe will be relevant to you and the instructional needs encountered in your classroom.

You will also find that, on occasion, an in-service workshop has been scheduled just for your school. This usually takes place immediately after school and is designed at the request of the principal and, hopefully, a representative committee of teachers who reflect your need requests and those of other teachers. This type of in-service usually occurs after a full day of teaching and requires an enthusiastic, well-informed speaker and an increase in your blood-sugar level to be successful. The more informal such sessions can be, the better. Opportunity for questions and interaction with the speaker is a must, either during or following the presentation.

Staff development projects, however, will take place all during the school year. This type of project provides ongoing and continued contact with the instructional leader, whether this is your school principal, school district personnel, or an outside curriculum innovator. The staff development project usually takes the form of focusing on a problem of major concern at the local school or district-wide level. For example, should your school have a large population of children who have limited English speaking skills, the staff development focus could increase understanding of this problem and provide ongoing opportunities to develop a reading and writing curriculum to meet the needs of these children. This could take the form of discussions led by school district or outside area specialists, demonstration teaching by highly successful teachers, and development of instructional materials or adaptation of existing materials to meet the special instructional needs of the children.

Continued Professional Development

Other examples of ongoing staff development at your school or district-wide level include adoption of new reading or literature textbooks, development of a new instructional approach such as a literature-based approach, and production of a new evaluation approach such as Portfolio Assessment. We recommend that you take every possible opportunity to participate in such staff-development projects. You will find that you not only build an important understanding of curriculum change but will be greatly enriched by the opportunity to explore and discuss new ideas with teachers at your own and other schools.

PROFESSIONAL ORGANIZATIONS

One hallmark of the professional teacher is knowledge and understanding of the most recent thinking and instructional ideas in the field. This knowledge and awareness can be developed in a variety of ways. One of the most effective, however, is through professional reading and literacy organizations.

At least two major professional organizations provide opportunities to explore the latest thinking and applications in reading and writing. The first is the International Reading Association (IRA), which has over one thousand local reading councils spread throughout every part of the United States, its territories, and Canada, and affiliates in approximately thirty other countries. Through the IRA, you have access to local council activities that sponsor local and national speakers on a wide variety of reading and literacy topics. Your attendance and participation in local council events will be welcomed by the local council officers and membership. Most state councils of the IRA hold a large state-wide meeting each year. The IRA produces *The Reading Teacher*, a journal (nine issues per year) for preschool and elementary teachers, that emphasizes instructional approaches and strategies reflecting the latest thinking in the field. This journal also includes reviews of the most recent children's books, professional books, evaluation approaches, and research. The organization also publishes *The Journal of Reading* specifically for teachers at the middle school and secondary level. IRA also sponsors an annual convention and regional conferences, held in different parts of the United States and Canada. A World Reading Congress is held on even-numbered years and usually meets in foreign countries, ranging from Sweden to Australia to Argentina. The publication division of the organization has a prolific output of professional books that develop the most recent concerns and issues in the field. Information on membership, the local council closest to your teaching location, and publications can be obtained by writing to:

International Reading Association
800 Barksdale Road
P.O. Box 8139
Newark, DE 19714-8139

or by calling
1-800-336-READ.

The second literacy organization that holds excellent potential for your professional growth is the National Council of Teachers of English (NCTE). This organization has members throughout the United States and Canada and has provided important leadership in encouraging integration of language arts skills. NCTE publishes *Language Arts* (eight issues per year), which is designed for the elementary school teacher, and is just now introducing *Voices from the Middle*, a journal for middle grade teachers. These journals emphasize theory and instructional practices and strategies, and publish reviews of the latest children's literature, professional books, and research. The NCTE publication for secondary English teachers is *The English Journal*. NCTE holds two major conventions each year in different parts of the United States, as well as regional and state conferences. Information on membership and publications can be obtained by writing to:

National Council of Teachers of English
1111 Kenyon Road
Urbana, IL 61801

or by calling
1-800-369-NCTE.

One special-interest professional organization formed in recent years is the Whole Language Umbrella (WLU). This organization focuses on whole language theory and curricula with the intent of improving learning and teaching at all levels of education. WLU serves as an umbrella organization that connects teacher support groups and individuals interested in whole language in the United States and Canada. The support group consists of five or more teachers who meet to share and discuss information and ideas. WLU publishes two newsletters and two updates each year for its membership. The organization holds one annual conference involving nationally recognized speakers who present theory, research, and teaching ideas related to holistic literacy development. Information on membership can be obtained by writing to:

WLU Membership (U.S.)
P.O. Box 2029
Bloomington, IN
47402-2029

WLU Membership (Canada)
#6-846 Marion Street
Winnipeg, Manitoba
R2J OK4

or by calling
1-812-846-8280

or by calling
1-204-237-5214

You will find many advantages in membership in reading and literacy professional organizations. Not only will you have the opportunity to encounter and explore the most recent thinking and ideas for early innovation in your classroom, but you will also be updated on the most current children's literature, professional books, and research. Your active attendance and participation in local professional councils and state, regional, and national conventions will enable you to hear and meet the individuals who have strong influence on reading and literacy trends across the nation. Finally, your professional involvement will enable you to meet other professionals like yourself and establish friendships, while visiting major cities in the United States and other countries of the world.

CONTINUING EDUCATION

As you enter the teaching profession, or even if you have several years of experience, you should give careful consideration to continued professional growth through higher education. If you feel the desire to develop greater understanding of reading and literacy development and possess the desire to pursue your ideas in depth, you should begin to explore what higher education degree programs are available to you in your immediate region. Inquire about the nature of the program, what higher degrees are awarded (M.A.? M.Ed.? Ed.D.? Ph.D.?), the faculty who will be available to you, and the reputation of the program. Your information search should include discussions with other teachers, professors at the college or university of interest to you, and close examination of bulletins and programs of study provided by these institutions.

Most M.A. programs require twenty-four to thirty-six units of credit for completion. Some programs require the completion of a thesis problem studying a specific aspect of reading and literacy development, while others require a comprehensive examination covering the work taken. Many M.A. and M.Ed. programs can be completed in one year of full-time study or part-time study over two years when combined with one or two summer sessions.

Doctoral degree (Ed.D., Ph.D.) programs vary in length and requirements, ranging from three to five years of study. These higher degrees also require the completion of a dissertation problem researching some aspect of reading and literacy development.

As you continue in the profession over several years' time, you will feel the desire to gain more professional knowledge in order to better understand the instructional needs of your children. When this occurs you should explore your continued professional development through higher education.

SETTING YOUR INFLUENTIAL TEACHER GOALS

At this point we turn to you for self-reflection and introspection on your own teaching. We encourage you to reflect on your classroom teaching experiences over the last year. This may include tutoring, student teaching, or responsibility as a full-time classroom teacher. Based on this reflection and introspection, identify, first, your strengths and, second, the areas of emphasis that you believe important for your increased teaching effectiveness. Use the checklist in Table 14-3, based on our discussions of influential teaching (Chapter 1) and reading and literacy areas (Chapters 2 through 13), to assist and stimulate your reflective thinking and ideas. Jot down any brief ideas that come to mind related to your "strengths" and "emphasis desired" under the "reflective notes" heading.

Based on this reflective analysis of your teaching, identify three influential teacher or instructional areas that represent your greatest strength in teaching:

1. _____

2. _____

3. _____

Congratulations! Reflect for a moment on what factors contributed to your development of these strengths. Make a few notes to represent these ideas below:

_____

_____

	STRENGTHS	EMPHASIS DESIRED	REFLECTIVE NOTES
1. INFLUENTIAL TEACHER CHARACTERISTICS			
1) Personal characteristics (energy, caring, self-expectations)			
2) Learner potential (understand student needs, learning expectations)			
3) Attitude toward teaching (enthusiasm, intellectual excitement)			
4) Life adjustment (concern for academic and personal problems)			
5) Quality of instruction (make material personally relevant, strategy oriented, engage students in intellectual discovery)			
2. READING AND LITERACY AREAS			
1) Reading and literacy process			
2) Early reading and literacy development			
3) Reading comprehension			
4) Vocabulary development			
5) Literature and reader response			
6) Writing development			
7) Word analysis			
8) Content-area literacy			
9) Language and cultural diversity			
10) Evaluation reading and literacy development			
11) Instructional approaches			
12) Classroom organization			

— **TABLE 14-3** —

Self-Reflection and Introspection Teaching Checklist

_____

_____

Now, identify three influential teacher or instructional areas that you believe need the greatest emphasis to increase your teaching effectiveness:

1. _____

2. _____

3. _____

Think for a moment on action you can take or a plan you can formulate to increase your teaching effectiveness in each of these areas. Record these ideas below:

_____

_____

_____

_____

_____

_____

_____

_____

This process of reflection, introspection, and planning moves you into the personal change process as you confront, examine, and adapt ideas to increase your teaching effectiveness. Your participation in this process suggests that you possess confidence in your self, are internally motivated to increase your teaching effectiveness, and hold high expectations for your self—all characteristics of the *Supportive-Productive* teacher style discussed earlier.

You have just established important self-derived goals that will lead to your becoming an *influential teacher*. Your awareness of your strengths and the areas you desire to emphasize to increase your teaching effectiveness form the basis for your professional growth. Your plan of action for your self-identified emphasis areas may range from observations of influential teachers presenting instruction in these areas and opportunity to try out new ideas in these areas to participating in in-service workshops and special professional convention sessions focusing on these areas. We encourage you to become reflective in your teaching and constantly to examine not only your successes but also ways that you can increase your reading and literacy teaching effectiveness with your children. If you can do this, you are well on the way to becoming an influential reading and literacy teacher.

DOUBLE ENTRY JOURNAL

*Go back to the list of areas for continuing profes-
sional growth and change that you made before
reading this chapter. Choose two or three areas
you listed and for each jot down resources available to you for (1) immediate and (2) long-range
action. What are some possible issues or constraints that might affect growth and change in
these areas? If you feel comfortable doing so, share
your list with a friend.*

A Concluding Personal Note

We have shared many ideas in these chapters based on our own teaching experiences, our observations of and discussions with influential
teachers, and our research and careful review of the ideas of other teachers and researchers. From the very first chapter, our central goal in sharing these ideas has been to assist you in becoming an *influential reading
and writing teacher.* We are convinced that the professional change
process leading to influential teaching requires self-reflection on your
own teaching, risk-taking as you try out new ideas, self-tolerance of mistakes, and self-fulfillment and professional pride in your successes. It is
important to remember that in becoming an influential teacher, your
learning process will be ongoing throughout this school year and those to
come. Teaching children has always been, and still is, a noble profession.
We wish you every success in becoming an influential teacher and in your
contribution to the literacy development of children.

Supporting Activities

1. Review our discussion on "Understanding Personal Change and Growth." Reflect on major change events in your life. Select one of these and examine the processes and stages that you experienced in this change. Do you find parallels to our three-step change process? Differences? Discuss your reflection and self-analysis with a class partner.

2. Examine the four teacher styles, related characteristics, and change potential for each identified in Table 14-1. Which style and characteristics most closely resembles your own personal teaching style? What factors in your life have influenced you in the development of this particular style? Do you perceive yourself as being open to change and readily willing to explore new ideas with the possibility of incorporating them into your teaching belief system? Why or why not?

3. Review our discussion on "Finding Support Through School Connections." During this review make notes on key ideas that you believe will be of value to you during your first year of teaching. Arrange for an interview with an elementary school teacher at the grade level of highest interest to you and explore the topic of "How to Establish School Connections." Use your summary notes to create a series of questions for your interview. Be sure to include such areas as influential peer teachers, the principal, and supportive parents. Summarize the information from your interview and share your findings and conclusions with a class partner.

4. Talk to your professor and obtain information on one of the following: (1) the local reading council monthly meetings in your area; (2) the annual State Reading Association Conference (affiliated with the International Reading Association); (3) the State English Teachers Conference (affiliated with the National Council of Teachers of English); (4) or a Whole Language Umbrella conference. You may also wish to call the numbers listed above for similar information (note that two of these are toll-free numbers). Arrange to attend one of these meetings and select program presentations that are of high interest to you. Be sure to inquire about student discount conference registration fees and student discount membership fees. Share your new conference teaching ideas with a class partner.

5. Review our discussion on "Setting Your Influential Teacher Goals." If you have not already done so use the checklist in Table 14-3 to identify your self-perceived instructional strengths and areas of emphasis that you wish to strengthen. Develop three specific personal goals and a plan to increase your teaching effectiveness in becoming an influential teacher. Share your goals and plan with a class partner.

California Commission on Teacher Credentialing. (1992). *Success for beginning teachers: The California new teacher project 1988–1992.* Sacramento, CA: California State Department of Education.

Gallagher, M. C., Goudvis, A., & Pearson, P. D. (1988). Principles of organizational change. In S. J. Samuels & P. D. Pearson (Eds.), *Changing school reading programs: Principles and case studies* (pp. 11–39). Newark, DE: International Reading Association.

McLaughlin, M. W., & Marsh, D. D. (1978). Staff development and school change. *Teachers College Record, 80* (1), 69–94.

Rogers, E. (1983). *Diffusions of innovations.* New York: The Free Press.

Ruddell, M. R. (1993). *Teaching content reading and writing.* Allyn & Bacon.

Ruddell, R. B. (1992). A whole literature and literature perspective: Creating a meaning-making instructional environment. *Language Arts, 69,* 612–620.

Ruddell, R. B., & Sperling, M. (1988). Factors influencing the use of literacy research by the classroom teacher: Research review and new directions. In J. E. Readence & R. S. Baldwin (Eds.), *Dialogues in literacy research* (pp. 319–329). Chicago: National Reading Conference.

Ruddell, R. B., & Williams, A. (1972). *A research investigation of a literacy teaching model: Project DELTA* (EPDA Project No. 005262). Washington, DC: Department of Health, Education and Welfare, Office of Education.

Smith, B. O., & Orlosky, D. E. (1974). Educational change: Its origins and characteristics. In R. B. Ruddell, E. J. Ahern, E. Hartson, & J. Taylor (Eds.), *Resources in reading-language instruction* (pp. 64–69). Englewood Cliffs, NJ: Prentice-Hall.

AUTHOR INDEX

References in **boldface** indicate authors of children's books

SUBJECT INDEX

References followed by t or f indicate tables or figures, respectively.

Credits

Page 39 (Figure 2-1) and page 324 (Figure 7-8): From J. C. Harste, V. A. Woodward, & C. L. Burke. (1984). *Language stories and literacy lessons.* Portsmouth, NH: Heinemann, pp. 94 and 96. Reprinted by permission. Page 42 (Figure 2-2): From C. Temple & J. W. Gillett. (1989). *Language arts: Learning processes and teaching practices.* New York: HarperCollins, pp. 41 and 43. Reprinted with permission. Page 47 (Table 2-1): From R. B. Ruddell & M. R. Ruddell. (1994). Language acquisition and literacy processes. In R. B. Ruddell, M. R. Ruddell, & H. Singer (Eds.), *Theoretical models and processes of reading* (4th ed.). Newark, DE: International Reading Association. Copyright 1994 by the International Reading Association. Reprinted with permission. Page 76 (Figure 3-1): Based on P. Harris. (1989). *First grade children's constructs of teacher-assigned reading tasks in a whole language classroom.* Unpublished doctoral dissertation, University of California, Berkeley. Used with permission. Page 80 (Figure 3-2): From E. Sulzby. (1985). Children's emergent reading of favorite storybooks: A developmental study. *Reading Research Quarterly, 20,* 464. Reprinted with permission of Elizabeth Sulzby and the International Reading Association. Page 82 (Figure 3-3): From W. H. Teale & E. Sulzby. (1989). Emergent literacy: New perspectives. In D. S. Strickland & L. M. Morrow (Eds.), *Emerging literacy: Young children learn to read and write.* Newark, DE: International Reading Association, p. 2. Reprinted with permission. Page 84 (Table 3-1): From D. S. Strickland & L. M. Morrow (1989). *Emerging literacy: Young children learn to read and write.* Newark, DE: International Reading Association, p. 161. Reprinted with permission. Pages 109 and 438: PEANUTS reprinted by permission of UFS, Inc. Pages 89-90: Text reprinted with permission of Jenny Sirell. Page 110 (Figure 3-5): From J. L. Davidson. (1991). *Illustrating and making books.* Cortland, IL: Prairie Publications.

Reprinted with permission. Page 115 (Figure 3-6): From L. M. Morrow. (1989). Designing the classroom to promote literacy development. In D. S. Strickland & L. M. Morrow (Eds.), *Emerging literacy: Young children learn to read and write.* Newark, DE: International Reading Association, p. 126. Reprinted with permission. Page 136: From *Charlotte's Web* by E. B. White. Copyright 1952 by E. B. White. Renewed c 1980 by E. B. White. Illustrations copyright renewed c 1980 by Garth Williams. Selection reprinted by permission of HarperCollins Publishers. Pages 161-167 (Figure 4-1): From R. B. Ruddell, D. L. Monson, & S. L. Sebesta. (1981). *Wingspan, Teacher's Edition.* Boston: Allyn & Bacon, pp. 89-95. Reprinted with permission. Page 175 (Figure 4-2): From Taffy E. Raphael. (1986). Teaching question-answer relationships, revisited. *The Reading Teacher, 39,* 519. Reprinted with permission of Taffy E. Raphael and the International Reading Association. Page 188: Text from A. S. Palincsar & A. L. Brown . (1986). Interactive teaching to promote independent learning from text. *The Reading Teacher, 39,* 771. Reprinted with permission. Pages 190-191 (Figure 4-3): From R. B. Ruddell & M. R. Haggard. *Thinking about reading: Focus on story comprehension.* Cleveland, OH: Modern Curriculum Press, pp. 5 and 6. Reprinted with permission. Page 211 (Table 5-1): From P. A. Drum & B. C. Konopak. (1987). Learning word meanings from written context. In M. G. McKeown & M. E. Curtis (Eds.), *The nature of vocabulary acquisition.* Hillsdale, NJ: Erlbaum, p. 76. Reprinted with permission. of Lawrence Erlbaum Associates, Inc. Page 212: Excerpt from *Little House on the Prairie* by Laura Ingalls Wilder. Text copyright 1935 by Laura Ingalls Wilder. Copyright c renewed 1963 by Roger L. MacBride. Selection reprinted by permission of HarperCollins Publishers. Page 212: Excerpt from *Sharks* by Gi' Berger. Christopher Santoro, Illus. Copyright c 1987 by Gilda Berger.